Mastering™
Maya® 3

John Kundert-Gibbs

Peter Lee

SYBEX®

San Francisco • Paris • Düsseldorf • Soest • London

Associate Publisher: Cheryl Applewood

Contracts and Licensing Manager: Kristine O'Callaghan

Acquisitions and Developmental Editor: Mariann Barsolo

Editors: Jim Compton, Marilyn Smith, Pete Gaughan, Carol Henry, Donna Crossman

Production Editor: Elizabeth Campbell

Technical Editor: Tim Coleman

Electronic Publishing Specialists: Publication Services, Maureen Forys

Proofreader: Publication Services

Indexer: Nancy Guenther

CD Coordinator: Erica Yee

CD Technician: Kevin Ly

Book Designer: Maureen Forys, Happenstance Type-O-Rama

Cover Designer: Design Site

Cover Illustrator/Photographer: Jack D. Myers

Library of Congress Card Number: 2001086864

ISBN: 0-7821-2835-1

Software License Agreement

Terms and Conditions

The media and/or any online materials accompanying this book that are available now or in the future contain programs and/or text files (the "Software") to be used in connection with the book. SYBEX hereby grants to you a license to use the Software, subject to the terms that follow. Your purchase, acceptance, or use of the Software will constitute your acceptance of such terms.

The Software compilation is the property of SYBEX unless otherwise indicated and is protected by copyright to SYBEX or other copyright owner(s) as indicated in the media files (the "Owner(s)"). You are hereby granted a single-user license to use the Software for your personal, noncommercial use only. You may not reproduce, sell, distribute, publish, circulate, or commercially exploit the Software, or any portion thereof, without the written consent of SYBEX and the specific copyright owner(s) of any component software included on this media.

In the event that the Software or components include specific license requirements or end-user agreements, statements of condition, disclaimers, limitations or warranties ("End-User License"), those End-User Licenses supersede the terms and conditions herein as to that particular Software component. Your purchase, acceptance, or use of the Software will constitute your acceptance of such End-User Licenses.

By purchase, use, or acceptance of the Software you further agree to comply with all export laws and regulations of the United States as such laws and regulations may exist from time to time.

Reusable Code in This Book

The authors created reusable code in this publication expressly for reuse for readers. Sybex grants readers permission to reuse for any purpose the code found in this publication or its accompanying CD-ROM so long as both authors are attributed in any application containing the reusable code, and the code itself is never sold or commercially exploited as a stand-alone product.

Software Support

Components of the supplemental Software and any offers associated with them may be supported by the specific Owner(s) of that material but they are not supported by SYBEX. Information regarding any available support may be obtained from the Owner(s) using the information provided in the appropriate read.me files or listed elsewhere on the media.

Should the manufacturer(s) or other Owner(s) cease to offer support or decline to honor any offer, SYBEX bears no responsibility. This notice concerning support for the Software is provided for your information only. SYBEX is not the agent or principal of the Owner(s), and SYBEX is in no way responsible for providing any support for the Software, nor is it liable or responsible for any support provided, or not provided, by the Owner(s).

Warranty

SYBEX warrants the enclosed media to be free of physical defects for a period of ninety (90) days after purchase. The Software is not available from SYBEX in any other form or media than that enclosed herein or posted to www.sybex.com. If you discover a defect in the media during this warranty period, you may obtain a replacement of identical format at no charge by sending the defective media, postage prepaid, with proof of purchase to:

SYBEX Inc.
Customer Service Department
1151 Marina Village Parkway
Alameda, CA 94501
(510) 523-8233
Fax: (510) 523-2373
e-mail: info@sybex.com
WEB: HTTP://WWW.SYBEX.COM

After the 90-day period, you can obtain replacement media of identical format by sending us the defective disk, proof of purchase, and a check or money order for $10, payable to SYBEX.

Disclaimer

SYBEX makes no warranty or representation, either expressed or implied, with respect to the Software or its contents, quality, performance, merchantability, or fitness for a particular purpose. In no event will SYBEX, its distributors, or dealers be liable to you or any other party for direct, indirect, special, incidental, consequential, or other damages arising out of the use of or inability to use the Software or its contents even if advised of the possibility of such damage. In the event that the Software includes an online update feature, SYBEX further disclaims any obligation to provide this feature for any specific duration other than the initial posting.

The exclusion of implied warranties is not permitted by some states. Therefore, the above exclusion may not apply to you. This warranty provides you with specific legal rights; there may be other rights that you may have that vary from state to state. The pricing of the book with the Software by SYBEX reflects the allocation of risk and limitations on liability contained in this agreement of Terms and Conditions.

Shareware Distribution

This Software may contain various programs that are distributed as shareware. Copyright laws apply to both shareware and ordinary commercial software, and the copyright Owner(s) retains all rights. If you try a shareware program and continue using it, you are expected to register it. Individual programs differ on details of trial periods, registration, and payment. Please observe the requirements stated in appropriate files.

Copy Protection

The Software in whole or in part may or may not be copy-protected or encrypted. However, in all cases, reselling or redistributing these files without authorization is expressly forbidden except as specifically provided for by the Owner(s) therein.

To Kristin, Joshua, and Kenlee.
JKG
To John, David, and my loving parents.
PL

Acknowledgments

While *Maya* is a word for illusion, there is no illusion to how a book like this gets done: the hard work and effort of a number of very dedicated, talented people. While everyone who had any part in this book deserves credit, we have room to mention only a special few.

First thanks go to Perry Harovas, who guided the creation of this book's predecessor, *Mastering Maya Complete 2*. Perry not only defined the structure and the scope of this book (and contributed some interviews); he also inspired us with his enthusiasm for Maya and the teaching-by-example approach we have followed.

We would next like to thank the hard-working, inspired people at Alias|Wavefront for making such fantastic tools for us. We are especially indebted to Chris Ford, Mark Sylvester, Richard Kerris, Duncan Brinsmead, Russell Owen, Jackie Farrell, Sharon Zamora, Mike Stivers, Katriona Lord-Levins, Tracy Hawken, and Vic Fina. We thank Rick Kogucki (Senior Product Specialist) and Cory Mogk (Maya Product Specialist, Games and Interactive) for their technical feedback and advice. Their contributions to this book have been invaluable.

We are privileged to thank Ellen Pasternack, Miles Perkins, Habib Zargarpour, and Craig Lyn from Industrial Light & Magic, who were always willing to help and went beyond the call of duty with their time and effort. We would also like to thank Yumi Ozaki and Robin Akin at Square USA for their invaluable help in getting those *Final Fantasy* images into the book. Thanks too to all the folks at Big Idea Productions—especially Steve Byrd and Joji Arnett for the wonderful *3-2-1 Penguins!* images. We'd also like to recognize Haeyoung Moon at Storydale Inc. for his contribution of several of the wonderful images in this book. Thanks also to Chihoon Lee and Namwoo Noh at Cinepix for their assistance.

We would also like to thank the acquisitions, editorial, and production team assembled by Sybex for their insightful, timely and professional management of the evolving work, especially Jim Compton, Mariann Barsolo, Cheryl Applewood, Tim Coleman, and Elizabeth Campbell. Marilyn Smith, Pete Gaughan, Carol Henry, and Donna Crossman also contributed greatly to the editing. On the production side, Jan Fisher and her colleagues at Publication Services displayed their usual skill and resourcefulness in turning the edited manuscript into a finished book. Dan Mummert obtained copyright permissions for material on the companion CD-ROM and in the color insert. Erica Yee and Kevin Ly made the CD-ROM a reality.

Without the generous support and freedom our employers have given us, this book could never have been written. A special thanks to the faculty and staff at the University of North Carolina at Asheville, especially James D. Lee, who helped rewrite Chapter 3; Jonathan Fischoff, who researched using the Trax editor for lip-synching; Chancellor James Mullen; and Vice Chancellors Tom Cochran and Jim Pitts.

Our loved ones have been with us throughout this book's production, and have given their time and energy to this work as much as we have. From this large group, John Kundert-Gibbs would like to give special thanks to Joan and Lee Gibbs and Kristin, Joshua, and Kenlee Kundert-Gibbs. Peter Lee would like to thank Tim Kim, Heesun Choi, Sharon Park, Danny Han, and Eunjoo Lee, who provided much needed love and support throughout.

Contents at a Glance

Contents

Foreword

Welcome to the wonderful world of Maya. Little did I realize more than fifteen years ago that I would be writing the foreword to a book about a product that is the result of an idea I had in 1984—to do something with computers and art.

I can imagine how excited you must be. You have the book, the software, and a hot computer; and now you are going to get busy and educate yourself in the many disciplines that it takes to be an accomplished Maya animator. I am happy and excited for you. The investment you are about to make in yourself is worth every minute you put into it—and every hour, week, weekend, and holiday that you work through as you baby-sit that final render or rush to make a 9 A.M. deadline. There are thousands of people just like you who have dedicated themselves to becoming world-class experts at Maya. This book is now a part of your continuing education program.

When we started Wavefront in 1984, we had a vision of how an artist would use our tools to create amazing images. That vision attracted many like-minded people to our way of doing things. Coincidentally, during that same spring in 1984, two other companies were having the same conversations: in Paris the early developers of Explore from Thomson Digital Images (TDI) and in Toronto the founding team at Alias Research. Each of the companies had attracted like-minded artists and animators that gravitated to our approach to the computer graphics problem. Now those various methodologies, features, functions, and workflows are represented in our next-generation application, Maya.

Maya is the combination and, in many ways, a culmination of hundreds of man-years of effort at creating a computer graphics system that meets the demanding requirements of users, from the ultrahigh-end film studios to the start-up animation companies that are springing up in garages around the planet. Maya effectively brings together the best thinking of all three systems plus new technologies, workflow, and usability features that were impossible to imagine 15 years ago. There is a lot here to learn. Nevertheless, diligence, patience, and an open attitude will help you succeed as you go through the exercises in this book. Challenge yourself.

Learning Maya is a lot like learning the Japanese game of Go. They say it takes minutes to learn and a lifetime to master. You can get through the Alias|Wavefront tutorials in a couple of days. However, that just gets you to beginner status. You obviously want to improve your skills beyond this—you purchased *Mastering Maya 3* to move beyond Maya's beginning tutorials. Your ability to utilize the skills that you learn in this book in creative ways will enable you to develop unique solutions to your future graphics problems. It is only after years of grappling with tough visual problems that you achieve expert status. Remember, there are usually more than a few ways to solve the same problem within Maya. Everything can be combined with everything else, and this is one of the most powerful aspects of the software.

This book will get you acquainted with Maya Version 3. When we started work on Maya in 1995, after the merger of Alias and Wavefront, we wanted to deliver a software system that would change the way computer animation was created by challenging established ways of working—even those we pioneered ourselves. In Version 1, we set our goals high, and we met most of them. Version 3 now completes our original design plans for the software and its architecture. Software is never actually done, just as a great painting always seems to need "just a little more—if I only had the time."

I had the chance to review a few of chapters of this book while they were still being edited, somewhat like getting a look at alpha software. The great thing about a book not written by a product's manufacturer is that the authors can take certain liberties. They can have fun with the lessons and their comments. I am sure you will appreciate the tone the book uses as you are led though lessons that will reinforce your knowledge of each of the various aspects of Maya. The lessons build upon themselves, which is great for taking you through the process incrementally. I have always enjoyed learning this way. The best part of the book is the enclosed CD. This way, you know you have a safety net; if you make a mistake, you can always reload the lesson examples.

Once you have gotten a good feel for the software and its potential, it will be time to meet others who share your enthusiasm for Maya. Internet News Groups, Online Chats, Maya Rings, and the various Alias|Wavefront and Maya Web sites are all good forums to meet others and discuss specific aspects of the software, its uses, and how much this book helped you in getting more out of the software. I encourage you to take time regularly to interact with other users. See if there is a user group in your community and make sure you plan a trip to Siggraph each year for the Global Users Association's annual meeting.

Well, enough about how great life will be once you have learned Maya; it is time to get to work and start exercising your gray cells. I hope that this book becomes just one more part of your investment in lifelong learning and continuing education. This is just the beginning. Have fun. I still do—every day!

Ride the wave,
Mark Sylvester
Ambassador
Alias|Wavefront
Santa Barbara, California
January 2001

Introduction

Welcome to *Mastering Maya 3*! If you're new to Maya and this series of books, *Mastering Maya 3* will lead you through the wonderful, deep riches that are Alias|Wavefront's 3D animation universe, Maya. If you already own Maya and use *Mastering Maya Complete 2*, rest assured that this new version has been thoroughly updated and revised with new content to allow you to continue your exploration of this wonderful, evolving piece of software. (See the "What's New" section below for some highlights of new material in this edition.)

Whether you are new to Maya (and even to 3D animation) or have spent years working with Maya and other 3D software, *Mastering Maya 3* will help you create better, more challenging images and animations than you have before. Whether you work through the examples in this book step by step or use the book as a reference guide, you will find new techniques, shortcuts, and software capabilities throughout the book, letting you get the most out of the investment in time and money you have put into Maya.

Regardless of whether you work in the trenches of a large animation-and-effects house or are starting up a studio of one, the knowledge you gain by reading through this book will allow you to realize your visions more fully and more rapidly. Digest the book, experiment with the software as you go, play, and above all, take joy in what you're creating with Maya. After all, there aren't many people who have the privilege of realizing their dreams and visions!

What You Will Learn from This Book

Maya is an amazingly rich, full-featured 3D graphics and animation package that uses the tremendous power of today's computers to produce amazing images and animations. Maya's dynamics engine, for example, puts the "real" world of gravity, wind, collisions, and such on your computer, allowing you to create very realistic (or not so realistic) animations in a straightforward manner. While Maya has amazing power and depth, it presents this in a user interface that is both logical and consistent enough for you to learn quickly, and flexible enough to adapt to the needs of your particular workflow.

Mastering Maya 3 is a comprehensive, practical guide to every major aspect of the program. Rather than work through what every radio button or check box does without grounding this knowledge in practice, this book presents Maya's tools in a hands-on manner, showing not only what everything does, but why you would want to use a tool in a specific way. Additionally, through a number of real-world projects, you will learn how to use Maya efficiently for your creative needs, so you won't have to figure out optimal workflow on your own.

You'll begin with a tour of the user interface and its tools for optimizing your workflow. Then you'll learn the basics of computer modeling and the major types of modeling available in Maya: NURBS, polygon, and subdivision surfaces. You'll next work through different modes of animation, including Maya's new Trax nonlinear animation. After this, you'll learn how to texture, light, and render scenes out to take best advantage of Maya's rendering engine. Finally, you'll learn about Maya's advanced tools: particle dynamics and the Paint Effects tool.

Who Should Read This Book

This book is intended for a range of Maya users, from beginners to experts, and there is something in *Mastering Maya 3* for everyone, but we expect most readers will be in the advanced beginner or intermediate range. We assume that most people who invest in a professional-quality 3D graphics program (and the hardware on which to run it) are serious about 3D animation. We assume you have already done some work with 3D modeling, animation, and rendering, and are now ready to hone your skills and take advantage of the breakthroughs that Maya makes available. You may be working in a production environment already, or in a training or educational program, or in a related field and preparing to make the jump to 3D modeling and animation. In any case, whether you're a neophyte or guru, you will certainly learn something here, whether it's how to use the Maya interface or some cool new way of performing a complex task.

If you're a relative beginner, or feel your background in the fundamentals of Maya and 3D animation has a few holes in it, you should start from the beginning and work through the first sections of the book. Here you will learn how to create a human model from the ground up, texture it, add a skeletal control system to it, and animate and render it. You will also learn how to create a living environment, a pet dog, and everyday objects for your character to interact with.

Users at the intermediate level will find plenty of interest beyond the fundamentals. Two chapters introduce the MEL scripting language, giving you the key to unlocking Maya's full automation power. As you'll see, you don't need to learn the entire language to customize your workspace and automate repetitive tasks to make your workflow more efficient. The last five chapters provide an introduction to the Paint Effects 3D modeling tool and an in-depth look at Maya's particle dynamics.

Even if you're beyond the beginner level, you can find valuable information in practically every chapter. Scan through the table of contents to find the topics that interest you most, or check through the "What's New" section below for a list of the most significant new features of Maya 3, along with references to the chapter in which we introduce these new features. No matter what level 3D artist you are, you will find valuable, even exciting projects, tips, and techniques. As an added attraction, we have collected 24 pages of wonderful Maya art, including the results of projects from this book, as well as images from professional studio projects. All of this material should inspire you to create better, more challenging work than you might have believed yourself capable of.

How to Use This Book

Mastering Maya 3 is not just a reference manual. As working animators and 3D artists, we knew from the beginning that simply explaining the settings of menus and dialog boxes would not be an effective way for you to learn how to use the software—or for us to share insights and experiences. We knew that "hands-on" would be the best approach for learning this complex software—and for retaining that knowledge the next time you need the information. Therefore we've built each chapter around examples and tutorials that let you try out each new feature as you're studying it.

To implement this approach, we've created a fully integrated book and CD-ROM. The companion CD contains working files—Maya scene files, sketches, TIF images, and MEL scripts—that will get you started with each exercise, as well as rendered images and animations you can use to check your progress as you go. (The CD also contains some illustrations that are best viewed in color, along with some bonus material.)

Many of the exercises are intended to create production-quality work, but most can be done by anyone with a little 3D experience—and of course some patience and persistence! A few exercises are intended for more advanced users, and are identified as such.

Several of the more ambitious projects in the book (like creating and texturing a human model) span several chapters, allowing you to build up knowledge in a step-by-step manner. Even so, you do not need to read the chapters through from beginning to end: we have provided intermediate scene files that will allow you to "step into" the process at any point you wish. As with any how-to book, you can focus on the subjects that interest you or the tasks you need to accomplish first, particularly if you are already an experienced animator. However, should you find the book hard to put down once you start reading it, we won't complain!

What's New in This Edition

If you have Maya 3.0 or higher, there are a number of new features—from very small to impressively large—that grace the newest version of Alias|Wavefront's software. As you read through *Mastering Maya 3,* you will see a "New" icon (like the one at the left) any place there is a new or changed feature in Maya 3. While many of these new features are relatively small, here are some highlights of significant changes in Maya 3:

- Creating lights is now done via the Create menu, which makes the process of creating lights analogous to creating geometry, cameras, or other Maya objects. See Chapters 1 and 20.

- A new Help menu command searches for menus by keyword. See Chapter 1.

- Area light allows for light emitting from areas rather than points. See Chapters 1 and 20.

- A Performance Settings window allows for optimization of scene responsiveness. See Chapter 3.

- A pop-up shelf menu allows for quick switching of shelf tabs and access to shelf settings. See Chapter 3.

- You can now select and duplicate NURBS patches in much the same way as polygon faces. See Chapter 4.

- You can now fully model, bind, texture, and render subdivision surfaces with numerous additional functionalities. See Chapters 6 and 8.

- Subdivision surfaces can now exist in either hierarchical or polygon proxy mode. See Chapters 6 and 8.

- Artisan now includes a Paint Textures tool, for painting color, transparency, bumpiness, and other texture attributes. See Chapter 7.

- The new Trax Editor performs nonlinear animation. Creating complex, repetitive motion for games, animation series, and other purposes is where Trax really shines. See Chapter 14.

- The Automatic Mapping and Move And Sew UVs commands have greatly increased the efficiency of creating clean UV maps. See Chapter 19.

- A Movie Texture node now allows movie files to be assigned to surfaces. See Chapter 18.

- With the Transfer command, you can copy vertex or UV information from polygon to polygon. See Chapter 19.

- The displacement mapping algorithm has been greatly improved in displacement quality and tessellation efficiency. See Chapter 19.

- A Layered Texture node can add layers of textures directly and more efficiently than Layered Shader. See Chapter 19.

- Paint Effects brush strokes can be instanced as particles, allowing for random placement and movement of Paint Effects objects in a scene. See Chapter 21.

- Particles now have a built-in random lifespan setting, providing a more straightforward way to create particles that die off at random times. See Chapter 22.

- Particles can now be emitted in a volume of space, rather than from a point or from a surface. See Chapters 22 and 24.

- Fields can now be applied on a per-vertex basis, allowing fields to be associated with individual vertexes of an object or with individual particles in a particle system. This supplants the previous "add field" option when creating fields. See Chapter 25.

How This Book Is Organized

Depending on your interests and skill level, you can either study each chapter from beginning to end or start with what you need to know first. Here's a quick guide to what each part and chapter covers.

Part I: Maya Fundamentals introduces Maya and its tools with the following topics:

Chapter 1: The Maya Interface introduces the elements that make up models, windows, menus, and other parts of Maya, with quick examples of how to use these elements.

Chapter 2: Your First Maya Animation uses a hands-on example—building and launching a rocket ship—to solidify understanding of the basic elements of Maya: modeling, texturing, lighting, animation, dynamics, and rendering. This provides a good foundation if you aren't accustomed to using Maya.

In **Chapter 3: Techniques for Speeding Up Workflow,** we introduce Maya tools that allow you to work quickly and efficiently, saving screen real estate, organizing your work, and using tricks to speed up tool selection and repetitive tasks.

Part II: Modeling offers a detailed exploration of Maya's modeling techniques:

Chapter 4: Modeling Basics uses relatively simple objects to introduce basic modeling concepts and Maya's way of implementing them. The example projects are a great way to learn about construction history and other aspects of Maya's modeling tool kit.

In **Chapter 5: NURBS Modeling** we open up the world of NURBS modeling, showing what elements make up a NURBS curve or surface, how to edit them, and finally how to apply these concepts by modeling an aftershave bottle and a human face.

Chapter 6: Polygons and Subdivision Surfaces explores the basic ingredients for creating and editing polygons and subdivision surfaces. Various techniques are employed to create a hand in polygons; then another project deals with completing the human head from the previous chapter as a subdivision surface.

In **Chapter 7: Working with Artisan**, you will be given a guided tour of Artisan. You'll learn why it's such a useful set of tools and what you can do with it besides just "denting" your models, and you'll get a preview of MEL scripting in Artisan's MEL script painting function.

All the work you've done so far leads up to **Chapter 8: Organic Modeling.** In this chapter, we show you how to take a dog from a sketch to a finished NURBS patch model, and we finish building the human character using subdivision surfaces.

Part III: Animation shows how to add motion to the models you've created:

Chapter 9: Animating in Maya is where you will learn all you need to know to get started creating, controlling, and editing animation in Maya. The hands-on project will teach you how to animate fingers by using Set Driven Keys.

In **Chapter 10: Paths and Bones** you are introduced to setting up skeletons correctly, and how to animate cameras and objects quickly with motion paths. The hands-on project sets up the human character for animation.

Chapter 11: Deformers shows how to use the many deformers in Maya to aid in modeling and animating efficiently. You will also discover how to create facial animation, learning in that process how to create proper facial expressions and phonemes.

Chapter 12: Binding introduces you to the two different skinning processes available in Maya for binding a character to skeletons. The hands-on tutorials will take you through binding the human character and the puppy model created in earlier chapters.

Chapter 13: Character Animation Exercises introduces and explains walk cycles, both two-legged and four-legged, going through the fundamentals of animation in the process. In addition to a walk cycle, we teach you how to animate a run cycle and catching and throwing a ball. The Maya Character setup feature is also covered in detail.

Chapter 14: Nonlinear Animation Using the Trax Editor introduces the new Maya 3 Trax Editor and shows how to use this new tool to create poses and "clips" of animations that can then be used as often as needed to create everything from walk cycles to facial animations and lip synching.

In **Chapter 15: Working with Rigid Body Dynamics** you will learn about animation using Maya's dynamics engine instead of traditional keyframing techniques. You'll learn what rigid bodies are and how to control them, and you'll put them to use in real-world examples like animating a pair of dice being tossed. You will learn how to use fields and forces for different results, and how to "bake" the animation when you are done, speeding up interactivity and ensuring that no discrepancies occur during batch-rendering.

Part IV: Working with MEL shows how to make the Maya Embedded Language work for you, even if you're not a programmer:

Chapter 16: MEL Basics is a jumping-off point for beginning MEL users, ending with examples that put the theory into practice.

Chapter 17: Programming with MEL takes MEL scripting further, showing you how to create, debug, and edit full-blown MEL scripts and MEL interfaces.

Part V: Rendering takes you through the details of producing rendered images and animations:

Chapter 18: Rendering Basics explores the way Maya defines a rendered image, how to use IPR (Interactive Photorealistic Renderer), image planes, and proper use of Depth of Field. You will also learn how to set up multiple-pass renders that allow changes to be made quickly and without rerendering the entire animation.

With **Chapter 19: Shading and Texturing Surfaces** you will learn how to texture surfaces correctly the first time using the Hypershade and how to create a number of effects using various networks of render nodes. Polygon texturing and UV mapping are also extensively covered. As hands-on exercises, we texture the dog model and the clothing and skin of the human model from previous chapters.

Chapter 20: Lighting examines the Maya lighting system, the shadow types available, how to add effects to lights, and proper studio lighting of your subjects. You will learn how to balance speed and quality with Depth Mapped shadows and when to use raytraced shadows, as well as how to create fog, light color, glow, and halo effects.

Part VI: Advanced Maya Effects extends your Maya skills to work with particles and soft bodies, as well as the Paint Effects tool:

Chapter 21: Paint Effects takes you into the world of Maya's tube-based scene-generating tool. You will learn what's possible with Paint Effects and what the hundreds of attributes mean, to help you understand and use Paint Effects to its fullest potential. The tutorial that ends the chapter takes you step-by-step through adding real hair to the child model.

In **Chapter 22: Particle Basics** we introduce you to Maya's dynamic particles engine. You will learn what particles are, how and when to use them, and how to control them. Throughout the chapter are a number of practical examples that are built upon in the next chapters.

Then, in **Chapter 23: Particle Rendering,** we show you the different ways to render particles, the differences between hardware and software rendering, and why each type of particle render has its own place in your rendering pipeline.

With **Chapter 24: Using Particle Expressions and Ramps** we expand our understanding and control of particles, as we show you how to add expressions and ramps to grow and move the particles, as well as to define their radii and other particle attributes, and how to control what happens to particles at death.

Chapter 25: Dynamics of Soft Bodies takes the particle and rigid body knowledge you have gained in the previous chapters, and puts it to use in soft body simulation. We cover Goal Weights, springs, constraints, and more. The chapter concludes with two great uses of soft bodies: simulated water ripples from a fountain and a water tentacle out of science fiction.

Finally, the **Appendix** offers some food for thought as Perry Harovas and John Kundert-Gibbs interview luminaries in animation and computer graphics.

You'll learn about how Maya was created and the challenges it faces; and how Maya was and is being used at Industrial Light & Magic for movies such as *Galaxy Quest*.

Conventions Used in This Book

Throughout the book, the following symbols will help you find specific information when you need it and accelerate your ability to learn Maya.

This is a Tip. Tips are helpful hints that demonstrate efficient, effective procedures to accomplish your task.

This is a Warning. Warnings alert you to bugs, hazards, and other potential problems or areas where you need to proceed with caution.

Throughout the book, this symbol flags the places where you can take advantage of files on the CD-ROM—project files or starter sketches for the hands-on exercises, color versions of selected illustrations, and animation clips.

This symbol identifies features that are new in Maya 3. If you're familiar with previous versions of Maya and want to skim a topic for the latest changes, look for this marker.

This Is a Sidebar

Sidebars develop specific ideas and expand upon information that is akin to the chapter's primary information. Sidebars also present related troubleshooting techniques and sources for additional information.

Hardware and Software Considerations

While computer systems continue to improve dramatically year after year, Maya is one of the most demanding applications you can run on a desktop machine; it thus requires specialized system configurations to maximize Maya's performance. Maya 3 is available on Windows NT and 2000, and IRIX, and will shortly be available on Mac OS X (a batch rendering engine is available for the Linux OS). Alias|Wavefront has been able to implement the same feature set and user interface on each platform, so all of the information in this book applies to both Windows and IRIX platforms. (Because the Macintosh version is not yet released, we cannot speak to how completely Maya translates to this platform, but Alias|Wavefront's stated goal is to have feature and interface parity.) The CD-ROM accompanying the book, however, has only been tested on Windows, so we cannot guarantee that all parts will work exactly as described on IRIX or Mac systems.

Alias|Wavefront provides a qualification chart in the printed documentation and on its Web site (`www.aliaswavefront.com/en/Community/Jump/qual_charts.jhtml`), certifying particular combinations of processors, operating system versions, graphics cards, and drivers for operation with Maya. Before purchasing any new system to run Maya, be sure to check this chart for your configuration.

Alias|Wavefront lists the following *minimum* hardware requirements for running Maya on Windows; to work at a comfortable level of interactivity, you'll probably want more processor speed, RAM, and disk space.

- Pentium II processor

- 128MB RAM (256MB strongly suggested)

- CD-ROM drive

- High-performance graphics card. See the qualification chart for an up-to-date list of acceptable cards.

- Hardware lock or Ethernet lock provided by Alias|Wavefront with Maya

- Three-button mouse with proper mouse driver software

- Sound card (optional)

- Graphics tablet (optional)

- Disk space as follows for an NTFS file system (space requirements are much greater on a FAT system):

  - 220MB for Maya Complete

  - 300MB for Maya Unlimited

  - 15MB or more temporary space on the install drive to start the installation process

The following are minimum software requirements for Windows.

- Windows NT 4.0 (with Service Pack 4 or greater) or Windows 2000

- TCP/IP network software (for batch rendering and other features)

- Web browser: the latest version of Netscape Navigator or Internet Explorer suggested

- The latest graphics card driver software (available from the card manufacturer's Web site)

- Appropriate driver software for optional hardware (like a tablet)

The Next Step

By the time you finish *Mastering Maya 3*, you'll be well on your way to mastery of Maya 3. A number of chapters offer suggestions for further reading related to animation and 3D graphics, and to some of the most important Web sites in the field. Be sure to check these sites, as well as the Sybex Web site (www.sybex.com) for updates on Maya 3, as well as for bonus materials and further information.

As you work through this book and begin exploring Maya on your own, you'll probably think of topics you'd like to see us cover in future editions of this book, as well as other improvements we might make. You can use www.sybex.com to provide feedback; or you can send feedback directly to the authors: John Kundert-Gibbs (jkundert@unca.edu) and Peter Lee (peterlee3d@yahoo.com). We welcome your feedback and look forward to hearing from you!

Now it's up to you to make the most of the tools that Maya offers. Have fun, work hard, and remember that the most important tool you have as an artist is your imagination—so get out there and make yourself proud!

Part I
Maya Fundamentals

In This Part

Maya (from the Sanskrit word for "world of illusion") is a program designed to produce groundbreaking, photo-realistic models and animations. Built into this program are an abundance of tools and "subtools" that can overwhelm even the most wizened old 3D artist. To make all of Maya's tools work together in a logical, consistent, and intuitive manner is a monumental task that continues with version 3 of the program. Still, the basic structure of the Maya interface is not only solid enough for most users to quickly learn and use, it is so intuitive that several other 3D software manufacturers are busy copying much of Maya's look.

In Part I of this book, you will learn the fundamentals of interacting with Maya's user interface. If you are already very familiar with the Maya interface, you may wish to skim these chapters; however, we will cover several aspects of the program that have changed in version 3, so a little time spent leafing through these pages may help you get up to speed with the new release. If you are new to Maya, reading these three chapters should help you better understand how you can work effectively with Maya and its interface. After working through this section, you should be well prepared for the more advanced parts of this book.

The Maya Interface

MAYA

Chapter 1

3D modeling and animation are among the most challenging tasks a person can do. Trying to get your vision of a universe transferred into pixels is part science, part art, and a great deal of perseverance. Fortunately, the engineers at Alias|Wavefront have spent a great deal of time and energy making Maya as helpful and transparent to use as a complex program can be. Still, with a program as large and complex as Maya, a good introduction to the program's components can be very helpful in getting the most from your work as quickly as possible. This chapter explores Maya's user interface, examining each element of the work environment in turn. After reading through the chapter, you should have a good understanding of the major parts of Maya's GUI (graphical user interface), as well as how to utilize these parts in your modeling and animation work. Topics include:

- Introducing Maya 3
- What's behind the Maya interface?
- Scene windows
- Scene objects
- Window layouts
- The hotbox
- Menus
- Shelves
- The Outliner and Hypergraph
- The Channel box/Attribute Editor
- The Timeline
- The Command line/Feedback line and the Script Editor

What's New in Maya 3

While the Maya interface may at first glance appear much as it did in version 2, there are a number of subtle changes to it, evidence of the growing maturity of Maya's user interface. Here are some highlights of the revised interface:

- The Create menu now allows you to create lights, in addition to cameras, utilities, and geometry.

- A new Find Menu item (Help ➜ Find Menu) allows you to search for a menu item you cannot find.

- The Display menu now consolidates all display elements (e.g., UI element display) into one menu.

- Maya Complete now contains global stitching, area lighting, and volume particle emitters, and particles can accept Paint Effects brush strokes for texturing.

- Maya's Status line now contains Render and IPR Render buttons, and groups of buttons can be minimized by clicking their dividing lines.

- The numeric input box (on the Status line in Maya 3) has a pull-down menu with several options, including text-based object selection (using wildcard characters), renaming, and relative and absolute positioning of selected objects.

- A tab selector and pull-down menu on the shelf allow faster access to shelf options and tabs.

What's Behind the Maya Interface?

What makes Maya different? First, interacting with it is a straightforward process, for several reasons. All scene windows, plus the Hypershade and Hypergraph windows, are easily navigated via the same keyboard and mouse combinations for zooming, tracking, and rotation (rotation only works in perspective camera views). Because navigating works the same way in all windows, you only have to learn one set of commands to get around Maya's world. Moving objects around a Maya scene window is similarly intuitive: select the Move, Scale, or Rotate (or any other) tool, grab a manipulator handle (or the center box, to move on all axes simultaneously), and alter the object. To try out an example, you can create a new scene in Maya, add a ball (by clicking the sphere object in the toolbar, or by choosing Create ➜ NURBS Primitives ➜ Sphere). Now rotate around the ball by holding the Alt key down and pressing the left mouse button. This type of rotation is known as *camera*, or *scene* rotation. To rotate the ball itself, choose the Rotate tool from the toolbar (or simply press the E key on the keyboard), and then choose any of the manipulator rings around the ball and rotate it by dragging with the left mouse button, as in Figure 1.1. To move an object, choose the Move tool (or press the W key). To scale, choose the Scale tool (or press the R key).

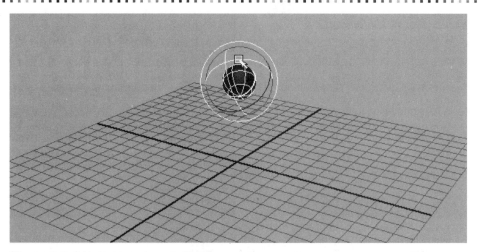

Figure 1.1 *Rotating a sphere in Maya*

Three-Button Mouse Conventions in Maya

Maya makes extensive use of all three mouse buttons. This book—as well as the Maya manuals—uses a shorthand notation to describe the basic mouse operations:

Click, or **LM click**, means to click (press and release) with the left mouse button.

Drag, or **LM drag**, means to click the left mouse button, hold it down, and drag.

Shift+click means to LM click, hold down the Shift key, and click another item.

Choose means to either click or hold down the left mouse button and choose an item from a menu.

MM drag means to click and drag with the middle mouse button.

RM choose means to hold the right mouse button down (in a specified area) and choose an item from the pop-up contextual menu.

Rotate (Tumble) view means to rotate the (perspective) camera; that is, hold the Alt key and the left mouse button down, and then drag in the perspective window to rotate the view.

Move view means to move (any) camera; that is, hold the Alt key and the middle mouse button down, and then drag in any scene window to move the view.

Scale view means to scale—or zoom—(any) camera; that is, hold the Alt key and the left and middle mouse buttons down, and then drag in any scene window to scale (or zoom) the view in or out.

Another powerful difference between Maya and other packages lies in how you interact with Maya's user interface. There are nearly always two or more ways to accomplish a task—called *workflows*—in Maya. For example, if you prefer not to use menus on top of the screen, you can use Maya's hotbox (which is itself customizable) to access all menus, or any grouping therein by merely pressing and holding the space bar, as in Figure 1.2. (The Cloth and Maya Live menus shown in Figure 1.2 are available only in Maya Unlimited; Maya Complete users won't see them.)

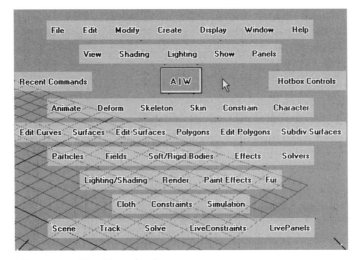

Figure 1.2 The Maya hotbox

You can also, as noted before, create items via the toolbar or, equivalently, via menu commands. Most impressive, however, is that Maya will let you decide how you interact with it. If you are not satisfied with Maya's interface, you have many ways in which you can alter it, including creating marking menus, toolbar buttons, and hot keys. All of these can be created fairly quickly (especially the toolbar buttons) but can contain extremely complex instructions.

For more on how to tune Maya's GUI for your own work, see Chapter 3, "Techniques for Speeding Up Workflow," or Chapter 16, "MEL Basics."

Finally, Maya's plug-in architecture (its API, or application programming interface) and especially its built-in scripting language, MEL, are very open and comprehensive. Because of Maya's API, plug-ins (like the built-in Artisan and FX) fit seamlessly into the program, so much so that it is often difficult to determine where the main program stops and the plug-in begins. While the API is fairly complex and is best left to knowledgeable programmers, MEL (or *Maya Embedded Language*) is a reasonably simple scripting language that gives just about anyone with a bit of programming experience access to nearly all of Maya's very powerful features in the graphical user environment. Not only can you create specialized, time-saving scripts with MEL, you can also create entire windows, or even a whole new GUI for the program (because Maya's entire GUI is built on MEL scripts in the first place). This feature can enable, for example, a technical director to create a custom interface for her artists, allowing them to deal with character animation without their having to know anything about the low-level details of the construction and "stringing" (or animation setup) of the character.

As should be obvious from these features, Maya provides a very modern, intuitive, and customizable environment for you. Whether you have a shop of one person or one hundred, Maya's adjustable interface will get you building complex animations far more quickly than other—even more expensive—packages. Let's now take a more thorough tour through the Maya interface, looking at several important areas of the GUI.

Interface Elements

Although there are many elements composing Maya, they can be grouped into about nine categories. We will quickly examine each category in turn.

Scene Windows

The scene windows are your primary interface with the objects (and lights and cameras) you create. When you open a new Maya scene, it opens the default configuration, which is one large scene window (the default perspective camera), alongside the Channel box, similar to what is shown in Figure 1.3.

 If you prefer, you can have the Channel box toggle with the Attribute Editor (rather than having the Attribute Editor float in a separate window). Should you wish to toggle the two windows, choose Window → Settings/Preferences → Preferences, and select the Open Attribute Editor In Main Maya Window radio button.

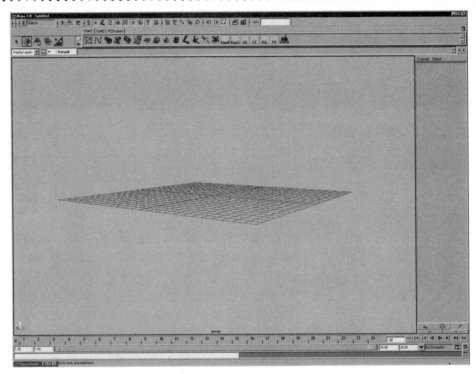

Figure 1.3 *The Maya user interface*

Once the default window is open, you can make the perspective view the active window by clicking anywhere inside the window. When this (or any) window is selected, its borders turn blue. At this point, you can rotate, scale, or translate the view to adjust what you see in this window (for specifics on how to do this, please see the earlier sidebar on mouse conventions). The default scene window is called the *persp* (for perspective) view and is simply the view from the default perspective camera that Maya builds upon opening a new scene.

You can build other perspective cameras by choosing Create ➜ Camera. To view the scene through this new camera, choose Panels ➜ Perspective ➜ camera1.

In addition to the default perspective camera, Maya also creates three *orthographic* views—top, side, and front—that you can also see (in what's called a "four view" window) by selecting the perspective window and then quickly pressing and releasing the space bar, as shown in Figure 1.4.

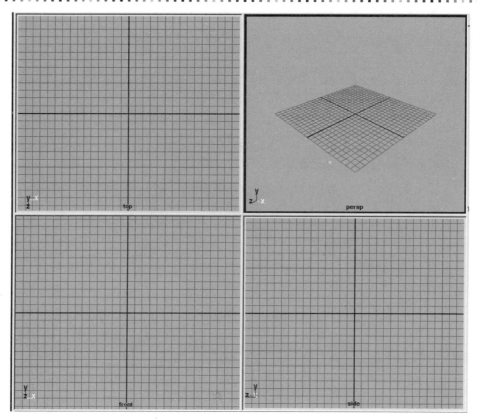

Figure 1.4 *The four-view display*

Orthographic and Perspective Views

An orthographic view is a nonperspective view from a 90 degree (or orthogonal) angle. Because these are not perspective views, they do not reduce the size of objects as they move away from the camera. A perspective view of a row of columns, for example, would show the back column as smaller than the one nearest the camera. An orthographic view, on the other hand, will show all columns as the same size, as there is no scale reduction (perspective) in this view. An orthographic view may be thought of as similar to a blueprint drawing, while a perspective view is like a camera picture.

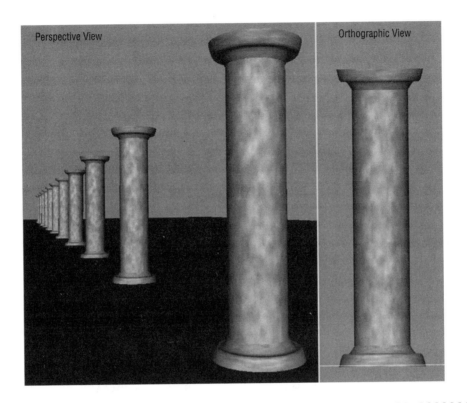

To make one of the orthographic views fill the screen, click in it (to select this window), and press and release the space bar again. Being able to switch quickly between different view layouts and window sizes greatly speeds up your workflow in Maya, as no extensive menu selection process is required to rapidly change views.

To switch views in Maya without losing your current selection, MM click in the view you wish to activate (e.g., the front view), then press the space bar.

Moving in Scene Windows

Moving around scene windows is fairly straightforward, once you learn the key and mouse combinations for doing so. Additionally, because you move in all scene windows (plus the Hypergraph, Hypershade, and Trax windows) using these same commands, once you learn how to move in one window, you can move in all. As the perspective window has the most options (you can rotate, or tumble, the view as well as zoom and translate), let's quickly look at how to maneuver around the default perspective window.

Open a new scene in Maya; then hold down the Alt key and the left mouse button and drag the mouse around. The scene should spin around as you drag the mouse.

If the scene does not rotate as you drag (you may see the cursor become a circle with a line through it), you may be in an orthographic view, which does not allow rotations. To move to a perspective view, hit the space bar to show the four-view layout; then click in the perspective window (top right) and hit the space bar again.

To translate a scene (move up/down or left/right), hold the Alt key down once again, hold down the middle mouse button (MMB), and drag the mouse around. You will see the scene move around with the mouse movements. (Note that the camera is actually moving opposite to your mouse movements: as you drag right, the camera moves left, so the objects appear to move right. You can see this clearly if you make cameras visible and look at the camera in a different view as you drag.)

To scale your view (zoom the camera in and out), hold down the Alt key once again, hold down both the left and middle mouse buttons, and drag. As you drag right, the scene grows larger (you're zooming in); as you drag left, the scene grows smaller (you're zooming out). If you wish to quickly zoom into a specific area of your scene, hold down the Alt and Ctrl keys, then drag (with the left mouse button only) a box around the area of the scene you are interested in, starting on the left side. When you release the mouse, the scene will zoom in, covering the area you outlined. If you drag the mouse from right to left, the scene will zoom out so that the entire scene window you start with fits into the box you drag (the smaller your box, the further out you zoom). If you now open the Hypergraph or Hypershade (Window ➔ Hypergraph or Window ➔ Hypershade), you can use the same key/mouse combinations to scale or move around either of these windows. You will note, however, that you cannot rotate either of these views, as this would accomplish nothing useful.

You can think of the Alt key as the "scene movement key." Whenever you hold down the Alt key, you are in scene manipulation mode, rather than in object manipulation (or some other) mode. The consistent use of the Alt key for scene movement is just one more example of the thought that has gone into the Maya interface.

Scene Objects

Scene *objects* (geometry, curves, cameras, and lights) are the fundamental building blocks from which you create a Maya scene or animation. The procedure for creating and manipulating any object is generally the same: create the object (most often in the

Create menu), choose a manipulation tool (like Translate or Rotate), and alter the object. You can also adjust the pivot point (or "center") of an object, and you can manipulate the individual components of geometric objects.

Creating Scene Objects

Because most scene objects are created in very much the same fashion, we'll go through a few representative examples here, rather than a thorough examination of how to create all possible objects in Maya. Should you have specific questions about creating a type of object that is not covered here, you can always check Maya's online documentation (accessed via the Help menu).

Maya's built-in help files are a great (and easy) resource. To access them, just choose Library (or the specific aspect of the program you are interested in) from the Help menu. You can also press F1 to access the main Help library. After opening the Maya Library window (which will open in a Web browser, as it is an HTML document), you will be able to search for a term, browse through a complete index of all Maya documents (the index alone is nearly 2MB of data!), or read any of the Maya manuals in electronic form.

To create a piece of geometry (a sphere or cone, for example), you choose the type of geometry you wish to create from the Create menu. For a simple three-dimensional object (like a torus or a cube), you can choose from either polygonal or NURBS primitives. Using the NURBS option, you can also select a two-dimensional (non-surface) square or circle. When you create an object, you can either use the last saved settings or open the Creation Options window and adjust the object's settings to what you desire before creating it.

NURBS (or Non-Uniform Rational B-Spline) objects are created via a series of curves (or "isoparms") that are mathematically derived from several points (control vertices, or CVs). NURBS surfaces are more complex to calculate, but they can be warped and twisted more before they show excessive unnatural creasing. Polygonal surfaces, on the other hand, are created by placing many small triangular or rectangular surfaces together. Polys are simpler to calculate—at least for simple surfaces—but tend to show their constituent blocks if they are bent or distorted too much—especially if the surfaces are created with a minimal number of polygons, or facets. NURBS surfaces tend to be better suited to organic forms (like bodies), while polygonal surfaces generally work better for more mechanical objects (like space ships); but this is by no means a hard-and-fast rule.

As an example, let's create a default polygonal sphere, and then use the option box to create a NURBS cylinder. To create the poly sphere, simply choose Create ➜ Polygon Primitives ➜ Sphere. On releasing the mouse, you should see a sphere appear at the center of Maya's default grid. If you look closely, you will note that the sphere consists of many rectangular objects (more accurately called quadrilaterals) that butt up against each other, forming the sphere. Now move the sphere aside (press the W key and move the sphere away from the center of the grid) and create a NURBS cylinder with nondefault options. To access the option window of the NURBS cylinder, choose Create ➜ NURBS Primitives ➜ Cylinder ❏ (choosing the ❏ symbol—the *option box*— in a Maya menu item always brings up an option window). Upon releasing the mouse button, you should see the window shown in Figure 1.5.

This window provides a great number of options. You can define any of the following:

- the pivot point

- the axis the cylinder will use as its long axis

- the start and end angles of the cylinder

- the radius

- the height-to-radius ratio (a higher number will make a taller cylinder)

- the number of spans (vertical pieces) and sections (horizontal pieces) the cylinder has

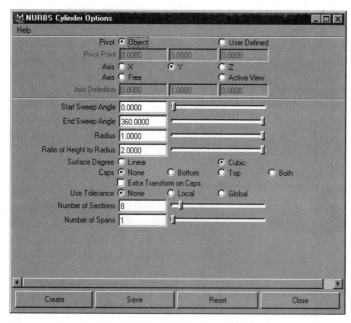

Figure 1.5 *The NURBS Cylinder Options window*

For the purposes of this little example, try setting the End Sweep Angle to 270 (this will create a three-quarters cylinder), the Height to Radius to 4 (making the cylinder taller), and set the Caps option to Both (creating a cap on both the top and bottom of the cylinder). When you click the Create button at the bottom, you should get the object shown in Figure 1.6.

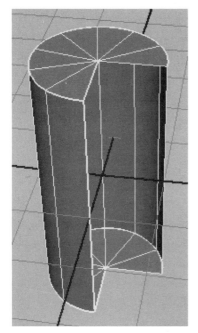

Figure 1.6 *A cylinder created using custom options*

You can almost always reset an object's creation settings to their default values by choosing Edit ➜ Reset Settings in the options window.

To see the object smooth shaded with textures (instead of a wireframe), press the 6 key on your keyboard (not the numeric keypad). To view an object at a higher interactive resolution, press the 3 key (pressing these keys will not affect how the object renders, only how it is displayed). Figure 1.6 uses these settings to display the cylinder.

Creating a camera object is as simple as creating a geometry object. Choose Create ➜ Camera and a new perspective camera (initially called camera1, camera2, and so on, until you save them with more specific names) is created. To adjust the camera's options as you create it, choose the option box (□), and change the camera's settings. While all the settings in the camera option window are a bit much for an introductory chapter, most are fairly self-explanatory to anyone familiar with photography or 3D animation.

For more on camera options, please see Chapter 18, "Rendering Basics."

Some notable options are that you can make any new camera orthographic (as opposed to perspective), you have control over near and far clipping planes (where the camera stops "seeing" objects that are too far away or too close), and you can choose to have two or three nodes on the camera (allowing you to manipulate where the camera is looking, for example, via a manipulator handle outside the camera itself). Try creating a camera with two nodes (under Animation options). When you create this camera, shown in Figure 1.7, it will automatically have a second manipulator handle for a new view node that you can move (by pressing the W key and dragging the handle around), and the camera follows where the manipulator handle goes.

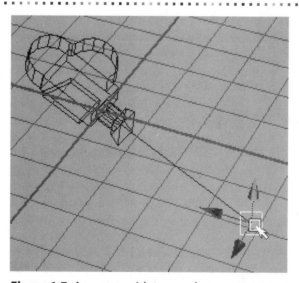

Figure 1.7 *A camera with two nodes*

To create lights, choose Create ➜ Lights and select the type of light you wish to use. When creating lights, you can choose from Ambient (a light that fills all space evenly, like indirect sunlight in a room), Directional (parallel light rays from one source, mimicking direct sunlight), Point (radial light like that from a bare light bulb), Spot (light as from a theatrical spot light), and the new Area Light (light emitted from a rectangular area that imitates a block light source like a window). For example, create a spot light (Lights ➜ Create Spot Light ❏) with the following options: Intensity 1.5, Cone Angle 50, Penumbra 10, and Color a light blue (click the default white color chip to bring up the color picker; then choose a light blue color). The penumbra controls how quickly your spotlight "fades out" around its edges: a value of 0 means that the spotlight goes from full intensity to 0 at its edges (not a very natural look); a value of 10 or 20 degrees makes the spotlight fade out from full intensity to 0 over that number of degrees. If your spotlight were aimed at a simple plane, the rendered image would look something like the light on the right in Figure 1.8 (the one on the left is a spotlight with a penumbra of 0).

Figure 1.8 *Two spotlights: the left-hand one has no penumbra, while the right has a Penumbra setting of 10 degrees.*

To see how an area light works, create a sphere, stretch it out, and add an area light (be sure its direction vector is pointing at the sphere). Stretch the area light out, and in the Attribute Editor set the light's decay rate to Quadratic. As you move the light (very) close to the sphere, you will see an oblong of light appear on the sphere, shown in Figure 1.9, matching the points where the light is closest to the sphere. Use the IPR renderer (click the IPR icon in the status bar) to see the light's effect change as you adjust its attributes.

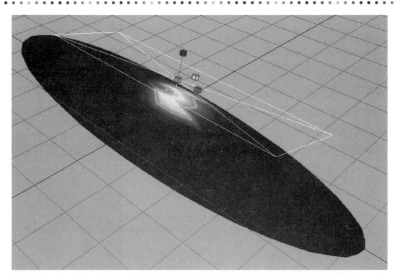

Figure 1.9 *A new area light shining on a distorted sphere*

For more on creating and using lights, see Chapter 20, "Lighting."

You can also create either CV (control vertex) or EP (Edit Point) curves via the Create menu (Create ➜ CV Curve Tool or EP Curve Tool). The CV Curve tool creates a CV with each click of the mouse. The EP Curve tool creates edit points as you click the mouse button. Control vertices lie off the curve they control, while edit points lie on the curve. Each type of curve tool is useful under certain circumstances—the basic rule of thumb is that for smoother curves, you should use the CV Curve tool, while for more tightly controlled curves use the EP Curve tool. In Figure 1.10, matching a CV curve and an EP curve created with identical mouse clicks, note that the CV curve (on the left) is smoother, its extremes much less pronounced than the EP curve (on the right), as the CV curve is not forced to pass through each point you define, whereas the EP curve must.

For more on creating and using curves, see Chapter 6, "Polygons and Subdivision Surfaces."

After an EP curve is created, it is automatically converted into a CV curve. You can see this by switching to component mode and noting that the edit points have changed into CVs, and that their position is no longer the same.

To create, say, a CV curve, choose Create ➜ CV Curve Tool (or click the CV Curve Tool button on Shelf1), and then click several times in the scene window with the mouse. You can also drag the points around as you create them, and you can

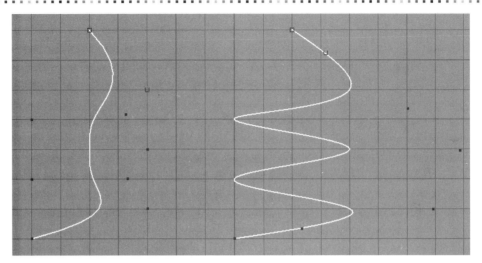

Figure 1.10 *A curve produced with the CV Curve tool on the left, and one produced with the EP Curve tool on the right*

erase points by hitting the Delete or Backspace key, or by pressing the Z key to undo the last action. When you are satisfied with the curve, hit the Enter key, and the curve is constructed.

Moving Scene Objects

Once you have created an object, you will probably wish to move, rotate, and/or scale it. Because the procedures are the same for all objects (and lights, cameras, and curves), let's just use a cylinder as an example here. Create a new cylinder with default options (Create → NURBS Primitives → Cylinder ❏; then choose Edit → Reset Settings, and click the Create button). To move this cylinder, press the W key on the keyboard—you should now see a *Move tool manipulator handle* that allows you to move the cylinder on any or all axes, as shown in Figure 1.11.

If you do not see the manipulator handle, be sure the cylinder is highlighted, by clicking (or click+dragging) it.

To move the cylinder on the X axis only, click and drag the red arrow; to move on the Y axis, click and drag the green arrow; to move on the Z axis, click and drag the blue arrow. To move the object freely in all directions, click and drag the yellow box at the center of the manipulator handles. Try moving the object up a little on the Y axis and to the right on the X axis.

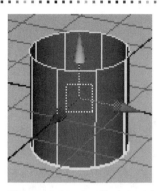

Figure 1.11 *A cylinder with Move tool manipulator handles*

All manipulator handle colors are consistent with the axis marker, on the bottom-left of a scene window—X is red, Y is green, and Z is blue. This consistency lets you know what axis you are adjusting, no matter from what angle you are viewing the scene.

To scale the cylinder, press the R key, and then scale the object on the X (red), Y (green), or Z (blue) axis—or click and drag the yellow box at the center of the manipulator to scale on all axes simultaneously. Try scaling the cylinder up on the Y axis and then out in all directions, until you get something like Figure 1.12.

To rotate the cylinder, press the E key, and then rotate around the X (red), Y (green), or Z (blue) axes—or click the yellow circle on the outside to rotate on all axes at once (rotating on all axes at once is difficult to control and therefore not advisable). Try rotating clockwise on the Z axis and then counter-clockwise on the X axis, as in Figure 1.13.

Manipulator controls have their shortcut keys arranged so that they follow the top row of a QWERTY keyboard—Q for Select, W for Move, E for Rotate, R for Scale, T for the Manipulator tool, and Y for the Last Used tool (like the CV Curve tool, for example). This layout makes the manipulator tools very easy to access, and it's easy to remember their shortcut keys.

Finally, it is possible to move the pivot point of your cylinder (or any object) so that it is not in the object's center. To move the pivot point, press the Insert key on your keyboard (turning the manipulator handle into the pivot-point handle); then move the handle to where you want the object's center of rotation, movement, or scaling to be. Try moving the pivot point of the cylinder to its bottom, as shown in Figure 1.14, so that any further rotation will occur from that point.

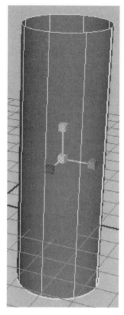

Figure 1.12 *A moved and scaled cylinder*

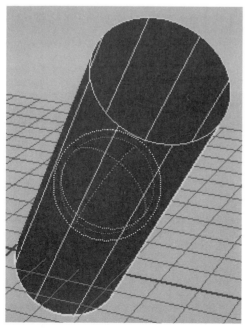

Figure 1.13 *The cylinder, rotated*

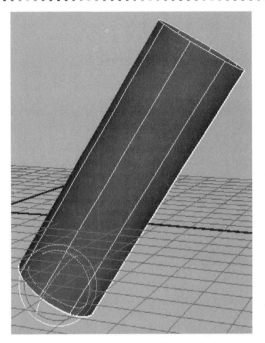

Figure 1.14 *The cylinder, with its pivot point moved to the bottom*

Once you have moved the pivot point, you must return the manipulator to its "normal" state by pressing the Insert key once again.

Objects versus Components

All geometric objects are made up of component elements. When you are in object mode, clicking or dragging any part of an object selects the entire object. In component mode, however, you can choose specific pieces of an object to manipulate. Using the cylinder from the last section as an example (just create a default cylinder if you've deleted it), select the object (so it turns green) while in object mode and choose the Select By Component Type button in the Status line (or just press the F8 key) to change to component mode. You will now see the CVs that make up the cylinder, as shown in Figure 1.15—if you had created a polygonal cylinder, you would see the points defining the edges of the polygonal facets.

As shown below, the Select by Component Type button is on the Status line, just to the right of the word *Objects*. The leftmost of these three buttons is Select by Hierarchy; the middle button is Select by Object; the right button is Select by Component Type.

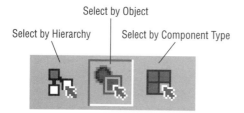

Select by Object

Select by Hierarchy   Select by Component Type

Figure 1.15 *The cylinder, with CVs displayed in component mode*

You can adjust components of an object just as you would an object itself by using the Move, Rotate, and Scale tools. Try selecting the top row of CVs on the cylinder (LM drag a square around them), then moving them up some, scaling them out on the X and Z axes, and rotating them around a bit, as shown in Figure 1.16.

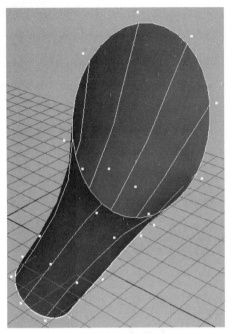

Figure 1.16 *The cylinder, with several CV components manipulated*

To select several components (CVs, facets, vertices, etc.) at once, you can drag a selection marquee around them (a selection marquee is the square box that you see when you drag in a Maya scene window). To add more components, hold down the Shift key and drag (or click) more points. (If the points are already selected, Shift+clicking or dragging them will deselect them.) Remember that you can always maneuver around the scene window (hold down the Alt key as you drag the mouse) to make selection easier.

If you now switch back to object mode, you will once again be able to choose and manipulate the entire object. Modeling (and even animation) is often a dance between object-mode and component-mode manipulation of your objects, and remembering that the F8 key switches between these two modes can be a real time saver.

Selecting by Component Type

One of the trickier aspects of Maya (at least for some) is picking the proper component of an object when in component mode. There are many types of components you can select, including CVs, hulls, faces, edges, and so forth (and there are usually several options in each of these choices), but there are only two ways to make these selections. One method is more thorough; the other is better suited to quick selections of the most common component types.

The quicker, easier method for selecting specific component types is to use a contextual menu while your mouse is over an object. To try this, create a sphere in an empty scene and then, with your mouse over the sphere, hold down the right mouse button, as shown in Figure 1.17. You will be presented with several options for component masking, plus a menu of actions you can perform on the object (such as templating or untemplating it).

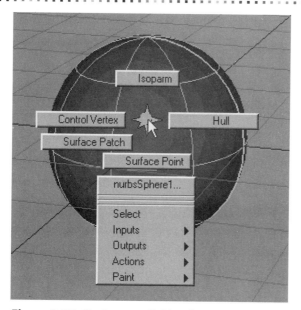

Figure 1.17 *Options available when RM clicking on a NURBS sphere*

By selecting Control Vertex (for example) from this pop-up menu, you can easily move into component selection mode for CVs, and begin manipulating your CVs as you wish. To return to object mode, press the F8 key twice.

While the contextual menu method is quick and easy, it does not give you access to all the component types you might wish to choose from. To choose a component type that's not listed in the pop-up menu, you need to use the Status line. To the right of the Object/Component text field and Hierarchy/Object/Component icons is a set of eight blue icons, each representing a class of components you can enable or disable in your selection process. To the left of these icons is a black triangle; this displays a drop-down menu where you can enable or disable all objects for selection. The component types you enable here will then be available when you drag your mouse over an object in component mode.

If you turn off all components, you will not be able to select anything in the scene window—including objects in object mode! This is a good place to look first if you discover you cannot choose any objects in a scene.

If you hold down the right mouse button on any of the blue icons, you will see a menu of subtypes you can either enable (check) or disable (uncheck) for component selection. Enabling or disabling component types is known as *selection masking,* and it's a great way to simplify the task of picking a specific object or component in a complex scene. If you are not familiar with components or selection masking, try playing around with these options in Maya before going on.

Window Layouts

In addition to the default window layout (the perspective view plus either the Channel box or the Attribute Editor), Maya provides many other built-in layouts, and—as is consistent with the Maya interface philosophy—if you wish, you can create your own.

Built-in Layouts

Maya offers two types of built-in layouts: generic layouts and prebuilt, or saved ones. Generic layouts are just basic layout elements (like a four-view layout), while saved layouts are useful combinations of the basic elements prebuilt into layouts for different purposes. To begin with, let's look at how to access a generic layout. Under the Panels → Layouts menu (accessed either via the Panels menu in the scene panel, or, as shown in Figure 1.18, from the hotbox) are several layout choices for your scene windows.

Choosing the Four layout (the first choice) will place the view you currently have active (often the perspective view) in the upper-left quadrant of a four-view layout. (Note that this is different from the layout you get by pressing the space bar, as the perspective view—or whichever view you have active—ends up in the top-right quadrant when using the space bar, but in the top left in this case). The 3 Top/Left/Right/Bottom Split views place the active window on the top (or left/right/bottom) half of the screen, then split this view into two; the other half of

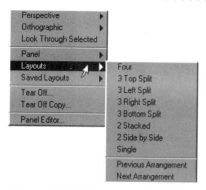

Figure 1.18 *The menu choices for generic layouts*

the screen has a single view window. The 2 Stacked or Side by Side layouts are similar, except that they don't split the active view in half (thus the active view and one other view share the screen space evenly, either top-and-bottom or left-and-right). There is also a single view, which is the same as selecting a view and pressing the space bar to make it fill the entire screen.

While the generic views can be useful (especially for building your own layouts—discussed below), the prebuilt layouts are more commonly used because they fulfil specific needs. To access the saved layouts, choose Panels ➜ Saved Layouts, as in Figure 1.19, and then select a saved layout to use.

The Single Perspective View and Four View options are the views you are already familiar with. Rather than look at each saved layout in a list, let's examine just a few— once you understand a couple of the saved layouts, the rest are fairly self-explanatory. Persp/Graph/Hypergraph is a generic Three View (as described above) with the top half split between the perspective view and the Hypergraph, while the bottom half of the screen is occupied by the Graph Editor. This view was created from the generic 3 Top Split view by changing each panel to the Perspective/Hypergraph/Graph Editor view and then saving it. The Hypershade/Outliner/Persp view is a 3 Bottom Split, with the Hypershade occupying the top half of the screen and the Outliner and perspective view splitting the bottom half. Another useful layout is the Persp/Relationship Editor layout, which stacks the perspective view on top of the Relationship Editor. If you have Maya Unlimited and the Maya Live plug-in active, there are several layouts specifically for use with Maya Live toward the bottom of the menu, including Maya Live Setup, Track, Solve, and Manual MatchMove.

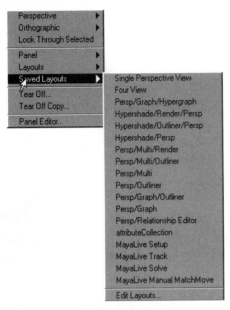

Figure 1.19 *The Saved Layouts menu*

Building Your Own Layout

If the prebuilt Maya layouts don't quite fit your needs, never fear: the final choice in the Saved Layouts menu (Edit Layouts) lets you create and save your own layout for later use. You can even erase any or all of the prebuilt layouts from the menu.

Don't erase a saved layout unless you are sure that neither you nor anyone else working on your machine is interested in using that layout any further. To get the layout back, you'll either have to reconstruct it manually or reinstall Maya.

As an example of how to create your own layout for later use, let's create a layout with the perspective view filling half the screen on the top, and the bottom split between the Hypergraph and the Hypershade. (This can be a useful layout if you need to connect several materials to several objects at a time, as selecting the objects in the perspective window can become tedious.) As with most things in Maya, you have a choice about how to create your new layout: you can either start from a generic layout or modify one of the prebuilt ones. Although starting from a prebuilt layout is often simpler, we will start from a generic layout in order to describe the whole procedure.

1. Choose Panels ➜ Layouts ➜ 3 Bottom Split.

2. Make sure the top half of the window is occupied by the perspective view (if not, select the top half and then choose Panels ➜ Perspective ➜ Persp).

3. Now select the lower-left quadrant and choose Panels ➜ Panel ➜ Hypergraph. This should turn the lower-left window into a view of the Hypergraph.

4. Finally, select the lower-right quadrant and choose Panels ➜ Panel ➜ Hypershade, turning this corner into a view of the Hypershade.

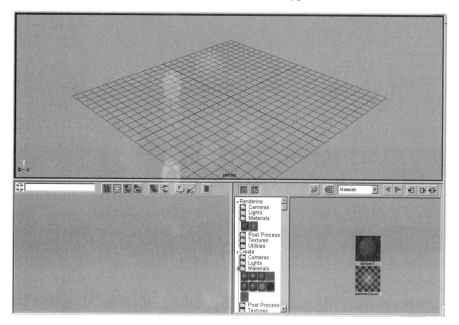

5. To save our new layout, choose Panels ➜ Saved Layouts ➜ Edit Layouts, which brings up a window with several tabs.

6. The Layouts tab should be selected (if not, choose it).

7. In the layouts tab, choose New Layout, then rename the layout from its default name (Panel Configuration 20) to something more memorable, like Persp/Hypergraph/Hypershade, and hit the Enter key to change the name.

On closing the window, your new layout will be placed at the bottom of the Saved Layouts menu. If you later choose to discard this new layout, return to the Edit Layouts menu, select the new layout, and press the Delete button.

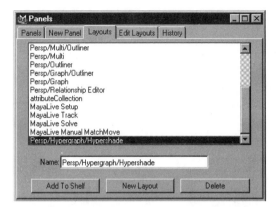

You can actually build a custom configuration directly inside the Edit Layouts menu, by using the Panels and Edit Layouts tabs. This method is more difficult than the one outlined above, however, so our recommendation is to stick with the above method.

The Hotbox

The hotbox in Maya is a tool for displaying all of the menus relevant to your work at a given moment, without taking up any screen real estate when it's not in use. While you can do everything you wish in Maya without ever using the hotbox, once you get used to the way the hotbox conserves space and puts nearly all of Maya's tools in easy reach, you'll wonder how you ever got along without it. To access the hotbox, just press (and hold) the space bar. In its default configuration, you will see something like Figure 1.20.

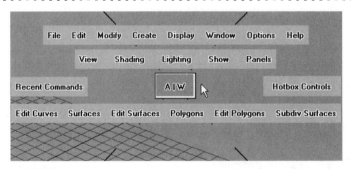

Figure 1.20 *The hotbox in its default configuration*

The top row of the hotbox always shows the general menus (the menus that are available in all menu sets), like the Window, Options, Create, and Modify menus. The second row replicates the menu set of the active panel (in this case, the perspective view), with menu items such as View, Lighting, and Panels. The third row has a Recent Commands menu (showing the last 15 commands you performed) and a Hotbox Controls menu, which allows you to fine-tune how the hotbox and general menus display their information. The bottom row of menus is, in this case, the Modeling menu set, with specialized menus for editing curves, surfaces, and polygons. In the very center of the hotbox (where the A|W logo sits) is a quick way to change views from perspective to front to side to top, as well as an options menu for how the hotbox displays. Access to all these menus is the same: press (and hold—the hotbox menus will not remain open when you release the mouse button) the left mouse button over the menu; then drag inside the new sub-menu that appears (called a *marking menu*) to select the item you wish, as in Figure 1.21, releasing the mouse when it is over your selection.

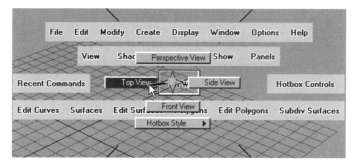

Figure 1.21 *Selecting the top view using the hotbox*

In addition to the menus you can see, there are four regions, called zones (defined by the four lines extending from the hotbox at 45-degree angles), which have special functions. The top zone allows you to quickly select from several saved layouts. The right zone allows you to toggle elements of Maya's GUI on or off (we will discuss customizing your workspace in Chapter 3). The bottom zone lets you change the selected window to any of several useful views (like the Hypergraph or the Hypershade). The left zone lets you toggle between object and component mode (mimicking the F8 key), and it also lets you toggle on and off several masking modes.

While you can use the hotbox in its default configuration, it is more useful (if a bit more cluttered) when you turn on all menu sets (Modeling, Rendering, and so on) at once. In the Hotbox Controls menu, choose Show All, which displays all menu sets at once, as shown in Figure 1.22.

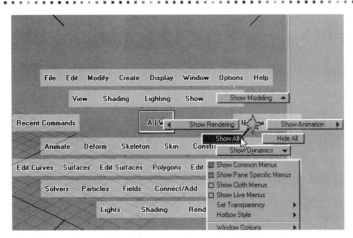

Figure 1.22 *Selecting the Show All option in the hotbox*

In this configuration, you have access to nearly all of Maya's tools in one place, and it's all available at the press of the space bar. If you are not familiar with using the hotbox, try forcing yourself to use it for all your menu choices for a couple of hours of work; you likely find that you soon prefer using the hotbox over the standard menu selection method.

Menus

While we have discussed menu sets on and off throughout this chapter, let's take a moment to look at how Maya's menus are organized. The top row of menus (or the top row in the hotbox) is split into two parts: the menus that are always present (the constant menus) and those that change according to the mode the program is in (the mode menus, like the Animation menu set, for example). Always present are File, Edit, Modify, Create, Display, Window, and Help. To change the variable menus, choose the menu set you want from the Status line (just below the menus—or under hotbox controls in the hotbox). The sets you can choose from are Modeling, Animation, Dynamics, and Rendering.

In addition to the general menus, nearly every view window in Maya has a built-in menu. The perspective view, for example, has the following menus: View, Shading, Lighting, Show, and Panels (the Show menu allows you to show and hide different types of objects). The Hypergraph view contains these menus: Edit, View, Bookmarks, Graph, Rendering, Options, Show, and Help. For perspective and orthographic views, you can either access their menus from the top of the window pane or use the second row of menus in the hotbox. For views like the Hypergraph or Hypershade, pressing and holding the right mouse button will bring up the menus (or you can use the menu across the top of the window). There are also menus for the Channel box and Attribute Editor.

Generally speaking, most windows in Maya have their own menu set, which explains why Maya doesn't just use one menu bar across the top of the screen: there are at least 100 individual menus, and there would be no space to place all these menus across one screen. Attempting to nest all these menus, on the other hand, might have taken 10 or more levels of nesting to fit all the menus into one menu bar, making the task of picking any individual menu item both laborious and baffling. Given the complexity of the task, organizing Maya's windows into contextual subsets was both a necessity and a more elegant solution to the problem.

Even so, it is often difficult to locate a menu item you have not used in a while. Fortunately Maya 3 provides a menu search function as well. Choose Help → Find Menu, then type the text of the menu (a partial name is fine) and hit Enter. For example, if you enter **sm** in the text box, the menu search will find all occurrences of *smooth*, *smoothness*, *smart*, and *smoke*. This is a very handy new feature, and one worth trying out.

Shelves

While we have not touched on shelves much in this chapter, they offer a convenient way of grouping your most frequently used commands and tools together in one place. The shelf bar is one of the most noticeable features of Maya's GUI, and it appears just below the Status line. The left side of the Shelf line contains the manipulation tools that we have discussed above. Additionally, there are several icons, organized into a tab called Shelf1 (and Shelf2, etc.) that perform useful commands. For example, to create a NURBS sphere, you merely click the blue sphere button; to create a spotlight, click the spotlight button; to create a CV curve, click the CV curve button (the leftmost button on the right side of the shelf). New to version 3 of Maya are two widgets just to the left of the shelf icons. By clicking the top one (a gray tab icon), you can quickly navigate to any tab (useful if you have created dozens of tabs). Clicking the bottom widget opens a menu of common shelf commands, plus access to the shelf editor.

You can customize shelves and shelf icons to suit your needs. For more on how to do this, see Chapter 3 or Chapter 16.

Having these buttons available on a shelf makes the process of creating each item much more straightforward than having to find them in a hierarchical menu set.

The Outliner and Hypergraph

While we will cover the inner workings of the Outliner and the Hypergraph later in this book, let's take a quick look at these two scene management windows. The basic purpose of the Outliner and the Hypergraph is the same: to allow you to see an abstract (or outline) of the scene. The way the two display a scene's outline, however, is very different.

If you have used a 3D animation program in the past, you probably will be familiar with a scene management tool like the Outliner, shown in Figure 1.23. From top to bottom, the Outliner (Window ➜ Outliner) lists all objects in your scene, including cameras (note that the orthographic views—top, side, and front—are just cameras listed in the Outliner), lights, curves, and geometric objects. If you have objects that are parented to one another (a leg, for example, is parented to a body so that they move together), the Outliner will indicate this by a twirl-down arrow to the left of the parent object (the body in this case). Clicking the arrow will show the child object (the leg) which, because it is the child object, is tabbed in under the parent. The Outliner menu contains several options, which will be discussed further in Chapter 3.

Figure 1.23 *The Outliner, showing a leg object childed to a body object*

The Hypergraph, by contrast, is probably like nothing you've seen before. It is, essentially, a linked (or hyperlinked) outline of your scene, showing not only your scene elements, but how they are connected. While the Hypergraph may at first appear bewildering, its fashion of laying out a scene can prove invaluable. Figure 1.24 shows how the scene shown in the Outliner, above, would look in the Hypergraph.

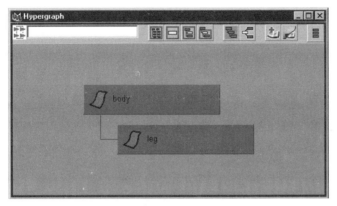

Figure 1.24 *The Hypergraph with leg and body*

If you're interested, you can learn much more about the Hypergraph and Outliner in Chapter 3.

The Channel Box/Attribute Editor

The Channel box (to the right of the main scene window) and Attribute Editor are related windows that give you access to just about every aspect of the objects and materials in your scene. The Attribute Editor (accessed by pressing Ctrl+A) gives you access to all an object's attributes, while the Channel box gives a more simplified view of only the object's *keyable* (or animatable) attributes. As these two panels are counterparts, it makes sense for them to be grouped together, and you can set the two to toggle (the Attribute Editor replacing the Channel box on the right side of the window) by choosing Window ➜ Settings/Preferences ➜ Preferences and then, in the Interface section, clicking the Open Attribute Editor In Main Maya Window radio button.

The Channel box is so named because elements that can be animated in a 3D program have often been termed "channels." To animate a ball going up and down, you would animate its Y-axis channel (by setting several keyframes over time). While Maya uses the term attribute for anything that could potentially be keyable in a scene, those that have actually been set to keyable are placed in the Channel box.

As you'll see throughout this book, the Attribute Editor and Channel box are your keys to controlling all of an object's attributes, including numerical inputs for translation, rotation, scale, and visibility, as well as its construction history, like spans of CVs and the radius of a circular object. The Attribute Editor, in addition (via its tabbed windows), allows you to access materials, tessellation criteria, and other features. To toggle between the Channel box and Attribute Editor, just press Ctrl+A.

(Materials? Tessellation? If you're new to 3D animation, don't worry about absorbing all the jargon right away. The following chapters introduce all the essential concepts in a logical and straightforward way.)

If you click on the name (not the text box, but the actual name—see Figure 1.25) of an attribute in the Channel box and then MM drag in the scene window, you will get a "virtual slider" that controls the number next to the channel name, as shown in Figure 1.25. This is a very powerful, time-saving feature in Maya.

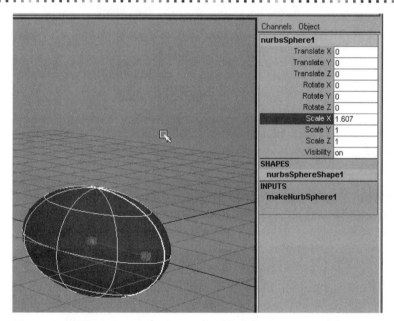

Figure 1.25 *Creating and using a virtual slider*

The Timeline

The Timeline, just below the main scene window(s), is the key to animation in Maya.

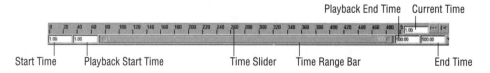

The numbers on the Timeline by default are set to frames (and by default, frames per second is set to film rate—24—so 24 frames equals one second of animation). To the right of the time slider is the current time marker (probably set to 1.00). To change the current time in your animation, you can either drag the time marker in the time slider or double-click the current time field and enter a number (like **5**). You will then see the time marker move to that frame. Larger numbers (like frame 20) are, of course, later in the animation. Below the time slider is a range marker (the gray bar with a 1 on one end and a 24 on the other) that lets you control the range of the time slider within a larger animation. To change the position of the time slider while maintaining the same range (24 frames by default), just drag the range bar by its middle. To change the starting point of the range, drag the left square left or right. To change the ending point, drag the right square to the left or right.

To the left of the time range bar are two numeric fields. The left-most field sets the animation start frame (often people will set this number to 0 for the first frame instead of 1). The field to its right sets the starting frame of the time range (changing this number is equivalent to dragging the left square of the time range slider). To the right of the time range bar are two more fields; the left one sets the ending time of the animation range (equivalent to dragging the right square on the time range bar), while the right field controls the end point of the animation (set to 48 frames as a default).

To change the settings for the time slider, open the animation preferences window (either click the Animation Preferences button, to the right of the key icon at the bottom right of the screen, or open it by choosing Window ➜ Settings/Preferences ➜ Preferences, then choose the Settings/Timeline category). In this Preferences section, shown in Figure 1.26, you can control how tall the Timeline is (useful when sound files are imported), set playback to normal or free (the latter required for playback of dynamics), and even adjust animation beginning and end points and so forth. Under the Settings section, you can change your slider units from the default film (24fps) to PAL, NTSC, seconds, minutes, or even hours.

To play back an animation, you can either use the VCR-like controls to the right of the time line, or press Ctrl+V to start and stop the animation, and Ctrl+Shift+V to reset the animation to its starting frame.

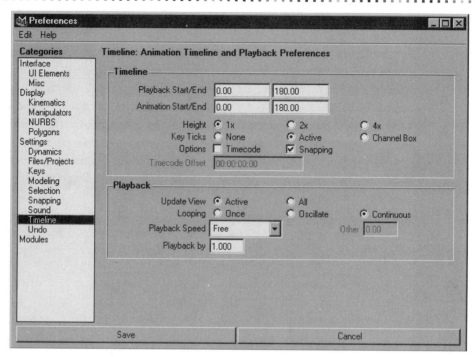

Figure 1.26 *The Animation Preferences window*

The Command-Line/Feedback-Line and the Script Editor

At the bottom of the Maya screen is the Command/Feedback line. The two halves of this line function in tandem and are simply the last lines of the Script Editor's input and history windows, respectively. Therefore, let's first take a quick look at Maya's Script Editor. While most of your interaction with Maya is via the GUI, most of what you actually tell Maya to do is passed to it via MEL (the Maya Embedded Language). The selections and other actions you make in the GUI are recorded as MEL commands. Creating a NURBS sphere, for example, is simply the command sphere followed by several optional flags. To access the Script Editor, either click the Script Editor icon just to the right of the feedback line (at the bottom right of the screen), or use the menu (Window → General Editors → Script Editor). The Script Editor, shown in Figure 1.27, is split into two halves. The top, which is the history window, probably has several lines of code in it (these would be the last commands you have issued to Maya). The input window at the bottom awaits any MEL commands you might wish to give to Maya.

Figure 1.27 *The Script Editor window*

For information on how to use MEL commands with the Script Editor, please see Chapter 16.

To see how the Script Editor works, type **sphere** (in lowercase letters) into the input window and press the Enter key on the *numeric keypad* (not the alpha keyboard). You should see the line

```
// Result: nurbsSphere1 makeNurbsSphere1 //
```

appear in the history window (telling you what Maya has done to complete your command), and a sphere will appear at the origin of your scene.

In version 3 of Maya, you can now press Ctrl+Enter (on the main keyboard) to execute your command.

Because the Command line is just the last input line in the Script Editor, you don't have to open the Script Editor for a simple command. Try closing the Script Editor and then, in the Command line, type in **cone** (all small letters), and press either Enter key. A cone should appear in your scene, and the Feedback line (to the right of the Command line) should now read

```
Result: nurbsCone1 makeNurbsCone1
```

This lets you know what actions Maya has taken to complete your command.

To "focus" on the Command line when you are in a scene window (so you don't have to click in the Command line field with your mouse), just press the ` (reverse apostrophe) key on your keyboard.

Summary

This quick tour has shown that, while Maya is a very deep and complex program, a great deal of thought has gone into making the interface as intuitive as possible. Consistent interface elements (like using the Alt key and mouse drags to move around many different windows), grouping tools together, and even placing clues about your orientation in space and the type of tool you're using directly in the scene windows—all of these features work together to ease the new user's entrance into this complex environment.

More important, the interface is completely customizable, from its smallest to its largest detail, so that you can tailor the program to meet your needs. As you grow more comfortable with using Maya, you will want to optimize its interface to allow you to work more quickly with less clutter; in Chapter 3, we will explore exactly this issue, looking into built-in options, creating buttons and menus of your own, and making the best use of some of Maya's organizational windows (like the Outliner and Hypergraph). If you are new to Maya, spend a bit of time playing with the interface after reading this chapter. Otherwise, move on to the next chapter, where you can put your understanding of the Maya interface to good use while creating a complete animation from scratch!

Your First Maya Animation

MAYA

Chapter 2

Now that you have an overview of how Maya works, let's put this knowledge to practical use. In this chapter, you'll get to try out modeling, keyframing, texturing, and using Maya's built-in dynamics, all in one animation that shows off the power of Maya's interface and renderer. You'll also get a chance to practice the basics of maneuvering around a Maya scene, and you'll start to see where adjusting various options would lead to different results.

While we won't deal with theory or do a lot of explaining in this chapter (that's what the rest of the book is for!), if you follow along, you should get a very good idea of many of the major parts of Maya.

If you are already familiar with other 3D animation packages, going through this chapter should get you ready to use Maya proficiently. If you are new to the whole world of 3D animation, this animation will be challenging yet rewarding. Don't get too discouraged if things don't turn out perfectly the first time you try. Just remember to save your project often, and under different names, and you can always go back a step or two and try again.

But enough talk—let's do some animating!

- Setting the scene: modeling
- Texturing your models using the Hypershade window
- Lighting the scene
- Animating the rocket
- Creating a follow camera
- Rendering the animation
- Advanced topic: adding exhaust

Setting the Scene: Modeling

In this chapter, we're going to build, texture, light, and animate a little rocket ship that takes off, loses power after a couple of seconds, and crashes back to earth.

While this modeling and animation project is a bit simplified, it is definitely a real-world example of work you can do in Maya. Remember that you can return to this project as you progress through the book, refining your work. Given a bit of time and practice, you should be able to get this project looking very good—even if you've never done 3D work before! To give you an idea of what you're working toward, see Figure 2.1 for a still shot from the completed animation. (To get the full effect, see the Color Gallery and the 02rocket movie on the CD.)

Figure 2.1 *The rocket taking off*

As described in the Introduction, the companion CD is designed to be an integral part of this book. It contains working files for all the exercises, along with finished versions of many projects. For this chapter's project, you'll find the complete animation, along with the rocket.ma *project file.*

The first step to almost any animation in Maya is to build your scene elements; therefore, we'll build the rocket (and ground) as our first step. To build our little ship, we'll use just a couple of the many different modeling techniques Maya has available for you.

1. First, we need to create a project and save our file into this project, so it has a home. Open Maya by double-clicking its desktop icon. Now, from the File menu, choose File ➔ Project ➔ New. In the New Project option window, click the Use Defaults button, type in a name for your project (something like **rocketProject**) in the Name text box, and click Accept to accept these choices. You now have your project saved in your default directory on your hard drive. You also need to save your scene. To do that, choose File ➔ Save Scene As, and then choose an appropriate name for the file (like **rocket1**).

Saving Maya Project and Scene Files

Your project consists of several folders (or directories) of information about the scene (which is where your scene file is stored), any rendering jobs, source images, output images, textures, and so forth. Whenever you first create a new scene in Maya, there are *two* steps to saving: first, save your project (which contains all the proper places for Maya to store your project's information), and then save the actual scene file.

A new feature of the Windows NT version of Maya 3 is that you can choose to browse for your new project's file location. With the New Project window open, click the Browse button next to the Location text field and use the standard file browser to choose the location of your project.

Maya is based on the Unix operating system, which means you *must never use spaces* in your filenames—even if you're running the NT version of Maya. If you do, Maya will give you an error when you try to open your scene later, and you won't be able to access your earlier work! The NT operating system will allow you to save according to its filename conventions, but Maya's file system will have problems recognizing names with spaces.

It is a very good idea to append a number to the name of every scene (for example, **rocket1**). As you work, you will want to save your scene often, in case you run into any problems, and, rather than just saving over your old scene, you should save a new scene each time, numbered sequentially (**rocket2**, **rocket3**, and so on). Every time you are told to save in this project, remember to save a new file with a higher number. If you are concerned about disk space on your hard drive, you can erase earlier versions of your project as you work through later ones. It is usually enough to save the last four or five versions, and then start trashing the earlier ones.

2. Once you have saved your project and file, change your scene window from the default perspective view to a "four view" of the scene by first clicking the scene (large) window and then pressing and releasing the space bar quickly. Your scene window should change to four smaller panes, each labeled for its view perspective (top, side, front and persp-perspective). Select the side view by clicking your mouse inside this pane; then press and release the space bar quickly again to make the side view take up the entire viewing pane (see Figure 2.2).

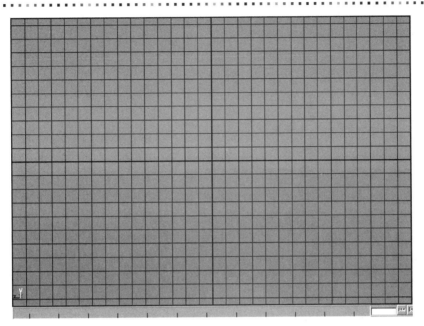

Figure 2.2 *The side view pane*

To create the body of the rocket, we'll use an EP (Edit Point) Curve tool to define four points that make up the rocket's outline, and then "revolve" this curve into a surface.

3. Pick the EP Curve tool (Create ➡ EP Curve Tool); your cursor should turn into a cross, indicating that you're now using the EP Curve tool. Because we want the first (top) point of the curve to lie directly on the X axis (the thick vertical line at the center of the pane), we need to turn on the "snap to grid" feature before we create the first point on the curve. Click the Snap to Grid button on the Status line in Maya (the topmost toolbar).

You can also use a keyboard shortcut to enable grid snapping: hold down the X key on the keyboard while clicking, and each point you click will snap to the nearest grid intersection.

4. A little below the top of the window, where the Y axis meets one of the other grid lines, click once (with your left mouse button) to create your first point. Now turn off the Snap to Grid button (click it again), and create three more points, approximately like the following image. If you hold down the mouse button when you click to create a point, you can move that point around until you like its positioning; you can also hit the backspace key to remove the last point you made. When you are satisfied with the shape of the ship, hit the Enter key to save the points (the line will turn green).

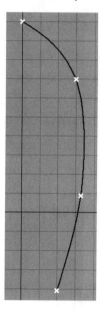

5. Our next step is to create a surface from our outline. Be sure Modeling is showing on the Status line (at the far left top of the screen). If not, choose it from the pop-up menu there. Now revolve the curve by choosing Surfaces ➜ Revolve ❑.

The ❑ symbol in Maya is known as an option box. Selecting this box with your mouse will open a window where you can change the options of your command—in this case, the Revolve command.

6. In the Revolve option window, choose Edit ➜ Reset Settings and then set the segments to 16 (instead of the default 8). Click the Revolve button. You should now see your curve transformed into a squat rocket ship body! To see your

rocket ship shaded, hit the 3 key (on the main keyboard; not the numeric key-pad) and the 6 key—the 3 key changes your view to high resolution, while the 6 key turns on flat shading mode (instead of wireframe).

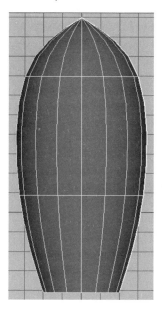

In Maya 3, most option windows close when you click the *item-name* button (in this case, Revolve). To keep the window open (to create other objects, for instance) click the Apply button instead of the Revolve (or other) button.

7. Rename your object (shown in the Channel box, at the right of the main win-dow) from revolvedSurface1 to something more appropriate, like **body**: click once on the name (revolvedSurface1) and type in your new name, replacing the old one. Save your work now.

If you don't see the object name listed (and a Channels menu directly above it), try holding down the Ctrl key and pressing the A key. This should change your view to the Channel box view.

If something goes wrong on this or any step in the project, remember that you can always hit the Z (undo) key to move back one or more steps in your work.

8. Now we need to build our rocket engine exhaust nozzle. We'll create this from a revolved curve that we'll drag up into the rocket, leaving only its broad base visible. We'll use the same method we learned to create the rocket itself: choose the EP Curve tool (or hit the Y key, which will reselect the last used tool for you), and then click several points to form the outline curve that you'll rotate into an exhaust nozzle shape.

To make the size (scale) of the curve easier to see, try creating the exhaust nozzle directly below the rocket body.

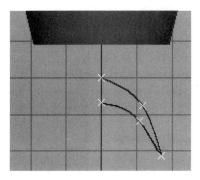

9. When you are satisfied with the look of your curve, hit the Enter key and, while the curve is still selected (green), choose Surfaces ➜ Revolve to revolve it into a nozzle. (Note that we don't have to use the options this time; this revolve operation will use the same options you set for the rocket body last time.) Hit the 3 key to smooth out the view of the engine nozzle; then rename the object (in the Channel box) from revolvedSurface2 to **nozzle** and save your work.

10. We now need to move the nozzle into the base of the rocket. Choose the nozzle (if it's not green, click or drag a selection marquee on the nozzle—be sure not to highlight the rocket body or the original curve you used to revolve the nozzle); then press the W key to enter Move mode. You should see several colored arrows (above the nozzle) around a yellow box. Click and drag up on the green arrow until the nozzle is where you want it to be.

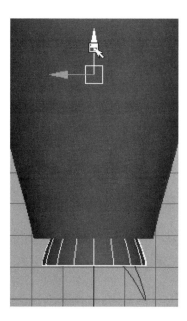

Maya Shortcut Keys

The QWERTY keys (across the top left of your keyboard) are shortcut keys. Memorize these keys now—using shortcut keys is one secret to getting work done in Maya quickly! Here's the function for each one:

Q Puts Maya into select mode (where you can only select, not modify, scene elements).

W Places Maya in Move mode.

E Places Maya in Rotate mode.

R Places Maya in Scale mode (not rotate mode!).

T Places Maya in Manipulator mode (we won't deal with this tool in this chapter).

Y Places Maya in whatever mode—besides Move, Scale, and Rotate—was last chosen (the EP Curve Tool, in our work).

You can also adjust the display of objects in the scene using the 1–7 keys on your alpha keyboard (not the number keypad).

1 Changes the display of any selected object into low-resolution display (increases interactivity with the program, but the objects look blocky).

2 Changes the display of any selected object into medium-resolution display.

3 Changes the display of any selected object into high-resolution display (which looks much better, but can slow down how responsive Maya is).

4 Changes the display of any objects in the scene (not just selected objects) to wireframe display (faster interactivity and the ability to see through objects).

5 Changes the display of any objects in the scene to flat-shaded display (basic coloring is visible).

6 Changes the display of any objects in the scene to texture-shaded display (the basic look of a texture is visible on objects).

7 Changes the display of any objects in the scene to textured-shaded and lit display (so the basic effect of lights can be seen).

11. Now let's create a cockpit for our ship from a default sphere. Click the Sphere (ball) button on your tool shelf, or choose Create ➔ NURBS Primitives ➔ Sphere (remember to press the 3 key to display the sphere in hi-res mode). You won't be able to see the sphere, as it is currently inside the rocket body, so change to Move mode (press the W key) and move the sphere to the right of the rocket body. Now change to Scale mode (the R key) and stretch the sphere up until it is about twice as tall as it is thick. Finally, change back to Move mode (the W key) and move the sphere into position near the front end of the rocket body. Be sure to change the name of the object (in the Channel box) from nurbsSphere1 to **cockpit**, and save your work.

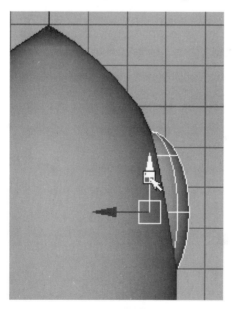

12. No 1950s-era space ship would be complete without some fancy fins. We'll create one fin using a default cone, and then adjust its points to make it look more like a fin. Choose Create → Polygon Primitives → Cone ❏, choose Edit → Reset Settings, set the Subdivisions Along Height option to 5 (instead of 1), and click Create; then name the cone **fin1**. Set Maya to Move mode, and then move the cone out so it is below the cockpit. Now change to Rotate mode (the E key) and rotate the cone so it points away from the side of the ship. To do this, grab the outermost (yellow) ring of the Rotate tool and drag to the right.

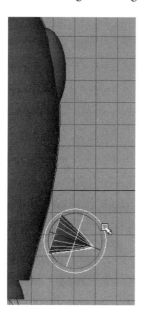

13. The fin is almost correctly placed, but it's currently much too small. Change to Scale mode (the R key), and then scale the whole cone out (click the yellow box in the center, and then drag to the right) until it is the right size. We're getting closer, but now the cone has been scaled out in all directions. To fix this, change to four-view mode (press the space bar quickly), and, in front or top view, click on the red (X-axis) scale box at the end of the scale manipulator and scale the fin so it is thin in that dimension.

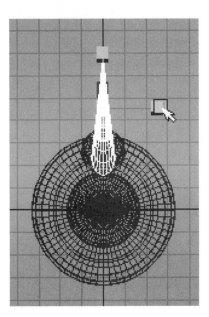

14. Now that the cone/fin is thin, return to the side view (click in the side view, and then press and release the space bar). Highlight the fin so it is green; then press the F8 key to go into Component Selection mode. Drag a selection marquee around the point at the tip (it will turn yellow), and then press W (Move mode) and move that point down so it is about as low as the exhaust nozzle—don't worry that it looks very angular right now. Next, draw a selection marquee around the second row of points in from the tip (be sure to select only this row), and move them down some as well. Finally, choose the bottom set of points on the next three rows in (toward the body), and move them up a bit. You should now have a curved fin. Save your work.

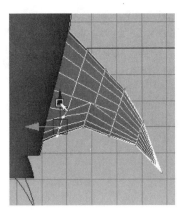

15. When you like the shape of the fin, press the F8 key again to return to Object mode. While the fin is nice, it could use some smoothing. Be sure the fin is still selected (green), and then choose Polygons ➜ Smooth to smooth out the angles between polygon facets. With Maya 3, the cone will jump to Component mode when you use the smooth tool. To change back to Object mode (where you can manipulate the cone as a whole, instead of its individual polygons), press the F8 key. At this point, you might wish to move the fin in toward the body more, so that the fin sticks partway into the body.

We have one fin; now we need to make two more. Rather than model these new fins, let's make Maya do the work. First, we need to move the pivot point of the fin (the point around which it rotates) to 0 on the X and Z axes, and then we'll just tell Maya to make two duplicates and rotate them.

16. Click on the fin to highlight it, press the Insert key on your keyboard, click the blue handle (it may be difficult to see), and drag it to the center line. To more accurately center the pivot point, hold down the X key while dragging, forcing the pivot point to snap to the grid. When the pivot point has been moved, press the Insert key again to return to normal Move mode.

You may find it easier to move the cone's pivot point if you shift to wireframe display mode momentarily. To do so, just press the 4 key on your keyboard (not on the numeric keypad).

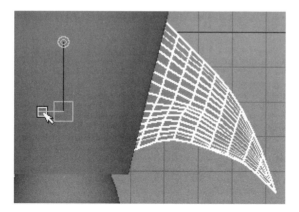

17. Now choose Edit ➜ Duplicate ❑ and, in the option window, set Rotate Y (the middle box) to 120 (120 degrees, or one third of a circle), set Number of Copies to 2, and click Duplicate. You will now have three fins spaced evenly around the body of the ship—Maya even names the other fins fin2 and fin3 for you!

18. As a last step, we need to make some ground for our rocket to take off from. Choose Create ➜ NURBS Primitives ➜ Plane ❑, choose Edit ➜ Reset, and then set the Width to 100 (so the ground is very big). Click Create, then rename the plane **ground**. You'll note that the plane is right in the middle of the rocket. Using the Move tool, move the plane down until it is a significant distance below the ship—don't let the rocket body, fins, or nozzle touch the plane, or you will have big problems later in this chapter!

100 is the maximum width you can make the plane using the option window. To make the plane bigger, you can either scale it using the Scale tool, or click the makeNurbsPlane text in the Channel box and set the width to a larger value (like 1000) there.

19. Now that we have all of our pieces, we need to get rid of the construction history for each of them, and then erase the curves that generated them (otherwise we'll have problems later on in the animation process). First, select everything in the scene (or RM choose Select All in the scene window); then choose Edit ➜ Delete by Type ➜ History. Now find the curves you used to build the body and nozzle of the rocket (you can choose any component of the rocket and then use the right and left arrow keys to "scroll" through all the components—or you can use the Outliner or Hypergraph to find the curves). When you have each curve selected, just hit the Backspace key to delete them all.

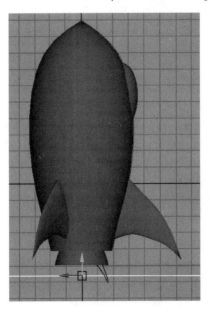

As a last step, we need to make all our rocket components into one object (we'll call it rocket), and move the pivot point of our rocket down to the ground plane (the reason for this will be apparent as we animate the ship).

20. Drag a selection marquee around the ship and all its components (be sure not to include the ground, though!); then hold down the Ctrl key and press G. This creates a new group (called group1) that contains all the pieces of the rocket we have modeled. Rename this group to **rocket**.

Should you accidentally highlight the ground plane with the rocket components, just hold down the Shift key and click anywhere on the plane to deselect it.

In the future, if you click on any component of the rocket (the body, say) and press the up-arrow key, Maya will automatically choose the rocket group for you.

21. Be sure the rocket group is still selected (check to see that its name is showing in the Channel box); then press the Insert key. Move the pivot point down (using the green handle) until it is below the bottom of the nozzle. Moving the pivot point will be important when we animate the scale of the ship (otherwise the ship will scale around its middle, instead of its bottom). Be sure to press the Insert key again when you are done moving the pivot point. Save your work.

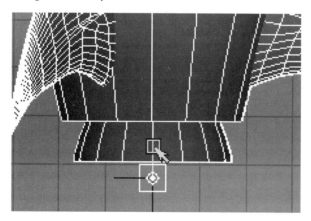

22. Let's take a look at our handiwork. Change to perspective view in the scene panel (remember the space bar trick), change to Shaded mode (press the 6 key), and then rotate around your ship by holding down the Alt key and the left mouse (LM) button and dragging around the scene window.

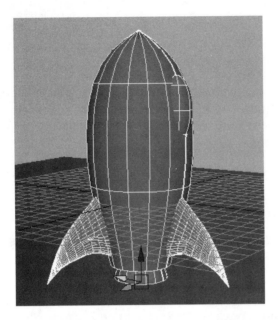

If your results are very different from those you see in the book, you may wish to return to the area that is different and rework it until you are satisfied with the results.

Save your work and take a break—good job so far!

Texturing Your Models Using the Hypershade

You might find the model you've created so far a bit… well… *gray*. Let's remedy that situation now by adding materials to the different model elements, giving them a bit more color and interest. Materials in Maya are the general container for a shading network, which gives an object its color, transparency, reflectivity, and so forth. Normally, you create a material and then edit the material's settings or add textures (images or procedural textures) to get the look you want. Think of materials in Maya as your own virtual paint can.

To create these materials, we'll use the Hypershade.

1. Select the cockpit and then choose Window ➜ Hypershade, opening the Hypershade window.

2. To create a new material, look down the left-hand side of the Hypershade (called the Visor) until you find the Create section. Open the Materials folder, choose the Phong shader, and with your middle mouse button drag (MM drag) the Phong material into the window on the right (the Hypershade window). Name the material **cockpitPhong** by holding down the Ctrl key, double-clicking the default name (**Phong1**), and then typing in the new name.

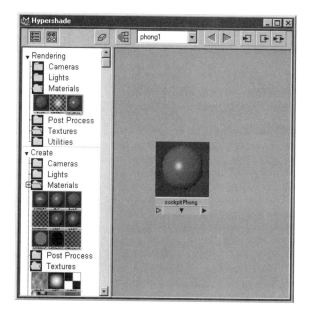

3. To assign this new material to the cockpit, just MM drag the material ball onto the cockpit in the scene window. Because the Phong material is still gray, you won't see much difference yet.

4. To adjust the color of the new material, double-click it in the Hypershade. This will open the Attribute Editor with several options you can control for color and other attributes.

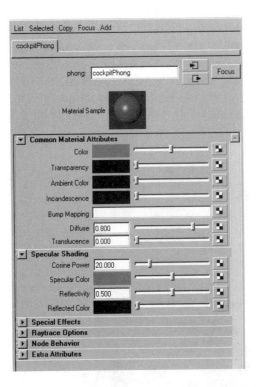

5. All we're interested in for the cockpit is its color. Click on the gray rectangle next to the word *color*, and, in the color picker that pops up, choose a very dark blue (almost black) color. You can watch the cockpit itself change as you adjust the color. When you get a color you like, click the Accept button.

6. Let's make another Phong material for the body of the rocket. MM drag a Phong material onto the right side of the Hypershade window, and then rename this material **bodyPhong**. Now MM drag the material ball onto the body of the rocket.

7. In the Attribute Editor, adjust the color of the new material to a very pale blue-gray (the color of brushed aluminum). To make this work right, you'll need to set the saturation of your color very low (we set it to 0.075).

8. When you accept the color, you'll probably notice that the specular highlights (the shiny areas) on the rocket body are big and ugly. Fortunately, we can compensate for this. In the Specular Shading area of the Attribute Editor, set Cosine Power (the size of the highlight) to a large number, like 75, and set Specular Color to a darker gray (drag the slider to the left). When you finish, you should have a more pleasing highlight.

9. To create the ground shade (we don't want a specular highlight on the ground!), let's use the lambert shader, which does not create highlights. MM drag a lambert material (top right) onto the right side of the Hypershade; then rename it **groundLambert**. Then MM drag the new material onto the ground plane, assigning it to the plane. (You may need to go into perspective view to see the ground plane.)

10. In the Attribute Editor, set the color of the ground plane to a dusty orange-yellow (a desert dirt color).

11. The last two materials we'll make will be a bit more interesting. First, let's create a material with a procedural texture for the nozzle. Create a new Phong shader, name it **nozzlePhong**, and assign it to the nozzle.

12. Instead of assigning a color to the new material, click the little checkerboard next to it (to the right of the slider). This will bring up the Create Render Node window. Click on the Checker button, and your material will have a checkered pattern to it.

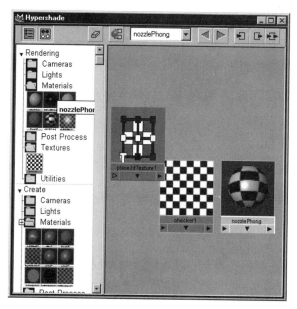

13. While this texture as it currently is might be all right for playing checkers, it's not what we're after. In the Attribute Editor, make both of the colors in the checkered pattern a shade of gray (drag the sliders next to the color swatches). Finally, decrease the Contrast setting to about 0.7. These changes will make the pattern much subtler.

14. Now click on the place2Dtexture1 tab (at the top of the Attribute Editor) and set Repeat UV to 16 and 0.5, respectively. This will give the nozzle the ringed appearance common to rocket nozzles.

15. Finally, let's create the fin material, using a ramp to get our effect. First, create a new Phong material (called **finPhong**), and assign it to all three fins. You will probably have to rotate the scene panel in order to see all three fins so you can do this.

16. In the Attribute Editor, click the checker box next to Color again, to bring up the Create Render Node window. Choose Ramp from the list of 2D textures. You should see a Ramp Attributes window with a default ramp appear, and all the fins should have the colors applied to them.

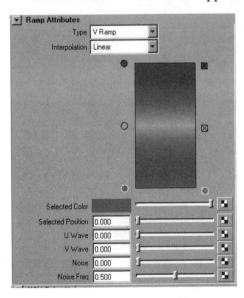

17. While the smooth transitions of the default ramp are nice, they're not what we need for our fins. From the Interpolation pop-up menu, choose None. This turns off the smooth interpolation of the colors, making the ramp a series of color bars.

18. To change the ramp colors, select the ramp color marker (the circle to the left of the color bar) and then click inside the Selected Color swatch (below the ramp sample) to bring up the color picker. To create a new color in the ramp, just click in the ramp sample where you want that new color. To move a color up or down, drag the color marker circle on the left of the color bar. Finally, to remove a color, click the check box to the right of the ramp sample. You can use whatever colors you like for the ramp, but when you are finished, you should have something like Figure 2.3, a color version of which is on the CD.

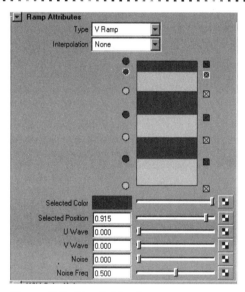

Figure 2.3 *The finished ramp*

We now have a fully textured ship and ground plane. While none of these materials is terribly complex, they give the ship some color and add to the cartoonish feel of the world we're creating. To be able to see our ship when we render it, we'll next need to add some lights to the scene.

Lighting the Scene

To light this scene, we'll add four lights: one ambient light to shade the whole scene and three spotlights. This lighting setup will give the scene a nighttime quality, which is a bit more fun than one big light for the sun. Additionally, we'll make two of the lights "track" (or aim toward) the ship at all times.

1. First, let's create our ambient light. Choose Create ➜ Lights ➜ Ambient Light ❑. In the option window, set the intensity to 0.2, click the color swatch and set the color to a pale blue, and then click Create.

To see how the scene is lit so far, press the 7 key on your keyboard to go into lighted mode (the scene should be almost dark). Press the 6 key to return to flat-shaded mode.

2. Now let's create our spotlights. Choose Create ➜ Lights ➜ Spot Light ❑. In the Option window, choose Edit ➜ Reset Settings, set the penumbra angle to 10 (this fades the edges of the spotlight), and then click Create. Rename this light **frontSpot** (if the Channel box isn't open, press Ctrl+A to toggle it back on). Press the W key to get into Move mode, and then move the light up and away from the ship, toward the camera. Be sure the light is above the rocket by a significant amount; otherwise, it won't light the ground below the ship (which gives depth and solidity to the scene).

To move your lights, you will need to use the top and side views (use the space bar to see these views). Scale these views out by holding down the Alt key, along with the left and middle mouse buttons, and dragging to the left in each window pane.

3. Because we want this spotlight to aim at the ship at all times, let's add an aim constraint to it. First, click on any part of the ship; then press the up-arrow key (be sure the Channel box says *rocket* in its title area). Then, holding down the Shift key, click (or drag around) the light, highlighting it as well. Finally, from the Animation menu set (choose Animation from the top-left pop-up menu),

choose Constrain ➜ Aim ❏. Choose Edit ➜ Reset Settings and then change the three aim vector text boxes to read 0, 0, and –1. Click the Apply button and check that the spotlight is pointing toward the rocket (the cone should open toward the rocket body). If the spotlight is "looking" in another direction, try the following settings until one works: 0,0,1; 1,0,0; or –1,0,0. (The aim vector of a spotlight—like that of the camera we'll add shortly—is determined by where you place the lights in relation to the rocket. As your rocket may be aligned along a different axis, you will have to try these settings until you discover the proper axis for your scene.) Once you have determined the proper aim vector, the spotlight will be locked onto the rocket, wherever it goes.

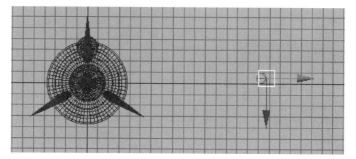

4. We now need to create another light, this one off to the right side of the ship. Create a new spotlight (Lights ➜ Create Spot Light), call it **rightSideSpot**, and move it off to the right of (and above) the ship.

5. We want this light to follow the ship as well, so we'll do the same trick again: first, select the rocket (remember to press the up-arrow), then Shift+select the

rightSideSpot light. Finally, choose Constrain ➜ Aim to force the light to point at the ship. You should not need to open the option window this time, as the proper aim vector should be set now. If your light is not aiming in the right direction, undo the last step, open the Aim Constraint option window, and repeat the end of step 4, above.

6. Finally, let's create our last spotlight (which will stay pointed at the launch area). Once again, create a spotlight; then name the new light **leftSideSpot**, and move it to the left and above the rocket.

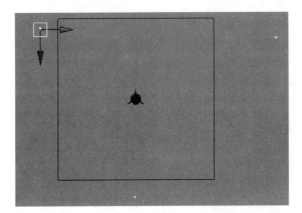

7. As we won't be auto-aiming the light, we'll need to do it manually. In the top view (with the light still selected), from the Panel menu at the top of the top view panel, choose Panel ➜ Look Through Selected to change the view to show what the light sees (nothing at this point). Rotate the view until the rocket is centered in the view (hold down the Alt key and drag with the left mouse button). To return to top view, choose Panel ➜ Orthographic ➜ Top.

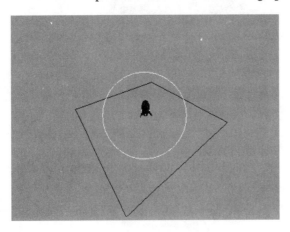

8. To see how your scene is lit, press the 7 key again. It should be well (and evenly) lit across the ship and the ground near it. If not, try moving your lights around, or increasing their intensity.

9. Save your work and take a break. Good job so far!

 It is often difficult to see how well lit your scene is using the flat (openGL) renderer. To get a better view of your scene, choose Render → Render into New Window from the Rendering menu set (the top-left pop-up menu). This will create a quick little rendering of your scene.

Animating the Scene

If things haven't been interesting enough so far, we're really going to have fun here: we'll animate our little ship, and use some of the power of Maya's dynamics engine to launch it and bring it back to earth.

Keyframed Animation

First we need to create a keyframe animation of the ship about to take off. Keyframe is an old animation term for important moments in an animation (key frames). In digital animation, you tell the computer which frames are important (the keyframes), and the computer "in-betweens" the rest of the frames between these key frames, creating an animation.

For our simple animation, we'll only animate the scale of the ship as it squashes, getting ready for takeoff, and then stretches as it "leaps" off the ground. This is classic cartoon anticipation and overshoot—you'll recognize the effect from any old Tex Avery cartoons you run across.

1. To create our first keyframe, first be sure you're on the first frame of the animation (use the VCR-like controls at the bottom-right of the screen to rewind, and check to see that the timeline marker is at 1).

2. Next, select the rocket (be sure it's the whole rocket group, and not just the body); then, in the Channel box, drag your mouse over the text of the three scale channels (scaleX, scaleY, and scaleZ), highlighting them. Then, with the mouse over the selected channels, use the right mouse button to choose (RM choose) Key Selected from the pop-up menu. The channels for scale should turn orange, indicating that they're now keyframed.

3. Once you have created your first keyframe manually, you can make Maya automatically keyframe your channels from that point on. Check to be sure the Auto Key option is on by verifying that the key icon at the bottom-right of the screen (below the VCR-like time controls) is red. If it's not, simply click it to turn it red.

4. By default, our animation runs for 24 frames, or one second. (Maya defaults to 24 frames per second—film speed.) So we need to make our animation longer. In the number field for the end time (to the right of the time range slider), set the frame range to 100 frames—a bit over four seconds.

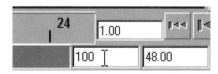

5. Move the time marker (the gray bar in the time slider) out to 48 frames (2 seconds) by dragging it across the time slider—or just click about where the 48th frame would be. Be sure your rocket is still selected, and then enter Scale mode (R key) and scale down the Y (green) axis so that the rocket becomes shorter (a scale of about 0.7 on the Y axis channel should do). You may notice that this simply shrinks the rocket; we also need to scale out the X and Z axes to make the rocket appear to maintain a consistent volume as it squashes. While we could do this via the X and Z scale handles, it is easier to do so in the Channel box itself. Click in the scaleX text box, and then enter a value of 1.4. Do the same in the scaleZ box. Your rocket should now look squashed rather than simply shrunk.

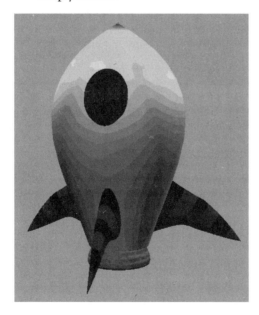

6. We now need to hold this squashed look for some frames (a *hold keyframe*). Move the time marker to frame 60, select the scale X, Y, and Z channels again, and RM choose Key Selected (alternatively, you could reenter the numbers you had before, forcing Maya to create a new keyframe via the Auto Key option).

7. At this point, it's a good idea to play back your animation to see how it looks so far. Click the Rewind button on the VCR-like controls (or press Alt+Shift+V); then click the Play button (or press Alt+V) to play the animation. The rocket should squash down and hold its appearance—and then the animation loops and repeats itself.

8. Now let's make the rocket stretch out, as if stretching to take off from the ground (don't worry for now that it's not moving up). Move to frame 70 and set the X, Y, and Z scales to 0.7, 1.4, and 0.7, respectively (the rocket should look stretched out now).

9. We need another hold keyframe (with the rocket stretched out), so move to frame 78, choose the scale channels, and RM choose Key Selected once again.

10. Now move to frame 90 (close to four seconds), and reset all the scale channels to 1—the ship will now return to its original shape at 90 frames. When you play back the animation, you should see the rocket squash, preparing for take-off, then stretch up (as it takes off—don't worry, we'll take care of that next!), and finally return to its original shape. If you don't like how the animation runs, you can Shift+click on any keyframe in the timeline (highlighting it in red), and then drag that keyframe left or right on the timeline, thereby adjusting the speed of the animation between each keyframe.

Using Dynamics for Animation

We've completed the keyframing for this animation project. Now let's make Maya do the rest of the work. We'll make the ship rise into the air by giving it a force (or impulse), and then drag it back down using gravity. Finally, we'll make the ground and rocket collide. To do all this, we'll use what is known as rigid body dynamics to tell Maya what forces act on our object (the rocket). As explained in Chapter 15, Maya (specifically, its dynamics engine) will use our input to do all the calculations necessary for realistic movement.

1. First, we need to make both the rocket and ground rigid bodies, so they'll react to each other and the forces we apply to them. Select the ground plane, and then change to the Dynamics menu set (from the pop-up menu at the top left of your screen). Choose Soft/Rigid Bodies ➜ Create Passive Rigid Body ❑. (Be sure not to select Active!) In the option window, set the Static and Dynamic Friction to 0.5, and set the Bounciness to 0.2. Click Create to create the rigid body.

2. Now let's make the rocket a rigid body. Select any of the rocket's body parts and press the up-arrow (be sure *rocket* is the name selected in the Channel box). Choose Soft/Rigid Bodies ➜ Create Passive Rigid Body ❑. In the option window, set the rocket's mass to 1000, set the Impulse Y to 5000, and set the Impulse Position Y to 12 (this forces the impulse to be above the rocket's body, so it won't spin around when you launch the rocket). Click Create.

If you get an error when you try to create the rocket's rigid body, check (using the Hypergraph or Outliner) to be sure you have erased the two curves for the nozzle and body of the rocket. If you haven't, do so—this should take care of any error messages.

3. With the rocket still selected, choose Fields ➜ Gravity ❑. In the option window, set the magnitude of gravity to 25 (this setting is far heavier than Earth's gravity, but it makes the animation look better!), check to be sure the Y direction of gravity is set to –1 and that X and Z are 0, and then click Create. Because the rocket was selected when you created the gravity field, it will be "attached" to gravity (that is, affected by it).

4. If you play back the animation now, you will see that it looks just the same as before. That's because our rocket is still a passive rigid body (meaning that nothing can affect it). What we have to do is keyframe the rocket to be an active rigid body just at the frame where it should take off. Select the rocket, and then move to frame 62. Under the Shapes/RigidBody2 node (in the Channel box), you should see a channel called Active (toward the bottom) that is set to *off*. Click the text once (the word Active), and then RM choose Key Selected to set a keyframe. Now move to frame 63, click in the text box that says *off*, and type in the word **on**. This will set a keyframe, setting the active state of the rocket's rigid body to *on*, so it can now be affected by forces.

5. Before you play back the animation, you'll want it to run longer. Set the playback length to 1000 instead of 100. (Type **1000** in the end-time number box, just to the right of the time range slider.) The frame range should now go from 1 to 1000. Rewind and play back the animation; you should see the rocket zoom off into parts unknown.

 If the rocket gets stuck in the ground, you've got a rigid body interpenetration error, a problem you'll learn more about in Chapter 15. To fix it, move the ground down a bit and run the animation again.

 When playing back dynamics animations, it is extremely important to rewind the animation before you play it back each time. If you don't, Maya will become confused about its calculations, and you will see very strange results!

6. To make our ship stop going up and up, we need to turn off our impulse. Go to frame 104 (with the rocket still selected), select the channel for impulse Y, and RM choose Key Selected. Move to frame 105, and type 0 in the impulse Y number field (setting the impulse to 0 from this point on). When you play back the animation, the rocket should rise out of sight, and then, around

frame 450, crash back down into the ground, bouncing around until it comes to rest.

To see the animation better, try zooming your camera back (press Alt with the left and middle mouse buttons, and drag left)—this is called scaling the view. Also, if you don't like the way the rocket bounces off the ground, you can set the ground's bounciness setting to lower (or higher), and you can change the rocket's impulse setting from 5000 at the start to some other very similar number (like 5001). This small change will make the bounces go in very different ways.

You should now have a complete rocket animation, using keyframes for part of it and making Maya do the calculations for the rest. Next, we'll discuss how to make a new camera and have it aim at the ship at all times; then we'll talk about how to render the whole animation out.

Save your work and take a break. Good job!

Creating a Follow Camera

As you may have noticed, the default perspective camera's view of this animation leaves something to be desired. What we need is a camera that follows the rocket into the air and back again—we need to aim our camera at the ship, just as we did with the lights.

Auto-aiming a camera at an object would *not* be a good idea if we wanted realistic animation. It is generally better to keyframe the camera to follow the object's motion, as this introduces "human" errors into the camera tracking (making the motion look like a person operating a camera instead of a computer operating one). For our cartoonish animation, having a camera follow the rocket is acceptable; however, if you wish, you are welcome to keyframe the motion instead.

1. Create a new camera (Create ➜ Camera) and name it **followCamera**. Using the four view panes, move the camera down the X axis (to the right in the top view), and then move it up a bit off the ground plane. Do not rotate the camera at this point!

2. Select the rocket, and then Shift-select the new camera. In the animation menu set, choose Constrain ➜ Aim to force the camera to point at the rocket.

3. To look through your new view, choose a panel (the top view, say), and choose Panels ➜ Look Through Selected. Make this your sole viewing pane (press the

space bar), and then play back the animation. You should see the camera follow the rocket up into the air, and then back down again.

4. Save your work.

If the camera is too close to the action, or too far away, just zoom your view (Alt+LM and RM buttons and drag) to get a better view.

Rendering the Animation

While watching the animation play in your scene window is great, it's probably a bit bumpy (especially if you have a slower machine). There are two ways to render a cleaner view of your animation: playblasting and final rendering (batch rendering). While a final rendering gives very high-quality results, it takes a great deal of time to produce these results. Playblasting, on the other hand, produces a rougher (flat shaded) look, but goes as fast as your video card can spit out images. Thus, for a quick look at the animation, playblasting is a far better choice than a final rendering.

Playblasting the animation is one step: choose Window ➜ Playblast and watch as Maya creates an animation for you, using the basic shading mode of your computer. Once the animation is complete, you will be able to view it in its own little movie window, as in Figure 2.4. You'll learn more about playblasting in Chapter 10.

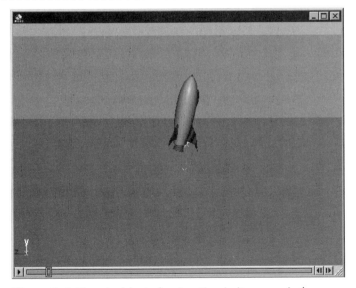

Figure 2.4 *The playblasted animation in its own window*

Rendering the final product is a bit more complex and takes much longer. Essentially, a final (batch) rendering creates a high quality "snapshot" of each frame of the animation, using all the lighting, material, and animation information your scene can provide. The results of a final rendering can be excellent, but it is a fairly slow process, as your computer has to do many calculations for every pixel of every image. Thus, you will only want to proceed with these steps when you're sure you're happy with your animation.

1. Choose Window ➜ Render Globals to open the Render Globals option window. In the Image File Output section, set the Frame/Animation Extension to **name.ext.#**, set the end frame to about 700 (you want to be sure it's a large enough number that the rocket has come to rest first), set the Frame Padding to 4 (this adds zeroes before your frame number, so the frame will be numbered render.0001, render.0002, and so forth, instead of render.1, render.2, etc.), and set the active Camera to followCamera (otherwise Maya will use the default persp camera, and you will waste your rendering time).

2. Twirl down the Resolution arrow, and set the Render Resolution to 320 × 240.

3. Twirl down the Anti-aliasing Quality arrow, and set the Presets field to Intermediate Quality (this makes for a fairly fast render time, but with decent quality).

4. When you have finished changing your settings, close the Render Globals window, and open the Rendering menu set (the top-left pop-up menu). Choose Render ➜ (Save) Batch Render. Type in a name (like **rocketRender**) in the File box, and click Save/Render.

5. Maya will render out all 700 frames of the animation (which will take some time). You can view the progress of each frame in the Feedback line (at the bottom-right of the screen), or, to view the current frame that is rendering, choose Render ➜ Show Batch Render. To cancel the render at any time, choose Render ➜ Cancel Batch Render.

6. When the rendering job is finished, you can view it using the fcheck utility. In Irix, type **fcheck** in a shell window; in NT, choose Run (from the Start menu) and type **fcheck** in the text field. A window will open, letting you navigate to your images directory (it should find this for you automatically). Choose the first frame of your animation and hit OK. Fcheck will cycle all frames into memory and then play back the animation at full speed.

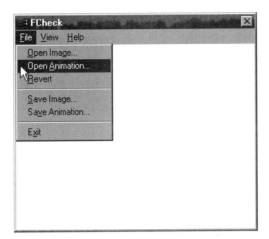

Congratulations! You have modeled, textured, lit, animated, and rendered an animation in Maya. If patting yourself on the back isn't your style, you can move on to the "advanced" section (next), where you will learn how to create a particle exhaust trail for the rocket. If this was enough practice for a start, just skip right on to the next chapter and save particles until the end of the book.

Advanced Topic: Adding Exhaust

If you've worked extensively with other animation packages, what we've done so far may seem fairly straightforward. In that case, you're probably ready to explore another area of Maya dynamics, namely particles. We'll use a particle emitter to create a shower of particles, and then texture them to look like smoke and flames. To make it appear that the "exhaust" is powering the rocket, we'll turn the emitter on and off (via keyframes) at the appropriate moments.

1. First, we need to create our emitter. In the Dynamics menu set (top-left pop-up menu), choose Particles ➜ Create Emitter ❏. In the option window, make the name of the emitter **exhaustEmitter**, set the Emitter Type to Directional, set the Rate to 0, and, under the Distance/Direction section, set the Spread to 0.3 and DirectionY to −1 (so the emitter points downward). Twirl down the Basic Emission Speed Attributes arrow and set the Speed to 60. Finally, click Create. You now have a particle emitter, which needs to be attached to the nozzle of the rocket.

2. To attach the emitter to the nozzle, first move the emitter (which should still be selected) down into the base of the nozzle. With the emitter still selected,

shift-select the nozzle and press the P key, making the nozzle the parent of the emitter (so that the emitter will travel along with the rocket as it moves).

3. If you play back the animation right now, the particle emitter will shoot out no particles, because its rate is set to 0 particles per second. Just before the rocket takes off (frame 63) we need to turn on the "engine"—our particles. Go to frame 59, select the Rate channel for the emitter, and RM choose Key Selected to set a keyframe at 0 for this frame.

4. Now go to frame 60 and set a rate of 500 so there are suddenly many particles shooting out from the ship. If you play back the animation now, a shower of particles (points by default; we'll fix that in a moment) will shoot out from the exhaust nozzle.

5. Now we need to turn off our rocket. Go to frame 104 and set a keyframe for the Rate at 200 (select the Rate text, and RM choose Key Selected). Now, at frame 105 (where the impulse turns off as well), set a new keyframe for Rate at 0. When you now play back the animation, the particles will stop coming out of the rocket at frame 105—however, the particles hang around forever (they never die). We need to give our particles a life span so they will die off like good flames should.

Maya 3 makes it much easier than previous versions to control how particles live and die (see Chapters 22–24).

6. With the emitter still selected, press Ctrl+A to turn on the Attribute Editor. Once in the Attribute Editor, click the particleShape1 tab at the top; then, in the Lifespan Attributes section, choose Random Range for the Lifespan Mode. Leave the Lifespan at 1 (second), but change the Lifespan Random to about 0.3. Setting these two attributes this way makes each particle live 1 second, plus or minus 0.3 seconds (or in a range from 0.7 to 1.3 seconds). When you now play back the animation, you should see the particles die out approximately a second after they are created (thus the trail of particles follows the rocket up as it takes off). Save your work.

7. Now that we have a good trail of particles to work with, let's change the rendering type from points to something more interesting. In the Attribute Editor (with the particleShape1 node still selected), under the Render Attributes section, set the Render Type to Cloud (s/w—for software rendered). Next, click the Current Render Type button to add the attributes that belong with the Cloud render type.

8. In the new fields, make the Radius 1.5, the Surface Shading 1, and the Threshold 0.5. When you play back the animation (which will now run significantly slower), you should see that the exhaust particles are now spheres. To see what they would look like in a real rendering, choose Render ➜ Render into New Window (from the Rendering menu set).

9. Now we're closing in on a good exhaust cloud. The last piece of the puzzle is to create a texture for the particles. Play the animation to a frame where the particles are showing; then open the Hypershade (Window ➜ Hypershade). To create a cloud texture, we need to create a volumetric texture. To do so, scroll down the left-hand window until you reach Create: Materials, and click the + sign to the left of the Materials folder. A Volume folder will appear below the materials swatches, and clicking on it will open the Volume materials. MM drag the particleCloud material (the light blue ball) onto the right-hand window of the Hypershade, and then rename the material **exhaustVM**.

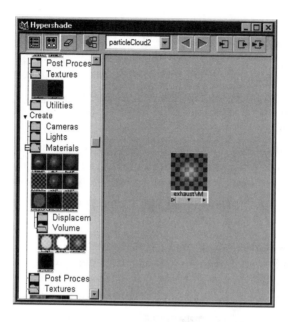

10. Select the exhaust particles, then right-click the material (in the Hypershade) and RM choose Assign Material to Selection. Move over to the Attribute Editor, and set the color of the material to a bright yellow. Set the Transparency to a light gray (by moving the slider to the right), and set the Glow Intensity to 0.5. Test-render your current frame—the exhaust should now glow a bright yellow as it is emitted from the nozzle. If you're not satisfied with the look of the exhaust, try adjusting some of the material settings, or the render attributes of the particleShape1 node. Save your work again.

When you are satisfied with the look of your exhaust, you can render out the entire animation sequence (see the "Rendering the Animation section," above) to see how things look with your exhaust plume. To compare your work with ours, you can take a look at `02rocket.mov` on the CD-ROM.

Summary

Congratulations! You have completed a real-world animation project your first time out. If your work does not look the way you would like it, that's all right. It can take quite a while to get an animation package to produce just what you had in mind. No matter how you did, you can always return to this project as you continue through this book.

You may find that after a few more chapters, you'd like to give this project another try. In that case, you should use this chapter as a reference, not a guide. In other words, try to do the work by yourself, and read the directions here only when you get stuck. In this way, you'll make the project your own, and you'll learn even more from it.

Whether you tried this rocket animation with years of digital 3D experience under your belt or it was your first foray into the wonderful world of 3D, you should be able to see how powerful the Maya environment can be. Now that you have an idea of what Maya can do, it's time to learn more about why and how Maya does what it does. Throughout this book, we'll give you a great deal more explanation about what we're doing than we did in this chapter, but you'll still be working on real-world projects, refining both your understanding of and skill with Maya. You've taken your first step into the world of Maya—now use this book as your guide to a journey through your new and exciting world.

Techniques for
Speeding Up Workflow

MAYA

Chapter 3

In Chapter 1, we examined many of Maya's interface features. Here, we will look at ways in which the default Maya interface can be adjusted to optimize the ways you interact with the program. From adjusting basic interface options to using hotkeys, shelves, and marking menus, and on to proper use of the Outliner, Hypergraph, and other windows, this chapter will show you how to customize Maya to do what you want quickly and easily. Finally, we will end with a quick demonstration of how to use Maya's tools to perform a modeling task with a minimum of pain and effort. Topics include:

- Adjusting interface options
- Using the hotbox instead of menu sets
- Shelves
- Hotkeys
- Marking menus
- Working in layers
- The Outliner
- The Hypergraph
- The Connection Editor
- The Hypershade
- Building an arm

Adjusting Interface Options

The first and most obvious place to start customizing Maya's interface to optimize your work is via the general interface options. Changing these options can make the interface cleaner—allowing you to work with fewer distractions—and also give over more space to the main scene view.

Most interface options (or preferences) are now under Window ➜ Settings/Preferences ➜ Preferences. Within the new Preferences window, most user interface (UI) preferences are (fittingly enough) under the Interface section of the Categories list, to the left of the window, as in Figure 3.1.

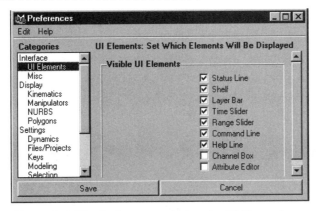

Figure 3.1 *The Preferences window for UI Elements*

If you choose the Interface category, you can turn off the title bar and main menu bar. Doing so removes the blue border at the top of the screen (which contains the title of the scene) and the menu set at the top of the main window, saving about 30 or 40 pixels of space for your scene window, and cleaning up the interface look a bit. You can also tell Maya to either remember or forget where you position your windows, whether menus should appear in panel windows, whether the focus (the cursor) will stay on the command line after you execute a MEL command from it, and whether the Attribute Editor appears in a separate, floating window or replaces the Channel box when Ctrl+A is pressed.

You can also turn off the main menu bar and/or pane menus under the Hotbox Controls menu in the hotbox: display the hotbox and choose Window Options ➜ Show Main (or Panel) Menu Bar.

The Interface/UI Elements category allows you to turn all components of the window (except the main scene window) on or off. If, for example, you are only modeling for a while, you could turn off the time and range sliders, freeing up more space for your scene. The Interface/Misc category allows you to specify how the main scene window will first appear when you open a new Maya scene (it defaults to Single Perspective view), as well as how existing files will be opened and saved, and how help is displayed in your Internet browser.

There is also a new Performance Settings window (Window ➜ Settings/Preferences ➜ Performance Settings), which allows you to adjust the settings for Stitching, Trim Display, Flexors, Blend Shapes, and a number of other options. You can set these calculation-intensive Maya elements to be on or off by default, or set them to work on an interactive basis, in which Maya ceases trying to update calculations while you work in the scene window (during mouse actions). Under the Dependency Graph Evaluation section, you can also tell Maya to update scenes while dragging (the default), when the mouse button is released, or only on demand (when a button is pressed in the scene window). For complex scenes, adjusting some or all of these settings may significantly help the speed with which you can interact with a Maya scene.

Using the Hotbox Instead of Menu Sets

As we discussed in Chapter 1, using the hotbox instead of dealing with all of the different Maya menu sets can really speed up your work, as well as clean up your Maya environment. Many professionals turn off all menu bars (main and panel), and use the hotbox to choose menu functions. To turn off menus, either use the Preferences menu (as described in the previous section) or uncheck the Main and Panel menus under the Hotbox Controls menu (Hotbox Controls ➜ Window Options ➜ Show Main (Panel) Menu Bar). Once Main and Panel menus have been turned off, to access menus just press and hold the spacebar to bring up the hotbox. Any or all menu sets can be displayed in the hotbox, depending on your choices under the Hotbox Controls menu. Generally speaking, advanced users tend to display all menu sets (Animation, Modeling, Dynamics, Rendering, and Maya Live, Cloth and Fur, if those are available) at once, making the hotbox fairly complex to look at, but once you find where all the different menus are, it's only a one-step procedure to access any menu from that point on.

For more on how to use the hotbox and how to set its options, see Chapter 1, "The Maya Interface."

Shelves

While we briefly discussed shelves in Chapter 1, they might have appeared to be only marginally useful. What makes shelves really useful is not what appears on them by default, but the fact that you can easily add new buttons to any shelf. You can, for example, make any menu item a shelf button, or even place MEL scripts on the shelf, allowing you to perform complex tasks at the click of your mouse. Additionally, as you can create and use multiple shelves, you can make a shelf specific to a task. For example, one shelf could be devoted to just MEL scripts, and another could be given over to common tasks for a specific project you're working on. To create a new shelf, choose Window ➜ Settings/Preferences ➜ Shelves, select the Shelves tab, and click the New Shelf button.

To switch to a new shelf (shelf2, for example), simply click its tab on the shelf bar, or select the shelf from the new pop-up shelf menu (the gray "folder" button to the left of the shelf), as shown below. (You can also customize shelf settings using the pull-down menu: the black triangle just below the shelf menu tab.) To create a new shelf button from a menu item, hold down the Ctrl, Alt, and Shift keys (all together), and choose the menu item from the menu bar (*not* the hotbox). A new button will appear on the active shelf, and clicking this button will be the same as selecting the menu item you had chosen.

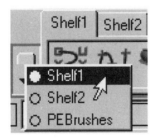

You must create shelf buttons from the main (or panel) menu bar, not the hotbox. As many users turn off these menu bars, it is a bit of a pain to create new shelf buttons—you first have to reactivate the menu bar, then create the button, and finally turn the menu bar off again.

To delete any shelf button, just MM drag it to the trash can at the top right of the shelf bar. To move an item to a different place on the shelf, simply MM drag it to the place you wish it to be. Other shelf items will adjust themselves to the new placement.

As an example, let's create a button that automatically creates a NURBS cylinder, and place it just next to the NURBS sphere button on shelf1. First, be sure you have shelf1 selected by making sure its tab is frontmost (or click the Folder button, as described above). Next, hold down the Ctrl, Alt, and Shift keys and, from the main menu bar, select Create ➜ Nurbs Primitives ➜ Cylinder. A new button icon should appear at the far right of shelf1. Finally, just MM drag the new button between the sphere and cone icons on the shelf. Voilà, one more primitive you can now create without resorting to the menu bar!

You could also create a NURBS cylinder button that automatically brings up the options window. Just hold down Ctrl+Alt+Shift and choose Create ➜ Nurbs Primitives ➜ Cylinder ❏.

You can create as many of these buttons as you wish (though you might have to scroll through the list if you create too many on one shelf), and/or delete any of the default buttons Maya provides for you, thus customizing your shelves to contain buttons that are the most useful to you. Buttons for items like the Hypergraph and Hypershade are very nice to place on shelf1 for easy access.

You can also turn MEL scripts into shelf buttons. To see how this works, let's create a very simple example. Open the Script Editor (click the Script Editor icon at the bottom right of the screen, or choose Window ➜ General Editors ➜ Script Editor). In the input (bottom) section of the window, type in the following:

```
sphere -n ball -r 2;
```

Highlight this text (drag over it, or triple-click the line), MM drag the text up to the shelf, and a new button will appear. Now, whenever you click this new button, a new NURBS sphere named ball, with a radius of 2, will appear at the origin of your scene. Even this simple example makes it clear how powerful a little MEL scripting can be; clicking one button not only creates a sphere but names it and gives it the radius you wish. You could even build a whole shelf for geometric primitives, with a group of buttons for each primitive type, each button having a different option set.

Hotkeys

After using Maya for a short time you should be familiar with many of its hotkeys, which are simply shortcuts to commands (or command modifiers) that are accessible by a keystroke. Accessing the Move tool, for example, is a simple matter of pressing the W key. As with most of Maya's interface, you are not limited to the built-in hotkeys. You can design your own, modify, or even delete the Maya default hotkeys.

As an example of how to create a hotkey, let's make a keyboard shortcut to bring up the Hypergraph. First, open the hotkeys option window (Window ➜ Settings/

Preferences ➔ Hotkeys). In this window, scroll down until you reach the Window Menu set, then find HypergraphWindow and highlight it, as shown in Figure 3.2.

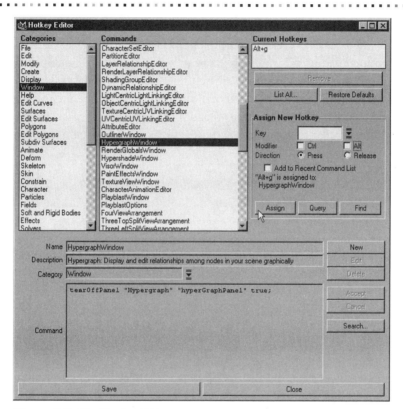

Figure 3.2 *The Hotkey Editor*

First, we need to find a key that is not currently mapped to any other hotkey. Under Assign New Hotkey, in the Key text field, type a lowercase **g** (G is different from g for hotkeys!), be sure the Press radio button is enabled, and check the Alt box (which means the hotkey will be Alt+g, not just g). If the key is not queried automatically (telling you the key is or is not assigned), click the Query button to see if any hotkey currently uses this combination. You should see a message just above the Query button telling you no command is currently mapped to this key (if one is, try another key/modifier combination). To enable the new hotkey, click the Assign button; you should now see (in the Current Hotkeys section) that Alt g has been assigned to the Hypergraph command. Press the Save button to save your changes. To test the new button, close the Hotkey Editor window, then press Alt+g in the scene window. The Hypergraph should pop right up for you!

Marking Menus

In addition to shelves and hotkeys, you can also create entire contextual menus (called marking menus) that appear either in the hotbox or when you press a hotkey combination.

For example, let's create a marking menu that will create a sphere using one of four options: radius = 1, radius = 2, radius = 3, radius = 4. First, open the Marking Menus option window (Window ➜ Settings/Preferences ➜ Marking Menus). In this window, you will see listed several marking menus that have already been created for Maya, including the region menus that appear to the north, east, south, and west in the hotbox, similar to what is shown in Figure 3.3 (for more on this, see Chapter 1).

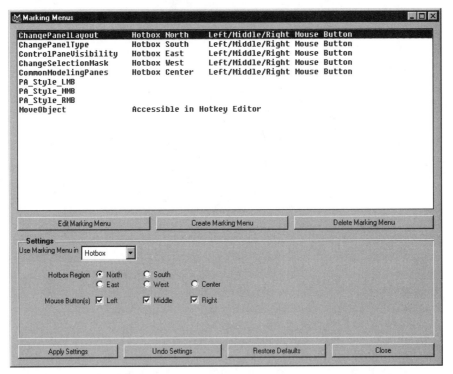

Figure 3.3 *The Marking Menu option window*

For our purposes, we want to create a new marking menu, so click the Create Marking Menu button. This brings up the Create Marking Menu window, with several blank boxes that we will use to create our own marking menu, shown in Figure 3.4.

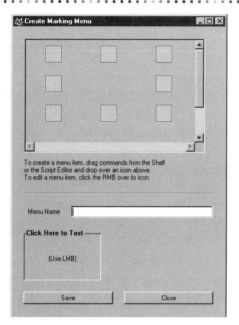

Figure 3.4 *The Create Marking Menu window*

First, give the marking menu a name, such as CreateSpheres. Because we will create a marking menu with four options, it is logical to use the top, right, bottom, and left boxes as our menu positions. There are a couple of ways to assign a command to a menu item: you can MM drag a shelf button that you have made (or one of the default buttons, like the cone button) onto a menu box; you can MM drag MEL scripts or commands to the menu item; or you can RM click on a menu item and choose Edit Menu Item (the option we will use here). Starting at the top center box, shown in Figure 3.5, RM choose Edit Menu Item, and in the window that pops up, type **Sphere radius 1** in the Label field, and type **sphere -r1;** in the Command(s) field (be sure the sphere command is in lower case!). Finally, click Save and Close to save your changes.

Now move over to the right center (east) box, RM choose Edit Menu Item, and repeat the steps from above, but this time label the button **Sphere radius 2**, and make the MEL command **sphere -r2;**. Move to the south and west boxes, and repeat the steps, making the south box create a sphere of radius 3, and the west box create one of radius 4. When you are finished, your Create Marking Menu window should look like Figure 3.6.

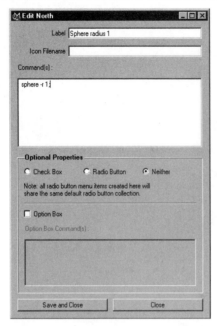

Figure 3.5 *Editing the "north" marking menu box*

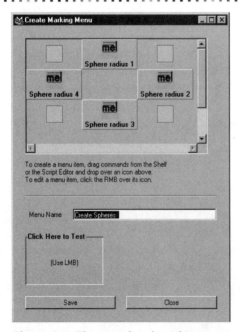

Figure 3.6 *The completed marking menu*

To test the buttons, click the Click Here to Test box. You should see all your menu options appear, as in Figure 3.7, and if you choose an option, an appropriately sized sphere should appear in your scene window.

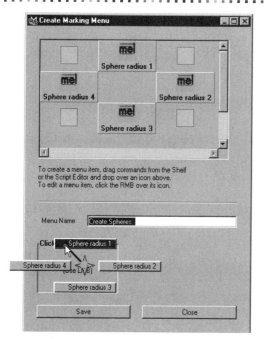

Figure 3.7 *Testing the new marking menu*

Once you have your menu working as you want, click Save and then Close to return to the Marking Menus Options window. Your new CreateSpheres menu should now appear at the bottom of the list, highlighted (if it's not highlighted, do so). We now have our menu, but we can't access it from the scene window. To do so, we need to choose whether we want the menu to be part of the hotbox or accessible via a key-stroke. This time, let's create a marking menu that will appear when we press a special key: under Settings, choose Hotkey Editor from the pop-up menu and then click the Apply Settings button. To the right of the CreateSpheres item in the list at the top of the window, there should now be the message *Accessible in Hotkey Editor,* meaning that we can now make a hotkey for our new menu.

Close the Marking Menu Options window and open the Hotkeys Options window (Window ➜ Settings/Preferences ➜ Hotkeys). Scroll all the way to the bottom of the Categories list and click on the User item. You should see CreateSpheres (Press) and CreateSpheres (Release) in the Commands pane.

The press and release states are important to a marking menu: while you are pressing the hotkey (the press state), the menu will appear; when the key is released (the release state), the menu disappears. If you forget to define a release state for your menu, it will not disappear when you release the hotkey!

Now we just follow the steps we used in the last section to define a hotkey. First, select the Press item: CreateSphere; then query a key—Ctrl+R should be open for your use. When you have found an open key combination, be sure your Action radio button is set to Press; then click the Assign button. You should get a menu asking if you want to create a Release state as well for your hotkey—answer yes to this. When the key is assigned, you should see that CreateSphere (Press) is now set to Ctrl+R Press in the Current Hotkeys pane, while CreateSphere (Release) is set to Ctrl+R Release.

To test your new marking menu, hold down Ctrl+R, and press the left mouse button. As Figure 3.8 shows, you should see your marking menu, ready for use!

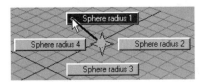

Figure 3.8 *The marking menu, ready for action*

There are many steps involved in creating a marking menu, so you probably wouldn't create one for a quick, simple task. But consider the power a marking menu gives you: it's a complete new menu with multiple items (and even subitems) that you can access anywhere in the scene window at the click of a key. Marking menus are relatively easy to create, and a great idea for tasks you repeat often—especially if they have multiple options.

This discussion of customizing shelves, hotkeys, and marking menus is very basic. Because MEL scripts are the most efficient tool for customizing these interface elements, you'll find a much more thorough discussion of these topics in Chapter 16, "MEL Basics."

Working in Layers

Working in layers can be particularly useful when you are modeling a multiple-part, complex object (for example, the inner workings of a mechanical clock, or a complex creature like a human or dog). By placing groups of objects in layers (fingers in one layer, hand in another, arm in another), you can easily hide, display, template, or otherwise adjust large groups of objects all at once, rather than tediously selecting each object and then changing it—or, even worse, being unable to select one object that is hidden behind another.

The Layer bar is a quick visual reference for working in layers, so if you have it turned off, turn it back on again (choose Window ➜ Settings/Preferences ➜ Preferences; then choose Interface/UI Elements and click the Layer Bar check mark). As shown below, the Layer bar should appear just above your scene window, with the Default layer already selected (the Default layer is where all objects that have not been assigned to other layers are stored). To create a new layer, just click the layer icon (the icon to the far left of the Layer bar that looks like three sheets of paper). If you double-click the default layer name (layer1), a dialog box will open, allowing you to rename the layer. Once your new layer is created and named, make a couple of simple objects (like a sphere and a cylinder). Select your objects and, using the triangle button to the left of the layer name, choose Assign Selected. The objects you had selected are now part of your new layer. Return to the scene window, deselect your objects, and (again from the Layer pop-up menu), choose Select All in Layer. Now you see that your objects are selected, as they are a part of this new layer.

To get a better view of your new layer, choose Edit Membership from the layer pop-up menu. This brings up the Relationship Editor, shown in Figure 3.9, with all layers on the left side, and all objects on the right side.

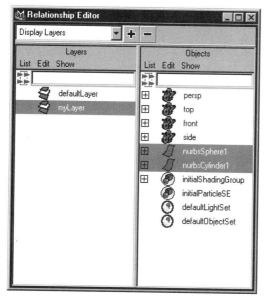

Figure 3.9 The Layer Relationship Editor

When you click a layer name, all objects in that layer become highlighted on the right (highlighting signifies inclusion in the layer). You can then click any object on the right side, toggling its inclusion in the layer. Each object can only belong to one layer. Therefore, if you highlight your sphere in the default layer (for example), it will be un-selected from your other layer. You can quickly change which layer you are working with, and which objects are included in each layer, by using this window. Try placing one object in your layer and another in the default layer.

You can also adjust each layer's attributes by choosing Layer Attributes from the Layer pop-up menu.

To quickly hide or show all objects in a layer, check the Visible box in the Layer pop-up menu. This menu can also change the state of each layer: the Standard state is your normal working state. The Template state turns the objects into templates (they cannot be selected or moved, and they turn a pinkish orange). The Reference state makes the layer a reference layer, once again making all objects in it unselectable, but keeping their display properties.

In Maya 3, you can see when a layer (aside from the default layer) has its visibility set to off: there is now an X to the left of the layer name if the layer is invisible.

While working in layers for a simple scene like our example may seem a waste of time, as we move on to more ambitious projects you'll see how useful it is to select, hide, template, or otherwise alter several objects in a complex scene. If you have not used layers before, try modeling an intricate object that has many overlapping pieces, such as a stapler, and you'll appreciate how much layers can speed up your workflow.

For more information on layers, see Chapter 4, "Modeling Basics."

The Outliner

There are two basic ways to view all of the information in your scene: the Outliner and the Hypergraph. While the Hypergraph is the more flexible and powerful of the two, the Outliner is usually easier for a new Maya user, and it performs several tasks in a more straightforward fashion than does the Hypergraph. Conceptually, the Outliner is exactly what its name implies: an outline of the scene you are working on.

To open the Outliner, choose Window ➜ Outliner from the main menu set (or hotbox). If you had created a default sphere, and it was selected, the Outliner window would look like Figure 3.10.

The first four items in the Outliner are the four default cameras (plus any other cameras you might have created). Next are listed geometric objects (like the sphere). Finally, sets (groupings of objects, like the default light and object sets) are listed. Any highlighted objects (in gray) are selected in the scene, and vice versa. You can rename

Figure 3.10 *The Outliner with a sphere selected*

any object listed in the Outliner by double-clicking its name. You can also bring up the Attribute Editor and focus it on any object in the Outliner by double-clicking its icon.

There are several viewing options available in the Outliner, accessed either via the Outliner's menu or by holding down the right mouse button anywhere inside the Outliner window. Among the more important options are showing only specific types of objects, like geometry (Show ➔ Objects ➔ Geometry), showing shape nodes for objects, or showing all objects, rather than just the DAG (Directed Acyclic Graph—a technical term for the common objects you see in the scene) objects. If, for example, you turn on Show Shapes, a plus sign appears to the left of any object in the scene that has a shape node (as a sphere or other geometric object would have). By clicking the plus sign, you can expand the outline to see the shape node; in the case of our sphere, this would reveal the nurbsSphereShape1 node, as in Figure 3.11.

Figure 3.11 *The Outliner showing the shape node*

The Outliner can be used in several ways, but there are two that are probably the most appropriate: to get a quick look at the scene as a whole, and to access objects in a complex scene without having to pick the object. The first use for the Outliner—getting an overview of the scene—is the function of any good outline (from the outline of a term paper to the schematic outline of an electrical circuit). Because you can show or hide any type of object in the Outliner, you could, for example, look only at the lights in a scene; this would allow you to see quickly how many lights there are, and, by double-clicking the light icons, you could just as quickly bring up the Attribute Editor to examine or adjust their options.

The second main use for the Outliner—allowing quick selection—flows from the first. As the Outliner provides easy access to any or all objects in the scene, you can rapidly choose, alter (via the Attribute Editor), or rename objects in a convenient list form, rather than having to hunt through a scene to find them, never knowing for sure if you have forgotten an object. In complex scenes, the ability to choose objects becomes even more important. Consider an object like a Christmas tree with a hundred ornamental lights on it. The tree itself might consist of two or three dozen objects (branches, base, and so on), and the hundred lights would be intertwined in the tree, making them very difficult to select for modification. In the Outliner, however, this job would be easy. First you would choose to show only light objects (Show ➜ Objects ➜ Lights) and then move down the outline of the scene, selecting and adjusting lights at will. As should be apparent, this method of interacting with your scene can be a real lifesaver.

Maya 3 has the option of splitting the Outliner window, so you can see two places in a large scene. To split a window, simply place the cursor over the bottom of the Outliner window and drag the mouse up into the window somewhere. To move the divider around, drag it up and down. To remove the split, drag the divider down off the bottom of the window.

The Hypergraph

If you come to Maya from another 3D package (as many of us have), you are probably familiar with a window like the Outliner, which helps you keep track of objects in your scene. On the other hand, it is unlikely that you have run across anything quite like Maya's Hypergraph. The Hypergraph performs many of the same functions as the Outliner, but it uses a completely different interface design. This tool is worth studying at length in a chapter on interface optimization; use of the Hypergraph can radically reduce the time you spend hunting through the scene and other windows, thus speeding up your workflow.

While the Hypergraph may seem confusing on its surface, once you understand that its interface was designed to parallel Maya's scene window interface—and once you see the many different ways in which the Hypergraph can function—you will wonder how you ever got along without it. Even if you consider yourself an experienced Hypergraph user, you may find that this section will reveal a few tips and tricks you didn't previously know.

What Is the Hypergraph?

The Hypergraph is a hypertext-like view of your scene (thus the name). If you have worked with an HTML authoring tool, you will recognize the Web-like appearance of linked objects in the Hypergraph. Every element visible in a scene is represented by a text box, and any linked objects have a line that connects them together, showing their connection in the scene. Passing your cursor over the line, you'll see which elements of each object are connected. Besides displaying the relationships between objects and elements in a scene, the Hypergraph also lets you create or modify those relationships—for example, you can parent two objects together or break an input connection directly in the Hypergraph, rather than having to go to the scene window or Relationship Editor. Moreover, the types of objects visible in a scene depend on the filtering choices you've made using the Hypergraph's Options ➜ Display menu. In essence, the Hypergraph is your scene; with it and the Channel box, you can do pretty much everything you can do in a scene window, and more. The difference is that the Hypergraph is represented as text boxes instead of the objects you would see in the scene windows. While the Outliner is probably more familiar, the Hypergraph is more aligned with Maya's general interface philosophy, and, more important, it allows quick tracking and focusing across hundreds of scene elements, so it can be much more efficient than the Outliner in complex scenes.

Getting to Know the Hypergraph

Because the Hypergraph offers so much information, it takes a bit of effort for most people to feel comfortable with it. We will therefore work through the Hypergraph piece by piece in the following pages, using examples to clarify certain concepts, but mostly just showing how the interface works. By the time you finish this section, you should feel comfortable enough with the Hypergraph to begin using it in your work (if you don't already).

Navigating the Hypergraph

Open a new scene in Maya, and create two objects—say a sphere and a cone. Now open the Hypergraph, by choosing Window ➜ Hypergraph from the main menu set. In the Hypergraph window, you should see icons for the objects you created, as illustrated in Figure 3.12.

Figure 3.12 *The Hypergraph, showing a sphere and a cone*

Because you will probably access the Hypergraph many times while working in Maya, it is a good idea to create a button on your shelf for it, or use the hotkey (Alt+G) we created earlier in this chapter. To create a shelf button, from the menu bar (not the hotbox), choose Window ➜ Hypergraph while holding down the Ctrl, Alt, and Shift keys. A new button will appear on the shelf for the Hypergraph.

If you compare Figure 3.12 to a view of the same scene in the Outliner, you can see that the Hypergraph is actually less complex (as it doesn't show the cameras or default sets), but it is organized in a side-to-side manner, rather than top-to-bottom.

You will also notice that when an object is selected in a scene, the corresponding box in the Hypergraph turns yellow; if the object is not selected, its box remains gray (similar to the default shading color of all objects in Maya). Clicking an object box (or node) in the Hypergraph is the same as selecting the object in the scene window: the box turns yellow (indicating it is selected) and the object in the scene is highlighted in green. It is worth noting that you can choose to display only certain objects in the Hypergraph (Show ➜ Objects ➜ NurbsObjects, for example), or show object components like shape nodes (Options ➜ Display ➜ Shape Nodes).

Where the Hypergraph really shines is in its ability to navigate (zoom or track) like any of the scene windows in Maya. To zoom, hold down the Alt key and the left and middle mouse buttons—dragging to the left zooms out, while dragging to the right zooms in. To track across (or up and down) the Hypergraph window, hold down the Alt key and the middle mouse button, and then drag the mouse around to track through the window. By tracking and zooming, you can quickly move through even a large scene, finding the nodes you're interested in. Additionally, you can use two hotkeys to frame the window around a selected object or around all objects in the Hypergraph. To focus the window on one or more selected objects (highlighted in green or white in the scene window), press the F key. To expand the view to fit all graphed objects, press the A key. If you try this with our example scene (with the cone selected), pressing F will fill the Hypergraph window with the cone node, while pressing A will expand the view to fit both the sphere and the cone.

The A and F keys work in any scene window—pressing F will focus the window on the selected object(s), while pressing A will make the entire scene fit in the window.

If your scene is complex, and you find yourself consistently hunting for a particular object (or group of objects) in the Hypergraph, you can save yourself a great deal of time by bookmarking any or all views you are likely to need at a later point. Although our example scene is too simple to warrant using bookmarks, let's see how the process works by creating three bookmarks: one focusing on the sphere, one focusing on the cone, and the third showing both objects. First highlight the cone and press the F key (or just zoom and track until the cone box fills the Hypergraph window). Then choose Bookmarks ➜ Create Bookmark ❏ from the Hypergraph menu set. Choosing the option box will open a window that lets you name the bookmark (if you don't open the window, Maya will choose a default name for you). In this case, type **cone** and click the OK button. You now have a bookmark for this view arrangement, which you can return to at any time. Next, select the sphere object and press the F key; then create a bookmark for it (name it **sphere**). Finally, create a bookmark for the complete view of the scene (press the A key to jump to a complete view of the scene) and name it **all**.

To test your bookmarks, zoom and track the window to a completely different view, and then choose Bookmarks ➜ Cone (or Ball or All) from the Hypergraph menu set. The view should jump back to the one you defined for that bookmark. To edit your bookmarks (add a new one, delete a bookmark, or rename one), choose Bookmarks ➜ Bookmark Editor, select the bookmark you wish to edit, and choose the appropriate action from the Bookmark Editor's Edit menu.

You can also create bookmarks for different types of views (with the Hypergraph in different modes—as discussed later in this chapter). This functionality can really save time, as you can avoid having to continually reset the Hypergraph's view modes as you switch between different aspects of your project.

One other nice feature of the Hypergraph is that it shows you when an object is keyframed, by changing its box shape in the window from a rectangle to a parallelogram. If you keyframe the ball shape, for example, its Hypergraph representation will change to give you a visual indication that it is now a keyframed node, as shown in Figure 3.13.

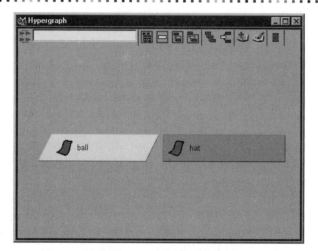

Figure 3.13 *The Hypergraph with the ball node keyframed*

Doing Work in the Hypergraph

Besides viewing selected objects in the Hypergraph, you can also select any object simply by clicking its box. To select the sphere in our example, click its box, turning it yellow (and selecting it in the scene window as well). To select multiple objects, you can either Shift-select them or drag a selection marquee around the boxes representing all the objects you wish to select. To deselect one selected object, Shift+click it. To deselect all objects in the scene, click anywhere in the Hypergraph window outside a text box. To rename an object in the Hypergraph, Ctrl+double-click the name in the box, and then type in the new name and press Enter. For example, we could rename the sphere ball and the cone hat in our practice scene.

In the Hypergraph, *parenting* one object to another (the child object will then follow its parent's movements, rotations, and scaling) is just a matter of MM dragging the child object on top of its parent-to-be. In our example, MM drag the ball (sphere) onto the hat (cone). As Figure 3.14 indicates, the ball will now appear beneath the hat—with a line connecting the two—showing that it is now the child of the hat.

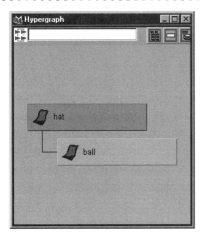

Figure 3.14 *The ball as child of the hat*

If you now select the hat, you will notice that the ball also becomes highlighted (in the scene window), and that any transformation you apply to the hat is automatically applied to the ball. To unparent (disconnect) the two objects, MM drag the ball into an empty space in the Hypergraph window. The objects will once again appear side by side (with no interconnecting line), indicating that they are independent of each other.

Nodes and the Hypergraph

The underlying structure of a Maya scene is based on nodes and attributes. A node is the fundamental element of a scene, and most of the time an object in a Maya scene window (or in a shader network or the like) has several nodes. An attribute is a behavior (or characteristic) of a node, and each node can have many attributes, including custom attributes that you create yourself. Some common nodes would be the nurbsSphere1 and makeNurbsSphere1 nodes created when you make a default NURBS sphere. The attributes of the nurbsSphere1 node include translateX, Y and Z, rotateX, Y, and Z, scaleX, Y and Z, and Visibility. Attributes of the makeNurbsSphere1 node include radius, start and endSweep, and spans.

Nodes are connected together, either by default when you create, say, a geometry object (which has a shape and a transform node connected together), or when you manually connect two objects (for example, by parenting one object to another, or by attaching a new texture to a material group). Most attributes that are of the same data type (for example, floats or vectors) can be attached to each other across two nodes.

If you are not used to working with Maya, the entire concept of nodes may seem pretty frightening. While the theory may seem difficult, however, nodes and attributes are fairly easy to understand in practice: nodes are anything that can be shown in the Hypergraph (or a bold-faced name in the Channel box, or a tab at the top of the Attribute Editor), while attributes are what appears in the Channel box or Attribute Editor when a node is selected.

In the Hypergraph, all you see are nodes, and changing Hypergraph display modes just changes which nodes you are looking at.

To see how changing display modes changes the nodes you see in a scene, let's again look at our simple example scene (the ball and hat). From the Hypergraph menu set (or by holding down the right mouse button inside the Hypergraph window), choose Options ➜ Display ➜ Shape Nodes. Now that shape nodes can be seen in the Hypergraph, you will see the ballShape and hatShape nodes, as in Figure 3.15, which are separate from the ball and hat nodes. (The ball and hat nodes are called *transform* nodes, and are in control of where the object is, its rotation, and its scaling, while the shape nodes are in charge of what the object looks like.)

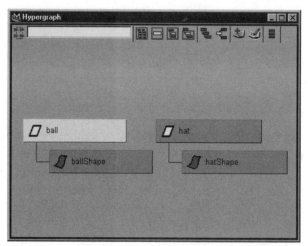

Figure 3.15 *Ball and hat with shape nodes showing*

You can also show all nodes (many of which are normally invisible) that lead into and out of an object node, revealing the hidden depths of what Maya is doing when you create a "simple" object. Select the ball node and choose Graph ➜ Up and Downstream Connections from the Hypergraph menu set (or click the Up and Downstream

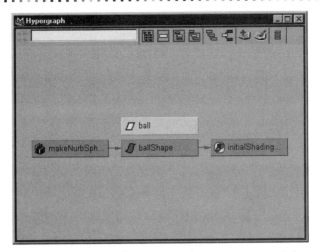

Figure 3.16 *The ball node, showing upstream and downstream connections*

Connections button at the top of the menu bar). You will then see all of the input and output nodes connected to your ball, as shown in Figure 3.16.

In this layout, the ball transform node sits atop the others, while the bottom three nodes show the flow of information for this object: the makeNurbsSphere1 node (where you control radius, U and V isoparms, and so forth) outputs to the ballShape node, which then outputs to the initialShadingGroup node, where the ball is given a texture and made visible.

No objects in Maya are visible unless they are attached to a shading group. While the underlying structure of an object is contained in its shape and transform nodes, it is only in the shading group that the object is given a color and texture—therefore, without its connection to a shading group, you could not see the object.

If you wish to dig even deeper, choose the initialShadingGroup node, and display the up and downstream connections again. This time, as Figure 3.17 shows, you will see the shapes (plus a lambert shader—the default one) that feed into the initial shading group, plus the shading group's output to the renderer and lights. To return to your original view, just choose Graph ➜ Scene Hierarchy—or choose one of the bookmarks you had previously saved (a nice time-saver!).

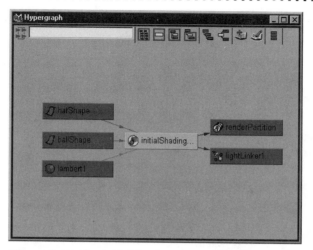

Figure 3.17 *The InitialShadingGroup with up and downstream connections showing*

Because Maya is constructed on nodes, and the Hypergraph can show just about any node grouping (based on your filtering choices), you should begin to see how valuable a tool the Hypergraph can be as you work through the different stages of your animation process. From modeling to texturing to lighting to animation, the Hypergraph is flexible enough to display the data you need—and even *only* the data you need, should you wish—for each stage of your work. Just keep in mind that the Hypergraph shows nodes, and Maya is built on nodes, so all you have to do is figure out which nodes you want to see for any given stage of your animation process, and you can get the Hypergraph to display them for you.

Know Your Nodes

While there are a great number of nodes in Maya, they tend to fall under one of these general categories:

- Transform nodes (containing items like Translate X or Rotate Y)
- Shape nodes (containing items like the makeObject inputs)
- Invisible nodes (like default cameras)
- Underworld nodes (nodes that are created, for example, when a curve is drawn on a surface)
- Material nodes (like lambert or phongE)
- Texture nodes (colors, procedural textures, or image files used to alter the behavior of a material node)

- Texture placement nodes (used to place textures on objects)
- Light nodes (lights, like a spotlight)
- Utility nodes (which provide a utility to a shader network, such as the multiply/divide node)

Menus and Buttons: Where the Action Is!

While the Hypergraph's default view is very useful, it is just a first step to viewing your scene in the Hypergraph. By using the Hypergraph's menu choices (the most common of which are repeated in buttons across the top of the Hypergraph), you can make the Hypergraph show you just what you need in an organized, concise manner.

The Edit Menu

The Edit menu contains several ways to control the display of selected items (or edit those items). First, you can rename an object—this is the same as Ctrl+double-clicking the object's name. You can also collapse or expand a hierarchy; for example, if the ball has its shape node showing, you can collapse the shape node, hiding it beneath the ball's transform node. A red triangle reminds you that there are collapsed nodes beneath the visible one, as in Figure 3.18. To expand the nodes again, just choose Edit ➜ Expand.

You can also collapse and expand nodes by simply double-clicking the top node of the group you wish to hide or reveal.

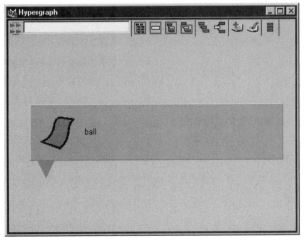

Figure 3.18 *A Ball node, showing it has children hidden by the downward arrow*

If you have several groups of collapsed nodes beneath a parent node (for example, if you have several child objects, all of which have collapsed subnodes), you can expand all nodes at once by choosing Edit → Expand All. The option Show Selected displays items that are selected in the scene window (or Outliner) but have been filtered out of the Hypergraph display. For example, if you have turned off display of NURBS objects in the Hypergraph, but choose a NURBS sphere in the scene window, you can force the Hypergraph to show it by choosing the Show Selected menu item. The Attributes menu item brings up the Attribute Editor for the selected item (the same as selecting the item and pressing Ctrl+A). Finally, you can choose to clear your Hypergraph view, if your view has gotten too complex.

The Edit menu also offers a couple of options for use with the freeform layout, as we will discuss shortly.

The View Menu

Under the View menu, you can choose to change the Hypergraph to the last view you used—or the next, if you have moved backward and forward in views. This command can be useful if you move a great distance through the Hypergraph in a complex scene and wish to return to where you were previously. The Previous and Next View commands function in a similar manner to bookmarks but change according to the Hypergraph view. You can also frame your selection (this has the same effect as the F key), frame all (the same as the A key), frame the hierarchy, or frame a branch of the hierarchy.

These four framing options (Frame Selection, All, Hierarchy and Branch) can be accessed by the four leftmost buttons in the Hypergraph toolbar, which is located atop the Hypergraph window, as shown here.

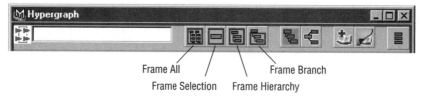

Framing a hierarchy focuses on the selected object plus any other objects in that hierarchy. Framing a branch frames the selected object plus any objects *below* it in the hierarchy. If the ball is the child of the hat in our example scene, selecting the ball and then framing the hierarchy would focus the window on the hat and ball nodes; framing the branch would focus the window only on the ball (and any child nodes it might have).

The Bookmark Menu

The Bookmark menu lets you create and edit bookmarks for any layout or view you wish to save in the Hypergraph. We discussed bookmarks earlier in the chapter, so here we need only note that two buttons on the Hypergraph toolbar are related to the Bookmark menu: the Add Bookmark button (a book with a red plus on it) and the Edit Bookmark button (a lifted leaf with a book below it). The Add Bookmark button simply adds a bookmark for the current view, while the Edit Bookmark button opens the Bookmark Editor window, allowing you to rename, delete, or add bookmarks.

The Graph Menu

The Graph menu controls the general parameters of what the Hypergraph shows. You can graph the upstream connections for an object (all nodes that feed into the selected object), the downstream connections for an object (all nodes that the selected object feeds information into), and both the up and downstream connections for that object. Because choosing one of these options changes the view from the default scene hierarchy, once you have chosen an upstream/downstream graph, you can also choose the Scene Hierarchy view to return to the scene hierarchy.

The graph Up and Downstream Connections and Scene Hierarchy menu items are also available as buttons on the Hypergraph toolbar, as shown here:

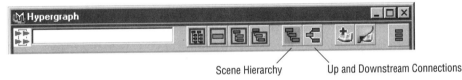

Scene Hierarchy   Up and Downstream Connections

Should your graph get behind your scene window (an unlikely event, but possible), you can force the Hypergraph to rebuild itself by choosing Graph → Rebuild. By using this command, you can be sure the Hypergraph is up to date if you ever suspect it is not. Finally, the Layout command in the Graph menu lets you change (or reset) the arrangement of items when you are looking at upstream or downstream connections. Arranging these nodes may allow you to make more sense of them or to move unwanted nodes off screen while you work.

When you graph the up and/or downstream connections in the Hypergraph, you are displaying what is known as a dependency graph. Put simply, a *dependency graph* shows the connections between nodes (like shading network elements) in a Maya scene, allowing you to see the flow of information from one node to another—in other words, how each node depends on the others to which it is connected.

The Rendering Menu

The Rendering menu lets you focus the Hypergraph on materials, textures, shading groups, lights, and images. You can also use the Rendering → Create Render Node command to create a render node directly in the Hypergraph, rather than having to use the Hypershade or the Multilister to do so.

With the advent of the Hypershade, the Rendering menu set in the Hypergraph is less useful than it once was. It is still very convenient, however, to have all shading information accessible in the same window as the scene hierarchy, especially when you just want to take a quick peek at a shading item rather than work with it extensively.

The Options Menu

The Options menu gives you control over how the Hypergraph displays nonstandard (invisible, shape, or underworld) nodes, and also how the Hypergraph as a whole is laid out. Of the Options submenus (Display, Orientation, Layout, Transitions, and Update), the one you will probably use the most is Display. The Display submenu lets you choose which types of nodes and connections will be displayed in the Hypergraph window. As we have already seen, you can show shape nodes (which control the structural options of an object); you can also display invisible nodes (such as the cameras or any objects you have hidden) and underworld nodes (these are nodes generated by objects such as surface curves, which have their transform nodes in a local rather than a global space). You can also turn on or off the display of expression, constraint, or deformer connections. For example, Figure 3.19 shows that if you aim-constrain the ball to the hat in our example scene (Constrain ➜ Aim), you can display the connections Maya makes between the ball, the hat, and the new aimConstraint node.

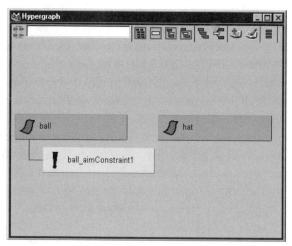

Figure 3.19 *The Hypergraph displaying constraint connections*

You can also display a background image for the Hypergraph window if you are in freeform layout mode (see below) by choosing Options ➜ Display ➜ Background Image (in freeform) from the Display submenu.

The Orientation submenu of the Display menu lets you toggle between horizontal (the default layout) and vertical layout modes. If you like working in an Outliner-like fashion (with nodes stacked on top of each other), you may prefer the vertical orientation mode. The Layout submenu allows you to choose automatic (default) or freeform layout mode—the freeform layout mode lets you move nodes around into any shape you wish, while the automatic mode places the nodes in a predetermined order next to one another. The Transitions submenu enables you to create an animated transition between views when you choose View ➜ Previous or Next View. By default, the view changes instantaneously, but by checking the Animate Transitions box (and then choosing how many frames the transitions will be), you can force the Hypergraph window to scroll from one view to the other. While they are cute, transitions are more of a time-waster than anything useful—unless you need to figure out where one view is in relation to another. The Update submenu lets you choose when to update the Hypergraph window; you can choose to update on a selection, on a node creation, on both (the default), or on neither.

The Show Menu

The Show menu lets you make very specific choices about the objects you wish to see in the Hypergraph window. Under Show ➜ Objects, you can show (or hide) geometry, lights, sets, and cameras, to name just a few. You can display all objects by choosing Show ➜ Show All. You can select several objects (in the scene window or the Hypergraph), and then show only those and other objects with the same type as your selected objects (Show ➜ Show Selected Type(s)). You can also invert the types of objects you display (Show ➜ Invert Shown). If, for example, you were working on a scene with 10 lights and 20 geometry objects, you could display only the lights while you worked on lighting the scene and then invert the selection filter to show all your other objects while you tweaked your models or animated the scene.

Making and Breaking Connections in the Hypergraph

One of the most interesting features of the Hypergraph is its ability to make and break data connections between nodes. To see how this works, take our example scene (the ball and hat), and add a lattice deformer to the ball (select the ball node, then choose Deform ➜ Create Lattice). Select the ball node again, and choose Graph ➜ Up and Downstream Connections. In this new view, you will see connecting arrows between the nodes that make up the lattice-ball group. By passing your cursor over one of these arrows, you can see the output/input data connections between nodes, as illustrated in Figure 3.20.

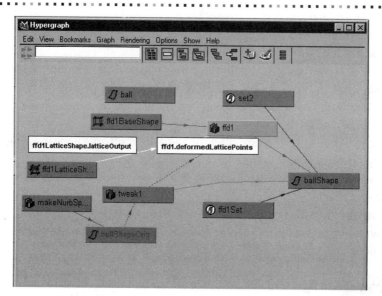

Figure 3.20 *Hypergraph showing deformer input/output connections*

To break one of these connections, just click one of the arrows (highlighting it yellow) and hit the Delete key. You can, for example, break the deformer connection between the lattice and the ball if you highlight the arrow that shows the ffd1Lattice-Shape.latticeOutput to ffd1.deformedLatticePoints connection (shown in Figure 3.20). If you alter the deformer (scale it, say), you will immediately see the ball return to its original shape once you have deleted the connection.

As should be obvious, it is dangerous to go around deleting connections between nodes—especially if you don't know what you're doing. This is not to say you shouldn't experiment; just save your file before you do start deleting connections, so in case you can't get what you want, you can at least return to a good version of your project.

To make a connection between nodes, just MM drag one node on top of another (the node that will output a value will be the one you drag; the one that will accept an input value will be the node you drag onto). Once you have completed the drag operation, the Connection Editor will open, allowing you to choose which attributes to connect. If, as in Figure 3.21, you MM drag ffd1Lattice onto the ball node, you might connect the lattice's visibility attribute to the ball's visibility (click each of these attributes on the right and left of the Connection Editor to connect them). Then, when you hide the lattice, the ball will hide as well. To confirm that the connection has been made, you will see a new arrow in the Hypergraph showing the connected attributes.

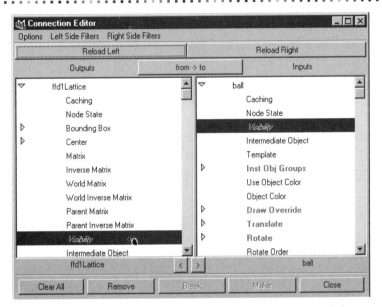

Figure 3.21 *The Connection Editor showing connected visibilities*

In general, most people use the make-break connection ability of the Hypergraph (and Hypershade)) primarily to make and break connections between shader nodes in a shader network, such as the luminance output of a texture being fed into the transparency of a material node. While the connected attributes differ between types of scene elements, the method of making and breaking connections is the same as described above.

The Ins and Outs of the Connection Editor

The Connection Editor is an extremely useful Maya feature. Essentially, it lets you connect any output of one node to any matching (that is, of the same data type) input of another node. The Connection Editor can do some amazing things, connecting even the most bizarre attributes (as long as their data types match). This ability to manipulate connections at such a low level gives you creative control over anything from ramp texture colors to object rotation order based on another object's position (or that of another node on the same object), visibility, node state, or whatever else you can dream up. In shader networks, the output color of one node (like a fractal map) is often automatically input into the input color of another node (like a phongE texture) when you create a texture map. With the Connection Editor, you can also plug the output color of one node into the bump map node—a node that controls how "bumpy" a surface looks—of a texture (which is the same as MM dragging the node onto the bump map channel of the texture), or even control the intensity (or height) of a different bump map based on the output of this node.

While the number of attributes available to connect via the Connection Editor can be a bit overwhelming, the window's controls are fairly straightforward. Let's take a look at how the Connection Editor works.

Using the Connection Editor

To make a connection, first load the left and right sides of the Connection Editor (Window → General Editors → Connection Editor) with the two nodes you wish to connect (or, alternatively, MM drag one node onto another in the Attribute Editor to automatically open and load the Connection Editor). Then click the output attribute you wish to use and, from the list of attributes with matching data types (not grayed out), choose the input node.

Some data types, like color, have arrows next to them, allowing you to access their component attributes—in the case of color, it would be the red, green, and blue components of the color. Thus, while color (a vector) may not be a match (and is thus grayed out) for the X scale of an object, you *can* connect the red component of color to the object's X scale; depending on the direction of this connection, the object's redness would be controlled by its X scale, or the object's scale would be controlled by its redness.

The Connection Editor Controls

The controls in the Connection Editor's window are easy to use. The buttons at the top enable you to reload the left or right side of the window (thus changing which node is loaded on each side of the window). By clicking the "from -> to" button, you can change the direction of the input/output of the two nodes (making it "to <- from").

The Right and Left Side Filters menus let you display only those attributes you are interested in—this can be a great way to reduce the clutter of available attributes to a more manageable number.

Under the Options menu, you can change the default behavior of the Connection Editor—which is to make and break connections automatically as you click the attributes in the left and right windows—to a manual mode. If manual mode is selected, you must press the (now enabled) Make and Break buttons at the bottom of the window to create (or disconnect) the connection between two attributes.

The Clear All button removes all connections, and the Remove button removes the loaded nodes.

Finally, the two arrow keys just below the left and right windows allow you to step through all nodes on an object (for example, the shape to the transform node of a geometric object), saving you a trip back to the Hypergraph to highlight a new node, and then reload it into the Connection Editor. To disconnect the two attributes, just click a connected attribute on one side of the window to unhighlight it.

The possibilities for using the Connection Editor are so many and varied that the best advice is just to open a new project, create some objects and shader networks, and play with different connections, so you can get a feel for the different ways you can control one node via another. This way, when you are faced with what might appear to be a difficult problem in a "real world" situation, you may see that some clever use of the Connection Editor will do the trick nicely.

Freeform Layout Mode

There is one last way you can modify the Hypergraph to make the data in it even more understandable: the freeform layout. This layout mode allows you to place your nodes anywhere you wish in relation to each other (above, beside, around, and so forth). This can be a real help when you build a complex character like a human, as you can arrange the nodes for the hands, say, where the hands of a figure would be. You can even import an image as a background plate for the Hypergraph window (perhaps a sketch of your figure) to serve as a reference in the freeform layout mode.

To enter freeform layout mode, either choose Options ➡ Layout ➡ Freeform Layout or click the Freeform Layout toggle button on the toolbar in the Hypergraph (the button farthest to the right). Once you are in freeform layout mode, you can drag nodes anywhere in the Hypergraph window that you wish, perhaps shapes or figures. To load a background image for your new layout, choose View ➡ Load Background Image and browse to find your image. You can also reset your freeform layout to its default arrangement by choosing Edit ➡ Reset Freeform Layout. Thus, no matter how much mess you make of your node arrangement, you can always return to a clean view at the touch of a button.

As an example of using the freeform layout, let's build a human figure in the Hypergraph (we won't actually build a character in the scene window, but if you have one you've already built, feel free to use that figure instead of our random assortment of primitives). First create 20 or 30 scene primitives. If you wish, you can lay them out in the scene window in the form of a person, or you can just arrange them in the Hypergraph. In the Hypergraph, be sure you are in freeform layout mode, and then drag nodes up to the head region (renaming them things like "skull," "nose," "right eye," and so on), the body, the arms, and the legs. When you're finished, you should have a graph like Figure 3.22 that looks something like a person, where every node is intuitively related to its (supposed) function in the scene window. Obviously, arranging nodes like this in a complex scene can save you a great deal of time when it comes to finding a particular node (the right eye, for example) that you wish to manipulate.

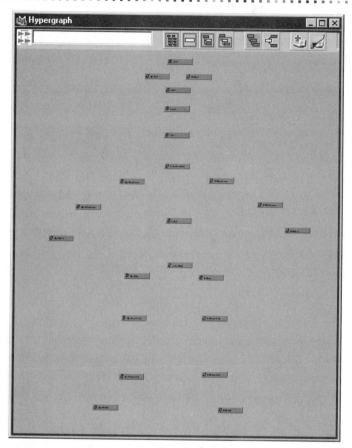

Figure 3.22 *Freeform layout representing a person*

The Hypershade

While you can still use the Multilister (Window ➜ Rendering Editors ➜ Multilister) from version 1 of Maya, the Hypershade (introduced in version 2) is now the de facto standard for working with materials and other render-related objects. Using a similar convention to the Hypergraph, the Hypershade not only shows you interactive previews of what a material or texture will look like, it shows how the elements of a shader network are connected, giving you a great deal of information in an intuitive interface. As with the Hypergraph, you can zoom and track the Hypershade like any Maya scene window, and use the F key (frame selected) and A key (frame all) to quickly focus on any element(s) you wish, making it easier to navigate scenes with large numbers of shading groups.

To open the Hypershade, choose Window ➜ Hypershade. You'll see the display shown in Figure 3.23. On the left is the Visor window, which is similar to the Outliner but contains graphic icons of textures and allows you to create, as well as view, any material node you wish. On the right is a Hypergraph-like window with all materials listed—in a new scene, there will only be two materials listed, the lambert1 shader (the default shader for geometry) and the particleCloud1 shader (the default shader for software rendered particles).

To make either the Visor or the Hypershade take over the entire Hypershade window, click the two top left buttons in the Hypershade window (the left one toggles the Visor on and off, while the right one toggles the Hypershade).

To select a material, simply click it; yellow highlight will indicate it is selected. You can then view that material's upstream connections, its downstream connections, or both by clicking the appropriate button at the top right of the Hypershade window, as shown in Figure 3.23—or by choosing Graph and the connection type from the Hypershade menu. The particle cloud, shown in Figure 3.24, has several inputs and outputs that appear if you click the Show Up and Downstream connection button.

An upstream connection is any hypershade node that "feeds into" the selected node (its output is fed into the currently selected node; it is upstream in the data flow). A downstream connection is any node that the currently selected node feeds data into—thus it is downstream from the selected node in the data flow.

To get back to a general view of materials, choose Materials from the pop-up menu at the top left of the Hypershade window.

You can also view shading groups, utilities, lights, cameras, and so on, by choosing the item from this pop-up menu.

In addition to looking at materials, textures, and such, you can also create them directly in the Hypershade in one of two ways. To create a material graphically, find the Create subsection of the Visor (below the Rendering section), click the Materials folder to open it (unless it is already open), and MM drag a material ball into the Hypershade side—try the phongE material, for example. After dragging, you will get a new phongE material in the Hypershade, ready for you to adjust. To assign this new material, you can just MM drag it on top of any object in your scene window. (Or you can RM

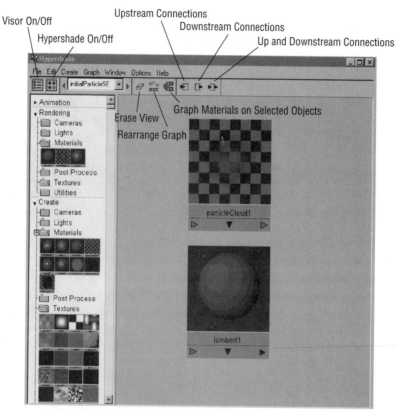

Figure 3.23 *The Hypergraph, in its default state*

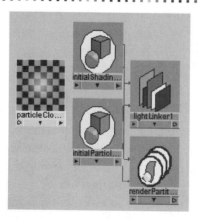

Figure 3.24 *The Hypershade graph of the particle material*

choose Assign Material to Selected with the cursor over the material; this is a good method of assigning the material to several objects at once.) To change the material's attributes (color or transparency, for example), double-click the material ball to bring up the Attribute Editor, and then make any changes you wish to the material. The ball in the Hypershade, as well as any objects that have this material assigned to them, will be automatically updated with your changes. The other method for creating a new material is simply to choose Create Material from the menu in the Hypershade— Create ➔ Materials ➔ phongE, for example. This produces a new material in the Hypershade window, just as MM dragging the material icon from the Visor does.

To assign a texture to your new material, you can again choose to create the material via menu commands (Create ➔ Textures ➔ 2D ➔ Fractal, for example), or just MM drag a swatch from the Create: Textures folder in the Visor on top of your material, as shown in Figure 3.25.

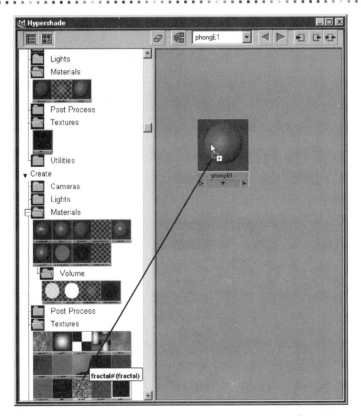

Figure 3.25 *MM Dragging a fractal texture onto a phongE material*

Once you finish dragging, a menu will open, letting you select which element of the material (that is, which input) you wish to assign the fractal (or other) texture to. The most common choice is simply Color, so choose that. The Hypershade window will be updated to show that the fractal1 texture is connected as input to the phongE material ball (coming from the left is input; going to the right is output). This ball and any other objects with the phongE material in your scene will update to show the new texture.

While there are many other functions the Hypershade can perform besides the basics we have covered here, the centralized power of being able to create, modify, connect, and disconnect materials, textures, and so forth, should be obvious from the quick tour we have taken. It is worth the effort to get to know the new Hypershade, as it will save you a great deal of time and effort later in your work with Maya's shader networks.

For more on rendering with the Hypershade, see Chapter 18, "Rendering Basics."

Hands-On Maya: Building an Arm

Let's take all the interface/optimization information we've gathered together thus far and put it to use in a practical example. Over the next few pages, we'll model an arm, and then "string" it to bend at the elbow, using an Inverse Kinematics (IK) chain. (You'll learn more about IK modeling in Chapter 13, "Character Animation Exercises.") Throughout this example, we'll put our understanding of Maya's interface to good use, making our modeling task easier.

1. Open a new scene in Maya.

2. Either sketch out a top and side view of an arm and scan them into your computer, or use the sketches included on the CD-ROM (ArmTop.tif and ArmSide.tif).

Working from Sketches

Sketching your image before you model is *always* a good idea—even if you have no skill at drawing. It is much easier to see what you're creating by quickly drawing it on paper than it is to try to create an object in 3D space out of your head. You will find that sketching an object before modeling it, far from taking extra time, will save you a great deal of time, and give you better-looking results as well.

When you sketch an object for use as a background image for modeling, it is important that your two views (top and side here) are exactly the same size. Graph paper is very useful in these circumstances, as it is easy to see the exact measurements of your image on this type of paper.

3. As we will use these sketches to make our model, they need to be loaded into Maya's top and side views so we can reference them as we build our arm. First, open the Outliner and select the top camera icon, double-clicking it to open the Attribute Editor. In the Attribute Editor, click the Environment triangle, and then click the Image Plane: Create button to create an image plane for the top view camera. When you click this button, the Attribute Editor will focus on the image plane (imagePlane1), but you still need to assign your arm image to the plane. To do so, scroll down to the Image Name line (in the Image Plane Attributes section) and click the Browse icon that looks like a folder. Find your top arm image (or use the ArmTop.tif image on the CD) and choose it. Repeat this process for the side view, using the side arm view image instead. When you are finished, your four view should look like Figure 3.26.

   In order to keep from accidentally selecting one of these planes as we continue to work, let's put them on their own layer and make that a reference (unselectable) layer. From the Layer bar, click the Create a New Layer button, rename this layer ImagePlanes, select both image planes, and choose Assign Selected from the Layer menu. To make the layer a reference layer, choose Reference from the pop-up layer menu.

   There are several good modeling techniques to use from this point on, but we will use a common, fairly painless, method that produces good results quickly: lofting a series of circles into a shape.

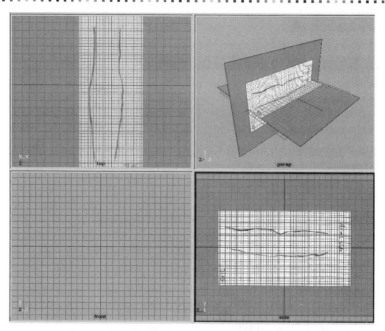

Figure 3.26 *The Arm sketches as image planes*

Lofting creates a shape in something like the way a wooden ship hull is laid (or lofted) over a skeleton of wood that defines the shape the hull will have once the lofting process is complete.

First, create a new layer (click the New Layer button in the Layer bar) and name it Circles—we will assign our circles to this layer to keep them separate from our eventual lofted surface. Next, expand one of the views (the top, say) to fill the screen (click in that pane, and then press the spacebar quickly). Choose Create ➜ Nurbs Primitives ➜ Circle ❑, and in the option window, change the Normal Axis setting to the Z axis. (From our angle, the circle will now appear as a line, as it is lined up with the arm's axis.) Click the Save button (to save the settings) and close the window. We could create our circles by going to the menu each time, as we just did, but let's speed up our work-flow by quickly making a button on the shelf to make our circles. Hold down the Ctrl, Alt, and Shift keys and, from the main menu bar (this won't work from the hotbox!), choose Create ➜ Nurbs Primitives ➜ Circle; a new button should appear on your shelf, and clicking that button will create a circle.

Now we're ready to build our arm. In the top view (don't worry about the side view yet), click the Circle button, move the new circle down to the bottom of the arm, and scale it to the same size as the bottom of the sketched arm, as shown in Figure 3.27. Remember that you can zoom your view in to see how accurately you're placing the circles.

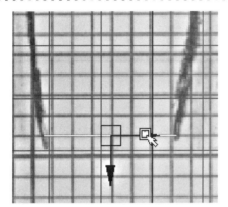

Figure 3.27 *The First Circle, moved and scaled to the proportions of the arm sketch*

If you find the background image too dark or distracting, select the camera (top here), open the Attribute Editor, click the imagePlane1 tab, and (under Image Plane Attributes) reduce the alpha gain to about 0.5. As the alpha channel here corresponds to how opaque the images is, this adjustment will fade the image back a bit, giving you a clearer view of the circles you are creating.

To build the outline of the arm, create several circles and position and scale them to fit the sketch of the arm in the top view. Be sure to place more circles around the elbow area, as that area will eventually bend (as any good elbow should), and therefore needs more definition. When you are finished, your "arm" should look similar to Figure 3.28.

When you have finished with the top view, you will now need to switch to the side view, this time scaling and moving the circles so they fit from this view as well. (Don't move them along the X axis, however, as this will destroy the work you've done in the top view.) Your completed side view should look similar to Figure 3.29.

If you find you need a new circle to help build the shape in the side view, add one—just be sure to go back to the top view and adjust it there!

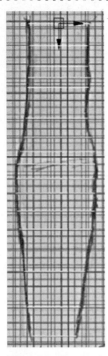

Figure 3.28 *Circles complete the top of the arm.*

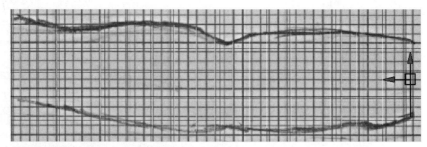

Figure 3.29 *Side view of the completed arm*

We now have the outline of our arm finished—it's time to create the arm itself! We need to select all the circles that will make up our arm and then loft them. But don't just drag a selection marquee around the circles: the Loft tool depends on the order in which you select your circles, so we need to be careful about the order in which we select them. Starting at either end (the top or bottom of the arm), Shift+click each circle in order, until all are selected. Before we loft these circles, first assign them to the Circles layer for later use (choose Assign Selected from the Circles layer menu). Now let's see how we did: loft the circles into a surface (Surfaces ➜ Loft). You should see an arm-like tube appear in your perspective window, as Figure 3.30 shows. Because of the image planes, it's a bit difficult to see the arm. To quickly get rid of the image planes now (as you won't need them from now on), go to the ImagePlane layer's pop-up menu and uncheck the Visible box.

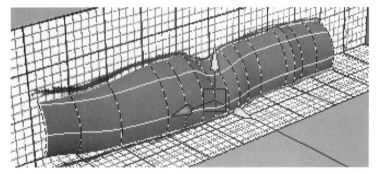

Figure 3.30 *The arm, lofted*

You will probably find that the arm doesn't look quite realistic yet. Fortunately, because Maya remembers construction history, you can go back and tweak the position, scale and rotation of the circles (using the same techniques we used to create the circles, above) to get the arm to look the way you want it. When you like your arm, turn off the circle layer's visibility, so you can see the surface more clearly, as in Figure 3.31.

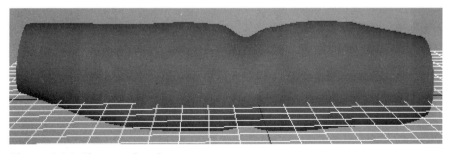

Figure 3.31 *The completed arm*

Templating the lofted surface (Display ➜ Object Components ➜ Templates) so you can't accidentally select it is a real time saver. To "untemplate" the object when you are finished with adjustments, select the lofted surface in the Outliner or Hypergraph, and choose Display ➜ Object Components ➜ Templates again. Or you could simply create a layer, assign the lofted surface to that layer, and then make the layer a reference or template layer.

Now we need to string our arm with an IK chain so we can move it around like a natural arm. Make the side view fill your workspace, and then choose the IK Joint tool from the shelf (or choose Skeleton ➜ Joint Tool). Starting at the top (shoulder), click (or drag) the tool where the shoulder joint should be, then click again where the elbow should be, and finally click where the wrist would be, as in Figure 3.32. If you don't like where your joint is, undo the last click (press the Z key) and try again. When you are satisfied with the look of the joints, press the Enter key to confirm the new joint.

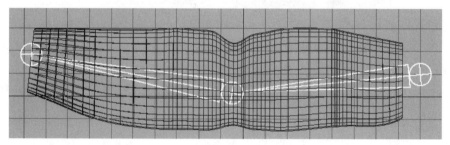

Figure 3.32 *Arm with skeleton joint*

Be sure not to make all three joints follow a straight line. Maya's IK solver uses the direction of the joint's initial bend to determine which direction it will bend later. If you make the joints straight, Maya won't know which direction to bend the arm, and you will get bizarre results.

We could now manipulate the joints using the Rotate tool, but it is generally easier to create an IK chain to make the moving simpler. To do so, choose the IK Handle tool on the shelf (or choose Skeleton ➜ IK Handle Tool) and click first on the shoulder joint and then on the wrist joint. (Skip the elbow joint, so that the kinematics chain will go through the elbow, allowing it to bend with the wrist movements.) You should now see a green line connecting the shoulder and wrist joints. If you wish, you can now move the joint around by drag-selecting the wrist IK handle and moving the arm—however, only the joint moves at present; we need to attach the arm to our new joint.

If you move the joint around before attaching the arm to it, be sure to undo (press Z) back to the original position before attaching the arm.

The final step, attaching the arm surface to the arm joint, is a process of selecting the joint and surface and binding them together. First, select the root joint of the arm skeleton (the shoulder joint), and then Shift-select the arm surface. Finally, choose Skin ➜ Bind Skin ➜ Smooth Bind to bind the two together. To see your beautiful new arm at work, drag-select the wrist joint's IK handle and use the Move tool to move the wrist around. The skeleton (and arm surface) should follow the wrist where you drag it, as in Figure 3.33.

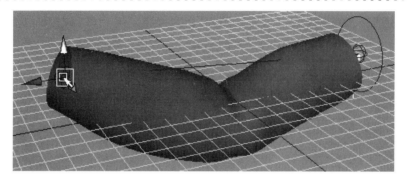

Figure 3.33 *The arm, bent*

You may notice that the elbow doesn't bend properly (it folds too much). You can use the Artisan tool to adjust the joint goal weights of the arm to make the bend far more realistic looking. For more on how to do this, see Chapter 7.

Summary

In this chapter, we went over many elements in Maya you can either adjust or use as-is to get the most out of your work. Looking at general options, shortcuts, organizational windows like the Hypergraph, the Hypershade, the Outliner and the Connection Editor, as well as working in layers, we saw how much you can adjust Maya's default interface to improve your workflow. The final working example—building a movable arm—took many of the workflow lessons we learned in this and the previous chapters and put them to real-world use. We created a shortcut button, worked in layers, and used hotkeys to choose the Scale, Move, and Rotate tools, all of which increased the speed with which we completed a reasonably complex task.

Even if much of what you have read in this chapter is a bit confusing to you now, try to remember, as you begin working on more complex projects, the little tricks and shortcuts we have discussed here. With a bit of practice, many of the techniques discussed in this chapter will become second nature to you, and your Maya skills and products will reflect this.

Part II
Modeling

In This Part

Part II of this book will take you through all the different methods of modeling in Maya. Before anything can be textured, animated, or rendered, you must build visible surfaces. In the following five chapters, you will learn how to do that by creating and editing primitives, curves, NURBS, polygons, and subdivision surfaces. By progressing through exercises that build a living room, a hand, a puppy dog, and a full human character, you will begin to master the various techniques used to build any object you can imagine inside Maya.

Of special interest to advanced users will be the discussion of subdivision surfaces and the accompanying tutorials. Although it is included only in the Unlimited version of Maya 3, subdivision surface modeling has developed into a very attractive and convincing alternative to the more traditional modeling methods, and we have accordingly given in-depth coverage in this book.

Modeling Basics

MAYA

Chapter 4

This chapter introduces the basics of modeling. The first section is devoted to the concepts you will need to become familiar with before plunging fully into the modeling tools and actions in Maya 3. A good understanding of the general principles of modeling will enable you to use your time wisely and efficiently as you work.

In the following pages you will have an opportunity to try out some of Maya's modeling aids as you learn some modeling fundamentals, and then you will create some furniture using Maya's primitives. You will begin to master:

- What is modeling?
- What makes a model good or bad?
- Different modeling methods
- Maya's modeling aids
- Modeling with primitives

What Is Modeling?

Let us begin with a working definition of what modeling is in computer animation: 3D modeling is the process of creating three-dimensional surfaces using a computer, for the purpose of rendering them into a picture or a sequence of pictures. In fields such as the automobile industry or engineering, the digital models are actually built with specific products in mind—their purpose is the creation of a physical model or prototype, and ultimately a working automobile or a building. Rendering is only a stage they go through in order to get to their ultimate destination. For 3D artists working in computer animation, however, the ultimate destination for the models they build is pictures that exist in TV, videos, or celluloid—all 2D environments.

This difference gives rise to an important principle, which determines how we should build models for computer animation: *The only thing that really matters in modeling is the picture(s) people will see.* Modeling anything that will not be seen, in other words, is a waste of time.

Creating an Illusion

Digital space is a world of facades. If only the back and right walls of a room (as in Figure 4.1) will be seen, it makes no sense to build the front or the left side. Modeling for the computer animator is all about creating illusions for the eye to feast on—build only what the eye (the camera) will see. This is the reason why careful preproduction planning is so crucial, and why well-organized production teams will create detailed storyboards before they commit to building anything.

Are You a Modeler?

A professional sculptor or an architect will usually have a much easier time modeling on the computer than a person with no such background, just as a painter or a photographer will find it easier to do texturing or lighting in a digital environment. Many of the skills that are used in these fields transfer immediately into the computer environment, and other skills soon follow, as you become familiar with your surroundings.

But don't be too discouraged if you want to become a modeler but have no such background. Computer animation is a different world, and the computer is a different tool. There are skills specific to digital modeling that must be learned.

Digital modeling should be viewed as a separate and independent artistic medium—as different as painting is to sculpting, for example, each with its own sets of rules and technical skills. One must feel as comfortable with the computer as a painter would with a brush, or a sculptor with clay. And just as some painters know nothing about sculpting but still are great painters, so can one be a great 3D modeler without being a sculptor or an architect.

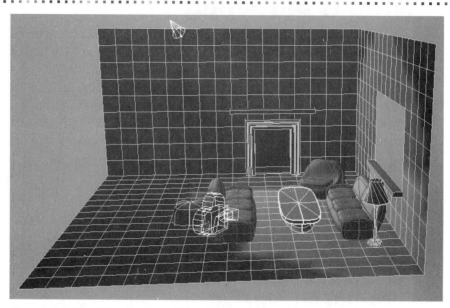

Figure 4.1 *The living room we'll begin creating in this chapter*

Good Models and Bad Models

Good models look good when rendered, and bad models look bad. It's that simple. The catch, of course, is that it takes a lot of time and care to produce models that look good, and always a lot of sweat and effort to produce great-looking models. Tight schedules and deadlines often make this a very difficult—if not an impossible—task.

There are other, less obvious, factors in the production environment that determine whether a model is good or bad, and these are just as important as how great it looks. The two criteria for good modeling most frequently used in animation are how computationally *heavy* or *light* a model is and how well it can be set up for animation.

Improperly built models often end up being heavy, meaning they are built with too much geometry and can cause numerous problems for the animators, or lose precious production time in rendering. A heavy model makes the computer's CPU work harder than it would otherwise need to. A light model, in contrast, does not have a lot of geometry for the computer to calculate and thus allows the animator to act more interactively with it, producing better animation in shorter time. It generally renders faster, too.

If a model is going to be deformed in a certain way—in other words, to bend and stretch as it animates—the modeler needs to build the model with that in mind, putting the necessary points where they will deform properly. Generally, extra isoparms should be inserted around joint areas such as elbows, knees, or fingers. The isoparms should also run along the way the surface will stretch or crease. In some cases, not having points in certain areas is actually better. It takes up a lot of time to create different facial shapes for lip-syncing, and if the face has a lot of CVs or vertices, the work becomes exponentially more time-consuming. Compare the faces in Figure 4.2: which would be easier to work with in creating different facial shapes?

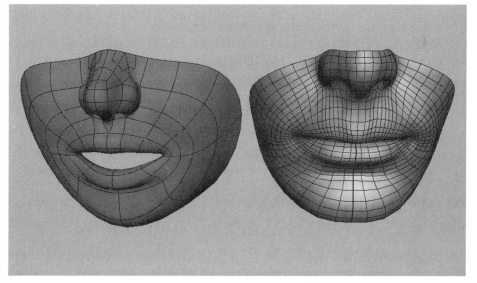

Figure 4.2 *A face created using subdivision surfaces (left) and one created using NURBS surfaces (right)*

Different Methods of Modeling

Maya provides many different ways to model: you can model with NURBS, polygons, and/or subdivision surfaces. How do you decide which method would best serve your modeling needs? This question is all the more significant because with Maya 3 Unlimited (and we hope Maya Complete will soon have it, too), subdivision surfaces have truly become a legitimate way to model and animate.

The conventional wisdom is that NURBS models are good for smooth, organic, deformable surfaces, whereas polygons are good for sharp-edged, rigid structures. This is an oversimplification, and though different situations may ideally call for the use of one or both methods, you can pretty much accomplish anything you want with either approach—there are die-hard enthusiasts on both sides. The advantage of NURBS surfaces is that they are smooth, whereas polygons are faceted. On the other hand, polygons allow arbitrary topology, whereas NURBS surfaces are restricted to four-sided patches. (*Topology* is a mathematical concept that deals with those properties of objects that are not affected by changes in size or shape. In Maya, topology refers to the way points interconnect to create a surface.)

What is revolutionary about the subdivision surfaces in Maya is that they combine the strengths of both NURBS and polygon modeling, minus their weaknesses. They are smooth like NURBS surfaces, but they can also be built on arbitrary topology similar to polygons. You can create one smooth and continuous subdivision surface in building almost any organic model, bypassing the sometimes tricky situation you can run into with NURBS patches of trying to keep tangency along the seams. In Figure 4.3, the NURBS patches on the left are smooth, but they can't be joined in the middle. The polygon surface shown in the center is joined but is faceted. The subdivision surface on the right is both joined at the middle and smooth.

Does this mean that subdivision surfaces are better than NURBS surfaces or polygons? That we should use them over the other two methods? Not necessarily. As you can see from Figure 4.3, if you want to create a diamond, clearly you should work with polygons. To build a wine bottle, you would want to work with NURBS surfaces. For complex organic models, such as a human head, subdivision surfaces seem to be a good choice. The models you'll be building in this and the following chapters will generally try to incorporate all three methods: build the rough shapes with NURBS, tweak as polygonal surfaces, and then insert finer details as subdivision surfaces. Chapter 5 is an in-depth lesson in NURBS modeling, and Chapter 6 provides a similar look at polygon and subdivision surface modeling.

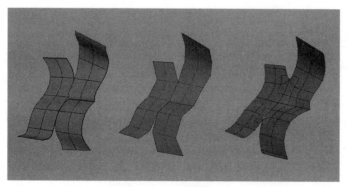

Figure 4.3 *The advantage of using subdivision surfaces*

Modeling Tools

Let us now look at some of Maya's modeling features available to us. Maya has a vast array of tools that can aid us in modeling. Here are some of the more basic and useful functions we will be covering in this chapter:

- Templates
- Layers
- Isolated selection
- Pick-masking
- Snapping
- Freezing transformations
- Construction history

Templates

In Maya, templates are mainly used as guides for modeling. Objects that become templates remain visible but cannot be selected like other objects. The standard way to turn an object into a template is to select the object and then select Display ➜ Object Display ➜ Template. You can also open the Attribute Editor (Ctrl+A), choose Display, and toggle on Template.

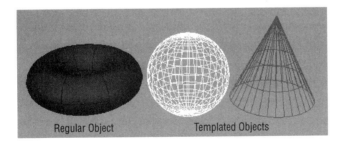

Regular Object   Templated Objects

Because the templated object cannot be selected in the usual way by dragging, in order to untemplate it, you must either select it in the Outliner or the Hypergraph editor, or use a selection mask (see "Pick-Masking" later in the chapter), and then toggle it back with Display ➜ Object Display ➜ Untemplate.

There is another way to template objects, and that is by using the Layer bar. A layer also has templating capability, and it is generally the more efficient way to template objects because it can handle groups.

Templating using layers is a bit different from templating using the method just described. A regular template can be picked using Selection Mask for templates, but templates created from layers can be selected only from the Layer menu.

The Layer Bar

Chapter 3 introduced the Layer bar, an extremely useful tool for modeling. Originally created for Alias Power Animator, it came back in its original form in Maya 2 and has become even better with Maya 3. A layer creates an exclusive collection of objects that can be selected, hidden, or templated together. Essentially, it acts as a directory or a folder for objects to aid in organization and work efficiency.

Be sure you are familiar with the basic techniques presented in Chapter 3 for working with the Layer bar and its Relationship Editor:

- To display the Layer bar if it has been turned off, select Display ➔ UI ➔ Elements ➔ Layer Bar.

- To work with layers in the Layer Editor, choose Window ➔ General Editors ➔ Display Layer Editor.

- To create a new layer, click on New Layer in the Layer Editor or click the New Layer button on the Layer bar—it's the button to the left of the Default layer.

- To add an object or a group of objects to a layer, first select them. Then click the down arrow next to the layer name to display the Layers menu, as in Figure 4.4, and select Assign Selected. You can RM over the layer to display the menu, as well.

- To move an object from one layer to another, simply select the object and assign it to the other layer.

You can also move objects between layers using the Relationship Editor; and by using the Layer bar or Layer Editor, you can hide a layer's objects, template them, or reference them. In Maya 3, the color box on the left side of each new layer will display T for Template or R for Reference, and the box will be crossed with an X when layer's visibility is turned off, as in Figure 4.4. Objects in a Reference layer are just like regular objects in that they can be used for snapping (see the section "Snapping" below) and can be shaded, but they cannot be selected. Removing a layer does not delete its member objects, but only the layer itself.

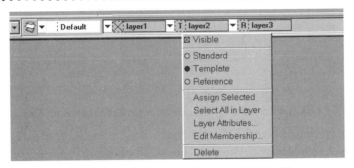

Figure 4.4 *The drop-down menu for an individual layer*

Use the Layer Colors palette to identify different groups of objects as belonging to a layer. Double-click on the color box in the Layer bar to pop open the Layer Colors palette and assign a color, or use the Layer Editor to do the same. Using different colors can not only make things much easier to work with in very complex scenes, it can also make the scene a bit more interesting to look at, as in Figure 4.5 (also available in the Color Gallery on the accompanying CD).

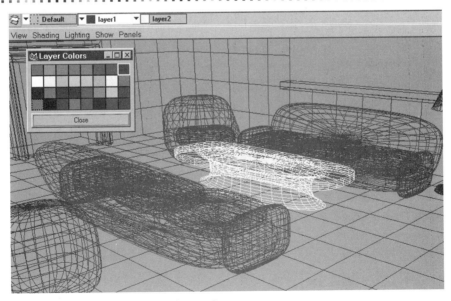

Figure 4.5 *Using the Layer Colors palette*

Isolate Select

New in Maya 3 is the ability to display only the objects, or parts of an object, that you want displayed within a view panel. Select objects (or their CVs or faces) that you want to isolate for viewing; then, in the view panel menu, select Show → Isolate Select → View Selected. See the result in Figure 4.6. You can also add or remove objects for viewing inside the panel with the other menu options, such as Add Selected Objects and Remove Selected Objects. This new feature can be a lifesaver when working with heavy, complex models, especially with dense polygonal surfaces. Remember, Isolate Select affects only the screen display, and only the specific viewing panel that has View Selected turned on.

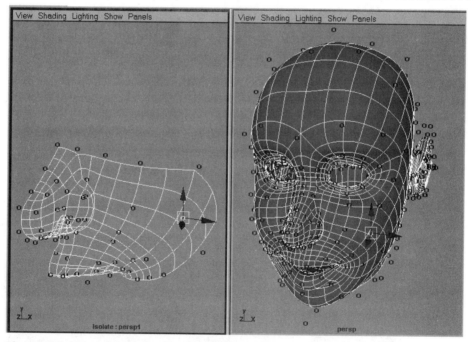

Figure 4.6 *Using the new Isolate Select function*

Pick-Masking

One of the most elegant features of the Maya interface is its ability to limit selection to specific types of objects, components, or hierarchical elements. This function is also known as creating a pick mask or selection mask. (Maya uses the terms interchangeably.)

You can RM choose an object to pick-mask elements that specifically apply to that object, or you can use the buttons on the Status line to pick only the elements you want to select.

When you put the mouse arrow over the buttons on the Status line, Maya tells you what they are. If you RM click on the button, a submenu pops up which lists the different elements that button will select. You can turn off the ones you do not want selected.

When you RM choose an object you are working on, Maya automatically figures out which marking menu selections should become available for that specific object type and gives you the appropriate choices. For a curve, you get a different set of items from the one used for a NURBS surface, as you can see in Figure 4.7.

The really cool thing about this feature is that depending on the pick mask you choose, Maya adjusts the display of control vertices, edit points, and hulls so that you will only select what you want to select, and hides the rest. For example, if you pick-mask Control Vertex from the curve's marking menu, Maya will automatically go into the component selection mode and display only the CVs for you to select. Or if you pick-mask Hull, it will show only hulls. Figure 4.8 illustrates the difference.

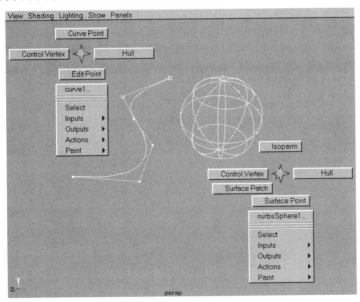

Figure 4.7 *Pick-masking displays a different marking menu for a curve than for a NURBS surface.*

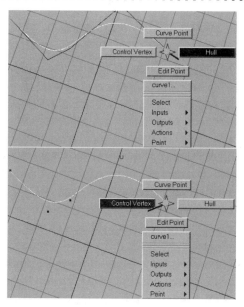

Figure 4.8 *Pick-masking to display a curve's hull (top) and its control vertices*

Maya 3 has an addition to its NURBS surface selection mask called Surface Patch. It allows you to select individual NURBS patches the way you would select a polygon face. This selection option is used with another new command, Edit Surfaces ➔ Duplicate NURBS Patches. See the "Hands-On Maya" tutorial in Chapter 5 for an example of its usage.

You can create various selection masks using the Status line in three different levels. You can limit your selection by *component types,* such as CVs, Edit Points, Faces, Edges, and so on:

You can also create Selection Masks to pick only *object types,* such as Curves, Surfaces, Joints, and so on:

And finally, you can limit selection by *hierarchy types,* such as pick-masking only the root or leaf level of a hierarchy. When you are in the hierarchy mode, you can create a pick mask to select only templated objects, as well.

When you are limiting selection by hierarchy types, the marking menu's component selection masks do not work, because Maya is only allowing root or leaf nodes to be selected.

Note that when several elements are active in the selection mask, Maya has a *priority list* that causes certain elements to be selected before others. Maya's default selection mask is set to select by object type with all the different object types turned on, so when you drag over a NURBS surface and a joint at the same time, it should select both objects. But because Maya's default selection priority list has "joints" before "NURBS surfaces," it will select the joint and leave the NURBS surface unselected. If you want to see the selection priority list, go to Window → Settings/Preferences → Preferences, and go to Setting → Selection to see the dialog box in Figure 4.9.

Do not change the default priority list or turn it off unless you have a good reason to. The priority list was defined with careful deliberation, and you will find as you work your way through the various stages of a production in Maya that the default priorities make a lot of sense and are very efficient.

Snapping

The snapping tools allow you to transform an object or a component to snap to grids, curves, points, view planes, or a surface. These elements become targets, or magnets, when activated. You can access these tools in the order they were listed in the Status line as snapping toggle buttons:

You also can use Maya's default hotkeys for snapping to grids, curves, or points. These are the hotkeys that come with Maya's default setting:

- Press X and click or drag to snap to a grid
- Press C and click or drag to snap to a curve
- Press V and click or drag to snap to a point

Let's briefly try out these tools. Create two curves as shown in Figure 4.10. Select Create → CV Curve Tool and X+click on the grid. Click eight times and press Enter to complete the first curve, on the left. Type **y** to access the CV Curve tool again and draw the second curve, on the right.

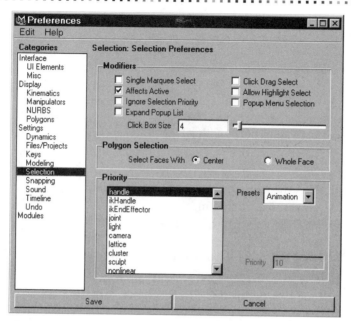

Figure 4.9 *The selection priority list in the Preferences window*

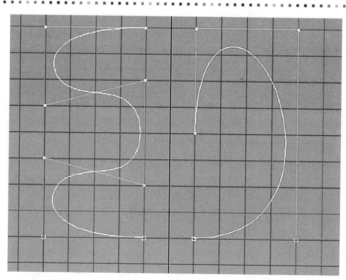

Figure 4.10 *Two curves, snapped to a grid*

RM choose to pick-mask CVs over the second curve. Then select the first CV at the bottom, select the Move tool by pressing the **w** key and V+drag to the first CV of the first curve. It should snap to the CV, as in Figure 4.11. Now try to C+drag the last CV of the second curve to the first curve. It's not snapping, because snapping to a curve is distance sensitive. Drag the selected CV over to the first curve, making sure it's right over the curve. Now C+drag the CV again, back and forth. It should stay on and along the curve, as in Figure 4.11. Snap-to-curve also snaps to curves on surface and surface isoparms.

You can also snap the manipulator to stay locked on one of the manipulator handles when you are in the perspective view, restricting the manipulator's movements to XY, XZ, or YZ handles, just as if you were in an orthographic window. Just Ctrl+click on the manipulator handle where you want the snap to happen, and the square plane at the center of the manipulator facing the camera will rotate to face the manipulator handle. Note that the constraint applies only when you drag the manipulator's center, not one of its axis handles. To release the constraint, Ctrl+click the center of the manipulator (this actually snaps the manipulator to move along the camera view plane).

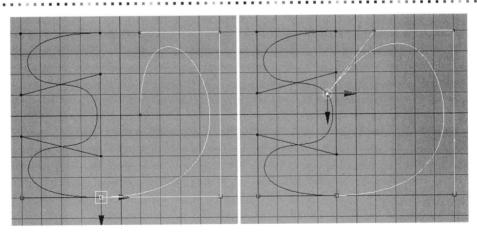

Figure 4.11 *Snapping a CV to a point and a curve*

Maya also has point-to-point snap capabilities. Under Modify ➜ Snap Align Objects, you will see the options Point to Point, 2 Points to 2 Points, and (new in Maya 3) 3 Points to 3 Points. The object containing the first selected point or set of points will snap to the second selected point or set of points. These points can be CVs or vertices, but note that it is the object controlled by the selected points that moves, not the points themselves.

Making an Object Live

Yet another way to snap objects or components is to make an object live. A live object acts as a construction aid in modeling, a magnet for other points. Any point you move will snap to the live object's surface. This useful modeling aid can be applied to any single object.

To do this, choose Create ➜ NURBS Primitives ➜ Sphere, and then select Modify ➜ Make Live, or click the Make Live button (with the magnet icon) on the Status line. You'll see that the sphere has turned green, and if you are in shaded mode, the sphere is no longer shaded. It has become *live*, a magnet for other elements, and while it is in that mode it cannot be selected. Select Create ➜ EP Curve Tool and try clicking a few times in the perspective window. All the edit points snap to the sphere surface. Hit Enter to complete the curve and try translating it. The manipulator now shows only X and Y handles, as in Figure 4.12, which are actually U and V handles that move the curve along the parameters of the sphere surface. Toggle the Make Live button off, and the curve should translate into the XYZ 3D space again.

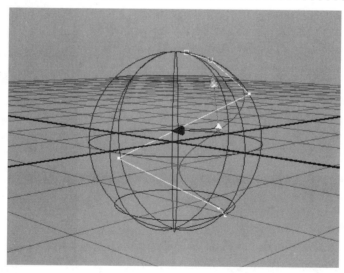

Figure 4.12 *Because this sphere is live, the curve's edit points snap to its surface*

Using the Construction Plane

Maya also has a special construction plane under the Create menu. It does not render and, with the default setting, is displayed as a 24-unit plane in the XY axis, but it's actually infinite in size, like the ground plane in the perspective window. It exists primarily to be made live and to aid in the construction of curves as an alternate ground plane. To appreciate how the construction plane differs from a regular NURBS plane in the way it behaves as a live object, try the following short exercise.

Start a new scene. Select Create ➜ CV Curve Tool, and X+click to snap the CVs for a curve on the ground plane, as shown below. Do not press Enter yet. Choose Create ➜ Construction Plane ❏, click Apply with everything at default, then set the Pole Axis to YZ and click Apply again. Close the option window. You should see the planes intersecting, as shown in Figure 4.13.

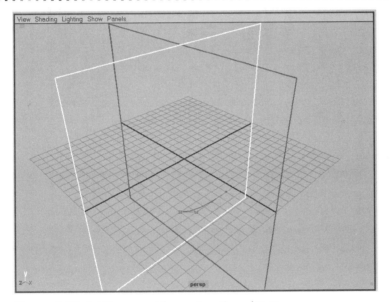

Figure 4.13 *A CV curve with construction planes*

Select the hotbox (space bar) ➜ North Zone ➜ Persp/Outliner. In the Outliner, select plane1 and then select Modify ➜ Make Live. Continue to X+click CVs on plane1 as shown in Figure 4.14, until the curve being created comes to the grid next to the intersection point of the two construction planes. Since plane1 is now live, the CVs snap to the plane's grid. Only construction planes allow the CVs to continue to build in this way.

In the Outliner, select plane2 and then select Modify ➜ Make Live. Start X+clicking the CVs on plane2 until the curve being created comes to the grid above the ground plane. Toggle off the Modify ➜ Make Live option and finish X+clicking the CVs once again on the ground plane, as shown in Figure 4.15. Press Enter to complete the curve!

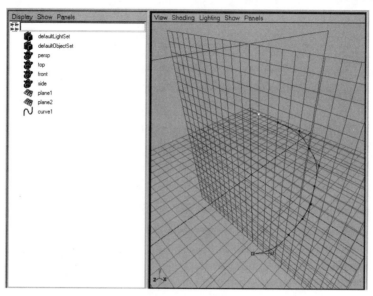

Figure 4.14 *The CV curve on the first construction plane*

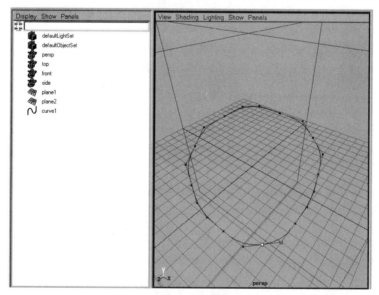

Figure 4.15 *The CV curve completed with construction planes*

If you are transforming an existing object to a live plane, you have to move the manipulator's center, not one of its axis handles, to make it snap to the plane.

Freeze Transformations

When you create any object, it is initially placed at the origin, or (0,0,0) in the world space. As you work with the object, transforming it in various ways through translation, rotation, and scaling, there may be times when you want the point where you've placed the object to become its local origin, or (0,0,0), even though it is not the world space origin. To do this, select the object, and then select Modify ➜ Freeze Transformations.

But what if you wanted to freeze only the translation values of an object, and leave its rotate and scale values intact? A new feature in Maya 3 is an improved option window for Freeze Transformations that allows you to do precisely this. You can now choose to freeze only the Translate, Rotate, or Scale values of an object. Figure 4.16 shows the new Freeze Transformations option window.

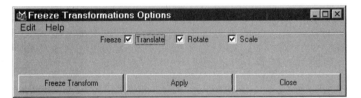

Figure 4.16 *The Freeze Transformations option window*

How Maya Handles Construction History

Maya's handling of construction history is much more powerful than in its predecessors, Alias Power Animator and Studio. Its procedural structure allows construction history to be maintained much longer in the model-building process than was previously possible, which means you have more control and greater freedom to explore alternative modeling possibilities. Because it makes the scene complex, however, in certain situations you may want to have the construction history turned off. You can do this by toggling the History button off in the Status line.

You can also delete a specific object's construction history by selecting Edit ➜ Delete by Type ➜ History. You will see more examples of construction history in the next chapter's tutorial.

Modeling with Primitives

Finally, we are ready to begin modeling! Although Maya provides us with many different ways to do what we need to do, often the fastest and easiest way to get the job done is to use *primitives*—ready-to-use basic shapes like those shown in Figure 4.17. Maya has a wealth of NURBS and polygon primitives: spheres, cubes, cylinders, cones, planes, and toruses. Maya also has a NURBS circle and square, which are made of curves.

Figure 4.17 *Examples of primitives*

Although they are all different in form, many of these primitives are created involving similar variables, an example of which we will see a bit later. By starting with the primitives, you can immediately create simple objects, which then can be manipulated in various ways to produce more complex surfaces easily and quickly.

Building a Staircase

Let's begin exploring primitives by building a spiral staircase. In the example below, we will start with a cube to represent an individual step in the staircase, and then copy it many times.

1. Start a new scene, and select Create ➔ Polygon Primitives ➔ Cube.

2. Manipulate it as follows: in the Channel box, type **–6, 0**, and **0.5** for Translate X, Y, and Z respectively, and **5, 0.5, 1** for Scale X, Y, and Z. You should now see the cube placed as follows:

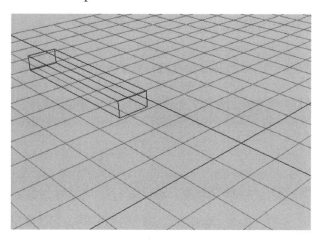

In the Channel box, the default naming convention is set to Nice. For example, you read "Translate X" in the first line of the Channel box. If you are a beginner, this is very helpful, because everything is clearly stated. But you can also change this to Short format by RM choosing Channel Names and selecting the Short setting. The first line should now read "tx," which looks cleaner and gives a bit more space for the modeling windows.

3. Keeping the cube selected, go to Edit ➔ Duplicate Options. Set the numbers in the dialog box as follows: Translate **0, 0.5, –1**; Rotate **0, –10, 0**; Number of Copies, **35**; Geometry Type, **Instance**.

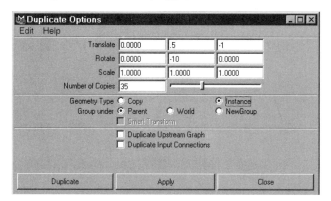

4. Click the Duplicate button, and voila! You should now have a spiral staircase. Note that the duplicates here are *instances,* which means any manipulation of the shape of the original cube will be applied to the duplicates as
well. Go to the top view, RM choose Vertex over the original cube, select the
four vertices at the top side of the cube, and then rotate and translate them
until they overlap the duplicated cube at the bottom side, as below.

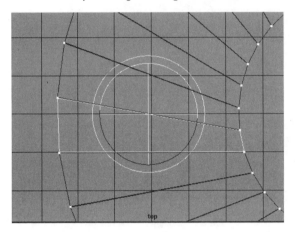

5. You can also get different shapes for the spiral staircase, as shown here, by
selecting all the vertices of the original cube and translating them in X and Z.

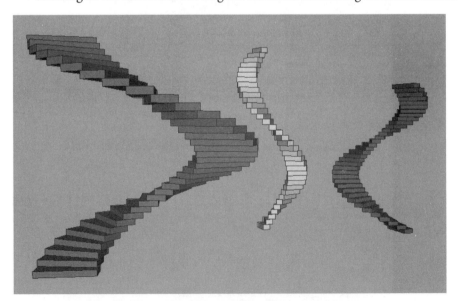

In situations like the example given here, you will find that it is better to use instances rather than copying the original geometry. Instances are computationally much lighter (less taxing on the CPU) than copied duplicates, and you can manipulate the shape of the instanced duplicates with the original geometry.

A Look Inside a Primitive: Torus

The torus is a good example of Maya's primitives, so let's look at its properties in detail. A torus is basically a revolved circle, a donut-shaped surface that is closed on both U and V parameters.

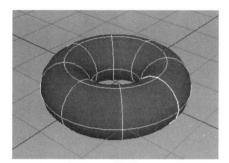

Choose Create ➜ NURBS Primitives ➜ Torus, and in the Channel box, under INPUTS, click makeNurbTorus1. You will see the various variables that form the shape of the torus:

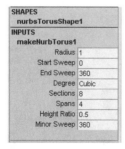

You can also get to these same variables before you create the object via the Torus ❑ dialog box, or after you create the object via the Attribute Editor.

Try doing the same with some other primitives, like the cylinder and the sphere. Note that many of the torus primitive's properties have exactly the same counterparts in the other primitives—you should go over those variables with the other primitives as well, in order to see the various possible shapes they can form with different settings.

Now let's experiment with some torus settings. Click on Radius; then, inside the modeling window, MM drag slowly and see what happens to the torus. The radius measures the distance from the center of the geometry to its circumference. In the case of a torus, it measures the center of the circle revolving around it, which effectively means that the Radius setting controls the size of the torus.

Start Sweep and End Sweep determine in degrees where the torus starts and where it stops revolving along V.

For the Degree section, click on Cubic and you will see a pull-down menu with Linear as the other degree choice—this setting will give sharp edges to the torus as shown by the torus on the left side in Figure 4.18. Sections subdivide the torus along V, and Spans subdivide it along U.

Sections and spans should all be finalized before any CVs are pulled, as changing them afterward will produce unpredictable results.

Height Ratio is the ratio between height and radius; this effectively determines the thickness of the torus.

And finally, Minor Sweep determines in degrees the amount of surface (along U) the circle revolving around the torus will have, as shown by the torus on the right side in Figure 4.18.

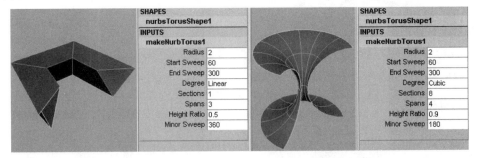

Figure 4.18 *Different settings for a torus can produce radically different results.*

Primitives are useful not because of what they are, but because of what they are capable of becoming—because of the way they can help us create the final surfaces we want, as we will see in the next tutorial.

Hands-on Modeling: Creating a Living Room Scene with Primitives

In this tutorial, we will start building a living room scene with primitives. Remember the principle, build only what the camera will see? The first thing we need to do, then, is to visualize what you want to see at the end. Picture the camera capturing a living room at an angle, with a sofa set, a table, a lamp, and a dog by the window! (You'll find the rendered image in the Color Gallery on the CD. It's called `livingroom.tif`.)

We will get to the lamp and the dog later, but for now we can build the rest with three simple primitives that Maya provides.

1. Create a new scene. Drop a sphere into the scene: either click on the sphere icon in Shelf1 or select Create ➜ NURBS Primitives ➜ Sphere. Go into Side View, pick-mask Control Vertex, and drag to select the top two rows of CVs. Type **w** to use the Move tool.

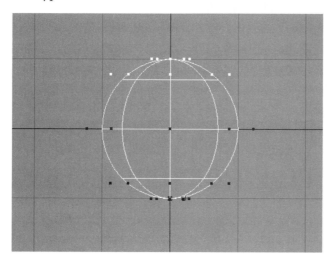

2. Snap the CVs to the first grid above the ground level by X+dragging the Y handle to that grid. Make sure you are not dragging the center of the manipulator, or all the CVs will snap to one point. If the grid isn't displayed, select Display ➜ Grid to

make it visible. Repeat the same action with the two bottom rows of CVs to the grid below ground level, as below.

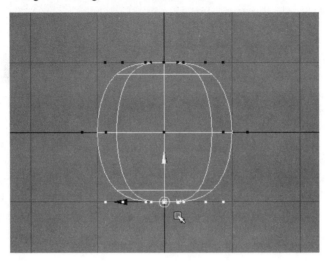

3. Go to the top view, and again snap the edge rows of CVs to the unit grids on each side of the sphere, as shown below.

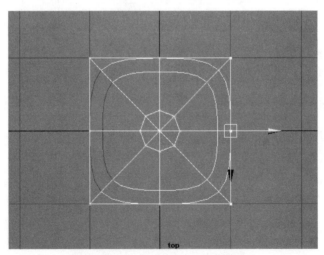

4. Take the sphere, which now looks more like a cube with round edges, and duplicate it several times (Edit ➜ Duplicate), scaling, translating, and rotating it to make the sofa, as shown here.

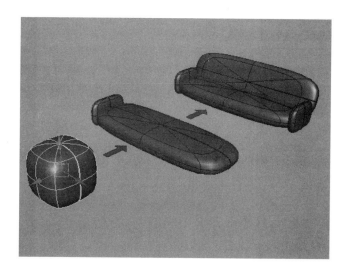

When you are building several objects, it is good form to build each object at the origin and then move it out of the center when it is finished. As long as you do not freeze its transformation or change the pivot, you can always transform it back to its original position for further modifications.

5. For the cushions, copy the sphere, pull the top row of CVs (which looks like a single point) down just a bit, scale and translate it to be on the sofa, and make two more copies to cover the whole sofa. When the sofa is done, select all of its elements and select Edit ➜ Group. This makes it a lot easier for us to work with the sofa as one entity. We can hide the sofa for now while we move on to the table and the chair. Select Display ➜ Hide ➜ Hide Selection.

6. For the table, select Create ➜ NURBS Primitives ➜ Cylinder ❑, set Caps to Top and click Create. This will become the table top. Move it to one side for now. For the table base, select Create ➜ NURBS Primitives ➜ Torus, and set the Height Ratio to 0.2 and Minor Sweep to 190 degrees. Translate the cylinder to the top of the torus, and scale and translate each object to form the table shape you see below. Group the cylinder and the torus; then translate them to the ground level.

7. Select Display ➜ Show ➜ Show Last Hidden to make the sofa visible again. Place the sofa and the table roughly in the positions shown here.

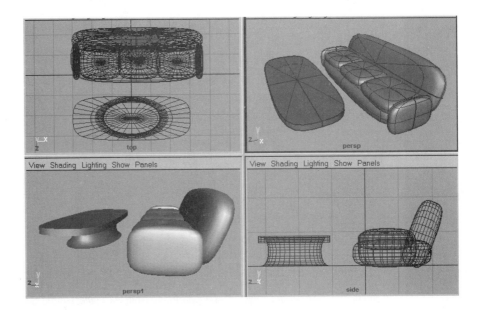

8. To select a group node in the modeling window, select one object in the group and press the ↑ (Up Arrow) key. If there are branches in the group hierarchy, repeat the ↑ key until you reach the root level.

9. The chair is a bit trickier. Copy the sphere, and hide all the rest. Translate the sphere to (0.5, 0, 0.5) using the Channel box. Switch to top view, and snap the middle CVs to the grid for each side of the sphere as shown:

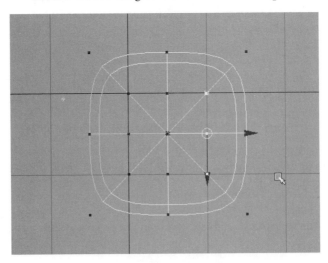

10. In the side view, grab the two rows of CVs at the right bottom corner and snap them to the Y axis. Grab the rows of CVs at the left side and snap them to the second grid to the left. Grab the CVs at the top-left corner and drag them down as shown below:

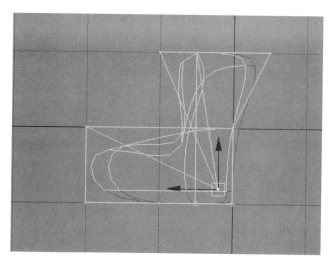

11. In the perspective view, select the CVs as shown and push them back in Z a little. You can also select the CVs at the chair's side and scale them out to make the chair look rounder. If you are having a hard time seeing the right CVs, toggle the hulls to be visible by choosing Display ➜ NURBS Components ➜ Hulls.

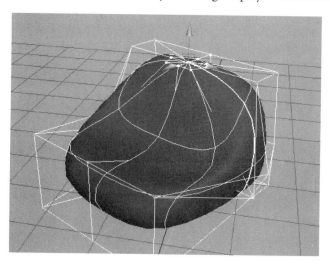

12. To finish, copy one of the cushions from the sofa and put it on the chair. Group the chair and the cushion. Select Display ‹ Show ‹ All. Create three planes by selecting Create ‹ NURBS Primitives ‹ Planes for the floor and the two walls, then arrange the "furniture" as you see fit. Shown below is the final textured and lit living room. We will come back to this scene later to add more interesting pieces.

Summary

This chapter introduced the basic concepts of modeling and the tools that Maya provides to aid you in creating and editing surfaces. You also learned how to use primitives to build more complex objects such as a staircase or pieces of furniture.

In the next two chapters, we will delve in more depth into three major types of modeling: NURBS modeling, polygon modeling, and subdivision surfaces modeling.

NURBS Modeling

MAYA

Chapter 5

This chapter covers modeling with NURBS curves and surfaces. It begins with an explanation of the basic theory and concepts involved in modeling curves. The goal is simply to give you a basic understanding of what you are doing as you work with NURBS in Maya. If you are familiar with these concepts, you may wish to skim through this section. The chapter then introduces the tools that Maya provides for working with curves and for creating and editing surfaces. It concludes by demonstrating these tools in two hands-on exercises: one that creates an aftershave bottle and one that creates a human head. The second tutorial is quite advanced, in the sense that the operations are more involved and the instructions are not as detailed as in basic tutorials; it assumes that you have more working familiarity with Maya's interface and basic techniques. Although it will take time to work through this and other advanced tutorials in this book, you should by all means go through them, as those tutorials are where all the really fun stuff happens—where the artist in you can come to the fore. Topics include:

- Curve and surface concepts
- Creating curves
- Editing curves
- Creating surfaces
- Editing surfaces
- Hands-on Maya: aftershave bottle
- Hands-on Maya: building a character I (advanced)

Curve and Surface Concepts

Part of the genius of Maya is that it makes the highly complex mathematics of modeling and animation almost completely transparent to the user. You don't need to know much about what Maya is doing behind the scenes when you use its tools, but it is useful to know a little about it. Not everyone wants to know what *NURBS, B-splines,* or *parameterization* means. When you are striving for artistic expression, mathematical concepts may not be something you want to delve into. These concepts may seem to you like unwelcome relatives at a hip party—you invite them in and exchange pleasantries ("How are you? How are the kids?") but want nothing to do with them afterwards!

Nevertheless, these and other "techno-words" are built into the very fabric of what computer animation is. Maya is, after all, computer software—the better grounded you are in these "esoteric" concepts, the deeper and farther you will be able to go in mastering your art. But be assured that as dry (or exciting!) as things may get in the following sections, nothing overly technical will be thrown at you.

If you find it difficult to understand some of the concepts being presented in the next few sections, just skip them for now. You can come back later when those topics have become a bit more relevant to you.

Curves Are Equations

The curve you draw in the computer is actually a curve segment or a continuous series of segments. One segment is called a *span*. A curve span is a digital representation on the screen of a mathematical concept called a parametric equation. Because the equation is describing a position in 3D space, it always has three variables (x, y, z), and the power of the variable with the highest degree in the equation determines the classification of the curve. Hence, a first-degree curve is a linear equation, which is a straight line. A second-degree curve is a quadratic equation, or an arc. A third-degree curve is a cubic equation, which can actually twist in 3D space. There are two higher-degree curves: fifth- and seventh-degree curves, which can actually twist twice in one span. Maya has all these degree options in its curve-creation tools, but for most practical purposes, the cubic curve is almost always used. In Maya, the default curve is cubic (see Figure 5.1).

Curves Are Also Splines

A Control Vertex (CV) is a point in 3D space that determines the shape of the curve it is attached to by defining and influencing its equation. The CVs and the curve segments they control are collectively known as *splines*.

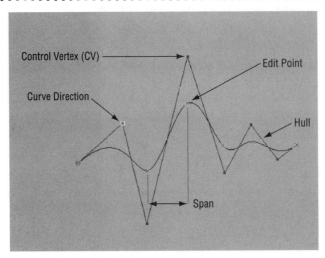

Figure 5.1 *The anatomy of a cubic curve*

Historically, a spline was a plank of wood bent to form part of a ship's hull by forcing it between pairs of posts, known as "ducks." The placement of these ducks determined the shape of the plank's curve, just as the placement of CVs determines the shape of a curve in computer graphics.

There are different ways to calculate how the CV positions are interpreted into curve shapes, and these different methods—types of equations or formulas—distinguish the splines further into Bezier curves, B-splines, or NURBS. NURBS, the focus of our attention in this chapter, stands for *Non-Uniform Rational B-Splines*. (Don't worry about understanding the meaning of all the components of this daunting acronym. The important thing to understand is how a NURBS curve behaves.)

The advantage a NURBS curve has over the other types of splines lies essentially in the way it can be cut and joined. Regular splines cannot be cut and joined at arbitrary points along the curve, only where their control points are. A NURBS curve, however, can be cut and joined anywhere, because any point on the curve can be calculated and located. This advantage carries over into surfaces as well. NURBS surfaces can be attached to other NURBS surfaces with different numbers of spans, or *isoparms*, for the same reason.

Edit Points (EPs) are points where curve segments join to form one continuous line. They are also called *knots*. Maya has a CV Curve tool and an EP Curve tool for creating curves. The two tools create curves differently, but both create NURBS curves (see Figure 5.2).

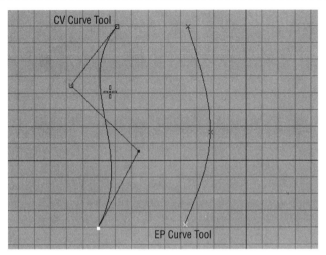

Figure 5.2 *The CV Curve tool and the EP Curve tool*

Surfaces and Parameterization

Curves cannot be rendered; only surfaces can. In modeling, curves are always created to help in the creation of surfaces. This means that at the end of the day, no matter how many curves you create, only surfaces matter. Any discussion about surfaces, however, needs to include the concept of parameterization—yes, here comes another unwelcome relative.

To best understand parameterization of surfaces, we need to examine it with curves first. Parameterization of a curve is the calculation of where knots (edit points) are placed along the curve, enabling any point on the curve to be assigned a parameter value. The variable representing this value is defined as *U*, and the curve is given a direction as a result.

To see this at work, create a default curve made of four spans: either seven clicks of CVs or five clicks of EPs. Now pick-mask Curve Point and try dragging along the curve. At the top of the Maya window you should see the curve parameter value changing as you drag. The start of the curve is assigned a parameter value, U[0]. The second edit point of the curve is assigned the value U[1], the third edit point, U[2], and so on. The halfway point between the fourth edit point of the curve and the last edit point is assigned a value of U[3.5], as shown in Figure 5.3. Any point on the curve can be similarly assigned a parameter value this way. This method of calculating the point values along the curve is called *uniform parameterization*.

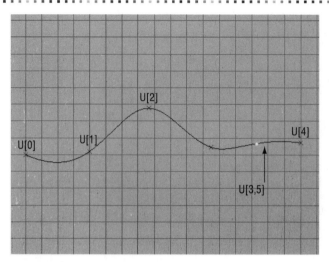

Figure 5.3 *Uniform parameterization*

Another calculation method in Maya is called *chord-length parameterization,* and the way it assigns the *U* value to a point on the curve is more complicated. We needn't go into exactly how the calculation is done, but the value assignment is dependent on the distances between successive edit points of the curve, not the number of edit points. So two curves with the same number of edit points but drawn differently will end up with different parameter values at those edit points. The difference between chord-length and uniform parameterization can be seen in Figure 5.4. The curve in Figure 5.4 is drawn in exactly the same way as the curve in Figure 5.3, but the values assigned to the points on the curve are different because it is a chord-length curve. Note that the third edit point of this curve has a value of U[8.5012].

How does all this relate to surfaces? A surface is an area in 3D space defined by the parameterization of two variables, *U* and *V*. The area is calculated in such way that at any point on the surface, a UV coordinate can be given, and the area is given UV directions. This is exactly the same situation as with the curves, except now you have the *V* parameterization as well. It's important to understand the difference between the *UV* coordinate system and the XYZ world space coordinates. The latter system identifies any point in Maya's 3D world space, whereas the former deals only with a 2D surface area.

Uniform parameterization produces more predictable values for curves and surfaces than chord length and is therefore the preferred choice for modeling in general and the default setting in Maya. The advantage chord-length parameterization has is in texturing: it allows more evenly distributed textures on uneven surfaces than the

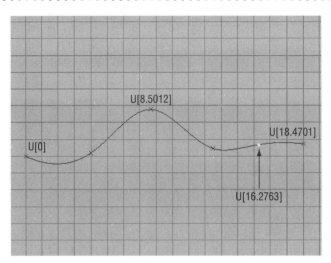

Figure 5.4 *Chord-length parameterization curve with values at different points*

Figure 5.5 *The bottle on the left was rendered using chord-length parameterization, and the bottle on the right with uniform.*

uniform method. The bottles shown in Figure 5.5 are revolved from curves that have exactly the same CV placements, except that the one on the left uses chord length and the other uses uniform.

You will generally want to use uniform surfaces rather than chord-length surfaces. As we will see in Chapter 19, Maya now provides a Fix Texture Warp option in the Attribute Editor for all NURBS surfaces that distributes UV textures using the chord-length method. Nonetheless, the chord-length concept is worth knowing about, as it is still a part of Maya's program. Many command options mention chord length.

Surface Normals

In addition to having UV directions, a surface also has a front side and a back side, determined by its *normals*. A normal is essentially a vector shooting out perpendicularly from a point on the front side of a surface. In other words, it extends in the direction that the surface point is directly facing. The concept of surface normals is important for using certain modeling tools, as well as for texturing and rendering, and you should become comfortable with it.

You can use the "right-hand rule" illustrated in Figure 5.6 to determine which side of a surface is front, or which way the normals are pointing. If the thumb points to the increasing U direction, and the index finger points to the increasing V direction, then the middle finger bent perpendicularly to these two fingers is the direction of the surface normals.

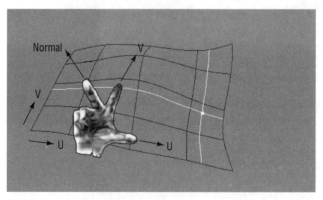

Figure 5.6 *Using the right-hand rule to determine surface normals*

You can see the surface normals of an object while in shaded mode by selecting the object and then selecting Display ➜ NURBS Components ➜ Normals (Shaded Mode).

Surfaces, like curves, are made up of spans, or rather they span a given number of span areas. The area covered by one UV span is called a *patch*. The flowing lines separating the patches are called *isoparms*. These are the surface equivalents of knots, or edit points. Figure 5.7 illustrates the terminology of surfaces.

Isoparms
UV[0][4]
UV[4][4]
V
Patch
UV[0][0]
U
UV[3.3015][1.7154]
UV[4][0]
Span

Figure 5.7 *The anatomy of a surface*

Pick-masking the Isoparm element allows you to select any flowing *isoparametric* curve that has either a U or a V value on the surface, just like selecting a curve point on a curve. With surfaces, you can also pick-mask Surface Point, which enables you to select any point on the surface with a UV parameter value, or Surface Patch, which enables you to select patches such as polygon faces.

When you select a surface point and choose Edit Surfaces ➔ Insert Isoparms, both U and V isoparms are inserted.

Open, Closed, and Periodic Curves and Surfaces

A curve or surface can be open, closed, or periodic. If a curve's form is open, its start knot and end knot are not together. A closed curve has its start knot and end knot occupying the same position, called the seam, and tangency can be broken at this point. A periodic curve is distinguished from a closed curve in that none of its CVs occupy the same position as the knots. It has a seam, but tangency is unbroken. Surfaces are always open at least in one direction. The only exception is the Torus, which is periodic on both U and V.

Creating Curves

Maya has several tools for creating curves, and also a Text tool. As mentioned already, Maya can create curves either with edit points or with CVs.

Generally, if the curve needs to pass through a specific point, then the EP Curve tool would be a better choice, as the edit points actually lie on the curve. The CV Curve tool should be preferred in most other situations because it is better at controlling the curve shape.

Using the CV Curve Tool

Go to front view and select Create ➜ CV Curve Tool ❑. In the resulting option window, you can see that the default settings are Cubic and Uniform. Leave everything at the default setting and X+click near the origin. Draw the curve on the left in Figure 5.8. Oops! The last CV placement was a mistake. No problem. Because you haven't pressed Enter yet to complete the action, you can still control the CV's placement after you've created it. Just MM click and you can X+drag the CV back to where it should be placed, like the curve on the right.

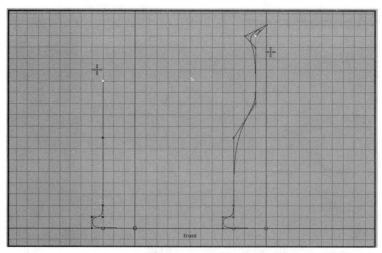

Figure 5.8 *Using the CV Curve tool you can easily correct mistakes.*

Once you have completed the curve, you can revolve it to create a wine bottle like the one shown in Figure 5.5.

You can also edit CVs or EPs while you are creating a curve by pressing the Insert key. With this method, you can select multiple points for repositioning. To continue creating the curve, just press the Insert key again.

Using the Pencil Curve Tool

Pencil is another great curve-creation tool in the Create menu, especially if you have access to a digitizing tablet. It may look like it is producing a thousand edit points when you are using it, but with a simple rebuild command, Edit Curves ➜ Rebuild Curve, you can get an elegantly simple curve. Rebuild Curve ❏ has a Number of Spans setting for Uniform Rebuild Type that you can adjust.

Each time you release the mouse, the Pencil tool completes building the curve. As a result, you will often end up with several separate curves when the drawing is done. Again, you can easily attach these curves using Edit Curves ➜ Attach Curves. In Figure 5.9, raw curves on the left have been rebuilt and attached to create the curve on the right.

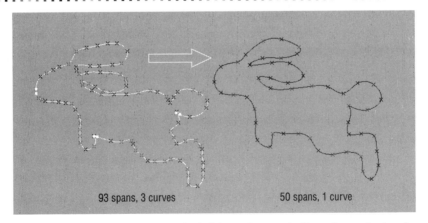

93 spans, 3 curves   50 spans, 1 curve

Figure 5.9 *The raw curves on the left have been rebuilt and attached to form the curve on the right.*

When using the Pencil tool, it's far better to end up with several separate curves that better represent what you wanted to draw than to try to draw everything as one curve.

Using the Arc Tools

In contrast to the free form of the Pencil tool, the Arc tools enable you to create circular arcs of various angles. There are two types: the simple two-point circular arc and the three-point circular arc, which has one more control point. Figure 5.10 illustrates both types.

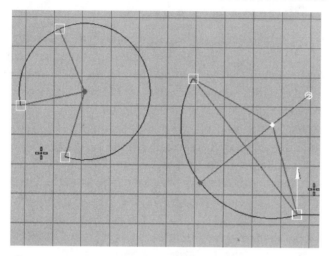

Figure 5.10 *A two-point circular arc (left) and a three-point circular arc (right)*

Once you've created a three-point circular arc, for example, you can still manipulate the arc edit points. First select Modify ➜ Transformation Tools ➜ Show Manipulator Tool (or press the "t" hotkey) and then, in the Channel box, under Inputs, choose makeThreePointCircularArc. The three points should be visible now.

Duplicating Surface Curves

Yet another curve creation method is Duplicate Surface Curves, which is actually not part of the Create menu but appears on the Edit Curves menu. It can be a very efficient and powerful curve generator, especially with its ability to duplicate all the isoparms of a surface. To try this tool for yourself, create a default cylinder, pick-mask Isoparm, select an isoparm anywhere on the surface, and select Edit Curves ➜ Duplicate Surface Curves. Figure 5.11 shows the result: a curve with the same number of spans as the cylinder has been duplicated.

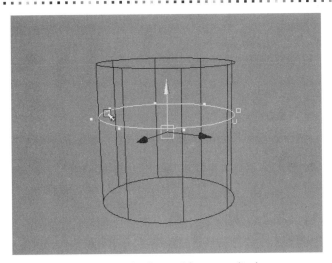

Figure 5.11 *A curve duplicated from a cylinder*

Now translate the duplicated curve out of the cylinder. Select the cylinder, and repeat Edit Curves ➜ Duplicate Surface Curves. This time, as shown in Figure 5.12, all the isoparms of the cylinder are duplicated. You can set the options so that only U or V will duplicate. The default is both.

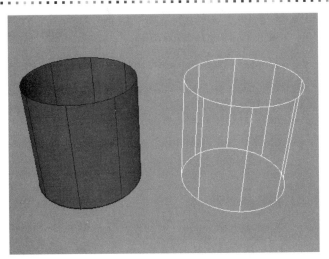

Figure 5.12 *Selecting the cylinder before duplicating surface curves duplicates all of its surface isoparms.*

The span of the duplicated curves will be the same as the cylinder's, but the number of curves being duplicated will match the number of isoparms being displayed on the screen—if the cylinder's NURBS smoothness is set to fine, you will get more curves than if the smoothness is set to rough.

Editing Curves

Once you have created the curves you need, Maya provides various actions and tools to edit them. In this section we'll go through attaching and detaching curves, aligning curves and surfaces, rebuilding curves, inserting knots, adding points to a curve, cutting and filleting curves, and offsetting curves.

Attaching and Detaching Curves

The Attach Curves option requires that you pick two curves or curve points. For most situations, Maya can automatically figure out which ends of the curves are being attached, and you only need to select curves as objects. In situations where the ends being attached are not correct, you can select curve points to force the proper ends to attach. To pick curve points, pick-mask Curve Point, and then drag the curve point to the curve end you want, as shown in Figure 5.13.

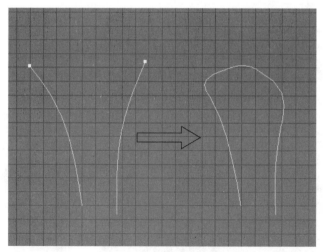

Figure 5.13 *Attaching two separate curves to form a new curve*

When selecting curve points on two or more curves, first select the curve point on one curve, then pick-mask Curve Point on the other curve, and Shift+click the second curve point. The first selection stays selected.

When both of the correct end curve points are selected, select Edit Curves ➜ Attach Curves ❏. Blend is the default attachment method, and Blend Bias 0.5 means both curves will meet halfway. This is the ideal setting when you need to maintain symmetry. When Blend Bias is set to 0, the first selected curve will attach itself to the second curve.

If you find the curve shapes are changing too much when you attach them, try clicking Insert Knot in the option window. For situations where you absolutely need to have the curves maintain their original shape, you can change the Attach Method setting to Connect. For this to work properly, however, the curve ends have to be touching already. Figure 5.14 shows the effect of these different attachment methods.

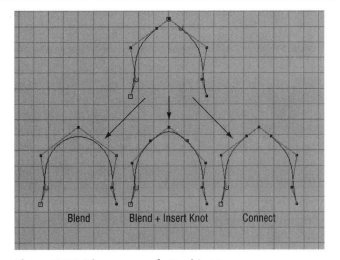

Figure 5.14 *Three ways of attaching two curves*

When attaching curves or surfaces, if the construction history is on, make sure the Keep Original option (the default setting) is toggled on as well. Odd behavior may occur if it is toggled off and the attached object is modified later.

Detaching connected curves is simple. You just select curve points, or edit points, or both, as shown in the three curves in Figure 5.15, and then select Edit Curves ➜ Detach Curves. This works on multiple curves as well.

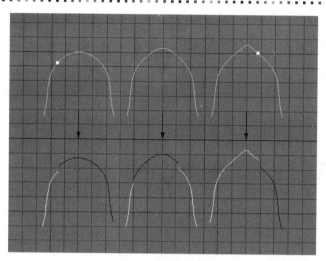

Figure 5.15 *Detaching curve segments*

Curve and Surface Alignment and Continuity

When two separate curves or surface ends are not touching, they are said to be *discontinuous*. Once they are touching, there are three possible levels of continuity between the two: *position continuity, tangent continuity,* or *curvature continuity*. In creating a smooth, continuous surface out of patches, you need at least tangent continuity between the connected patches. In this section you'll work with two example curves to get an understanding of the concept of these degrees of continuity.

To set up the example curves, create two CV curves as shown in Figure 5.16, using X+click to snap them to the grid. Make copies and translate them aside.

Position continuity, also called zero-order continuity (C0), occurs when the two end CVs are placed in the same 3D space. Select the two copied curves and select Edit Curves → Align Curves ❑. Set Continuity to Position, and modify Boundary to Both. Then click Align to see the result shown in Figure 5.17.

Tangent continuity, also called first-order continuity (C1), occurs when the tangents at the ends of the two curves have the same slope in addition to position continuity. Practically speaking, this occurs when the two end CVs of the curves all line up. Select the two original curves, change Continuity to Tangent in the option window, and click Align to see the result shown on the left in Figure 5.18.

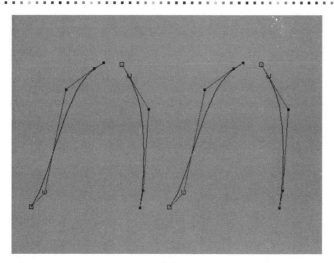

Figure 5.16 *Two curves and their copies*

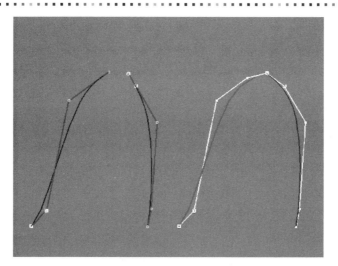

Figure 5.17 *Curves aligned with position continuity*

Curvature continuity, also called second-order continuity (C2), occurs when curves that have tangent continuity also "curve" away from their end points in the same way. Another way of saying this is that the radii of the curvatures of the two curves are the same. Practically speaking, this means that in the curve being modified, the third CV from the end point (in addition to the second CV) is also translated to accommodate

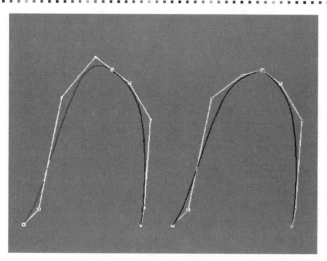

Figure 5.18 *Position alignment (right) and tangent alignment (left)*

the curvature change. Select the copied curves again, the ones with point continuity alignment, change Continuity to Curvature, then click Align again. Notice, as shown on the right in Figure 5.19, the changes in the positions of the second and third CVs from the end. There are few tools in Maya that give options for curvature continuity. Align is one, and the other is Project Tangent, which is not covered in this book.

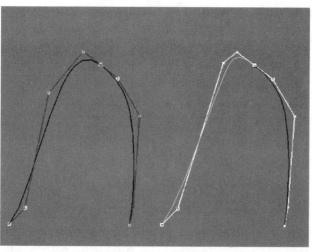

Figure 5.19 *Tangent alignment (left) and curvature alignment (right)*

The default setting for Align Curves and Surfaces (they are the same action) is Modify Position First, which means the first curve selected will move in its entirety to align itself. After you have performed the Align, try playing with the various optional settings in Channel box ➜ Inputs to get a better idea of the options.

Rebuilding Curves

The Rebuild Curves tool allows you to rebuild curves in various ways. Rebuilding curves is important for creating good surfaces. When you work with curves for a while, they can end up with unnecessary CVs, or CVs bunched up unevenly. You can clean them with the Rebuild Curves tool. Remember that from cleanly built (or rebuilt) curves come clean surfaces. To try this tool, create a curve using the Pencil Curve tool. With the curve still selected, select Edit Curves ➜ Rebuild Curve ❑.

When the Rebuild Type is set to Uniform, which is the default setting, you have to manually state how many spans the curve should have. The default is set at four spans, but the number you need to use will vary depending on the complexity of the required shape.

The Reduce setting simplifies the curve according to the Global or Local Tolerance level you set, as illustrated in Figure 5.20. The Match Knots setting requires two curves to be selected; it reparameterizes the first curve to match the number of knots in the second curve. The No Multiple Knots setting gets rid of multiple knots, which are sometimes created when curves are attached or knots inserted. A multiple knot occurs when more than one knot, or edit point, occupies the same position on a curve. The Curvature setting redistributes and inserts more edit points in areas of higher curvature according to a tolerance level, just like the Reduce setting. To change the Global Tolerance setting for the Reduce or Curvature options, go to Window ➜ Settings/ Preferences ➜ Preferences and click on Settings to open the Tolerance section.

Let's cover one more option: the Keep CV option allows you to rebuild the parameter of the curve while keeping the CVs in their original position. When you insert knots, as described next, the span of the curve increases and more CVs are created, but the parameterized values of points along the curve stay the same as before the insertion. The Keep CV option recalculates the curve parameters to include the inserted knot, while keeping the CVs in the same position.

Inserting Knots

The Insert Knot command allows you to add more edit points or CVs to further edit a curve. To use Insert Knot, select a curve point on the curve where you want the extra edit point to be created and then choose Edit Curves ➜ Insert Knot. Note that another

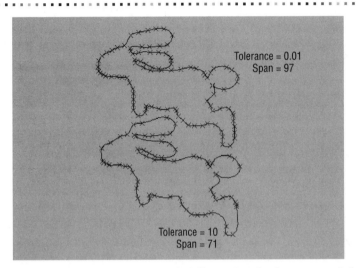

Figure 5.20 *Curves rebuilt with different local tolerances and thus different numbers of spans*

CV is created as well. A useful option for Insert Knot, also available for Insert Isoparms for surfaces, is the Between Selections option. Select two edit points; then select Edit Curves ➜ Insert Knot ❑, click the Between Selections option, and click Insert. As shown in Figure 5.21, another edit point is added exactly halfway between the two selected edit points.

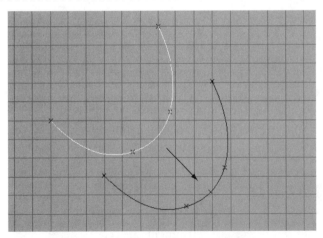

Figure 5.21 *A curve with a knot (edit point) inserted between two existing edit points*

If you select two curve points with this option, these two curve points will also turn into edit points, along with the new edit point you've inserted in the middle. This may not be the result you desire.

Adding Points to a Curve

Once the curve has been created and you want to add more curve to it, you can use Edit Curves ➜ Add Points Tool. If you want to add points, not from the last CV but from the start of the curve, select the curve and then select Edit Curves ➜ Reverse Curve Direction. If you want to add additional edit points instead of CVs, just RM choose the curve and pick-mask Edit Point. Then, when you select Add Points Tool, it will be set to add edit points and not CVs. Note the difference between Insert Knot and Add Points: the former adds more points inside an existing curve, whereas the latter actually creates a longer curve segment.

Using the Curve Editing Tool

Usually you can manipulate a curve by translating the CVs. But at times you may want an edit point to stay in position while the CVs around it move to change the curve shape. The curve editor is useful in such situation.

Create a curve, and then select Edit Curves ➜ Curve Editing Tool. Grab the Parameter position handle (as shown in Figure 5.22) and move it along the curve while keeping V pressed to snap the editor to edit points. Once it's on the edit point you want, you can modify the curve tangent direction and scale around the edit point without moving the edit point itself.

Cutting Curves

Edit Curves ➜ Cut Curve is another very useful curve editing function. It takes multiple curves and detaches them where they intersect. The default option setting for Find Intersections is In 2D And 3D, which finds the intersections for the curves even if they are not actually touching in 3D space, but only seem to touch in one of the active 2D views. In Figure 5.23, a group of circles that were created from a cylinder have been cut by a large circle, with the cutting done in the side view panel. Notice how the large circle isn't touching any of the cut curves in the actual 3D space.

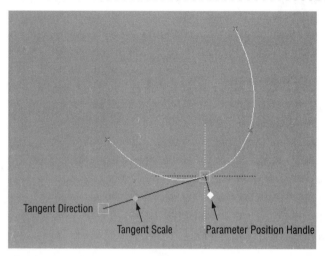

Figure 5.22 *Manipulating a curve with the Curve Editing tool*

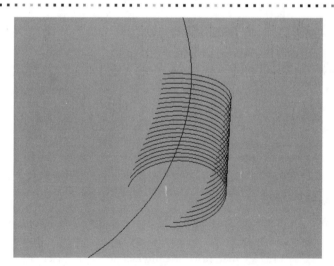

Figure 5.23 *A group of circles that have been cut with a large circle*

Filleting Curves

Curve Fillet takes two intersecting curves and creates a fillet. Unlike Cut Curve, which can be projected from a 2D view, the fillet curves actually have to be touching. The default setting creates a circular fillet from the two curves. Where the lines are intersecting, sometimes the fillet occurs at the wrong corner. In such case, you need to cut the curves first, and then select the curves you want to fillet. The Trim and Join settings in the option window can also save you a lot of time by trimming the curves and attaching the segments into one curve. See Figure 5.24.

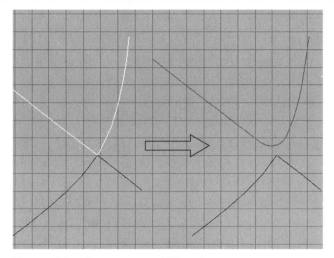

Figure 5.24 *Curves cut and filleted*

Offsetting Curves

Offset Curve duplicates a curve with an offset distance that you set in the option window. There is an important difference between offsetting a curve and copying and scaling a curve. When a curve is duplicated and uniformly scaled, it maintains the curve shape, whereas a curve created from the offset maintains the distance between it and the original curve, though not necessarily the original shape. Figure 5.25 illustrates the difference.

Creating Surfaces

Once the curves are all prepared, Maya provides us with various ways of creating surfaces from them. We will now cover these surface creation actions and tools in Maya's Surfaces menu, and the Text tool under the Create menu as well, which is closely related to the Bevel tool.

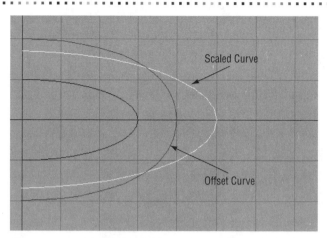

Figure 5.25 *Scaling and offsetting a curve*

Revolve

The Revolve tool on the Surfaces menu takes selected curves and revolves them around a designated axis, which you set in the option window. The default revolve axis is vertical, or Y. The other settings are X, Z, and Free. The last option makes available the Axis boxes, which use the translation values of the Show Manipulator axis handle. This allows you to change the revolve axis interactively after creating a surface, by manipulating the Show Manipulator tool.

For a simple example, let us build a lamp to go in the living room we built in the previous chapter.

1. Start a new scene and select CV Curve Tool. Draw curves in the front view as in Figure 5.26.

2. With the curves selected, select Surfaces ➡ Revolve. The default setting works fine for our purpose, and we see a revolved lamp. But wait: the lamp cover seems a bit lacking in design. Let's see if we can make it look a bit more stylish, like the lamp in Figure 5.27.

3. Select the lamp cover, go to Channel Box Input, and click on revolve2. Change Degree to Linear, and Sections to 12. Now select the profile curve for the lamp cover and, again in Channel Box, translate it (1, 2, –2), rotate it (–25, –25, –25), and scale it (1, 2, 1).

Figure 5.26 *A curve profile for the lamp we'll create*

Figure 5.27 *The finished lamp*

4. Put a simple sphere inside the lamp cover and deform it like a light bulb and the model is ready for texturing. The Chapter 5 Color Gallery on the CD-ROM shows the finished version. We can add this lamp to the living room later on, so save the file as Lamp for future use.

Lofting

Lofting is without a doubt the most often used function in surface creation, and hence the most important. The Loft command creates a surface using selected curves, isoparms, or trimmed edges. The settings for Maya's Loft command are simple, and the default settings need not be changed for most occasions. You can loft any combination of curves, isoparms, and even trimmed edges. One thing you must always be careful about, however, is the order of the curves you pick for lofting. The first curve selected defines the U direction of the lofted surface, and since the surface is lofted in the same order the curves are selected, the way you select the curves is important. Sometimes you will encounter a situation like that illustrated on the left in Figure 5.28, where if you marquee-select a group of curves and loft them, the resulting surface is not what you want. In such a case, you could either select the curves one by one in the proper order, or move them in the Outliner as we've done on the right in Figure 5.28, so that the order in which they are listed matches the order in which you want the lofting to occur.

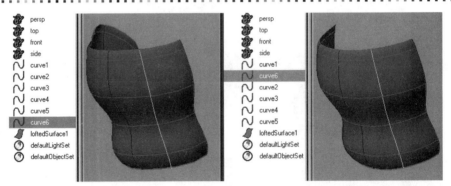

Figure 5.28 *Using the Outliner, you can place curves in the correct order for lofting.*

If the curves being lofted are uniform curves and have the same number of spans, then the resulting lofted surface will retain the same uniform parameterization and the same number of U spans as the curves. If the curve spans are different, you will generally end up with a surface that has many more U spans. The number of V spans of the surface will equal the number of the curves being lofted minus 1, assuming you are using the default settings.

In Maya 3, the Loft command now has an option called Section Spans, which can increase the number of spans between curves being lofted. This can be a time saver when you want to create a surface with several sections but have only two or three curves to work with.

An excellent example to use for lofting is the torus primitive. Create a default torus, and while it's still selected, open Edit Curve ➔ Duplicate Surface Curves ❑, click on *V*, and click Duplicate. Select just the torus and delete it. You are left with eight circles to loft. Select all of them and loft with the default setting by selecting Surfaces ➔ Loft. You end up with seven-eighths of a torus, as shown on the left in Figure 5.29. Select the surface and check the Attribute Editor. Note that it has seven spans in V, its Form V is Open, and from the top view, its span direction for V is clockwise.

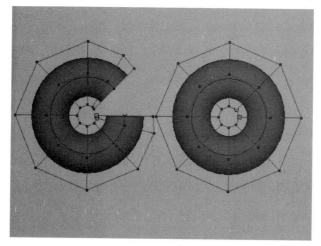

Figure 5.29 *Open loft and periodic loft of a torus*

Undo with Z until you have only the curves again. This time, select the circles individually counterclockwise, and in the Loft option window, click on the Close setting. Select Surfaces ➔ Loft again, and you should get a complete torus as on the right in the figure. Note that now the *V* span is 8, its Form V is Periodic, and its span direction for V is counterclockwise.

Extrude

The Extrude command extrudes a surface from selected curves, or curves on a surface, or isoparms. Extruding isn't complicated, but it can get confusing because there are so many buttons you can click in the Extrude option window.

Extruding usually involves two or more curves, or curves on a surface, or even isoparms. The first curves are the Profile curves that will be extruded, and the last one is the Path curve that will guide the extrusion. The Extrude command provides several settings that control the shape of the surface being extruded:

- The Tube setting in the option window makes the profile curve turn with the path.

- The Flat setting lets the profile curve maintain its own orientation as it moves along the path.

- The Distance setting requires only one curve, and it activates the Extrude Length slider. With Distance, you can determine the direction of the extrusion with either the Specify setting, in which different axis choices are listed, or the Profile normal, in which the extrusion goes along the direction of the profile curve's normal.

- The Result Position option lets you either make the path come to the profile curve, which is the At Profile setting, or make the profile go to the path, which is the At Path setting.

The following example illustrates a general method that should work well as a way to create extrusions. Let's say you wanted to build a frame for the fireplace in the living room from Chapter 4. Start a new scene. With the EP Curve tool set to Linear, create the fireplace frame path using a construction plane as shown in Figure 5.30. Then, in the top view, create the profile curve for the frame.

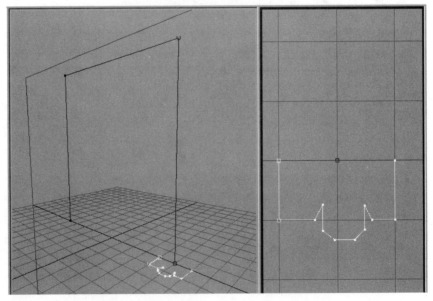

Figure 5.30 *The frame profile and the frame path curves*

Now select the profile, move its center to one of the ends of the path curve and select Surfaces ➜ Extrude with everything at the default setting. We should now have a frame shape like the one in Figure 5.31. Note that you can adjust the shape of the surface by manipulating the curves.

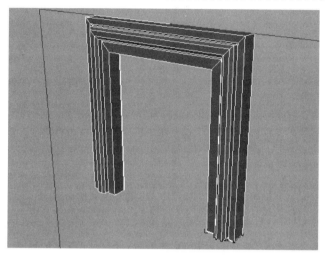

Figure 5.31 *The finished frame shape*

Working with Planars, Text, and Bevel

An object is *planar* if can be wholly mapped to a plane; that is, if it is a 2D object in 3D space, if it has length and width, but doesn't have depth. A true planar object, then, cannot be twisted in three directions. As soon as it is, it ceases to be planar. A planar surface is an efficient way to create trimmed surfaces from closed curves, assuming those curves themselves are planar. Planars are especially useful when it comes to creating text in Maya; in fact, there is actually a Trim option setting for creating text, which creates planar surfaces.

For a quick example of a planar, create a circle and apply a default planar to it by selecting Surfaces ➜ Planar to get a trimmed surface. Pick-mask on the circle and try moving a CV up and down. The trimmed circle surface will disappear and come into existence only when the CV is perfectly on the ground plane.

To better understand planar objects, let's create a simple letter M. Start a new scene, select Create ➜ Text ❏, and type **M** inside the Text field (we are being economical here). Although the Trim option is available here for creating a planar surface, we will create it another way. Leave everything at its default and click Create. A planar curve outline of the letter M is created. Go to the Perspective window to see the planar curve letter in 3D. You should see the picture (a) in Figure 5.32.

Figure 5.32 *Creating the letter* M *: (a) as a planar curve; (b) with a default bevel; (c) with bevel properties adjusted; and (d) with a planar surface added*

Beveling is almost the opposite of planar in that it usually creates depth in flat things. It is a very flexible and powerful function that can take a curve, an isoparm, or even a trimmed edge and create bevels, or sloping edges.

Let's bevel the planar outline of the letter M you created in the previous section. Select the M curve and select Surface ➜ Bevel ❑. The options here are not complicated, but they can be a bit confusing because of the orientation: Top Side bevels the back of the letter, Bottom Side bevels the front, and Both bevels front and back.

When the text is created in Maya, it is facing front. If you have trouble relating Top to back, Bottom to front, and Height to extrusion depth, just imagine the letters lying face down on the ground.

You can make the bevel corners Straight or Circular, and you can have the bevel edges remain straight, arc in (Concave) with sharp definitions, or arc out (Convex) smoothly. You can leave the Bevel Width, Depth, and Height at default settings—we'll be interactively adjusting them afterwards. Click Bevel, and you should see picture (b).

If you want to change the default settings for corners and edges, go to the Channel box, Input section and click bevel1 to get at those settings. Hit T to activate Show

Manipulator for Bevel history. You should see three blue dots connected with lines. If you don't see these, go to the Input section and click bevel1 again, and they should appear.

These blue dots are handles with which you can manipulate Bevel Width, Depth (the depth of the bevels, or the sloping edges), or Height (the depth of the actual extrusion of the text curve). Manipulate them until you are satisfied with the shape of the letter M; then pick-mask Isoparm and select the front edge of the bevel surface, as in picture (c) in Figure 5.32. Select Surface ➜ Planar and you should see the front side of the M now covered, as in (d). You can use the letter to decorate the living room later. Save the file.

Boundary

The Boundary function is most easily described when compared to lofted curves. When two curves are lofted, the result is a four-sided surface, two of whose opposing edges are defined by the curves. The other two edges are automatically calculated to be straight lines going from one curve to the other. When more than two curves are being lofted, the other two edges can become curved, but these, too are interpolations between the curves being lofted. A boundary function, in contrast, enables the four sides of a surface to be created from four curves, thus giving the artist more control over precisely how the surface edges should be defined.

To see how boundaries work, start a new scene. Create four different curves with two or three spans each. Place them so that their ends intersect, like the curves on the left in Figure 5.33. You can select the curves in any order you want, or drag-select them all together, but the first curve picked determines the UV parameterization of the boundary surface because the surface U parameters are determined by the curve's own U parameters. So if the UV direction for the boundary is important, then you should keep that in mind when you are building the first curve.

Once the curves are all selected, select Surfaces ➜ Boundary with the default settings. You should end up with a surface that has three or four UV spans, like the one on the right in Figure 5.33. Save this file; you can use the same curves for working with birails in the next section.

As shown in Figure 5.34, the Boundary function can also create surfaces with only three curves. This type of surface created with the boundary is not really a surface with three edges, but rather a surface with one zero-length edge. The order of picking is significant in this case because the pinched zero-length edge (also called the degenerate surface) occurs between the first two curves picked. This is important in situations where the surface patch needs to be attached to another surface patch.

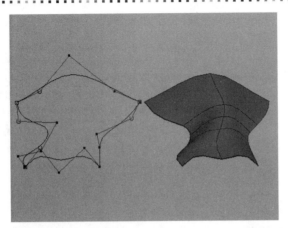

Figure 5.33 *The four curves on the left define the boundary of the surface on the right.*

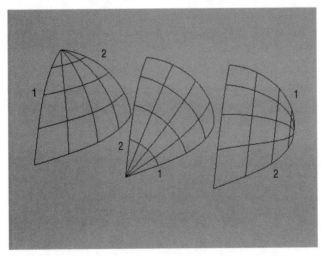

Figure 5.34 *Surfaces created with the Boundary function from three curves, selected in different orders*

Note that Maya also offers a Square tool, which works much like Boundary in that it takes three or four curves and produces a surface patch. The way it creates tangency, however, is more complex, and Square is considered an advanced tool.

Birails

Birails are functions much like boundaries in that they work to determine the four sides of a surface. Essentially, birails extrude one or more profile curves along two rail curves, or paths. The parameters of the profile curve(s) define the V parameters of the birailed surface, and the two rail curves define the U parameters of the surface.

Let's see how birailing works. Get the curves you built for testing the boundary function. Select Surface ➡ Birail ➡ Birail 1 Tool. (We will delve into the options a bit later.) Maya asks you to select the profile curve; select one of the curves. Now you are instructed to select the two rail curves; select the two curves adjacent to the first picked curve. The birail surface is created.

You can try this again with different selection orders and see how the surface differs in each case, and how it also differs from the boundary surface. The fourth curve of the boundary is basically ignored, being replaced by the profile curve. Let's look at the other birail tools.

Click the Birail 2 Tool option, and again leave all the settings at their defaults. You are instructed to select two profile curves now. Select the two parallel curves. Then pick the two rail curves. A birail is created. Notice how this surface looks much like the boundary surface? That is because the same four curves are used to create the surface.

For the Birail 3+ Tool, we need another curve to act as a profile curve. It would be good to build a curve with two or three spans like the other curves, and you should make sure the newly added profile curve is touching the rail curves. You should have something like the curves shown in Figure 5.35.

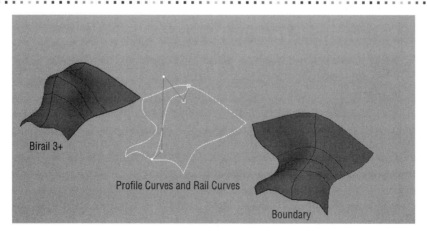

Figure 5.35 Three profile curves and the rail curves

The Birail 3+ tool works a bit differently—you select all the profile curves first, hit Enter, and then pick the two rail curves. The birailed surface appears. Birail 3+ is basically a high-level loft, with the U parameter surface edges following the rail curves, and you can have control of the inner areas of a surface with the Birail 3+ tool that you cannot get with Boundary or the other birail tools.

Let's look briefly at a few option settings. All three types of birails have Nonproportional or Proportional settings under Transform Control. The first setting modifies only the parts of the profile curve that change when it birails, whereas the proportional setting maintains the shape of the profile curve—hence the name proportional. So if the rail curves grow wider, the nonproportional setting will only stretch the profile sideways, but the proportional setting will enlarge the entire profile.

The Rebuild option also allows the curves of the birail to have their own rebuild options, which may in some situations give us much lighter surfaces. For the rebuild settings, refer to "Rebuilding Curves" earlier in this chapter.

Editing Surfaces

Once a surface is created, you will often need to manipulate it to produce its final form. Maya's many surface editing tools and actions generally behave in exactly the same way as their curve counterparts, which we discussed earlier; so we'll go through most of them pretty quickly. Some others require a closer look, such as the Trim tool. We will also focus more on modeling techniques using these tools.

Attach and Detach Surfaces

These actions work exactly the same as their curve counterparts. With curves, you were pick-masking curve points, whereas with these surface actions you pick-mask isoparms.

Working with Construction History

Start a new scene. Select Create ➜ NURBS Primitives ➜ Cone. Focus in on it by pressing F, and select its isoparm about halfway up. Now choose Detach Surfaces with the default settings. Select the top half, move it up a bit, apply Attach Surfaces, and translate it to the side. You should see something like picture a) shown below. Now grab the top part of the cone again and try transforming it in various ways while observing the effect it has on the new surface. Figure 5.36 shows more examples of the various effects produced on the new surface.

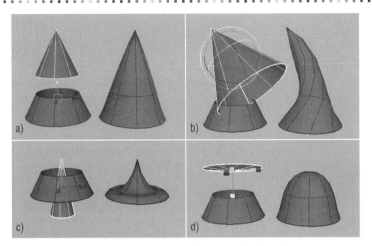

Figure 5.36 *A detached cone and reattached surfaces*

The Surface Editing Tool

Maya 3 provides a new surface editing tool, much like the curve editing tool for curves. You'll find it on the Edit Surfaces ➜ Surface Editing submenu, and like its curve counterpart, it provides a good alternative to surface modeling with CVs. Using the Manipulator positioner, you can move the editor along the surface without disturbing it and you can deform the surface by dragging the Move manipulator or using the Tangent manipulators, as shown in Figure 5.37.

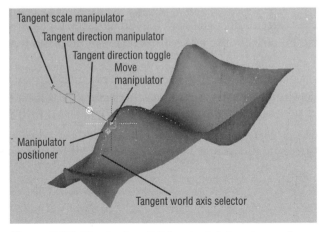

Figure 5.37 *The Surface Editing tool deforming a plane*

Inserting Isoparms and Aligning Surfaces

The Insert Isoparms command is the surface-editing equivalent of Insert Knots for curves, but using it can be trickier if you choose (in the command's option window) to insert Between Selections. Selecting isoparms is not always as easy as picking edit points. Make sure you are clicking right over the isoparm rather than click-dragging, or you may end up highlighting an isoparametric curve between the isoparms, in which case that curve will be inserted as an isoparm as well.

You can also check the Feedback line just above the Layer bar to see if what is highlighted has a neatly rounded parameter value (assuming it is a uniform surface). If it does, it usually means you have selected an isoparm.

Align Surfaces is the surface equivalent of Align Curves. They actually use the same option window. In most situations, simply attaching or stitching (see Chapter 8, "Organic Modeling.") creates the continuity we desire, but in those cases where you specifically want surface curvature continuity, you would want to use Align Surfaces first.

Extend and Offset Surfaces

Extend Surfaces and Offset Surfaces are both Maya 3 Unlimited actions. The first action extends a surface's edge(s) according to a set distance. It can either extrapolate the direction to the way the surface was curving at the edge, or simply go off in a tangential direction.

To try this option, first create a torus. Go to Inputs, click makeNurbTorus1, set its variables as shown in Figure 5.38, and you should see a quarter-formed torus. With the torus still selected, select Edit Surfaces ➜ Extend Surfaces. Open the Attribute Editor, select the extendSurface tab, and set Extend Side to Both and Extend Direction to V.

The Offset Surfaces option is the surface equivalent of Offset Curves, with simpler settings. In its option window, the Surface Fit setting calculates the distance of the offset from the surface, whereas the CV Fit setting calculates the distance of the offset from the CVs. Select the extended torus and apply Offset Surfaces. Go into the Inputs window, click Distance, and then, in the modeling window, MM drag to interactively adjust the distance of the offset. A good distance is –0.2. You should see something like the picture in Figure 5.39.

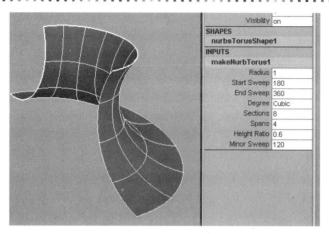

Figure 5.38 *You can use the torus shown here to test the effects of extending and offsetting surfaces.*

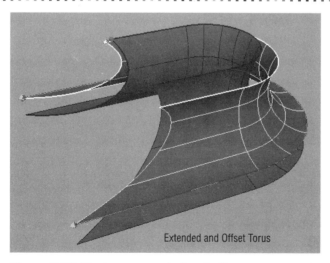

Figure 5.39 *The torus extended and offset*

It's often better to use editing functions at default settings, and then interactively change the settings by using the Attribute Editor or the Channel box with Show Manipulator.

Offsetting can be used with lofting. Try offsetting a curve from one of the top edges, lower it a bit, and use it with the two surface edge isoparms to create a loft between the two surfaces. Repeat for the bottom edges, and you should see something like Figure 5.40.

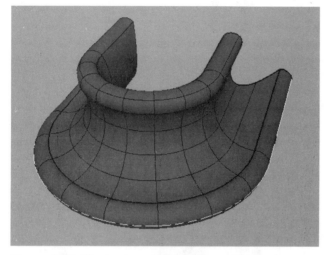

Figure 5.40 *The torus extended, offset, and lofted*

Trim and Round

Trimming is a way to cut surfaces into desired surface shapes using curves on surfaces (see below). Trimming indiscriminately can produce heavy models because it can create a lot of unnecessary isoparms, and that is always a factor to keep in mind when using the Trim functions. At the same time, a well-applied trim can save a lot of work in producing the models you want.

Projecting Curves On Surfaces

In order to trim a surface, you need *curves on surfaces* first. This is Maya's term for curves that are mapped to the UV parameters of the surface they are on, rather than to the XYZ coordinates of world space. Maya can let us project curves, curves on surfaces, isoparms, or trimmed edges to a designated surface and create curves on that surface. Let's look at this with an extended example.

Let's try building a spherical opening protruding from a wall. We will use projections, trimming, and filleting to do this.

1. Create a NURBS sphere, scale it uniformly to 2, and rotate it 90 degrees in X.

2. Create a NURBS circle, which should appear right inside the sphere.

3. Go to top view, select both, and select Edit Surface ➜ Project Curve On Surface, with the default setting.

4. Go back to the Perspective window, and you should see two curves on surface on the sphere (as in the image on the left in Figure 5.41).

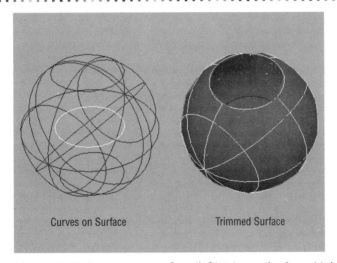

Curves on Surface   Trimmed Surface

Figure 5.41 *Curves on a surface (left), trimmed sphere (right)*

The Trim Tool

Now you're ready to try trimming:

1. Select the bottom curve on surface (you should be able to select it just like a regular object) and delete it.

2. Select Edit Surface ➜ Trim Tool.

3. Select the sphere, and it should turn white. Click on the middle of the sphere to designate that as the part of the sphere you wish to keep. Hit Enter. You should see a trimmed hole as in the image on the right in Figure 5.41.

4. Select the sphere and scale it up to (3, 3, 3). Notice that the hole on the sphere is keeping its size. When you move the circle, the hole follows it.

5. Select the sphere and apply Edit ➜ Delete By Type ➜ History to erase the procedural relationship between the circle and the trimmed hole.

Untrimming Surfaces

Oops! We made a mistake: we wanted to make a hole at the front of the sphere, not at the top—but since we deleted the history, we can't move the hole. How do we fix this situation? Curves on surface can be deleted like objects, but not trimmed edges. There is an action specifically for untrimming surfaces, which is Edit Surfaces ➜ Untrim Surfaces. You can choose to delete only the last trim or use the default setting, Untrim All. Select the sphere and apply Untrim Surfaces.

Projecting with Surface Normal

Project Curve On Surface has another option we haven't used yet—projecting based on surface normals. To try this, open the Project Curve On Surface option window. The default setting is Active View, which means the curve is projected onto the surface from the camera of whatever view is active. The other option is Surface Normal, which determines the projection of the curve by the normals projecting from the surface. Here the projection is actually done the opposite way. Click on Surface Normal, keep the option window open, select the circle and move it to (0, 0, 4), rotate it (–60, 0, 0), and scale it (3, 3, 7). With the circle still selected, select the sphere and click the Project button. You'll see the results shown in Figure 5.42. Notice that you only see one curve on surface created near the circle and not on the other side. That is because the normals on the other side are not seeing the circle. Trim the sphere, and delete the circle.

Intersect Surfaces

As well as projecting curves and isoparms, Maya can also create curves on surfaces when NURBS surfaces intersect. The Edit Surfaces ➜ Intersect Surfaces with default settings creates curves on surfaces on both intersecting surfaces. To try this tool, create a NURBS plane, rotate it 90 degrees in X, translate it –1 in Z, and scale it uniformly to 30. This will be the wall. Drag-select both the sphere and the plane, and select Edit Surfaces ➜ Intersect Surfaces. You should see curves on surface on both surfaces. Select the plane and trim out the circle. Trim the sphere as well, and you should see something like Figure 5.43.

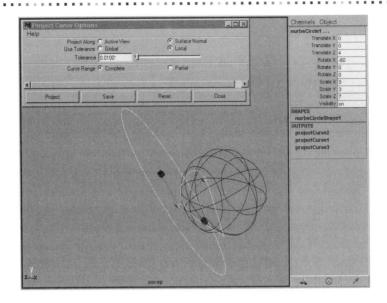

Figure 5.42 *Projecting a curve based on surface normals*

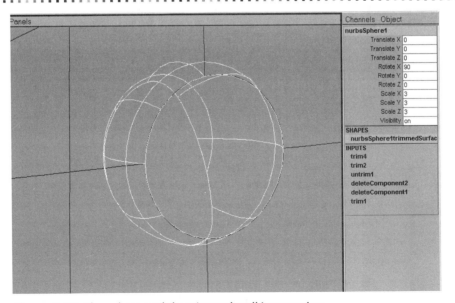

Figure 5.43 *The sphere and the trimmed wall intersecting*

Fillet and Round

Fillet and Round are similar functions, but Round is considered a more advanced tool. Let's try both, starting with Fillet. Drag-select the plane and the sphere. Select Edit Surfaces, Surface Fillet, Circular Fillet. The default setting works well here. In other situations, you may have to go into Input and fiddle around with Primary or Secondary Radius to get the fillet to curve the right way. The result should look like the upper image in Figure 5.44. The option window also has a Create Curve On Surface setting for further trimming.

Now, to try out Round, undo the fillet action. To use Round, we must have two edges. Select Edit Surfaces ➜ Round Tool, and select the trimmed edges. You should see the yellow Round radius manipulator indicating the fillet radius. You can interactively change the radius by grabbing the end handles of the manipulator. The default is 1, which is fine for this example. Press Enter, and you'll see the fillet created once again, as in the lower image in Figure 5.44. But with Round, the surfaces are also trimmed so that the fillet actually joins the trimmed edges of the surfaces. You can offset the sphere and loft the trimmed edges of the spheres to get some thickness, and create a tunnel into the wall, as in the right picture in Figure 5.44.

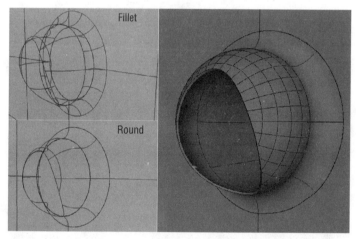

Figure 5.44 *Filleting and rounding, and the final opening in the wall*

Trim Convert

A new option for Rebuild Surfaces in Maya 3 Unlimited is Trim Convert. It can rebuild single-region trimmed surfaces as nontrimmed surfaces. This means the trimmed half-sphere in Figure 5.44 can be trim-converted, but the wall cannot, because it has a hole inside it. Select the trimmed sphere, select Edit Surfaces ➜ Rebuild Surfaces ❑, set the

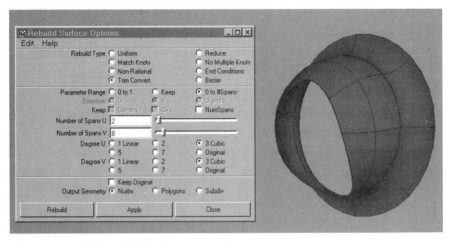

Figure 5.45 *Using the Trim Convert option*

options shown in Figure 5.45, and apply. The sphere becomes a regular NURBS surface again. You can proceed to attach the sphere to the round surface if you wish.

Hands-On Maya: Aftershave Bottle

Our discussion of NURBS modeling has covered a lot of ground. An extended hands-on exercise will help you see how to use these tools effectively together. Let's try building an aftershave bottle.

1. Start with edit points building straight lines. Make sure you are in top view, and X+click the edit points as shown here:

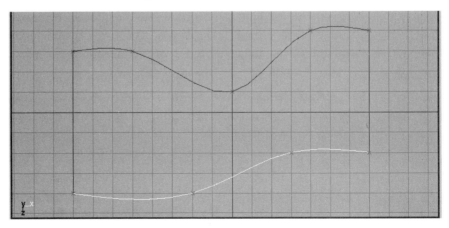

2. Select two adjacent curves, and apply Edit Curves ➜ Curve Fillet with the Trim option turned on. Do the same for the other three corners. If the curve fillet fails, change the curve direction of one of the curves with Edit Curves ➜ Reverse Curve Direction, and try again. If the angle of intersection for the curves is too wide, Maya will also have trouble calculating the fillet.

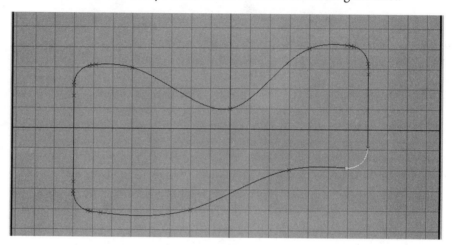

3. Attach the resulting eight curves with the options set to Connect Attach Method and Remove Multiple Knots. If the last two curves attach at the wrong ends, pick-mask Curve Point to force the curves to attach at the bottom right. Then use Edit Curves ➜ Open/Close Curves to close the loop, making it *periodic*. Rebuild the curve with the options set to Uniform and Keep CVs. The curve should now have a parameter range of 32 spans or something similar. Edit the CVs until you're satisfied with the shape.

4. Using the marking menu, get into the persp/outliner view. Although there is now only one curve, you will notice there are a lot of invisible nodes because of the construction history. Since we no longer need them, select the curve and Edit ➜ Delete By Type ➜ History.

5. Select the curve, select Edit Curve ➜ Offset ➜ Offset Curve ❑, set Offset Distance to 0.5, and reduce Max Subdivision Density to 0. This is important in keeping the same number of curve spans for the offset. Click Offset, and check the Attribute Editor (Ctrl+A) to make sure the new curve has the same number of spans as the original curve. Translate the curve up in Y to 1. Now duplicate the curves as shown here:

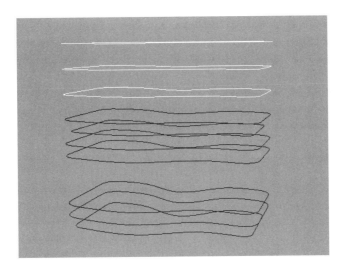

6. Select the curves (in proper order) and apply Edit Surfaces ➜ Loft. Delete all the curves. Duplicate the lofted surface, and enter −1 for Scale Y in the Channel box. Translate it up, and you should see something like image (a) below.

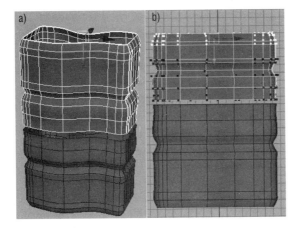

7. Pick-mask Control Vertex over the top surface and, in the front view, translate the points down in Y and closer together. You should have something like image (b) above.

8. Select the edge isoparms and select Edit Surfaces ➜ Attach ❑, check off Keep Originals, and click Attach. We now have the body of the aftershave bottle. Select the top edge isoparm of the surface, select Edit Curves ➜ Offset ➜ Offset Curve ❑, set Offset Distance to −0.5 and Max Subdivision Density to

0, and click Offset. An offset curve is created as shown below. Loft between the surface edge isoparm and the offset curve. Then select the offset curve again, and apply Surfaces ➜ Planar with the default settings. You should have the surface's top covered, as shown below.

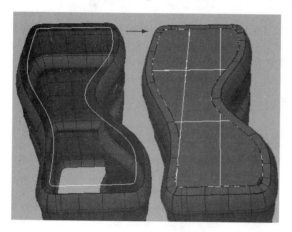

9. Attach the lofted surfaces together. Put a cylinder and a sphere at the top as the bottle cap. You may want to squash the bottom of the sphere a bit. The modeling part is done. You can find the finished version in the Chapter 5 Color Gallery on the CD-ROM.

Hands-On Maya: Building a Character I (Advanced)

We will be creating a character in several tutorials throughout this book. There is no one standard way to create characters; the approach taken in this book is only one of many possibilities. In this tutorial, we will cover the NURBS part of building the character's head. Building a realistic human head used to be more difficult, but with the arrival of subdivision surfaces, things have become considerably easier.

The face we'll create appears as `face_reference.tif` in the Chapter 5 Working Files directory on the CD-ROM.

1. Start out with a sphere that has 14 sections and about 16 spans. Cut out the front—the front will be the mouth, and the back will be the top of the head. Shape the sphere into a very rough figure of a human head, as shown next.

 It's always a good idea to have a sketch or a picture as reference when building models—a front view and a side view, as above.

2. Cut the head in half in the middle. Refine the head more, pulling out the chin and roughly sculpting the mouth. Insert isoparms where you need them and delete rows of CVs where you do not need them. You want the following minimum number of isoparms or patches for the face: three rows and columns of patches for the eye area, and three isoparms (or two patches) each for the mouth corner and mouth bottom. Duplicate curves from the mouth edge and loft as below to create the oral cavity. Attach the oral cavity to the face.

It's always better to start out with a minimum number of CVs and insert more isoparms as needed, rather than starting out with too many CVs and having to delete them later. Remember, it takes only three points (isoparms) to curve a surface. It's a very simple rule, but one that is often overlooked in modeling.

3. If you want to see the other half of the face as you are modeling, duplicate the half face, then make the scale value of the resulting surface negative along the X axis so that it becomes a mirror image of the face. Open the Connection Editor. Select the first face's shape node (select the geometry and then hit the down-arrow key) and load it into the Output window. Load the second face's shape node into the Input window. Connect World Space to Create as below. Now the second face, on the right, deforms when the CVs of the first face, on the left, are moved.

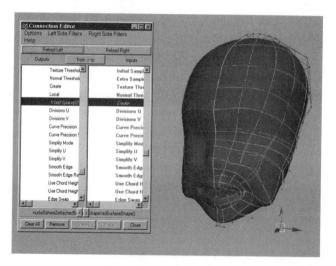

4. Pick-mask Surface Patch to select the nine patches for the eye area, then duplicate the patch with Edit Surfaces ➡ Duplicate NURBS Patches. Place a sphere around where the eyeball would go, and project a curve to form an outline of the eye on the sphere, as in (a) next. Duplicate several curves from the curve on surface and loft to get the eye area, as in (b). Cut the new surface into four pieces, then rebuild them in *U* so that they are 3 spans each, as in (c). Loft between the edges of the duplicated patch and the edges of the four cut pieces, as in (d).

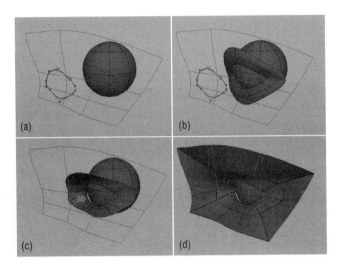

(a)   (b)

(c)   (d)

5. The NURBS part of the eye area is done. The refinement of the eye area, as well as the nose and the neck areas, will continue in Chapter 8. The eyes can be as simple as a plain sphere or a bit more sculpted, as is the one below. There are two spheres—the inner one deformed for realistic pupils, and the outer one transparent and used for specularity only.

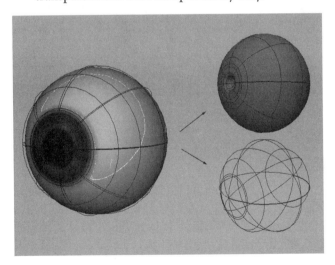

6. The method for building the ear is similar to that for the eye area. Select the four surface patches on the head as below in (a), and then select Edit Surfaces ➜ Duplicate NURBS Patches to duplicate the area where the ear will be attached. Place a sphere with eight spans and sections near it as below in (b). Later, once

converted to polygons, the eight sections of the sphere will be connected to the eight-span area of the head. Cut the sphere in half, and start sculpting it into an ear shape as below in (c). Insert more isoparms along V as needed, but keep U sections the same number. Otherwise, we will have problems connecting the ear to the head later. Once the ear is sculpted as in (d), you could cut it into four pieces the way we did with the eye area and loft with the duplicated patch, but in the case of the ear, we'll keep it simple and connect it to the head as a polygon in Chapter 6.

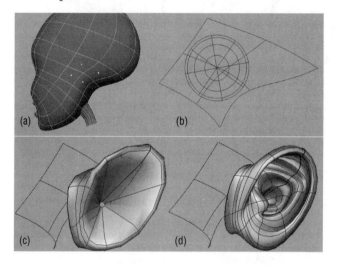

(a)   (b)   (c)   (d)

The NURBS part of the modeling is done. Save the scene with all the parts. In the next chapter, we will come back and work with polygons and subdivision surfaces to finish creating the head.

Summary

This chapter covered a lot of material. We learned to create and manipulate NURBS curves and surfaces, and we saw examples of building things with them. We also started an advanced tutorial on building a human face, which takes a lot of practice for you to become good at. The next chapter will also be quite substantial, introducing the world of polygons and subdivision surfaces. We will continue building the human head in the next chapter. Then we will come back to modeling with NURBS again in Chapter 8, where we will proceed to build a puppy dog in patches and continue our character modeling.

Polygons and Subdivision Surfaces

M A Y A

Chapter 6

Polygons are still the preferred modeling and animation choice for many gaming companies. If you are interested in going into that field, you should be particularly interested in this chapter. Because subdivision surfaces are so closely related to polygons, they are presented in the latter part of this chapter as well.

Alias|Wavefront has made some major changes to polygon modeling in Maya 3. The polygon code was rewritten to improve general performance, speed, and stability in working with large polygonal data. In addition to a number of new commands, the polygon menus have been significantly reorganized. Many existing commands that were located in the Edit Polygons menu in Maya 2.5 are now in the Polygons menu, and vice versa.

We will begin with some polygon terms and concepts, and then learn how to create and edit them. We will then introduce subdivision surface modeling concepts and show how to work with them. The chapter ends with a pair of tutorial exercises, the first building a polygon hand and the second continuing our character modeling tutorial begun in the previous chapter.

New

- Polygon faces, solids, and shells
- Techniques for creating and displaying polygons
- Polygon selection and editing tools
- Working with subdivision surfaces
- Hands-On Maya: building a polygon hand
- Hands-On Maya: building a character II (advanced)

Polygon Concepts and Terms

The word *polygon* is derived from a Greek word meaning "many angled." In mathematics, a polygon is defined as a closed figure formed by a finite number of coplanar segments that are not parallel and intersect exactly two other segments only at their endpoints.

As far as we are concerned, polygons are triangles, rectangles, pentagons, and other many-sided line drawings. Each endpoint is called a *vertex*, each line is called an *edge*, and the area inside is called the *face*. Figure 6.1 shows these and other terms used with polygons.

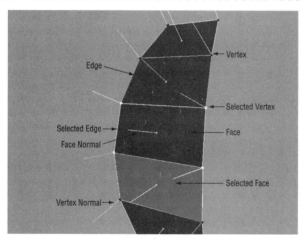

Figure 6.1 *Anatomy of a polygon*

Polygon Faces

Faces have a front side and a back side, like NURBS surfaces. The most basic polygon surface is the triangular face. The front side of a triangular face has only one normal vector, because triangles are, by definition, planar. Quadrangular polygons (quads) are four-sided faces, which may or may not be planar. You also can create faces that have five or more sides, called *n*-sided faces, but as a general rule, polygon surfaces should be kept as triangles or quads.

A triangular face is the building block of all modeling. Every type of surface geometry is eventually converted into triangular faces (a process known as tessellation) *before it is rendered.*

Polygon faces are usually connected (attached to each other), sharing common vertices and edges, but they can be *extracted* with their own unshared edges and vertices while still being part of the polygon surface. Unshared edges are also called *border edges*, and they cannot become *soft edges* (see the Reverse and Soften/Harden commands in the "Editing Polygons" section). Figure 6.2 illustrates the difference between shared and unshared edges.

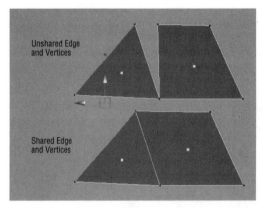

Figure 6.2 *Shared and unshared faces*

Polygon Solids, Shells, and UV Values

Polygons are classified as either solids or shells. A polygon *solid* is made up of connected faces that form an enclosed volume, where each edge is shared by two faces. A polygon *shell* is a collection of connected faces that leave some of its edges open as border edges. A polygon object can have more than one shell, as illustrated in Figure 6.3.

By default, faces have UV values assigned to them when they are created. As explained in Chapter 5, "NURBS Modeling," a surface in 3D space is defined by the parameterization of the variables U and V. A UV coordinate can be given at any point inside the area, and the area is given UV directions. UVs are needed for texturing purposes. Polygon UVs are difficult to distinguish from the regular vertex points, but they turn bright green when they are selected. We will come back to UVs when we come to texturing polygons in Chapter 19, "Shading and Texturing Surfaces."

Nonmanifold Surfaces

When working with polygons, you will sometimes end up creating surfaces that have an edge without a face, an edge shared by three or more faces, faces with opposite normals, or faces that are shared by a single vertex and no edge. Illustrated in Figure 6.4,

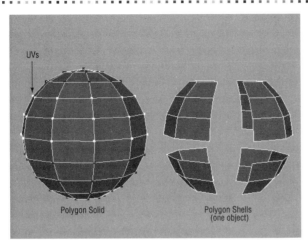

Figure 6.3 *A polygon solid and shells*

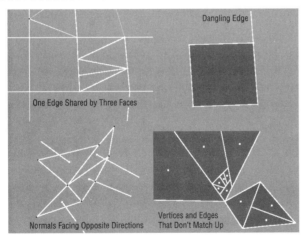

Figure 6.4 *Examples of nonmanifold surfaces*

these are called *nonmanifold* surfaces, and they are considered poor polygon surfaces, as they can lead to unpredictable results. Be careful not to create these topologies, and get rid of them when they do occur.

Maya 3 has a new option in its Polygons ➜ Cleanup command to get rid of nonmanifold geometry.

Creating Polygons

You can create polygons by clicking vertices to generate edges, much as you create curves. Two or more edges create a face, which contains face normals and vertex normals. You can also create polygon primitives or convert NURBS into polygons.

Using Polygon Primitives

As with NURBS, Maya provides several default polygon primitives you can use as starting points for creating more complex polygonal surfaces. When you select Create ➜ Polygon Primitives, you'll see a list of primitives much like the NURBS primitives.

Note that the polygon cube, cylinder, and cone surfaces are all one-piece solids, unlike their NURBS counterparts, which are made up of several pieces.

As an example, select Create ➜ Polygon Primitives ➜ Sphere ❑. In the option window that appears next, the Subdivisions Around Axis attribute is equivalent to the Sections attribute of the NURBS sphere, and Subdivisions Along Height is the same as the Spans attribute of a NURBS sphere. You also can choose the axis for the sphere's vertical direction. The Texture setting, which is turned on by default, maps UV values to the sphere being created. Click Create.

You can try editing the sphere's radius and subdivision attributes in the Channel box's Input section or in the Attribute Editor's polySphere tab. In the latter, you can also edit the Axis setting to change the sphere's orientation. The examples in Figure 6.5 show spheres with different settings.

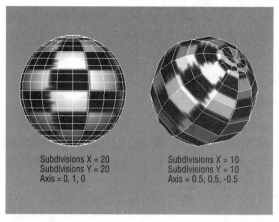

Figure 6.5 *Two spheres created with different settings*

Creating Faces

We can use Create Polygon to draw faces. Let's try a quick example:

1. In the side view, select Polygons ➜ Create Polygon Tool ❑.

2. Set all the options to their default values by clicking the Reset Tool button, and then change the Limit Points setting to 3.

3. Click in the modeling window in a counterclockwise direction as shown below. On the third click, a triangular face is created.

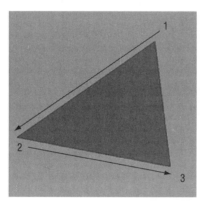

4. Change the Limit Points setting to –1 (the default). Then click again, as shown below. Press Enter after the fourth click to create a quadrangular face.

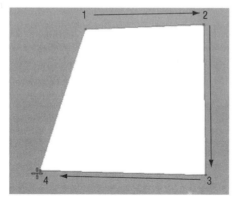

 If you leave the Limit Points setting at its default of –1, then after you've entered the desired number of vertices, you can just press Enter to complete the action.

5. Choose Display ➜ Custom Polygon Display ❏. Click the All button at the top of the dialog box to set the display for both faces. Check the Normals box in the Face section and the Vertices box in the Show Item Numbers section. Switch to perspective view, and you will see that the normal directions for the faces are opposite, as well as the directions of their vertex numbers, as shown below.

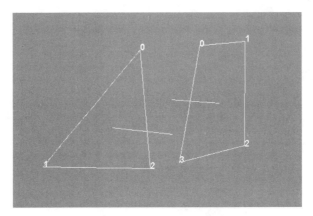

The direction in which you create vertices determines the direction of the normal: the front side of a face is created by clicking counterclockwise.

Faces that are not triangular may or may not be planar. If you want to make sure the faces you are building remain planar, you can select the Ensure Planarity option for the Create Polygon and Append To Polygon tools. This option forces the face being built to remain planar.

Adding Faces

The Append To Polygon tool is the same as the Create Polygon tool, except that it adds faces to existing faces rather than creating new ones. Let's add some faces to our triangular face:

1. Switch to side view and select Polygons ➜ Append To Polygon Tool.

2. Click within the triangular face to select it. You can tell it's selected because the border edges appear thicker.

By default, to select a face, you need to click or marquee its center. If you want to be able to select a face by clicking anywhere within it, choose Window ➜ Settings/Preferences ➜ Preferences, go to Settings, Selection section, and change the Polygon selection from Center to Whole Face.

3. Select the edge on the left side, and you will see pink arrows going clockwise around the triangular face. Also, a bright green dot appears at the zero vertex. That is where the appending begins.

4. Click two more times, as shown below. Then press Enter. You now have a quadrangular face attached to the original face. Notice that the vertex numbers are 3 and 4. You can continue to add faces this way.

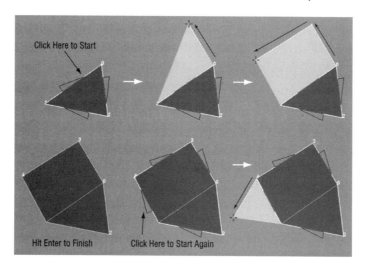

You can set the Append To Polygon tool to continue adding faces by setting the Limit Points option to 4. You can try this with the quadrangular face, as illustrated in Figure 6.6. After the second click, another quadrangular face is created, and you are still in the Append mode. You can build polygonal strips in one round of clicking this way, as illustrated. You also can create a triangular face by pressing Enter after the first vertex placement, but that will exit Append mode. Another technique, illustrated on the right in Figure 6.6, is to click one edge and then click another adjoining edge to create a face that is attached to those two faces, and continue to attach the face to more edges as you go. Follow the direction of the pink arrows to create the extra faces.

You can reposition a vertex while you are creating it, just as you can with curves (see Chapter 5), by MM clicking or pressing the Insert key.

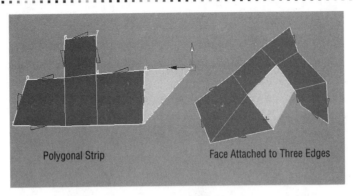

Figure 6.6 *Polygonal strips and attaching faces to edges*

Creating Faces with Holes

With the Create Polygon or Append To Polygon tool, you can easily create polygon faces with holes. After you've positioned the desired number of vertices with the default tool settings, do not press Enter. Instead, press Ctrl, and then place vertices inside the surface area. With the third vertex, a hole is created inside the surface, as shown in the upper right of Figure 6.7. If you want to create another hole, Ctrl+click to start again. When you're finished placing the holes, press Enter to complete the action. Because you cannot apply the Split Polygon tool on a face with holes, if you want to further subdivide the region, you should apply Polygons ➜ Triangulate first, as shown at the bottom left, and then clean it up by deleting edges and/or vertices.

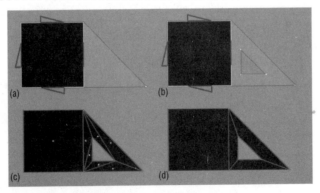

Figure 6.7 *Creating faces with holes*

Converting NURBS to Polygons

Maya has an efficient NURBS-to-polygon conversion capability. The default is set to triangles and the tessellation method, with a standard fit, but you will often change the settings to suit your needs.

Select Polygons → NURBS to Polygons ❑ to open the option window. Quadrangles usually convert more cleanly than the triangles, and they make editing easier. The Count option lets you control the total number of faces the converted surface will have. The Control Points option creates vertices that match the position of the NURBS CVs; you always end up with quadrangles with this option. The General option lets you control how isoparms are turned into faces. As we will see later, the Control Points and General options often offer the best conversion method. Figure 6.8 illustrates various conversion options. After the conversion, you can also edit the conversion settings in the Attribute Editor or the Channel box.

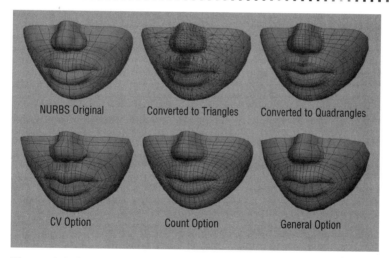

Figure 6.8 *A NURBS original converted to polygons using different settings*

Editing Polygons

This section focuses on the tools for working with polygons. You have many options, ranging from moving polygon components to manually softening or hardening a polygon's edges. Maya 3 also offers numerous ways to display polygons and selecting various components. As we do throughout the book, we will focus on the functions and the option settings that you are likely to use most often. Consult the Maya documentation if you need a complete list of the functions and their option settings.

Displaying Polygons

Maya provides many different ways of modifying the display of polygons:

- From Display → Polygon Components, which is an easily accessible submenu

- From Display → Custom Polygon Display ❑, which provides more details and the ability to control the display of more than one polygon

- From Window → Settings/Preferences → Preferences (in the Display Polygons section), which also lets you control multiple polygons, similar to the Custom Polygon Display dialog box

- From the Attribute Editor's Shape tab (in the Mesh Component Display section), which focuses on the selected polygon

The following sections describe the display options for the polygon surfaces that are available through these dialog boxes.

Displaying Vertices

You can set vertices so that they are visible even when the polygon is not selected. Vertex normals can also be made visible. The Backface Culling option for vertices is turned on by default in the Custom Polygon Display Options dialog box (shown in Figure 6.9), but it has no effect if the Backface Culling option is set to Off.

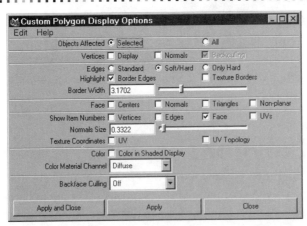

Figure 6.9 *The Custom Polygon Display Options dialog box*

There are three degrees of backface culling, and they can be very useful when you need to select only the front side of a surface (the Attribute Editor and Custom Polygon Display Options dialog box have slightly different wording for these options):

- Wire (or Keep Wire) mode blocks you from picking vertices and faces of the back surface, while still enabling you to select edges. Wire mode displays the back faces.

- Hard (Keep Hard Edges) mode works like Wire mode, except that it doesn't display the back faces.

- Full (or On) mode does not display the back side at all, and you can't select anything at the back of the shape.

Figure 6.10 illustrates these three modes.

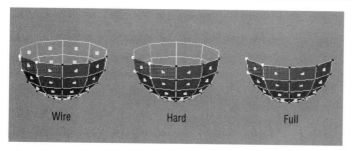

Figure 6.10 *The three modes of backface culling*

As mentioned in Chapter 4, "Modeling Basics," the new Isolate Select tool is also a great aid in displaying only the parts of the polygon surface that you are working on.

Displaying Edges and Borders

The settings in the next area of the Custom Polygon Display Options window control how edges and borders are displayed. Edges can be displayed in three ways:

- The Standard setting displays all the edges.

- The Soft/Hard setting displays the soft edges as dotted lines.

- The Only Hard setting displays only hard edges.

Soft edges do not render as sharp edges, whereas hard edges do. For more discussion on these edges, see the "Reverse and Soften/Harden" section later in this chapter.

The Border Edges setting is off by default. When you turn on this setting, you can see the border edges in thicker lines. The default width for border edges is 2, but you can increase the thickness. The dialog box also offers a Texture Borders option, which represents the starting point and endpoint for the texture UV placement. Figure 6.11 illustrates the effect of different display options for edges and borders.

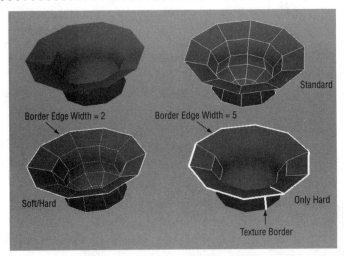

Figure 6.11 *Different edge settings and border widths*

Displaying Faces

In the Custom Polygon Display Options window, the choices for displaying faces are Centers, Normals, Triangles, and Warp. The Triangles option is available if the faces are not triangular, and it displays the faces in triangles made up of dotted lines. (Note that the Triangles option for face display is different from the Triangulate function, which actually adds the edges to the faces. With the Triangles option, the surface itself does not change; it only displays triangles.) When Warp is turned on, it detects any face that is warped, or nonplanar. Figure 6.12 illustrates the effect of different settings for displaying faces.

You can also choose to display face normals, as well as vertex normals, and set different length lines to represent them.

Displaying Numbers

We've seen that the order in which faces, edges, and other elements are created can affect the way Maya works with them. Using the Custom Polygon Display Options

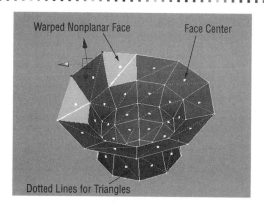

Figure 6.12 *The effect of different display settings for faces*

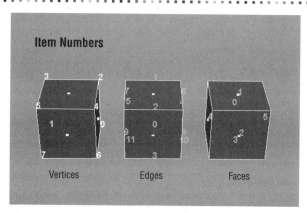

Figure 6.13 *The effect of different number displays*

dialog box, you can display numbers representing the order of creation for vertices, edges, faces, and UVs of polygon surfaces. Figure 6.13 shows examples of item numbering for vertices, edges, and faces.

Coloring Vertices

You can color vertices in Shaded mode by checking the Color In Shaded Display option in the Custom Polygon Display Options dialog box. To apply color to vertices, select them and choose Edit Polygons ➜ Colors ➜ Apply Color ❑. In the option window, you can create the color you want for the vertices, and then click the Apply Color button to see the result shown in Figure 6.14.

Figure 6.14 *Colored vertices*

Displaying the Polygon Count

Another display function that is useful in working with polygons is Display ➜ Heads Up Display ➜ Poly Count. In many game productions, keeping a model's polygon count below a certain number is crucial in maintaining real-time interactivity of the game.

As illustrated in Figure 6.15, Poly Count shows the following statistics:

- The numbers in green on the left show the total polygon count in vertices, edges, faces, and UVs for all the visible polygon surfaces inside the window.

- The numbers in white in the middle of the list show the numbers for visible selected polygonal objects.

- The numbers in white on the right side of the list show the total polygon count for the selected components.

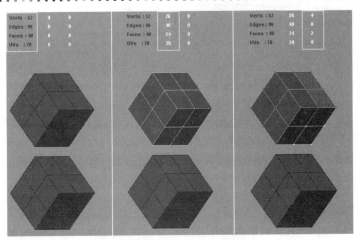

Figure 6.15 *Displaying Poly Count statistics*

Selecting Polygons

Before you can edit and manipulate your polygons, you need to select them. As usual, Maya offers several ways to accomplish this task. You will most often select components using the selection mask, by RM choosing over the surface you're working on. Alternatively, you can use hotkeys and the tools on the Polygons ➜ Selection menu.

Selecting with Hotkeys

You can use the following hotkeys for selecting components of polygons:

F8 Toggles between object and component selection

F9 Selects vertices

F10 Selects edges

F11 Selects faces

F12 Selects UVs

Ctrl+F9 Selects vertices and faces

To select more than one component, select a component, pick-mask to another selection mode, and then Shift+select the other component. Figure 6.16 shows the marking menu list for the various polygon components.

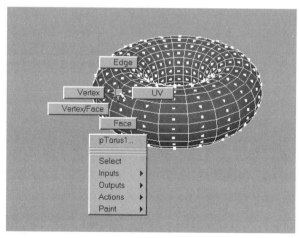

Figure 6.16 The marking menu for poly components

Using the Selection Tools

Maya also provides some tools to aid you in selecting components, as you can see in Figure 6.17. Select Edit Polygons ➜ Selection to see a submenu with selection tools. The Grow Selection Region function increases any selected component elements by one unit. Shrink Selection Region does the opposite. Select Selection Boundary leaves only the boundary of the selected component elements active and deselects the rest.

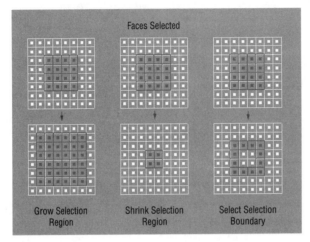

Figure 6.17 *The effect of the Grow, Shrink Region, and Select Boundary tools*

You can also convert any selected component element to another component type by using the Convert functions on the Selection submenu. As you can see in Figure 6.18, conversion is not cyclical—converting the selected vertices to UVs will give a larger region of UVs than the one you started with.

Constraining Selections

At the bottom of the Selection submenu is an advanced tool called Selection Constraints. Here are some examples of what you can do with this tool:

- You can constrain the selection to specific locations, such as border components or inside components.

- You can have only hard edges selected or only soft edges selected.

- You can select only triangular faces, only quads, or only faces with more than four sides.

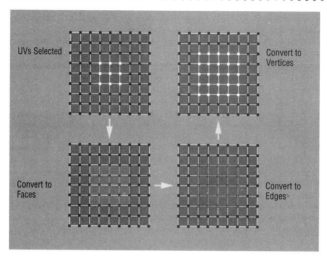

Figure 6.18 *Convert Selection functions*

- You can select components with a set amount of randomness.

- You can expand or shrink a selected region, or select the selection's boundary.

Figure 6.19 shows some examples of polygon selection constraints. You may notice that the *n*-sided faces look like they are quads or triangles. It's easy to confuse the two, but when you count the vertices or the edges, the selected *n*-sided faces have more than

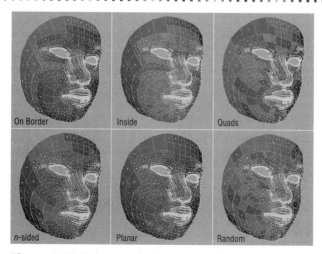

Figure 6.19 *Polygon selection constraints*

four. All the *n*-sided faces have smaller adjacent faces that divide their sides into two edges and three vertices. Another way to tell if a face is *n*-sided is to turn on the Triangles option in the Custom Polygon Display Options dialog box.

The contents of the Selection Constraint dialog box depend on the types of components being constrained. A good practice is to pick-mask the component you wish to select, and then open the dialog box. Another is to make sure to click the Constrain Nothing button before you close this dialog box.

Moving Polygon Components

You can move, rotate, and scale polygon components using the manipulator handles. Additionally, you can use the Move Component function under the Edit Polygons menu to translate, rotate, and scale the components.

The Move Component function has a local mode and global mode. You can switch between these modes by clicking the toggle handle, as shown in Figure 6.20. In local mode, the Z axis is always pointing in the direction of the surface normal.

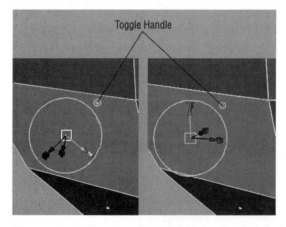

Figure 6.20 *The move manipulator in local and global modes*

Extruding and Duplicating Faces

When working with faces, you can use the Duplicate Face and Extrude functions on the Edit Polygons menu. With both of these functions, you can either keep the resulting faces together or have them remain separate by toggling Polygons ➜ Tool Options ➜ Keep Faces Together. Figure 6.21 illustrates all four options. Note that the duplicated faces are discontinuous from the original faces, and they become separate objects from the original polygon object. You can turn off the Separate Duplicated Faces setting in the option window, which will keep them as components of the original polygon object.

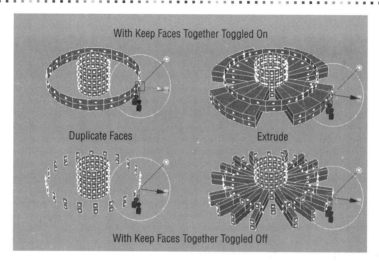

Figure 6.21 *Extruding and duplicating with Keep Faces Together toggled on and off*

A new addition to Maya 3 is the Extrude Edge command, in the Edit Polygons menu, which works the same way as Extrude Face, except that it works on edges. This command is especially useful for extending border edges, to give thickness to polygon shells. In Figure 6.22, the edge of the surface has been extruded twice and then converted to a subdivision surface.

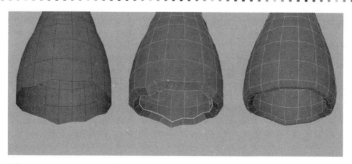

Figure 6.22 *Extruding an edge to give thickness to a polygon shell*

Making and Filling Holes

You can use faces to create holes in other faces. The examples in Figure 6.23 were created by duplicating the face and then selecting Edit Polygons ➜ Make Hole Tool. With its default settings, the Make Hole tool creates an extrusion with the second face becoming a hole for the first. Alternatively, you can produce holed surfaces by selecting Merge settings in the option window. If you do not want to disturb the position of the original surface, set Merge to First.

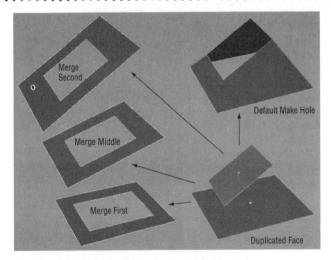

Figure 6.23 *Different ways of making a hole*

To get rid of unwanted holes in surfaces, select edges around the hole, and then use Edit Polygons ➜ Fill Hole. Figure 6.24 shows the result.

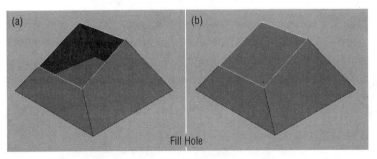

Figure 6.24 *Filling the default hole created in Figure 6.23*

Performing Boolean Operations

You can perform simple Boolean operations—such as union, difference, and intersection, as illustrated in Figure 6.25—on polygons at the object level. These simple functions can aid you greatly in working with polygons. You'll find them on the Polygons ➜ Booleans submenu.

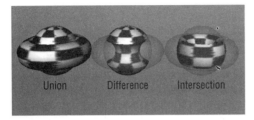

Figure 6.25 *The result of three different Boolean operations*

 At times, two polygonal objects may intersect in some way that makes it impossible for Maya to carry out the necessary Boolean calculations. You may get an error message, or the two surfaces may disappear. In such a case, move one of the objects slightly and try again. At other times, the objects may need to be cleaned up first, such as deleting faces with zero area.

After a Boolean operation, the vertices will often end up not matching well, requiring cleanup. For example, in the Difference operation, the first selected object remains, minus the intersecting part. In the operation shown in Figure 6.26, the torus ends up with a messy surface area at the intersection point, which will need to be cleaned up.

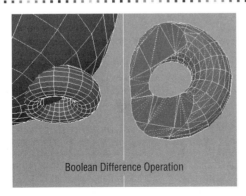

Figure 6.26 *After a Boolean difference operation, this torus requires some cleanup.*

Combining, Extracting, and Separating Polygons

The Combine function on the Polygons menu is similar to the Boolean union operation, but there are differences. The Combine function takes any collection of polygonal surfaces and turns them into one object, as the Boolean union does, but as you can see in Figure 6.27, it does not trim away the unnecessary parts. You also can see that the union operation actually attaches the edges and vertices of the objects being joined together, whereas the Combine operation leaves them unshared, or extracted.

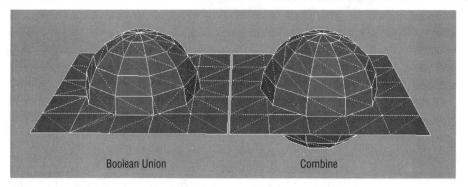

Figure 6.27 *The Boolean Union and the Combine operations*

Combining polygon objects is simple, but dividing one polygon object into separate objects is a bit more involved. Before any faces of a polygon object can become separate objects, they must be extracted to become different shells.

 An object that was created through the Combine operation already has extracted pieces. Thus, you can simply apply the Edit Polygons ➜ Separate operation to undo the Combine action; you don't need to use Extract.

The Extract function, also on the Edit Polygons menu, does exactly what it says: It extracts the selected faces from their neighbors so that the edges and vertices of the extracted faces are no longer shared. Figure 6.28 shows the result. The default setting separates any extracted faces automatically, so they become separate objects. If you want to extract faces but keep them as part of the original object, toggle off the Separate Extracted Faces setting in the Extract command's option window.

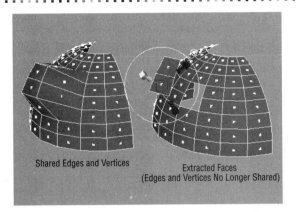

Figure 6.28 between the graphics labels:
Shared Edges and Vertices

Extracted Faces
(Edges and Vertices No Longer Shared)

Figure 6.28 *Extracting selected faces*

In Maya 3, the new Edit Polygons ➜ Split Vertex option performs a function similar to the Extract command. It applies to vertices, and makes each vertex split into
unshared vertices, also splitting adjoining edges into unshared edges, or border edges.
It has as its opposite the Merge Vertices command, discussed in the next section.

Merging Vertices and Edges

Merging is the opposite of extracting. Whereas the Extract function separates vertices
and edges so that they are no longer shared, the Merge function makes them shared by
faces.

Edit Polygons ➜ Merge Vertices function merges vertices so that instead of there
being several overlapping vertices at one point, only one vertex is shared by the edges,
and the edges become shared edges. Often, you will not see any difference until you try
moving the edges or faces, as shown in Figure 6.29.

The Edit Polygons ➜ Merge Edge Tool merges border edges. When you select the
tool, the border edges become thicker. Click on the first edge, and then the second edge.
Both edges turn orange. When you click again, the two edges merge. There are three
Merge mode options:

- Middle, the default mode, makes the first and the second edge merge at the
  halfway point.

- First makes the second edge snap to the first edge.

- Second makes the first edge snap to the second edge.

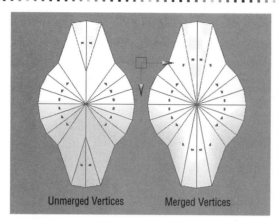

Figure 6.29 *Merging vertices*

After the merge, you are still in the merge mode, and the tool asks for another first edge to be picked. You can keep merging this way, as in the two faces on the left side of Figure 6.30, or if the edges to be merged are obvious, you can use the Merge Multiple Edges command. Select the edges near the area where the merging will occur, as in the top-right image, and then apply Edit Polygons ➜ Merge Multiple Edges to get all the border edges to merge. As you can see in the face on the bottom right, this command sometimes leaves a few edges unmerged. You can merge those with the regular Merge Edge tool.

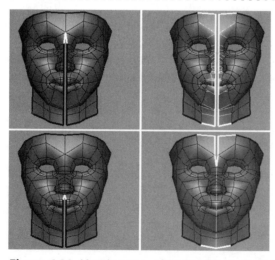

Figure 6.30 *Merging two adjacent objects: (left) by merging individual pairs of edges and (right) by using Merge Multiple Edges*

If merging edges produces weird connections, undo the operation and check the normals of the faces whose edges are being merged. If the normals are not consistent, you need to reverse some of them (see "Reverse and Soften/Harden" below).

Deleting and Collapsing Polygon Components

Although deleting polygon components is straightforward, there are a few things to keep in mind:

- You can delete only corner vertices, or vertices that are joined by only two edges (called *winged* vertices).

- You cannot delete border edges.

- You can always delete faces.

When you delete edges, be sure to delete the winged vertices that often get created in the process. You will see them when you pick-mask Vertex over the surface.

The Edit Polygons ➜ Collapse function does not work like Delete. Instead, it allows you to collapse faces and edges so that the remaining vertices are shared, as illustrated in Figure 6.31.

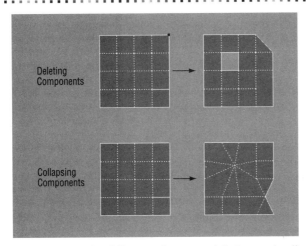

Figure 6.31 *The difference between deleting and collapsing components*

Splitting Polygons

The Edit Polygons ➜ Split Polygon Tool is probably one of the tools you'll use most frequently as you work with polygons. With this tool, you can divide faces into smaller pieces. (Do not confuse the Split Polygon tool with the Append To Polygon tool on the Polygons menu. The latter creates faces at the border edges of a surface, whereas the Split Polygon tool divides existing faces.)

Let's go through an extended example of modeling with a simple cube. Create a cube, and select Edit Polygons ➜ Split Polygon Tool. The mouse cursor changes into an arrow. Click on one of the top edges, and a bright green dot appears, representing a vertex. Click on the other edges as in Figure 6.32, and make the last click on the first green dot to complete a triangle of edges. Note that you can move the last dot along the top edge. Press Enter to complete the action. Select the three corner edges in front and delete them, and you will end up with the corner of the cube chopped off.

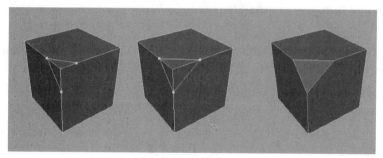

Figure 6.32 *A cube with a split polygon*

Now what if you wanted to repeat the process on another corner of the cube, but this time make the split polygon put vertices exactly at one-third the length of each edge? Maya doesn't provide us with such an option (yet) with the Split Polygon tool, but it can subdivide the edges to help us.

Edit Polygons ➜ Subdivide automatically and evenly divides an edge or a face into equal parts. The default setting is Subdivision 1, which divides an edge into two edges or divides a face into four quads or triangles. If you want to refine a rough polygon shape, subdividing provides you with a quick way of gaining more control points. Note that Subdivide should not be confused with subdivision surfaces, discussed later in this chapter.

To try the Subdivide option, select the three edges on a different corner of the cube, select Edit Polygons ➜ Subdivide, choose Subdivision Levels 2, and click Subdivide. Pick-mask Vertex, and you should see two extra vertices placed evenly apart on each of the three edges, as in the second image in Figure 6.33. Now you can proceed with Split Polygon, and then by deleting the corner edges, cut another corner of the cube.

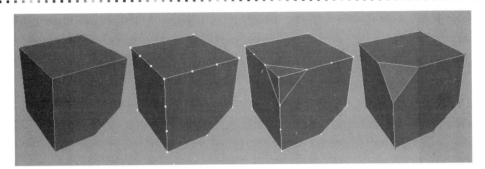

Figure 6.33 *Using Subdivide to facet a cube*

When you want to place a vertex at the end of an edge, don't click the endpoints of that edge. You may select the wrong edge that way. Instead, click the middle of the edge you want and drag to the endpoint.

When we look at the cube now, we see that it has triangles, quadrangles, and *n*-sided faces. We can delete the winged vertices easily, and to make the cube "clean," we can split the triangles and *n*-sided faces further into quadrangles. First subdivide the triangle faces, as seen on the left in Figure 6.34, and then split polygons to turn all the faces of the cube into quadrangles, as shown on the right.

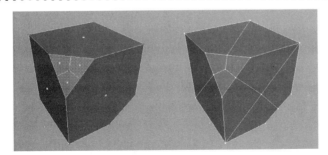

Figure 6.34 *Further splitting*

To make sure different splitting polygon edges intersect each other correctly in the middle of a face, set to 2 the Subdivision setting in the Split Polygon tool option window for the first split polygon going across the face. This creates an extra vertex right in the middle.

Smoothing Polygons, Averaging Vertices, and Beveling Edges

Smoothing is a simple but indispensable function that you will use over and over again with polygons. The Smooth tool on the Polygons menu subdivides a surface, or selected faces of a surface, according to the division setting in the option window (the default setting is 1) to create as smooth a surface as its division setting will allow. Unlike the Subdivide command, it actually moves the vertices to make the faces appear smoother (see Figure 6.35). It always produces quads, and you should generally leave the subdivision setting at the default. If you are going to apply Smooth more than once, you will usually want to tweak the surface before applying it again. We will see Smooth in action in the hand tutorial later.

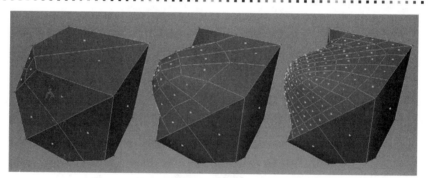

Figure 6.35 *Using the Smooth tool*

Polygons ➜ Average Vertices smoothes a surface without subdividing the faces into smaller pieces. It keeps the same surface topology, and essentially produces the same result as the Sculpt Polygons tool's Smooth option. (See Chapter 7 for more about this and other Artisan tools.) It can be used with the Transfer command to produce clean UVs on complex models (see the polygon texturing section in Chapter 19). In Figure 6.36, the middle face has Average Vertices applied once, and the one on the right has it applied five times.

Edit Polygons ➜ Bevel enables you to smooth sharp corners and edges very easily. In Figure 6.37, a simple cube's corner edges were selected, and then Bevel was applied. The middle cube's bevel has its Segment option set to 4. This produces an *n*-sided face, which you can clean up into quadrangles, as in the third cube.

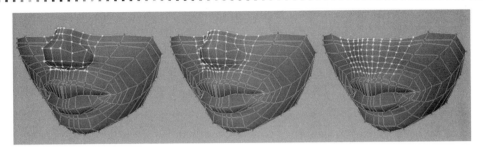

Figure 6.36 *Using the Average Vertices option*

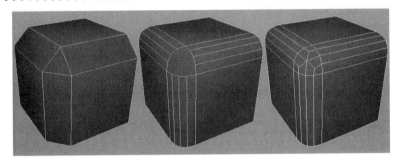

Figure 6.37 *Beveling*

Mirroring Geometry

One more polygon modeling tool needs to be introduced: Polygons ➜ Mirror Geometry. It's like copying the left half of the face in Figure 6.38, scaling it –1, putting it on the other side, and then merging all the border edges, all in one step. But it's better than that, because mirroring also takes care of the normal flipping, keeping the copied side's

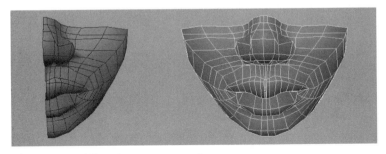

Figure 6.38 *Mirroring to create a face*

normals the same as the original side. Mirroring makes it easy for you to concentrate on modeling just one side of a human face, and then to see quickly how it'll look as a whole face. (Looking carefully at the face on the right, you'll see a slight gap in the upper lip. Mirroring doesn't always do a perfect job.)

Reverse and Soften/Harden

Finally, normals play a significant role in editing polygons in Maya. A surface needs to have all its normals on the same side. When you're working with various polygonal objects, separating and attaching them, you may find that normals on some of the faces have become inconsistent. This may cause problems such as the border edges not merging properly or textures being mapped incorrectly. The Reverse function, found on the Edit Polygons → Normals submenu, reverses the front and back sides of the selected faces, reversing their normal direction as well. The Reverse and Propagate option not only reverses the normals of a selected face, it also "propagates" to other faces, reversing their normals as if they are facing the same side of the surface as the first selected face. It was formerly a separate action but in Maya 3 became an option inside the Reverse command.

Soften/Harden, another function found on the Normals submenu, can manually determine whether a polygon's edge is to be hard (edgy and sharp) or soft (smooth and rounded). Let's try out this tool:

1. Create a polygon sphere and set its subdivisions to 10.

2. Select Display → Custom Polygon Display ❑. In its dialog box, turn on both Vertex Normal and Face Normal.

3. Zoom in to look closely at the vertices of the sphere in Shaded mode. You should see normals, as shown below.

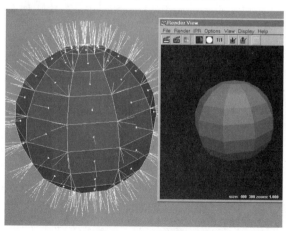

4. It may appear messy, but if you look carefully, you can see that each vertex has four normals coming out of it, with each normal parallel to its corresponding face normal. Pick-mask Edge and select the upper half of the sphere.

5. With the upper sphere's edges still selected, select Edit Polygons ➔ Normals ➔ Soften/Harden ❏.

6. Click the All Soft (180) button, then the Soft/Hard button. Each vertex on the upper half of the sphere now has only one normal coming out, which is not parallel to any of its face normals, as shown below. The other vertex normals are not shown because the edges are now soft edges. Notice that the upper half of the sphere is rendered smoothly.

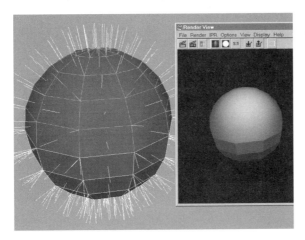

7. Open the Attribute Editor for the sphere and go to the tab called polySoftEdge1.

8. Open the Poly Soft Edge history. You'll see the Angle slider set at 180. Try moving the Angle slider down. From around 35 degrees and lower, you should see the deleted vertex normals popping back in, and the edges becoming hard edges again.

Subdivision Surface Modeling

The Catmul-Clark's B-spline subdivision surface scheme was first introduced as a geometric modeling technique over twenty years ago, but only recently has the technology for using subdivision surfaces been developed enough for use in commercial computer animation software such as Maya Unlimited.

Major improvements in Maya 3 Unlimited have made it possible to use subdivision surfaces not only for modeling, but also texturing, animation, and rendering, making it a real alternative to using NURBS or polygon techniques. Subdivision surfaces are useful for the following reasons:

- They can exist on arbitrary topology, like polygon surfaces, bypassing the difficulty of creating a form in four-sided patches.

- They are smooth and continuous, like NURBS surfaces. They do not have the problem of creating a faceted look, as polygons do.

- They allow a hierarchy of up to 13 levels of detail, which allows isolated areas of highly detailed modeling, and binding at the base levels.

Creating Subdivision Surfaces

There are no stock subdivision surfaces in Maya. They are created from polygon or NURBS surfaces. When you convert NURBS surfaces to subdivision surfaces, the conversion doesn't recognize trimmed areas, and it will treat chord-length surfaces as if they were uniform surfaces. Also note that converting NURBS surfaces directly to subdivision surfaces produces the same result as first converting the NURBS surface to polygons using the NURBS To Polygon command with the Control Points tessellation method, and then converting to subdivision surfaces, as in Figure 6.39.

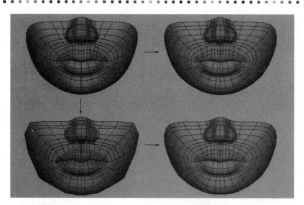

Figure 6.39 *Two ways of creating subdivision surfaces*

Conversion from polygon to subdivision surface requires that the polygon surface meet the following conditions:

- The surface cannot have nonmanifold topology, such as three or more faces sharing an edge, or faces sharing a vertex but no edge.

- There can't be any winged vertices.

- No adjacent faces can have opposite normals.

In addition to these requirements, keep in mind some guidelines that will help you produce good and efficient subdivision surfaces:

The polygon or NURBS surface should be light.   Using subdivision surfaces makes the most sense when the surface being converted is simple. The subdivision surface smoothness contrasts with the polygon edges. If the polygon is heavy, it may appear smooth already, so there is less reason for using subdivision surfaces. Because subdivision surfaces are heavier to move and render than a smoothed polygon with the same topology, if the polygon looks smooth enough, it should be the preferred choice. In Figure 6.40, the smoothed cube (top center) still looks faceted, as opposed to the subdivision surface (top right), but the monster, when smoothed (bottom center), looks very smooth with no noticeable difference in the subdivision surface (bottom right). You may want to use the smoothed polygon in such a case, and not the subdivision surface.

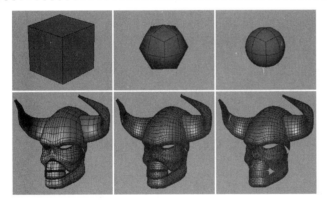

Figure 6.40 *Converting a simple polygonal object to subdivision surfaces is much more efficient than converting a complex object that already appears smooth.*

The polygon should be quadrangles.   With NURBS conversion, the resulting subdivision surfaces are clean, because NURBS surfaces are by definition four-sided. Converting nonquadrangular faces of polygons, however, creates what are called *extraordinary points*–points connected by less than or more than four edges, as seen in the pictures in Figure 6.41. Note that the triangle and the five-sided faces on the cube produce subdivision surface points connected by either three or five points. These points make the subdivision surface unnecessarily heavy, and could make the area appear bumpy. The cube at the bottom left in Figure 6.41 is heavier than the one at the top left because it has more edges, but the resulting subdivision surface is actually lighter, because the extra edges have changed the triangle and the five-sided faces into quadrangles.

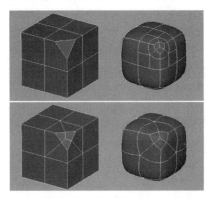

Figure 6.41 *Extraordinary points resulting from triangle and five-sided faces, and the corrected subdivision surface*

As with NURBS and polygon modeling, whether to use subdivision surfaces depends on the model you want to build.   Subdivision surfaces are ideal for creating organic models. When dealing with sharp, rigid edges, polygons would still be more efficient, because they are lighter and come with edges already. If you want to create perfectly circular objects, like mechanical parts, again, you may want to use NURBS modeling. The sphere on the left in Figure 6.42 is a subdivision surface created from a cube, and a circle is surrounding it. The right sphere is a default NURBS sphere, also surrounded by a circle. If you look carefully, you will notice that the subdivision surface sphere is not perfectly circular.

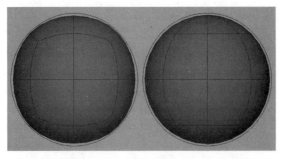

Figure 6.42 *Unlike the NURBS sphere on the right, the subdivision surface sphere on the left is not perfectly circular.*

Working with Subdivision Surfaces

There are many ways to refine and edit subdivision surfaces. You can work in hierarchy mode or polygon proxy mode, transforming components of subdivision surfaces such as points, edges, and faces the same way you would with polygons. You can add detail in isolated areas or collapse levels of detail, create creases, mirror or attach surfaces, or convert them back to polygons.

Hierarchy Mode

This is the default mode for subdivision surfaces. To try it, create a simple sphere out of a polygon cube, and then RM click it to show the pick-mask menu. As with polygons, the components displayed will depend on what you pick, as illustrated in Figure 6.43. You can travel the different levels of hierarchy with the Finer and the Coarser commands. A newly created subdivision surface has only two levels: level 0, called the base mesh, and level 1.

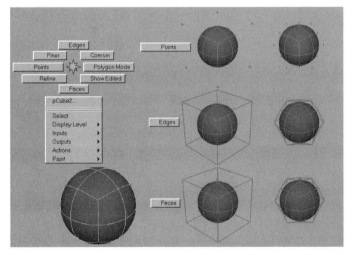

Figure 6.43 *The pick-mask menu for a subdivision surface sphere*

Pick-mask Point to display points, and then pick-mask Finer to travel to the level 1 display of points. Select a point as shown in Figure 6.44 step (a), and pick-mask Refine. That point becomes an area of nine points (b). Repeat the process again to show level 3 points. Select a point at the end, as in (d), and select Subdiv Surfaces ➜ Expand Selected Components. Note that level 3 points expand to cover more areas (e). Pick another level 3 point at the end and move it out, as in (f), and the same number expansion happens again.

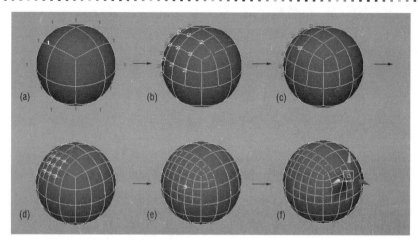

Figure 6.44 *Working with hierarchy levels*

Once the point has been pulled out, the sphere retains this as level 3 edited point information. If you go into the polygon proxy mode and come back to hierarchy mode, you can pick-mask Point again, and go back to level 3 to where you left off. Note that you would only see level 3 points in the area affected by the edited point. You can toggle Show Edited/Show All to see more precisely which are the edited points. If no points were edited, when you go into polygon proxy mode and come back, the sphere will show only levels 0 and 1 again because no change in any of the levels was recorded.

On rare occasions, switching to polygon proxy mode will delete the edited point information of levels 1 and higher. This should not happen; but if it does, undo, save the file, exit Maya, and start it up again. The edited points should now stay edited when you switch.

You can edit points up to 13 levels of hierarchy, but you would usually not want to go anywhere above level 2 or 3, as the hierarchical connection can significantly slow down the system. As we will see later in our tutorials, there is also an argument to be made for not tweaking anything—even in level 1.

One thing you cannot do in hierarchy mode is delete any points, edges, or faces, or change the underlying topology of the surface. In level 1 or higher, if you select some edited points, edges, or faces and "delete" them, the edit information disappears, and they move back to their original unedited positions. If you move a point in the base level, however, that tweak is permanent and will only disappear with an undo. If you want to delete points or change the underlying structure of a subdivision surface, you need to switch to the polygon proxy mode.

If you switch to polygon proxy mode when you are in a high level of hierarchy and no points have been edited, when you come back to hierarchy mode, you may not be able to display any points, edges, or faces. In such a case, select the surface, go to the Shapes section of the Channel box, and switch the Display Level to 0 or 1. This should make things display properly again.

Polygon Proxy Mode

Polygon proxy mode allows you to edit a subdivision surface as if it were a polygon. To switch into polygon proxy mode, RM over a subdivision surface and pick-mask Polygon Mode. This creates a polygon that matches the base-level control mesh of the subdivision surface, with its edges displayed surrounding the surface. The polygon is procedurally connected to the subdivision surface, so that whatever changes you make to the polygon also occur on the subdivision surface. This enables you to edit the surface just as if it were a polygon object by editing the polygon *proxy*: deleting points, edges, faces, appending or splitting polygons. You can perform almost any polygon operation on the subdivision surface when you are in this mode.

You can switch back and forth between polygon mode and hierarchy mode at any time by toggling the pick-mask Hierarchy Mode and Polygon Mode. Note that every time you switch from proxy mode back into the hierarchy mode, you delete all the history that accumulates with polygon operations. Frequent switching back to hierarchy mode is actually recommended, as it "bakes" the polygon operations and makes the changes a permanent part of the subdivision surface.

For example, in the simple subdivision surface you have from a cube on the left in Figure 6.45, you cannot create a hole on one side in hierarchy mode. Switch to polygon mode, extrude twice, and then delete the extruded face. The result is as you see in the third image. In order to make this topological change more stable and permanent, switch back to hierarchy mode, deleting the history of the polygon operations in so doing.

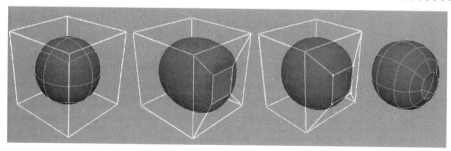

Figure 6.45 *Working in hierarchy and polygon modes*

Because the proxy mode can change the topology of the subdivision surface under it, if there are edited points under or near a change, they may disappear or produce unpredictable changes. Try to make all the changes having to do with the topology of the surface before you start editing in the higher levels of the hierarchy mode.

If you are not changing the topology of the subdivision surface but only transforming the base points, edges, or faces, do it in the hierarchy mode rather than polygon mode, as hierarchy mode is the more direct and efficient method.

Displaying Subdivision Surfaces

The Display menu has Subdiv Surface Components and Subdiv Surface Smoothness submenus for working with subdivision surfaces. The Components submenu lets you display subdivision points, edges, faces, and normals. When you are pulling points of a subdivision surface, you will find it helps a great deal if you can see the edges displayed at the same time.

The smoothness of the subdivision surface display can be changed in the same way as with NURBS surfaces: 1 for Rough, 2 for Medium, and 3 for Fine display, as in Figure 6.46. When Smoothness is set to Fine, subdivision surfaces display extra faces, which are there for display purposes only. The Smoothness submenu also contains the Hull setting, which displays subdivision surfaces like polygons. This can increase the interactivity quite a bit when working with heavy subdivision surface models.

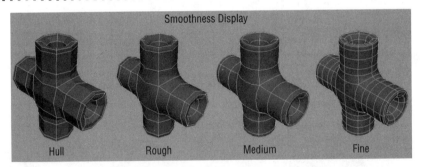

Figure 6.46 *Display smoothness settings*

You can also use the window panel's Show ➔ Isolate Select ➔ View Selected with subdivision surface faces. When you are in the Polygon proxy mode and you use View Selected, only the selected polygon faces will stay visible and the subdivision surface will not be displayed.

Extract Vertices and Tessellate

Rather than switching to polygon mode, you may want to convert subdivision surfaces to polygons. Maya's Extract Vertices and Tessellate commands perform that function. Using Tessellate with the default setting converts each face of the subdivision surface to a polygon face, as in the left picture in Figure 6.47. Extract Vertices, on the other hand, converts the surface's mesh points to the polygon vertices. The default setting converts the base level points to vertices, as in the right picture. The middle picture shows Extract Vertices with the level 1 option setting. Notice that although the resulting shape is similar to that of the tessellated polygon, the shape is a bit bigger.

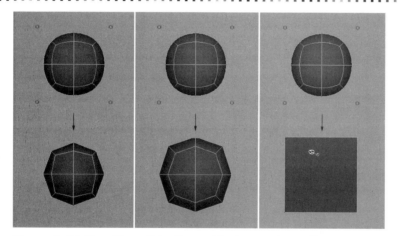

Figure 6.47 *The effect of the Extract Vertices and Tessellate commands*

The Extract Vertices command with the default level 0 conversion setting is especially useful, as it converts a subdivision surface to polygons the same way as switching it to polygon proxy mode. This means that whatever editing you want to do in the proxy mode, you can also do with the converted polygon, and then reconvert it back to the same subdivision surface again. The advantage of doing this is that the polygon surface is much lighter than the proxy mode. This makes it more efficient to work with, particularly for doing texture work, as we will see in the later chapters. The limitation of such a process is that Extract Vertices destroys higher-level edit information. Any detail work done in level 1 and higher will be lost in the conversion.

 When a polygon has been extracted from a subdivision surface, it carries an invisible polySurfaceShape node, which can cause problems with commands such as Polygons ➜ Mirror Geometry. If you need to perform such a command, first select the polygon, then go to the Hypergraph and turn on Invisible Nodes display (or go into Up and Down Stream Connections display), and then delete the invisible node.

Creasing Edges and Vertices

In hierarchy mode, you can create creases with edges or vertices, or you can uncrease the existing ones. In Figure 6.48, four edges were selected, then Partial Crease Edge/Vertex was applied twice on the third shape, and Full Crease Edge/Vertex was applied on the fourth shape. Partial creasing creates soft edges, whereas full crease creates sharp ones. To uncrease the edges, just select the same edges again and apply the Uncrease Edge/Vertex command. The crease information behaves the same way as higher-level edit points. The information is kept when the surface switches to the proxy mode, but it is deleted when the surface is converted to polygon via Tessellation or Extract Vertices.

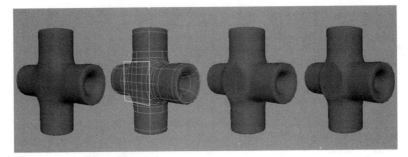

Figure 6.48 *Partial and full creasing*

Mirror and Attach

A common technique for modeling is to build only one side of a model, and then duplicate it and scale it –1 on the necessary axis, thus creating a mirror image of the model. For subdivision surfaces, you should use the Subdiv Surfaces ➜ Mirror command instead. If you use duplicate and negative scale technique, the results will disappoint you. You should be in hierarchy mode when using this command.

Once a subdivision surface has been mirrored as in Figure 6.49, you can choose Subdiv Surfaces ➜ Attach to complete the process. Again, you need to stay in hierarchy mode in order to attach. Note that the crease and edit information carries over into the mirror and attach actions.

Remember that you can always switch to polygon proxy mode and edit subdivision surfaces like polygons. If attaching does not completely attach all the edges, you can use Edit Polygons ➜ Merge Edge in the proxy mode to complete the attachment.

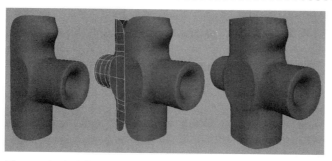

Figure 6.49 *Mirroring and attaching*

Hands-On Maya: Building a Hand

It's time to practice using the tools and actions we've covered in this chapter by building a polygon hand. Hands are usually built as polygons because it's difficult to build a NURBS hand that is not heavy and at the same time deforms well.

Building the Rough Hand

We begin by building the rough hand, starting with a poly cube.

1. Start a new scene. Create a poly cube. Select a face on the X axis and extrude it four times. Scale it until you see something like the image shown below. Delete the faces at the back side.

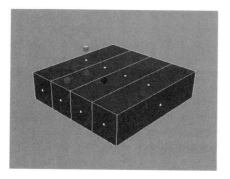

2. Select Polygons ➜ Tool Options and turn off Keep Faces Together. Select the four front faces and extrude them three times, as shown below. These

will be the fingers. As you are extruding, scale the faces down a bit each time to taper them. At every point, you should be tweaking the vertices to try to form a rough hand shape. For example, try to roughly round the wrist area at the back.

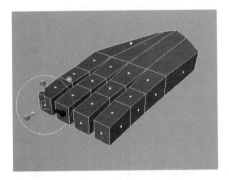

 Turn on the Backface Culling option's Keep Wire setting. This will help you to avoid accidentally selecting vertices or faces at the back side of the hand.

3. Push back the pinky finger, pulling it away from the ring finger to the side, and pull the middle finger out a bit. You can select faces to do this; however, in this situation, moving vertices seems to work best. Push up the two vertices where the knuckles should be.

Creating the Thumb

Building the thumb is one of the trickiest things you'll do in this tutorial. We'll use the Split Polygon tool to create the shape.

1. On the left side of the hand, draw two edges using Edit Polygons ➜ Split Polygon Tool. Next, at the bottom (the palm of the hand), draw four more edges. Pull out the vertex at the side and the one at the bottom beside it, and then pull them down. Select the face that sticks out with the vertices, and extrude it twice, turning and scaling it as you do. (See the illustration below for guidance.) This is going to be the thumb. Save the file as **hand_one**.

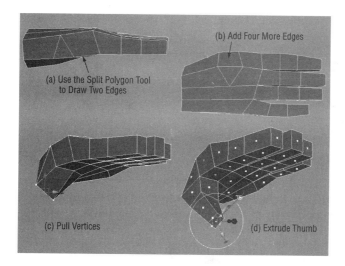

(a) Use the Split Polygon Tool to Draw Two Edges

(b) Add Four More Edges

(c) Pull Vertices

(d) Extrude Thumb

2. Add two lines of edges going around the hand using the Split Polygon tool. Use the tool to place extra faces around where the thumb bends into the hand, and move the triangular face further into the palm.

3. For the wrist, select the border edges, apply Edit Polygons ➡ Fill Hole to create an *n*-sided face, select it, and then extrude the face at the back, as shown below. After you extrude it, delete the face again.

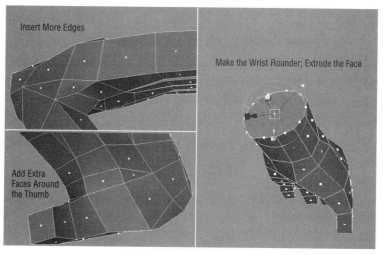

Insert More Edges

Make the Wrist Rounder; Extrude the Face

Add Extra Faces Around the Thumb

Keep the faces you are creating limited to quads and triangles. They should also run smoothly along set lines and not be placed haphazardly.

4. Scale out the hand to make it wider. Bend the thumb into the palm at an angle, as shown below.

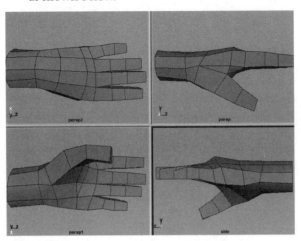

5. A lot of history has accumulated on the hand by now. Delete the history from the object and save the scene as **hand_two.**

Creating a Procedural Connection

The rough hand is now ready for smoothing. Once smoothing is applied, however, the hand becomes more difficult to shape because there are many more vertices to deal with. To make things easier, we'll use the rough hand as a lattice around the smoothed hand.

1. Make a copy of the hand and scale it up a bit. We'll call this the rough hand and call the original one the smooth hand (it isn't yet, but it soon will be).

2. Using Hypershade, assign a material to the rough hand, and make it totally transparent. In the Shaded mode, the rough hand should still display as a wire-frame, as shown below.

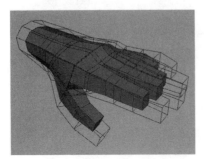

3. Select Window ➜ General Editors ➜ Connection Editor. Select the rough hand, press the down-arrow key to select its Shape node, and load it to the Outputs window by clicking the Reload Left button. Load the smooth hand's Shape node to the Inputs window the same way.

4. Scroll down in the left window until you find World Mesh and select it. Scroll down in the right window until you find In Mesh and select it. Both attributes become italicized, and World Mesh becomes World Mesh[0], as shown below. When you select the rough hand, the smooth hand turns pink to show that the hands are procedurally connected.

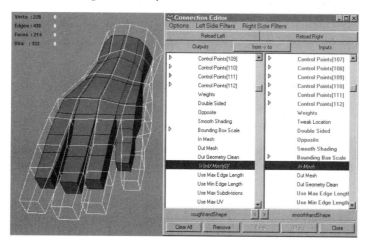

5. Select and move some vertices on the rough hand, and the smooth hand should deform along with the rough hand. Note that you can also move the smooth hand's vertices independently. Save the scene as **hand_three**.

Smoothing, Layering, and Rough Tweaking

Now we need to smooth and tweak the hand. We will need to do this in two stages, beginning with applying Smooth and fixing some problems.

1. Select the smooth hand and apply Polygons ➜ Smooth to it with the default setting. Some things immediately stand out as needing improvement, such as consistency in the width and the direction of the fingers. We need to fix these problems before we can apply Smooth again.

2. Before we start to tweak, let's put the smooth hand and the rough hand on different layers. Once the smooth hand is in a layer, select the Reference setting for the layer. The Template setting will only display the hand as a wireframe,

but the Reference setting will display the hand in Shaded mode, while still disabling it from being selected.

3. Tweak the rough hand until you are comfortable with the shape it has created in the smooth hand. You can hide the rough hand for now, and move back to the smooth hand by switching from Reference to Standard in the Layer menu.

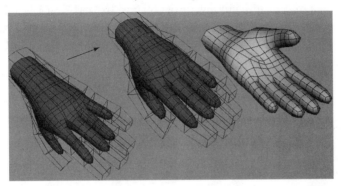

Fine Tweaking, Smoothing, and Applying Artisan

Now we will do some tweaking to prepare the hand for another smoothing. We will also use the Sculpt Polygons tool to get more surface definition and smooth out any unwanted creases.

1. Place vertices around the fingers and the thumb where the joints will bend. Think ahead to how another edge line will be placed between every line with the second Smooth. The area between the fingers needs to have a bit more space, and the knuckles should stick out more as well. (Don't worry too much about creating hard edges or creases at this point.)

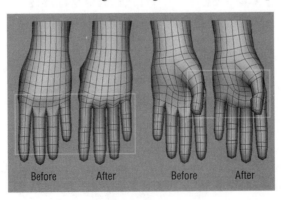

Before   After   Before   After

2. The thumb area needs special attention. Get rid of the extra edges, as shown below. Make sure that there are no winged vertices left behind. If you need to make adjustments that require moving a whole area, use the rough hand. Save the scene as **hand_four.**

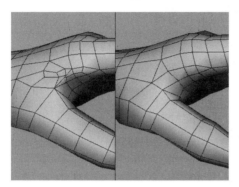

3. Apply Smooth one more time. At this point, the density of the surface calls out for the Sculpt Polygon tool. But such areas as the finger joints and fingernails should still be modified by selecting vertices. Notice the vertex placements around the finger joint areas and fingernails shown below.

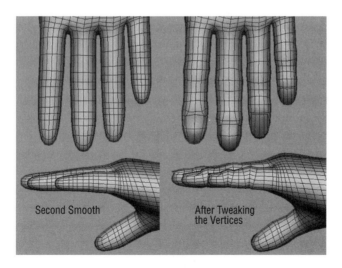

Second Smooth

After Tweaking the Vertices

4. Using Polygons ➜ Sculpt Polygon Tool (see Chapter 7, for more information), start pushing and pulling to get more definition for the hand, especially the palm, the knuckles, and the wrist area. Smooth out where the thumb joins the

hand as well. If you want to build a more mature-looking hand, you can try making the bones protrude along the back of the hand, and put more space between the fingers.

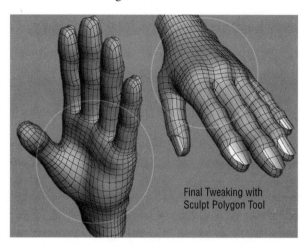

Final Tweaking with
Sculpt Polygon Tool

Change the Radius setting according to the specific area you are sculpting, and always set the Opacity low. It may be frustrating to need to click many times, but retaining control of the tool you are using is important.

The hand model is pretty much finished at this point. We will come back to this hand in Chapter 8, "Organic Modeling," when we resume our character tutorial.

Hands-On Maya: Building a Character II (Advanced)

In the previous chapter, we built a NURBS head, an eye and patches surrounding it, and an ear. In this tutorial, we will continue from where we left off, and finish building the head by converting these elements to polygons, editing them, and then refining them as subdivision surfaces.

1. Get the Character_NURBS.mb file from the Chapter 5 Working Files directory in the CD-ROM. This file incorporates all the work we did on the character in Chapter 5.

2. Duplicate the NURBS head, scale it –1 in X, and then attach it using Blend. Apply Open/Close Surfaces to make the head periodic in V. You can

edit the attached head until you're satisfied with the way it looks. If the number of isoparms going around the mouth is more than the isoparms of the head below, you should proceed with getting rid of the extra isoparms.

3. Convert the head to polygon surfaces using NURBS to Polygons, with Tessellation Method set to Control Points. You should see a polygon head like the one below. Don't mind the pointy chin.

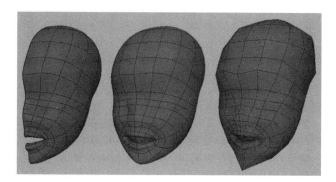

4. Delete the faces of the head on the right side, and also the nine faces around the eye, as selected below. The head_parts layer, which contains the various parts of the head, is set to Invisible, so RM over it and make it visible.

5. Convert the NURBS eye area patches (all eight patches) to polygon pieces, this time with Tessellation Method set to General and the U and V Type set to Per Span # Of Iso Params. You should have polygon surfaces with three faces on each of the four sides. Check to make sure all the surfaces have the same normal direction, using Reverse to correct any wrong normals.

6. Combine and then attach the faces using the Merge Edge tool, making sure there are no border edges separating faces in the eye area.

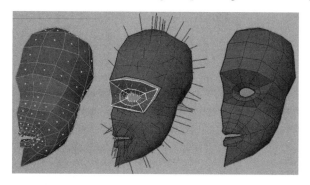

The options Control Points and General with Per Span # of Iso Params produce different results. The Control Points method produces extra faces at the open edges because of the extra CVs there, and you may need to clean them up, whereas the Per Span method does not. But on the other hand, polygons from the Control Points conversion become subdivision surfaces that more faithfully conform to the NURBS original. In this example, it was important to keep the shape of the head, so we used the Control Points method for that. By contrast, for the eye patches, it was more convenient to have the converted polygons' border edges match the number of edges surrounding them, so we used Iso Params.

7.   At the back of the head, delete four faces where the neck will join. Get a polygon cylinder with 12 faces in Axis and 3 faces in Height. Delete the top and the right half of the cylinder, and shape them roughly like the one below. Repeat the attaching procedure of step 2 to merge the neck to the head. If you set the Merge Edge tool's Merge option to First, and click the head edge first and the neck edge second, the results will be more satisfactory. Remember to always keep an eye on the form as you work, moving points whenever necessary to keep shaping the head.

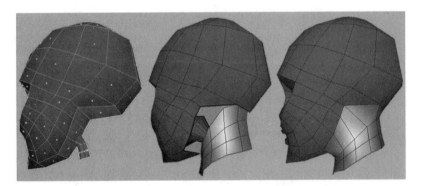

8.   Repeat the same procedure with the ear. If the NURBS ear is not periodic in *V* for some reason, make it so. Convert the ear with the Control Points option because we want to keep the shape of the ear. Delete four faces where the ear should join, as below. Four faces produce eight border edges, and our converted polygon ear should have the same number. The vertices should move to make the ear area rounder, but don't do any careful tweaking for now, as that can be done on the subdivision surface.

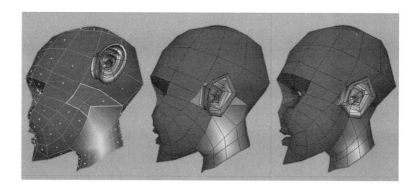

9. Mirror the head and merge the edges. Create a subdivision surface to see what the head looks like. You will notice that there are extraordinary points at the top of the head, because of the triangles at the pole area. Extract vertices to get the polygon surface again, and delete every other edge at the top as below. The result will be cleaner topology. You can go back and forth between polygon and subdivision surfaces and tweak the shape of the head.

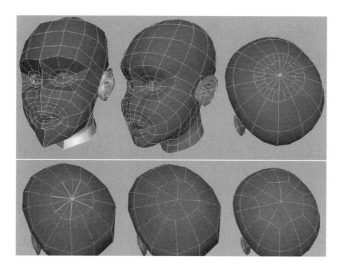

10. For the nose area, you could work either in polygons or in the polygon proxy mode of subdivision surfaces. Grab three faces where the nose would be, and apply Extrude Face. Translate in Z and scale according to the shape you are aiming for. The second Extrude should include extra faces to create the shape for the nostril area. As you work, continue to tweak the nose shape, as below.

After the rough shape is created, do another extrude for the nostril. You are really shaping just the left side of the nose, as the right side will be mirrored later, but extruding and tweaking the right side along with the left side is helpful in judging the overall shape of the nose.

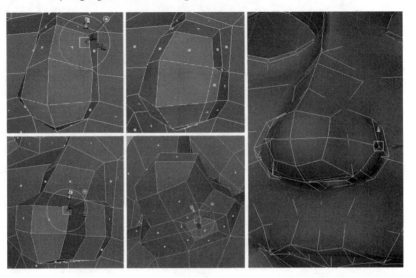

The mouth and the eye areas should be built as lightly as possible, as they will be deforming for animation—fewer points make it that much easier for animation. The ear and the nose areas, however, can be heavier, because they take little or no part in animation.

11. The head is almost done. All that is left now is tweaking. Stay in the base level for all your tweaks, as this enables you to go back and forth between subdivision surface and polygon heads. Place the eye in the proper place on the left side of the head, and tweak the eye area to fit the eye. Also tweak the left side of the head, around the ear, the nostril, the mouth, and other spots that need to be detailed. Delete the right side, mirror the head, and merge any border edges that remain. Duplicate the eye for the right side, too, and the head modeling is done. You can find the completed `character_head.mb` file in the CD-ROM Chapter 6 Working Files directory. We will create hair in Chapter 8, along with the body for the character.

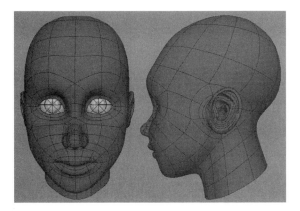

Summary

In this chapter, you were introduced to polygons and subdivision surfaces. You learned what polygons are, how to create them, and how to work with them with the tools and actions in Maya. You then learned how (and when) to work with subdivision surfaces. The first major exercise used polygon techniques to build a hand, and the second used subdivision surfaces to continue our advanced level character modeling tutorial.

In Chapter 8, we will go back to a specific kind of NURBS modeling, called *patch modeling*. We will build a dog model in many separate NURBS patches, covering several relevant advanced modeling concepts as we go. We will then complete the final part of the character modeling tutorial.

Working with Artisan

MAYA

Chapter 7

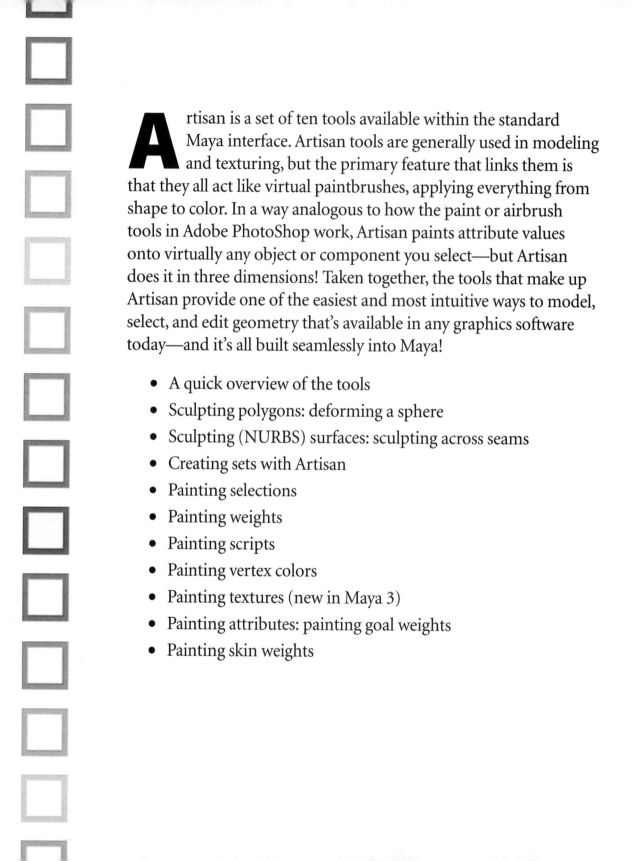

Artisan is a set of ten tools available within the standard Maya interface. Artisan tools are generally used in modeling and texturing, but the primary feature that links them is that they all act like virtual paintbrushes, applying everything from shape to color. In a way analogous to how the paint or airbrush tools in Adobe PhotoShop work, Artisan paints attribute values onto virtually any object or component you select—but Artisan does it in three dimensions! Taken together, the tools that make up Artisan provide one of the easiest and most intuitive ways to model, select, and edit geometry that's available in any graphics software today—and it's all built seamlessly into Maya!

- A quick overview of the tools
- Sculpting polygons: deforming a sphere
- Sculpting (NURBS) surfaces: sculpting across seams
- Creating sets with Artisan
- Painting selections
- Painting weights
- Painting scripts
- Painting vertex colors
- Painting textures (new in Maya 3)
- Painting attributes: painting goal weights
- Painting skin weights

The Tools: a Quick Overview

Here is a quick run-down of the 10 tools in Maya Artisan, with a brief description of what they do and how to open them.

Sculpt Polygons   This tool allows you to sculpt polygonal shapes as if they were made of virtual clay. To open this tool, choose (from the Modeling menu set) Polygons ➡ Sculpt Polygons Tool.

Sculpt Surfaces   This tool allows you to sculpt NURBS surfaces as if they were virtual clay. To open this tool, choose (from the Modeling menu set) Edit Surfaces ➡ Sculpt Surfaces Tool.

Paint Set Membership   This tool allows you to paint on membership in sets, rather than having to pick each point and assign it. To open this tool, choose (from the Animation menu set) Deform ➡ Paint Set Membership Tool.

Paint Selection   This tool allows you to select vertices on a NURBS or polygonal surface by painting on the surface, rather than selecting points individually. To open this tool, choose Edit ➡ Paint Selection Tool.

Paint Weights   This tool allows you to set the weights of clusters of vertices by simply painting on a surface. To open this tool, choose (from the Animation menu set) Deform ➡ Paint Weights Tool.

Script Paint   With this tool, you can paint the output of a MEL script onto an object using your mouse or graphics tablet, instead of manually running the script at each point. To open this tool, choose Modify ➡ Script Paint Tool.

Paint Vertex Color   This tool lets you paint colors directly onto individual polygons on a surface. To open this tool, choose (from the Modeling menu set) Edit Polygons ➡ Colors ➡ Paint Vertex Color Tool.

Paint Textures   This tool, added in Maya 3, lets you paint color, transparency, bump map, incandescence, and other attributes directly on NURBS or polygonal surfaces. To open this tool, choose (from the Render menu set) Lighting/Shading ➡ Paint Textures Tool.

Attribute Paint   This tool allows you to paint any (paintable) attribute onto your selected model. You can paint on colors, goal weights, or other attributes that you assign to be paintable. To open this tool, choose Modify ➡ Attribute Paint Tool.

New

Paint Skin Weights After smooth binding skin to bones, you can use this tool to modify the weights of the bound points to each joint in your bone chain, resulting in smoother, more natural skin motion. To open this tool, choose (from the Animation menu set) Skin ➜ Edit Smooth Skin ➜ Paint Skin Weights Tool.

Because they work as paintbrushes, Artisan tools are most efficiently used with a graphics tablet. In this book, for the most part, we're assuming a "plain vanilla" configuration that doesn't include a tablet, so the instructions in this chapter show how to use Artisan with a mouse and keyboard as the only input devices. If you do have a tablet, it should be configured (for the most part) automatically when you launch Maya. For more information on how to use your tablet with Artisan, see the online documentation under *Basics: Artisan*.

Sculpting Polygons: Deforming a Sphere

Let's begin our work with Artisan by modifying a polygonal object using the Sculpt Polygons tool. Open a new scene in Maya and create a polygon sphere (Create ➜ Polygon Primitives ➜ Sphere). Don't just click the sphere button on the shelf, or you'll get a NURBS sphere, and the Sculpt Polygons tool won't be very effective! Then follow these steps:

1. In the Channel box, under Inputs: polySphere1, set the subdivisions X and Y to 40, as in Figure 7.1.

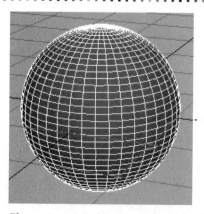

Figure 7.1 *A Polygon sphere with 40 divisions in X and Y*

When using Artisan sculpting tools, it is always important to have a large number of points to work with—either vertices (for NURBS surfaces) or facets (for polygon surfaces). If you do not provide enough points for Artisan to work with, it will not push and pull the objects' surfaces in ways you expect.

2. With the sphere selected, choose Polygons ➜ Sculpt Polygons Tool ❑ (from the Modeling menu set). This brings up the Tool Settings window shown in Figure 7.2, which is generally the same for every Artisan tool. (As most tool settings are the same from one tool to another, we will introduce them here and refer back to them in later sections of this chapter.)

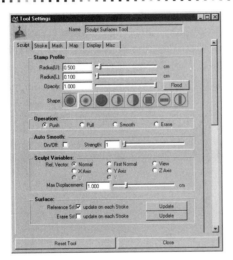

Figure 7.2 *The Polygon Sculpting tool option window*

3. In this window (be sure you're in the Sculpt tab), change the Radius U and L to about 0.3, set the Operation mode to Push, and set the Maximum Displacement to around 0.5. When you move your mouse over the sphere now (don't click anything just yet), you will see a red circle with an arrow pointing inward (toward the center of the sphere) and the label *Ps*.

The circle shows your brush's radius of influence, the arrow indicates both the direction of the effect and the amount of influence it will have (longer arrows mean bigger pushes and pulls), and the *Ps* stands for *push,* the current mode of the brush.

4. To see how this feedback works, try changing the radius of the brush to a smaller value in the Sculpt tab; the red circle will diminish to match. You can also change the direction of the effect: under Sculpt Variables, choose the X-axis radio button. As you now move the mouse around, you will see that the arrow always stays pointing down the X axis. You can try the other settings here as well—when you're done, set Ref. Vector back to Normal.

If you have a tablet, you can set the pen pressure to interactively change the radius of the brush—go into the Stroke tab and click the Radius radio button. You can also use the pen to adjust the opacity of the effect you are working on by clicking the Opacity radio button, or you can alter both elements at the same time by clicking Both.

5. Now that you have a feeling for some of Artisan's settings, try clicking and dragging the mouse over the surface. You should see the sphere dent inward as you drag your mouse across its surface, the dent always pointing inward toward the center of the sphere (because the brush option is set to Normal). If you make a few drags across the sphere, you will end up with something like Figure 7.3.

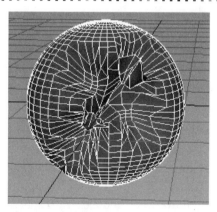

Figure 7.3 *A dented polygon sphere*

6. If you don't like what you have (or just to see how this works), you can erase your work. Click the Erase radio button (under Operation); then paint over the parts you don't like. If you want to reset the entire sphere, click the Flood button near the top right of the window. This will "flood" the entire sphere with the Erase command, thus resetting the sphere back to its original shape.

The Flood button can be used with any operation, such as push and pull, to apply a certain value to an entire object. You can then fine-tune specific parts of your surface by painting on them as normal.

You may notice that, as you make several strokes on top of one another, the polygon facets will tend to get very jagged looking (as if the sphere were made up of crinkly paper instead of clay). To smooth out your strokes, there are two options: the Smooth operation or the Auto Smooth option. Let's start with Smooth.

7. Once you have several strokes deforming your sphere (try pulling the points out this time), switch over to the Smooth operation by selecting its radio button on the Sculpt tab. Now brush over the sphere, concentrating on the sharpest edges. You'll see these edges move back toward their original positions on the (undeformed) sphere, and the strokes you have made will smooth out.

The Smooth operation "relaxes" whatever you paint over, making it tend to return to its original position, and thus smoothing the shape back out.

8. Now erase your sphere back to normal, check the Auto Smooth option, and set the Strength slider to about 5. As you paint strokes over the surface of the sphere (be sure you're in push or pull mode), you will notice that the polygons don't become as jagged as they did when the Auto Smooth option was off. To create smoothly organic shapes, always use a combination of the Auto Smooth option and the Smooth operation mode.

Besides adjusting radius, modes, and other options, you can also change brush shapes, using the row of Shape buttons near the top of the Sculpt tab—the graphic on each button shows its stamp shape. *Stamping* is simply clicking and releasing your mouse button (without dragging). The brush creates a "stamp" of its shape right on your object's surface. When you drag over the surface, you are laying down a series of stamps. You can see this effect if you drag very quickly over your object's surface: if the mouse is moving quickly, each stamp will be noticeably separate from the others, rather than all running together.

9. Erase the sphere back to normal, and then try stamping the sphere with each of the brush shapes to see how they compare.

As the Sculpt tool is set up right now, every time you make one stroke on top of another, the sphere will deform more and more (as if the effect were layering on top of itself—see Figure 7.4). That's because you have the Surface: Update on Each Stroke option turned on.

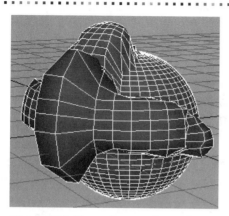

Figure 7.4 *The polygon sphere, showing the layering effect of Update On Each Stroke*

10. To set a maximum amount by which your strokes can deform the sphere, just uncheck the Update on each stroke option. The same strokes will then produce something like Figure 7.5.

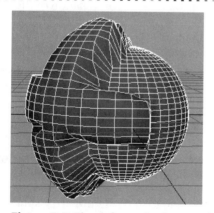

Figure 7.5 *The deformed sphere, with Update On Each Stroke turned off*

As you have probably noticed, you can also set the *opacity* of your brush. Opacity refers to the percentage of a tool's total effect that each application of it will have on your object. As an analogy, consider a real-world paintbrush: if the paint you're applying is highly opaque, one coat may be enough to cover your wall, whereas a semi-transparent paint would take several coats. In Artisan, if you have your brush set to Push with a maximum displacement ("push in") set to 1, and your opacity is 0.5 (or 50%), when you click on the surface of your sphere, the brush will only push in about 0.5 units, instead of 1. You can use the opacity setting to reduce the effect of your strokes, making each one subtler, thus allowing you to deform your objects in smaller increments than we have done so far.

Before we leave this introductory section, you should note that when an Artisan tool is active, you can bring up a marking menu with several Artisan options by simply holding down the U key and pressing the mouse button, as shown in Figure 7.6.

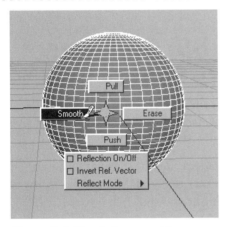

Figure 7.6 *The Artisan marking menu*

In addition to the settings available in the marking menu, there are hotkeys defined for several of the most common tasks, and you can create your own hotkeys for most Artisan settings.

 To modify the upper brush radius, hold down the B key while dragging your mouse left or right. Max displacement is mapped to M plus mouse-dragging right and left. To find out how to map other tool settings to hotkeys, see the Maya help files, or Chapters 3 and 16 in this book.

Once you are familiar with Artisan's marking menu and hotkeys, you do not need to keep the option window open for most operations. While you are starting out, however, it is a good idea to keep the window open. Throughout this chapter, we will access all Artisan toll settings via the option window, though experienced users may find it more efficient to access them through the marking menu or hotkeys.

If you have a graphics tablet, you can set the pressure of the stylus to map to brush radius or displacement amount, or both, using the Stylus Pressure setting in the Stroke tab. See the Maya help files if you have problems with your stylus, which should work automatically with the Artisan brushes.

For a complete list of Artisan's hotkey functions (and those that are not yet mapped), choose Window ➜ Settings/Preferences ➜ Hotkeys, choose the menu set for your Artisan category (Brush Tools: Modify UpperRadius, for example), and click the command in which you're interested. If you map any new hotkeys, be sure to save your preferences for future use (press the Save button at the bottom of the Hotkey Editor window).

Sculpting (NURBS) Surfaces: Sculpting across Seams

We're now going to look at Maya's Sculpt NURBS Surfaces tool, and use a NURBS head model (7head on the CD) to see how Artisan works with complex issues like surface seams.

1. First things first: we don't want to alter the shape of the person's ears or eyes, so hide them from view (select each one, and then choose Display ➜ Hide ➜ Hide Selection). The resulting head is shown in Figure 7.7.

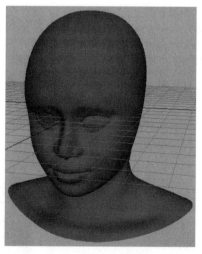

Figure 7.7 *A basic NURBS head without ears or eyes*

2. Drag-select the remains of the head, and then open the Sculpt Surfaces tool (Edit Surfaces ➜ Sculpt Surfaces Tool ❑). The entire surface of the head will now be available for sculpting. (If you had selected only one portion of the head, it would have been the only part available for sculpting.) You will see yellow bands where each surface is stitched to the others—if you see all the surfaces' isoparms, go to the Display tab and uncheck Show Active Lines.

Because there are stitched seams in this model, it will be bit more challenging to sculpt this surface without pulling apart the seams. (Seams—which will be dealt with in detail in the next chapter—are a highly complex surface structure. While Artisan does a great job of treating the object as a whole, you have to know how to adjust the Sculpt Surfaces tool settings to get it to work as well as possible. For the present, think of seams as stitched areas between different NURBS patches.)

3. In the Sculpt Surfaces Tool window, select the Seam tab and adjust Seam Tolerance and Min Length to 1. Setting these a bit higher than their defaults allows Artisan to "see" the common edges more easily as you work with the tool.

 Before you start deforming the face shape, it is a good idea to save a temporary version of the project file. If your settings get too messed up, it's easier to go back to that file than to go back to the original and hide the eyes and ears again.

One problem you will run into (if you let your brush stray too far) is that the upper head will not deform correctly—it has too few isoparms to deform well with Artisan. If we were planning to model the upper head next, we would need to insert more isoparms. But since we are not, we can just leave it alone for now (you can even deselect it if you want to be safer).

Let's create a heavier pair of eyebrows, using the Pull operation. We don't need to pull out each brow individually, because Artisan has a Reflect option that will allow us to do both sides simultaneously.

4. Click the Stroke tab, turn the Reflection option on (check the box), and set the reflection mode to V Dir (Horizontal). When you now pass your mouse over the head, you will see two brushes, mirrored around the centerline of the head.

5. Now turn back to the Sculpt tab, set the Operation mode to Pull, and adjust the radius of the brush(es) to something that looks appropriate for eyebrow size. Turn the opacity down to about 0.5, and set Max Displacement to about 0.5 as well.

By holding down the B key and moving the mouse left and right, you can interactively adjust the brush size and see the changes in the brush right on the face. (The range of sizes the brush can take on is determined by the brush minimum and maximum settings in the Sculpt Surfaces option window.) This is a much faster way to adjust brush size to a desired radius.

6. Starting close to the center, pull a stroke along the top of the eyes (where the brows are), and pull out a heavier eyebrow, as shown in Figure 7.8. You'll notice that both sides pull out with just one stroke—a great time-saver!

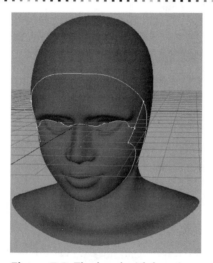

Figure 7.8 *The head with heavier eyebrows*

If you don't like your work, remember that you can erase your model back to its original state with the Erase function.

7. Once you have eyebrows you're pleased with, let's try creating an indentation below the cheeks that goes back toward the ears—specifically, across the seam boundary between the face and cheek patches of the face. Set your brush to Push and paint some strokes.

This is a well-modeled face: the stitches occur in places that would normally get no tweaking by tools such as Artisan (even though we're going to do that here). Placing seams in areas that won't move is very good practice; even though Artisan works well with stitches, it is not perfect. Whenever possible, it is better if you don't have to tweak stitched surfaces in the first place.

You will probably get unsatisfactory results at this point (and you may have to reopen your saved temp file; even erasing sometimes fails to set the stitches back to normal). The two surfaces are obviously not working as one, each one deforming a different amount under the brush's pressure. The solution here is to increase the number of surfaces the tool looks for as it works. (Be sure to get a clean copy of your head to start from first!)

8. Click the Miscellaneous tab, set the number of surfaces to two or more (or just click the Infinite radio button), and turn on the Use Common Edge Info option. With these new settings (and a bit of practice—try starting with the brush completely on one surface, then moving it to the other), you should get a nice "sunken cheek" look, as shown in Figure 7.9. Save this project for use later in this chapter.

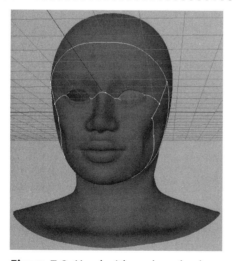

Figure 7.9 *Head with sunken cheeks*

Although this was a fast and simple introduction to real-world modeling using Artisan, it should give you an idea of just how powerful the tool can be for making subtle adjustments to your models. All it takes is a bit of practice and some knowledge of what the Sculpt Surfaces tool can do.

You can actually stitch surfaces using the Sculpt Surfaces tool. For more information on how to do this, see Maya's online help (Essentials: Chapter 12).

Creating Sets with Artisan

An Artisan tool that is sometimes useful is Paint Set Membership tool. With this tool, you can edit the set membership of points—for grouping with bones, for example—without having to pick individual points. (And if you've ever had to do that, you know why this is a useful tool!)

Let's use our base head from the last section, and create a few sets of points on it (or you can use 7head on the CD-ROM).

1. First drag-select the entire head, then open the Paint Set Membership tool (Deform ➜ Paint Set Membership Tool ❑). With the Paint Set Membership-tool open, the head should now be made up of several colors, each representing one of the sets that has been created for the head.

2. In the Set Membership tab, select set2 as the Set to Modify, and you should see the CVs in the lip area, as shown in Figure 7.10 (in color in the Chapter 7 Color Gallery on the CD).

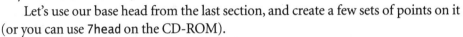

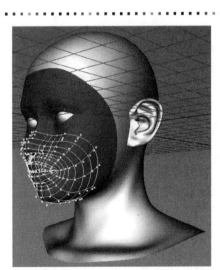

Figure 7.10 *The head with set memberships colored*

If you do not see a colored face, click the Display tab and be sure the Color Feedback and Display Active Vertices options are on. While here, you can also (if you prefer) turn off Active Display Vertices, which hides the isoparms and CVs on the head.

The Paint Set Membership tool works in three modes: Add, Transfer, and Remove. Add adds the painted points to the selected set, Remove deletes points from the selected set, and Transfer transfers points to the selected set. It is important to understand the difference between Add and Transfer. Add places the painted points into the selected set but *does not* remove them from membership in any other sets. Transfer both adds points to the selected set and removes them from membership in any other sets. The set you select in the Paint Set Membership Tool window is the set the points will transfer *to*. Points from any other set will be moved into your selected set.

You will notice that there is no opacity setting; all points are either in a set or not—there is no in between.

3. Let's add some points from the top of the head to the shapesSet that has all face points in it (in the Set Membership tab, select shapesSet under Set to Modify). With your brush mode set to Add (you can adjust the radius just as you did previously), paint some points on the top of the head into the shapesSet. The newly added points will change color as they are added to the set, as shown in Figure 7.11 (in color on the CD).

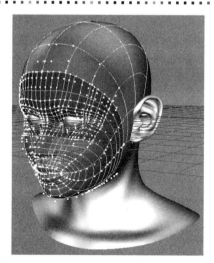

Figure 7.11 *Painting new points into the shapeSet set*

4. Now let's remove some points from set3 (the set around the jaws). Set your Paint Set Membership tool to Remove and paint out some of the points. As the CVs are removed, they disappear from view, as shown in Figure 7.12 (in color on the CD).

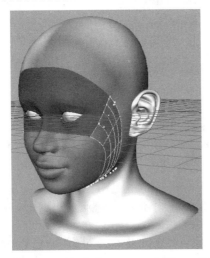

Figure 7.12 *Points removed from the jaw set*

5. Finally, let's transfer some points from one set to another. With the Paint Set Membership tool set to Transfer, select set2 (the set of CVs around the mouth), and then paint over the area below the eyes. You will notice that the points change color as they are transferred from their old set to set2, as in Figure 7.13 (in color on the CD).

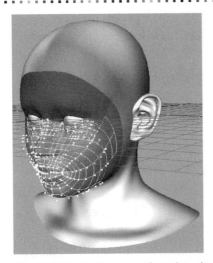

Figure 7.13 *Points transferred to the jaw set*

The Paint Set Membership tool can be very useful if you have several objects (such as this head) and you wish to form selection (or deform) sets across object boundaries for use in later deform processes, or just for ease of selection. Instead of carefully picking out points (and taking pains not to accidentally pick points on the back side of the object), you can intuitively paint these points into your sets with a brush.

Painting Selections

Akin to the Paint Set Membership tool, the Paint Selection tool allows you to pick vertices (or polygon facets) that you can then manipulate in standard ways. To see this tool in action, take the following steps:

1. Open a new scene, create a NURBS plane, scale it out a bit, and set its U and V patches to around 50 each (to give Artisan enough points to work with).

2. Now open the Paint Selection tool (Edit ➡ Paint Selection Tool ❑). The selection types here are Select, Unselect, and Toggle (which selects unselected points, and vice versa). There are also global Select, Unselect, and Toggle buttons.

3. To quickly see how Select works, pick out a brush shape and paint over part of the plane to select its points. You can now use the Move, Rotate, or Scale tools to alter just these points.

The advantage of being able to paint selections onto objects may not be obvious with a simple plane, where you could just as easily drag out selections with the Marquee tool. But on something more complex, like our head model, the Paint Selection tool can be a great asset.

1. Once again, open your neutral head project (7head on the CD-ROM).

2. Now, using the Paint Selection tool, select points around the mouth. Make the face smile by using the Move tool and the Scale tool. You will probably have to move back and forth between the Paint Selection tool (changing the points selected) and the Move and Scale tools. A resulting smile is shown in Figure 7.14.

Remember that the Reflect mode allows you to select points on both sides of the head simultaneously—cutting your selection time in half.

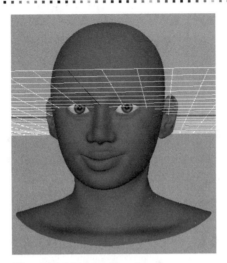

Figure 7.14 *A smiling head*

Painting Weights

If selecting CVs via painting doesn't give you enough control over the points you're manipulating, you can use the Paint Weights tool to set the goal weight (the amount of effect a manipulation will have on a given vertex or facet) of each CV in an intuitive manner. (There are several other ways to set CV weights, but the Paint Weights tool is so easy to use, it's often not necessary to go beyond this tool.)

To see how this tool works, let's create an Aztec (stair-stepped) pyramid just by painting different weights on a simple NURBS plane.

1. Open a new scene, create a NURBS plane with about 50 U and V patches, and scale it out to about the size of the scene grid (for easier viewing).

2. There is one step before we can use the Paint Weights tool—we must first make the plane's CVs into a cluster so their weights can be manipulated. Select the plane, and then choose Deform ➜ Create Cluster. If you forget this step (which is very easy to do), you will be extremely confused by the lack of responsiveness the tool has!

3. Now drag-select both the cluster and the plane it is mapped to, and open the Paint Weights tool (Deform ➜ Paint Weights Tool in the Animation menu set).

You should see the plane turn white, indicating that its goal weights are all set to a value of 1. If this doesn't happen, be sure you created a cluster from the plane, and then check to see if Color Feedback is on (it's under the Display tab of the tool). It may be hard to see the color with the plane's isoparms showing, so turn off Show Active Lines as well.

Next, we need to flood the entire plane/cluster with a goal weight of 0, or no influence (CVs with a 0 weight won't react to any manipulation).

4. Set the operation mode to Replace (which replaces the old goal weight with your selection), set the Value (of the goal weight) to 0, and click the Flood button. The entire plane should turn black, indicating it now has a goal weight of 0. This is the base of our pyramid, which will not move.

5. Now we need to paint our stairs. Choose the square brush option (the button that looks like a blue square), and change the value to 0.1 instead of 0. This next part is a neat trick: instead of having to increase the goal weight value manually each time, we can place the Paint Weights tool into Add mode (by clicking that radio button), and each brush stamp will increase the goal weight by 0.1. Thus, the more times you click on a spot, the higher the goal weight goes, and the lighter the area's shade of gray will become.

This tool also has Smooth and Scale operation modes. The Smooth mode smooths transitions between areas of different goal weights. The Scale mode scales (or multiplies) the object's goal weight by the number in the Value box.

6. With the square brush chosen, set the radius of the brush larger than the edges of the plane, center the brush around the origin, and stamp a higher goal weight onto a large square area of the plane. (You will probably find this easier to do in the top orthographic view.) You should see a large square portion of the plane become a slightly lighter gray than before.

In general, you can set the orientation of any brush that's not round. In the Stroke tab, you can choose from Up Vector (default), U and V Tangent (horizontal and vertical aligned), and Path Direction (which changes the orientation, depending on your stroke).

7. Make the brush radius a bit smaller and repeat the stamp; now a smaller portion of the plane should get just a bit lighter. Continue this process until you are at the center, with a very small radius. Your plane should look similar to Figure 7.15.

Figure 7.15 *A plane with stair-stepped goal weights*

8. To make your pyramid, switch to the Move tool, select the cluster weight *only* (not the plane—you may need to do this in the Hypergraph or Outliner), and then move it straight up the Y axis. You should see something that looks like a stair-stepped pyramid, as Figure 7.16 shows.

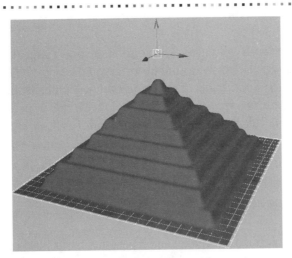

Figure 7.16 *The completed pyramid*

As a further exercise, try making a hilly terrain by using a simple plane, a cluster, and painted goal weights.

Weighting Clusters for Realistic Character Animation

Let's now return to our favorite head—either open your own file or use 7head from the companion CD—and examine how to weight the mouth clusters to allow for better manipulation of facial expressions when the character is eventually animated.

1. With the head showing, select only the lower face section (with the mouth) and create a cluster out of it.

2. Shift-select the cluster and mouth, and then open the Paint Weights tool. (You should see the area turn white, indicating a goal weight of 1 for all points.) As before, first flood the area with a goal weight of 0 (so the areas we don't want to move, won't).

3. Using the Add (or Replace) and Smooth modes, paint the areas around the lips, giving the corners of the mouth, and the cheeks above them, the highest weighting.

4. Try to imagine where the skin bends and stretches the most as you smile and frown (or look in the mirror to see), and then paint these creases onto the mouth. You may find it necessary to move the mouth and then repaint the goal weights to get the effect you want. Figure 7.17 shows the results of painting on these goal weights.

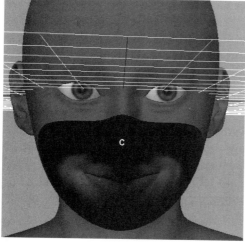

Figure 7.17 *Painted weights in the mouth area*

Remember that turning on Reflection will cut your work in half.

5. When you are finished, try making the face smirk (as in Figure 7.18), purse its lips, and then frown. You should find that this method of creating facial animations can—after a bit of practice—become a very powerful tool in your character animation bag.

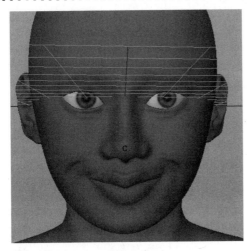

Figure 7.18 *A smirking face*

Chapter 25, "Dynamics of Soft Bodies," has a section describing how to use Artisan to paint goal weights for soft body hair.

Painting Scripts: Volcanoes on an Asteroid

The Paint Scripts tool lets you paint a MEL script onto your selected surface. MEL (or Maya Embedded Language) scripts are commands that can simplify complex or repetitive tasks. For more information on MEL scripts and how you can create your own, see Part IV: "Working with MEL." Maya provides several predefined scripts in the AW\Maya3.0\scripts\others (Windows NT) or ~Maya/3.0/scripts/others (Irix) directories, or you can create your own for use in a project.

The predefined scripts include painting on geometry, particle emitters, and soft body goal weights. For our purposes—placing a number of particle "volcanoes" on an asteroid—we'll use the emitterPaint script.

1. Open a new project and create a basic sphere at the origin. You may wish to distort the sphere some (try using the Sculpt Surfaces tool) to make the object look more asteroid-like.

2. Now open the Script Paint tool (Modify ➜ Script Paint Tool ❏) and click the Setup tab. In the Tool Setup Command text field, type **emitterPaint,** and hit the Enter key. This will bring up a window with options for the emitterPaint.mel script, as shown in Figure 7.19.

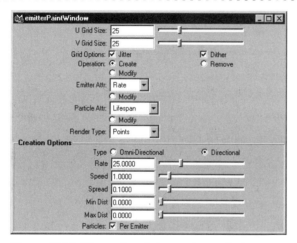

Figure 7.19 *The emitterPaint options window*

3. Leave the grid size at 25 in each direction (this sets how closely spaced the emitters will be), leave the Operation at Create, and be sure the Jitter box is checked (this randomizes the placement of emitters). Set the Type to Directional, the Rate to a low number like 10, the Speed to about 5, and the Spread to about 0.3, and be sure Particles: Per Emitter is checked. Close this window.

4. Now set the brush opacity to a low value like 0.1 (this will create fewer emitters, speeding up your interaction with the program), and paint a couple of strokes on the asteroid. When you finish, you should see several circles on the sphere, indicating that you have painted emitters onto the asteroid.

5. If you now click the Play button (at the lower right of the monitor), you will see particles being emitted from these emitters, as if volcanoes were exploding on the surface of the sphere, as in Figure 7.20.

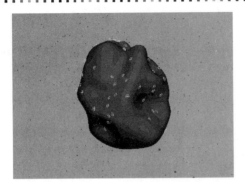

Figure 7.20 *Emitters on an asteroid sphere emitting particles*

*If you wished, you could go back and paint over the emitters, modifying the emitter rate, particle lifespan, and so on. Go back to the Setup tab of the Script Paint tool, type in **emitterPaint** again and hit Enter. In the emitterPaint window, you can change the operation from Create to Modify, and then adjust the Emitter, Particle, or Render type attributes. See Chapter 22, "Particle Basics," for more on how to create and use particles.*

Painting Vertex Colors

An Artisan tool that has a more limited use is Paint Vertex Color. This tool allows you to paint colors directly onto any polygonal surface, using the now-familiar Artisan brush. To try it, first create a polygon cone with about 40 divisions in each direction (so there are plenty of facets for Artisan to work with). With the cone selected, open the Paint Vertex Color tool (Edit Polygons ➜ Colors ➜ Paint Vertex Color Tool). Set your brush radius to whatever you wish; then click the color swatch next to Color Value and select a color. All that's left to do is paint on some color! Figure 7.21 (in color on the CD) shows an example.

The Paint Vertex Color tool is simply a series of presets of the Attribute Paint tool. The Paint Textures tool, discussed next, is a more robust and useful painting tool.

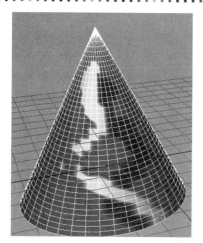

Figure 7.21 *A polygon cone, painted*

Painting Textures

New in Maya 3 is a very useful Paint Textures tool, which allows you to paint color, transparency, bump, incandescence, or other texture attributes directly on NURBS and (well-formed) polygon surfaces. This tool supplants and extends the Paint Vertex Color tool, so we will discuss it more fully.

When you create or modify a texture using the Paint Textures tool, Maya creates a new file texture (or renames one that already exists) for the selected material and paints on that file texture. Any scene objects that have this material applied to them will then be updated when you save the brush strokes out.

For more on textures and rendering, please see Chapter 18, "Rendering Basics."

Let's begin with a simple example: we'll paint some colors on a standard NURBS sphere.

1. In a new scene window, create a NURBS sphere (Create → NURBS primitives → Sphere), change it to high resolution, and set texture shading (press the 3 and 6 keys on your main keyboard).

2. Now let's assign a material to this sphere: open the Hypershade (Window → Hypershade), look under the Create section, and open the Materials folder (if it's not already open). Then MM drag a phongE material onto the right-hand window, as shown in Figure 7.22.

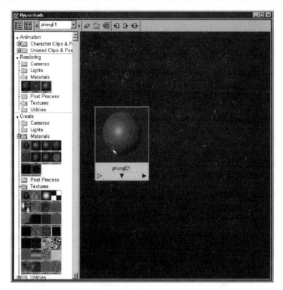

Figure 7.22 *Creating a new phongE material*

3. Now MM drag the texture onto the sphere in your scene window.

4. If you want to check to be sure the material is applied, open the Attribute Editor (double-click the phongE1 material in the Hypershade), and alter the color in the Common Material Attributes section. You should see your sphere update with the same color. If not, go back and MM drag the material onto your sphere.

We have a basic material applied to our sphere; now let's do some painting!

5. First, save your scene if you haven't before (otherwise, the Paint Textures tool will remind you to do so—it needs your scene name to name its textures), then select your sphere and choose Lighting/Shading ➜ Paint Textures Tool ❏. You will get an Artisan window similar to those you have worked with in this chapter. It has a few different features, some of which are shown in Figure 7.23.

6. Click on the Misc tab, and choose the UV Texture Paint mode. (Projective paint is better for multiple-part surfaces, like stitched bodies, but UV mode is better for single surfaces.) Also, be sure the AutoSave On Stroke check box is *off*. Under the Display tab, you might wish to turn off Show Active Lines. Under the Stroke tab, you can turn Reflection on (if you want to paint symmetrically on both sides of the sphere), and also set how your stylus will paint, if you have a stylus.

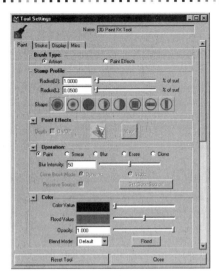

Figure 7.23 *The Paint Textures tool option window*

The AutoSave On Stroke option might seem like a good idea—especially if you plan to use IPR (Interactive Photorealistic Rendering, discussed in Chapter 18) to watch your texture update via the Rendering window. However, AutoSave On Stroke disables the undo feature, so if you make a mistake, you're stuck with it. Unless you are very confident of your painting abilities, it is better to save the image manually (as described below).

7. In the Paint tab, leave Texture Attribute To Paint at its default, Color. (But feel free to check the pop-up menu for other attributes you can paint.)

8. Now try to paint on your sphere. Nothing happens, because you have not yet assigned a file texture to your phongE material.

9. To rectify the situation, click the Assign Textures button (bottom of the Paint window), and, in the Assign File Textures window that pops up, set a size and image format for your texture, as in Figure 7.24.

Your file texture must always have a size ratio of a power of two (128 × 256, or 512 × 512, for example). If not, Maya will automatically convert the texture to such a ratio. This is important to remember if you create a texture in a paint package and intend to use it as a basic file texture to paint over later in Maya.

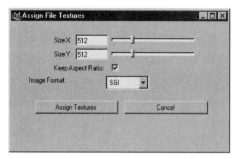

Figure 7.24 *The Assign File Textures window*

10. Before you paint strokes, try clicking the Flood button (in the Paint tab). You should see the entire sphere's surface update to the color you have chosen in the Color Value section of the Paint tab.

11. Once you have flooded the sphere, change the color (either adjust the slider or click the color chip and choose a new color there) and paint several strokes on your sphere, as in Figure 7.25 (in color on the CD). You have just painted colors directly onto your sphere!

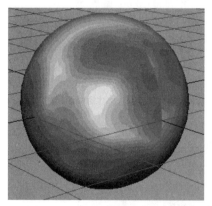

Figure 7.25 *Painted texture strokes on a white sphere*

If you now undo your painting (press Z, or choose Edit ➜ Undo), you will see that the sphere reverts *all the way* back to its original color. You have not saved the texture; and thus when you undo the painting, you undo *all* the painting, rather than just the last brush stroke. Because of this, you will want to save the texture manually—whenever you are satisfied with the current state of your painting—by clicking the Save Textures button in the Paint tab.

Remember that once you save the texture, you can no longer undo back to an earlier state of painting—so save only when you are sure you like what you have thus far.

Now let's try a bit more advanced example: we'll paint the front of a polygon cube so it looks like a cartoon adobe house with a door and window.

1. Create a new scene and save it; then choose Create ➜ Polygon Primitives ➜ Cube ❏. In the Option window, set the subdivisions along Width and Height to around 40 (you can set the Depth subdivisions too, but we won't be using them), and create the cube.

2. Rotate your view so you can see the front of the cube, as in Figure 7.26, and with the cube selected, choose Lighting/Shading ➜ Paint Textures Tool ❏. You may wish to turn Show Active Lines on (under the Display tab), as we'll be using the faces of the polygons to mask our painting.

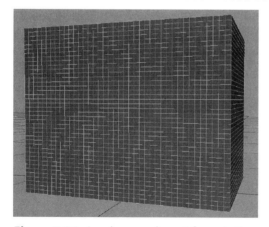

Figure 7.26 *A polygon cube, set for painting*

3. Under the Paint tab, choose Assign Texture, give it a resolution of 1024 × 1024, and click the Assign Texture button.

4. Switch to the Misc tab and set the paint method to Projective Paint. Now change the color to your "base coat" color for the house, and click the Flood button. Your entire cube house should now be the base color (we chose an off-white).

5. Now let's paint on a door. First, we need to mask out the polygon faces we'll use as the door. Go into select mode (or press the Q key), then RM choose Faces with the cursor over the cube. Shift-select a number of faces on the front of the cube that will become the door area, as in Figure 7.27 (in color on the CD).

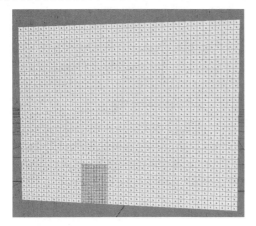

Figure 7.27 *The door faces selected*

6. Switch back to the Paint Textures tool (or press Y), choose a new color for your door, and paint over the door faces. If you wish, you can reset the brush to a very small size and paint a doorknob on as well. Figure 7.28 shows a close-up of the finished door.

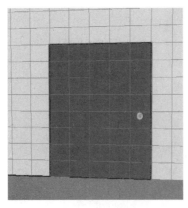

Figure 7.28 *A close-up view of the door and doorknob*

Do not click the Flood button. That will cause the entire surface (even the faces that have not been selected) to be painted the new color.

Now let's paint a window into the house. First, we'll paint a transparency map onto the windowpanes, so they are semitransparent; then we'll paint a color over the top, where the crossbars of the window would be.

7. Select a group of faces on your cube that will be the window area—a good-sized picture window, as in Figure 7.29 (in color on the CD), will do nicely.

Figure 7.29 *Faces selected for a picture window*

8. Under the Paint tab, select Transparency for the Texture Attribute to Paint, then click the Assign Textures button and assign a 1024 × 1024 texture to the transparency map. You will see the cube turn a light gray.

9. Set the Color Value to black (completely opaque) and click the Flood button, making the entire cube opaque. Now raise the color to a very light gray (color doesn't matter for transparency, only shades of gray) and paint into your window area with a large brush. You may wish to go back with a smaller brush and paint some streaks of "dirt" on the window, where it won't be as transparent— or you can wait and do this when you paint on your colors, next.

10. Now choose Color for the Texture Attribute To Paint (your house will become mostly white again), choose a very small brush, and paint in crossbar supports for your window, as in Figure 7.30. You may wish to go back to the transparency image and paint on the dark crossbars there as well, so they don't render semi-transparent.

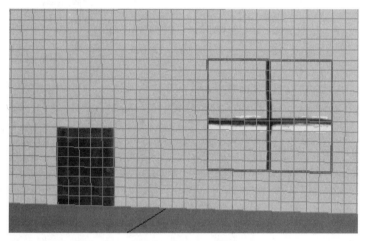

Figure 7.30 *Window crossbars painted in*

11. Finally, render out a test image to see what your cube house looks like. If you don't like the look, just return to the Paint Textures tool and adjust to your heart's content.

Obviously, there are many more features you can paint on using this new tool—specularity maps are a good example. All the other texture attributes you can paint, however, behave just like color and transparency, so you should now find using them very easy.

Painting Attributes: Painting Goal Weights

The Attribute Paint tool is very useful, as you can use it to paint any "paintable" attribute onto a surface. For our work, we're going to use this tool to paint on the particle goal weight of a soft body, making a simple cylinder into a bendable fishing rod. Soft bodies are collections of Maya particles that look like solid objects. They are very useful for creating malleable objects like fat on a body—or a flexible fishing pole. For information about creating and working with soft bodies, see Chapter 25.

We could also use the Script Paint tool to do this; it has a predefined script, paintGoalPP, that will do the same thing.

1. Open the file 7rodSB, on your CD-ROM (or build a skinny cylinder, animate it, and make it a soft body). If you play back the animation, you will see that the entire "fishing rod" moves back and forth as one solid piece—we're going to change that by reducing the goal weights at the top of the rod.

2. Select the rod and open the Attribute Paint tool (Modify ➜ Attribute Paint Tool ❏).

3. Click the Attr (attribute) tab and then, under Paintable Object Type, expand the particle selection (click the plus sign) until you see goalPP and highlight it. The goalPP attribute (which defines the per-particle goal weight—or how closely the soft body will cling to the original object when it is moved) will now be placed in the Paintable Object list.

4. Highlight the goalPP text; then click the right arrow, moving it over to the Selected side, as shown in Figure 7.31.

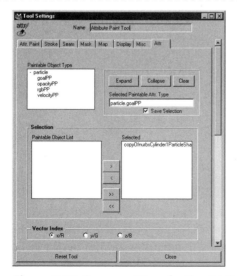

Figure 7.31 *Proper settings for the Attribute tab*

5. Finally, click the Save Selection check box so you don't have to repeat these steps if you change tools.

6. Move back to the Attr. Paint tab, set the Operation to Replace, the Value (goal weight) to 0, and the Opacity to 1, and click the Flood button. This sets all goal weights to 0, meaning that the soft body will not move with its (invisible) animated parent anymore—you can play back the animation to test this, if you wish.

7. Once you see how the Goal Weight attribute works, flood the entire rod with a value of 0.5 so there will be some connection between the rod and its animated parent.

8. Once you have the entire rod set to 0.5, set your mode to Add and set your Value to 0.1. We're going to increase the goal weight as we go down the rod by simply painting on a lighter color. Set your brush radius fairly large, so it wraps around the whole cylinder—you can also change the brush shape to square if you prefer. To get a smooth transition from dark to light, you will probably need to use the Smooth mode as well as the Add mode. Run a couple of frames of the animation frequently to see how you are progressing. Figure 7.32 shows the rod (on its side for space reasons) in motion.

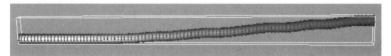

Figure 7.32 *The weighted rod in motion*

 A very good method for getting smooth transitions on an object like this is to start at the bottom and make a series of upward brush strokes, each one going up a bit farther.

 You must rewind animations using soft bodies before playing them back. If you don't rewind, the animation will start giving you bizarre results.

While it can take a bit of practice to paint goal weights onto objects effectively, learning how to do so can really improve the control you have over soft body animations, allowing you to create much subtler variations of motion than would be feasible without such a paint method for applying goal weights.

Painting Skin Weights

If you are working with smooth-skinned, jointed characters, the Paint Skin Weight tool is just what you need for precise control over how your character's skin bends in relation to joint movement. We will use a simple setup of a cylindrical arm and an elbow joint to examine how to use this tool. You can either create this scene on your own or use the 7arm file on your CD-ROM.

1. With your project open, try moving the joint up and down (drag-select the bottom IK handle, and then use the Move tool to move it—and the arm—up and down). You will notice that although the bound skin moves with the joints, the elbow area doesn't respond correctly—it needs to crinkle just a bit more.

2. Select the cylinder and open the Paint Skin Weights tool (in the Animation menu set, choose Skin ➜ Edit Smooth Skin ➜ Paint Skin Weights Tool ❑). You should see a grayscale image of the cylinder and, in the Skin Paint tab, you will have a choice of your three joints (joint1 at the shoulder, joint2 at the elbow, and joint3 at the wrist). If you select joint1, as in Figure 7.33, the color of the cylinder will show how heavily bound to the shoulder joint each point is. White represents a bind weight of 1, fully affected by any joint motion, and black is a bind weight of 0, not affected at all.

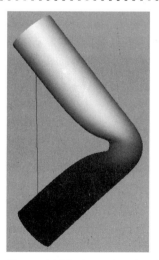

Figure 7.33 *Arm, showing joint1's influence*

If your cylinder is not colored, be sure Color Feedback is on (under the Display tab), and also be sure your scene is set to Shaded mode (press the 5 or 6 key on the keyboard).

3. You can see by looking at the color feedback that the inside of the elbow is very dark when either joint1 or joint2 is selected, indicating it is not being influenced by either joint very much. Let's paint slightly higher values into this area.

4. First, bend the arm some so you can see your results as you work. Next, select joint1 in the Tool Settings window, set your brush mode to Add, set Value to about 0.1, and set Opacity fairly low (like 0.1 or 0.2). Set your brush to a fairly small radius, zoom in on the elbow area, and start painting higher goal weights on, switching between joint1 and joint2, and watching what happens. Your goal is to get a nicer crease between the upper and lower arm here, and setting higher goal weights at and just above (*below* for the elbow joint—joint2) the elbow will increase the joint's influence, making it pull the elbow area into more of a crease.

If your strokes make the elbow area too lumpy, use the Smooth mode to smooth the lumps out—you may not want to smooth out all the lumps, however, because skin does wrinkle as it bends!

Once you have worked a while, you should end up with something like Figure 7.34.

Figure 7.34 *Arm with goal weights adjusted*

The effect here is subtle, but subtlety is what this tool is all about. The difference between the two images above is not great, but the second is far more appealing and realistic than the first—and getting this elbow bend without the Paint Skin Weights tool would be very difficult and time-consuming. Once again, Artisan makes a difficult, painstaking task a lot easier.

Summary

This chapter has presented all the Artisan tools and, while the review was fairly brisk, you should have a good feel for how Artisan works by now. Keep in mind that all the tools operate in a similar manner, but with different options. You may be thinking at this point that virtual painting is something of an art to master (hence the name Artisan), but don't be intimidated. Consider this: how would you accomplish any of the tasks we have done in this chapter without Artisan tools? Only when you imagine working without these tools is their power really evident. Artisan's tools take highly complex tasks that used to require custom programming and/or hours of dull, painstaking work and place all of these jobs in easy reach. Artisan is also highly intuitive, especially if you use a stylus with it: after all, just about anyone understands how paintbrushes work. After reading this chapter, you may save yourself hours of time and frustration if, the next time a job seems too difficult, you try Artisan on the problem.

Mastering Maya 3

Color Gallery

Take a stroll through our gallery to see some of the most creative ways Maya is being used in games, animated films, multimedia theater works, and more. You'll also find rendered versions of many of this book's hands-on projects.

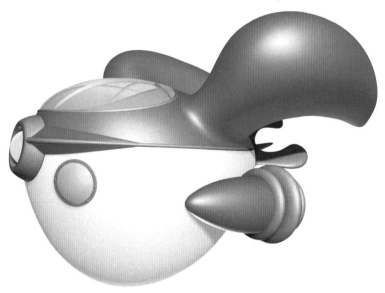

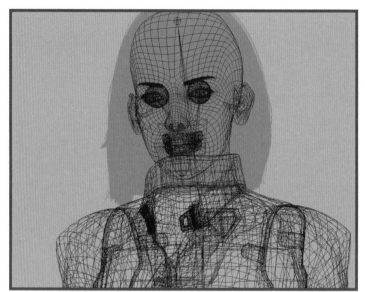

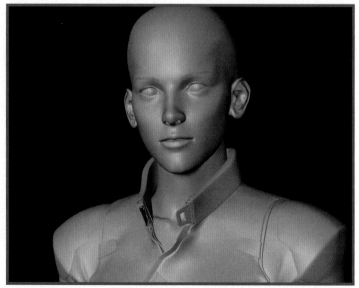

The model of Aki is constructed entirely in Maya. To simulate facial and clothing deformations, a struc-ture of influence objects is created to simulate muscles. Pose changes during animation automatically drive the cloth simulation with minimal adjustments.

Aki's hair is created through a custom Maya simulation plug-in. Dynamic simulation drives panels of geometry to approximate hair collisions with her face and outfit. At render-time, Renderman's curve rendering is used to generate tens of thousands of hair follicles resulting in a dense full head of hair with shadows. Hair is usually composited as a separate layer. Textures are painted in Photoshop and StudioPaint.

The eye and lip images are close-ups of the Aki model. The models are built in Maya and rendered using Renderman. Close attention is paid to the resolution in which the character will be displayed. In these examples, the texture resolutions areas high as 5000 × 5000 pixels for print purposes. A custom skin shader was created to render the flesh.

Bowlin' Fer Souls

The bowling pins, the Devil, and his Cadillac were modeled in Maya. Thanks to Maya's flexible node structure, the modeling, texturing, effects, and character animation were all done simultaneously between the two main artists. MEL scripts were used to automate tasks such as importing/exporting hundreds of shaders between scenes. This efficient Maya pipeline allowed the three-minute animation to be completed in just three months.

*SuperGenius Animation (*www.supergenius3d.com*) is a collective of two, Tim Coleman and Oliver Wolfson. "Bowlin' Fer Souls" is running in Spike and Mike's Sick and Twisted Festival of Animation. Accolades for "Bowlin' Fer Souls" include the 2000 3D Design magazine grand prize "Big Kahuna" award as well as Eveo.com's $25,000 Spring Contest grand prize. A copy of "Bowlin' Fer Souls" is available on the CD-ROM.*

The Puppy

The finished version of the dog begun in Chapter 8 and completed in Chapter 19. This simple puppy was built from NURBS patches, which were assembled using the Stitch tools and bound with Smooth Bind. The textured, constrained, and weighted model is also included in the Chapter 19 Working Files directory on the CD-ROM.

The Living Room

The finished living room scene, built in stages beginning in Chapter 4 and completed in Chapter 19. It includes the furniture, the lamp, the letter M, and the puppy. An Env Sky was used as the environment texture, and glow was applied to selected shaders.

Water Head

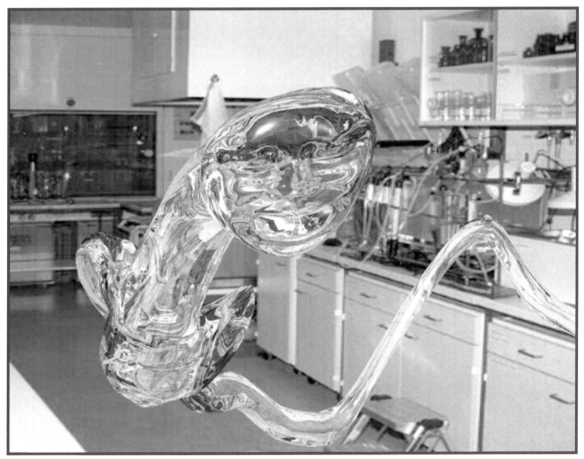

Copyright © 1999 John L. Kundert-Gibbs (head model by Peter Lee)

In this image created by author John Kundert-Gibbs, the pseudopod and head are an example of several concepts from this book, from facial modeling to blendshape animation to soft bodies and texturing. This is an enlarged still from the animation available on the accompanying CD-ROM.

Fountain

The fountain, created by author John Kundert-Gibbs, is a marriage of modeling, dynamics, texturing, raytracing, Paint Effects, and a bit of tricky compositing. Because of the level of complexity in the scene, the three passes required to create this still image took over two hours of rendering on a dual 550MHz Pentium III machine. An animated version of this scene is available on the accompanying CD-ROM.

Telaira

Telaira is Kevin Chu's first attempt at making a human character and was created as a test of his Maya modeling skills. She is made entirely from tweaked NURBS primitives. The fur lining was created with Maya Fur. Kevin is a student of the 3D arts and has devoted the past 14 months to learning Maya.

Mission to Nobody

This still image, taken from the animated short "Mission to Nobody," is from the opening sequence as the girl (Robbie Walker) and robot exit the car and contemplate the battle they are about to engage in. The short is the culmination of a group class project done by University of North Carolina at Asheville students. Elements were rendered in several passes, including a background layer, the car and robot, and the live actress.

The environment was created in 3D Studio Max. Models were created in Maya and then brought into Max (via the .obj format) for texturing and rendering. Live video was shot with a BetaSP camera, digitized, and composited in After Effects.

Production team: Jeff McCoy, Nick Morgan, Michael Bender, Russell Barker, Chris Hewatt, Carl Gibbs, Keoki Trask, and Robbie Walker as "the girl."
Adviser: John Kundert-Gibbs.

Blast Off!

A still frame from the rocket model and animation project in Chapter 2, this shot shows how effective even a simple project can be. By building simple model parts, using some keyframed and some rigid body animation, and the addition of lights, textures, and glowing particles, we've made the cartoon-style rocket appear to leap off the pad for parts unknown.

Floating

The corridor was built by Haeyoung Moon, at Storydale. The lights were used in combination with glow effect, and the glass sections in the walls were created using grid texture and incandescence. The character was lit using area lights exclusively linked to the character to create the long specular highlights.

Stairs at Sunset

The shadows were positioned to create the impression of a sunset. The brick texture was retouched in Photoshop to make the bricks look more random.

Maya Boy

The finished character begun in Chapter 5 and completed in Chapter 19. He was raytraced to create the proper shadows for hair. File images used for color, bump, and specular maps were created using Deep Paint 3D. Texture maps for the body were created by Haeyoung Moon, at Storydale. The textured, constrained, and weighted model is also included in the Chapter 19 Working Files directory on the CD-ROM.

A Dagger of the Mind...

In Shakespeare's Macbeth, *the title character sees a bloody dagger that swims before him, urging him on to kill the current king. An animation of the knife seen here (an excerpt is available on the CD-ROM) was projected onto screens of tobacco cloth (providing a ghost-like effect) during a production of the play at the University of North Carolina at Asheville.*

This knife was modeled using subdivision surfaces, and the particles of blood were animated using forces and constraints so they would "sweat" into existence, and then drip off the edges of the knife.

Search Lights

Copyright ©2000 John L. Kundert-Gibbs

This still image of helicopter search lights pouring over an open field is from an animated background plate, composited under filmed actors, and then displayed behind a live actor. It was used in an adaptation of Harold Pinter's short play, The New World Order, presented at the University of North Carolina at Asheville. The play is an exposition of mental torture, and this televised background, which ran under chromakeyed video of the torturers, was an insight into the imaginings of the tortured man—the live actor—while he was being tortured.

The spot lights were given visible cones of fog, and then animated using expressions guided by keyframed animation. The trees and grass are customized PaintEffects brushes painted directly onto a ground plane.

From the beginning, the overall visual concept for 3-2-1 Penguins was to adhere to a classic 2D aesthetic, while still taking advantage of 3D's qualities of depth and volume. The rich appearance is achieved by relying on building detail through more geometry, rather than added texturing.

The tight schedule and small staff required the development of innovative, time-saving approaches to many aspects of the production process. Lighting has been streamlined through the use of separate rigs applied to each character and location, providing flexibility and freedom from resetting lights for each new camera angle. The chore of adjusting the rim-light-to-camera angle from shot to shot is automated, yet adjustable, and the majority of the lighting setup is quickly and easily tweaked. The custom character UI,created with MEL scripting, allows the artist to work intuitively with selected parts of the character while concurrently viewing the animation curves and timeline ticks of other, unselected pieces.

Basement

Glows were added to the staircase and the walls to imitate a sunny day above in contrast to the dark basement.

Mason & Dixie

These mushrooms are in the process of auditioning for parts in a fictional TV show. The characters are both made with NURBS surfaces and their movements are controlled by expressions and set-driven keys. The most difficult part of creating these characters was developing a way to attach the eyes to the body in such a way that body deformations did not deform the eyes. With high-level controls on the characters, and using the Trax editor, the animation process is greatly simplified.

Production team: Jonathan Fischoff, James D Lee, Charmie Tate, and Andrew Shearer.
Adviser: John Kundert-Gibbs.

Organic Modeling

MAYA

Chapter 8

The types of modeling covered in previous chapters—
NURBS, polygons, and subdivision surfaces—are techniques
based on specific Maya tools and their underlying math.
Organic modeling, by contrast, is a process that embraces various
techniques and is defined by its subject matter: organic forms, especially people and animals. These forms are typically more complex
than mechanical forms, and they usually deform as they move,
which makes this chapter a fitting preparation for the animation
techniques that follow in Part III. Topics include:

- Isoparm selection and insertion
- Surface division into patches
- Stitching preparations
- Parameter rebuilding
- Stitching tools
- Mirroring and attaching techniques
- Hands-on Maya: building a character III (advanced)

This is a fun chapter. It demonstrates the various organic modeling procedures by working through two projects. First is a real-life project, in which we will build a NURBS dog from scratch to finish. Then, for the advanced hands-on Maya tutorial, we will complete the third and final part of the character modeling project. This more advanced tutorial uses a combination of subdivision surfaces, polygons, and NURBS techniques. Hands-on exercises are the best way to get down to the nitty-gritty details of organic modeling.

At the same time, this is a difficult chapter. The time required to build these models will vary depending on your skill level and familiarity with organic modeling, but you shouldn't build the whole dog, for example, in one session. It is also important to keep in mind that you are not producing a work of art at this point. Focus on learning the tools and techniques of organic modeling. (And you can always use the prepared model found on the accompanying CD instead of building it from scratch.)

As with any real-life project, things may get messy as you work your way through this chapter. It is important to practice good work habits. Save your work often, name things carefully, and take regular breaks to clear your head. Always consider *why* you are doing each step, instead of blindly working through them. You will learn much more that way.

Laying the Groundwork for Modeling

One of the *worst* ways to start your modeling process is to plunge in without knowing how you want your model to look. Such an approach will make your work sloppy and waste valuable time. For our work, we'll use a sketch of a puppy (Figure 8.1) as a background image.

Figure 8.1 *A reference sketch for the modeling project*

The next thing we need to know is what this dog is going to be doing. Let's say the dog will be walking or running, so we only need to concern ourselves with the movements of the dog related to those specific actions. (Walking and running are fairly easy to set up.) If the dog were also to move in more complicated ways, such as sitting or rolling on the ground, then we would need to build the dog accordingly to account for those movements as well.

In studio productions, models are not considered complete until they have gone through many extreme poses to test their suitability for animation. The designer may need to modify the model if it fails to hold its shape under certain extreme poses at the testing stage. In some cases, different versions of the model may be required for different animation situations.

Building the Head and Body

Let's start at the top, with the head and body. Building a good body piece with the minimum number of isoparms and proper isoparm distribution is important, as it will influence the shape and the placement of the legs.

1. Create a new scene and go to side view. To bring in the image of the dog from the accompanying CD, in the window panel, select View ➜ Camera Attribute Editor, go to Environment and click the Image Plane Create button. You can use the Image Name field to browse for the image puppy_sketch.tif on the CD.

2. Create a NURBS sphere, rotate it 90 degrees in the X axis, and scale it out. Go to the Channel box, open makeNurbSphere1, and set Sections to 10 and Spans to 20. Translate the sphere to about where the puppy's body is, as shown next. Delete the history of the NURBS sphere by applying Edit ➜ Delete By Type ➜ History.

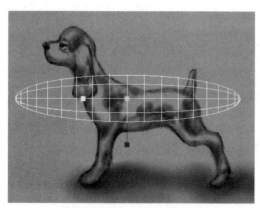

If you find the image plane too bright, you can darken the picture by lowering the Color Gain setting in the Image Plane Attributes section of the Attribute Editor.

3. Pick-mask the sphere's CVs or hulls and transform them using translate, rotate, and scale procedures to get the same profile form as the dog in the picture. Space the isoparms as shown and explained below.

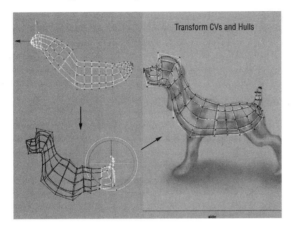

Transform CVs and Hulls

The Face Two rows of CVs should do for the nose area, because we will place a sphere for the nose later. Also, since we are not including eyelids or a mouth, we can use a minimum number of isoparms for the face—three rows of CVs will do.

The Body Use three rows of CVs for the back of the head and the neck, and three more for the chest area. Use one row for the stomach area, and three rows for the back leg area. Note that the stomach shape is actually created by three rows of CVs; the row for the stomach area works together with the last row of the chest area and the beginning row of the back leg area.

The Tail Two rows "tie" the tail to the back of the torso, and two more make the tail curve tightly toward the end. The last three rows shape the endpoint of the tail—they are one more than we need, so select the third row of CVs from the end of the tail and press the Delete key to remove it. Scale the last two rows out to fit the profile of the tail.

It's important that the deformed NURBS sphere has no history when you delete its row of CVs. Otherwise, upon deletion of the CVs, the whole shape of the object will change.

4. Switch to a two-view layout by selecting Window ➔ View Arrangement ➔ 2 Side by Side (you can also use the marking menu and select Panels ➔ Layouts ➔ 2 Side by Side). Make one window perspective view and the other top view.

5. Select hulls again, and scale in the X axis to make the shape look more like a puppy. The hulls may be scaled in the Y or Z axis as well, to fine-tune the profile shape. You should end with something like the shape shown below.

Use the arrow keys to go up and down the UV parameters with the selection of CVs. This technique is especially useful when you are selecting hulls.

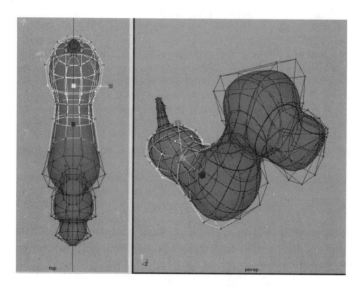

Cutting Up the Body

Now that we've defined the basic shape of the head and body, things are going to get a bit more complicated. To add legs, we need to make holes for them, which means we need to cut the body into pieces. But first, we need to put in more isoparms in select places for smoother stitching later on.

How Many CVs Do You Need?

As you are building your model, always ask yourself how many CVs you need to get the shape you want. Remember, it takes only three CVs to curve a line. It follows that only three rows of CVs are needed to curve a surface. When you study models with this rule in mind, it's surprising to see how often unnecessary isoparms are placed for simple curvatures on surfaces.

You might want to add one more row to "tie" a curve, making it very tight and edgy. Another way to tighten a curve is to increase the CV weights, instead of adding more CVs. The drawback to this technique is that sometimes the weight information gets lost when models are transferred to other programs.

Be a minimalist when you are starting out. The fewer CVs you have, the easier it is to control the surface area. You can easily insert more isoparms to refine your model, but it is more difficult to get rid of them without disturbing what you've already built. Having fewer CVs also lets you concentrate on the big blocks of the model you are creating and ignore the details, which is a good drawing and sculpting principle to follow.

Selecting and Inserting Isoparms

To insert isoparms, you need to select existing isoparms and specify where you want to put the new ones.

1. In perspective view, select the Select tool from the Minibar. Pick-mask Isoparm and click the first vertical isoparm going around the nose area. In the Help line (below the Command line), you should read "U Isoparm 19.000." When you select the next isoparm, it should say "U Isoparm 18.000," and so on.

2. Click the horizontal isoparm around the eye level. You should see "V Isoparm 9.000" in the Help line. The isoparm around the mouth level should be "V Isoparm 1.000," and so on. If your isoparms show opposite numbers, such as 1.000 in place of 19.000, you can reverse the parameter values by selecting Edit Surfaces ➔ Reverse Surface Direction ❑, setting the Surface Direction to V, and then clicking the Reverse button.

When selecting isoparms, if the number ends neatly, such as 1.000 or 1.25, it usually means you have selected the proper isoparm. If the number ends not so neatly, such as 9.01 or 15.476, it usually means you've missed the isoparm. One way to be sure is to select any U or V isoparm near the isoparm you want, and then enter the exact value for the isoparm in the numeric input field in the far right corner of the Status line. To do this, you need to switch from selection mode to numeric input mode.

3. Shift+click U isoparms 13, 12, and 11. Then choose Edit Surfaces ➜ Insert Isoparms ❏, select Between Selections, and click Insert. You should see two U isoparms inserted: 12.5 and 11.5.

4. Repeat the procedure for V isoparms 7 and 8 to insert an isoparm 7.5.

5. Insert three isoparms between V isoparms 2 and 3 to get 2.25, 2.5, and 2.75. The inserted isoparms should be placed as shown below.

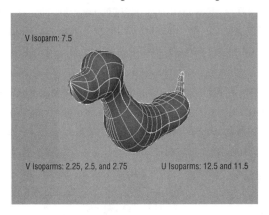

Dividing the Surface into Patch Regions

Now we're going to cut the puppy in pieces. Yes, this seems cruel, but it will help us a great deal in reducing the amount of work we need to do.

1. Select the V isoparms 2.5 and 7.5, and then choose Edit Surfaces ➜ Detach Surfaces. Delete the right half. The image should look like the one shown below.

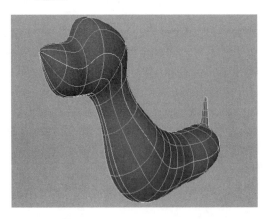

2. Select the V isoparms that will be cut to create the holes for the legs shown below. (The V isoparm values may be either 2.375 and 1.875 or 2.25 and 1.25, depending on the way you split the body into two pieces.) Choose Edit Surfaces ➜ Detach Surfaces again to detach those areas. Now there are three pieces. We need to divide these into 15 separate regions.

3. Select the U isoparms 12.5, 11.5, 9, and 7 along the three pieces and detach them. You may want to do this in several steps. Get rid of the patches where the legs will be. We end up with two holes and 13 patches.

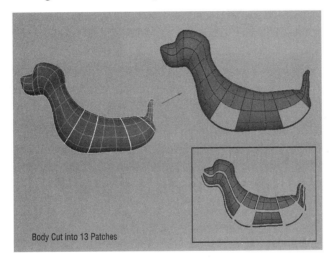

Body Cut into 13 Patches

4. This is a good place to pause and clean up. Group the 13 pieces and name them if you wish. If you haven't saved the file yet, do so now. While you are in the middle of building a model, the object names and their groupings are simply for your own convenience, and they don't need to be organized too carefully. The scene name, however, should describe what you've done, such as Dog_13pieces, or where you are in the modeling stage, such as Dog_model_1.

It is simplest to rename objects in the Outliner. Just double-click the node and type in the name. When you are naming a series of nodes, such as obj1, obj2, obj3, and so on, you can also copy one name and paste it repeatedly—the numbers will be updated automatically.

After you've cut up the surface, the smaller patches retain the parameter values they had before they were detached. They must be parameterized again using Rebuild Surfaces before you can apply stitching. If you don't do this, the results will be unpredictable. We will deal with this a little later in the chapter, in the "Rebuilding Parameters" section.

Building the Legs

Because we are now dealing with only half of the puppy's body, we need to come up with just one front leg and one back leg. Later, we'll duplicate these to add the other two legs.

1. Create a layer, name it Dog Body, and assign the 13 patches to it. We can hide them or turn them into templated objects later when we are working with the legs.

2. Create a sphere and set its spans to 20. Detach it in the middle to get a half sphere with 10 spans. Delete the top half. Use move, rotate, and scale procedures to transform the bottom half to the position shown below.

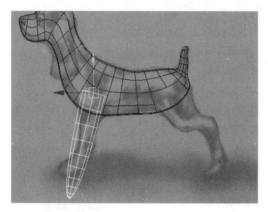

3. Select hulls and build the leg in side view (in the same way that we built the profile of the dog's body). Note the way that the rows of CVs are distributed in the side view shown next. Then scale the leg to the proper size in the X axis in the perspective view or the front view.

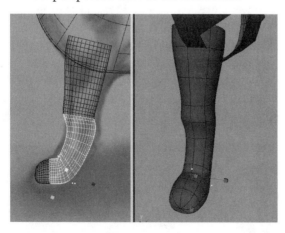

4. Move the leg to where it should be on the dog, a bit to the side, and tweak the CVs to place the top opening of the leg near where the hole is on the dog's body, as shown below. It is important to try to place the two spans of the leg geometry next to the two spans of the hole on each side, so they will stitch smoothly. How well the leg is being positioned for stitching with the body pieces involves some guesswork. After you gain some experience in stitching, your guesses will become more accurate.

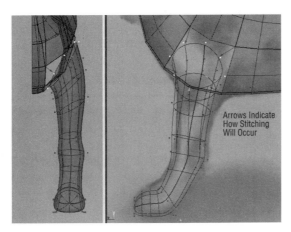

Arrows Indicate
How Stitching
Will Occur

Typing in numbers to position items is often not possible when you are building models. Organic modeling in particular is both fun and frustrating at the same time because you need to trust your artistic sense more and "guesstimate," as opposed to being precise. Do not think of guessing as being sloppy. It is doing things roughly now, knowing that you will be tweaking later.

5. Create a layer and name it Dog Legs. Assign the front leg to it and turn off its visibility.

6. Build the back leg the same way you created the front leg. Ten spans of isoparms are enough. You now should have something similar to the illustration shown below. Notice how the isoparms are placed around the joints as you are moving the hulls and the CVs. Also, the top end of the back leg is a bit higher and farther back than the hole on the body. This was done intentionally in preparation for stitching.

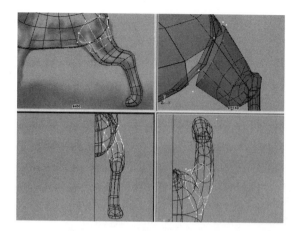

7. As a final step, we need to cut the legs into four pieces. Select V isoparms 1, 3, 5, and 7 and detach them. For both the front and the back legs, the isoparm values should be the same. Group them accordingly, name them, and assign them to the Dog_Legs layer.

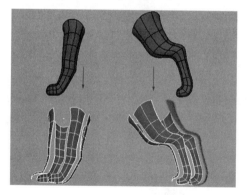

Rebuilding the Parameters

Now that we have the patches all built, we are almost ready to stitch them together. However, first we need to rebuild the parameters. Currently, the smaller patches still have the same parameter values they had before they were detached. We need to reparameterize so that we can have the proper calculations between the patches for stitching.

1. Select Edit Surfaces ➔ Rebuild Surfaces and make sure the settings are as below. The Keep CVs box should be checked. Don't close this dialog box.

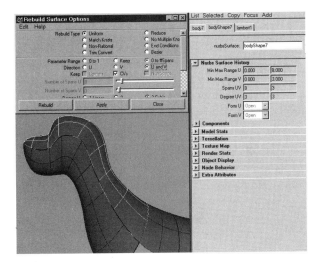

2. In the modeling window, press Ctrl+A to open the Attribute Editor. Select the top patch of the dog's head, and look at the Nurbs Surface History of the geometry. In the Spans UV field, the values are 8 and 3, but the Min Max Range for U and V have different numbers. We need to reparameterize the patch to get the Max Range numbers to match the Span values.

3. Select all the geometry pieces in the modeling window and click Rebuild. You should see slight changes in the isoparm placements. Although the changes may seems insignificant, they are necessary for proper calculations between the patches to take place. Select the dog's top head patch again. The Max numbers for UV should now match the corresponding Span values.

Stitching the Model

The next stage of building our puppy model will be to stitch together the parts we've created. Stitching involves a set of Maya techniques and tools that we haven't used in earlier exercises, so before we continue, let's take a brief break from building the puppy and see how stitching works in Maya.

Stitching Basics

Maya has three types of stitching available from the Edit Surfaces ➜ Stitches submenu: Stitch Surface Points, Stitch Edges Tool, and Global Stitch. We will use the Stitch Edges tool to put together the different parts of the dog and continue to shape its body, and then use the Global Stitch function to keep the patches seamless.

Stitching Surface Points

Stitch Surface Points is a simple tool used to join CV points from different surfaces. To use this type of stitching, select one CV you want to stitch from each of the surfaces and apply Stitch Surface Points. The points should snap together, meeting each other halfway as shown on the left side of Figure 8.2.

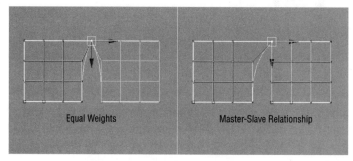

Figure 8.2 *Two ways of stitching surface points*

Another way to use Stitch Surface Points is to open its option window and turn off the Assign Equal Weights setting. Then, when you select CVs and apply the stitching, the first point will stay where it is, and the other points will snap to the first point, as on the right side of Figure 8.2. The points in this setting are said to be in a *master-slave relationship*. The point that does not move is the master, and the point that moves is the slave.

Stitching Edges

The Stitch Edges tool is used to join two surface edges together. The default setting joins the edges in a master-slave relationship, as shown in the upper half of Figure 8.3. When you open the option window for this tool, you will see that Weighting Factor On Edge1 is set to 1 and Weighting Factor On Edge2 is set to 0. This means the first edge isoparm you picked will not move, and the second edge isoparm you picked will snap to the first edge, as in the top right of the figure. If you want to apply equal weighting for both edges so that they will both move to meet in the middle, adjust the Weighting Factor settings to 0.5 for both edges, as shown at the bottom left. The edges will then meet halfway, as shown on the bottom right.

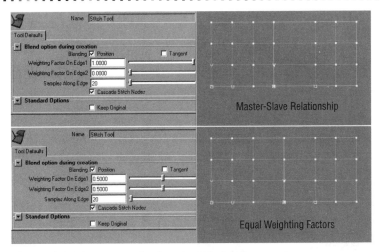

Figure 8.3 *Two ways of using the Stitch Edges tool*

Global Stitching

Global Stitch can stitch all of the edges of adjacent surfaces together. It automatically gives all the surface edges being stitched equal weights, and holds the pieces together like rubber. For Global Stitch, the edges of the surfaces must be closer together than the Max Separation setting in the options, or it will not apply to the surfaces correctly.

For both the Stitch Edges tool and the Global Stitch function, you have the option of maintaining C0 continuity or C1 continuity, also known as tangent continuity, between the stitched edges. See Chapter 5, "NURBS Modeling," for more information about the degrees of continuity.

Stitching between Two Edges

Now it's time to put the pieces of the dog together into a seamless whole. For the following procedures, you may want to get into the wireframe or the x-ray viewing mode, because either of these modes makes it easier to pick isoparms. To switch to the x-ray viewing mode, go to the modeling window and select Shading ➜ Shade Options ➜ X-Ray.

First, we'll attach the legs to the dog's body by stitching the leg edges.

1. In perspective view, select the front leg and press the F key to center the geometry so that you can rotate around it. Select Edit Surfaces ➜ Stitch ➜ Stitch Edges Tool ❑ and click the Reset Tool button to make sure you're using the default settings. Then check the Tangent setting and close the option window.

2. Select the top-edge isoparm (it's also called a *surface boundary* isoparm) of the leg patch. Then select the patch edge located at the top side of the hole. The patch edge should snap to the leg patch, and the two patches should turn bright green. (You don't need to press Enter to complete the stitching process at this point.)

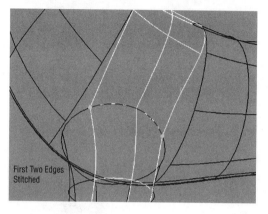

First Two Edges Stitched

3. Go to the next boundary isoparm of the leg and repeat the stitching with the side edge of the hole.

4. Repeat the process with the next two edges. You should have a cross shape of green patches coming out from the body to the leg patches, as shown below.

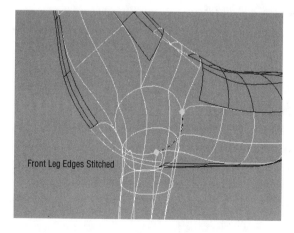

Front Leg Edges Stitched

5. Press Enter to complete the action.

In addition to pressing Enter to complete the stitching action, you can press any of the tool hotkeys, such as Q for the selection mode. To repeat the stitch action, press Y.

6. Repeat the procedure with the back leg, as shown below. Make sure to select the leg boundary isoparm first and the body boundary isoparm second, because the order of selection determines the master-slave relationship. The slave edge snaps to the master edge, and it is important that the leg patches function as master edges.

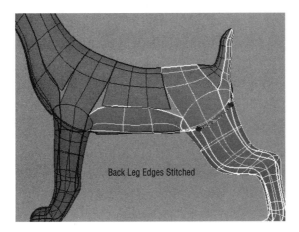

Back Leg Edges Stitched

Stitching the Corners

So far, we've stitched seven body patches to the legs. There are still six corner patches that need to be stitched. Let's try stitching one of the head patches as an example.

1. To stitch the top patch of the dog's head to the adjacent patches, select Edit Surfaces ➜ Stitch ➜ Stitch Edges Tool (leave the default settings). Select the boundary edge of one of the adjacent patches, and then select the edge of the head patch, as shown below on the left. Complete the action by pressing Enter. Then repeat the procedure with the other adjoining patch as shown below on the right. Even though the head patch may look like it is lined up after the first stitching, you still need to stitch it to the second adjacent patch to make sure that the patches are lined up properly.

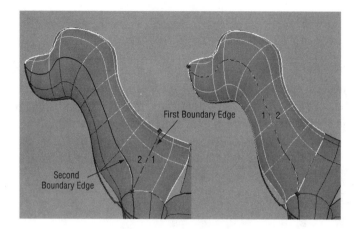

2. Repeat the procedure to stitch the corners on the other five patches. Following is an example of one of the patches that must be stitched three times. The patch represented as number 2 needs to be stitched to three other number 1 patches. Pick the number 1 patch boundary isoparms first each time, and then select the boundary isoparm of the number 2 patch being stitched.

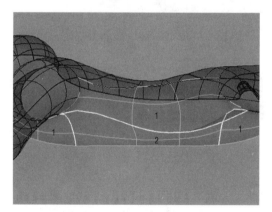

Tweaking the Stitched Surfaces

When you look at the final stitched surface in shaded mode, you will probably notice creases. The places where the creases occur and their severity will vary with how you've built your own model. At this point, yours should look similar to the model shown below. Unfortunately, there is no easy way to get rid of these creases.

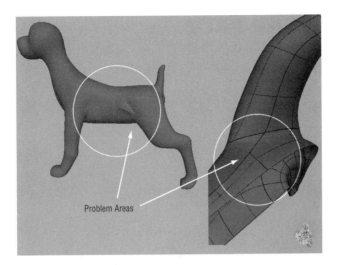

Where the stomach meets the back leg, the isoparm has actually folded (as shown on the right side above). In such situations, you need to tweak the CVs of the master edges (the leg patches in our example) to get rid of the creases. Shown below are some of the ways CVs have been pulled and rotated to correct the problems. Generally, you should move two CVs from the master edge to keep control of the surface tangency. Where the four patches are being joined at the corner as in the top-left picture, you may want to move the four CVs on each of the two master patches, eight CVs in all, together in order to maintain their tangency. When you move the CVs on the master edges, the slave edges will follow to keep the tangent continuity between the surfaces.

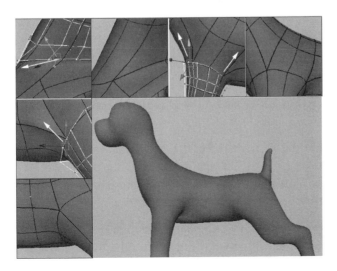

Building the Face

In contrast to the elaborate modeling that went into building the body, we'll keep the dog's face simple. Use spheres for the eyes, nose, and ears, as shown next.

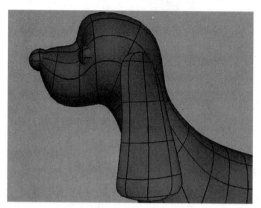

Place the eye and the nose in the appropriate positions, and pull in a couple of the CVs on the head to make room for the eye (but don't touch the two end CVs along the boundaries). You can create the ear by deforming the hulls of another sphere.

Mirroring and Attaching the Model

Mirroring is a common modeling technique. As its name implies, mirroring duplicates the selected items as a mirror image of the original items along a selected axis. Again, the symmetry of human and animal bodies means that we can take advantage of mirroring to greatly reduce the work of modeling such a body. We will use mirroring to duplicate the right half of the puppy.

1. Select all the objects in the modeling window except for the nose. Group them. This sets up the surfaces for mirroring because the pivot point for the group node is at the origin. Select Edit ➜ Duplicate ❏, set Scale X to –1, and click Duplicate. You should have a mirrored group of objects.

2. You now see the whole model of the dog. Before you attach the middle patches, make sure you like what you see. Are the body parts proportional? Are the legs too close or too far apart? If you want to modify any parts of the dog, undo the duplication and make the necessary changes before continuing.

3. When you are satisfied with the way everything looks, select the edge isoparms of all the patches that meet at the middle, or the Y axis, and attach them using

the default settings. You should end up with ten attached pieces making up the profile of the puppy.

The left side patches of the puppy are still stitched together, while the right side patches are not. This is fine, because the modeling is now all done, and we no longer need the stitches. Your puppy at this point should look as shown below.

Cleaning Up the Model

Now we can clean up our model by deleting the history and the transformation information. We can also group the model parts. Note that in our particular project, the history and the transformation information of the patches are no longer needed, so we can delete them. In other situations, however, this information may be important. For example, you may want to animate a complex object procedurally, by controlling a simpler node that carries the history or the transformation information of the complex object. So, you'll need to decide whether to delete or retain this information on a case-by-case basis.

1. Select all the patches in the modeling window and select Edit ➜ Delete By Type ➜ History.

2. Select Modify ➜ Freeze Transformations.

3. Group the legs and name them. Give the group nodes sensible names, such as Front_Legs, or L_frontleg. You may not feel you need to name the leaf nodes. However, it is a good idea to rename everything, rather than leaving a node named something like leg33detachedSurface2detachedSurface2.

4. Group the body and the face, renaming them appropriately.

5. Put the face and body pieces into the Dog_Body layer. Put the leg pieces into the Dog_Legs layer.

Globally Stitching the Model

Finally, we should apply global stitching to the puppy. Unlike regular stitching, global stitching doesn't have a master-slave distinction; all the pieces are held together with equal weight. When we were building the model, we needed the control provided by the regular stitch; namely, the master-slave relationship of the edges being stitched. Now that the model is put together seamlessly with first-order continuity (C1) among the patches, we can easily stitch all the pieces together with one command.

1. Select all the pieces except for the face objects, and then select Edit Surfaces ➔ Stitch ➔ Global Stitch ❑.

2. Click Reset to set everything to the default settings. Then click Global Stitch. Now if you move any of the patches, you will notice that they behave like rubber, stretching to keep themselves together.

3. The model is now ready to be set up for animation. Save the final scene as dog_model.mb. You can find this finished version in the Chapter 8 Color Gallery on the CD.

The puppy was built in NURBS to illustrate the patch modeling techniques. It would be easy for us to take the NURBS puppy at this point and turn it into a subdivision surface puppy, using the same techniques that were used in building a character's head in the previous chapter.

Hands-On Maya: Building a Character III (Advanced)

In Chapter 5 we began the project of building a character, a young boy, using NURBS modeling techniques to create the face. Then, in Chapter 6, "Polygons and Subdivision Surfaces," we continued the project using polygons and subdivision surfaces to finish building the head. In this tutorial, we will combine various techniques to create the character's body, hands, feet, and hair.

1. We are going to take advantage of subdivision surfaces again to build a seamless body, using basically the same techniques that were used for building the

head. First build a rough outline of the body with a cylinder as below, with 15 U spans and 12 V spans. Cut it in half, keep the left side, and add another V isoparm to where the arm will attach. The selected surface patches on the right below will be where the arm will attach. The number of spans will be 3 for top and bottom and 2 for front and back, so the arm should have 10 spans to fit the body cleanly.

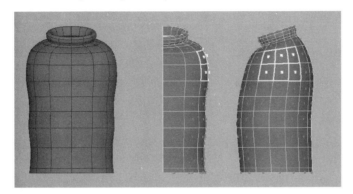

2. Convert the body to polygons, and delete the six faces where the arm will attach. You may also want to delete unnecessary faces at the bottom or the top. Roughly tweak the vertices to make the hole round, as on the left below. Build the arm from another cylinder, with 10 U spans and about 10 V spans for the length of the arm. Place the arm near the hole on the body as on the right below, convert it to polygons, and then combine the two surfaces.

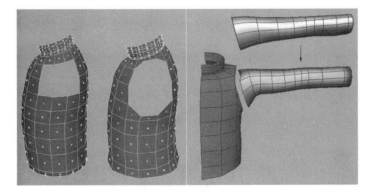

3. Once the two are combined, they can be merged using the Merge Edge tool. Once the arm has been attached, more tweaking is needed. For the hand, we can use the smoothed polygon hand we built in Chapter 6, but for the purposes of this tutorial, let's also make a subdivision surface hand. Either one will work well, although

for close-up shots of the hand, the subdivision surface hand would render more smoothly. Take the polygon hand before smoothing, and edit the edges and vertices to turn all faces into quadrangles, as below. You can put in extra edges where the fingernails will go, and then use Full Crease Edge/Vertex command to create sharp edges around the fingernails as in the third hand below.

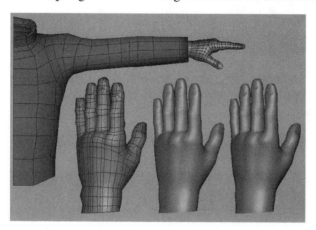

4. The leg is a bit tricky. Start with a cylinder. Down the length of the leg could be about 14 or 15 U spans, and around the leg should be 10 V spans. Deform the CVs to make it look like half of the lower torso and the leg, as on the left below. Turn the cylinder into polygons using the Control Points setting, delete the extra edges and vertices at the middle, and select the top four faces. See how the hole that would be created from deleting the four faces matches up with the body.

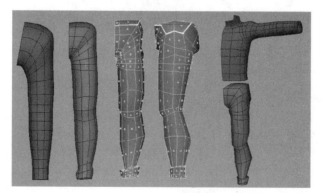

5. Because the body has three faces for the side but the leg only has two for its side, it needs one more edge to match the body. Split three of the faces as in the second image below. Because one of the top faces now has five vertices, when

the top four faces are deleted, the leg now has an open space with nine edges. Tweak the vertices to make it look more like the last leg below. The leg should now match up cleanly edge for edge with the body.

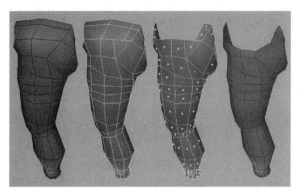

6. Combine the body and the leg; then merge them. You'll see the image on the left below. Tweak the vertices, taking care to raise the waist line and pushing the circle of the shoulder line further into the body, as in the middle image below. Mirror the body, merge the edges, and tweak more until you are satisfied with the way the body looks. Convert the polygons into subdivision surfaces to get something that looks like the right image below.

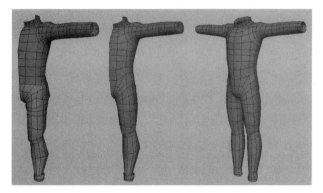

If the Create Subdivisions command gives you an error message and does not convert the polygon, the polygon count may be too high. In that case, go to the option window and increase the value of Maximum Base Mesh Faces. Or it could mean there are winged vertices that you forgot to delete.

7. You can go back and forth at any time between polygons and subdivision surfaces, work with half a body for a while, and then mirror and merge again. You should also fit the head into the neck area by scaling the body and tweaking the vertices. To put the finishing touch to the body, select the top nine faces on the shoulder area, as shown on the left below, and then extrude them twice. When converted to subdivision surfaces, the extrusion becomes a shoulder pad, as shown on the right.

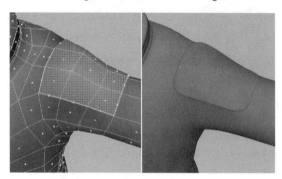

8. The shoes and hair are left to model. Start with a NURBS sphere and get a rough shape of the shoe. Convert it to polygons, and edit the tip of the shoe to get rid of the pole as in (a) below. Extrude to create the bottom part, as in (b). Look carefully at how the edges have been edited to create quadrangles in (c) below. The areas where the edges are placed closely together are there to get sharp edges. Extrude the top two rows of faces twice to get more detail, as in (d). Convert to subdivision surfaces and tweak the top area to fit around the ankle, as in (e).

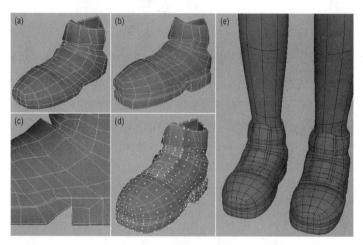

9. Finally, the hair on our character is composed of many simple NURBS strips. Try to place them as if they were tufts of hair, and layer them so you won't see any "bald" spots from any normal camera angle. In Chapter 19, "Shading and Texturing Surfaces," we will texture them with transparency maps to simulate hair strands.

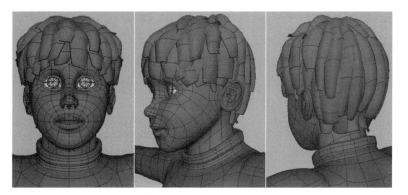

The character model is now done. You can see the final version of the model (`character_model.mb`) in the Working Files folder and a rendered image in the color insert section of the book. The next step is to set up the character for animation, and then bring him to life.

Summary

In this chapter, we stepped through building a complicated patch model of a dog, from scratch to finish. In addition to learning one specific method of building a dog in patches, we also covered the concepts and techniques for building complex models in general. These techniques included rebuilding surfaces, mirroring and attaching parts, and stitching to create seamlessness.

We also finished our character modeling project, building a seamless body, arms, and legs, with simple shoes and what will hopefully be considered stylish hair. We will come back to our models for character setup tutorials in Chapter 13, "Character Animation Exercises."

Part III

Animation

n Part III, you will learn all about animating in Maya. To make things move and come alive inside the computer—that is what a computer animator does. In the following seven chapters, you will cover the basics of keyframe animation, and you'll learn to animate with paths, skeletons, and deformers. You will also learn to bind surfaces using different methods, set up a character hierarchy for animation, and then practice different ways to make that character come alive by applying various principles of animation and by using a new feature in Maya 3, the Trax Editor. You will also be introduced to ways of realistically simulating physical forces acting on objects using rigid bodies.

Animating in Maya

MAYA

Chapter 9

This chapter introduces you to animating in Maya. We will go over the fundamental concepts of keyframing in Maya, the various interface controls, and the tools for creating and editing keyframes. The tutorial in this chapter demonstrates how to use Maya's Set Driven Key tool. The techniques you'll learn in later chapters are quite challenging, so be sure to get a firm grasp of the basic tools in this chapter, as they will help you to get through those upcoming chapters more smoothly. Topics include:

- Keyframe animation
- The Time Slider and Range Slider controls
- Techniques for creating keyframes
- Techniques for editing keyframes
- Hands-on Maya: Animating a finger

Keyframe Animation

Animation, at its most basic level, is change over an interval of time. In Maya, almost anything can be changed over time; in other words, almost anything you create in Maya can be animated.

You've learned how Maya has a node-based structure. Any attribute within the node that has a numeric value is *keyable*. Keying, or *keyframing*, in Maya is the act of assigning a numeric value to a node attribute at a specific time frame. As the frames change, so can the attribute value. For example, the basic attribute Visibility actually has a numeric value of either 1 (for on) or 0 (for off), so it can be keyframed and animated.

Keyframing is a concept taken from classic 2D animation. Senior animators draw important "key" poses of characters being animated at certain frame intervals, called *keyframes*. Then the junior animators take over and draw all the frames between the keyframes, which are called *in-betweens*. The same thing happens when you are animating in Maya, as shown in Figure 9.1. You are the senior animator who establishes the key poses of whatever it is you are animating, and the computer is the whole department of junior animators drawing the in-betweens for you.

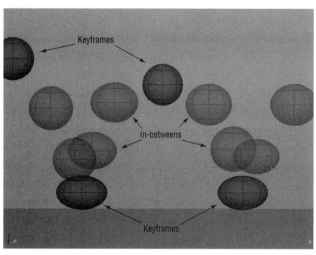

Figure 9.1 *(key poses for sphere with the in-betweens)*

Other kinds of animation you may decide to explore on your own in Maya include rotoscoping, which is actually a kind of keyframe animation, and motion capture, a process of creating function curves from live actors' performances.

Are You an Animator?

There are different levels of animating. At the most basic level, you are moving things from A to B, which almost anyone can do. The next level of animating involves learning and intelligently using certain animation principles, such as squash and stretch, anticipation, key posing, and so on. The 2D cell-animation schools are still the best places to learn these principles, although computer animation schools are beginning to offer classes in this area. If you want to be an animator, there is no way around it—you must learn them.

The ability to bring life to a character, however, requires more than just following animation principles. A successful animator also has a good sense of timing, which belongs to the realm of performance. Timing is a skill you are born with as much as something that is learned, and certain individuals are naturally better at animating than others, just as some people are naturally better dancers or singers than others. In fact, the ability to create authentic emotions and pathos in animated characters requires great acting skills.

A good way to discover whether you are an animator or not is to go through a whole animation project, and ask yourself which parts of the project you enjoy spending time on the most. An animator's focus will generally be different from that of the other 3D artists. Modelers and texture artists, for example, are usually interested in how things look; they want to create beautiful images, evoking certain feelings. Animators are usually most interested in telling a good story.

Animation Controls

Before we go further into keyframing, let's look at some animation control tools: the Time Slider and the Range Slider. These and the other tools discussed in this chapter are in Maya's Animation module.

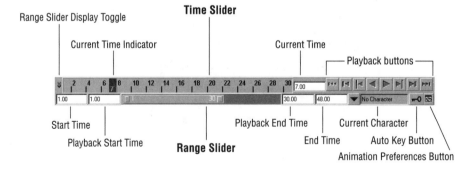

Playing Back and Updating Animations with the Time Slider

The Time Slider comes with playback buttons, which look like those on a video player control panel. You can also use the following hotkeys to control the playback:

Alt+V   Toggles between play and stop

Esc   Stops the playback

. (period)   Moves to the next keyframe

, (comma)   Moves to the previous keyframe

Alt+. (period)   Moves to the next frame

Alt+, (comma)   Moves to the previous frame

You can click or drag in the Time Slider to do various things. When you click a frame number, that frame becomes the current time. If you drag the mouse, the animation updates interactively, which is called scrubbing. Scrubbing is great for viewing animation if the scene is light, as the object(s) being animated will update almost real-time, but it loses its effectiveness as the scene becomes heavier.

When you MM click or drag, the current time indicator moves to where the mouse is without updating the animation. This is a valuable function when you want to quickly keyframe the values of one frame to other frames. MM dragging is also used for scrubbing only the audio, as opposed to scrubbing the whole scene.

The Time Slider can also become a virtual Time Slider inside the modeling window, the Graph Editor, or the Dope Sheet. To display it this way, press the K key at the same time you press the mouse buttons. By K+dragging in any window, you can scrub the animation. By K+MM dragging, you can move the current time without updating the scene, and scrub only the audio. This technique can be especially useful when you are editing function curves in the Graph Editor. The Graph Editor and Dope Sheet are discussed later in this chapter, when we get to the topic of editing keyframes.

RM choosing inside the Time Slider opens the Key Edit menu. This menu offers the standard key-editing functions, which we will discuss later in the chapter in the "Editing Keyframes" section. It also provides access to several useful submenus:

- With the Set Range To submenu, you can control the playback range in various ways. One option here is the Sound Length setting, which you can also use to discover the length of an audio file.

- With the Sound submenu, you can show, hide, or rename any of the audio files that have been imported.

- With the Playblast function, you can preview your animation as real-time movie clips (the Playblast function is discussed in Chapter 10, "Paths and Bones").

In order to play an audio file, you need to set the Playback Speed setting to Normal in Animation Preferences, found under Options → General Preferences.

Controlling the Playback Range with the Range Slider

The Range Slider is a simple tool used to control the playback range of the Time Slider. You can set where the Time Slider starts and ends by sliding, shortening, or lengthening the Range Slider, and hide it by toggling the Range Slider Display button at the left of the Time Slider.

The Auto Key button on the Range Slider (the next-to-last item on the slider) lets you set keys automatically as you transform the selected object in the modeling window. Using Auto Key for keyframing is explained in the "Creating Keyframes" section of this chapter.

The Animation Preferences button on the right end of the Range Slider lets you view the animation settings in the Preferences dialog box. The animation settings include options that let you adjust the Time Slider. For example, setting the Height to 2× or 4×, as shown below, can help you see the audio waves more clearly, which is helpful when you are scrubbing audio files.

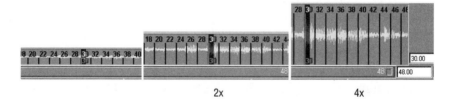

2x   4x

You can also go to the Settings section of the Preferences dialog box and adjust the Time setting under Working Units. The default setting is 24 fps (frames per second).

Creating Keyframes

There are many ways of creating keyframes in Maya. You can use the hotkeys, the Set Key or Set Breakdown function in the Animate menu, the Channel box, the Graph Editor, or the Attribute Editor. All of these methods are described in the following sections.

Using Hotkeys for Keyframing

Several hotkeys are useful for keyframing:

S Keyframes a selected object at a specified frame (same as Animate ➜ Set Key, discussed in the next section)

Shift+W Keys the translations

Shift+E Keys the rotations

Shift+R Keys the scales

Keyframing with Set Key

The standard way to keyframe a selected object at a specified frame is to select Animate ➜ Set Key. In the command's option window, the default setting is Set Keys On All Keyable Attributes. With this setting, when you click the Set Key button in the Set Keys Options dialog box (or press the S hotkey), all the attributes displayed in the Channel box are keyed. This setting may not be practical for situations where you need to set keys to only a few attributes, such as the translation attributes, for example.

Set Key Settings

When you change the Set Keys setting to All Manipulator Handles, all the manipulator values are keyed. When the setting is Current Manipulator Handle, as shown in Figure 9.2, only the active manipulator handle is keyed. This is a useful setting if you want to restrict the keying to the attribute values you are changing, such as the Y-axis translation.

Figure 9.2 *The Set Key Options window*

The Prompt setting lets you set keyframes at multiple frames. If you select Prompt, when you click the Set Key button (or press the S hotkey), you are prompted for the frames to keyframe. Enter the frame numbers you want keyframed and click OK.

Keyable Attributes

All keyable attributes are displayed in the Channel box. The default attributes are Translation, Rotation, Scale, and Visibility.

In Maya, each object can have its own keyable attribute settings. You can add or remove the keyable attributes of an object by using the Channel Control. Select an object, and then choose Window ➜ General Editors ➜ Channel Control to open the dialog box shown in Figure 9.3.

The Channel Control shows a long list of nonkeyable attributes on the right and a list of ten default keyable attributes on the left. When you select an attribute in either list, the Move >> or the <<Move button becomes active, and you can move the selected attribute to make it keyable or nonkeyable. Any changes you make in the Channel Control are reflected in the Channel box. The Channel Control also has a tab for Locked attributes. When an attribute becomes locked, its value becomes static and nonkeyable. The fields for the attribute also become gray.

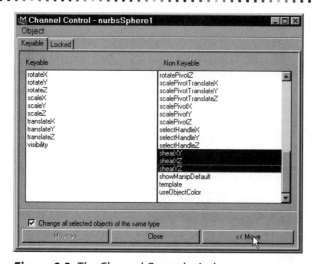

Figure 9.3 The Channel Control window

Some people find using the Channel box to lock attributes easier than the Channel Control or the Attribute Editor.

Keyframing with Set Breakdown

Set Breakdown works the same way as Set Key, except that instead of setting keys, it sets *breakdowns*. What distinguishes breakdown frames from keyframes is that when regular keys are inserted into a breakdown curve, the breakdown frames become "bound" by the regular keys, and the breakdowns maintain a proportional time relationship to those keys.

To get a better idea of how breakdowns differ from keys, you can try the simple exercise in the "Working with Breakdowns" section later in this chapter. First, however, you need to become familiar with some further tools for controlling animation, particularly the Time Slider and the Graph Editor.

Keying Attributes in the Channel Box

You can key different attributes in the Channel box. Select an object, open the Channel box, select any attribute(s), and RM choose over the attribute names. A long menu pops up, offering many key-editing functions.

The Key Selected command keyframes the attributes that are selected in the Channel box. Key All keyframes all the keyable attributes for the selected object. The Breakdown Selected and Breakdown All commands work the same way for breakdowns. The Lock and Unlock commands work on selected attributes.

Keying Attributes in the Attribute Editor

You can also set keys in the Attribute Editor the way you do in the Channel box. A difference is that when you RM choose over the keyable attributes in the Attribute Editor as in Figure 9.4, you don't get as many functions in the menu that pops up.

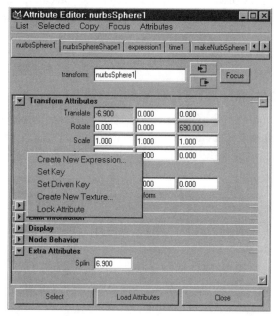

Figure 9.4 *The Attribute Editor with the pop-up menu for a selected attribute*

You can lock attributes and set keys, but the keys are set for all X, Y, Z values of translation, rotation, or scale attributes. One advantage of using the Attribute Editor is that you can easily access nonkeyable attributes and make them keyable using the editor.

Keyframing with Auto Key

Auto Key is an efficient way to keyframe in many situations. When you click the Auto Key button on the right side of the Range Slider, the key icon turns white and the background turns red. Once this feature is turned on, any change you make to the attributes of selected objects at any frame are automatically keyframed. The only precondition with Auto Key is that a keyframe must already exist for an attribute before that attribute can be auto-keyed. The Auto Key button is a toggle; click it again to turn the function off.

As an example of using Auto Key, follow these steps:

1. Create a sphere and set keys for its translation attributes at frame 1.

2. Click the Auto Key button to turn on the function.

3. Move to frame 10, and translate the sphere to a different position. The change is automatically keyframed.

4. Move to frame 20 and try rotating the sphere. Nothing is keyed because there are no initial keyframes for the rotation attributes.

 If you use Auto Key, make sure to toggle it off when you are finished or you may unknowingly keyframe objects and end up with a lot of undesirable animation.

Adding, Deleting and Renaming Attributes

Maya also allows you to create your own custom attributes, and to rename or delete them. To try out this feature, create a sphere and select Modify ➜ Add Attribute to open the dialog box. You can get to the dialog box through the Attribute Editor as well, by opening its Attributes menu at the top of the Attribute Editor window. In the Add Attribute dialog box, the Control tab allows you to create simple new attributes with values ranging from 0 to 1. The New tab gives you control over the new attribute's keyability, data type, and minimum, maximum, and default values, as shown in Figure 9.5.

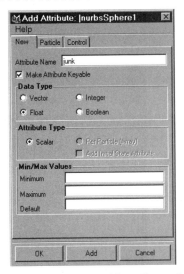

Figure 9.5 *The Add Attribute dialog box*

Make sure the sphere is selected and create an attribute called Junk with the default settings; and you should see the additional attribute for the sphere in the Channel box. The added custom attributes can be very useful in setting up set-driven keys or expressions, as we shall see in the hands-on Maya tutorial later.

You can rename custom attributes with the Modify ➜ Rename Attribute command. You can also delete them by going to the Channel box, RM-clicking next to the custom attribute, and selecting Delete Attributes. (You may need to deselect and select the object again to update the Channel box.) Only the additional custom attributes you assign to nodes can be renamed or deleted, not the built-in attributes that are assigned to nodes by Maya.

Editing Keyframes

After you've created the keys or breakdowns, you can edit them using the Edit ➜ Keys submenu, Channel box, Graph Editor, Dope Sheet, or Time Slider. We will cover the Graph Editor first, because it is the most important keyframe-editing tool, and you will want to use it most often.

Working with Animation Curves in the Graph Editor

When you create a series of keyframes in the Timeline, these keyframes can be represented as function curves, or animation curves, inside the Graph Editor. The Graph Editor works like a regular orthographic window in that you can use hotkeys like A and F for viewing the function curves, the Alt+MM drag to track, and the Ctrl+Alt+LM or MM marquee for zooming. However, the settings for the Move and Scale tools change in important ways when the Graph Editor is the active window.

If you are not familiar with animation curves, the Graph Editor may look complicated to you at first. It is more complex than most other editors in Maya, but it is very important that you learn to work with the Graph Editor and the animation curves. Experienced animators know how to "read" animation curves, visualizing how an object will move differently when the curves are edited a certain way. This alone can often separate the good animators from the bad ones.

To see how the Graph Editor works, let's create some animation curves:

1. Create a sphere. Key translation and rotation animation to it over 30 frames.

2. Using the marking menu hotbox, select Persp/Graph View. The top window should now show perspective view, and the bottom should display the Graph Editor, as in Figure 9.6.

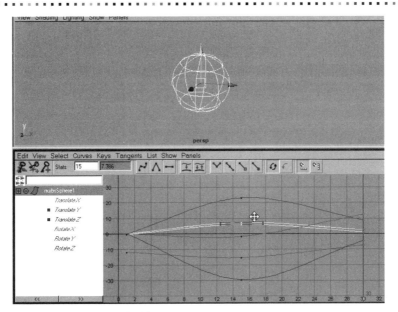

Figure 9.6 *The Graph Editor*

3. Press A to fit all the curves to the window. You should see six animation curves, one for each channel of the six attributes.

4. Marquee-select a few keyframes near the current time indicator. Notice that the graph outliner to the left shows which curve keys were selected. Move them, and you will see the sphere update interactively.

5. You can also work with only the curves you want by selecting those curves in the graph outliner. Select the translate curves, and only those curves are displayed.

6. The options for the Move tool change when it's used inside the Graph Editor. Either double-click the Move tool icon above the Layer bar, or select Modify ➜ Transformation Tools ➜ Move Tool ❏ to open the option window. Then click inside the Graph Editor to make it the active window, and you will see the options change. As shown below, listed under MoveKey Options are moveOnly and moveOver. The default moveOver setting lets you move selected keyframes over other keyframes. The moveOnly setting allows you to move the keyframes only between other keyframes.

7. Open the Scale tool's option window. Again, you'll see settings that are different for the Graph Editor. The default Gestural setting sets the pivot point for scaling the selected keys to where you place the mouse. The Manipulator setting lets you create a box to move and scale, as shown in Figure 9.7. This may be the preferable setting for many situations.

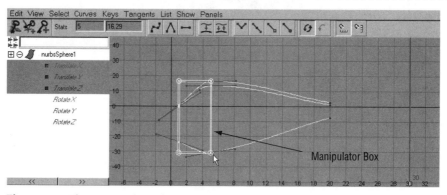

Figure 9.7 *The manipulator box*

Using the Graph Editor Tools

The Graph Editor provides many toolbar tools to help you edit curves.

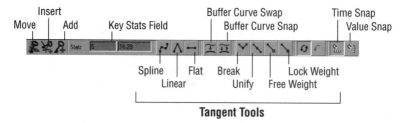

The Time Snap and Value Snap Tools

The Time Snap tool, which makes the keyframes snap to frames, should always be turned on, because it makes editing keyframes so much easier. You will have fewer occasions to use the Value Snap tool, which snaps the keyframes to the nearest integer value of the attribute you are keying. Before moving on to the other tools, turn on Time Snap. Instead of working without the snap function and then needing to snap the keyframes later, it is much better to have the Time Snap tool on from the beginning.

There are Time Snap functions in the Graph Editor, the Dope Sheet, and the Time Slider. You can also access Time Snap in the Preferences dialog box, under Settings → Timeline → Options, where Snapping is On by default.

The Move Nearest Picked Key Tool

The Move tool in the Graph Editor is actually the Move Nearest Picked Key tool, and it works differently than the standard Move tool (above the Layer bar). These two similar yet different tools can sometimes cause frustration if their functions are confused. The Move tool moves all selected keyframes or their tangent handles, while the Move Nearest Picked Key tool moves only one keyframe or tangent handle at a time—the one nearest the mouse pointer. It will not move curves. You can constrain the tool using the Shift key for horizontal or vertical movements, just as you can constrain the regular Move tool.

The Insert Key and Add Key Tools

The Insert Key and Add Key tools are similar. Insert Key inserts a key on the curve at the selected frame. Add Key adds a key to whatever value and frame you are clicking, changing the curve shape accordingly.

The Tangent Tools

The tangent tools let you change the shape of the curve around the keyframes. The Spline (the default shape), Linear, and Flat tools let you pick those shapes. You can see other types on the Tangents menu. Select a few keyframes and play with the types to see how they behave.

In situations where you want to break the tangent or increase the roundness of the curve at specific keyframes, you can use the Unify or Break tool (also available from the Keys menu), with the results shown in Figure 9.8.

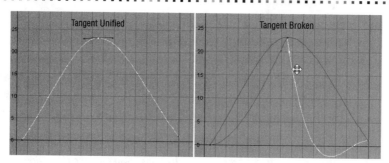

Figure 9.8 *A smooth tangent and a broken tangent*

Before you can free a keyframe's tangent weight and change it, the tangent of the keyframe must become weighted. Select the keyframe (you can also select the entire curve) and select Curves ➜ Weighted Tangents. The tangent handles change as shown on the left in Figure 9.9. You can then unlock the weights, using the Free Weight tool, and change the curve shape as shown on the right. After you are finished adjusting the curve shape, you can use the Lock Weight tool to lock the tangent weights of the keyframes.

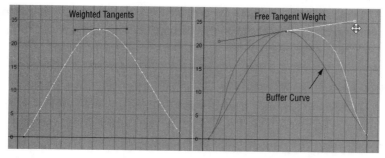

Figure 9.9 *A keyframe with weighted tangents (left), and with unlocked weighted tangents*

The Buffer Curve Snapshot and Swap Buffer Curve Tools

The Snapshot and Swap tools are similar in function to the Undo command. When you turn on View ➜ Show Buffer Curves and you edit a curve, changing its shape, the original shape remains as a buffer (as shown in the Figure 9.9 example of the free tangent weight). The Swap Buffer Curve tool snaps the changed curve to the original buffer curve. The Buffer Curve Snapshot tool makes a new buffer curve from the changed curve.

The Key Stats Fields Tool

The Key Stats Fields tool lets you enter precise values for keyframes. It is especially handy when you need to assign the same values for multiple keyframes. When the values of the selected keyframes are not the same, the field turns purple, but it turns white again when those keyframes are assigned the same value.

Using the Graph Editor Menus

The Graph Editor menus provide some of the same tools as the toolbar, as well as some other useful functions.

Cut, Copy, and Paste Functions

Using Edit menu functions, you can cut, copy, and paste selected keyframes. Before you paste, however, make sure to set the proper option settings, or unexpected results could occur. Go to Edit ➜ Paste ❏, for example, and look over the different settings.

The curves shown in Figure 9.10 were copied from the original curve (shown in white), and then pasted with different option settings back to the original curve. The first example shows a curve inserted into the current time with the Connect setting checked. Notice that the curve being pasted has moved up so that its starting point connects to the original curve at the current time indicator. If you turn off the Connect setting, you get the second example shown in Figure 9.10. The pasted curve is still inserted into the original curve, but it is not translated vertically to connect with the original curve. The Merge setting produces the third example, where the curve being pasted merges with the original curve. Note that the last keyframe of the resulting curve is the same as the pasted curve. The fourth example is pasted with the Time Range set to Start and the Time Offset set to 30. Note that, in this case, you would get the same result if you set the Time Range to Clipboard and Time Offset to 29, because the copied curve on the Clipboard starts from frame 1.

When using functions that offer numerous optional settings, you will often have different ways of achieving the same result. Different situations will make different settings optimal for those situations. In order to know which settings are optimal for a particular purpose, you need to have a clear understanding of what the settings do. It's frustrating to discover that a function that works for one situation will not work for another because different settings are required, and you don't know what those setting changes should be.

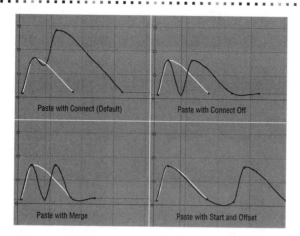

Figure 9.10 *Curves pasted with different settings*

Pre and Post Infinity Cycles and Extrapolations

View ➜ Infinity displays the curve values before and after the first and last keyframes, to infinity. Under the Curves menu, you can select Pre and/or Post Infinity cycles or extrapolations, as shown in Figure 9.11.

- The default setting is Constant, which means the values for the first and last keyframes are maintained.

- The Linear setting takes the slope of the tangent.

- The Cycle setting repeats the curve segment, where the first keyframe of the next cycle occupies the same frame as the last keyframes of the current cycle. This can lead to jerky, skipping motion if the first and last keyframes don't have same values.

- The Cycle with Offset setting takes the last keyframe value as the starting point for the next cycle.

- The Oscillate setting mirrors the cycle before it.

The Add and Remove Inbetween Functions

Two other nifty functions are Add Inbetween and Remove Inbetween, found on the Keys menu. These are simple functions that either add or remove a frame at the current time, causing all the keyframes after the current time to move one frame forward or backward.

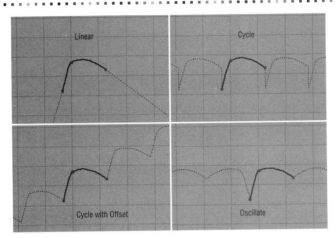

Figure 9.11 *Various cycles and extrapolations*

The Auto Load Option

In some situations, you may want to deselect one object and select another but still maintain the keyframes of the first object. In such a situation, you can turn off the Auto Load function on the List menu.

Editing Key Times with the Dope Sheet

The Dope Sheet has many of the same editing functions that are available in the Graph Editor. To open the Dope Sheet, select Window ➜ Animation Editors ➜ Dope Sheet; you'll see the window in Figure 9.12. Because the Dope Sheet edits only key times, it is designed to allow you to move easily around keyframes, curves, and whole groups of curves.

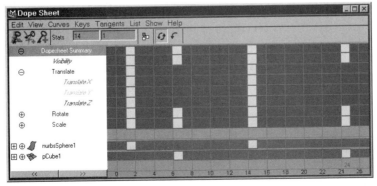

Figure 9.12 *The Dope Sheet is an alternative to the Graph Editor.*

The Dope Sheet also has a Dopesheet Summary line, which selects all the keyframes of the selected objects for editing. Alternatively, you can open the summary to select all of the specific keyable attributes of the selected objects for editing. For example, you can select the Move tool, select all objects in the modeling window, select the Dopesheet Summary in the Dope Sheet, and move all the keyframes for the entire scene. You can also open the Dopesheet Summary, select Rotate, and then move only the rotation keyframes of all the selected objects in the scene.

Editing Keys in the Channel Box

Key editing in the Channel box works the same as in the Graph Editor or the Dope Sheet, except that you don't have access to the option windows. The Cut, Copy, Paste, and Delete functions, when RM chosen in the Channel box, are performed with the default settings.

The difference between Delete and Cut is usually not significant, but it is worth knowing. Cut puts the keyframes into the Clipboard; Delete simply deletes them. If you have keyframes in the Clipboard that you want to keep, use Delete to remove animation from the selected attributes so that you don't replace the Clipboard items.

Using the Keys Submenu

You can access several key-editing functions from the main menu by selecting Edit ➜ Keys. The functions on this submenu work differently than those with the same name in the Graph Editor, and it's important not to confuse these functions. The functions in the Keys submenu edit keyframe curves at the object level. They are used mainly to transfer animation curves between objects.

Cut Keys and Copy Keys have the same option settings. Select Edit ➜ Keys ➜ Copy Keys ❑ to open the Copy Keys Options dialog box shown in Figure 9.13. The Hierarchy setting Selected copies only the animation curves of the selected object. The Below setting copies all the animation curves of the selected object plus all the objects on the hierarchy below it. You can also control the time range of the curves being copied by clicking Start/End and typing values in the Start Time and End Time boxes.

The Paste Keys options are the same as the Graph Editor's Paste options. If you copy animation curves from a hierarchy, you can paste them into the same hierarchy as well as into other similar hierarchies.

You can cut or copy curves from multiple objects. The objects' selection order is important in this case because the curves are copied in the same sequence. Also, when you are pasting to multiple objects, their selection order needs to be the same as the order in which the objects were selected for the Copy Keys function.

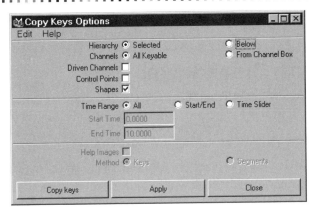

Figure 9.13 *The Copy Keys Options window*

Working with the Time Slider

The Time Slider has several key-editing functions, which you can access by RM choosing an object that has keyframes. When you do this, the Time Slider displays key *ticks*—red vertical lines showing where keyframes are, as illustrated in Figure 9.14. (Breakdowns are displayed as taller, narrower green ticks.)

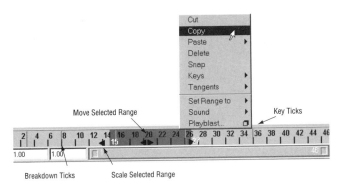

Figure 9.14 *The Time Slider*

By Shift+clicking and dragging, you can select a frame, or a range of frames. This range is displayed in a red block with arrows at the start, in the middle, and at the end of the block. You can then move the frame or frame range by dragging the arrows in the middle of the block, scale it by dragging the arrows at the side, or edit it by selecting functions with RM choose.

The Cut, Copy, Paste, and Delete functions are the same as those in the Graph Editor, without the options. The Paste function has Connect set to Off. The Paste Connect function works like the Graph Editor's Paste with the default settings.

Working with Breakdowns

Now that you've worked with the Time Slider and Graph Editor, we can move on to the topic of breakdowns. This short exercise demonstrates how breakdowns work in Maya.

1. Create a sphere and keyframe it in the X axis at frame 1.

2. Translate it in the X axis to 5 at frame 20, and 0 again at frame 30, setting breakdowns. You can set breakdowns by RM choosing in the Channel box or by selecting Animate ➜ Set Breakdown. Everything should be the same as if keyframes were used, except that the ticks in the Time Slider are red at frame 1 and green at frames 20 and 30.

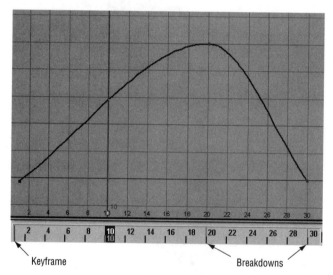

3. Set a keyframe at frame 10 with the X-axis translation value of 10.

4. Open the Graph Editor, select the keyframe at frame 10, and try moving it to frame 15. Note that the breakdowns at frames 20 and 30 move as well, maintaining their curve shape with respect to the keyframe being moved, as below. This is what is meant by breakdowns being "bound" by keyframes.

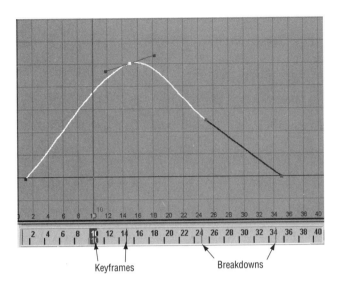

Keyframes   Breakdowns

Hands-on Maya: Animating a Finger

In some cases, when one object's attributes change, another object is affected accordingly. For example, consider the way that fingers fold: Whenever the second joint of a finger folds, the third joint generally folds as well. Or whenever a button is pressed, a light may be turned on or a door open. It would be nice if you could make such process automatic. The Set Driven Key tool enables you to do this. You can open the tool from the Channel box, Attribute Editor, or Animate menu (select Animate ➜ Set Driven Key ➜ Set ❑). Its function is to link attributes to each other in a master-slave relationship. The attributes that influence the other attributes are called *driver* attributes; the ones that are influenced are called *driven* attributes.

We will use the partial hand in the file finger_setup.mb, as shown in Figure 9.15, for our tutorial, but if you want to, you can create a simple joint hierarchy like the one we'll be using (for a full discussion on creating joints, see Chapter 10).

Using One Driver Attribute

We will start by using the Set Driven Key tool with a single driver attribute.

1. Open the file finger_setup.mb from the CD-ROM, under the Chapter 9 Working Files directory. It's a simple setup of a partial hand that has been smoothed, skinned, and weighted to a hierarchy of joints.

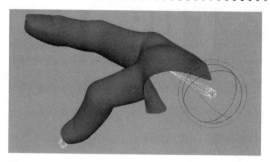

Figure 9.15 *Use this partial hand as the starting point for an exercise in setting driven keys.*

2. In the Outliner, select all the joints in the hierarchy, and open Window ➔ General Editors ➔ Channel Control. In the Channel Control window, select all the attributes on the left side except the rotation attributes, and click the Move>> button. This leaves us with joints that can only be keyed in their rotation attributes, as below.

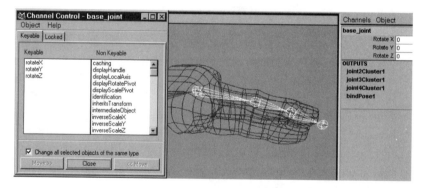

3. Select base_joint, mid_joint, and end_joint; then select Animate ➔ Set Driven Key ➔ Set ❑. The three joints are listed as Driven and the Driver list is empty. Click the Load Driver button, and the three joints will load as Driver items as well. Select base_joint from the Driver list and mid_joint from the Driven list. Their rotation attributes appear on the right side, as shown below. Select rotateZ on both lists, and hit the Key button. Select just mid_joint; in the Channel box, you will see that the Rotate Z attribute field has turned orange. This indicates that the attribute has animation, but there are no red ticks showing in the Time Slider, because there are no explicit keyframes. The mid_joint Rotate Z value is now driven by the base_joint Rotate Z value.

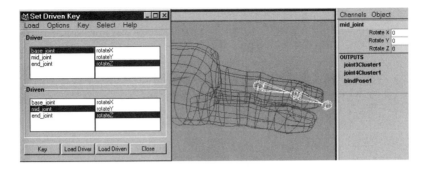

4. Select base_joint and in the Channel box change its Rotate Z value to 90; then select the mid_joint and change its Rotate Z value to 100. Hit the Key button again in the Set Driven Key window. Now, whenever you rotate the base_joint to 90 degrees, the mid_joint will be driven to rotate 100 degrees. With mid_joint selected, open the Graph Editor. You will see a curve representing the way base_joint drives the mid_joint, as shown below.

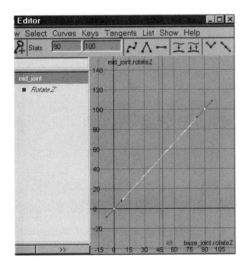

5. Because the values before the first key and after the last key are constant by default, if you rotate the base_joint to a negative value or a value greater than 90 degrees, the mid_joint will remain at 0, or at 100. If you want the mid_joint to be driven by the base_joint for all values, select the curve, open the Curves menu in the Graph Editor, and set the Pre Infinity and Post Infinity values to Linear, as shown below. Now the mid_joint will be driven by the base_joint for all values. Repeat the same procedure with the end_joint as

well, except perhaps you may want to make the end_joint rotate 80 degrees when the base_joint rotates 90 degrees, as the end joint tends to rotate a bit less than the middle joint.

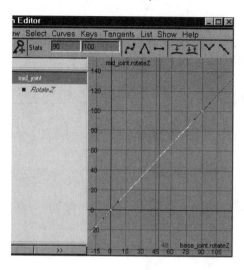

As you can see from this example, using Maya's Set Driven Key feature is not difficult at all. One limitation, however, is that once the mid_joint and the end_joint have become driven objects, they can't be keyframed. What if you wanted to have a finger bending as in Figure 9.15 above (as you would when snapping your fingers)? Because the end_joint is already constrained to the rotation value of the base_joint, trying to rotate the end_joint the other way doesn't seem possible. We can solve this problem by using multiple driver attributes.

Using Multiple Driver Attributes

While the end_joint cannot be keyframed, it can be driven by more than one driver. Although you can set up another driver to drive the end_joint in any node, logic dictates that we use the same base_joint node for the second driver.

1. Select the base_joint and open Modify ➜ Add Attribute window. In the New tab's Attribute Name field, enter **reverse_rotation,** leave all the settings at their defaults, and click OK. In the Channel box, you should see a new attribute with the same name. You can use this attribute to drive the end_joint.

2. Select the base_joint and end_joint, open the Set Driven Key window, and load those objects as drivers as wells. Select base_joint Reverse_rotation as the driver attribute, end_joint rotateZ as the driven attribute, as below, and click the Key button to set your new keys.

3. In the Channel box, make the reverse_rotation value 90, do the same for end_joint rotateZ, and click the Key button in the Set Driven Key window again. With the end_joint selected, go to the Graph Editor and set the Pre and Post Infinity to Linear for the curve representing the new connection to the Reverse_rotation attribute. You can now use the base_joint's attributes, Rotate Z and Reverse_rotation, to animate the fingers more freely, as below. Note that the final Rotate Z value of the end_joint is roughly 40 minus 80, which is about –40 degrees.

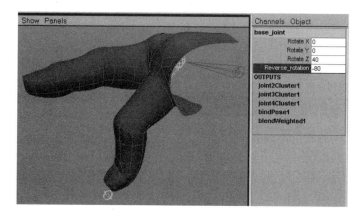

Summary

In this chapter, we covered the basic concepts of keyframe animation and the tools Maya offers for creating and editing keyframes. Some of the interfaces are more challenging than others, especially the Graph Editor if you are not already familiar with function curves. It is the Graph Editor, however, that you will come to love using as you become more familiar with animating in Maya. The next few chapters are going to be challenging, so by all means, take a break!

Paths and Bones

MAYA

Chapter 10

I n this chapter, we will continue our examination of animation in Maya by exploring path animation and skeleton construction. Our examples include a chair drifting at sea with a camera following it, a dummy human being built with a skeleton and spheres, and a hierarchy of nodes to set up a character model for binding and animation.

- Path animation
- Skeletons with bones and joints
- Forward and inverse kinematics
- Constraints
- A hierarchy for animation

Path Animation

Path animation is essentially animating objects along a designated path created with a curve. With the proper settings, the objects can move differently and even deform as they follow the path. This type of animation is ideal for animating things like roller coasters, ships, and moving cameras.

Attaching an Object to a Path

For path animation, you attach an object to a path. To see how this works, let's try creating a simple path animation.

1. Create a curve and a cone, as shown below. Make sure that the Time Slider range is at 48 frames.

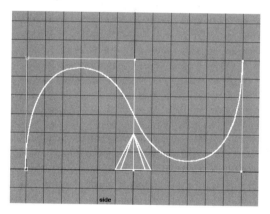

2. With the cone still selected, select the curve as well. Then choose Animate ➜ Paths ➜ Attach to Path ❑. Reset the options to make sure that you're using the default settings, and then click Attach. You should see the cone snap to the beginning of the curve. Try scrubbing through the frames (by dragging the mouse across frames in the Time Slider) and watch how the cone moves.

3. Under Inputs in the Channel box, you will see motionPath1. Click it, and you will see the U value, which is 0 at frame 1 and 1 at frame 48.

4. Go to frame 15 and check that the U value is 0.298. MM drag the current time indicator back to frame 1. The U value should still read 0.298. Click the U value, RM choose, and use Key Selected to keyframe that value at frame 1. Now the starting point has changed to U value 0.298, and the cone travels only about 70 percent of the curve from frame 1 to 48.

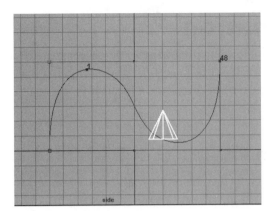

5. Open the Attribute Editor and click the motionPath1 tab. Change the setting to Follow. Additional options, including Inverse Up and Inverse Front, become available. Set Front Axis to X and Up Axis to Y. Scrub the Timeline on the Time Slider, and you will see how the cone moves differently. Click Inverse Up to flip the object vertically. Set Front Axis to Y and Up Axis to Z. Click Inverse Front to flip the object along the curve. Figure 10.1 shows the effects of setting different attributes for the motion path.

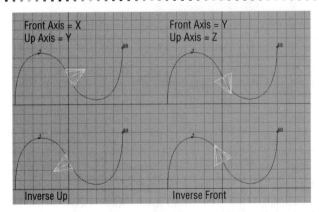

Figure 10.1 *Different settings for a motion path in the Attribute Editor*

Now that you have an idea how path animation works, we will try a more complex exercise next.

Making an Object Float

In this tutorial, we will create a short animation of a chair floating at sea. In addition to exploring further how to use path animation, we will also introduce using cameras and previewing in Maya.

1. Open the living room scene you created in Chapter 4, "Modeling Basics," and select the chair group node. Rename it to **Chair**, and then select File ➜ Export Selection and save the file as Chair.mb. (You can also find this file on the accompanying CD, in the Chapter 10 Working Files folder.) You've just exported only the chair hierarchy into a new file.

Maya's default Export function exports everything associated with the model(s) being exported, including its history, expressions, and animation. If you want to export only the model, turn the other settings off in the option box.

2. Start a new scene, create a NURBS plane, scale it to 100 uniformly, and increase the Patch UV spans to 30.

3. Switch to the Modeling module. Select Edit Surfaces ➜ Sculpt Surfaces Tool ❏ and click Reset Tool. Switch to the Map tab and load the Wave.tif file from the CD. You will see the plane become wavy, but it's not wavy enough. Click the Reload button three more times. Each time, you will see the waves become more pronounced, as the displacement is compounded.

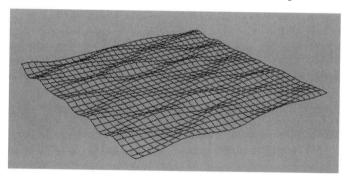

If you want to create the Wave.tif file yourself, create a plane and open the Hypershade window. Assign a Blinn material with the water texture and manipulate the variables until you see something like the Wave.tif file. Use the Edit ➜ Convert to File Texture command in the Hypershade window, and then convert the .iff file to .tif format using Fcheck. See the discussion of Hypershade in Chapter 19, "Shading and Texturing Surfaces," for details on shading and texturing surfaces.

4. Go to the top view and create a simple curve near the middle of the wavy plane. Select both objects and create a curve on the surface by selecting Edit Surfaces ➜ Project Curve on Surface.

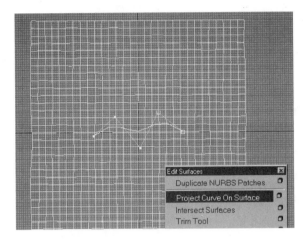

5. Hide the curve (make it invisible). It's better not to delete anything until you are sure you no longer need it. In this case, you may want to use the original curve to adjust the curve on the surface later on, when you animate the camera.

6. Import the Chair.mb file into the scene.

7. Set the Time Slider range to 240 frames. Select the top hierarchy of the chair, and then select the curve on the surface. Switch to the Animation module and select Animate → Paths → Attach to Path, with the default settings.

8. Open the Attribute Editor and click the motionPath1 tab. Click Follow and set World Up Type to Normal. Try different settings for Front Axis and Up Axis until the chair is sitting upright. (X for Front Axis and Y for Up Axis should work, but you may need to use different values.) Your scene should look something like the one shown below.

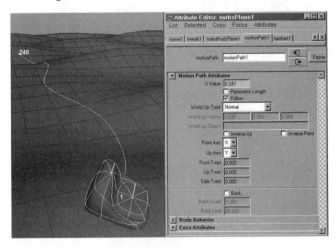

When you're using curves on a surface as the path, using the Normal for the World Up Type setting works well, because it makes the attached object's up direction the surface's normal. However, when you're using regular curves as the path, the Normal setting does not work as well, because a curve's normal will reverse if the curve's path goes from convex to concave. The attached object may end up flipping as it animates along the curve.

Moving the Chair

The chair is a bit too low in the water, but if you try to move it, it will snap back when you scrub the Time Slider because it's attached to the path. You can move the node below the top hierarchy to move the chair up, which would actually be the best solution, because the node below the top hierarchy isn't constrained to the path. However, for this tutorial, we will move the top node.

1. Select the top Chair node and press Insert to show the pivot manipulator. Drag the Y-axis handle down, and you will see the chair go up. This is because the pivot is constrained to the path.

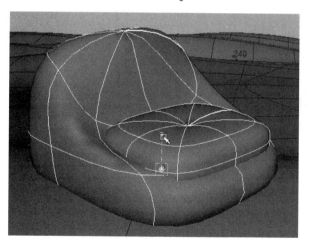

2. Press Insert again to turn off the pivot manipulator. Select the node that is one below the top Chair node and check to make sure that its Y rotation value is 0 in the Channel box. Then use Key Select at frame 1. Move to frame 240, enter **360** for Y rotation, and keyframe it.

3. Now as you scrub the animation, the chair should slowly rotate as it floats along the curve on the surface. View the animation to see how the chair moves.

Animating the Camera

The chair seems to be floating, but the water isn't moving. We can make it seem like it is by animating the camera.

1. In any modeling window, select Panels ➔ Perspective ➔ New to create the Persp1 view. This will be our animated camera.

2. With the Persp1 camera still selected, zoom in to the curve on the surface and Shift+select it. Select Animate ➔ Paths ➔ Attach to Path ❏. Choose Follow, X for Front Axis, Y for Up Axis, and Normal for World Up Type. Click Attach.

3. Switch to perspective view and press F to center in on the Persp1 camera. You should see the camera positioned as shown below.

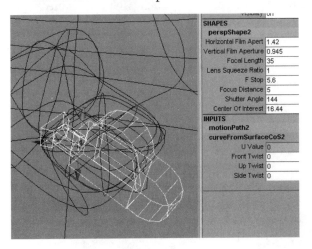

4. As you can see, the camera isn't looking exactly where it should be. We need to adjust its direction and also position it a bit behind the chair. Click motion-Path2 in the Channel box, and you will see the Front Twist, Up Twist, and Side Twist input variables. Select them one at a time and try MM dragging in the modeling window to see the effect each has on the camera.

If the Twist attributes are grayed out, you probably attached the camera to the curve on the surface a bit differently. This isn't a problem. Just select the grayed-out areas, RM choose, and select Unlock Selected to unlock the attributes and make them keyable.

5. Return the Front Twist and Side Twist values to 0, and set the Up Twist value to –90. The camera should now be looking along the curve.

6. Select the curve on the surface. In the Channel box, select motionPath1. This is the path animation for the chair. Go to frame 60, then MM drag the current time indicator back to frame 1. Select the U value, which should be at 0.247, and keyframe it using RM in the Channel box. If you scrub the Timeline now, the chair should start in front of the camera, as shown in the top picture in Figure 10.2.

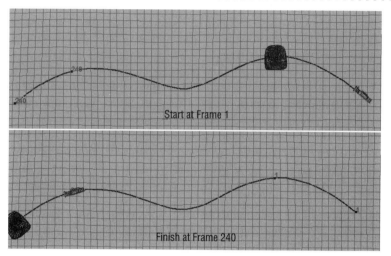

Figure 10.2 *Start and finish positions for the chair and the camera*

7. Select motionPath2. This is the path animation for the Persp1 camera. Go to frame 200, then MM drag to frame 240. Select the U value again, which should be at 0.8333, and keyframe it. Now the camera should finish behind the chair at the end of the animation, as shown in the bottom picture in Figure 10.2.

8. The only thing that remains for us to do is to adjust the height of the Persp1 camera. It's sitting too low on the surface plane. Go to Four Views layout, and make one window Persp1 camera view and another one the perspective view.

9. Select the Persp1 camera in the perspective view, select the Move tool, and press Insert to display the pivot manipulator. Grab the Y-axis handle and push it down to make the camera move up. You should scrub the Timeline back and forth to come up with the ideal height for the camera. You may even want to move the chair farther away from the camera.

10. When you are satisfied with the camera view, use Playblast, as described in the next section, to see how everything looks. Save the scene as `Wave.mb`. You may want to use it again later to try texturing the water and the sky.

You can find a finished version of the floating chair on the accompanying CD. It's named `cam_anim.mov`.

Previewing and Playblasting

When you are previewing an animation, even with powerful machines, you often cannot get real-time playback. Here are some suggestions (by no means exhaustive) to help you achieve faster playback speed:

- Before you play the animation, make the active viewing window as small as you can without losing important details. Select the Four View window setting, and then drag the active window to a smaller size.

- If you can see the animation well in wireframe, then by all means, preview it in wireframe.

- In the shaded mode, make the NURBS display Rough (Display ➜ NURBS Smoothness), or in the modeling window, select Shading ➜ Flat Shade All. Check if you can still preview the animation clearly. (Press Alt+V to play; press Alt+V again to stop.)

- For animation with joints, you can turn off the geometry display altogether, or use simple primitive proxy geometry to stand in for the more complicated geometry.

Playblast provides a quick way for you to view scenes as movie clips (or picture sequences, although you will rarely use that option). Select Window ➜ Playblast ❑, click Reset, adjust your Time Slider range to about 30 frames for testing purposes, and then click Playblast. Maya quickly captures the active window view for the duration of the Timeline and creates an `.avi` movie clip in your C:\Temp directory. This movie clip will be deleted automatically when you exit Maya.

Many of the Playblast options are self-explanatory, but a few are not so straight-forward:

- The default compressor for the movie player is the standard Microsoft Video 1, which you can change to suit your computer's own capacity by clicking the Compression button.

- Instead of using the From Window setting for Display Size, you can have a Custom setting of 320 × 240 or something similar in ratio, with Scale set to 1.0, to gain more control over the area of your active window that is captured.

- If you choose Fcheck, picture sequences are created instead of a movie clip. The Fcheck setting enables you to acquire wireframe renders for your model turnarounds in minutes. You can save the .iff picture sequences into any directory by using the Save to File setting, or convert them to other image formats using Fcheck's Save Animation option.

Making the Camera Move

In our next tutorial, we will set up a moving camera attached to a path that can remain focused on an object. We will continue working with our floating chair.

Animating Waves

Open the scene that you just created. The surface plane appears wavy, but it is not actually moving. Let's create some animated waves on it.

1. Select the plane and choose Deform ➜ Nonlinear ➜ Wave to apply Wave deformation (see Chapter 11, "Deformers," for more information about Maya's deformers).

2. Translate the waveHandle node to (−100, 0, 100) and scale it to 300 uniformly.

3. Set the Amplitude wave property to 0.005 and the Wavelength property to 0.1. Leave the other properties at their default values.

4. Keyframe translate X at frame 1. Keyframe again at frame 240 with the X value at −60.

The waves look more realistic now. The surface still needs smaller ripples, but that's a texturing matter (see Chapter 19 for details on texturing techniques).

Adding a Three-Node Camera

We will use path animation with a three-node camera to get the proper effect we want. The default camera Maya creates is a single-node camera, which is what you see in perspective view or when you create a camera from the Panels menu. A two-node camera also has a camera_view node, which determines the camera's center of interest. A three-node camera has an additional camera_up node.

1. Create another simple single-span curve above the surface to act as the camera path, as shown below. Observe carefully where the CVs are placed in relation to the floating chair. The CVs have been positioned so that the camera will be able to follow the chair from behind and gradually catch up from an angle.

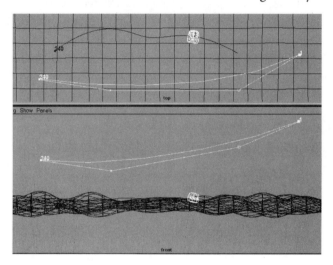

2. Select Create ➔ Camera ❑. At the bottom of the option box, click the Three for Nodes setting. Then click Create.

3. Select the camera_group node, and then select the curve. Use the Attach to Path function with the Follow and World Up Type Vector or Scene Up settings selected.

4. Select the chair, Shift+select the camera_view node, and then choose Constraint ➔ Point. The camera_view node should now be constrained to the chair (constraints are discussed in detail later in this chapter).

5. Scrub through the animation in camera view. You may find that the upper edges of the surface plane become visible for a few frames as the camera swoops down. You can try to fix this by accessing the motion path's properties and rotating the Front Twist setting, or by moving the CVs of the motion path curve.

6. Use Playblast to see how the camera moves. You may need to tweak the curve a few times to make the camera behave exactly the way you want it to.

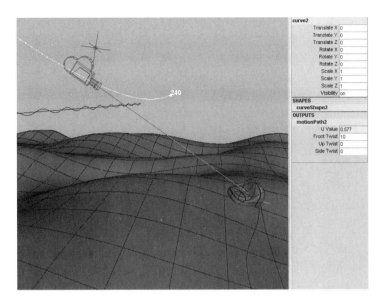

As you've seen in this example, path animation is relatively easy and can be useful when you want your animation to follow a particular route. Now we will turn to the more complex techniques of animating characters using skeletons and kinematics.

Skeletons and Kinematics

"The knee bone is connected to the hip bone…." Bones are connected, and together they make up a skeleton. A skeleton is a protective structure that houses the vital organs of animals, maintains their shape, and enables them to move about.

There are no vital organs in a digital character to protect (not yet anyway), but Maya does provide joints, which enable us to animate characters efficiently and maintain or deform their shapes properly. Using skeletons at a basic level is easy in Maya, but it can also become quite complex.

Skeletons are built with bones and joints. You select Skeleton ➜ Joint Tool, and then click to place joints in the modeling window, much as you would edit points for a curve. Maya connects the joints by bones.

In building skeletons, it's good to know the kinds of joints you should be creating:

- A ball joint can rotate in all three axes, like the neck bone. This is the default Joint tool setting.

- A universal joint can rotate in two axes, like the wrist bone.

- A hinge joint can rotate in only one axis, like the knee bone.

Some people find it better to limit the joints they create according to their functions, such as a universal joint or a hinge joint, because it means more efficiency in animation and fewer calculations for Maya to perform. For example, you might use universal joints for wrists and ankles and hinge joints for knees.

Using Forward Kinematics

Forward kinematics works well for free rotational motions, such as a character's arms swinging when she walks or her spine rotating when she turns. Our main concern with forward kinematics is setting up the joints correctly for animation. Let's use the Joint tool to build a human skeleton.

Building a Leg

We will begin by building our skeleton's leg. We need to place leg, knee, and foot joints.

1. Select Skeleton ➜ Joint Tool ❑. Click Reset Tool to set all of the options to their defaults, then choose Auto Joint Limits.

2. Go to side view and X+click the joints to snap them to the grid, as shown below. When you've created all of the joints, press Enter to complete the action.

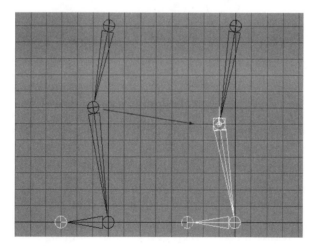

At any time during the creation of joints, you can MM drag to adjust the position of the last joint you created, or you can use the up arrow key to go back to other joints. Note that if you go back up a few joints and click with the left mouse button, you will add another bone branching from the joint.

3. Name the joints **Lleg**, **Lknee**, and **Lfoot** (*L* for left). You don't need to worry about the last joint in the chain, because that joint never takes part in the setup or animation of a character.

4. Go to the perspective view, select the knee or the foot joint, and try rotating it. You will see that you can rotate it only in the Z axis, and that there is a limit to the Z rotation. The Auto Joint Limit setting creates a hinge joint, which will not rotate past its parent joint or bend away from it more than 180 degrees, as shown below. It works well here with the knee.

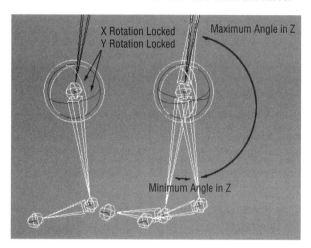

If you want the foot to rotate in the X or Y axis as well, you can set this up through the Attribute Editor. In the Joint section, select X and Y for the Degrees of Freedom setting. The joint limit for the Z axis will still apply, unless you turn off the Rot Limit Z setting in the Limit Information section.

In the leg you've created, notice that the bones were placed *at an angle*, not in a straight line. This is because the angles between the bones are needed to determine which way the bones will bend. Also, the default joint orientation in Maya is determined by the joint's relationship to the child joint. This means that when a joint is created, its local X axis points into the bone—to the child joint. The Y axis points toward the bending direction, perpendicular to the X axis. The Z axis is perpendicular to the bending direction and the X axis. A hinge joint, therefore, will rotate around only the Z axis. You can display a joint's local rotational axes, as shown in Figure 10.3, by selecting Display ➜ Component Display ➜ Local Rotation Axes.

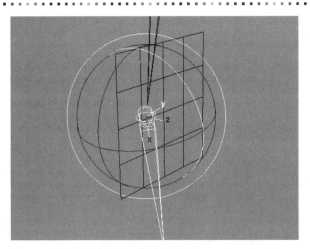

Figure 10.3 *Viewing a joints local rotational axes*

When joints are created with the default setting, the local Z-axis rotation will always bend the bones, and the local Y-axis rotation will rotate them from side to side. A corollary of this is that the window in which you decide to build the joints is important. You should figure out how you want the bones to bend, then build them accordingly in the proper window. For example, if your model is facing the front view, you should build her spine and legs in the side view. You will see examples of creating joints in different windows when we build the rest of the skeleton, which will be right after we mirror the joints in the next section.

Moving and Mirroring Joints

You can use the Move tool to move the joints you've created. If you select a joint and move it using the Move tool, the joints below its hierarchy will move with it. If you select the Move tool and then press Insert to show the pivot manipulator and move the pivot, only the selected joint will move. You can also use Maya's other tools on the Skeleton menu to edit the joints you've created (or are in the process of creating)—by inserting, removing, connecting, and disconnecting joints—and even to reroot a skeleton.

Now we can use mirroring to create the other leg. Because joints behave differently from regular object nodes, we need to use the Mirror Joint command to duplicate the right leg symmetrically.

1. Move the leg hierarchy to (2, 0, 0). Then select Skeleton ➜ Mirror Joint ❑, select YZ as the setting, and click Mirror.

2. Try rotating the left and right knee together. They should be rotating as mirror images of each other, as shown below.

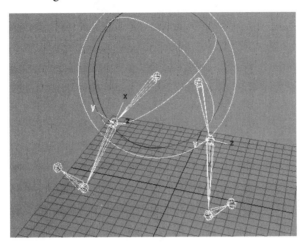

3. Name the mirrored joints **Rleg**, **Rknee**, and **Rfoot**.

As you saw in this example, when you mirror joints, the rotational limit information should copy into the mirrored joint. However, if the rotational settings are not activated, as sometimes occurs, open the Attribute Editor and activate them—the numerical information is already there. If some of the Rotate fields are grayed out but the joint is still rotating, click twice on the Degree of Freedom boxes to activate the lock.

If you find that the joints are not being mirrored properly, you can try grouping them under another joint, mirroring them, and then ungrouping them.

Building the Rest of the Skeleton

We will quickly go through the steps for adding the spine and shoulder hierarchy of joints.

1. Go to the side view and create the spine chain with the default Joint Tool option settings, as shown below. The spine joints need to be ball joints. From the top view, create the left shoulder chain, as shown below. (Remember that we're creating a simple skeleton.)

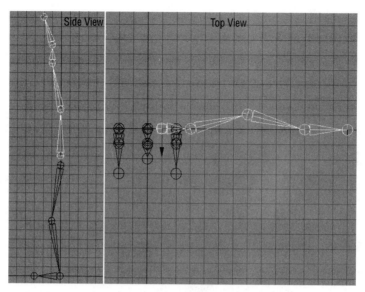

2. Name the spine hierarchy **waist, chest, neck**, and **head**. Name the shoulder hierarchy **Lshoulder, Larm, Lforearm**, and **Lhand**.

3. In the front view, translate the shoulder chain up until it's a little below the neck bone.

4. In the Hypergraph window or the Outliner, group the legs under waist, and the Lshoulder chain under chest. You should see something like the hierarchy and picture shown below.

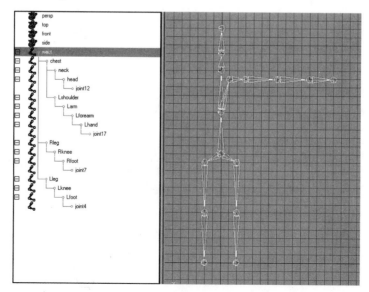

5. To put rotational limits on the shoulder joints, open the Attribute Editor and select the Lshoulder joint. The shoulder does not need to rotate in the X axis, so turn off X in the Degrees of Freedom setting. We want the Larm joint to rotate like a ball joint, so don't change its settings. Lforearm is a universal joint that cannot rotate in the Y axis, so turn off Y. Lhand is also a universal joint that cannot rotate in the X axis, so turn off X.

6. For these joints and others, you can also set specific minimum and maximum rotational limits. Let's do this for the Lforearm joint as an example. Select Lforearm. In the Attribute Editor, open the Limit Information, Rotate attribute. You will see three Rot Limit fields, with Y rotation grayed out. Put checks in the four Rot Limit X and Z boxes, and the Min and Max fields become unlocked.

7. In the top view, try rotating the Lforearm joint in the Z axis. When it's straight, the current degree reads about –28, so put in **–30** for the Min value. When it starts overlapping Larm, the degree is around 137, so enter **130** for the Max value.

8. For the X rotation, let's assume that the palm is facing straight down. In this case, Lforearm should be able to rotate about –90 degrees to make the palm face front, and about 45 degrees the other way. Enter those values for the Min and Max fields.

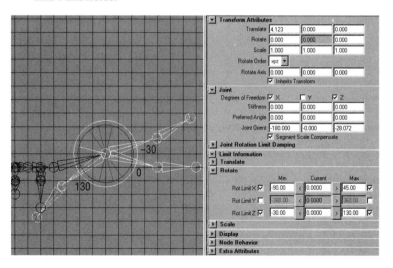

There are limits for Translate and Scale as well, which you may sometimes want to use. Maya also has Rotation Limit Damping settings, which allow the joints to ease in and out of the rotational limits.

9. Select the Lshoulder joint and mirror it. You should now have a complete, albeit very simple, human skeleton.

10. Scale, rotate, and translate the spheres to various positions and group them to their respective joints in the Outliner or Hypergraph window. It's not important exactly how the spheres are shaped or where they are placed, as long as they roughly represent the body parts being controlled by the individual joints. The final dummy human is shown in Figure 10.4.

11. Save this scene as Dummy_human.mb.

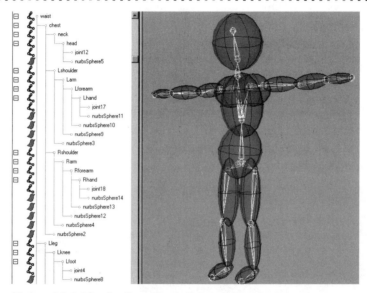

Figure 10.4 *The Outliner hierarchy and the sphere human*

Reorienting Local Axes of Joints

To gain precise control over how the joints rotate, you need to know how to reorient joints. In the skeleton you've just created, let's say you've translated the shoulder joint down one unit using the pivot manipulator. If you display the local rotational axes, you will see that the X axis is no longer pointing directly into the bone's center. It's off about −24 degrees.

To reorient the X axis, select the Rotate tool and switch to the component mode. RM choose the question mark button (Miscellaneous) and check Local Rotation Axes, then select the shoulder joint. You can rotate the Y-axis handle in the front view until you see the X axis pointing directly into the shoulder joint. You can also enter precise rotational values by typing in a MEL command in the Command Line field; for example, type `rotate -r -os 0 -24 0` to relatively rotate the local axes −24 degrees around the Y axis.

For those interested in MEL commands, there is also the `joint -e -oj xyz -zso` command, which reorients the local axes of a joint automatically. But be careful how you use this command, because it destroys the mirror properties of symmetrical hierarchies.

Animating the Dummy

As noted earlier, using forward kinematics mainly involves setting up the joints the right way. Now that we've created and grouped the joints and applied the proper limits to them, all we need to do is transform the joints and keyframe them. Work on the top hierarchy first, then move down to the lower joints until you achieve the poses you desire. Figure 10.5 shows some sample poses.

Figure 10.5 *Various poses for the dummy*

Using Inverse Kinematics

For goal-oriented motions, such as having a character plant her feet on the ground or reach out her hands to open a door, working with forward kinematics can be very difficult and tiresome. For these and other types of motions, you will want to animate using inverse kinematics (IK).

Inverse kinematics uses *IK handles* and *IK solvers*. An IK handle runs through the joints being affected, which are called the *IK chain*, and a handle wire runs through them. A *handle vector* starts from the start joint and finishes at the end joint, where the IK handle's *end effector* is located. The parts of an IK handle are illustrated in Figure 10.6.

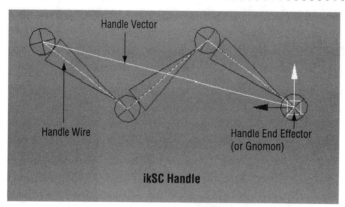

Figure 10.6 *Components of an IK handle*

An IK solver looks at the position of the end effector of an IK chain and performs the necessary calculations to make the joints rotate properly, from the start joint to the end joint of the IK chain, in such way that the end joint will be where the end effector is. When the end effector moves, the IK solver converts the translation values of the end effector to the rotational values for the joints, and the joints update accordingly. Usually, the IK chain will span only three joints, but it can handle more, as in the example in Figure 10.6.

Maya has three kinds of IK solvers: the ikRP (Rotate Plane) solver, the ikSC (Single Chain) solver, and the IK Spline solver. Each type of IK solver has its own type of IK handle.

Using the ikRP Handle

Since the ikRP solver is the default setting for the IK handle tool, let's see how that works first. As you work, refer to Figure 10.7, which shows the components of an ikRP handle.

1. In the side view, draw a simple joint chain (as in the inset on the upper-left corner of Figure 10.7).

2. Select Skeleton ➜ IK Handle Tool ❏ and reset the tool to its default settings.

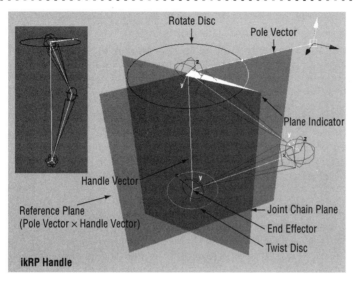

Figure 10.7 *ikRP handle components*

3. Click the first joint, and then click the last joint. You should see that an IK handle has been created. The circle at the top looks complicated (as shown in Figure 10.7), but it's actually a fairly simple setup, once you've learned what its components are.

The ikRP solver calculates only the positional value of the end effector, which means it ignores the rotational values of the end effector. The joints are rotated by the ikRP solver in such way that their Y axes are planar, their X axes are pointing to the center of the bones, and their Z axes are perpendicular to the bending direction. This is the default local orientation set up for joints. If you do not see the rotate disc, select the end effector and press the F key to display the Show Manipulator tool.

The plane along which the joints are bending is represented by the plane indicator. The plane itself is called the *joint chain plane*. You can rotate this plane about the handle vector using the twist disc, which rotates the IK chain. The Twist degree is measured relative to a reference plane created by the handle vector and the pole vector, which can be translated and keyframed.

At times, the way you want the arm to bend will cause the IK chain to flip with the default reference plane setting. To avoid this flipping, adjust or animate the pole vector.

In the Attribute Editor for the ikRP handle, you will see Snap, Stickiness, and Solver Enable settings. These are discussed in the "Switching between Inverse and Forward Kinematics" section, following the discussion of the ikSC handle.

The advantage of using the ikRP solver over the ikSC solver is that it offers more precise control over the rotation of the IK chain. The disadvantage is that it necessarily has more components to deal with.

Using the ikSC Handle

The ikSC handle is simpler than the ikRP handle. Let's experiment with it.

1. Go to the side view and draw another simple joint chain.

2. Select Skeleton ➔ IK Handle Tool ❑ as before, but this time, select the ikSC solver setting. Close the option box.

3. Click the first joint, and then click the last joint. You will see the ikSC handle.

4. Select Rotate and try rotating the IK handle. You will notice that only the local X and Y rotate handles seem to have any effect, and that they snap back to certain angles after you release the handles.

If you press F to display the Show Manipulator tool, you will see nothing, because there are no extra manipulators for the ikSC handle— everything is controlled by the IK handle. The ikSC solver calculates the rotational values of the end effector and rotates the IK chain in such way that all of the joints in the chain will have the default local orientation for joints. The joint chain plane exists in the ikSC solver, although you do not see any representation of it in the handle. As with the ikRP handle, the plane cuts across the chain so that the X and Y axes are lying on the plane, as shown in Figure 10.8.

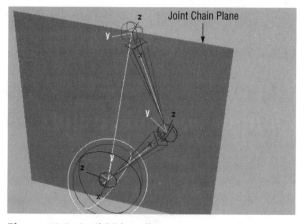

Figure 10.8 *An ikSC handle*

In the Attribute Editor for the ikSC handle, you will see Priority settings. The ikSC handles can have a Priority assignment when there are two or more chains overlapping. The handle with the Priority 1 setting will rotate the joints in its chain first, next the handle with the Priority 2 setting will rotate its joints, and so on. The Po Weight setting determines the handle's position/orientation weight. If the weight is 1, the end effector will try to reach only the handle's position; if the weight is 0, the end effector will try to reach only the handle's orientation. You should leave this setting at the default value of 1. The Snap, Stickiness, and Solver Enable settings are discussed in the next section.

The advantage of using the ikSC handle is that you need to use only the IK handle to control the IK chain. For situations where you do not need a great amount of IK chain rotations, this would be the more economical method of animating.

When you are using the ikSC handle to rotate IK chains, use the Graph Editor to interactively adjust the rotational values. It produces most predictable results. See Chapter 9, "Animating in Maya," for more information about the Graph Editor.

Switching between Inverse and Forward Kinematics

Maya allows you to switch back and forth between using ikRP or ikSC handles and rotating joints (forward kinetics). It's easy to do, and you may find it useful. Let's go through the technique using the ikSC handle we created in the previous section.

1. Go to frame 1 and turn on Auto Key. Without this setting, the process becomes cumbersome.

2. Keyframe the IK handle, move to frame 10, and translate the IK handle. You should have another keyframe automatically set.

3. In the Attribute Editor, turn off Solver Enable to locally disable the ikSC solver for this IK handle.

4. Select the two joints in the IK chain and keyframe them. Go to frame 20 and rotate the joints. Go to frame 30 and repeat the action.

5. Select the ikSC handle again. In the Attribute Editor, turn on Solver Enable to enable the ikSC solver. You will find that the IK handle acquired the keyframes for frames 20 and 30 in the same positions where the joints were keyframed.

In order for this switch to be possible, you need to have the IK handle's Snap setting on and the Stickiness setting off in the Attribute Editor. If Snap is off or Stickiness is on, then the IK handle will not snap to the end joint when the joints are rotated.

One more thing to be aware of in switching back and forth between inverse and forward kinetics is that the movements generated by the rotation of the joints and the corresponding keyframes of the end effector will not always match. They will be roughly the same, but you may need to tweak the end effector's animation.

If you build a chain in a straight line, ikSC or ikRP solvers will not be able to calculate and bend the chain. In order to fix this problem, first rotate the child joint(s) to make the chain angled—even a fraction of a degree should do. Then apply Skeleton ➡ Set Preferred Angle to the joints. Delete the existing IK chain and create a new one. Now the ikSC and ikRP solvers should be able to bend the chain.

Using the IK Spline Handle

The ikRP and ikSC handles are similar in their attributes, but the IK Spline handle is quite different in the way it functions. The IK Spline solver takes a NURBS curve as part of its handle and rotates the IK chain to follow the shape of the curve. The CVs of the NURBS curve, rather than the end effector of the handle, are animated. The IK Spline handle is ideal for animating curvy or twisty shapes, such as tails, spines, snakes, or tentacles. Let's try out this type of IK handle.

1. In the side view, build a joint chain, as shown below. For IK Spline handles, the joints need not be built at an angle, but the bones should be short to ensure the chain will move smoothly.

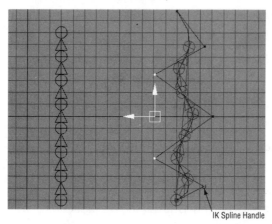

IK Spline Handle

2. Select Skeleton ➡ IK Spline Handle Tool ❑ and select Number of Spans 4. Leave the other options set to their defaults and close the option box.

3. Click the top joint, and then click the last joint. You will see the IK Spline handle.

4. In the Outliner, select the joint chain or the IK handle and try moving the joints. The joints have become attached to the curve, and the IK handle doesn't show a manipulator.

5. Display the CVs and move them around, as shown below.

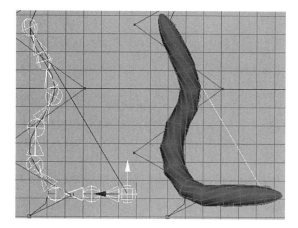

 You can also create your own NURBS curve and have the IK Spline handle use that curve. Turn off the Auto Create Curve setting in the IK Spline Handle option box. Click the root joint, the end joint, and then the curve to create the IK Spline handle.

6. Open the Attribute Editor for the IK handle. You will see the regular attributes and some specifically for the IK Spline handle. Try typing in numbers for the Offset, Roll, and Twist settings.

Offset translates the joint chain along the curve, with 0.0 as the start of the curve and 1.0 as its end. Roll rotates the whole joint chain. Twist gradually twists the chain from the second joint on. If the Root Twist Mode setting is turned on, the twist begins from the root joint. The Root on Curve setting constrains the root joint to the start of the curve. Turn it off, and you can move the root joint off the curve, but note that it is still constrained to the curve.

As you have seen, skeletons can be moved and rotated with forward or inverse kinematics to animate various parts of a character. In addition to the IK tools, Maya provides the Constrain menu in the Animation module. The constraints on this menu are often used in conjunction with the IK tools to set up a character for animation.

Constraints

Objects in real life are "constrained" in many different ways. For example, if you are holding a baseball, when your hand moves and rotates, the ball moves and rotates with it, because the ball is constrained by your hand movements. As another example, consider a tennis player whose eyes are always looking at the tennis ball. If you wanted to imitate these actions in Maya, it would be difficult and time-consuming to try to reproduce the motions of the baseball or the eyes by keyframing them. Instead, you can use constraints to automate such animation tasks.

Maya's Constrain menu offers Point, Aim, Orient, Scale, Geometry, Normal, Tangent, and Pole Vector constraints. All of the constraints work in the same way. You select two or more objects, and then select the constraints that you want to apply. The first objects you select act as the targets that constrain, and the last one is the object being constrained. When you select more than one constraint target, the constrained object is shared between the targets according to the weights you set for the targets.

Using the Point Constraint

The Point constraint makes the center of the constrained object stick to the center of the target object. When you have more than one target, the Point constraint places the object being constrained at a point between the targets' pivot points, with the placement determined by the average value of the weights of the targets, as shown in Figure 10.9.

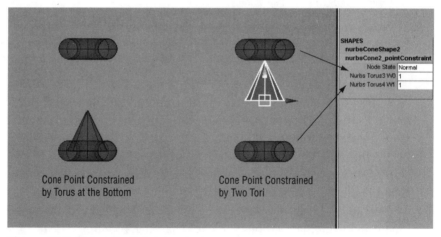

Figure 10.9 *Using the Point constraint*

Maya also has a Point on Curve Locator constraint (Deform ➜ Point on Curve Locator), which creates a locator at a selected point on a curve or an edit point. This constraint makes the locator position constrain the curve at that point, without breaking the curve's tangency.

Using the Aim, Orient, and Scale Constraints

The difference between the Aim and the Orient constraints can be a bit confusing. The Aim constraint creates an Aim vector (the default setting is the X axis of the object), which points the object being constrained to the *position* of the Aim target, as shown in Figure 10.10. In the example on the right in Figure 10.10, with two tori, notice the tilt toward the torus on the right. This is because that torus's weight input is 1, and the other torus's weight input is 0.7.

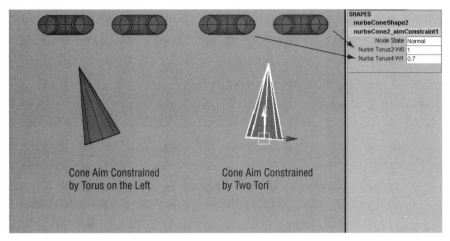

Figure 10.10 *Using the Aim constraint*

The Orient constraint causes the rotation values of the object being constrained to be the same as the *rotation* of the Orient target. In the example on the right in Figure 10.11, the cone has the average rotation value of the tori.

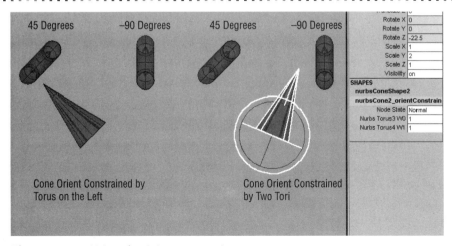

Figure 10.11 *Using the Orient constraint*

Aim constraints are especially useful for quickly making a character look at, or focus on, different objects. Orient constraints are great for controlling joints.

The Scale constraint functions the same way as the Orient constraint. The object being Scale constrained has the same scale values as the target object, or the average scale values of the target objects, as shown in Figure 10.12.

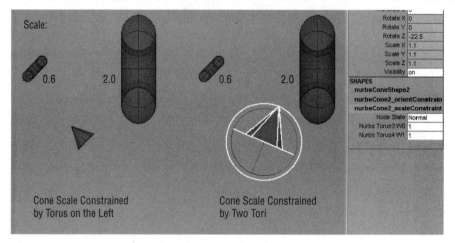

Figure 10.12 *Using the Scale constraint*

Using the Geometry and Normal Constraints

The Geometry constraint makes the center of the constrained object stay on the surface of the target object, as in the example on the left in Figure 10.13. It doesn't lock the attributes of the constrained object, allowing it to slide along the target surface.

The Normal constraint works much like the Aim constraint. The difference is that the aim vector of the object being constrained aligns itself with the normal vector of the surface that passes through the constrained object's center, as shown in the example on the right in Figure 10.13.

Using the Tangent and Pole Vector Constraints

The Tangent constraint aligns an object's aim vector to the tangency of the target curve, as you can see in the example on the left in Figure 10.14. It works in much the same way as the Aim and Normal constraints.

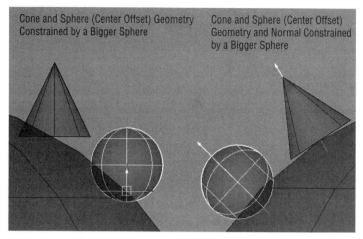

Figure 10.13 *Using the Geometry and Normal constraints*

The Pole Vector constraint is a Point constraint specifically designed to constrain the pole vector of an ikRP handle (ikRP handles were discussed earlier in this chapter). This constraint is shown in the example on the right in Figure 10.14.

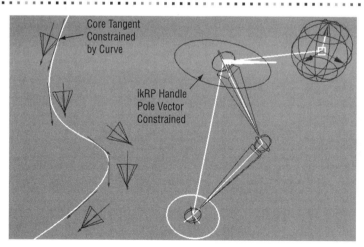

Figure 10.14 *Using the Tangent and Pole Vector constraints*

Hands-on Maya: Setting Up a Character for Animation

Let's build the skeleton for the character that we finished modeling in Chapter 8, "Organic Modeling." We will also put IK handles and constraints on him, and organize all of the nodes into a proper hierarchy to get him ready for binding and animation.

Creating the Skeleton

We'll begin by using Skeleton ➜ Joint Tool to give our character bones and joints. The root joint will be used to move the entire upper body. Two spine joints and the chest joint will be used to deform the body. The neck and head joints will animate the head.

1. Load the `character_model.mb` file, from the Chapter 10 Working Files folder on the CD.

2. Convert the head, body, and the shoes to polygons using the Extract Vertices command (polygons will be lighter to deal with). Since the hands have creasing information, they shouldn't be converted; otherwise, the information would be lost.

3. From the side view, use the Joint tool with the default settings to draw the backbones and the leg as shown below. Make sure that the knee joint is at the lower end of the knee area, and place the ankle joint down at the lower end of the ankle area. Once the leg chain is created, name the joints as shown below.

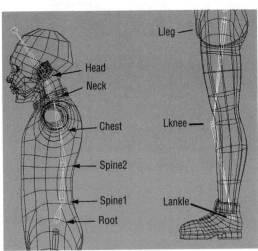

4. Create a joint chain for the foot, which will allow the character to rotate at two pivot points: the heel and the ankle. In the side view, draw the heel joint at the end of the heel, keeping in mind that this is where the foot will pivot. Then draw two more joints for the ball of the foot. Press the up arrow key twice to go back to the first heel joint, and create the next joint by snapping it (v+click) to the ankle joint of the leg. A joint with two branches is created. Name the joints as shown below. Do not confuse the Lfoot_ankle joint, which is part of the foot, with the Lankle joint, which is part of the leg.

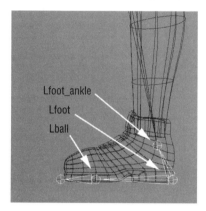

5. Move the leg and the foot joint chains to the left side, and group the leg joint under the root joint, as shown below.

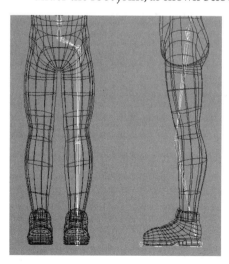

Animating the foot realistically is a complicated process. There are four pivot points to consider for true foot movement: the ankle pivots the foot when it's rotating in the air, and the toe, heel, and ball of the foot can all become pivots for the leg when the foot is on the ground. In the give and take of control versus efficiency, managing the animation of four pivot points is often not worth the effort. For those interested, however, Alias|Wavefront has a good tutorial on the Inverse foot, which allows control of these four pivot points.

6. We want the shoulder joint to primarily rotate up and down, so create it in the front view, as shown below.

7. Create the arm chain in the top view, because we want the chain to bend forward, as shown below. Note the Lforearm joint's placement; it doesn't matter exactly where the joint is placed, as long as it lies in a fairly straight line between the Lelbow and the Lwrist joints. We will be using this extra joint later to deform the forearm.

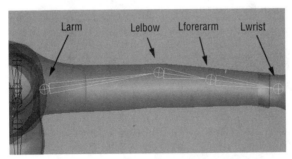

8. Open the Lforearm joint's Attribute Editor, Joint section, and turn off its Y and Z Degrees of Freedom, because we want it to rotate only in the X axis.

9. Group the Larm joint to the Lshoulder joint, and then group the Lshoulder joint to the chest joint.

10. Select the Lshoulder joint and all the joints below it, and choose Display ➜ Component Display ➜ Local Rotation Axes. Notice how the local axes for the shoulder joint and the other joints are different. This is because they were

created in different windows. We want the shoulder joint to rotate differently from the arm joints. That's why the shoulder joint is created in the front view, and the arm joints are created in the top view.

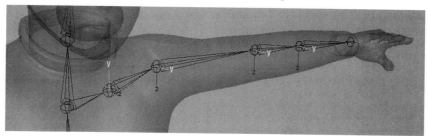

11. From the front view, create the first finger chain, as shown below. Creating finger joints must be done carefully if you want clean Z-axis rotations. To better see the joint placements, you may want to reduce the joint size by using the Display menu.

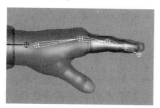

12. Create the other finger chains. You can move the index and index1 joints, but you shouldn't move its child joints, because that will complicate the finger rotation. You can also scale the joints in the X axis to make sure that the joints are placed exactly where you want them, but don't scale them in Y or Z. It may actually be better to create the other finger joints individually, rather than copying the first index finger chain and trying to make that fit the other fingers. You should end up with finger joints placed somewhat like the picture on the bottom right below.

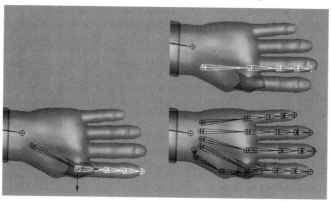

13. Select a finger joint and choose Display ➡ Component Display ➡ Local Rotation Axes. As with the shoulder joints, note how the local rotation axes are displayed on the finger joints. They should all be consistently pointing in the same direction.

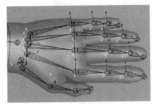

14. When you're finished creating the joints, name them appropriately, such as Lindex, Lindex1, Lindex2, etc., and group them to the wrist joint, as shown below.

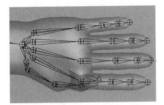

15. Select the Lshoulder, Lleg, and Lfoot joints, and then mirror them using the Skeleton ➡ Mirror Joint command. In the option window, make sure Mirror Across is set to YZ and Mirror Function is set to Behavior. You should see a skeleton like the one shown below.

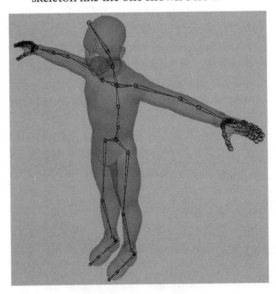

16. Assign the same names for the mirrored joints, but use the letter *R* for right in the prefix (instead of a *L* for left).

This completes the creation of the joints that we will use to animate our character. The `character_skeleton.mb` file on the CD (in the Chapter 10 Working Files folder) contains the completed skeleton setup.

Adding IK Handles and Constraints

Now we're ready to put IK handles on the arms and the legs of our character. We will then create foot and hand controls. Finally, we will add constraints for the eyes. This section is long and involved, so save your work often and take a break occasionally.

1. Select Skeleton ➜ IK Handle Tool. With the default setting, which gives us the ikRP solver, click from the Lleg joint to the Lankle joint. Repeat the process for the other side. Click also from the arm joint to the forearm joint for both sides (note that the end effector does not go to the wrist, but to the forearm joint). You should end up with four ikRP handles constraining the arms and the legs.

2. Create a circle and rotate it 90 degrees in the Z axis. Under Inputs in the Channel box, set Degree to Linear and Sections to 1. Freeze transformation and delete history. The circle should now look like a triangle. The triangle, and copies of it, will be used as Pole Vector constraints.

3. Translate the triangle to place it directly in front of the Lleg joint. Make a copy of the triangle and place it in front of the Rleg joint. Rename the triangles **Lleg_pole_c** and **Rleg_pole_c**.

Applying Leg Constraints and Attributes

Now that we have the IK handles set up, we can apply constraints and attributes. We will start with the legs.

1. Select Lleg_pole_c, then select the IK handle for the left leg, and apply the Pole Vector constraint. The pole vector line should appear from the leg joint to the triangle, as shown below. Repeat the process for the right side. (We will apply the same pole vectors for the arms, but a bit later.)

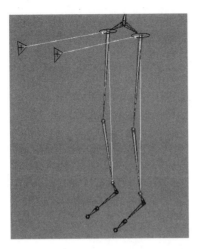

2. Create a locator and snap it to the Lfoot joint. Name the locator Lfoot_c (*c* for control), and group the Lfoot joint under it.

3. Parent the IK handle for the left leg under the Lfoot_ankle joint, and then make it invisible. Open the Attribute Editor for Lfoot_c, go to the Display section, and turn on Display Handle. This node will be used to move the left leg. Try moving and rotating the node to make sure the leg is moving with it, and that the foot is rotating with it as well, as shown below.

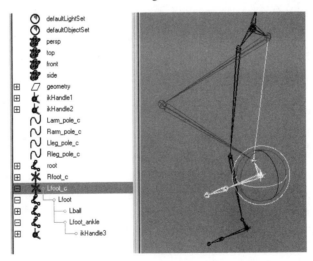

4. With Lfoot_c selected, choose Window → General Editors → Channel Control, and move the Scale and Visibility attributes to Non-Keyable. Close the window.

5. Select Modify ➜ Add Attribute, and add an attribute named **Ball_rotate**. We will use this extra attribute to rotate the ball of the foot.

6. Use the Set Driven Key window to make the Lball joint's Z rotation be driven by the Lfoot_c's Ball_rotate attribute for all values (see the finger animation tutorial in Chapter 9 for more details). With this setup, changing the value for the Ball_rotate will rotate the Lball joint, as shown below. You should also disable the Lball joint's X and Y rotations by turning off their Degrees of Freedom in the Attribute Editor.

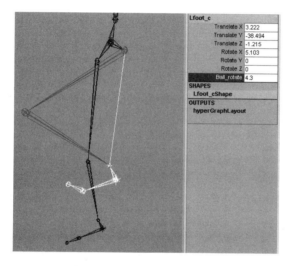

7. Repeat steps 2 through 6 for the right foot.

Applying Arm Constraints and Attributes

We will use a similar process to set up the node to control the arms and the hands, but things are a bit more complex. In rotating the hand, we need to solve a problem. The wrist rotates in the Y and Z axes, but the X rotation actually comes from the elbow. But since the elbow is part of the IK handle, we cannot control its X rotation. Even with a forward kinematics approach, we run into problems in terms of deformation weighting. To solve this problem, we inserted an extra joint we named the forearm joint, whose sole function is to rotate the hand in the X axis and to deform the forearm. Instead of using Set Driven Key to connect the locator to the forearm and the wrist joints, we will use the Connection Editor.

Although we created the IK handle between the arm and the forearm joint to enable the forearm joint to rotate in X, we will move the position of the end effector on the wrist. This will allow us to point-constrain the IK handle to the hand_c node, which makes animating the arm more efficient. Maya allows us to do this, using a neat pivot-editing technique, as you will see in the following steps.

1. Create a locator and snap it to the Lwrist joint. Open the Attribute Editor for the locator, go to the Display section, and turn on Display Handle. Rename the locator **Lhand_c**. This node will be used to move the left arm and rotate the hand and the fingers.

2. Open the Hypergraph window, select Lhand_c and the Lforearm joint, and go to the upstream and downstream connections mode. You should see the nodes shown on the left side below. MM drag the Lhand_c node over the Lforearm joint node, and the Connection Editor should open. Connect Lhand_c's Rotate X to the Lforearm joint's Rotate X, as shown on the right side below. Now whenever Lhand_c rotates in the X axis, the Lforearm joint rotates in the X axis as well. If you have not turned off the Lforearm's Y and Z Degree of Freedom in the Attribute Editor before, you can do it now.

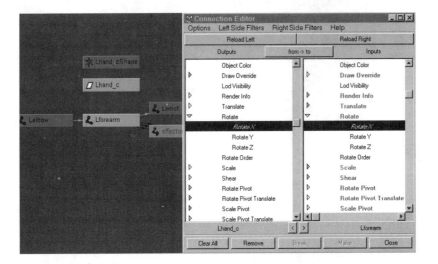

3. Follow the same procedure for the Lwrist joint. Connect Lhand_c's Rotate Y and Z to the Lwrist joint's Rotate Y and Z, respectively, using the Connection Editor, as shown below. Turn off the wrist joint's X Degree of Freedom in the Attribute Editor.

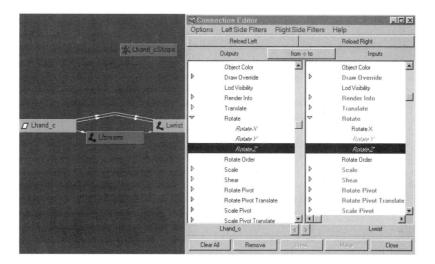

4. In the Outliner, go to the Larm hierarchy to select effector1. The effector isn't visible, but if you select the Move tool, you can see that it's positioned at the Lforearm joint. Press the Insert key to enter pivot edit mode, and snap the effector's pivot to the Lwrist joint, as shown below. Press Insert again to toggle out of pivot edit mode. Now if you select the IK handle, it is also positioned at the Lwrist joint.

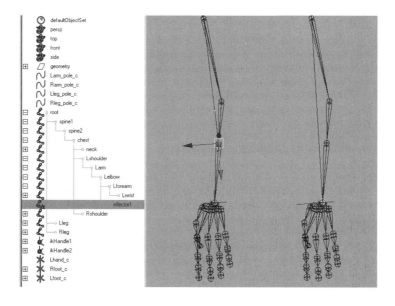

5. Select Lhand_c, then select the IK handle on the Lwrist, and apply the Point constraint. Hide the IK handle. You can now use Lhand_c to move the arm and rotate the Lforearm and the Lwrist joints.

6. The Pole Vector constraint for the left arm can also be applied now. Make a copy of the triangle and place it directly behind the Larm joint. Use it to apply the Pole Vector constraint for the arm IK handle, as shown below. Rename the triangle **Larm_pole_c**. It's placed behind the arm because the elbow bends the opposite way from the knee, as shown below.

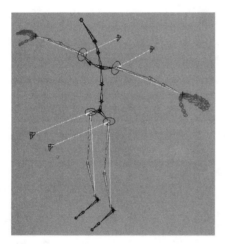

7. Let's add some attributes to the Lhand_c node to use as Set Driven keys for animating the fingers. Add attributes called **Fist** and **Grab**.

8. We want to set the driven keys with all the finger joints so that when the Fist value reaches 10, the fingers will be curled into a fist. Select the three joints of each of the five fingers below the Lwrist joint and load them as driven attributes. Load Lhand_c as the driver.

9. Select the Fist attribute from the Driver window. Select all of the joints in the Driven window, select the rotateZ attribute, and click the Key button, as shown below. This connects all of the joints' Z rotation to the Fist attribute.

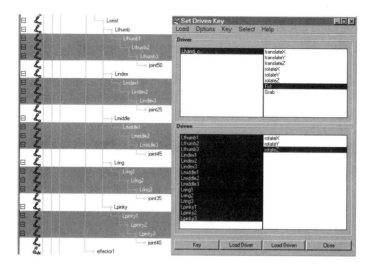

10. Select Lhand_c. In the Channel box, enter **10** in the Fist field. Rotate the finger joints in the Z axis to make a fist. Click the Set Driven Key window's Key button again. The Lhand_c node's Fist attribute is now set up to rotate the fingers into a fist, as shown below.

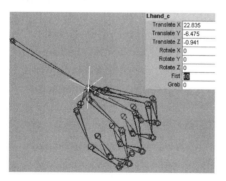

 You can refine the connection to include a negative value for the Fist attribute, which will stretch the fingers out. You may want to connect the thumb1 joint's Y rotation to the Fist attribute as well, to make a better fist. You might also want to add extra attributes in the individual finger joints to rotate the fingers separately.

11. Now we need to set the Grab attribute so that when the Grab value reaches 10, the fingers will seem to be reaching out to grab something. Select the Grab attribute in the Driver's window, and connect it to the rotateZ attributes of all the fingers in the Driven window, in the same way that the Fist attribute was connected. The Grab attribute is now set up to extend the fingers, as shown below.

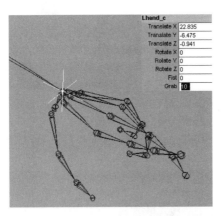

12. Repeat steps 1 through 11 for the right arm.

When you move the foot_c and hand_c nodes, you will notice a difference in the way that the feet and hands move. The feet keep the absolute rotation value of the foot_c node, whereas the hands rotate with the arms and rotate relative to the hand_c rotation values. For this reason, when you are rotating the hand_c nodes, you should keep in mind that the X rotation will always rotate the forearm, the Z rotation will rotate the hand up and down, and the Y rotation will rotate the hand sideways, no matter what position the hand is in. It's appropriate that the feet should move the way they do, because they need to stay planted on the ground. If you want the hand to move the same way as the feet, you can use the Orient constraint to connect the wrist joints to the hand_c nodes instead of using the approach outlined here.

Setting up the Eye Constraint

The last constraint we need to set up is for the character's eyes.

1. Copy two triangles from the pole_c nodes and rename them **Leye_c** and **Reye_c**.

2. Group Leye_c and Reye_c under a locator, as shown below. Rename the locator **Lookat**.

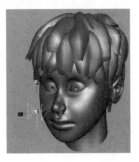

3. Apply the Aim constraint to the triangles, and template the triangles.

4. By scaling the Lookat locator, as well as moving it, you can have total control over how the eyes animate, as shown below.

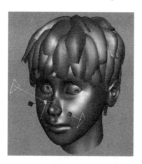

Setting up the Hierarchy

Finally, we need to place the different nodes into an animation-friendly hierarchy.

1. Select the root joint and choose Edit ➜ Group. Rename the top group node **Maya_Boy**. This node will be used to move the whole character in scene placements.

2. Under Maya_Boy is the root joint, which will control the upper-body movements. Place the foot_c and the leg_pole_c nodes under Maya_Boy.

3. Place the Lookat node under Maya Boy as well. You may think you should place the Lookat node under the head joint, so that the eyes will look where the head is turning to, but eyes that move with the rotation of the body joints tend to look dead, like those of puppets. In real life, people's gazes tend to stay fixed on specific objects, even if their bodies are moving about.

4. Depending on the kind of animation the character will be performing, you may want to place the leg_pole_c nodes under the root joint instead.

5. Place the hand_c and arm_pole_c nodes under the chest joint, because in most situations you would want the arms to be moving with the chest. But you may place these nodes under the root joint or Maya_Boy node instead, depending on the kind of animation you want.

6. If you find that hand_c flips when it's grouped under the chest joint, go to the Channel box and enter zeros in the rotation fields to fix the problem. You should see something close to the hierarchy shown below when you are finished.

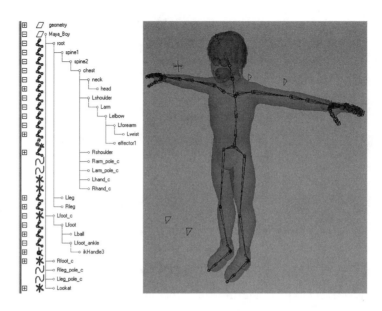

The character skeleton is now ready for animation. For your reference, a `character_setup_complete.mb` file is included in the Chapter 10 Working Files folder on the CD.

In your own work, it's important to remember that there is no one right way to build skeletons or place constraints to set up a character for animation. In each case, you need to consider what the character will be doing, how the body should deform, and how the limbs should rotate. Different situations call for different solutions. A properly prepared character will move well under close scrutiny, have the necessary range of movements, and be easy to animate.

Summary

In this chapter, you learned how to animate objects and cameras along paths, build skeletons properly, and create different kinds of IK handles on joints. You were also introduced to using constraints. Finally, you built a hierarchy of nodes involving joints, IK handles, and constraints to prepare the character modeled in the previous chapters for animation.

In the next chapter, we will cover how to use Maya deformers and prepare for facial animation.

Deformers

MAYA

Chapter 11

If the only way to model and animate were by pushing and pulling points, it would make life very difficult for modelers and be the bane of many animators' existence. Thankfully, Maya provides deformers, which let you bypass most of the menial work. With Maya's deformers, you can quickly build and animate deformed surfaces with a high level of control. Several deformers are indispensable for modeling and animating in Maya.

This chapter covers the following topics:

- Lattice deformation
- Cluster deformation
- Nonlinear deformation
- Sculpt deformation
- Wire deformation
- Blend Shape deformation
- Deformation editing
- Advanced facial animation techniques

Creating Deformers

Maya provides many types of deformers, which work in different ways. All of the deformers can deform anything with control points, including CVs on curves and surfaces, vertices on polygons, points on subdivision surfaces, and lattice points. Many deformers can also deform multiple surfaces, maintaining their tangency during the deformation process.

All deformers also work as sets, called *deformation sets*. You can edit the points being influenced by a deformation by changing their membership in the set, using the Relationship Editor, the Edit Membership tool, or the Paint Set Membership tool (discussed later in the chapter, in the "Editing Deformations" section).

All of the deformers and editing tools we will be covering in this chapter can be found on the Deform menu in the Animation module.

Lattice Deformation

Lattice is one of the most frequently used deformers. When you apply Lattice to an object, Maya creates an influence lattice and a base lattice around the object. When you transform the influence lattice or its points, the object inside the lattice transforms with it, or gets deformed by it, according to the degree of difference between the influence lattice and the base lattice.

Lattice allows you to control the deformation of complicated objects with fewer control points than you would need if you were deforming the objects directly. Because of this, the deformation is easier to create and the results are smoother.

Creating Lattices

You can apply Lattice deformation to a group of objects, only some points of an object, or points of a group of objects. You can even apply Lattice to points of a lattice, as shown in Figure 11.1, on the right. The lattice on the left in Figure 11.1 is made up of points from four objects. The shape in the middle is two tori, with the top torus latticed at the object level and the bottom torus latticed at its two top rows of CVs.

To apply Lattice, simply select the points or object(s) you want deformed and select Deform ➜ Create Lattice. You should see the influence lattice. The base lattice is also created, but it is hidden.

If you are animating the object being deformed, you will want the lattice to transform with the object. To make this possible, group the lattice and its base lattice under the deformed object. Grouping is available as an option setting when you are creating the lattice, or you can do it after you create the lattice.

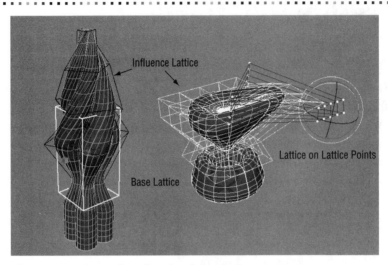

Figure 11.1 *Examples of Lattice deformation*

Lattice has its own local space, called STU space, which parallels the XYZ coordinate system. When you create or edit a lattice, you can adjust the STU divisions of the lattice, giving it more or fewer lattice points than the default setting.

Skinning an object indirectly with Lattice can be a great way to animate because Maya's lattice is so efficient, but sometimes you may run into a situation where an object is being transformed twice: from the lattice and from the skinning. See the discussion of the Relationship Editor later in this chapter for an example of how to deal with double-transformation problems.

Another way to adjust a lattice is through the Local Divisions setting, which is activated with the Local Mode setting. When Local Mode is turned on, each point exerts influence according to the Local Divisions setting, as shown in the left two examples in Figure 11.2. The default is 2, 2, 2, which means each point exerts influence up to two points away in STU space. When Local Mode is turned off, each point in the lattice exerts influence on the whole area. You usually want to leave Local Mode turned on.

The Freeze Geometry setting locks the object where it is being influenced. With this setting, when the object transforms, the deformed part of it stays fixed, as shown in the right two examples in Figure 11.2. You can activate Freeze Geometry in the Attribute Editor after lattice creation. You can also move the deformed object partially, then turn on Freeze Geometry, and the object will lock where it is.

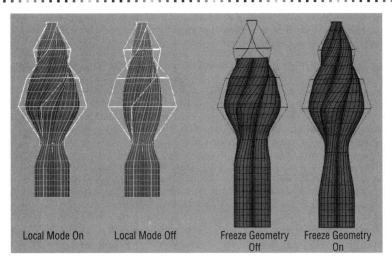

Figure 11.2 *Using Local Mode and Freeze Geometry with Lattice deformation*

Tweaking Lattices

To tweak a lattice, pick-mask Lattice Point over it, and you can manipulate its points in the same way as regular control points.

You can also manipulate the lattice to fit around an object better by transforming both the influence lattice and the base lattice. You can select the hidden base lattice in the Outliner. As long as the two lattices are being transformed together, no deformation occurs. When you are doing this, make sure that all of the control points of the object being deformed remain inside the lattice, or they will not deform with the lattice.

The lattice is created to fit an object's bounding box. If you find that some points are not deforming along with the lattice, try scaling up the influence lattice and the base lattice just a bit to make sure no points are straying outside the deformation.

If you've been tweaking the lattice points and you decide to start over from the original shape or to add more STU subdivisions, you can select Edit Lattice ➜ Remove Lattice Tweaks. If you want to undo the transformations you've applied to the lattice at the object level as well as the tweaks to the lattice points, select Edit Lattice ➜ Reset Lattice, which moves the lattice back to its original point of creation.

Cluster Deformation

Unlike the other deformers, Cluster produces a weighted deformation. When you apply cluster to an object, it creates weighted points in the cluster set. This is probably the most useful thing about using clusters.

The default weight of the clustered points is 1.0, but you can adjust their weights by using the Component Editor or the Paint Weights tool (Artisan). Let's try a simple exercise to see how to create clusters and adjust their weights.

1. Create a plane. Set it to span 10 patches in U and V.

2. Drag to select 25 CVs at the center of the plane. Select Deform → Create Cluster with the default settings.

3. A cluster handle appears as the small letter *c*. Select the Move tool and pull the *c* up. You should see something like the picture shown on the left in Figure 11.3.

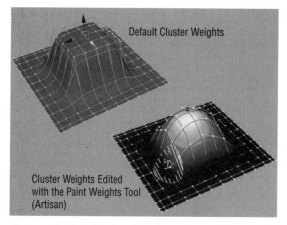

Default Cluster Weights

Cluster Weights Edited with the Paint Weights Tool (Artisan)

Figure 11.3 *Adjusting Cluster deformation weights with the Paint Weights tool*

4. Select the surface, and start the Paint Weights tool (from the Deform menu). Apply a bit of smoothing with low settings around the edges of the clustered points. You should be able to get a more rounded shape, as shown in the picture on the right in Figure 11.3.

5. Select the clustered points and choose Window → General Editors → Component Editor. Click the Weighted Deformers tab. Select the points being

deformed, and they should appear in a column called cluster1, with various values created by the application of the Paint Weights tool. You can type in lower weight values to round the cluster edges or use the slider at the bottom to interactively adjust the point values.

In general, when you want to have precise control over the percentage of the weighted points and the points are easy to pick in groups, the Component Editor is a good tool to use. When you want a more organic look or the surface is very dense, the Paint Weights tool (Artisan) is more efficient. (See Chapter 7, "Working with Artisan," for more information about using Artisan.)

When you are working with clusters, the cluster handle c has a default Select Priority Level of 2, which means that it is selected along with the surface it's deforming. You can open the General Preferences dialog box and change the Select Priority Level for the cluster handle, or you can open the Attribute Editor and choose Display Handle in the Cluster Handle Display section. A handle with the highest Select Priority Level will appear, which will allow you to select the cluster over the surface.

When you move an object that is clustered, you would expect the cluster handle to move with the object, but it doesn't. If you want the cluster to stay on the surface as it moves, group it under the object. First, open the Attribute Editor, click the Cluster tab, and make sure the Relative setting is on for Cluster Attributes. Next, if the object is at the origin, you can simply group the cluster under the object in the Outliner or Hypergraph window. If not, group the cluster to itself once to move the center to the origin, then group that node under the object. (Edit ➜ Parent will produce the same result.)

Nonlinear Deformations

The six deformers in the Nonlinear submenu all deform in, yes, nonlinear fashion:

- Bend bends an object along a circular arc.
- Flare flares and tapers an object.
- Sine curves an object into sine waves.
- Squash stretches and squashes an object.
- Twist twists an object.
- Wave creates circular ripples on an object.

These are all simple functions, but they are remarkably effective in creating their intended effects, as illustrated in Figure 11.4.

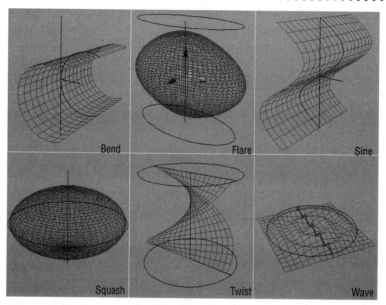

Figure 11.4 *The six nonlinear deformers*

Each of the nonlinear functions can deform just the selected points of objects, just like lattices or clusters. They can also deform multiple objects and maintain tangency between patches. The deformations start and finish along an axis line of your choice. The default setting is –1 and 1 of the local Y axis of the object being deformed, but it automatically transforms to fit the object. You can use the manipulator handles to interactively adjust the deformation attributes. Select the deformer in the Channel box Input section, open the modeling window, and press T to display the Show Manipulator option.

You can combine any number of deformers together. It's easy to create complex shapes by manipulating the deformer attributes of the different deformers. Note that when you use multiple deformers, their order of creation is important (see the "Changing the Deformation Order" section later in this chapter). You can animate the deformers, and you can also animate the deformed objects.

Let's try some examples with the nonlinear deformers. First, we'll use Bend and Sine to twist an object.

1.　Create a plane. Increase its subdivisions.

2. Apply Bend to it (select Deform ➜ Nonlinear ➜ Bend), with Curvature set to 3. Then rotate the plane about 15 degrees in the X axis. The plane twists, as shown in Figure 11.5.

3. Add Sine to it (select Deform ➜ Nonlinear ➜ Sine), with Amplitude set to 0.5. Transform the plane back and forth in the Z axis. The twisting now seems more random, as shown in Figure 11.5.

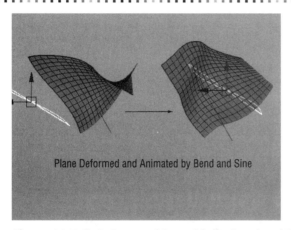

Plane Deformed and Animated by Bend and Sine

Figure 11.5 *Twisting an object with the Bend and Sine deformers*

4. Group the deformers and the plane. Now you can transform the deformers and the plane together as well.

You can quickly create a shape of a jet engine by applying Wave to a sphere, as shown in the left picture in Figure 11.6. You can start with any shape and play with the manipulator handles until you get the shape you want. Let's try creating an organic tree shape with the Flare, Sine, and Wave deformers.

1. Create a cylinder. Increase its sections and spans, and scale it up in the Y axis into a pillar shape.

2. Apply Flare to it (select Deform ➜ Nonlinear ➜ Flare). Flare out the bottom and taper the top.

3. Apply Sine to the object. Make the cylinder form about two waves.

4. Apply Sine again with a different wavelength and rotate it to make the cylinder wave more randomly.

5. Apply Wave (select Deform ➜ Nonlinear ➜ Wave), setting the Amplitude and Wave Length to about 0.1. Rotate the wave until the cylinder becomes gnarled like a tree, as shown in the middle picture in Figure 11.6.

6. Copy and scale the cylinder to make smaller branches, as shown in the picture on the right in Figure 11.6.

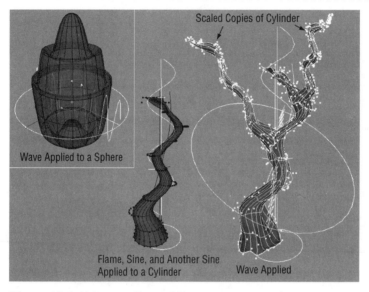

Figure 11.6 *Using nonlinear deformers to create shapes*

Sculpt Deformation

Sculpt deformation uses a sphere as a sculpting tool to make round or flat ring-shaped deformations. It can deform objects in three different modes—Flip, Project, and Stretch—using the appropriate settings as shown in Figure 11.7.

The Max Displacement and Dropoff Distance settings for Sculpt may seem similar, but they're not. The Max Displacement value determines the amount of strength with which the sphere can push or pull a deforming point. The Dropoff Distance setting determines the area of points that can be influenced.

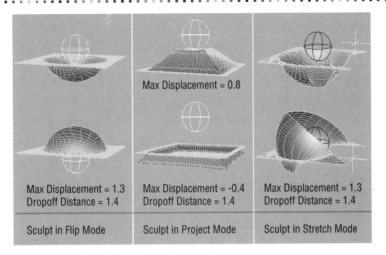

Figure 11.7 *Sculpt deformation modes*

Using Sculpt in Flip Mode

When Sculpt is in Flip mode, the sphere acts as if it has a force field, pushing points away from its center in the direction of the sphere's normal vector. If the sphere's center crosses a point, there is a "flip," because the point being pushed is suddenly pushed in the opposite direction.

Using Sculpt in Project Mode

Sculpt's Project mode is the opposite of the Flip mode. In Project mode, the sphere acts as a magnet, causing the influenced points to snap to it. A Max Displacement value of 1 causes the points to snap to the sphere's surface; values between 0 and 1 cause the points to travel a percentage between their original position and the sphere's surface. Notice that the deformation shapes produced by Flip and Project are quite different in Figure 11.7.

Using Sculpt in Stretch Mode

In Stretch mode, the sphere calculates its position relative to a Sculpt stretch origin locator, which is created with the sphere and stretches the affected points away from the locator. With the Stretch mode, you can group the stretch origin locator and the sphere and animate them together, as in the example shown on the left side in Figure 11.8. You can also change the Inside Mode setting to Ring or Even, as shown on the top right in Figure 11.8.

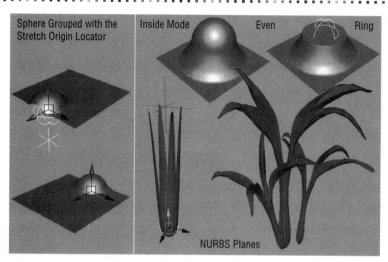

Figure 11.8 *Examples of Sculpt in Stretch mode*

Sculpt can be used in many creative ways. Just by sculpting a NURBS plane, you can easily fashion plant leaves, as shown on the bottom right in Figure 11.8. Once you've stretched the plane, scale out the CVs at the top, tighten the CVs in the middle, and tweak the CVs a bit to make the leaves asymmetrical.

Wire Deformation

Wire deformation works with an influence wire and a base wire, like Lattice deformation. The deformation occurs according to the relative distance between the two wires. Wire deformation is useful for creating facial expressions.

Applying Wire Deformation

Let's first try out Wire deformation on a simple shape.

1. Create a NURBS plane. Scale it out to 3, and make its patches U and V 16.

2. Place a circle on the plane, and draw a curve with one span inside, as shown in Figure 11.9 on the left side.

3. Select Deform ➜ Wire Tool and accept the default settings. Maya asks you to select shape(s) to deform. Select the plane and press Enter. Maya then asks you to select wire curve(s). Select the curve inside the circle and press Enter. If the deformer has successfully been created, the plane should turn pink.

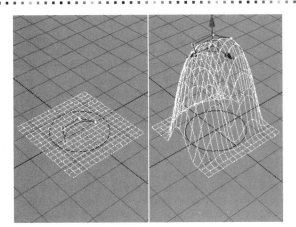

Figure 11.9 *Wire deformation*

4. The curve is now called a *wire*. Note that a hidden duplicate of the wire, called the base wire, has been created as well. Translate up the wire as shown in Figure 11.9 on the right side. Then try moving up the base wire. As the distance between the two curves decreases, so does the intensity of the Wire deformation.

5. Return the wires to their original position, select the plane, and delete history. The Wire deformer node disappears, but the base wire, which you need to delete manually, remains.

Using Holders

Let's repeat the process, but this time, we'll use the Holders option. Holders restrict Wire deformation by limiting the influence of the wires.

1. Select Deform ➜ Wire Tool ❏ and click Holders. As before, select the plane and press Enter. Then select the curve and press Enter.

2. Maya asks you to select a holder shape or clear the selection. Select the circle and press Enter. Maya now asks you to either select another wire (for more influence wires) or clear the selection. Clear the selection by deselecting all objects and press Enter to complete the wire creation. Notice that another invisible base wire is created.

3. Try moving the wire again and notice the difference. In the example on the left in Figure 11.10, the wire influence is overshooting the circle holder area.

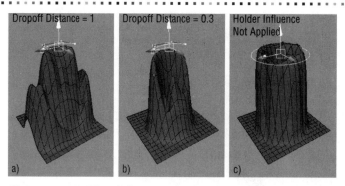

Figure 11.10 *Wire deformation on a plane with the Holders option*

4. In the Channel box, select wire1 under Outputs and decrease the Dropoff Distance setting to 0.3. The wire influence is now restricted inside the circle holder, as shown in the middle picture in Figure 11.10.

5. Try moving the circle up to see the difference between having a holder and not having one, as in the picture on the right in Figure 11.10.

Group all of the wires—the influence wire, the base wire, and the holder wire—under the object being deformed so that they will move with the object.

Using Dropoff Locators

Wire deformers have an additional control tool called Dropoff Locators, which can give you subtle localized control over the Wire deformation. Let's continue with our plane example to see how this tool works.

1. Move the wire down nearer to the plane surface. RM choose over the wire and pick-mask Curve Point.

2. Select a point near the second CV, and then Shift+select another point near the third CV.

3. Select Deform ➜ Wire Dropoff Locator with the default settings, and you should see something like the top-left picture in Figure 11.11.

4. Open the wire's Attribute Editor. There is now a Locators section, where you'll find sliders to control the locators' positions, their influence percentages, and

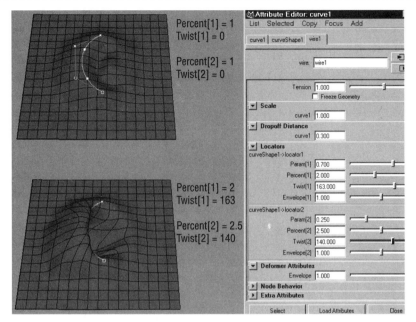

Figure 11.11 *Wire deformation with Dropoff Locators and the Twist setting*

their twist. The Twist setting simply twists the deformed points around the curve at the locator point.

5. Change the Locators settings as follows: Percent[1] to 2, Twist[1] to 163, Percent[2] to 2.5, and Twist[2] to 140. You should see something like the bottom-left picture in Figure 11.11.

Controlling Deformer Effects with Envelopes

For all the deformers, there is a general attribute channel called Envelope. Some deformers such as Blend Shape and Cluster actually have it as part of their option box. On all deformers, it can be accessed through the Attribute Editor, under the Deformer Attributes tab, or through the Channel box Inputs section.

The default Envelope value is always 1, but you can change it from −2 to 2. When the value is at 0, the deformer has no effect. At −1 the deformer produces the opposite effect. At 2, the deformer's effect is doubled. Such capacity can be useful for Blend Shapes, because its default sliders in the Attribute Editor or the Blend Shape Editor go from 0 to 1 only. When you increase the Envelope value to 2, the sliders' range essentially increases from 0 to 2.

Forming Facial Expressions

Now that we've experimented with a basic shape, let's look at how Wire deformation works on a face.

1. Open the Demo_Head.mb file from the Chapter 11 Working Files folder on the CD, or if you saved the one you created yourself in Chapters 6 and 7, open that file. Select the face and display the mesh edges and points by using the Display ➔ Subdiv Surface Components submenu.

2. Create a NURBS circle with the number of sections that matches the points going around the mouth, which should be 14 sections.

3. Use Isolate Select to view just the mouth area and the circle, as shown below. To do this, select the circle, select the subdivision faces around the mouth area, and then choose Show ➔ Isolate Select ➔ View Selected in the modeling window. Snap the CVs to the points around the mouth. This circle can be used as wire to give subtle control to mouth shapes.

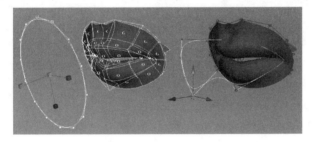

4. Create a curve that goes under the eye area and another one over the eyebrow area by snapping CVs to the points on those areas, as shown below.

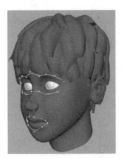

5. Use the Wire tool on the face (Deform ➔ Wire Tool), using the three curves as wires. In the Outliner, you should see base wires created for each wire curve.

6. In the Channel box, open wire1 and reduce the values of the three Dropoff Distance attributes for the three curves to about 0.5. You generally will want to localize the influence of the wires to only about this much or less. But try moving the curves, pulling CVs, and see what you think is the best setting for each of the curves. Remember that you can also animate the strength of the influence.

7. Try moving the CVs to see what facial expressions you can create, as in the picture below on the left. You can also create blend shapes with the wire curves and animate them as well, as in the picture on the right; the wires are hidden, and the curves beside the face are blend targets.

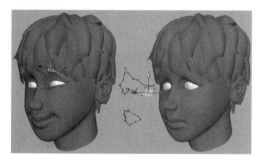

Blend Shape Deformation

Blend Shape is different from the other deformers. It is specifically designed to perform morphing tasks, and it has a separate slider editor. You can also access blend shape sliders in the Attribute Editor or through the channels in the Channel box.

Blend Shape is especially useful for facial animation. In this type of animation, a group of set shapes such as certain phonemes or facial expressions need to be readily accessible, editable and, as the name suggests, blendable.

Applying Blend Shape Deformation

Blending works best when the *target object* and the *base object* have the same *topology*, meaning they have the same number of CVs in the same order. Although Maya allows you to blend objects with different topologies, you may not always get the results you want.

To see what we mean, let's go through some examples.

1. Create two spheres. Change the first sphere's shape by pulling points, as shown below.

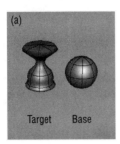

Target   Base

2. Select the first sphere, which will be the target, and then Shift+select the second, which will become the base. Choose Deform ➔ Create Blend Shape and accept the default settings.

3. Select Window ➔ Animation Editors ➔ Blend Shape. An editor opens with a target slider. A blendShape node is created, and the target slider is an attribute of that node. Maya 3 has a Horizontal orientation option, which displays the sliders horizontally. The default setting is vertical. Slide the vertical slider to 1, and the second sphere should morph into an exact replica of the first sphere, as shown below.

Default Blend Shape

4. You can also Blend Shape points. Select the first two rows of the first sphere (target) and the same for the second (base), then apply Blend Shape. You get something like the picture shown below.

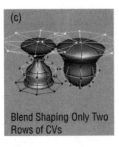

Blend Shaping Only Two
Rows of CVs

5. Notice that there is now another slider in the editor. Repeat step 4, but set the Origin setting to World in the Blend Shape option box. The blending calculates not only the relative translation of the target points, but their world space coordinates as well, as shown below. The morphing points of the base object translate exactly to where the target points are, no matter how the base object is transformed.

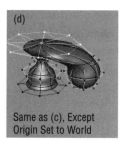

(d)

Same as (c), Except
Origin Set to World

6. Select the middle CVs of the second sphere and delete them, as shown below. The topology of the second sphere has changed; it now has eight fewer CVs than the first sphere.

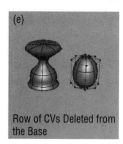

(e)

Row of CVs Deleted from
the Base

7. Apply Blend Shape to the spheres again, Maya replies with the message, "Error: No deformable objects selected." This is because the default Blend Shape setting checks to make sure the topology of the target object matches that of the base object. Turn off the Check Topology setting in the option box. Maya proceeds to morph the base object the best it can. The result is as shown below.

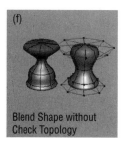

(f)

Blend Shape without
Check Topology

Blend-Shaping Hierarchies and Editing Shapes

When you are morphing a group of objects, you must make sure that the hierarchy of the target objects is the same as the base objects' hierarchy, or the morphing will not work properly.

In the picture shown in Figure 11.12, the face on the left is the base, and the one on the right is the target. The face is actually made up of four NURBS patches, as listed in the Outliner in Figure 11.12. Notice that the hierarchies of nodes are in the same order both under Face and Smile. Selecting Smile, then selecting Face, and then applying the default Blend Shape produces a slider named Smile. You can find an example NURBS_face.mb file with blend shapes in the Chapter 11 Working Files folder on the CD.

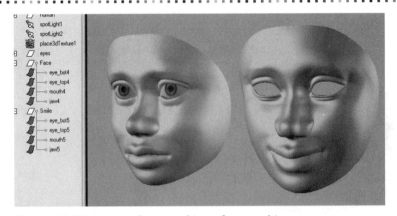

Figure 11.12 *Base and target objects for morphing*

To add more target shapes to a surface that already has a blend shape, create more target shapes, select them, select the base object, and choose Edit Blend Shape ➜ Add. If you see an error message saying you must specify a blendShape node, open the Add option box, choose Specify Node, and enter the name of the existing blendShape node.

Another way to add a shape is to open the Blend Shape Editor and click the Add button for that blend shape. This creates a copy of the base shape with the other blend shapes' influences on it. You can remove a target slider by selecting the same target shape you used to create that slider, then selecting the base, and then choosing Edit Blend Shape ➜ Remove. If you want to switch the order in which the target sliders are listed, you can do that two at a time by selecting two target shapes, then selecting Edit Blend Shape ➜ Swap.

You also can edit the target values in the Channel box or in the Attribute Editor, where the targets appear as sliders under the Weight section of the blendShape tab. Figure 11.13 shows some examples of target shapes, the blendShape tab of the Attribute Editor, and the Blend Shape Editor.

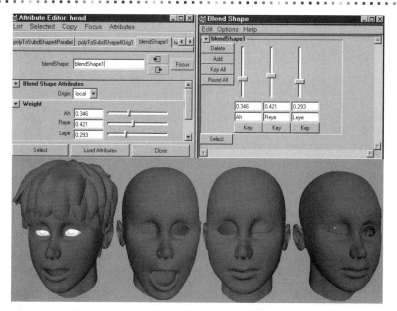

Figure 11.13 *Examples of facial targets for blend shapes*

Once you are satisfied with all the blendShape targets, you can delete the target objects to lighten the scene. This prevents you from further editing the target shapes, but the blending information remains with the base object, so you can always recreate a target geometry by copying it from the base object.

Editing Deformations

Deformations depend on the relationships among points and their groupings. The controls you can use for editing deformations include the Relationship Editor, Edit Membership tool, Paint Set Membership tool, and the Prune Membership function. You can also edit the deformation order.

Editing Deformation Sets

Whenever you create a deformer, Maya creates a deformer set of the same name. This set shows up in the Deformer Set Editing module of the Relationship Editor. You can use this editor to edit the membership of points in the deformer sets. The editor's Edit menu allows you to select any point in a set, add points to a set, and remove points from a set. It also lets you select or delete deformers. Let's go through a simple example.

1. Start a new scene. Create a cylinder.

2. Select the top two rows of its CVs and apply Lattice deformation with the default settings to the points (select Deform → Create Lattice).

3. Select both the cylinder and the lattice in the modeling window, and apply Cluster deformation with the default settings (select Deform → Create Cluster).

4. Try moving the cluster. You will see that you have a problem commonly known as *double transformation*, which is illustrated below. The points inside the lattice are being moved twice—once by the Lattice deformer, and again by the Cluster deformer. To solve this problem, the cluster should stop moving the points inside the lattice, because you want the lattice to still be able to affect the points on the cylinder.

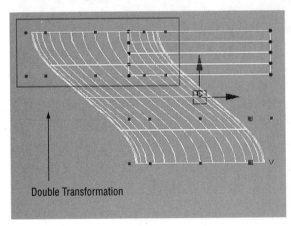

Double Transformation

5. Select Window → Relationship Editors → Deformer Sets. You should see the editor with two deformer sets on the left side: ffd1Set and cluster1Set. Click the plus signs to their left, and you will see a list of all the points that are being deformed by the lattice and the cluster.

6. Highlight ffd1Set and select Edit ➜ Select Set Members. You also can highlight the points inside the set and select Edit ➜ Select Highlighted. In the modeling window, the points become selected.

7. Highlight cluster1Set, and either click the minus sign button at the top of the window or select Edit ➜ Remove Selected Items. The selected points are no longer part of the cluster set, and they are not transformed twice.

When you are in the Relationship Editor, you can unclutter the right window by RM choosing over it and clicking Show DAG Objects Only. (DAG stands for Directed Acyclic Graph.)

Using Tools to Edit Membership

Maya provides a quick way to do what we just did in the previous section without using the Relationship Editor. You can use the Edit Membership tools to solve the double transformation and other deformation problems. Let's try it.

1. Use Undo to create the double transformation situation again (or repeat steps 1 through 3 in the previous section to recreate it).

2. Select Deform ➜ Edit Membership Tool. Maya asks you to select a set or a deformer. Our goal is to remove points from the cluster, so select it in the Outliner. All the points belonging to the cluster become selected.

3. Ctrl+click or marquee the points you want to remove. (If you want to add points to a deformer, you can Shift+click or marquee the points.)

The Paint Set Membership tool works in the same way as the Edit Membership tool. To use it in our example, you would select the cylinder, select Deform ➜ Paint Set Membership Tool ❑, select cluster1Set as the set to modify, choose the Remove operation, and brush over the cylinder, as shown in Figure 11.14. The advantage of using the Paint Set Membership tool is that it gives you color feedback, telling you which points belong to which deformer, which can be useful when you are editing rigid skinned objects. (See Chapter 13, "Character Animation Exercises," for more information about skinning techniques.)

Pruning Membership

With Lattice, Cluster, Sculpt, and Wire deformers, Maya provides a quick pruning function. The Deform ➜ Prune Membership function removes all the points of a deformer set that, at the time of the pruning, have not been moved from their undeformed positions.

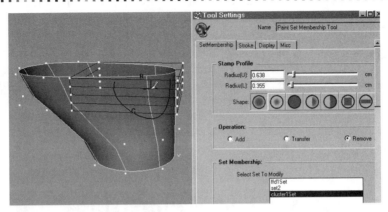

Figure 11.14 *Using the Paint Set Membership tool*

While pruning can lighten a scene by reducing deformer calculations, you may remove points that seem unnecessary from sets but later find that they need to be deformed after all. In such cases, you can always add those points to the deformer set again, using the editing tools described in the previous sections.

Changing the Deformation Order

Deformation order, or the deformation chain, refers to how multiple deformers affect a surface in order. Their order is usually determined by their order of creation, but you can use the advanced option settings to change their placement in the chain. You can also use the Complete List window for a selected object to edit the order. The best way to understand how deformation order works is to go through another simple example.

1. Create a NURBS cylinder. Scale it up to 5 in Y, and increase its spans to 4.

2. Copy the cylinder. Translate it out and deform it to look something like the one shown below.

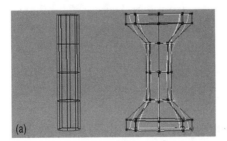

3. Apply Blend Shape to the original cylinder, as shown below. Set the Blend value to 0, and then delete or hide the copied cylinder.

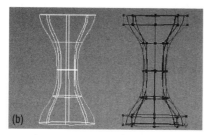

4. Apply Sine to the original cylinder, with an Amplitude setting of 1. You should see something like the shape shown below.

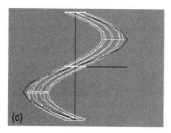

5. Increase the cylinder's Blend value to 1. You now see something like the shape shown below. If you want to see the cylinder morph into a shape like the one you produced in step 3, you need to change the deformation order assigned to Sine and Blend Shape.

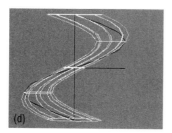

6. With the cylinder still selected, click the List of Operations button (adjacent to the Make Live button) and choose Complete List. You can also RM choose over the cylinder and select Inputs ➜ Complete List.

7. In the Complete List window, notice that history of the node chain starts from the bottom. MM drag the Non Linear node down to the Blend Shape node until you see a box appear around it, and then release the mouse button. The nodes' placements have switched. Now when you increase the cylinder's Blend value, it overrides the Sine shape, as shown below.

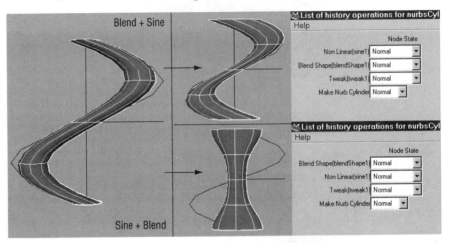

Advanced Facial Animation

A discussion of advanced facial animation techniques could quickly fill an entire book. Here, we will deal with only several basic points. At the simplest level, you can have a character talk with two shapes: open_mouth and close_mouth. Consider any muppet character, and you will see what we mean. For facial expressions at the simplest level, you need only close_eyes and open_eyes (and perhaps not even those). For a more realistic setup, however, the number of facial shapes, or targets, can quickly grow to dozens.

Creating the Teeth, Tongue, and Oral Cavity

Before you can work on facial shapes, you need to create the teeth and gums, as shown in (a) in Figure 11.15. The upper teeth do not move because they are fixed to the skull; the lower teeth should rotate with the jaw. You should use Set Driven Key to have the lower teeth driven by open mouth shapes such as *ah* and *oh*. Make sure the rotation pivot for the lower teeth is similar to the jaw bone's, around the ear area. (See Chapter 9, "Animating in Maya," for details on the Set Driven Key feature.)

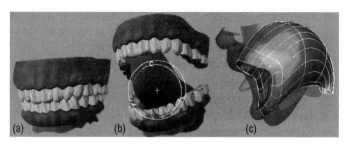

Figure 11.15 *Teeth, tongue, and oral cavity for facial animation*

If you are building a cartoony character, you may want to use a simple folded plane as teeth. It can actually look better on a character than more realistic teeth. The bugs in Pixar's A Bug's Life, *for example, have such simple teeth.*

You may also want a tongue, its tip clustered, to strike the back of the upper teeth for what the linguists, if not the dental experts, call the *alveolars* (*s, z, t, d, n, l*), or to the bottom of the upper teeth for the *th* sounds. An example is shown in (b) in Figure 11.15.

Another necessity is the oral cavity. A good way to proceed is to offset two or three curves from the boundary isoparms of the lips so you can maintain a procedural connection with the mouth shapes, create copies of those offset curves, translate them into the throat area, and loft. This is illustrated in (c) in Figure 11.15. You may want to wait until you have finished building the face before creating the oral cavity. It should become a morphing part of all the mouth targets.

Creating the inner mouth parts can be tricky and time-consuming. If you are not going to have close-up shots of a character's mouth, it may not be worth the effort. As an alternative, you can create a textured plane, curve it, and position it inside the mouth.

Creating Mouth Shapes

There is no fixed list of facial shapes you should create, nor is there a standard guide for how to set them up for facial animation. Specific projects call for specialized solutions, and animators will always experiment with different methods.

Setting up well-thought-out mouth targets may take longer, but it will save time in the long run, especially if you will be using the character repeatedly. Using Blend Shape for lip-synching and Wire deformation for fine tweaking and facial expressions will probably give the best results. Figure 11.16 shows a sample list of blend shapes for lip-synching.

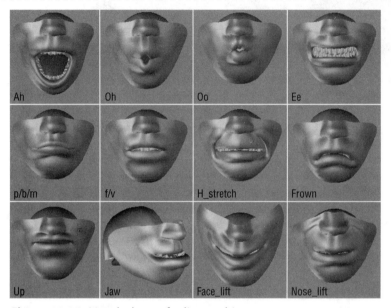

Figure 11.16 *Mouth shapes for lip-synching*

The *ah* and *oo* shapes are absolute necessities—*ah* because it opens the mouth and lowers the jaw, and *oo* because it can also be the shape for sounds such as *ch*, *sh*, and *w*, not to mention kissing and whistling.

You can get by using one shape for both *oo* and *oh*, but they are quite different shapes. The jaw drops for *oh*, creating a hollow space inside the mouth, whereas for *oo*, everything pushes up. The *ee* shape shown in Figure 11.16 is an extremely strong shape, which can double as an expression of anger or, combined with *ah*, screaming. For unaccented *ee* shapes, you may want to use the H(horizontal)_stretch instead.

For H_stretch, Frown, and Face_lift, you could separate them further into Left and Right targets. But be careful not to disturb the few middle CVs of the face, or you will get a double-transformation effect (described earlier in the "Editing Deformations" section).

For many of these shapes, if you build the targets carefully, you can also use their negatives. Figure 11.17 shows the negatives of some of the shapes.

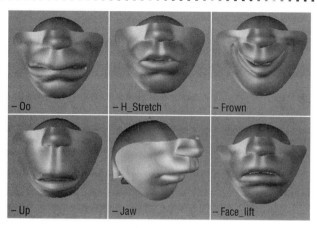

Figure 11.17 *Negative-value mouth shapes*

Note that the sounds discussed here have been spelled out like regular words; they are not accurately spelled phonetic sounds. For proper phonetic spelling, you should follow the IPA (International Phonetic Alphabet). Different dictionaries use slightly different spelling methods, but *ah* would generally be listed as [a:], *oo* as [u:], *ee* as [i:], and so on. Letters such as *c* are represented differently depending on how they are used. A soft *c* is [s]; a hard *c* is [k].

Setting Up Multiple Blend Shapes

One advantage of working with a face that's been built in patches, such as the one shown in Figure 11.18, is that when you are setting up your blending targets for the face, you can separate mouth shapes from facial expressions. This approach makes the setup more economical and efficient than throwing everything in together. You create two groups of blendShapes. The mouth and the jaw patches hold mouth shapes such as those described in the previous section. The eye patches hold facial expressions such as eyes closing and showing emotions—happy, sad, angry, and so on. Setting things up this way can be a bit more complex, however, and requires the use of the Set Driven Key feature.

In the example shown in Figure 11.18, Blend Shape was applied not to the top Face node, but to the Eye_area and Mouth_area nodes. This creates two blendShape groups: one for the mouth area and another for the eye area. The two targets, Ah and Eyeclose, are applied to the base objects, Mouth_area and Eye_area. The two shapes are independent of each other, so that when the eyes close, the mouth area is not affected, and vice versa. The third shape, Smile, however, is a combination of two target shapes: the

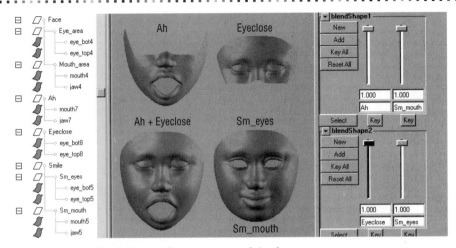

Figure 11.18 *Blend Shapes for two areas of the face*

Sm_eyes and Sm_mouth shapes. In the bottom-right picture in Figure 11.18, both shapes are at their maximum target value.

The two shapes must move together, or you can run into problems with patches overlapping or separating. When only the Sm_mouth slider is moved, creasing occurs, as shown in Figure 11.19. This is because the Sm_eyes slider does not deform the eye area, so there is overlapping. We can prevent this problem by making the Sm_mouth slider a driver for the Sm_eyes slider.

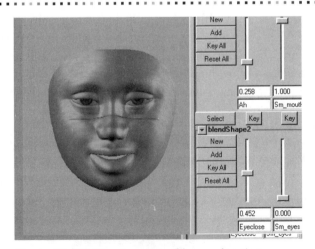

Figure 11.19 *Creasing caused by overlapping*

RM choose over a numeric input field in the Blend Shape Editor to pop up a menu. Select Set Driven Key. You can select the blendShape node in the Blend Shape Editor by clicking the Select button. Specify Sm_mouth as the driver and Sm_eyes as the driven. Key them at 0 and 1. Sm_mouth should now drive Sm_eyes, as shown in Figure 11.20.

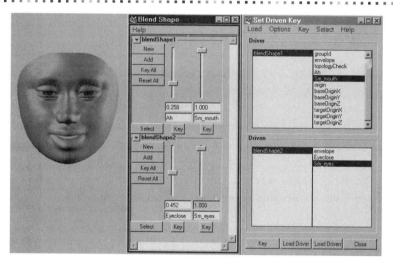

Figure 11.20 *Making the Sm_mouth slider a driver for the Sm_eyes slider*

Discerning Spoken Sounds

When you are setting up lip-synching, one of the worst mistakes you can make is to try to figure out the mouth shapes by going through the alphabet, spelling out what is spoken. It is better to reference a list of phonemes if you can, but better still to just follow the mouth shapes as the sounds are made. Here are a few rules that can help you to get started:

- Consonants are greatly affected by the sounds that surround them, which is a phonetic phenomenon called *assimilation*. For example, the consonant *d* in "how *do* you do?" and "how *did* you do?" forms two different mouth shapes, because the vowels that follow the *d* are different. A good rule to follow is to go through the vowels first, because they will often dictate how the neighboring consonants will be shaped. Once you figure out the vowels, the consonants will naturally fall into place.

- There is also a rule called vowel reduction or omission, which is a specific type of assimilation. For example, a phrase like "how did you do?" is often spoken "how ju do?". In a case like this, it helps to "unlearn" your reading skills; instead of trying to find sounds from the words, just listen.

- English is an intonational language. It's rhythmic, with regular beats of accented and unaccented syllables, and a few strong emphases punctuating different parts of sentences. You should listen to these emphases and figure out where the beats are falling. You can then skim through the unaccented segments and concentrate on nailing the accented syllables.

- For animation, you should be concerned only with what will be seen. If a character's back is toward you, for goodness sake, don't animate her face! If that seems obvious, then in the same way, you don't need to animate what goes on inside the mouth. Consonants such as *s*, *z*, *t*, *d*, *n*, and *j*, among others, can often be shown as just a slight up and down movement of the mouth. Consonants such as *k*, *g*, *ng*, and *h* matter only in that they fill time between vowel shapes. The *th* sounds (as in "*th*ing" and "*th*ey"), too, are indistinguishable in terms of shapes, and should be treated as one sound.

For many animators, lip-synch is not such an important part of facial animation. Far more important is creating proper facial expressions, especially in the eye area, and body poses that fit the action.

Keyframing and Tweaking Mouth Shapes

There are various methods of keyframing mouth shapes. You can use the Channel box, the Attribute Editor, or the Blend Shape Editor. It is generally not a good idea to keyframe individual shapes, because the shapes that are not keyframed may end up "floating" between their keyframes. A much more efficient method is to keyframe all of the shapes, then tweak them individually in the Graph Editor.

You can lock certain targets to exclude them from being keyframed if you know you won't be using them for a specific scene. For example, you might lock a smile target in a scene where you know the character isn't going to smile.

Keyframing with the Channel Box or Attribute Editor

The Channel box and Attribute Editor can be used to keyframe facial animation much like the Blend Shape Editor, although the Blend Shape Editor offers more functions.

In order to use the Channel box, you need to have the base object selected. The Attribute Editor has the Copy → Tear Off Copy function, which creates a copy window that still remains when the object is deselected. Another advantage of the Attribute Editor's torn-off copy is that it has sliders. The Channel box's targets are restricted to a value range of 0 to 1 for the targets, but you can set the Attribute Editor sliders to have a wider range of target values. Just type in numbers like –1 or 2 into the numeric input field, and the slider range will adjust accordingly.

You can use Key All in the Blend Shape Editor and in the Channel box, but not in the Attribute Editor. One way to get around this is to use the hotkey for setting keys. You may need to adjust the Set Key options to All Keyable Attributes in order to keyframe blended shapes. Figure 11.21 shows the Attribute Editor sliders and the Channel box being used to keyframe the blend shapes.

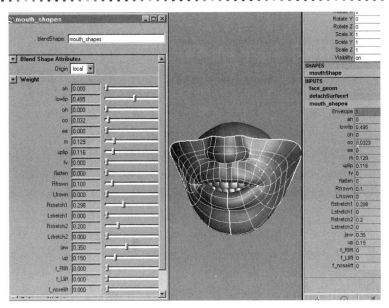

Figure 11.21 *Using the Attribute Editor and Channel box to keyframe blend shapes*

Tweaking with the Graph Editor

Once you've roughly animated the mouth shapes, you can use the Graph Editor to tweak the animation curves. You can also tweak using the Channel box or the sliders (turning on the Auto Key function will help), but only the function curves can give you a clear picture of how the shapes are moving through time. Figure 11.22 shows an example of the curves for the *oo* shape's rising and falling values in the Graph Editor.

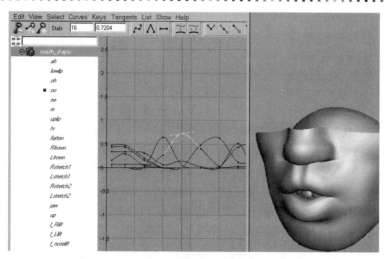

Figure 11.22 *Facial animation curves in the Graph Editor*

You would usually want to select either one or just a few different targets in the Graph Editor and focus on tweaking only those curves at one time, as shown in Figure 11.23. You may also want to turn off Curve in the Select menu if you are editing only keyframes.

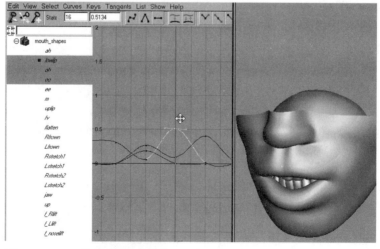

Figure 11.23 *Tweaking a curve in the Graph Editor*

When you're lip-synching a character's mouth movements to an audio file, the best approach seems to be to hit the sounds to the mouth shapes exactly, then at the end, move the keyframes about 2 to 4 frames backward on the Timeline. Lip-synching looks most natural when the target mouth shape is hit a bit before the sound is actually heard. Just remember this principle: Seeing comes before hearing.

Summary

In this chapter, you have learned how to apply various kinds of deformers to objects, or parts of objects. One of the wonderful things about deformers is that they can be combined in different orders to produce some remarkable effects. In particular, Wire and Blend Shape deformations allow you to produce high-level facial animation. Lattice can also be a very useful tool for both smooth and rigid skinning.

In the next chapter, we will cover the different ways of binding and weighting characters.

Binding

MAYA

Chapter 12

I n this chapter we will learn how to attach surfaces to skeletons and make them deform appropriately for animation. The attaching process is called *binding,* the bound geometry becomes the skeleton's *skin,* and the skin's deformation is affected by a process known as *weighting.* All of this terminology will soon become familiar as you go through the examples and exercises that follow. We will bind the character model, and then spend the rest of this chapter setting up and binding the puppy. Topics include:

- Rigid skinning
- Flexors and Artisan tools
- Smooth skinning
- Hands-On Maya: Binding a character
- Hands-On Maya: Binding a puppy

Skinning

We've already talked about how skeletons can bind objects and deform them properly as they move. The process through which skeletons do this is called *skinning,* and the objects that become bound to skeletons this way are called *skins,* or *skin objects.*

Like other deformers, skeletons can skin anything that has control points, such as CVs, NURBS curves, surfaces, polygonal vertices and objects, subdivision surfaces, and lattices. Although you will most often skin whole objects, it is worthwhile knowing that you can bind only a selection of points as well.

There are two kinds of skinning: *rigid* and *smooth.* Rigid skinning creates a joint cluster for every joint binding the objects. These clusters can contain points of multiple objects, and you can use flexors to smooth the bends. Smooth skinning creates a skin cluster for every object being bound; this cluster is shared by a set number of joints with different influence percentages. You can use influence objects to manipulate the deformation of smooth skins. For both kinds of skinning, you can use the Artisan tools to edit set membership and weights of the skinned points. When you are working with dense organic models, the difference between using Artisan and using the regular tools can be quite noticeable.

Rigid Skinning

Rigid skinning is called "rigid" because only one joint can influence a CV. There is no sharing of CVs as in smooth skinning, and the joint clusters that are created have a default influence value of 100 percent, which results in a rather rigid deformation when joints are bent. You can edit rigid skins by using flexors (a special type of deformer) or other deformers, or by changing skin point weights. All the tools we'll be using, unless stated otherwise, are available in the Skin menu in the Animation module.

Creating Rigid Skin

Let's start out with a simple example.

1. Create a cylinder and increase its sections to 10, its spans to 6, and its Height Ratio to 10.

2. In the side view, create a skeleton chain as shown in Figure 12.1 (a).

3. Select the cylinder and the skeleton—the order of selection here doesn't matter—and apply Skin ➜ Bind Skin ➜ Rigid Bind with the default settings. The cylinder turns pink to show that it is bound, or skinned, by the skeleton chain. Try rotating the second joint in Z by 90 degrees; you'll see that all the points bound by it rotate fully, or "rigidly," as in Figure 12.1 (b).

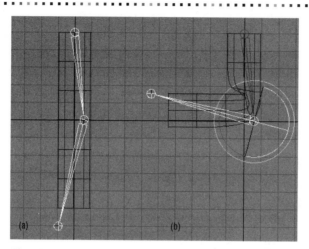

Figure 12.1 *A cylinder with rigid skin*

You can also skin selected joints in the same way you would complete skeletons. In the option windows for Bind Skin commands, change the setting to Bind to Selected Joints. You could then bind different geometries differently, such as rigid binding the hand, and smooth binding the body, for example. Using the Selected Joints option gives you more control over the binding process. If you want to skin one object separately to two or more joints in a hierarchy, bind the control points, as Maya will not allow you to bind at the object level twice. You can, however, bind an object to separate joint chains as different partitions.

Rigid Skin Editors

Open Window ➔ Relationship Editors ➔ Deformer Sets, and you will see two jointSets, one for each joint. The two sets contain all the points of the cylinder, and if you remove any of the points from the sets, those points will no longer be bound by the skeleton. Open Window ➔ General Editors ➔ Component Editor, and select the Joint Clusters tab. There are now two columns for the jointClusters. Select all the CVs of the cylinder and click Load Components in the Component Editor. You will see the points weighted under the joints they belong to. You can manipulate the weights here to make the bending smoother if you want to. For most situations, however, there are more elegant ways to make the bending smoother.

If you have trouble selecting CVs with a pick mask because the skeleton gets selected over the CVs, switch to component mode and select them. Skeletons are not selected in component mode.

Flexors

The easiest way to make joints bend smoothly is to use a *flexor,* a special type of deformer that works with rigid skinned joints. There are three types of flexors: lattice, sculpt, and cluster. You will usually want to use the lattice.

The Joint Lattice Flexor

To see how this tool works, select the skeleton and apply Go To Bind Pose. The cylinder is no longer deformed. Select the second joint and, from the Skin menu, apply Edit Rigid Skin ➜ Create Flexor. Leave everything at the default setting and click Create. A joint lattice (or flexor) is created with its orientation the same as the joint's local axes. Rotate the joint 90 degrees again, and you'll see that the bending is smoother—the flexor deforms the cylinder around the joint. You can further change the way the flexor is deforming by selecting it and editing its attributes in the Channel box. Notice how each attribute changes the way the flexor deforms the cylinder in Figure 12.2.

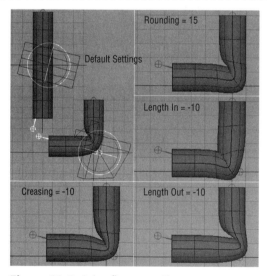

Figure 12.2 *Joint flexor attributes*

The Bone Lattice Flexor

You can also apply flexors to bones, but bone flexors are applied a bit differently. Their deformation is affected by the rotation of their child joint. Think of biceps and triceps bulging when you rotate your elbow. To try a bone flexor, select the first joint and apply Create Flexor. In the Create Flexor option window, turn off Joints and check At Selected Bones. Click Create, and a lattice is created around the first bone. Rotate the second joint 90 degrees, select the flexor, and, in the Channel box, change the values for the boneFlexor attributes. Notice that, instead of Creasing and Rounding, boneFlexor has Bicep and Tricep as the first two variables. You can easily get something like (a) in Figure 12.3.

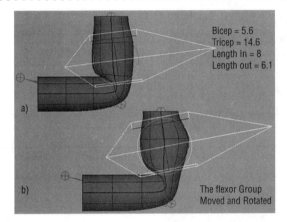

Figure 12.3 *The bone flexor in different positions*

You can move, rotate, and scale the flexors to adjust the way they are affecting the skin. In the Outliner, select the lattice group, which selects both the flexor and its latticeBase, and transform it. You can see the way the skin deformation changes while you are transforming the lattice group: Figure 12.3 (b) is the result of the lattice group being moved and rotated.

The Sculpt Flexor

You can also use a sculpt sphere as a flexor. It works just like a regular sculpt deformer, and there are no automated attribute controls as with lattice flexors. To have those controls, you need to use Set Driven Key. You can use the sculpt flexor as a bulging upper arm if you want, as shown in Figure 12.4, or as other parts of the body that regularly stretch with joint rotations, such as chest muscles. It can be applied as a joint flexor as well, although it is generally used as a bone flexor.

The Cluster Flexor

Cluster flexors have no options attached to them, and they exist only within joints. You can manipulate the smoothness of the joint's deformation, as well as the distribution of

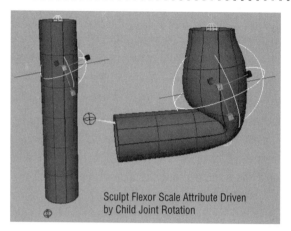

Figure 12.4 *The upper arm bulging*

the parent and child joints' deforming influences. Create a cluster flexor, then select the joint with the cluster flexor and press T to activate the manipulator handle. It shows two rings: one for the child joint, and another for the parent joint. The centers of the rings slide up and down the bones, changing the joints' Upper or Lower Bound values, and the radii of the rings change the Upper or Lower Value values. Figure 12.5 shows some of the ways you can change the bending with a cluster flexor.

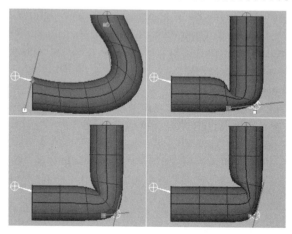

Figure 12.5 *A cluster flexor*

Go To Bind Pose

Do not confuse the Skin ➔ Go To Bind Pose command with Skeleton ➔ Assume Preferred Angle. The latter rotates the joints back to their creation positions, which can be changed with the Set Preferred Angle command. Bind Pose instead keeps track of not just the rotation but all the transformation values of the joints when the object was skinned.

If you decide to detach and reattach skinned objects, you would want to reposition the skeletons to their Bind Pose again. In order for Go To Bind Pose to work properly, the joints must not be locked. Often, however, some of the joints will become locked, because of constraints, expressions, or keyed IK handles. In such case, you can temporarily disable these nodes by going to Modify ➔ Disable Nodes and selecting the nodes that are causing the blockage.

Copy Flexor

The Copy Flexor function allows you to copy flexors to other joints. This is useful for creating flexors on mirrored joints or finger joints. Simply select first the flexor you want to copy and then the joint you want it copied to, and apply Edit Rigid Skin ➔ Copy Flexor. If you have many copies of the same flexors deforming something like finger joints, and you are comfortable using the Hypergraph, you can try setting up the connections so that one flexor node can drive all the lattice nodes. This would be especially helpful if you had to animate the attributes for all the flexors.

Edit Membership and the Artisan Tools

We've already been introduced to the Edit Membership, Paint Weights, and Paint Set Membership tools under the Deform menu. Rigid skin works with all of these tools.

Smooth skin does not work with these tools, because it has only one cluster set. It uses Paint Skin Weights (choose Skin ➔ Edit Smooth Skin ➔ Paint Skin Weights Tool) instead for weighting points.

As an example, let's return to the cylinder and the two joints. Delete all the flexors, go to Bind Pose, and apply Detach Skin. Select the skeleton and the cylinder, select Bind Skin ➔ Rigid Bind ❑, turn on Color Joints, and click Bind. Note that the joints are now colored. Rotate the second joint 90 degrees as before. Select Deform ➔ Edit Membership Tool, and the mouse arrow changes shape. Select the first joint, and all the points belonging to it are highlighted, as in Figure 12.6 (a). Shift+click the points at the bend to include them in the first joint, until you see something like Figure 12.6 (b). Remember that you should generally take care of editing membership before editing the weights of the control points.

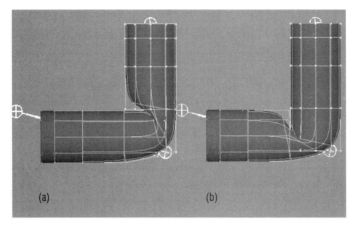

Figure 12.6 *Using the Edit Membership tool to add CVs to the root joint*

Select the cylinder, and select Deform ➔ Paint Set Membership Tool ❑. This tool performs the same function that Edit Membership provides. In the shaded mode, the cylinder shows two colors, representing the points that belong to the two joints. Because the joints themselves are colored, you can easily identify which joint is binding which part of the surface. Select the second joint, and you can add points to it with the paintbrush as shown in Figure 12.7.

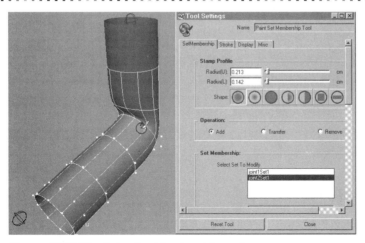

Figure 12.7 *The Paint Set Membership tool*

With the cylinder still active, select Deform ➜ Paint Weights Tool ❏. Set the Operation setting to Smooth, and select the second joint for the Clusters setting. Now the cylinder's color has changed again. The cylinder is black, except for the section bound by the second joint. The smoothing operation actually reweights the points in the second joint, as shown in Figure 12.8. You should always keep the brush at low settings, and it may take some practice, but once you get used to smoothing the weights, you can very efficiently smooth out the bend. Using these Artisan tools (introduced in Chapter 7) is definitely faster than using the Component Editor when dealing with dense models.

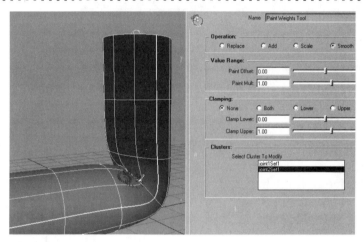

Figure 12.8 *The Paint Weights tool*

For fine control over deformations such as bending and bulging, you would want to use flexors and other deformers, but for simple smoothing tasks, or creating organic weighting around a surface, Artisan tools can be used. They create a lighter scene, without the extra deformer nodes.

Do not confuse the Artisan tools Paint Set Membership and Paint Weights. The first tool determines which cluster the points will belong to, and the second determines how much the points will be influenced by that cluster.

Smooth Skinning

For each object being skinned, smooth skinning creates one cluster set of points, which can be influenced by more than one joint. The main advantage of smooth skinning is that more than one joint can exert influence on the control point. This can also mean a bit more involved weighting process, but as we will see in the "Hands-On Maya" section, certain binding situations require smooth skinning to work. You can set the number of joints that can actually influence the points in the Smooth Bind option window, but all the joints in the skeleton can potentially influence the smooth skin.

You do not need flexors or the Edit Membership tool to edit points in the smooth skin cluster set. If you need that kind of deliberate control over the bends, you can always use deformers or influence objects, which are deformers specifically set up to work with smooth skinning. Artisan's Paint Skin Weights tool (Chapter 7) is especially useful with smooth skin.

Creating Smooth Skin

Let's get back to our cylinder. First use Go to Bind Pose, and then detach the skin. Select the cylinder and the joint chain, select Bind Skin ➜ Smooth Bind ❑, click Reset, and then slide Max Influences down to 2. The default Max Influences is 5, but you'd rarely need anything higher than 2 or 3. The default Bind Method is Closest Joint, meaning that joint influence priority is based on joint hierarchy. If you choose Closest Distance, joint hierarchy is ignored and whatever joint is closest to the skin point will have the greatest influence. Unless you specifically want the binding to be created this way, this is not how a hierarchically structured character deforms, and you should generally leave this setting at its default. Click Bind, and the cylinder is smooth-skinned. Rotate the second joint 90 degrees, and notice the difference in the way it bends as in Figure 12.9 (a): the skin deforms a lot more smoothly. Too smoothly, in fact. We want a bit more rigidity around the bending area than the default setting, something like the cylinder in Figure 12.9 (b).

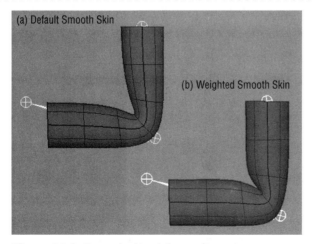

Figure 12.9 Smooth skin deformation

Weighting Skin Points

Before we address the lack of rigidity, however, let's see the differences between the smooth-skinned cylinder and the rigid-skinned one. Go to the Relationship Editor and choose the Deformer Set Editor, and notice that there is only one set. In the Component Editor, under the Skin Clusters tab, you will notice three columns of joints, including the very end one, and they all share in influencing the skin points. All the numbers in a row always add up to 1, meaning 100 percent influence. Select the cylinder, and select Edit Smooth Skin ➜ Paint Skin Weights Tool. Set the brush values low, set Operation to Add, and select the second joint to work on. The cylinder is black except for the area that is being influenced by the second joint. You can easily make the bend more rigid on the second joint, as in Figure 12.10. Repeat the process for the first joint. If you make a mistake, you can always undo it, and if you want to restart from the beginning, just select the object and apply Edit Smooth Skin ➜ Reset Weights To Default.

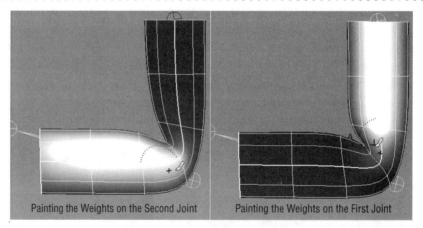

Painting the Weights on the Second Joint   Painting the Weights on the First Joint

Figure 12.10 *The Paint Skin Weights tool*

When you are in the Paint Skin Weights mode, you can also select different joints for weighting, by RM choosing Paint Weights over the joint you want.

Influence Objects

Let's say we want the biceps and triceps to bulge. We can use an influence object to accomplish this. Create a sphere and scale it to fit inside the upper arm. Select the cylinder skin, then the sphere, and apply Edit Smooth Skin ➜ Add Influence with the default settings. The sphere becomes an influence object, like a lattice deformer, with a hidden sphereBase object also created. You will generally leave the Base object alone, although you can optionally pull points of the Base object to change the deformation effect of the sphere. You can use Set Driven Key to automate the bulging by scaling up the sphere when the second joint rotates, as in Figure 12.11. The influence sphere and the sphereBase should be grouped under the first joint.

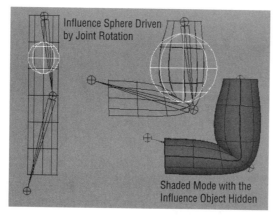

Figure 12.11 *The sphere as an influence object*

Do not delete an influence object the regular way, as it will mess up the smooth skin weighting. Select first the skin and then the influence object, and apply Edit Smooth Skin → Remove Influences.

We used a sphere, but we could have used any object with control points. The biceps and the triceps above look shapeless. Let's try the Influence object again, this time deforming a torus to get more definition for the biceps and triceps. Set up a torus as an Influence object with Minor Sweep at –180 and everything else at the default setting, as in Figure 12.12. Select the skin and, in the Channel box, open the skinCluster and set Use Components to On. An easy way to do this is to enter 1 in the field. When this is turned on, component-level deformation of the influence object will influence the skin as well. Sculpt the torus until the upper arm takes on the shapes for biceps and triceps as in Figure 12.12.

Keyframe the CVs, and move to a different timeline. Rotate the second joint, and sculpt the torus again until you see bulging biceps and triceps as shown in Figure 12.13. Copy the bulging torus.

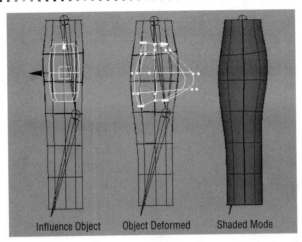

Influence Object   Object Deformed   Shaded Mode

Figure 12.12 *The influence object being sculpted*

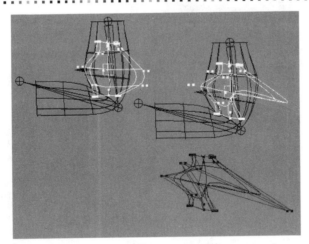

Figure 12.13 *Bulging torus when joint is rotated*

Move back to the frame where the torus CVs were keyframed. You can now delete the keyframe. Apply Blend Shape to the torus, making the copied torus its target. In the Channel box, open the blendShape channels, highlight the nurbsTorus target, and RM choose Set Driven Key. Make the blend shape driven by the joint rotation, as shown in Figure 12.14.

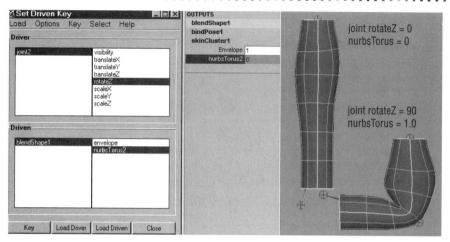

Figure 12.14 *Set Driven Keys causing upper arm to bulge*

Binding and Subdivision Surfaces

Before moving on to this chapter's exercises, we need to briefly discuss binding subdivision surfaces. The process of binding is exactly the same for NURBS, polygonal, and subdivision surfaces. For each situation, we are binding the control points that will be weighted to move and deform the surface appropriately. As we will see later with the NURBS puppy, it is not easy to bind multiple-patch NURBS surfaces, and we will use the lattice deformers to bypass the problem. The great thing about polygons and subdivision surfaces is that we do not have to worry about seams appearing at the edges, as they are usually single continuous surfaces. Unlike NURBS modeling, however, with polygons we cannot use the arrow keys to travel across the points in U or V, or select entire rows or columns. Weighting can become frustratingly tedious when you have to adjust weights on thousands of control points on a dense polygon model.

Binding subdivision surfaces is advantageous in that we do not have to worry about seams as we do with multi-patched NURBS surfaces, and because of its smoothing property, we usually end up binding a much smaller number of control points than we would with a comparable polygon surface. Again, as with modeling, we get the best of both worlds when we bind subdivision surfaces, as you can see in the bound cylinders in Figure 12.15. Cylinder (a) consists of four patches of NURBS surfaces, cylinder (b) is a comparable polygon surface with many more points, and cylinder (c) is a subdivision surface.

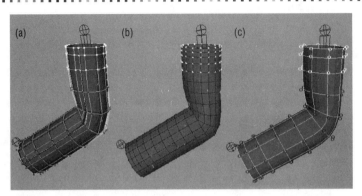

Figure 12.15 *Different surfaces bound*

Hands-On Maya: Binding a Character

In Chapter 10 we set up our character with a skeleton hierarchy. We will now proceed to bind the character to the skeleton. The binding procedure usually takes multiple steps, and different characters require different methods. For our situation, we will use rigid binding for the hands, body, and the head. For the shoes, we will use smooth binding.

Poly Proxy Binding

The straight approach to binding a subdivision surface is to bind the hierarchical surface at level 0. For our character, however, we will use an alternative "poly proxy binding" method: as the name suggests, the poly proxy mesh is bound to the joints and it deforms the hierarchical subdivision surface. This approach has a couple of advantages compared to binding the subdivision surface directly. As we will see in Part V, "Rendering," binding the polygon mesh allows us to easily change UV mappings without having to rebind the model or work with intermediate objects. Because the poly proxy mesh is much lighter than the subdivision surface it is connected to, you can weight it faster, especially if you are dealing with a heavy model. Also, the proxy mesh can be used as a rough proxy model to animate with once the binding is done. When we hide the hierarchical surface and leave the proxy mesh visible, the model can be more quickly animated.

1. Open the `character_ik_setup.mb` file from the Chapter 12 Working Files directory on the CD-ROM. It already has everything set up except for the binding. Open the Hypergraph window and turn on the Shape Nodes display option. You should see the subdivision shape nodes below

their transformation nodes, as in the left picture below. RM over the surfaces in the perspective view, including the body, the hands, the head, and the shoes, to go to poly proxy mode. In the Hypergraph window, you should see created extra poly proxy mesh shape nodes with names like *subD_bodyHistPoly* below the subdivision shape nodes, as in the right picture below. We will be binding these poly proxy mesh nodes.

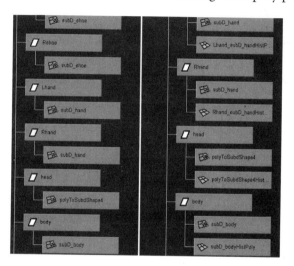

2. Select the subdivision shape nodes and hide them. The poly proxy meshes do not have any shading assigned to them yet, so connect them to a Lambert or Blinn material.

It's a good idea to group the subdivision shape nodes and the proxy polygon nodes to separate layers or sets, so that you can easily hide or show those shape nodes. If you create a set using the Set Editing Relationship Editor, the set will also appear at the bottom of the Outliner.

Binding Body Parts

Let's first bind the body.

1. Select the following joints in the skeleton hierarchy: the root, spines, chest, neck, shoulders, arms, elbows, forearms, legs, and knees. In other words, leave out the wrists and the joints below them, and the joints below the knee. With the appropriate joints selected, add the body poly proxy node to the selection, and select Skin ➜ Bind Skin ➜ Rigid Bind ❏. Make sure you have selected the body poly proxy node, the subD_bodyHistPoly node, and not the DAG node above it, as this will also select the hidden subdivision surface as well.

2. Set the Bind To setting to Selected Joints and click Apply. Make sure the clusters have been created, by testing to see if the body deforms with the joints.

Now we should edit the membership of the vertices. We can't go through all the sections of the body, so we will use the Lelbow joint as an example.

3. In the Animation module, select Deform ➜ Edit Membership Tool; then, in the modeling window, click the Lelbow joint. All the points that belong to the Lelbow joint become highlighted, as shown in (a) below. You want to transfer the membership of the points so that the rows of points above the elbow area also become part of the elbow joint's cluster set. This "overreaching" may seem improper when those points deform the way they do in (b) below, but such rearrangement of point membership is necessary if you want parts of the upper arm area to deform when the elbow joint rotates. Once the weighting has been properly assigned, the deformation will appear more agreeable, as in (c) below, where some of the points on the forearm have also been transferred to the forearm joint.

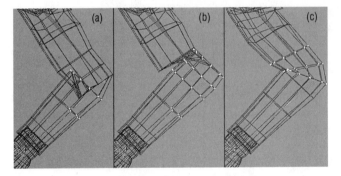

When you have completed all the membership assignments for a joint, it's a good idea to create a set for those points using the Relationship Editor for Sets. When you move on to weighting, this can help you greatly in selecting the relevant points.

4. Use the approach just described in assigning memberships for different joints. In particular, the membership for the knee joints should also include the lower thigh area above the knee, as we did with the elbow, and for the same reason. Keep in mind how the points will deform after you've lowered the weights. The shoulder area is tricky to weight properly, and carefully assigning the most appropriate points to the shoulder joints will go a long way in enabling the shoulder area to deform well. You may also have to reassign some points as you

go through the weighting process. The membership assignments for different sections of the body are shown below. For a closer examination of how the points were assigned, look at the character_bound.mb file in the Chapter 12 Working Files directory on the CD-ROM.

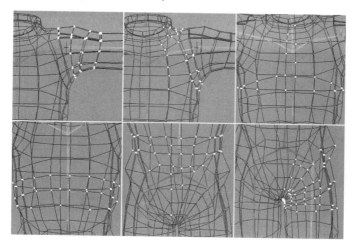

5. Select the head and the neck joints, add the head proxy mesh (not the DAG node above it) to the selection, and apply Rigid Bind. The membership assignment for the head and neck joints should be as shown below.

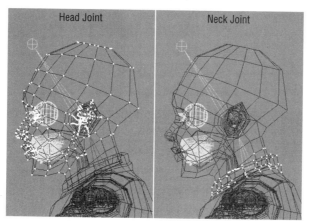

6. The head is the easiest part to bind and assign weights. The hand, by contrast, is probably the hardest part to work on. Select the Lwrist joint and the joints below it, add the Lhand proxy mesh node to the selection, and apply Rigid Bind. You will most likely want to adjust membership assignments as you are

weighting the points for the fingers. The first finger joints also deform the palm area, so they need extra attention and deliberation. The last two rows of the hand should be reassigned to the Lforearm joint. Again, the membership assignments for certain areas of the hand are shown below, but for a closer examination, refer to the file in the CD-ROM.

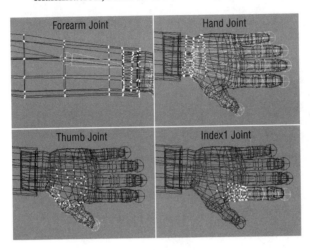

The shoes need to be bound differently. Since we created an inverse foot setup for the feet, the joint chain for the foot is separate from the leg joints. If we rigidly bind the shoes, then we have a weighting problem that cannot be solved—the knee joint and the foot joint will deform the ankle area from two separate pivot points, and choosing membership for one will exclude the other influence. What we need is for the ankle area to be influenced by both. We can make this area deform correctly by smooth-binding the shoes, which will enable the points to be shared by the knee and the foot joints.

7. Select the Lknee, Lfoot, and Lball joints, add the Lshoe poly mesh node to the selection, and apply Smooth Bind, making sure to set the Bind To setting to Selected Joints. Since the shoe is smooth-bound, there is no need to assign membership to its control points.

8. Before we move on to the weighting process, make sure the other parts of the head, such as eyes, eyelashes, hair, and teeth, are grouped under the head joint. Since these body parts need not deform with the joint rotation, they needn't be bound. You could bind them, if you wanted to, but it would only make the model heavier, without improving the setup.

Editing Skin Weights

This is the fun part of binding a character, where you get to punch a lot of decimal figures into a spreadsheet-like Component Editor. Using the Artisan tool is an alternative approach to entering numbers, but even with that, for final weighting refinements, you do have to make use of the Component Editor. Once you become used to using it, however, this tool really can become an interesting part of character setup. Let's do the knee area for a simple example.

1. First, keyframe the Lfoot_c control node to make the left knee bend over a span of frames. You can then drag along the Timeline to see how the knee will bend as you are assigning the weights to the Lknee joint. The default weights clearly do not do a good job of deforming the knee, as shown below.

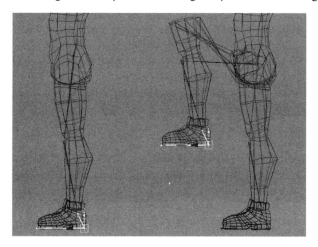

2. Display the hierarchical subdivision body shape node you had hidden, to see how the weighting affects the deformation. Select the points on the body mesh that belong to the knee joint, and open the Window ➜ General Editors ➜ Component Editor. On the Joint Clusters tab, scroll across until you come to a cluster column with the numbers showing. As you can see, the default numbers are all 1, meaning 100 percent influence. Edit the weights as follows: the points around the shin area should be assigned a value of 1, the next row, 0.9, and then 0.6, 0.3, 0.1, and 0.01. As you assign the values, notice how the deformation of the knee area changes, as shown next.

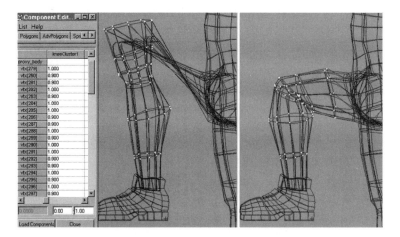

3. Surface areas such as the fingers and the neck are much like the knee area, and are fairly easy to weight. The head is the easiest—the whole head should remain fully weighted at 1 to the head joint, deforming starting from the neck area. But certain parts are much harder to deform properly, such as the thumb and palm area, the shoulders, and the legs. The legs, for example, can be weighted to move correctly to the front and back, but that will not necessarily improve their side up and down movements, or twisting from side to side. You should, therefore, keep your goal weights for the character's movements and try to reach for those specific movements as you are weighting the different sections of the character. As you weight the different areas to test various character poses, keyframe as many different movements as you can. What seems to be deforming well in one pose may not hold up well in another, or it may deform incorrectly while changing to another pose. Some example poses are shown below.

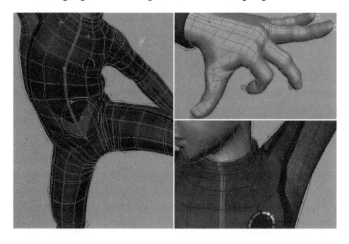

There is obviously a limit to the control you can achieve with point weighting. To aid you in getting exactly the shapes you want, you can also make use of deformers such as flexors, influence objects, or blend shapes. You will usually use Set Driven Keys or expressions to connect the deformers to the joint rotations.

4. With the shoe, the weighting is a bit more involved. Select some points on the shoe, and open the Component Editor. For smooth-skinned surfaces, the cluster values show up under the SkinClusters tab. As you can see in the Editor below, there are three joints that can potentially exert influence on each point, so you need to input more values per point.

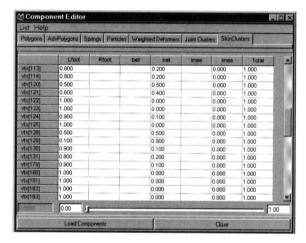

	Lfoot	Rfoot	ball	ball	knee	knee	Total
vtx[113]	0.800			0.200		0.000	1.000
vtx[114]	0.800			0.200		0.000	1.000
vtx[120]	0.500			0.500		0.000	1.000
vtx[121]	0.600			0.400		0.000	1.000
vtx[122]	1.000			0.000		0.000	1.000
vtx[123]	1.000			0.000		0.000	1.000
vtx[124]	0.900			0.100		0.000	1.000
vtx[125]	1.000			0.000		0.000	1.000
vtx[128]	0.500			0.500		0.000	1.000
vtx[129]	0.100			0.900		0.000	1.000
vtx[130]	0.900			0.100		0.000	1.000
vtx[131]	0.800			0.200		0.000	1.000
vtx[179]	0.900			0.100		0.000	1.000
vtx[180]	1.000			0.000		0.000	1.000
vtx[181]	1.000			0.000		0.000	1.000
vtx[182]	1.000			0.000		0.000	1.000
vtx[183]	1.000			0.000		0.000	1.000

5. A good way to proceed weighting skin cluster points is to give one joint 100 percent influence, and then subtract a certain value from it by adding it to another joint. For example, let's say we want to make the weighting at the top of the shoe 95 percent influenced by the knee joint, and 5 percent influenced by the foot joint. We can initially assign a value of 1 for those points under the knee joint column. The other two joints' influences drop to zero. Then enter a value of **0.05** under the foot joint. Now the values at the knee joint drop to .95, and the ball joint values remain at 0.0. The area below the ankle should generally be 100 percent influenced by the foot joint, as the shoe is a rather rigid object. Since the knee should not influence the ball of the foot area at all, begin weighting the relevant points by assigning a value of 1 to either the foot or the ball joint. The shoe should deform as shown next.

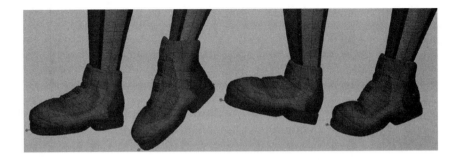

Cleaning Up

The character is now ready for animation. You should hide the subdivision surfaces and display only the poly proxy mesh surfaces. Some animators like using the Hypergraph window to select the control nodes, others the Outliner window. Still others prefer to keep only the modeling window open and select the handles inside the camera view. Use layers to convert the poly meshes into reference objects now that you don't need to select them. You can hide the geometry if you'd like and work only with the skeleton for even faster interaction. Display selection handles for the root joint and other control nodes if you want to pick them in the window. Some animators, however, prefer not to display anything but the geometry. You may also want to rename nodes to make them easier to identify, such as renaming subD_bodyHistPoly node to something like proxy_body. Delete anything that you no longer need, whether it's geometry, curves, history, or empty nodes, and save it as `character_bound.mb`. We will use the completed character in the next chapter to demonstrate various animation tasks.

Hands-On Maya: Binding a Puppy

Our final exercise in this chapter will be to set up and bind the multi-patched NURBS puppy we built in Chapter 8. We will briefly go through the skeleton setup, put on IK handles and constraints, and organize the hierarchy to get it ready for animation. Then we will apply smooth binding to the puppy to make it deform with the skeleton.

Creating the Skeleton

We'll begin by using the Skeleton ➜ Joint Tool to give the puppy bones and joints.

1. Bring in the file `dog_model.mb`, the final global-stitched model of the dog, from Chapter 8 Working Files directory on the CD.

2. In the side view, draw the backbone as shown below, starting from the hip area and finishing at the nose. Draw the tail. Draw the front leg and the back leg

with Auto Joint Limits turned on. Notice where the wrist is—that is where the IK end effector will be placed.

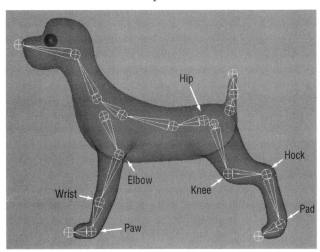

3. To make the back leg the proper shape, increase the grid division and use X+click. This is important because we will be using IK with the three joints of the leg. If the bones are not built as a "z" shape as in the picture below, they may not bend the way we want them to.

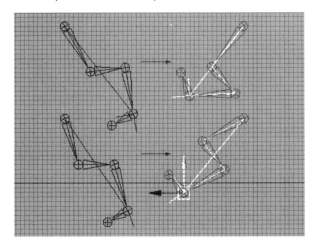

4. Name the joints. The backbone chain should be hip, back, chest, neck, and head. The tailbone chain should be tail1 and tail2. The front leg chain should be named Larm, Lelbow, Lwrist, and Lpaw. Finally, the back leg chain should be Lleg, Lknee, Lhock, and Lpad.

Adding IK Handles and Pole Constraints

Now we're ready to apply inverse kinematics to the puppy, using the Skeleton ➜ IK Handle Tool.

1. In the perspective view, move the leg joints to the left side so that they are placed properly as shown below. Put ikRP handles on them to test how they bend. For the back leg, try to keep the three bones that will use IK coplanar. Think also of how the skin is going to stretch with the skeleton as the joints are moving.

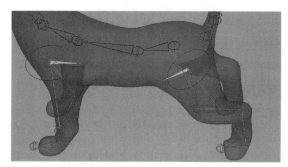

2. Mirror the front and back legs on the YZ axis. The ikRP handles should copy as well. Check to make sure the joint limits are working. If the ikRP's plane indicator for the mirrored leg does not mirror properly, try mirroring with the option set to Orientation instead of Behavior.

3. Group the front legs to the chest. Group the back legs and the tail to the hip joints. Name the joints properly, such as Rarm and Relbow. Name the IK handles Lfront, Rfront, Lbackleg, and Rbackleg.

4. Create four locators and place them as pole vector constraints for the legs. Two should go directly behind the front legs, and two should go directly in front of the back legs. Your drawing should look something like the following.

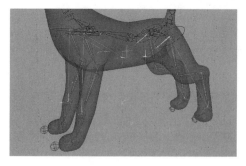

Constraining the Legs

We have a problem with the puppy's legs. We would like to have the paws planted on the ground when the dog walks, but because the IK chain is to the wrist, the rotation center is the wrist, not the paw. To a lesser degree, we have the same problem with the pads rotating when the body moves. We'll solve this problem by using locators and the Orient constraint.

1. Create four locators. Snap them to the paw and pad joints. Name them Lfront_c, Rfront_c, Lback_c, and Rback_c (the *c* stands for "control").

2. Select Lwrist (make sure you select this joint and not the Lpaw joint), then Lfront_c locator, and apply Constrain ➜ Orient. The locator should rotate to match the rotation values of Lwrist.

3. Repeat step 2 for the right side of the leg. Also orient-constrain the two back_c locators to the back pad joints. You should see them rotated and positioned as below.

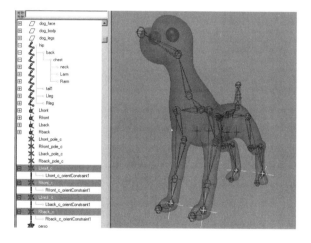

4. Open the Attribute Editor for the Lwrist joint. Click the X and Y Degrees of Freedom settings. They need to be activated before the joint can be constrained. Repeat this process for Rwrist and the two back pad joints.

5. In the Outliner, delete the constraint nodes under the four control locators. In the modeling window, select the Lfront_c locator first, and then Lwrist (not the Lpaw joint); then select Constrain ➜ Orient. Do the same for Rfront_c and Rwrist. The rotation attributes of the wrist joints are now constrained to the control locators. Repeat the process for the back locators and the pad joints.

6. In the Outliner, group the Lfront ikRP handle with the Lfront_c locator by MM dragging it to the locator node. Do the same for the Rfront ikRP handle and the Rfront_c locator. Now if you try moving or rotating the Lfront_c and Rfront_c locators, the legs should follow, pivoting around the paws. Place the IK handles for the back legs under the back_c locators as well.

    When you group the IK handle under the control locator, the handle may flip to a weird angle. This is not a problem; the IK handle just hasn't updated. After you've grouped all the IK handles, select the pole vector constraint locators, move them, and press Z to undo the move. The IK handles should snap back to their original angles.

7. Select the hip joint and group it to itself by selecting Edit ➜ Group with the default setting. This produces a parent node. Name the node Puppy, and group the pole vector constraints and the control locators under it. The Puppy node is the top node and will move the whole dog. Create an extra attribute channel in the front_c locator to rotate the paw joint via Set Driven Key. Hide the channels that will not be animated, such as the Translate attributes for the joints, using the Channel Control. In the Outliner, you should see a hierarchy like the one shown below.

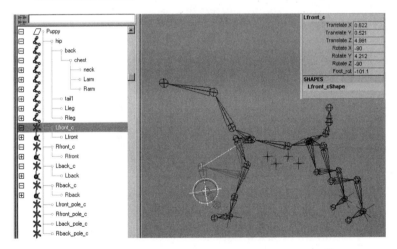

In your own work, it's important to remember that there is no one proper way to build skeletons or place constraints to set up a character for animation. In each case, you need to consider what the character will be doing, how the body should deform, how the limbs should rotate, and so on. Different situations call for different solutions. A properly prepared character will move well, have the necessary range of movements, and be easy to animate.

Binding the Puppy

In order to deal with the NURBS puppy's multiple patches, we are first going to create two lattices: one for the puppy's head, another for the body. Then we'll bind the two lattices plus the tail and the legs to the skeleton as smooth skin. The skeleton will deform the lattices, which will then deform the puppy's head and body. This method of indirectly moving the puppy using lattices is easier to weight, and it produces smoother deformation.

1. Create a skeleton layer to control the visibility of the skeleton, IKs, and constraints. Hide the layer for now. Select the head patches, eyes, ears, and nose; then go into component mode and select all the CVs, except the last two rows of the neck area, as shown below. Create a default lattice and increase its STU divisions to (4, 5, 5).

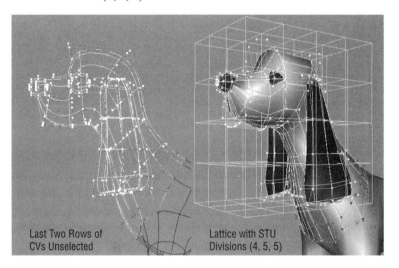

Last Two Rows of CVs Unselected

Lattice with STU Divisions (4, 5, 5)

We didn't have to include the eyes and the nose to the lattice deformer. We could simply group them to the head joint instead. If they are bound to the lattice, however, you have the choice of deforming them along with the rest of the head. For cartoon effects, you may want to weight the head lattice to something less than 100 percent.

2. Creating the body lattice is a bit more involved. You have to select rows of CVs from different patches, and it will help to create a set in the Relationship Editor to contain all the points for selection purposes. Select all the CVs of the body patches (a). Select the two rows of CVs from the neck area (b). Select the top three rows of the front leg patches (c). Select the top two rows of the back leg

patches. Finally, select the bottom three rows of CVs of the tail patches (e). The resulting lattice should look like (f) below.

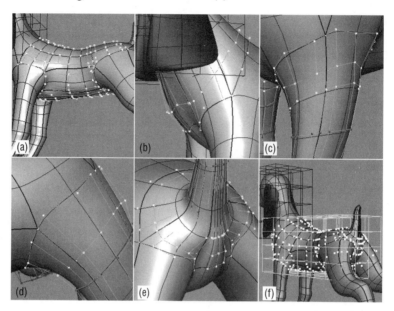

3. Try moving the lattices to see that none of the points that should be included have been left out. Select the lattices, the leg patches, and the tail patches. Unhide the skeleton, and include it in the selection as well. Apply Skin ➜ Bind Skin ➜ Smooth Bind ❑, click Reset, reduce Max Influences to 2, and click Bind. Maya starts to create a skin cluster for each of the patches and the lattices. Open the Relationship Editor and go to the Deformer Set Editing module. You should see 24 sets altogether. There are two lattice sets and 22 skin cluster sets: 16 for the leg patches, 4 for the tail patches, and 2 for the lattices. Remember, the lattices are now also smooth-skinned objects.

4. We have a double transformation problem with the lattices (discussed in "Editing Deformation Sets," in Chapter 11). Try moving the top skeleton joint node—some of the leg CVs and the tail CVs are translating further than they should because they are getting translated twice. There is a simple way to fix this problem. In the Relationship Editor window, highlight the body lattice set, apply Edit ➜ Select Set Members, and you should see the CVs for the body lattice get selected as below.

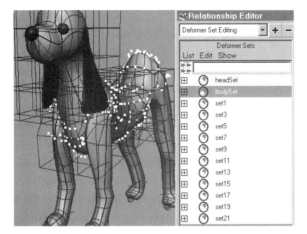

5. Highlight all the skin cluster sets (not the lattice sets) and click the minus button at the top, or choose Edit ➜ Remove to get rid of the selected items. The offending CVs are removed from the skin cluster sets, and the dog should look normal again.

Editing Skin Weights

We'll start weighting from the head. With lattices, you have to use the Component Editor to weight the lattice points.

1. Rotate the head joints and see how the integrity of the head shape holds up. The head area should mostly be fine with the default setting. For places where the deformation is occurring too much, such as the back of the head below, enter a higher value for the head joint in the Component Editor.

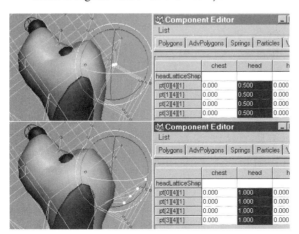

2. Create a cluster on the ears. Select the CVs as below, and apply Create Cluster with Relative mode on. Weight the points so that the bottom of each ear gets deformed the most. Group and parent it to the head joint. The ears should deform well enough within the lattice, but in cases where they are going through the head geometry, or for secondary animation, you can use the cluster to adjust the ears.

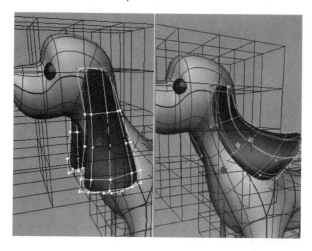

3. As you are weighting the different parts of the body and rotating the joints, you can always use Go To Bind Pose. But if you move the IK handles or the constraints, the Bind Pose will not work. One way to handle this is to keyframe those nodes. After you've tested them, you can return them to their original positions, after which the Bind Pose should work again.

4. Let's go through a simple example of lattice tweaking at the chest area. The four points below are being influenced by Rarm, Relbow, Larm, and Lelbow. The elbows, however, shouldn't be influencing the chest area, so enter 0 in the elbow columns. The arms are each assigned the value of 1 for two points. But the chest bone should be influencing the chest as well, so assign 0.5 in the chest joint. The value for the arm joints drops to 0.5 accordingly. As you can see, a lot of weighting actually consists of getting rid of unnecessary influences and thinking about which joints should be influencing the points. You may find it makes the process more efficient if you weight the point at 1 for one joint at the beginning, and then start adding influence values to the other joints.

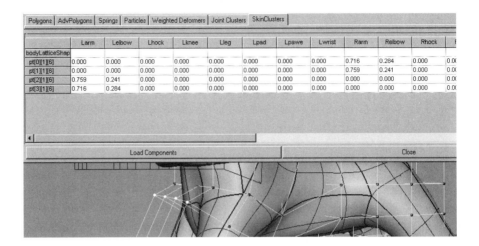

	Larm	Lelbow	Lhock	Lknee	Lleg	Lpad	Lpawe	Lwrist	Rarm	Relbow	Rhock	
bodyLatticeShap												
pt[0][1][6]	0.000	0.000	0.000	0.000	0.000	0.000	0.000	0.000	0.716	0.284	0.000	0.0(
pt[1][1][6]	0.000	0.000	0.000	0.000	0.000	0.000	0.000	0.000	0.759	0.241	0.000	0.0(
pt[2][1][6]	0.759	0.241	0.000	0.000	0.000	0.000	0.000	0.000	0.000	0.000	0.000	0.0(
pt[3][1][6]	0.716	0.284	0.000	0.000	0.000	0.000	0.000	0.000	0.000	0.000	0.000	0.0(

5. You can use the Paint Skin Weights tool for the legs and the tail if you want, but apply them only if you see the need. In our case, the default skinning has done a decent job of weighting. Once you are done with weight tweaking, save the file as dog_final.mb. You can try a four-legged walk cycle with it.

Summary

In this chapter we've covered rigid skinning and smooth skinning, using the subdivision surface boy character as an example of the former and the NURBS puppy as an example of the latter. We learned how to edit point set membership and weight the points using Component Editor. And that's it. No more tweaking CVs, applying IKs, or constraining. We are now ready to animate, and that is what we will do starting from the next chapter.

Character Animation
Exercises

Chapter 13

It's been a long time coming, but here we are, with a fully built model ready to be animated. In this chapter, we will use the character and the puppy we built to produce simple walk cycles. Then we will go through some more animation exercises, such as running and throwing a ball. Along the way, there will be selective presentations of a few of the more important classical animation principles.

In this chapter, you will find the following animation exercises:

- A step-by-step walk cycle
- A dog walk
- A run cycle
- Ball tossing
- A Maya character

Step-by-Step Walk Cycle

Walk cycles are often used as animation lessons because there is probably nothing more familiar than walking—just about anyone can go through the motions (or watch others walk). At the same time, a walk cycle requires you to be aware of and properly apply many fundamental animation principles. If you already have an animation background, this section may help you to get some needed sleep, but if you are just starting out, it may be quite educational. You should take time to read through the explanations and understand them fully.

For a more complete treatment of classical animation and its mysterious ways, you should try perusing The Illusion of Life: Disney Animation *by Frank Thomas and Ollie Johnston, which, after 20 years, is still the most enlightening, entertaining, and inspiring reference book for animators. For studies of how people and animals actually move in real life, Eadweard Muybridge's photo books are a great reference source for many artists.*

When creating a walk cycle, you can choose between two different types. The simplest type is a stationary walk, where the ground seems to be moving under the character. The other type is a more realistic walk in which the character actually moves forward. This second type is a bit more complex than a stationary walk but involves the same principles. We will be animating the simpler stationary walk, so that we can take more time dealing with the animation principles behind the movements. (You can see sample walk cycles in the Chapter 13 Working Files folder on the accompanying CD-ROM.)

Setting Up for the Walk Cycle

Animation is a very iterative procedure. You can try to animate everything at once, right from the beginning, and some people may prefer to work like this. But usually, you end up working at a much slower pace, and you can easily lose sight of the forest for the trees; that is, you may lose your perspective on how the character is animating overall because you are bogged down on translating and rotating so many control nodes.

It's much better to key in rough poses one or two nodes at a time, working on different parts of the character in stages, much like painting or sculpting. For the walk cycle, this will be our workflow:

- Animate the hip (root joint) and the left leg.
- Transfer and offset the animation to the right leg.
- Animate the spine joints.

- Animate the head.

- Animate the arms.

Once the rough animation is done, you can tweak and refine the function curves, and change subtle details of the walk to give it more personality. At every stage, you will want to do simple Playblasts to see how the keyframes make the character move in real time.

1. Select File ➔ Open Scene and bring in the `character_bound.mb` file from the Chapter 12 Working Files folder on the CD.

2. Create a plane and stretch it out. This will serve as the ground.

3. Translate the Maya_Boy node up or the ground plane down until you see his feet just on the ground, as shown in Figure 13.1.

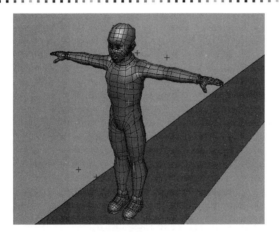

Figure 13.1 *The character on the plane*

4. Make sure the subdivision surfaces are hidden and only the poly proxy meshes are showing, because you want to concentrate on quickly creating rough poses. You can work with only the skeleton if you wish (as some animators do).

Animating the Hip and the Legs

Hip movement is probably the first joint you want to animate, because it is the most basic movement from which much of the other joints' movements spring.

An important decision is how many frames the walk cycle should be. Bigger and heavier characters tend to walk slower, and lighter characters walk faster, but you can infer more than just that. Different walks can reveal many things about a character. For instance, a slow walk done well can convey seriousness, dignity, and grace in a character, such as a king or a queen at a coronation. A fast, bouncy walk can convey the light-heartedness of a clown or the intense energy of a soldier. Long steps can imply confidence, energy, or urgency. Small steps can imply shyness, weakness, or leisure.

We'll do a very brisk walk and make it cycle in 18 frames. Generally speaking, it's better to make a character move faster, not slower, than what you would consider normal speed. Producing quick movements does not necessarily produce better animation, but it does discourage "floating" in your animation.

When animation is being examined, people often comment about there not being enough weight or enough snap to a character's movements, and comments like, "You know, this character just floats" usually sound the death knell for the animator.

The pelvic area moves in many different ways in a walk cycle. You need to translate the root joint up and down, but it also must rotate in the X and Y axis. (For the root joint created in the side view, the local X axis of the root joint spins the body, which is along the global Y axis; the local Z rotation bends the body forward and back; and the local Y rotation moves the body sideways.) You could translate the root joint in the X axis as well, for side-to-side movement, if you want. A female walk usually has greater X translation, making her hips sway; a male walk generally doesn't have any noticeable sway.

How far apart the feet are can change the look of the walk quite a bit. No one really walks with their feet straight below their shoulders, as in the left picture below, although this is a common mistake with beginning animators. You may, however, intentionally want a character's feet to be placed like this, to animate a Frankenstein walk, for example. Our character's feet will be placed together closely enough to be almost brushing against each other when they cross, as in the center picture below. This is probably the most natural distance for a regular walk. The feet can also come closer together, even cross each other in a walk, as in the right picture below. Such overlapping would produce a more feminine walk, like the way fashion models walk across a stage.

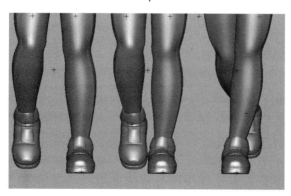

Before you begin, check to make sure that the animation speed is 24 frames per second by choosing Window ➜ Setting/Preferences ➜ Preferences, Settings section, and confirming the working unit for Time is Film (24 fps).

1. Rotate the root joint in the direction of the front leg. Since we want the left leg forward at frame 1, in the top view, rotate the body clockwise for about 15 to 20 degrees.

2. Repeat the keyframe at frame 19. At frame 10, it should be rotated about the same amount in the opposite direction.

3. You should see waves in the Graph Editor that look like the left picture in Figure 13.2. Use the Curves ➜ Pre Infinity and Post Infinity Cycle functions to make the waves repeat as in the right picture in Figure 13.2.

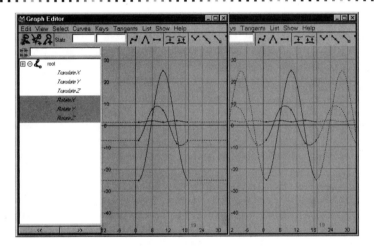

Figure 13.2 *Graph Editor function curves for the root joint*

When you are cycling function curves, use the tangent handles to get rid of sharp breaks that may occur.

Moving the Left Leg

We will set up the left leg first, and then copy its nodes for the right leg.

1. Translate the Lfoot_c node in the X axis to around 2.2. Move it forward in the Z axis, and rotate it in X to an extreme pose, as in the picture on the left in Figure 13.3, where the legs are widest apart. The heel is just touching the ground, and the toes are curled.

2. Copy the keyframe at frame 19 by MM dragging the current time indicator.

3. Go to frame 10, which is the halfway point in the cycle, and translate and rotate the control node and the toes to the back, as in the picture on the left in Figure 13.3. The toes at this frame are just about to leave the ground.

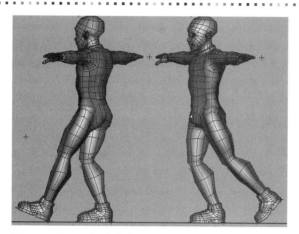

Figure 13.3 *The left-leg walk cycle*

4. Keyframe the in-between frames for the left foot, and adjust the root joint's values accordingly as shown in Figure 13.4. At frame 3, the left foot is planted solidly on the ground, and the body is at its lowest. At frame 6, the left foot passes under the body, and the body is at its highest. Around frame 8 is where the left foot actually pushes the body forward. Note how the root joint's Y translation values increase and decrease at different frames, as shown in Figure 13.4.

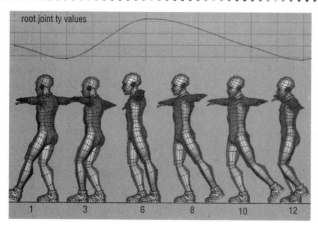

Figure 13.4 *The left leg in-between keyframes*

At frame 1, the front foot's heel touches the ground, but the weight of the body still makes it sink before it can spring back up. This is why the body is lowest around frame 3. Then, around frame 5 or 6, the body reaches its highest position. The heavier the body, the longer the recoiling will take. So if the recoiling process takes longer, the steps become a heavy, serious walk. If the body hangs around its highest position a bit longer, meaning the recoiling happens faster, the steps become a light, bouncy walk.

The Graph Editor below shows the root joint's Translate Y curves for different walks of another character. Just by looking at these curves, you should be able to tell that the first one is a fairly bouncy walk, the second is an extremely bouncy walk, and the third is a heavy walk.

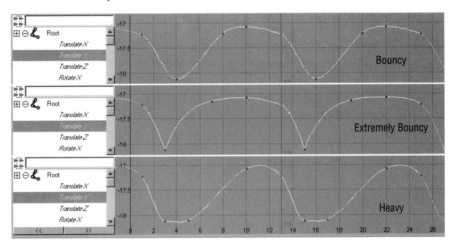

Moving the Right Leg

Now we can work on the animation for the right leg, but first we need to refine the root joint's rotations a bit.

1. Rotate the root joint a bit from the side view to make the body lean forward, as in the left picture in Figure 13.5. Also, at the extreme positions at frames 1 and 10, the hip is horizontal, but at frame 6 and 15, when the foot is passing the body (or rather, in reality, the body is going over the foot), the hip on the side of that foot should be lifted up by rotating the root joint in the front view, as shown in the middle and right pictures in Figure 13.5.

2. Now we need to copy the animation from the left leg to the right. Select the Lfoot_c node and choose Edit ➜ Keys ➜ Copy Keys, with the default settings. Select the Rfoot_c node and choose Edit ➜ Keys ➜ Paste Keys, again with the default settings. The right foot should snap to the left foot.

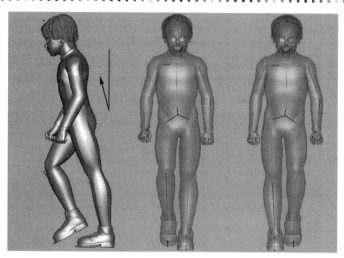

Figure 13.5 *Root joint's rotations*

Walking is often referred to as a continuous falling. When you walk, your body is pushed by the leg in the back position, and then the body leans and falls forward. If it weren't for the back leg speeding ahead of the body to break the fall, your body would actually fall to the ground.

3. Select both control nodes, open the Graph Editor, and choose View ➜ Infinity, then Curves Pre Infinity ➜ Cycle, and then Post Infinity ➜ Cycle. The two nodes should have identical function curves.

4. Now we need to change the Translate X curve values for the Rfoot_c node from positive to negative. In the Graph Editor, select the Translate X curve, choose Edit ➜ Scale ❑, change the Value Scale/Pivot setting to –1, and click the Apply button. The curve should now be a negative mirror of the original.

5. Select all of the Rfoot_c node curves and move them nine frames forward, so that the first keyframes are positioned at frame 10, as shown in Figure 13.6.

Now the legs should step and cycle indefinitely, with the right leg's animation trailing the left leg's by nine frames.

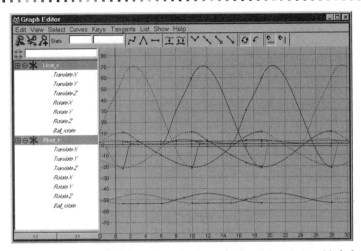

Figure 13.6 *Graph Editor function curves for the right and left feet*

Squash and Stretch, Rigidity, and Volume

One of the corollaries of a character (or anything) having weight is a principle called *squash and stretch*. In classical animation, this is considered one of the cardinal principles of animation. In our preceding example of the body sinking to its lowest recoil position in frame 3, the character is being "squashed" by the force of gravity and the resistance of the ground. When it bounces up, the body "stretches" to its highest point. What is a subtle movement in real life often becomes greatly exaggerated in animation. Especially in cartoony animation, squash and stretch in characters can become extreme.

In order to use the squash-and-stretch principle properly, you need to always apply it as a consequence of weight. Weight is force times mass (remember high school physics?), so something that has more mass will squash more; it will also squash more if more force is applied. This principle, however, needs to be balanced with another factor called *rigidity*.

In real life, rigid bodies such as tables or chairs do not squash or stretch at all, or so little as to not be noticeable. In animation, especially in cartoony animation, this physical reality is often overlooked, and you will see objects such as an anvil or a boulder being squashed and stretched as if they were made of rubber. But the fact is that the more rigid a thing is supposed to be, the less it should squash and stretch. Carelessly applying squash and stretch to what is supposed to be a rigid object (or character) can undermine its believability. A steel hammer, for example, even if it walks and talks, should stay mostly rigid if we are to believe that it is made up of steel—that it is a hard object. If it squashes and stretches like some soft, rubbery substance, its characteristics as a hammer are undermined.

When applying squash and stretch, another factor to keep in mind is consistency of *volume*. When a water-filled balloon is put on a hard surface, for instance, gravity causes the mass of the water to exert pressure on the rubber, causing the balloon to squash. But as it flattens, it also stretches out sideways because the volume of the water hasn't changed. Even cartoon characters need to have a sense of volume, and once a character's form becomes easily recognizable, that sense of volume must be maintained.

Animating the Upper Body

The upper-body movements in a walk cycle are mostly a matter of counter-rotating and counter-counter-rotating to balance the root joint's animation. In a natural walk, when the pelvis is rotating one way, the shoulders rotate in the opposite direction, moving to counterbalance the upper body against hip rotation.

Upper Spine and Chest Rotation

Much of the counter-rotation happens in the lower back area. The upper spine and chest joints' rotations are added to this to produce an "over-rotation." Because the face should always be looking straight ahead, the neck joint needs to be counter-rotated to correct the over-rotation, as shown in Figure 13.7.

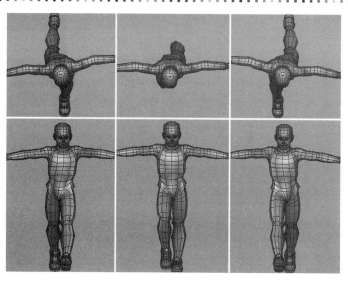

Figure 13.7 *Upper body rotations*

Note that the shoulder rotation in Figure 13.7 isn't as noticeable as the hip rotation. However, the rotation is a rather exaggerated movement in that you would rarely see this much shoulder rotation in real-life normal walks. You must also be careful to make the head as stationary as possible. If the spine and chest counter-rotations are not properly done, the head may noticeably move from side to side, which could make for a good cartoony animation, but generally is not found in normal walks.

Arm Movement

Arm movement follows the shoulder—specifically the shoulder rotation—transferring the motion like a wave starting from the shoulder and moving down to the fingers. First, you need to lower the shoulder joints about −15 to −20 degrees in the Z axis. Because the shoulder-bind position is for outstretched arms, when they come down, so should the shoulders. Move and roughly rotate the Lhand_c node, as shown in Figure 13.8. The poses are captured at frames 1, 5, 9, 14, and 18.

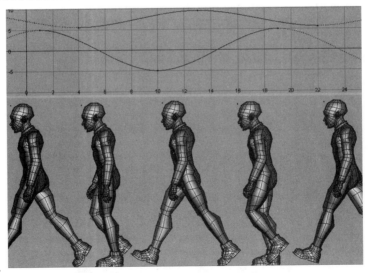

Figure 13.8 *The arm movements*

If you look at Figure 13.8 carefully, you will see that the arm is still in the process of swinging back at frame 1. The Lhand _c node follows the shoulder rotation about three frames behind; it reaches its extreme position at frame 4. This is called *follow-through* or *overlapping action* in classical animation. Loose limbs such as the arms do not stop when the object they are attached to stops moving, but rather continue to move for a few more frames, perhaps dangling a bit, before coming to a full stop. So when the shoulder rotation changes direction, the arms follow through and change their directions a few frames later. This is also called overlapping action because the change in the direction of the shoulders overlaps with the change in direction of the arms. The curves in Figure 13.8, the spine rotate.x curve, and the Lhand_c translate.y that follows illustrate this animation principle.

Hand Movement

Once you are satisfied with the way that the arms are moving back and forth, rotate the hand to make it follow through the arm movement about two frames behind. It may help to get rid of the rough rotations you had keyframed and start over from frame 6. The hand rotation in real life is usually nonexistent or very subtle. But again, as with the shoulder rotations, you may want to exaggerate the rotation to make it more noticeable. Examine the poses and the overlapping curves shown in Figure 13.9.

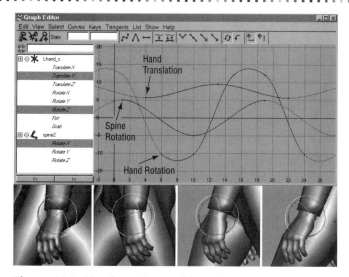

Figure 13.9 *Hand rotation and function curves*

Copy the animation from the left hand to the right hand control node, offsetting and adjusting the values as you did with the feet. Check to make sure that the curves are cycling properly, so that there are no broken tangents or values skipping at the start or the end of a cycle. Sometimes, an extra keyframe may lengthen a curve segment, causing it to not cycle correctly. One way to find out is to Playblast the animation over a few hundred frames. You can see a movie clip of the final walk in the Chapter 13 Working Files folder on the CD.

Exaggeration and Follow-Through

There is a fine line between keeping movements true to real life and exaggerating to achieve certain effects that you want. In our exercise, we noted that shoulder rotations are hardly noticeable in normal real life walks, yet we made the shoulders rotate more. We did this because when we try to imitate reality completely, we often end up with terrible animation. Exaggerating certain movements greatly improves the animation. This concept is clearer if you consider actors acting out a scene. Actors often exaggerate their movements to make their acting more "real" to the audience. Exaggeration, when properly executed, can communicate the meaning of the action to the viewers better than unexaggerated movements.

In animation, you can exaggerate in more varied ways, such as squashing and stretching characters and making them move in ways that are not physically possible. However, you do need to make sure that your exaggerations are serving to make the actions more "real" to the viewers, not less. Think of it as creating a caricature. If you draw a person, then exaggerate that person's distinguishing features, the resulting caricature makes us see who the person is more clearly. If you just exaggerate without a good reason, you end up with a bad drawing.

Another animation principle that often works together with exaggeration is follow-through, or overlapping action. Again, you have already seen an example of this with the arm movements of the walk cycle. Because the arm is dangling from the shoulder, when the spine and chest joints change their direction of rotation, the arm still moves in the same direction for a few more frames. It is following through, or overlapping with, the rotation action of the body. Follow-throughs and overlapping actions occur all the time in real life. Any situation where things are dangling or flapping, like appendages or soft body parts, require them. Follow-throughs are also the conclusion of any good, graceful motion. Anyone learning golf will be reminded of the importance of a good "follow-through" to his swing. In the same way, the follow-through motion of a character that occurs after the "hit," whatever that is, is just as important as the "hit" motion itself.

Creating More Interesting Walks

The walk the way it is now has all of the characteristics of walking, but it's rather boring. And boring in animation is synonymous with *dead*. But you can easily tweak the curves, now that you have them to play with, to create more interesting walk cycles.

For an example, let's edit our walk cycle to a happy walk. The walk we created is already fast, so just increase the bounce to be a bit snappier, a bit higher, which is more characteristic of a happy walk. Here are the modifications you can make:

- The front knee should be raised a bit more when the body is passing its highest point. Rotate the root joint forward, and then rotate the spine joints back so the spine will arch back.

- Rotate the neck as well so the character's chin will be pointing up.

- Animate the shoulders to lift a bit when the arm is forward. Bend the arms and lift them up more when they are forward, and make the elbow come out to the side by translating the arm Pole Vector constraints.

- You may also want to rotate the body more noticeably.

Of course, putting a smile on his face isn't a bad idea either, as shown in Figure 13.10. You can see a movie clip of the happy walk in the Chapter 13 Working Files folder on the CD.

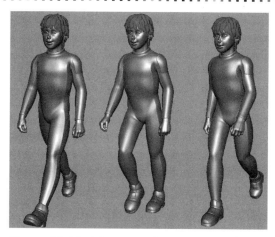

Figure 13.10 *A happy walk*

As you can see, once a walk has been established, it's very easy to edit the keyframes to create different walks. If you want a sad walk, slow the pace down, make the legs cover less ground, and rotate the back to be more hunched down. The head should be looking down as well, and the body should rotate less. Think of other kinds of walks you could create: a stiff, proud walk; a loose, drunken walk; an urgent walk; a leisurely walk; or a sexy, cat walk. Isolating and exaggerating the characteristics that will define such walks can be a useful exercise in character animation.

A Dog Walk

Now that we have gone through a step-by-step walk cycle, we can tackle a more difficult four-legged walk cycle. We'll also make the puppy move forward, to make the exercise more realistic.

A four-legged walk is basically two sets of two-legged walks that are offset by a frame or two. You will also find that the puppy is just good enough in terms of its weighting for a walk, but not much more, so you would want to keep an eye on how the dog's form holds up as you move it around.

In order to use the puppy for more extreme deformation situations, such as running or sitting, the model itself would need to be built more carefully. It would need more control points and better weighting. You would also want to use blend shapes and expressions to accommodate specific poses the puppy would assume.

Animating the Body

The first thing we want to do is to make the upper body move, then make the legs follow. The first several keyframes are necessarily rough guesses, the values of which will probably change as you animate and refine the other control nodes of the puppy. We'll make the walk cycle in 16 frames.

1. Open the Puppy_bound.mb file from the Chapter 12 Working Files folder on the CD.

2. Keyframe the hip joint at frames 1, 5, 9, 13, and 17.

3. In the Graph Editor, select the translate Z curve and delete the keyframes on it except for 1 and 17.

4. Move up the keyframe at 17 until you think the puppy has covered enough distance for two steps, or a cycle. When you work on the steps, it will become apparent whether you need to increase or decrease this value.

5. Take the translate Y keyframes at 1, 9, and 17 and lower the body a bit. This is when the puppy's steps are at their extreme positions.

6. Do the opposite of step 5 with keyframes 5 and 13, when the legs are crossing each other and the body position is at its highest.

7. Cycle the translate Y curve. For the translate Z curve, apply Cycle with Offset, or Linear. Your function curves should look like those in Figure 13.11.

Animating the Legs

Now we will make the legs move. In order to pull off this task of coordinating the legs and the body as the dog walks forward, we will need to work in the Graph Editor. Trying to keyframe in the modeling window or the Timeline for this type of work would be inefficient and frustrating.

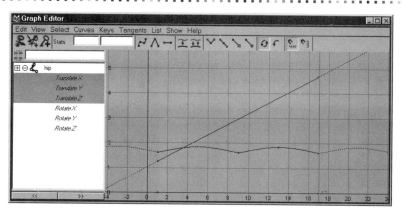

Figure 13.11 *Root joint translation curves*

1. Move the left legs, front and back (Lfront_c and Lback_c nodes), as follows and shown in Figure 13.12:

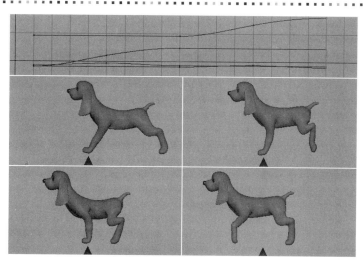

Figure 13.12 *The left legs move up*

- From frames 1 to 9, the front leg stays stationary, while the back leg moves up with the body, as shown in the left picture in Figure 13.12, with an extra keyframe at frame 5 to lift the leg.

- From frames 9 to 17, the front leg moves up with the body, with another keyframe at frame 13 to lift the leg, while the back leg stays stationary, as shown in the right picture in Figure 13.12 (the right legs are hidden for now).

- You should also rotate the legs appropriately. Note that the front leg's paw is controlled by the Foot_rot attribute.

2. Cycle all of the curves, but with the translate Z curves, apply Cycle with Offset.

3. With the left leg control nodes still selected, also select the hip joint.

4. In the Graph Editor, select only the translate Z curves to view them. Zoom out until you can see how the curves behave over a few hundred frames. You will probably see something that looks like the top picture in Figure 13.13, where the curves diverge over the Timeline.

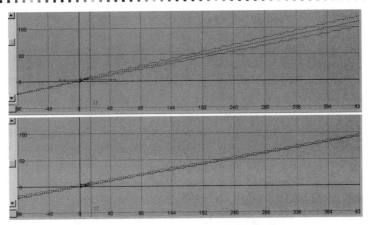

Figure 13.13 *Translate Z values of legs and hip joints*

5. Move the keyframes of the legs and/or the hip joint at frame 17 to adjust the values so that the curves will stay parallel over at least a couple of hundred frames, as in the bottom picture in Figure 13.13. It's important that the relative distances between the leg control nodes and the hip joint are not only maintained, but that the legs stay right under the body, so that it will look like they are supporting the body as the puppy walks.

6. Once the legs are cycling properly, we can copy the animation to their right leg counterparts. Copy Lfront_c's animation to the Rfront_c node, then move the curves back eight frames, so that their first keyframes will be at frame –7. The

most telling curve is the translate Z curve, and when you compare the values for the two front legs, you should see the translate Z curves crisscrossing, as shown in the top picture in Figure 13.14.

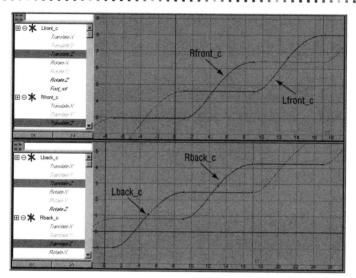

Figure 13.14 *Translate Z values for left and right legs*

7. Repeat step 6 with the back leg control nodes, except that this time, the copied curves should be pushed forward eight frames, not back. Again, see how the translate Z curves for the back legs crisscross in the bottom picture in Figure 13.14.

Refining the Walk

The legs are moving fairly well now, but something still doesn't quite seem right. There should be a couple of frames of delay between when the back leg comes up and the front leg moves forward. The back leg has to first push the puppy forward, which then makes it possible for the front leg to push off the ground as well. Select the front_c nodes, then in the Graph Editor, push all the curves forward two frames. These two frames of overlapping action make the movements of the four legs more natural.

The body moves in arcs, as you can see in the lines drawn above the pictures in Figure 13.15. The side-to-side rotation cycles once in 16 frames, with the body arching in toward the side where the back leg is coming up. The up-and-down rotation cycles once every eight frames, with every step, with the body arching down when the body is up. In exactly the same way as with the human walk, the back joint of the puppy counter-rotates to compensate for its hip-joint rotation. The chest joint rotates the body in the opposite direction, which the neck joint counter-rotates again to keep the puppy's head looking straight ahead, as shown in Figure 13.15.

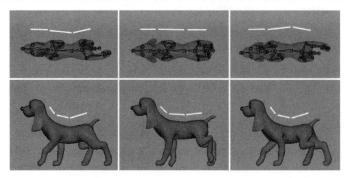

Figure 13.15 *Body rotations*

Finally, you may want to create and animate a camera so that it will keep up with the puppy as it moves forward. An easy way to do this is to copy the translate Z curve of the puppy's hip joint to the camera, and then move the entire curve up and down to adjust the camera view. You can see a movie clip of the final dog walk in the Chapter 13 Working Files folder on the CD.

A Run Cycle

From two to four legs, and now back to two legs again—after the previous exercises, doing another two-legged cycle should be pretty easy.

Running differs from walking in that when the body is at its highest position, both feet are actually off the ground; a slow jog is almost exactly the same as a very bouncy walk, except for that one fact. A runner is constantly leaping or bouncing forward, and as the run becomes faster, the body will lean forward more.

Setting the Distance

We'll cycle the run in 16 frames. As you saw with the puppy walk cycle, the most important thing to establish at the beginning is the distance covered.

1. Start out by keyframing the leg_c nodes and the root joint in an extreme pose, as shown in Figure 13.16. Keyframe the leg_pole_c nodes as well, because they will also need to move forward with the character as well.

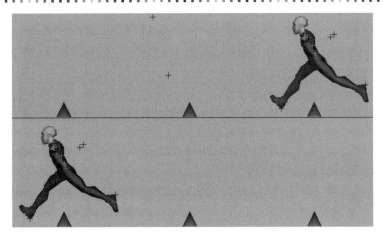

Figure 13.16 *Extreme running poses*

2. Go to frame 17, move the root joint, the leg_pole_c nodes, and the leg_c nodes in the Z axis up to a position that would cover the distance for two leaping steps, as shown in Figure 13.16. Cycle with Offset the translate Z curves. This distance will likely need to be refined later.

3. Keyframe the root joint at frames 5, 9, and 13. Get rid of the keyframes for the translate X and Z curves. Move the keyframes as follows to create the curve shapes shown in Figure 13.17.

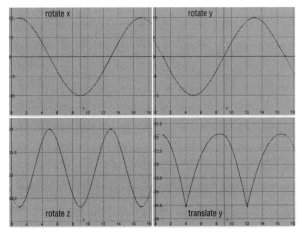

Figure 13.17 *Function curves for the root joint*

- Rotate X should rotate from about 20 to –20 degrees.

- Rotate Y should rotate between –10 to 10 degrees.

- Rotate Z should cycle every nine frames, rotating a few degrees.

- The tangents for translate Y should be broken at the bottom to make the bounce quick and snappy. Note that the keyframes for when the body is at its lowest have been moved to frame 4 and frame 12.

Animating the Run

We'll concentrate on keyframing the Rleg_c control node through the cycle, then copy the keys to the Lleg_c node.

At frame 1 (and frame 17), adjust Rleg_c's keyframes to accommodate the root joint's rotations. The root joint's translate Y value, on the other hand, should adjust to the leg. If the body is too low, it will keep the leg bent all the time; if the body is too high, it will stretch the leg too much. Each time you edit a keyframe at frame 1, make sure to move its counterpart at frame 17. Also, the right foot should be just touching the left foot, which means a translate X value of about –2.2.

Keyframe the Rleg_c as shown in Figure 13.18:

- At frame 1, the toes should be curling up.

- At frame 3, the foot should be planted on the ground.

- At frame 5, the body is passing over, and the foot should be starting to spring back.

- At frame 7, the foot is kicking off from the ground.

- At frame 9, move the foot so that it doesn't stretch or lag behind the body too much.

- At frame 12, the foot is passing the body, moving just above the ground.

- At frame 14, the knee is coming up and the foot is rotating in preparation to hit the ground again.

- Frame 17 should show the same leg position as frame 1.

Copy the keys from Rleg_c to Lleg_c. The Lleg_c node needs to be edited a bit:

- The translate X value should be the opposite of the right foot's, which is 2.2.

- Select all the curves, and then push them forward eight frames.

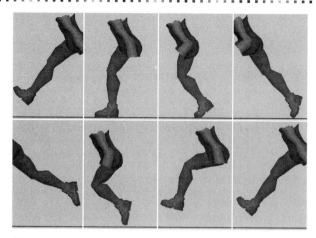

Figure 13.18 *Right leg poses*

- The first keyframes should start at frame 9.

- The translate Z curve needs to be pushed up, until it is crisscrossing with the Rleg_c node's translate Z curve, as shown in Figure 13.19. Do not, at this point, try to adjust individual keyframes of the translate Z curve, or the symmetry between the right leg's movement and the left leg's will be broken. Move the entire curve instead.

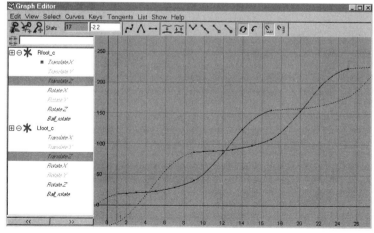

Figure 13.19 *Translate Z curves for the legs*

Note that there aren't any flat curve segments in translate Z curves for the legs. The flat segments occur when the foot is firmly planted on the ground for a while, which happens with walking. This doesn't happen with running.

Animating the Runner's Upper Body

By now, counter-rotating the spine and the neck joints to compensate for the hip movements should be a familiar task. In a run, the shoulders move, the body rotates more noticeably, and, of course, the arms swing much more dramatically. But for our character, let's try a bit of drama and have him keep his arms stretched out, perhaps trying to stop someone in front of him.

Rotate the shoulder joints down a bit and forward, and keyframe his arms stretched out. The rotations of the spine joints should be toned down to keep the chest looking straight forward, to keep the arms from swinging wildly from side to side. Aim for something like the poses shown in Figure 13.20 through the cycle.

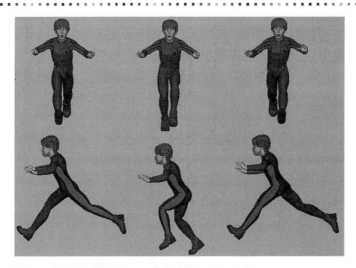

Figure 13.20 *Rotations of the runner's body*

If you want the arm movements to not repeat every 16 frames, try lengthening the cycle for the arms to something like 32 frames. This approach can make the movements seem more random. You can see a movie clip of the final run cycle in the Chapter 13 Working Files folder on the CD.

Arcs and Staging

Arcing is another important classical animation principle. In order to imitate life, you need to show motion as arcs, or waves. Nothing in this world moves in a totally straight line. Nature comprises arcs and waves, including all motion that occurs within it, as Tai Chi practitioners like to point out. We are told that even something as apparently straight as a ray of light is not perfectly straight. A run cycle, such as the one we just created, is all wave motions, as you can readily see in the Graph Editor.

But it's one thing to create wavy function curves and quite another to show them as wavy motions. Consider the often-used example of head-turning. Although the motion itself is an arc, depending on the angle from which you are looking at the head, the head-turning can appear as a straight-line motion. In order to show it as an arc movement, you need to either change the view or dip the head as it turns, and then bring it back up.

When you have roughly animated your character, get into the habit of going to the camera view and checking the lines the character's motions are creating. If you see a lot of straight lines even though the motions themselves are arcs, perhaps the camera view needs to be changed.

This brings up yet another important animation principle called *staging*. No matter how great the action is in a scene, it must be seen clearly to be appreciated. Staging a character involves making sure that the character's actions are being accurately transmitted to the viewers. The run cycle exercise, for instance, was shown in the side view because it best staged the motions of the body. If the same steps were captured in the front view, you would have a much harder time grasping what was going on. Classical animators will often only look at the silhouette of a character to determine whether the character's actions are being staged properly.

Staging also involves making sure that only one principal action is being presented at one time. If you want to show a character get up from a chair and also flash a smile, it would be poor staging to have her do both at the same time. It would be much better to have her stand up first and then flash a smile, or vice versa.

Ball Tossing

Animating a character interacting with things or other characters is always more challenging than working with a solitary character. Fortunately, it is more rewarding as well, because you can develop a character much more fully when she is acting and reacting in a more complex setting. But what may be an easy task in real life, such as two people shaking hands, can cause severe headaches for the person trying to animate such a scene.

Consider the perils of animating something like a battle between two sword fighters. How do you make them grasp their swords with both hands, clash blades, briefly stick the swords together, and then merrily continue in their deadly ways? Sorry, it's not for this book to figure out such things for you—you can tackle that one at a later date.

Here, we will go through a simple task of grabbing and throwing a ball by animating constraints, which is essentially the way you would solve more complex problems such as swordplay. You can see movie clips of this animation in the Chapter 13 Working Files folder on the accompanying CD.

Grabbing the Ball

We'll start by setting up the hand holding the ball.

1. Create a ball (sphere) scaled to 1.5 uniformly, and group it with itself, creating a parent node.

2. Select Modify ➜ Center Pivot to make sure the parent node's pivot point coincides with the ball's.

3. Place the character's hand on a table (a simple cube will do), illustrated in Figure 13.21.

4. Create a locator, scaled to 3 uniformly, group it under the Rhand_c node, and place it somewhere near the hand. Refer to the left picture in Figure 13.21.

5. Point-and-Orient constrain the ball's parent node to the locator, and the ball should snap to the locator positionally and orientationally, as in the middle picture in Figure 13.21.

6. Move the locator closer to the hand, and rotate the fingers to make it look as if the hand were holding the ball.

7. Keyframe the finger joints and the Rhand_c node at frame 15, as in the right picture in Figure 13.21. This is how the hand will be seen as grabbing the ball.

8. Select the ball's parent node, and you will see pointConstraint and orientConstraint attributes in the Channel box.

9. Select Node State, where it should say Normal for each attribute, and keyframe them at frame 15. In the Graph Editor, you can see that a value of 0 is created.

10. Go to frame 14. In the Channel box, click the Node State field to open the submenu, and select Block. Keyframe that for both attributes. You should then see a value of 2 created in the Graph Editor. (Note that the curve created is a stepped curve.)

11. Try moving the hand, and you will see at frame 14 that the ball is not constrained to the locator. Keyframe the ball where it is (at frame 15) just to make sure that the ball will be at that spot when the hand grabs it.

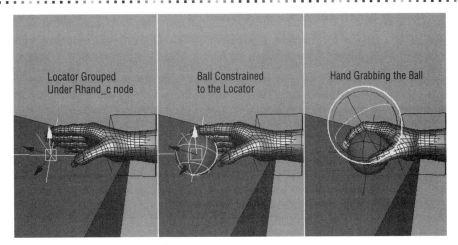

Figure 13.21 *The hand grabbing the ball from the surface of the table*

12. Now you can animate the Rhand_c node and the finger joints, starting from a distance at frame 1 and then swooping in to scoop the ball at frame 15, as shown in Figure 13.22.

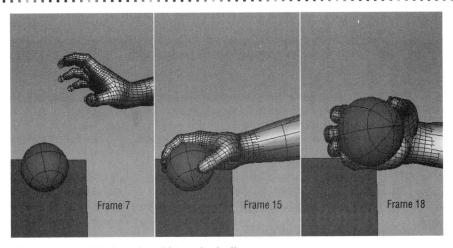

Figure 13.22 *The hand grabbing the ball*

Throwing the Ball

Animating throwing a ball is essentially the same thing as animating grabbing a ball, except that you are working backward.

1. Start out at frame 25 with the ball constrained to the hand. Swing the character's arm as if he were throwing the ball, and reach the point of release at frame 30. This means he should be flicking his wrist between frames 30 and 32. Finish the throw at frame 35.

2. Once you are satisfied with the throwing motion, go back to frame 30 and keyframe the ball where it is.

3. Go to frame 31, select the ball's parent node and, in the Channel box, change the Node State setting to Block for the Position and Orient constraints.

4. At frame 35, translate the ball to the direction where the ball has been thrown, and keyframe.

Now, when you move the Time Slider, the ball seems to be thrown from the hand at frame 31, and then shoots out from there, as shown in Figure 13.23.

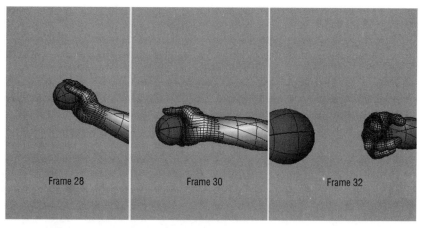

Figure 13.23 *The hand throwing the ball*

Maya Character Creation and Animation

All of the new developments in Maya 3, especially the introduction of the Trax Editor (covered in the next chapter), have made Maya's character node a useful aid in enabling animators to animate more intuitively. A *character,* as defined and used in Maya, is essentially a node under which you can collect all of the attributes you want to use to animate as a single entity. This usually will be the control nodes of a character you've created and want to animate. However, it could also be some very different collection of things that you want to animate together as a group, such as the lights and doors of a haunted house, for instance, or two different characters who are interacting closely.

Creating a Character

First, let's go through the steps for creating a character.

1. Bring in the `character_bound.mb` file from the Chapter 12 Working Files folder on the CD.

2. Select all of the major control nodes for animating the character: the root, spine1, spine2, neck, head, shoulders, hand controls, foot controls, and pole-vector controls for arms and legs. These should add up to a total of 15 control nodes.

3. Select Character ➔ Create ❑. The option window's default settings, as shown in Figure 13.24, include only the translation and rotation attributes for the selected nodes to the character node. You would rarely want to include the other attributes, which are selected for exclusion.

4. Click Create Character, and a node with a human icon named character1 should appear in the Outliner. You can rename it if you want.

5. Open the node, and you will see all the X, Y, and Z translation and rotation channels for the nodes you had selected, as shown in Figure 13.24.

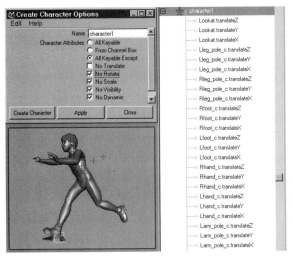

Figure 13.24 *The Create Character Options box and character node*

Editing a Character

Consider all of the attributes in the character1 node we just created. Perhaps certain attributes are not needed for the animation of the character, and maybe some extra attributes should be added. The Character menu in Maya 3 now provides the functions to perform this type of character node editing. For this example, we don't want the rotation attributes of the Lookat node to be part of the character1 node. Instead, we want to add its scale X attribute. First, the character1 node must be set as the current character, or the functions won't work.

1. Either select Character ➜ Set Current Character ➜ character1 or click the inverted triangle at the bottom right of the Maya window, beside the Auto Keyframe button. This opens the character pop-up menu. Pick character1 from the menu.

2. Select the Lookat node, select all of its attributes in the Channel box, and choose Character ➜ Remove from Character to remove them from the character's list of attributes.

3. Select the translate attributes, scale the X attribute of the Lookat node, and then select Character ➜ Add to Character.

The translation and the scale X attributes are part of the character node now. Why did we remove the translation attributes and then add them again? This was done to make the Lookat node's attributes stay together in the character node's list of attributes.

To quickly select all of the nodes included in the character1 node, you can select Character ➜ Select Character Nodes ➜ character1. To delete a character node, just delete the node using the Outliner or the Relationship Editor as you would remove any set. The attributes listed under it are not deleted.

Creating and Editing a Subcharacter

Maya 3 also introduces the ability to create a hierarchical structure within the character node, by creating a subcharacter node. A subcharacter node is created and edited in the same way as a regular character node. Let's try grouping the upper-body joints and control nodes together.

First, set the character1 node as the current character (as described in the previous section). Then simply select the nodes you want to group and choose Character ➜ Create Subcharacter, with the default settings. A subCharacter1 node is created inside the character1 node. You should see a hierarchical structure that looks something like the one shown in Figure 13.25.

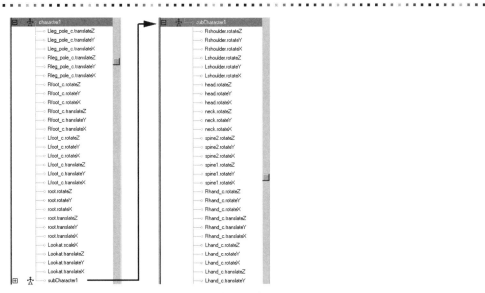

Figure 13.25 *A subcharacter node in the Outliner*

A subcharacter node is essentially another character node. If you want to add or remove attributes from it, you must set it as the current character. If you open the Set Current Character submenu now, you should see that character1 has an arrow beside it. It has itself become a submenu, containing the subcharacter1 node in it. When attributes are removed from a subcharacter, or the subcharacter node is deleted, they don't return to the parent character node. You need to put them back in manually.

Animating a Character

When using the character or the subcharacter in Maya, it's important to set the current character properly. Let's say that we want to keyframe Lhand_c node, and only that node, at frame 1.

1. Set Current Character to None. At the bottom right of the Maya window, the field should read "No Character."

2. Keyframe Lhand_c, and then select subCharacter1 in the Outliner. In the Channel box, you should see that only that node's translate and rotate attributes have been keyframed, as shown in the left side in Figure 13.26.

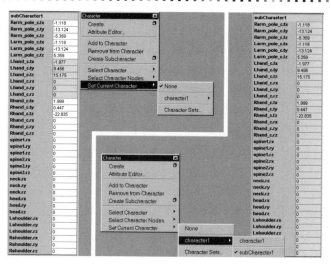

Figure 13.26 *The current character settings*

3. Undo the keyframe, set the current character to subCharacter1, and keyframe Lhand_c again. This time you should see that all of the attributes in the subCharacter1 node were keyframed, as shown in the right side in Figure 13.26.

4. If you keyframe Lhand_c with the current character set to character1, then all of the attributes under the character1 node, including the attributes in the subCharacter1 node, will be keyframed.

You can choose to keyframe only the attributes of a character or a subcharacter that you want by selecting them in the Channel box and RM clicking Key Selected, but this defeats the purpose of using the character node. It's much better to use the regular Set Key command and keyframe all of the attributes each time.

As we said at the beginning of this section, a character node collects all of the disparate elements from a character's setup into a single entity, eliminating the need to deal with a large number of controls—15 control nodes in our example. The real advantage is that the character node frees the animator to concentrate on animating the character. When you keyframe all of the attributes in the character node, it freezes the character into a pose, and thus encourages a "pose-to-pose" approach to animation, as shown below. Once you are in the character mode, you can forget about nodes and just animate!

Summary

In this chapter, we went through a simple walk cycle step by step, and then we examined more complicated animations such as a four-legged walk cycle, running, and grabbing and throwing a ball. We also covered the concept of character and subcharacter nodes in Maya and how they can aid animation.

In the next chapter, you will learn about the Trax Editor, which is a revolutionary nonlinear animation editing tool, introduced in Maya 3.

Animation Using the Trax Editor

MAYA

Chapter 14

One of the most anticipated new features of Maya 3 is the Trax Editor, a nonlinear animation editor that simplifies many of an animator's jobs and is especially useful for game developers. In essence, nonlinear animation helps resolve two problems common to keyframed animation: reusing keyframed motion and stacking keyframed motion.

While reuse of animation segments grew out of game development needs (in which short animations need to be reused and blended together), Trax, as this chapter will show, has advantages that go way beyond the gaming world. This chapter covers the following topics:

- Character and subcharacter creation
- Pose creation
- Clip creation
- Clip blending
- Clip sharing
- Walk Cycle creation with Trax
- Lip-synching using Trax

Characters

Before you can work with Trax in Maya, you must first create a character. A character can be anything from a single geometric primitive to a complex, fully functional virtual human, complete with skeleton and blend shapes. What ties a character's disparate objects together is that, once they are properly joined as a character, they are all grouped under a single node, and you can animate the appropriate channels on all of the objects in the character from one convenient place.

A character is not equivalent to a grouped set of objects for a very important reason: Character nodes are set nodes, not geometry or transform nodes. Because characters are sets, you can place other nodes in the set, or more important, *only certain channels* of other nodes. Thus, only channels that are relevant to animating a character need to be added to that character, eliminating much of the hunting through excess channels and extra keyframes that can occur when animating without using character sets.

Creating Characters

You create a character by selecting objects and choosing Character ➜ Create ❏ from the Animation module. In the option window, shown in Figure 14.1, you have the choice of giving your character a name (character1 is chosen by default), and you have three options for which object attributes to include in your character:

- The All Keyable option places all the attributes that appear in the Channel box into the character (often, this is too many).

- The From Channel Box option lets you select specific channels to include by highlighting them in the Channel box before opening the option window.

- The All Keyable Except option (the most generally useful, and selected by default) lets you pick which attribute groups to include in your character. For example, if No Scale is selected, the Scale attributes from your objects will not be included in the character.

Let's create a simple character and take a quick look at how character sets are actually structured in Maya.

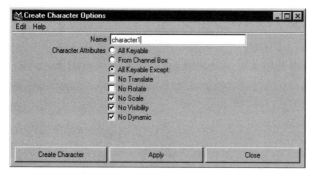

Figure 14.1 *The Create Character Options window*

1. In a new scene window, create a NURBS sphere and cone, and rename them **ball** and **cone**, respectively. You can move the scene elements around if you wish, but you don't need to for this example.

2. Drag-select both objects, and then choose Character ➜ Create ❑ from the Animation module. Choose Edit ➜ Reset Settings, and click the Create Character button to create your character. Your character, named character1, will be created, and the character name will appear to the right of the Range Slider at the bottom right of your screen.

Selecting and Examining Characters

By selecting the character and using the Channel box, you can quickly locate and animate the relevant attributes of all your objects in one place—which is the primary advantage of creating a character.

Now that we have a character, let's select it.

1. In the Outliner (unfortunately, set nodes, like character nodes, do not appear in the Hypergraph window in hierarchical mode), click character1 to highlight it.

2. Click the plus sign to the left of the character to see all of the nodes that are currently in the character1 set. Note that these nodes are the ones that appear in the Channel box when you select the character. Because we allowed only translation and rotation keyframes, those (for both the ball and cone) are all that appear in the set.

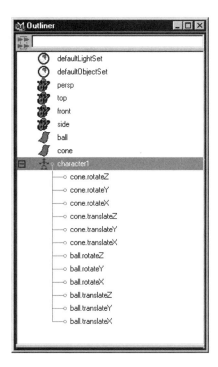

3. To see more clearly how the character is constructed (as well as how to add or remove attributes), open the character set's Relationship Editor by selecting Window ➜ Relationship Editors ➜ Character Sets. On the left side of the window, you see character1, just as in the Outliner. On the right side are all of the objects in the scene.

4. Highlight character1 on the left, and all scene objects that are part of this set will be highlighted on the right.

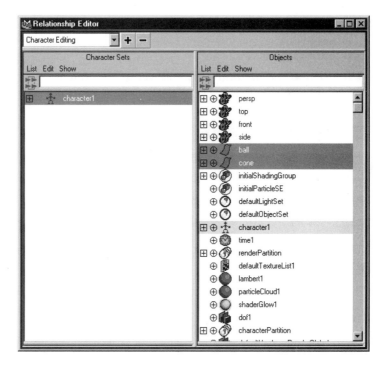

5. Click the leftmost plus sign by character1 on the right side to reveal all of the object attributes assigned to this set. This is the same as clicking the character1 plus sign on the left side (note that on the right, the attributes are all highlighted). Furthermore, both the ball and cone scene objects are highlighted, indicating that their nodes are (at least partially) in the character1 set.

6. Click the rightmost plus sign next to cone to see all of cone's attributes. Scroll down, and you will see that the translate and rotate attributes are highlighted, indicating that they are part of the character1 set.

Removing and Adding Character Attributes

Removing an attribute from a character is simple in the Relationship Editor: Find the attribute you wish to remove (the cone's translateX attribute, for example), and click it on the right side, unhighlighting it. You will immediately see that channel disappear from the character1 set, as well as from the Channel box (assuming character1 is still selected there).

To add an attribute, just highlight it on the right side while character1 is selected on the left. Even if you have already begun animating your character, you can still add or remove attributes from it. But be aware that if you remove a keyed attribute from a character, you lose any keyframes that attribute might have had.

You can also remove and add attributes via the Channel box and Character menu. Select a channel name (like cone.tx) and choose Character ➜ Remove from Character. To add an attribute this way, select the object and highlight the attribute you wish to add in the Channel box, and then choose Character ➜ Add to Character.

Setting a Working Character

To set a character to be the working character, you can choose the character from the pop-up menu at the right of the Range Slider, or you can choose Character ➜ Set Current Character ➜ *<character name>*. When you have set a character as the working one, setting keyframes will affect only keyable attributes of that character (those listed in the Channel box).

Let's see how this works.

1. Create a second character out of a simple cylinder (let it be named character2, which is the default).

2. Check in the character pop-up menu to be sure that character2 is set as the working character. Then choose *both* the cone and the cylinder, and set a key by pressing **s** (do not press the Shift key) on the keyboard.

3. Move the Timeline to, say, ten frames, and move both objects some distance away from their original positions. If auto keyframing is off (the key icon to the right of the character pop-up menu is not red), press **s** again to set new keys.

4. Rewind your animation. You should see the cylinder move between the two positions you keyed over ten frames, but the cone will stay where you last put it.

Why didn't the cone move? Because when you set keys, you set them on *only* the current character. Because the cone is part of character1, not character2, no keys were set as you moved the objects around. If you tried to set keyframes on the cylinder's Y scale, you would not be able to do so, because you did not define scale as keyable in character2. Although it may take a bit of time to get used to, the fact that Maya does not set keyframes on objects or attributes outside a character is a great way to avoid the numerous extraneous keyframes that always seem to crop up when doing animation work.

If you want to keyframe the cylinder's scale, but don't wish to add those attributes to your character, you can choose to turn off all character animation by setting the character pop-up menu (or Character ➜ Set Current Character) to None. Setting keyframes will then work for all scene objects and attributes.

Creating Subcharacters

Finally, you can create subcharacters that are part of your main character but can be animated and keyed separately. If, for example, you wish to animate a character's left arm separately from animation of the entire body, you can create a leftArm subcharacter, which will be hierarchically a child of the main character.

To create a subcharacter for a left arm, first create a character for the whole body (including the left arm), then with the body set as your character in the pop-up menu, select the elements of the left arm and choose Character ➜ Create Subcharacter ❑. Adjust the settings of the subcharacter to your liking and click the Create Subcharacter button. In the character pop-up menu, leftArm will appear as a submenu of the body character, indicating it is linked below the main body character.

You can also create sub-subcharacters: Set the subcharacter as your active character (leftArm in this case), select the objects you wish to be the subcharacter of the arm (left-Hand, for example), and choose Create ➜ Subcharacter. In this manner, you can have multiple subcharacters linked in a hierarchy.

Now that you have a good idea of what characters are and how they are constructed, let's create a couple of simple poses and use them in the Trax Editor.

Poses

By storing and applying poses to characters during the animation process, you can quickly return to any number of default configurations for your character. Poses can save you time if the character commonly returns to certain positions during an animation.

Creating Poses

Let's first create a pose for character1. If you still have your simple scene from the last section handy, use it for this example. If not, create one character called character1 and another called character2 (characters made of simple geometric primitives are fine for our present purposes).

1. Once you have your characters defined, set character1 as the working character using the character pop-up menu (or Character ➜ Set Current Character).

2. Open the Trax Editor by choosing Window ➜ Trax Editor. You will note that, as shown in Figure 14.2, character1 and character2 are listed on the left side of the window, and the right side includes tracks for each character (empty at this point) and a Time Slider at the bottom.

Frame Timeline Range
Frame All
Create Blend
Create Clip   Visor   Graph Animation Curves

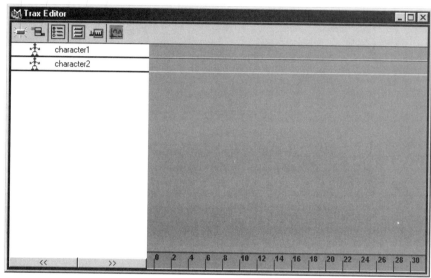

Figure 14.2 *The Trax Editor, with character1 and character2*

3. Select character1 in the Trax Editor so it appears in the Channel box (this is equivalent to picking the character in the Outliner).

4. In the Trax menu (or by RM choosing within the Trax window), choose Create ➜ Pose ❑.

5. Name the pose **startingPoint** and click the Create Pose button. You will not see any difference in the scene when you create this pose, but Maya has saved the position and rotation data of character1 in a clip in the Visor.

6. Open the Visor or Hypershade (Window ➜ Visor or Window ➜ Hypershade). At the top of the window, you will see a section called Animation.

7. Twirl down the arrow next to Animation, click the plus sign by the Character Clips & Poses folder, and then click the Poses folder. You will see that there is now a clip called startingPoint in this folder, which is the pose that you just saved.

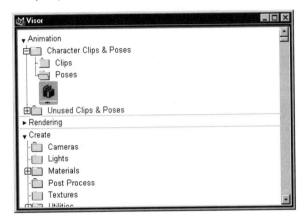

8. A pose works as you would expect. Try moving your character (or parts of it) to a different position, so it is not at the origin any more.

9. With the cursor over the pose in the Visor, RM choose Apply Pose. You should see your character return to its initial settings. (This pop-up menu also allows you to copy, instance, duplicate, or rename your clip or open the Attribute Editor.)

Note that if you were to adjust, say, the scale of one of your character parts, it would *not* return to its original scale when you applied the pose. This is because scale data was not included in the character, and thus is not recorded in the pose.

Placing Poses in the Timeline

Another use for poses is to place them in the Timeline. Placing poses in the Timeline can be beneficial in at least two ways. When working alone, you can place poses in the Timeline and move them around (by simply dragging them from place to place in the track) to get a quick "pose-to-pose" animation for your character, which you can go back to and refine later. In a multi-person production team, the lead animator could set poses for the most important frames in an animation (and adjust where those moments occur by moving the poses), and then the animation team could go in and create the in-between animation necessary to fill out the scene.

When you place a pose or clip into a track in the Trax Editor, you are actually creating an instance of the source clip stored in the Visor. When you drag the startingPoint clip, for example, into a track, it is called startingPoint1 (or 2 or so on), not just starting-Point. Because of this instance relationship, you can make any changes you wish to an individual pose or clip in a track without affecting the source clip's values. On the other hand, if you adjust the source clip's settings (via the Attribute Editor), all instances of the clip in tracks will be updated to reflect those changes. If you are familiar with a program like Director or Flash, you may recognize that the relationship between a source clip and a track clip in Maya is similar to that between a cast member and a sprite in Director, or a Library member and Symbol in Flash.

Let's try a simple pose-to-pose animation.

1. With the Visor and Trax Editor open, MM drag the pose from the Visor into the track for character1, pasting the pose into the track at a given frame, as shown below.

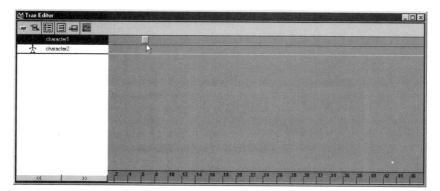

2. Move your character objects to a different place in the scene (and rotate them if you wish), and then create a pose with a different name (select Create ➜ Pose ❑ in the Trax Editor).

3. MM drag this new pose into the Timeline, as shown below.

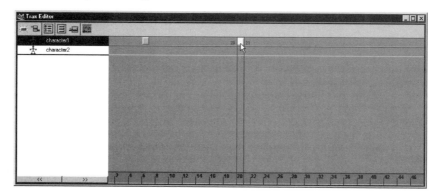

When you play back the animation, your character will "pop" from one pose to another, giving you a rough idea of the timing involved in the animation you would later create.

Clips

By allowing "clips" of animations to be stored in a sort of bin (akin to bins used in non-linear video editors), Maya lets you reuse animations as easily as pasting them into your scene work. Also, since animation is stored in clips, several different clips can be stacked on top of each other, or blended together, allowing you straightforward, nondestructive control over large- and small-scale animation of an entire character, without needing to find and adjust specific keyframes in several different character parts.

Creating Clips

Creating a clip is pretty much the same as creating a pose, except that instead of storing a single frame of position and rotation (and other) data, you store several keyframes of data. This allows you to create chunks (or clips) of an animation that can later be used in various places in a given track.

A clip can actually be composed of just one keyframe; however, a single keyframe clip can be difficult to use later, as it has no length to adjust or blend with other clips. This problem can be alleviated by selecting the source clip in the Visor, opening the Attribute Editor, and increasing the Duration of the source clip. However, it's easier just to create a multi-keyframed clip in the first place.

Once you have some sort of animation in your Timeline, you can create a clip in the Trax Editor by RM choosing Create ➜ Clip ❑. The Create Clip Options window, shown in Figure 14.3, allows you to choose how you wish to create and use your clip.

The Name field lets you name your clip (clip1 is the default name). The Leave Keys in Timeline check box lets you maintain the keyframes you use to create a clip in your Timeline. This can be useful if you wish to create several similar clips and don't want to reproduce all of the keyframes for each clip, but generally it is best to remove Timeline keyframes as you create a clip, so you don't get unexpected animation later.

The Clip radio buttons allow you to place the clip in the Visor only (if you don't plan to use it right away) or place the clip in the Visor and in a character track in the Trax Editor. The Time Range section provides four choices: use a selected time range (Shift+dragging in the Timeline), the start and end values of the Range Slider, the range of animation curves (from the first keyframe to the last for your character, which

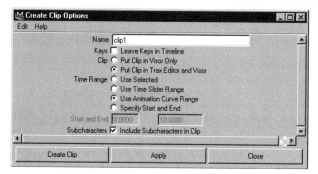

Figure 14.3 *The Create Clip Options window*

is the default method), or a manually specified start and end frame. Finally, you can choose to include subcharacter keyframes when you create a clip.

Let's create a clip.

1. In the Trax Editor, move character1 around some, set a keyframe, move the character somewhere else, and set another keyframe (you can continue this process with as many keyframes as you like). To set keyframes, simply press the **s** key after you move your character (be sure character1 is still selected, or you will not set keyframes on it).

 Remember that you can apply your predefined poses to help you set keyframes on the character.

2. RM choose Create ➔ Clip ❑. In the option window, name the clip anything you wish, set the clip to go in the Visor and Trax Editor, choose Use Animation Curve Range to set the length of the clip, and click Create Clip. As shown below, a new clip is inserted in the Trax Editor, ready for your use. In addition, in the Visor (under the Clips folder now, not the Poses folder) is a new source clip.

3. Click Play in the scene window, and you will see the time marker move across the Trax Editor Timeline as well. As it crosses the clip, your animation will play back, as it did when the keyframes were stored in the scene Timeline.

Once a clip is in a track, you can interactively change its position, length (or scale), and cycling options, as explained in the next section.

Modifying Clips

You can control the placement, length, cycling, and weight of a clip, as follows:

- To change the position (start and stop points) of the clip, just select the middle portion of the clip and drag the clip to a new point in the Timeline.

- To change the length (or scale) of the clip, drag on the top-right corner of the clip, as shown below. Alternatively, you can change the Scale value for the clip in the Attribute Editor. Changing the length of a clip means that the animation will take a longer or shorter time.

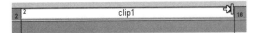

- To change the amount of times a clip repeats (its cycle settings), drag on the bottom-right corner of the clip, as shown below. Alternatively, you can set the Cycle number in the Attribute Editor. When there are multiple cycles of the original clip in your track, Maya places a black tick mark in the clip at each point where the original clip repeats.

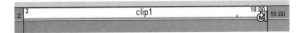

- To set the weight of a track, open the Attribute Editor and go to the Anim Clip Attribute section. Each keyframe in a clip is multiplied by the weight setting, so setting the weight of a clip to be greater than 1 means each keyframe will be exaggerated. Reducing the weight means a corresponding reduction in the level of each keyframe.

To change the scale of the Timeline in the Trax Editor (so you can see more or less of it), use the Alt+LM+MM drag method you use to adjust Maya's scene window. To move the range of time you are focused on, Alt+MM drag in the tracks area of the Trax Editor, just as you pan in the scene window.

Between controlling placement, length, cycling, and weight of a clip, you can fine-tune your animation to an exacting degree using the Trax Editor. If you want even more control over the shape of the underlying curves that make up a clip, you can graph the curves and adjust them as you would any animation curves in the Graph Editor. In the Trax Editor, choose View ➜ Graph Anim Curves (or click the Graph Animation Curves button in the toolbar, labeled in Figure 14.2). The Graph Editor will appear with all of the curves of your clip loaded in the window (you may need to press the A key to center the curves), as shown in Figure 14.4. You can then adjust the curves as you would any other animation curves, tweaking the motion until you are satisfied with it.

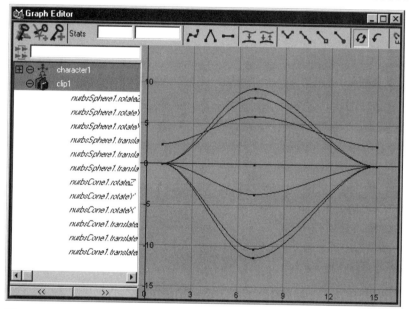

Figure 14.4 *A clip in the Graph Editor*

The animation curves of a clip loaded into the Graph Editor will *not* reflect any cycle, weighting, timing, or scale changes you have made to the clip. You will always see the curves from the original, unchanged clip in the Graph Editor. (For more information about using the Graph Editor, see Chapter 9, "Animating in Maya.")

Motion Warping: Adding Keyframes on Top of Clips

With Trax, you can also add keyframes over a track, tweaking the motion of a particular track while maintaining the integrity of the clip. This feature, called *motion warping*, allows a great deal of individual variation of a clip that might be used on several characters without affecting the underlying clip itself.

To create a motion warp, first set keyframes for the first and last frame on which the warp will occur (set these keys without changing the keyed values) to set the range of the warp. In the Trax Editor Timeline, the range of frames that set off the motion warp will be highlighted in blue, letting you know that a motion warp is in effect.

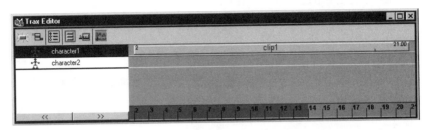

Once you have set a range, you can (within that range of keys) set any keyframes you wish on the character. As you make adjustments, Maya will *add* the keyframes you set to the clip animation, modifying the clip with the new keyframes. Since the effect of any keyframes you set is additive, it is best to set keys that affect movement in a fairly subtle way.

By using motion warping, you can alter one iteration of a clip cycle, make subtle adjustments to a particular motion on your character, or modify several characters that share the same clip animations, allowing each to behave in a slightly different way. (See the "Sharing Clips" section later in this chapter for details on sharing clip animations.)

Blending Clips

If adjusting one clip at a time in the Trax Editor is not enough for your animation purposes, never fear—you can blend animations between different clips or even between a clip and itself. For example, you might blend between a walking and standing clip or between a walking and running clip, reducing the need to keyframe complex transitional states in an animation.

To see how blending works, either use your simple character from the previous sections or create a character out of two primitives (such as a sphere and a cone), and create two clips: one clip with the sphere and cone moving in opposite directions along the Y axis, and the other with them moving in the X or Z axis in opposite directions.

You may find it easier to create the second clip if you disable the first one while you work on the other. To disable a clip, select the clip in the Trax Editor, then RM choose Enable/Disable Clip. A disabled clip's name is slightly grayed out, indicating it no longer affects the character's motion. Enabling and disabling clips can be a useful way to test individual motion on a character with multiple tracks of animation.

When you finish, the Trax Editor should have two tracks for character1, with both clips stacked on top of each other. Note that Maya has created a new track for character1 below the original one to accommodate the new clip.

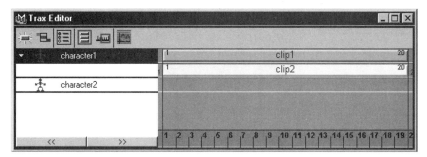

If you now play back the animation, the motions from both clips combine, so the sphere and cone travel diagonally opposite each other. To allow each clip to operate on its own, simply move one clip down the Timeline until it is no longer overlapping the other.

You can manually create new tracks by selecting the character and choosing Modify ➜ Add Track in the Trax Editor. To remove an unused track, select the character and choose Modify ➜ Remove Track (the bottom-most unused track is removed).

Clips are blended based on which clip is first in the Timeline. In other words, if clip1 starts on frame 20, and clip2 starts on frame 30, clip1 will hold the initial values (at 100%) for the blend, while clip2 will hold the final values (100%) of the blend. This system breaks down if both clips start at the same time on the Timeline, so avoid blending two clips that start at the same time.

Adding a Blend to Overlapping Clips

Partially overlapping clips will create additive animation during the frames when the two clips overlap. The trouble with the overlapped section is that the animation will "pop" when the new clip is introduced, as the values of the animated channels suddenly change.

To resolve the popping problem, you can add a blend to the clips, creating a smoother alteration from the values of one clip to the other. To create a blend, Shift+select the two clips and, with the cursor over one of the clips, RM choose Blend Clips. A curve will appear between the clips, as shown in Figure 14.5, indicating the animations of the two clips are now blended across the frames the two clips overlap.

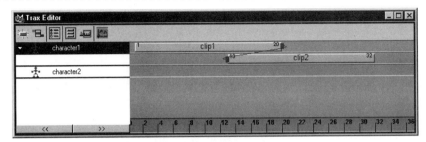

Figure 14.5 *Two animation tracks blended*

Modifying Clip Blends

To change the length of the blend (the number of frames over which the blend takes place), just slide one track relative to the other, changing the overlap. You can also blend tracks that are not on top of each other—the blend will occur between the last values of the first clip and the initial values of the second clip. Figure 14.6 shows a third clip (clip3) blended with clip2 in this manner.

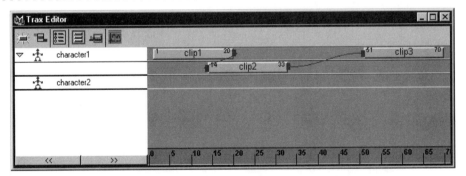

Figure 14.6 *A third clip, blended without overlapping with clip2*

To delete a blend that you no longer want, highlight the curve that represents the blend in the Trax Editor, and then press the Delete key.

For more control over blending clips, you can graph the blend. To do so, highlight the blend and choose View ➜ Graph Anim Curves from the Trax menu set (or click the Graph Animation Curves button in the Trax Editor's toolbar). The Graph Editor will open, showing the blend curve. As you can see in Figure 14.7, the default blend curve is just a straight line on a scale of 0 to 1 in both the horizontal and vertical axes. When the curve is at 0,0, the blend is completely weighted toward the first clip in the blend (that

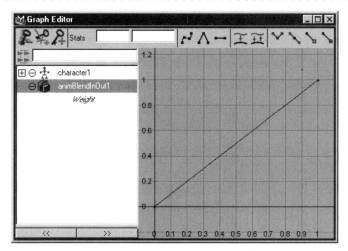

Figure 14.7 *The Graph Editor showing a default blend curve*

is, character channel values are 100% those of the first clip). When the curve is at 1,1, at the end of the blend, the blend is completely weighted to the second clip in the blend.

To create a different-shaped curve (for instance, to ease the blend in and out), simply adjust the tangent handles of the two blend keyframes, or add other keyframes into the blend shape. One possible curve shape is shown in Figure 14.8. (For details on using the Graph Editor, see Chapter 9.)

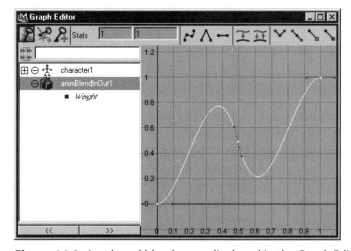

Figure 14.8 *An altered blend curve displayed in the Graph Editor*

Because the shape of the blend curve is independent of the length of the blend, you can adjust the shape of the blend and then increase or decrease the length of the blend in the Trax Editor (or vice versa), allowing a blend to be lengthened or shortened without changing its shape. This separation of curve shape from length is one of the workflow benefits of using Trax as opposed to traditional keyframe techniques.

Blending clips together allows for quick and easy transitions between different character animation states. Although these transitions aren't always perfect, they are generally very good, and they can be tweaked using the Graph Editor, by adjusting the blend lengths, or even by adding keyframes on top of the blend (using motion warping, as discussed earlier). Another advantage of using Trax is that it provides the ability to share clips and poses between characters in a single animation, or even in multiple, separate scenes.

Sharing Clips

Maya's ability to share animation clips and poses between characters provides for massive time savings in a complex, multi-character project or in several projects that can use each others' motion data. To see how sharing clips works, we'll first share clips within a single scene, then use a referenced scene to share clips, and finally use the import/export feature to share clips between scenes.

Sharing Clips in a Scene

You can share clips between characters within a single scene by copying and pasting clips from one character to another. If you have the simple project from the previous sections, you can continue to use it. If not, create a simple character with two geometric primitives and create two or three animation clips for it. Once you have one character animated with clips, create a second, similar character (for example, with two geometric primitives) and move it away from the first character in your scene, as shown below.

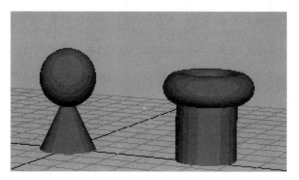

You can share clips between characters that are quite different from each other, but much of the animation of each clip may be lost in the transfer. Thus, it is generally better to share clips between similar characters.

There are two ways to copy a clip from one character to another. The simplest method (if the clip is already being used by the other character) is to copy and paste it from the first character's track into the second character's. To do so, RM choose Copy Clip with the cursor over the clip you wish to copy. Then, in the second character's track, choose Edit ➜ Paste, and the new clip will appear in the track for the second character.

The second way to copy and paste is to use the Visor. With character1 (*not* character2) set in the character pop-up menu, open the Visor and RM choose Copy with the cursor over the clip you wish to copy. Then, in the Trax Editor, place the cursor in a track for the second character and RM choose Paste, placing the clip into the track, as shown in Figure 14.9.

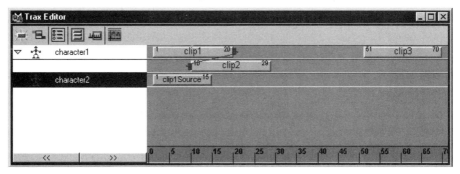

Figure 14.9 *A clip copied from character1 to character2*

Note that copying and pasting from the Trax Editor and from the Visor are not identical operations. When a clip is copied from the Trax Editor itself, any changes (to scaling, weighting, or cycling) you have made to that specific instance of the clip are transferred to the clip for the new character. When copy and pasting from the Visor, the original source clip is copied, with no modifications present. Depending on your design goals, one or the other method may prove more useful.

If you open the option box when pasting a clip, you have the option of pasting by attribute name, by attribute order, by node name, or by character map, as shown in Figure 14.10.

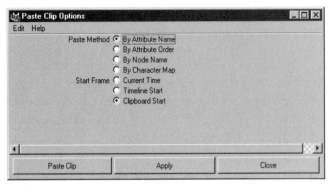

Figure 14.10 *The Paste Clip Options window*

Generally, you will want to use attribute name or attribute order to paste, because this will place the animation curves on attributes in the new character that are either of the same name or in the same order as in originating character. The By Node Name option will not work properly when the two characters are in the same scene (because two nodes cannot be named the same in a single scene). However, you could use this option when importing or copying clips into a new scene in which all of the nodes have names identical to those in the original scene. The By Character Map option creates a user-modifiable MEL script that maps the curves from one character to another. This method can be very powerful for pasting a clip from one character onto a very different one, but it is a fairly complex and specialized process, and not generally useful for the average Trax user.

For information about how to create and use a character map, see Chapter 13 of the online animation manual that comes with Maya.

You will likely find that your new character will move to *exactly* the same place as the first character (so the two overlap). If this behavior is acceptable, then you are finished with the pasting. If not, you have two ways to correct the problem:

- Activate the clip (bring its keys into the Timeline for editing by highlighting the clip, and then RM choosing Activate/Deactivate keys) and move the character to the proper position at each keyframe.

- Graph the animation curves (View ➜ Graph Anim Curves) and adjust the curves to move your character.

Graphing the animation curves generally tends to work more intuitively, because you can move the entire curve as a whole. Working with the individual keyframes in activate mode may lead to forgotten or misplaced keyframes, and thus to unwanted behavior.

Using a Reference Scene to Share Clips

To copy clips from one scene file to another, you can reference a source scene into a new one. Save your current scene (with clips intact), and then open a new scene and create another simple character. Now choose File → Create Reference and select the source scene you just saved. You should see the geometry from your old scene appear in the new one, and if you look in the character pop-up menu, you will see characters 1 and 2 (preceded by the scene filename) in the menu, in addition to the new character you just created.

In the Trax Editor, the two characters from your source scene will appear below your current scene character, as shown in Figure 14.11. You can then copy and paste clips as you wish, using the techniques described in the previous section.

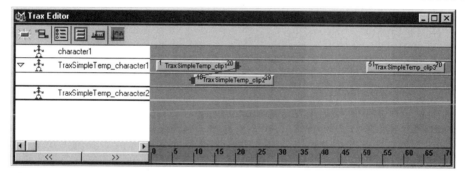

Figure 14.11 *Referenced clips in the Trax Editor*

When you are finished copying clips, remove the reference from your new scene. To do this, choose File → Reference Editor, then in the Reference Editor window, twirl down the arrow next to .\untitled, select the scene file you referenced, and choose Edit → Remove Reference. With the reference removed, all of the geometry and extra clips from the source scene are removed, and you are left with just the copied clips you wish to use in your new scene.

Exporting and Importing Clips

The third way to share clips is to export the clips themselves and then import them into a new scene. The exported scene will contain *only* animation clips (and poses), not geometry.

Reopen your old scene file (with the two characters) and open the Trax Editor (this method will not work from the Visor). Select all of the clips that you wish to export (only selected clips will be exported) and choose File ➜ Export Clip in the Trax menu. A dialog box will appear, allowing you to save the exported clips into a new scene file (stored, by default, in the clips directory of your project). Choose a name and export the file.

In a new scene file, create yet another simple character. In the Trax Editor, choose File ➜ Import Clip and import the clip file you previously exported. After the file has been imported, the clips from the other file are stored in the Visor of the new scene, under the Animation: Unused Clips & Poses folder. You can then use the Visor method of copy and pasting clips onto your new character, thus sharing the clips between files in this manner.

By exporting clips from scene files, you can create libraries of clips to be used later. For example, if you create walk, run, jump, sit, and stand clips for a character, you can save just the clip data to a scene file (or multiple files if you prefer), and then import this animation data into any other character file you create in the future, saving you the time of rekeying all of this motion data.

Using Trax to "create once, use many times" can drastically reduce the need to redo work, either in a single scene file or across dozens of scenes in ongoing projects. This, combined with the nonlinear, additive nature of Trax, makes it extremely useful for real-life animation work in which characters need to perform similar tasks many times, or where a number of characters need to share similar behaviors.

To finish this chapter, we'll take a look at two more complex examples of using Trax to create useful animation. First, we'll create a walk cycle for a simple character. Then we'll use Trax with blend shapes to provide for rapid lip-synching with multiple characters.

Hands-on Maya: Creating a Walk Cycle

In this first hands-on example, we're going to create a "Scooby-Doo" type walk cycle, where our character will glide across the ground rather than plant its feet as it walks (just check out any budget cartoon from the 1960s or early 1970s to see this effect). While the character and walk cycle generated here are simpler than that for a realistic human, for many cartoonish characters, a gliding walk style is perfectly acceptable. Additionally, most of the techniques used for this simple style of walking transfer well to more complex walk types (we will cover a few differences at the end of this section).

Creating the Character

We'll begin by creating a character and then creating subcharacters for arms and legs.

1. Open a new scene and create the "girl" character shown below using a sphere, a cone, and four cylinders. Be sure to move the pivot points of the arm and leg cylinders to where the shoulder and hip sockets would be (using the Insert key on the keyboard).

2. When you are finished creating the geometry, group all the parts into one group (select all, and then press Ctrl+G), and name the group **girlBody**.

3. Drag-select all of the body and choose Character ➜ Create ❑. In the option window, choose Edit ➜ Reset Settings. Name the character **girl** (she will have only translate and rotate elements keyable by default). Click the Create Character button to create the girl character.

4. With the active character set to girl (the name should appear in the character pop-up menu), select just the leg cylinders and choose Character ➜ Create Subcharacter ❑. In the option window, set the name of the subcharacter to **legs**, be sure the Attribute radio button is set to All Keyable Except, and choose the No Translate option (because the legs will only rotate, we don't need or want the translate channels in this subcharacter). Click the Create Subcharacter button to make the legs subcharacter.

5. In the character pop-up menu, set the active character back to girl (not legs, which will be selected now).

6. Select the arm cylinders and follow step 4 to create a subcharacter called **arms** (again with no translate channels). When you're finished, you should have a character (girl) with two subcharacters connected to it (arms and legs).

7. To create a pose of the girl, set the active character to girl, and then in the Trax Editor, choose Create ➔ Pose. We'll use this pose to reset the girl to a standing position later.

Animating the Character

To animate the girl, we'll first animate the legs rotating for the walking motion, then animate the body moving forward through space, and finally animate the arms moving back and forth in counter-motion to the legs. We'll create a 24-frame walk cycle, so each step will take 12 frames.

1. To animate the legs, set the active character to be the legs subcharacter (using the character pop-up menu). You can then select the legs subcharacter (using either the Outliner or Trax Editor) or just manually select each leg as you need it.

2. At frame 1, rotate the right leg forward about 40 to 50 degrees, and rotate the left leg back 10 to 15 degrees. (Don't forget to set keyframes as you go.)

3. At frame 6, set the rotation of the right leg to around 15 to 20 degrees, and set the rotation of the left leg to around –20 to –25 degrees.

4. At frame 12, key the left leg forward about 40 to 50 degrees, and rotate the right leg back about 15 degrees. (This is half way through the walk cycle, so the legs are essentially in opposite positions from frame 1.)

5. At frame 18, rotate the left leg to about 15 to 20 degrees, and rotate the right leg to about –20 to –25.

6. At frame 24, set the rotation of the two legs back to what they were at frame 1 (you may find it easier just to copy and paste the keys from frame 1 to frame 24).

At this point, you can either make a clip out of the leg animation you have created, or add body motion first, then create clips for legs and body simultaneously. We found it easier to create the body motion while the legs were still keyframed, so we opted for the latter approach.

7. To create the body motion, set the active character back to girl (not legs any longer).

8. At frames 1, 6, 12, 18, and 24, set the body position so that the girl's body moves forward as the legs rotate. (Don't worry if the motion isn't quite right yet; you can adjust it once the motion has been turned into clips.)

Creating the Clips

Now that we have body and leg motion, we can create the clips.

1. Choose Create ➜ Clip ❏ from the Trax Editor. Name the clip if you wish, choose to put the clip in the Visor and Trax Editor, use the animation curve range, and select the Include Subcharacters in Clip option so the leg clip is saved as well. Click the Create Clip button to create the animation clips.

2. In the Trax Editor, you will now have three clips: one for the girl character, one for the legs, and one for the arms (even though no keys have been set for the arms). Because we will create a separate clip for the arms, select the current arms clip and press the Delete key to get rid of it. You should then have animation tracks similar to those shown below.

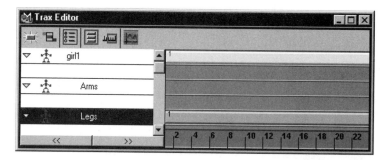

3. Now we need to create our arm animation. To make life easier (so the character doesn't walk away while you're animating the arms), disable the girl character clip by selecting the clip and, with the cursor over the clip, RM choose Enable/Disable Clip.

4. Set the character to the arms subcharacter in the pop-up window, then rotate the arms at frames 1, 12, and 24—24 being the same as frame 1—so that the arms move opposite to the legs (for example, when the right leg is forward, the right arm is back). We don't need to set keys at frames 6 or 18, because the motion of the arms is less complex than that of the legs.

5. In the Trax Editor, choose Create ➜ Clip ❏, name and create the clip using the settings described in step 1, except leave the Include Subcharacters in Clip option unselected (arms has no subcharacter).

6. With the three clips in the Trax Editor, reenable the girl clip (so she moves forward), and play the clips together. The first thing you will likely notice is that the arm swing is locked to the leg swing. The arms should drag a bit behind the legs as the girl walks.

7. To correct the locked arm and leg swing problem, drag the arm clip back 3 to 4 frames behind the leg and body clips, as shown below—a very simple solution indeed!

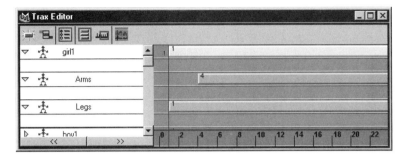

8. If you now wish to tweak the leg, body, and arm motions, you can graph the animation curves in the Graph Editor (in the Trax Editor, choose View ➜ Graph Anim Curves), and adjust them so the feet stick to the ground as nearly as possible, as shown below.

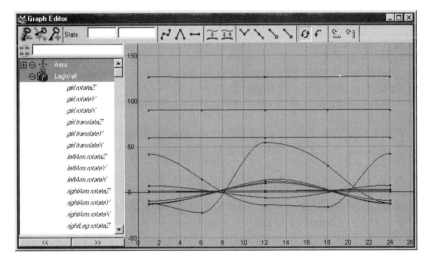

Creating the Walk Cycle

We now have one good step. To create a walk cycle, we need to repeat this motion. Fortunately, the Trax Editor makes this easy.

1. Double-click the girl clip in the Trax Editor to focus the Channel box (or Attribute Editor) on this clip.

2. Set the Cycle channel to a number like 3 instead of 1. Also, change the Offset setting to Relative instead of Absolute (otherwise, the girl will pop back to 0 between each step).

3. For the legs and arms clips, set the cycle to be the same, but be sure the Offset is Absolute, so that her feet and arms return to the same positions between steps.

The clips in the Trax Editor will update to show the cycle, and when you play back the animation, the girl will walk forward three complete steps.

You may notice that the girl's body gets ahead of (or behind) the leg motion as she walks, or that the legs or arms don't return to exactly where they were. This is because of minor errors in how the character has been keyframed. While these errors are too small to show up in one step cycle, they will appear as the cycles are added on top of each other.

To solve the problem of the body moving too far (or too little) for the legs, you can adjust the Weight setting of the body motion clip. By setting the weight a little greater (or less) than 1, you can adjust how far the body travels on each step, bringing the body back in line with the leg rotations.

To adjust problems with the legs and arms not returning to their rest positions, either change the Offset to Absolute (so the curves are forced to return to their exact starting values at the beginning of each cycle) or adjust the start and end keyframes for the rotations so they are exactly the same. Even small differences between start and end keyframes will add up over several cycles.

Blending the Clips

Once we have a walk we like, we can blend it with a standing clip to create a transition from walking to standing. First we need to create the standing clip.

1. Disable all of the clips in the Trax Editor by RM choosing Enable/Disable Clip.

2. Open the Visor, find the standing pose you created earlier, and RM choose Apply Pose to the character.

3. Key the values of the pose (be sure your character is set to girl), then move forward some frames, apply the pose again, and key the values.

4. In the Trax Editor, choose Create ➜ Clip ❏, give the clip a name (such as **Standing**), be sure that Include Subcharacters in Clip is selected, and create the new clip.

 Remember that clips of 0 duration (only one keyframe) are difficult to deal with. Even though both keyframes for the standing pose are the same, it is easier to create two frames for the clip than just one.

5. Blend the walking and standing clips by Shift+selecting them and RM choosing Blend Clips to produce a transition between the walking and standing states for the girl, as shown below (see the "Blending Clips" section earlier in this chapter).

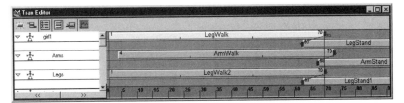

Sharing the Clips

As a last step, try creating a "boy" character, as shown below. Then apply the walk cycle from the girl to the boy by using one of the methods described in the "Sharing Clips" section earlier in this chapter.

To make things a bit more challenging, make the boy taller than the girl, so that you need to reweight the body motion to get the body to travel correctly with the motion of the legs (since longer legs travel farther when they rotate the same amount, the body must move more on each step).

A quick render of both characters' walk cycles is available on the CD-ROM as 14simpleWalk.mov, and the project file is also available (14simpleWalk).

Making a More Complex Walk Cycle

To move from the simple walk cycle we have created here to a more complex type is actually fairly simple (at least, once you have the nonslip foot setup working!). The only real adjustments that need to be made are as follows.

- Because the IK handles are manipulated for the legs (and often the arms as well), the legs subcharacter should consist of the IK handles rather than the leg bones.

- Since IK handles are translated through space rather than rotated, the legs (and arms) subcharacter should be set so that it has only translate channels (not rotation ones, as in the hands-on example).

- Because the IK handles actually move though space rather than rotating, the Off-set for the legs (and arms) subcharacter should be set to Relative, not Absolute. Otherwise, the character's legs will pop back to the origin at the start of every step.

Other than these adjustments, the method used in the hands-on exercise works quite well for realistic human walk cycles using nonslip foot techniques.

Hands-on Maya: Using Trax to Lip-synch

One of the most complex and tedious tasks facing a character animator is the task of lip-synching. The repetitive nature of continually recreating words for long-format animation is not a task for the weak of heart. Fortunately, Trax can greatly reduce the difficulty and tedium of creating lip-synching, while providing for a high degree of accuracy and flexibility. For our example, we will work with a cartoon character, but the same principles can be applied easily to the most realistic of 3D creatures.

We will not go through the steps to create eye clips and animation in this tutorial. However, the process for animating eyes is the same as for lip-synching, and creating eye animation with the included blend shapes is fairly straightforward.

1. Open the 14Tina project on the CD-ROM (you can also follow along with a character of your own if you wish). You will see a simple character (Tina) with an interesting hairdo.

2. In this scene, import the 14TinaSound file from the CD into your project (File ➜ Import). You may wish to copy the sound file into your *<scene name>*/Sound folder first, which will significantly increase response time.

3. To see the sound file in your scene, place your cursor over the Timeline and RM choose Sound ➜ 14TinaSound. You will then see the sound's waveform in the Timeline.

4. To see the waveform of the sound better, you can increase the size of the Timeline. Choose Window ➜ Settings/Preferences ➜ Preferences, and then choose the Timeline category. There you can set the Timeline to be default size (1✕), twice normal size (2✕), or four times normal size (4✕).

5. To hear the sound file while in your Maya scene, scrub through the Timeline while holding down the middle mouse button. The faster you drag, the more quickly the sound plays back.

The actual line that "Tina" says is: "What I'm gonna do? I'm gonna rock your world's what I'm gonna do. I got some singing and some dancing and a little bit of hoochy koochy thrown in too—oooh!" This line is part of a longer animation being created by a group of University of North Carolina at Asheville students (individual credits are given at the end of the 14Tina.mov *file on the CD-ROM).*

Creating Tina

First, we need to create a character (Tina) and three subcharacters (left and right eyes and mouth). Then we will add the scene's blend shapes to the subcharacters for eyes and mouth.

1. Select the Tina_Control node (select a body part and up arrow until you reach this node) and choose Character ➜ Create ❑. Name the character **Tina**, allow scaling for the character (plus translate and rotate), and create the character.

2. With Tina set as the character, deselect all objects (you don't need to select any body parts here) and create subcharacters called **REye_Tina**, **LEye_Tina**, and **Mouth_Tina**.

3. To add blend shape elements for the mouth, set the mouth to be the active character using the character pop-up menu, and then open the Blend Shape Editor by selecting Window ➜ Animation Editors ➜ Blend Shape. (For more information about blend shapes, see Chapter 11, "Deformers.")

4. In the Blend Shape Editor, find the Mouth_Tn blend shape node and click the Select button, as shown below.

5. In the Channel box, select all the Mouth_Tn attributes (starting with Envelope and ending with Tina_Closed), and then choose Character ➜ Add To Character to add these attributes to the mouth subcharacter.

6. Repeat steps 3 through 5 for the left and right eyes (be sure to set LEye_Tina and REye_Tina to be the active character first).

Creating the Word Clips

With the characters set up properly, it's time to start creating clips. Since Chapter 11 goes into detail about creating blend shapes, we'll cover just the process of converting them into clips here.

1. Be sure that Mouth_Tina is the active character, and then, using the blend shapes included, create a series of about four keyframes that create the "What" word. We found that the O_Close, E, Ah, Smile, and Closed blend shapes created a decent "What" in four frames, but you may find using other shapes works better.

You don't need to worry about how long a particular word is, as long as each mouth shape is held for the right relative length (a long vowel sound might be several frames; most consonants are about one frame). Since you will be able to adjust the length and weight of the animation clip later, you don't need to match the words to actual sounds yet.

2. Once you have a word you like, open the Trax Editor and choose Create ➜ Clip ❑. In the option box, reset the settings (Edit ➜ Reset Settings), name the clip **What**, and create the clip. You will now have the clip for "What" in a track for the mouth subcharacter, as shown next.

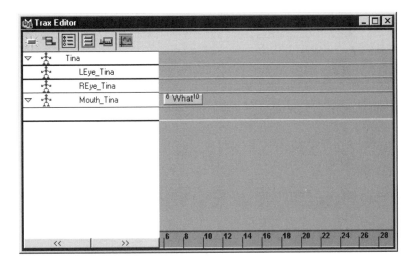

3. Move the word to around the start of the "What" sound in the Timeline (around frame 6 or 7), and scrub the animation (use the left mouse button in the Timeline, or hold down the K key and LM drag in the Trax Editor's Timeline). The scrub will play back fairly slowly, but you will be able to see the mouth update with the sounds as you scrub. You may find that you need to start the word earlier, or shorten it some to fit the sound track, because the word is very short as spoken here.

You can also use Playblast so you can hear and see the words as they are spoken. You may find, however, that the sound is not properly synchronized to the video track (we're not sure why this problem exists, and it happens only on some computers). If you do have this problem, the easiest way to view a quick render with sound is to hardware render the scene and then, in a compositing package (like Composer, Fusion, AfterEffects, or even Apple's Quicktime Player Pro), add the sound file to the rendered image sequence. This method takes a few extra steps, but it guarantees proper alignment of sound and video, which is pretty important here. See Chapter 18, "Rendering Basics," and Chapter 23, "Particle Rendering," for more information about hardware rendering.

4. When you are satisfied with your "What" animation, create clips for "I'm," "gonna," and "do." Then scale and move them into proper position as well.

5. At this point—a space of around ten frames without words—you might wish to create a neutral mouth clip for the character—a state where Tina's mouth would rest when she's not speaking. We chose to create a mouth shape with lips

slightly open and a medium-sized mouth width (a completely closed mouth for such short pauses seemed to make the character's mouth work too hard).

Remember to blend your clips (choose two clips, then RM select Blend Clips with the cursor over one of the clips). This will create a natural motion from one word to the next. Also remember that you can adjust the curve of the blend by graphing the blend in the Graph Editor, as explained earlier in this chapter.

6. Now we can start to save time by using clips. Tina's next two words are "I'm gonna," so you can just recycle those two word clips from before, placing them in the correct positions for the next words. You can copy and paste using any of the methods described earlier in this chapter, but the easiest way is to put the cursor over the clip, RM choose Copy, click in an empty area of the track, and RM choose Paste to paste the clip back in. You will likely find that you need to shorten the "gonna" word, because it's quicker the second time around (just click the top-right corner of the clip to interactively scale it, or use the Attribute Editor).

7. Continue either creating or reusing word clips until you reach the end of the sound file.

While it may take you a while to get really proficient, you should already see how rapidly you can create lip-synching using Trax. If we went ahead and animated several minutes of dialogue, the time savings would become even greater. This is because the character would repeat many words, allowing you to store and reuse a library of word clips instead of needing to re-keyframe each word as it came up. Additionally, because you can add keyframes on top of the basic mouth motion, expressions (smiles, frowns, and so on) can be layered on top of the speech. As you can see, using Trax is a pretty rapid and flexible way to animate character speech!

If you wish, you can look at a completed scene (with just mouth movement) by opening 14TinaAntimated on the CD. You can also take a look at a completed render (including eye and body motion) by opening 14Tina.mov on the CD.

One final step you can take when creating lip-synching is to transfer words from one character to another. To facilitate the transfer, you can create the blend shapes in the same order for another character; in other words, if Tina's mouth shapes are ordered as H, P_B_M, O_Close, etc., you could create Joe's blends in the same order. Then you can reference the Tina file (or export the clips, as explained earlier in this chapter), copy source clips from the Visor, and paste them into the new character's mouth subcharacter using the Paste By Attribute Order option. Thus, you can share libraries of words from one character to another, with obviously huge time savings. Additionally, if each character's blend shapes are slightly different looking (the smile blend, for example, being a sneer for an evil character), the words will look different for each character, because the source clips alter only the weights of the blend shapes, not what they look like.

Summary

Nonlinear animation has been an increasingly popular area of 3D animation over the past several years, and Maya's Trax Editor is one of the best, most robust NLAs (nonlinear animators) on the market. Using the Trax Editor, you can quickly produce animation from simple characters moving in simple ways to complex characters walking and talking.

By creating and reusing poses and clips, you can save a great deal of time in animating repetitive tasks. By blending clips, different animation states can fuse into one another, reducing the need for complex transition keyframes. With motion warping, keyframes can be added on top of existing clips for final tweaks, or to create individual motion for part of a character's animation. Finally, by sharing clips and poses between characters and scenes, you can leverage all of the work done for one character or one scene for use in other scenes and projects. Maya's nonlinear animation is so powerful, that once you begin using it, it's difficult to imagine complex character animation without Trax!

In the next chapter, we'll explore how to work with rigid body dynamics to produce physically accurate animation.

Working with Rigid Body Dynamics

MAYA

Chapter 15

I n this chapter, you will learn what rigid bodies are, when they can be useful, and how to apply rigid bodies to solve several situations where keyframing would either take too long or would not look realistic enough. Topics include:

- What are rigid body dynamics?
- Creating a simple rigid body
- Converting a body from passive to active mode
- Using fields to add effects to rigid bodies
- Using the Rigid Body Solver
- Using impulse and a Newton field to simulate orbital dynamics
- Converting (baking) a rigid body animation into keyframes
- Working with the Dynamics Simulator
- Adding constraints to a rigid body

What Are Rigid Body Dynamics?

If you've done any animation (either computer or traditional), you're familiar with the concept of keyframes, introduced in Chapter 9. Rigid body animation, on the other hand, is essentially a physics simulator built into Maya that tries to mimic (or exaggerate, if you want) what happens to real-world objects as they move under the influence of forces (like gravity or wind) and collide with other objects. If you've ever tried to keyframe even the simple motion of a ball bouncing on the ground, you realize how difficult it is to make a keyframed animation work in this type of situation. If you try something more difficult, like bouncing a cube off a wall, it can get really frustrating trying to make the collisions look realistic.

Fortunately, Maya has the answer for you: *rigid body dynamics* (often simply called *rigid bodies*). Using rigid bodies is pretty straightforward: you create one or more rigid bodies; create one or more fields that influence them (if you wish); give the rigid bodies an initial position, velocity, and impulse (if you wish); and play back the animation. Maya's *dynamics engine* does all the calculations to make the body behave realistically, based on your initial information; you don't need a degree in physics, just a bit of practice with the settings you have available.

Maya also uses its dynamics engine to create particle effects. See Chapters 22 through 25 to find out how Maya works with particle dynamics.

Rigid bodies come in two flavors: passive and active. Passive rigid bodies are *not* affected by fields and cannot be moved by collisions, though they can take part in collisions. Passive rigid bodies *are* keyframable (so you can move, rotate, and scale them via keyframes). Active rigid bodies *are* affected by fields, and will be moved by collisions. They are *not* keyframable (so you can't directly manipulate them).

Generally, a passive rigid body would be a floor, wall, or other object that is fixed to the world, while an active rigid body would be any kind of falling, moving, or colliding object (a basketball or a coin, for example). Although it would seem a great disadvantage that active rigid bodies cannot be keyframed, you can convert rigid bodies from passive to active at any time in an animation, allowing a rigid body to be passive for a time and then to become active. (We'll try an example of this shortly.)

Let's begin with a simple example to see how rigid bodies work.

Creating a Simple Rigid Body

In this example you'll create a simple rigid body—a bouncing ball—and experiment with a few settings that will affect the motion of the ball.

Start by creating a new scene in Maya. Create a NURBS plane and scale it out to about the size of the Maya grid. Now make a NURBS sphere with a radius of 1 and move it above the plane. Your scene should look like Figure 15.1.

Figure 15.1 *A sphere placed above a plane*

Now select the plane and choose Soft/Rigid Bodies ➜ Create Passive Rigid Body from the Dynamics menu. The plane is now a passive rigid body.

Next, select the sphere and choose Soft/Rigid Bodies ➜ Create Active Rigid Body from the Dynamics menu. The sphere is now an active rigid body.

To allow dynamics simulations to play back properly, the playback rate has to be set to Free, so that the physics engine can calculate what it needs to before going on to the next frame. Either select Window ➜ Settings/Preferences ➜ Preferences and choose Settings/Timeline or click the Animation Preferences button at the lower right of the screen to bring up the same window.

Animation Preferences

In the Animation Preferences window, choose Playback Speed: Free from the Playback area.

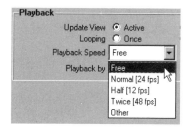

Close the window, rewind the animation, and play it back.

You must rewind any animation that contains dynamics—otherwise, the animation will not play back properly. You also cannot "scrub" through an animation by sliding the time marker back and forth. All dynamics data is calculated frame by frame, so if any frame is skipped, the calculations break down and the animation goes berserk. If this happens, just rewind the animation and start over—all will be well again.

To rewind, either click the Back button on the playback controller (located in the lower-right corner of the screen, it looks like a VCR control) or press Ctrl+Shift+V on the keyboard. To play the animation, either click the Play button on the playback controller or press Ctrl+V.

Nothing very interesting happened, right? Even though you have made two rigid bodies, you have not created any animation yet, because you have not added any fields (forces) or initial motion. Let's create a Gravity field to make things a bit more interesting.

From the Dynamics menu, choose Fields → Gravity. Now open the Dynamic Relationships window shown in Figure 15.2 (choose Window → Relationship Editors → Dynamic Relationships), choose the nurbSphere1 name in the Outliner on the left side of the window, and make sure gravityField1 is highlighted in the selection window on the right. If it's not, be sure to click gravityField1 to highlight it.

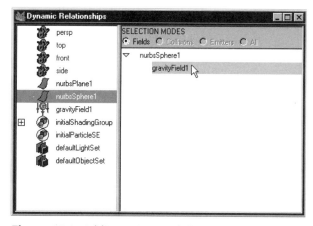

Figure 15.2 *Adding a Gravity field to the sphere in the Dynamic Relationships window*

If you select the sphere before creating gravity, the two will automatically be connected together. (If there are other active rigid bodies that you haven't selected, they will be unaffected by this force.)

Now rewind and play back the animation. You should see the ball fall toward the plane and bounce off it. If the animation is cut off too quickly to see this, increase the number of frames in the animation to 200 or more (type **200** in the text field to the right of the Time Slider).

Now let's examine the rigid body settings for our objects. In the Channel box, you'll see rigidBody1 (or 2, or whatever) listed under the shape node for the object you pick. For now, pick the plane and then click the rigidBody1 text.

Several text fields will pop down, giving you more control over the rigid body than you probably want. For now, just look down to these items: mass, bounciness, damping, static friction, and dynamic friction. Change the bounciness to 0.9 and replay the animation (remember to rewind first!). On the first bounce, the ball should bounce nearly as high as the height from which it was dropped, and it should take longer to settle to rest as the animation plays on. Now try setting the bounciness to 2. What happens? The ball bounces further up each time, soon disappearing from view—talk about a super ball! In our virtual world, not only do we get to simulate reality, we get to break the rules if we want.

Try playing with some other settings, like friction and damping—and remember to play with the settings for both the ball and the plane. You can also play with the mass settings, but a passive rigid body is defined to have an infinite mass, so the setting won't matter for the plane. Changing the mass of the ball won't make much difference at this point, either, because gravity is a universal force, affecting all objects in the same way. Later, we'll see where mass can be used more effectively.

Playing with the numbers is a great way to learn how rigid bodies work. Don't be afraid to try different settings for each of the channels of each rigid body—try to guess what your changes will do before playing back the animation.

Catapult! Converting a Body from Passive to Active Mode

Now let's create a catapult and see how easy it is to turn the active key on and off for a rigid body. Again, start with a new scene. Create a NURBS plane scaled to about the grid size. Now create a cylinder, rotate it so it lies along the X axis, and squash it nearly flat. Your scene should look like Figure 15.3. With the cylinder selected, press Ctrl+G to group the cylinder to itself (if you don't do this step, you may end up with strange behavior later on).

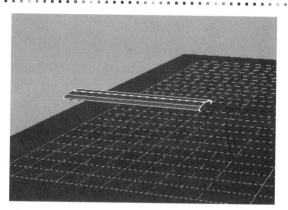

Figure 15.3 *A plane with a squashed cylinder*

Now move the insert point of the new group from the origin all the way to the right end of the cylinder.

 To move the insert point, select the Move tool, press the Insert key on your keyboard (which will change the Move tool's handle from one with arrows to one without), and move the new handle around. Don't forget to press the Insert key again when you're done, or you'll stay in insert mode!

Once you have this set up correctly, add a sphere of radius 1 and place it on top of the left end of the cylinder, as in Figure 15.4.

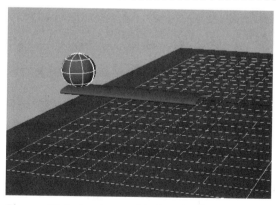

Figure 15.4 *A sphere added to the flattened cylinder*

Now select the plane *and* the sphere, and make them passive rigid bodies. In the Hypergraph or Outliner, MM drag the sphere onto the cylinder's parent group (probably called group1), making the sphere the "child" of the cylinder (so they will rotate together). Now set a keyframe at your first frame on the cylinder's rotation channels (select the rotation channels and RM choose Key Selected), move the Time Slider to about 15 frames, rotate the cylinder so it is close to upright, as in Figure 15.5, and keyframe this new setting.

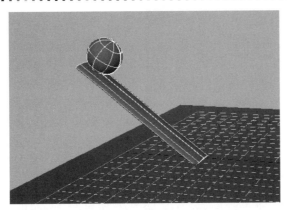

Figure 15.5 *The cylinder moved into an upright position*

Setting the Auto Keyframe button to On will make Maya automatically set a new keyframe whenever some channel changes—after you first manually set the first keyframe for that channel.

Play back the animation. You should see the cylinder (and its attendant ball) rotate up in a few frames, and then stay still.

Now let's make this ball fly! Select the sphere and, in the Channel box, find the Active channel (or attribute), located toward the bottom of the rigid body attributes. It should currently have a value of Off. Select the *name* of the channel (Active), set the Time Slider to around 12 frames, and RM choose Key Selected while pressing on the Active name. This will set a key (with a value of off, or false, or 0) on the Active channel. Now move forward one or two frames, click in the text next to the Active name, and type **On** in the Channel box. If the Autokey function is on, you'll automatically generate a keyframe; otherwise, select and manually keyframe this channel.

What you have done here is to force the sphere to become an active rigid body *just as the sphere is being pitched up in the air by the cylinder*. This timing allows us to take advantage of some clever programming by the Maya developers: the sphere will "inherit" speed and rotation from the movement of the cylinder, and so it will fly away from the cylinder the moment it becomes an active rigid body.

To test this, rewind and play back the animation. The sphere should go flying off to infinity. Of course, to finish this simulation correctly, we need to add gravity once again.

Select the sphere and then choose Fields ➜ Gravity (it should automatically connect to the sphere). Now play back the animation. The ball should (depending on how fast your cylinder rotates) either shoot or "plop" off the cylinder. If the ball flies off the catapult too slowly, try rotating the cylinder further at its last keyframe, or shorten the number of frames over which it rotates up. If the ball flies off too quickly, rotate the cylinder less at the last keyframe, or increase the number of frames over which it rotates up.

We've already played with the numbers on the rigid bodies in the last example. This time, let's play with gravity itself. In the Outliner or Hypergraph, select the gravity node you just created. In the Channel box, you'll see several settings for gravity, including Direction and Magnitude. Direction defaults to –1 in Y, or down, as gravity in the real world pulls down—a negative value—on the vertical axis. Magnitude defaults to 9.8 (that's 9.8 meters—or 32 feet—per second squared, the force of earth's gravity). Let's make things a bit heavier. Try setting gravity to, say, 200 or so. Now, when the ball comes off the cylinder, it should drop like a *very* heavy stone. Or try a value of 2—now we're on the moon!

Although the geometry in this scene is simple, the results are not: this same trick could be used as a character throws a ball at a can or bottle, creating a very nice mix of keyframed character animation and realistic physics.

Using Fields to Add Effects to Rigid Bodies

After you play with the gravity settings for a while, find a value for gravity that will give the ball a good long flight time, because now we're going to add some other fields to affect the ball's flight.

First, let's add some wind. Select the sphere, and then select Fields ➜ Air ❏. The Air Options window shown in Figure 15.6 opens, giving you several ways to adjust the Air field.

You'll see three buttons at the top (Wind, Wake, and Fan) that are simply preset options you can use to create the effect of wind, the wake of a passing car, or a fan. You can try all three buttons to see what settings each one changes. When you are finished experimenting, click the Wind button and the Create button. A new field, called airField1, will appear in your Outliner or Hypergraph.

Now play back the animation again. You should see the sphere get shoved right off the end of the plane (as the wind, by default, pushes in the positive X direction). Try changing the X component of the wind to 0 and the Y component to 1. Now the ball should fall more gently (like a beach ball). Next, increase the magnitude from 5 to a large number like 200. The ball will now "blow" up into the air, as the wind force is stronger than gravity. Set the wind back down to a reasonable number like 5 or 10.

Figure 15.6 *The Air Options window*

As another experiment with fields, try turning the wind on and off by keyframing its magnitude.

Now let's add turbulence. Select the sphere and choose Fields ➔ Turbulence. Play back the animation. With the default magnitude of 5, the effects on the motion of the sphere will be very subtle. If you set the Turbulence field's magnitude to 50, and turn the Attenuation down to around 0.1, you will see the sphere move about in random ways as the turbulence field affects its motion. Try different numbers for the channels of the Turbulence field and see what results from making these changes. With rigid bodies, fields, and particle dynamics, it is a very good idea to take a simple animation and experiment with what each channel does by changing the numbers and watching the results in the animation. It is only by this kind of experience that you can see how Maya's physics engine really works.

You can also attach a field to an object by selecting the field, Shift+selecting the object, and then choosing Fields ➔ Attach To Selected Object As Source. The field will then travel with its parent object and can be used to create a wake or turbulence as the parent object passes rigid bodies or particles.

We've seen how different fields can change a rather humdrum animation into something more interesting. Now let's make the simulation engine work a bit harder by creating more complex shapes.

Using the Rigid Body Solver

When you work with more complex shapes, you may find that Maya's default settings don't provide the speed or accuracy that you are looking for in your rigid body simulation. For such occasions, Maya allows you to adjust how it calculates rigid body simulations by using the Solver ➜ Rigid Body Solvers window. With the *Rigid Body Solver* you can adjust how Maya calculates the simulation, giving you the ability to fine-tune your simulation for speed or accuracy.

Let's look at the solver in action. Create another empty scene, add a plane and a sphere (at some height above the plane), and make the plane a passive rigid body and the sphere an active one. Add gravity and test the animation to be sure the ball bounces on the plane as it should.

Now let's make the shape a bit more complex. First, increase the U and V isoparms to 16 or more each (on the makeNurbSphere1 node). Then take the sphere and mold it into a bizarre, angular shape something like Figure 15.7.

· ·

Figure 15.7 *An angular shape, which will behave differently than a perfect sphere*

You can create this shape quite easily using Maya's Artisan utility (Edit Surfaces ➜ Sculpt Surfaces Tool ❑), as discussed in Chapter 7. Or you can just pull individual CVs out of the sphere.

When you play back the animation this time, Maya will probably go just a bit slower—this time, it has to keep track of a lot more surfaces! If you play back the frames one at a time (and look under the plane), you'll probably also be able to see a few points where some of the sphere's surfaces poke through the plane.

At full-speed playback, you probably won't notice these errors, but there are times when you might wish to correct problems like this—or perhaps speed up playback for a particularly complex simulation. In these situations, you can use the Rigid Body Solver menu to adjust how Maya calculates its rigid body simulations. Essentially, the Rigid Body Solver gives you some control over the way Maya's dynamics engine handles the mathematics involved in the movement and interaction of rigid bodies. As you've just seen, complex shapes interact in complex ways, and adjusting calculation options via the solver is useful when the result of using Maya's default settings isn't accurate enough or fast enough to look realistic.

You can get access to the Rigid Body Solver in one of two ways: either choose Solvers ➜ Rigid Body Solvers, or select a rigid body, open the Attribute Editor (Ctrl+A), and select the Rigid Solver tab. Either way, you'll see the window shown in Figure 15.8, which allows you to adjust the solver to meet your needs.

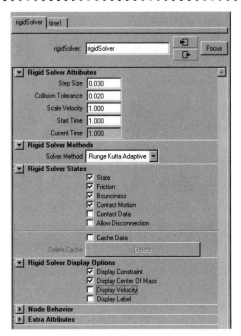

Figure 15.8 *The Rigid Body Solver window*

Notice the Rigid Solver States and Rigid Solver Display Options sections of the window. Here you can turn most major functions on and off. As an example, turn on the Display Velocity check box and play back the animation. You will see an arrow that points in the direction of the sphere's velocity; its length represents the speed of the sphere. If you turn off the State check box, the animation will do nothing, because clearing this check box turns off the solver. (This is a good way to quickly eliminate dynamics so you can concentrate on other elements of an animation.) If you turn off the Contact Motion check box, the sphere will fall, but it will no longer bounce, as dynamic interactions no longer work. Try turning off each of the check boxes in turn and see what effect this has on playback. When you're finished, reset the check boxes to their default state.

The Rigid Solver Methods section of the window offers three choices, though normally you will use the default method, Runge Kutta Adaptive. If you have a very complex simulation, however, and either wish to view it more quickly in interactive playback or don't care about the accuracy of the simulation for your final rendering, you can (temporarily) set the method to either Runge Kutta or to Midpoint. Midpoint is the least accurate but fastest. Runge Kutta is a compromise between the two extremes. For your dented ball, you probably won't see much difference between the three methods.

The Runge Kutta and Runge Kutta Adaptive options are named for the Runge Kutta solution, a mathematical method of solving an interlocking system of differential equations using first-order derivatives. In Maya, time is broken down into discrete steps (referenced through the Step Size field), and the integral of the equations is approximated at each step. Though the technique is mathematically complex, it is fast and accurate enough for most applications.

The top—and most useful—section is labeled Rigid Solver Attributes. Using the Step Size, Collision Tolerance, Scale Velocity, and Start Time fields, you can alter the way in which the solver simulates rigid body dynamics. Let's look at each option:

Using the **Start Time** box, you can alter when the Rigid Body Solver begins to function (e.g., if you set the Start Time to 50, the Rigid Body Solver will not start working until frame 50).

Scale Velocity is useful only if you have checked the Display Velocity check box in the section below—the Scale Velocity slider lets you scale the arrow that sticks out from the rigid body, making it fit within your window.

Step Size defines the "chunk" of time (measured in fractions of a second) the solver divides the Timeline into. A smaller step size means more calculations per second of animation, but it can also mean a more accurate simulation. If you have trouble with rigid body *interpenetration errors* (meaning that two bodies have "pierced" each other, as in our example), reducing the step size is a good place to start.

Collision Tolerance tells Maya how carefully to evaluate frames where collisions take place. A large collision tolerance will speed up playback but can become very inaccurate.

Try making the collision tolerance 0.8 and playing back your animation. You will notice that the sphere doesn't bounce correctly on the plane. Now set the tolerance to 0.001 (the smallest possible value). If you saw points at which the sphere's points stuck through the plane before, they should no longer appear (or at worst should poke through only a little bit).

Experiment with different step sizes and collision tolerances, and see how the changes affect the simulation. Often you can get away with making either the step size or the collision tolerance very large, as long as you keep the other element small. Finding a compromise between speed and accuracy for a complex simulation is often the key to using rigid body dynamics effectively.

Speeding Up Calculations with Additional Solvers

Each additional object a rigid solver has to keep track of can geometrically increase the calculation time. To compensate for this, you can speed up calculations by isolating different parts of a simulation from one another and assigning additional solvers to each part.

Let's see how this works, by making some changes in the deformed sphere scene you created in the previous example. (If you no longer have that scene, just create a ball and a plane, make the ball an active rigid body and the plane a passive rigid body, and then create gravity. Play back the animation to be sure the ball bounces off the plane.)

Now we're going to create a second Rigid Body Solver and assign the ball to it. Choose Solvers ➜ Create Rigid Body Solver. This creates a new solver, which will be called rigidSolver1 (or 2 or 3, depending on how many others you have created).

Now set the new solver as the default (so that all new objects will be assigned to this solver): choose Solvers ➜ Current Rigid Solver ➜ Solver*X*, where Solver*X* is the solver you wish to establish as the default. Since we have already created both of our rigid bodies using the same solver, we need to assign one of the two bodies (the ball) to the new solver—rigidSolver1. Unfortunately, there is no button to do this, but you can do it with a quick bit of MEL (Maya Embedded Language) scripting.

In the scene window, select the sphere and then, in the Command line (accessed by pressing the ` key while you're in a scene window), type the following:

```
rigidBody -edit -solver rigidSolver1;
```

This command tells Maya to edit the rigid solver for whatever objects are selected in the scene.

For more on MEL scripting, see Chapters 16 and 17.

Now play back the animation again. This time, the ball should pass right through the plane. Although the plane and ball are both still affected by gravity, they no longer interact with each other, as they "live" in different solver states.

If you wish to edit the settings of your new rigid solver, be sure it is selected (in Solvers ➜ Current Rigid Solver), and then select Solvers ➜ Rigid Body Solver. This will bring up the Attribute Editor with the rigidSolver1 selected.

Finally, with rigidSolver1 selected, you can create a new plane (or other object), make it a passive rigid body, and play back the animation. Because both the ball and the new plane share the same solver, they will collide properly.

Using Impulse and a Newton Field to Simulate Orbital Dynamics

Let's now see how rigid bodies can be used to create a realistic simulation of a rocket ship going into orbit. We'll use a small cone for the ship and a big sphere for the planet, but you can model just about anything you wish and substitute those objects in their places.

First, create a sphere with a radius of 25 units and name it **planet**. Scale your view out so you can see it clearly. Now, create a cone (named **rocket**) and scale it so it looks this size on the sphere:

It really doesn't matter how big the cone is, as long as it looks good to you (we just left it at its default settings).

Be sure to place the cone a little above the surface of the sphere, or you'll get rigid body interpenetration errors, like those we saw earlier.

Now make the sphere a passive rigid body (by choosing Soft/Rigid Bodies ➜ Create Passive Rigid Body) and make the cone an active rigid body (choose Soft/Rigid Bodies ➜ Create Active Rigid Body).

We could add a simple gravity field to these objects, but gravity pulls everything in the same direction. What we need here is a field that's centered on our planet; we'll use the Newton field (named after Sir Isaac). The Newton field creates a gravitational "well" in the planet that will attract all other active rigid bodies to it, its force depending on how far from the planet the object is.

Choose Fields ➜ Newton; then Shift+select the sphere and choose Fields ➜ Attach to Selected Object as Source. In your Outliner or Hypergraph you will now see a Newton field parented to the planet. Choose the cone and open the Dynamic Relationships Editor (Windows ➜ Relationship Editors ➜ Dynamic Relationships). In this window, click the Newton field to highlight it—this connects the cone to the Newton field.

Set the frame length to 1000 or more and play back the animation. The rocket should fall and land on the surface of the planet, bounce a bit, and stay there. If not, try turning the magnitude of the Newton field down to 5 or 6 and see if that helps.

Now we've got gravity; what we're missing is the thrust (or impulse) that every rocket uses to escape gravity. With the rocket selected, click the rigidBody2 text in the Channel box and set the rocket's impulse Y to around 5. Play back the animation. Most likely, the rocket will go flipping around out of control as it rises, just like those early V-2 rocket tests. The reason is that the impulse (or thrust) is coming from the bottom of the cone, so any slight error in thrust spins the rocket. In reality, this is a serious and very difficult aspect of rocket science. But in our virtual world, we have a quick fix: set the ImpulsePositionY to around 4 or 5, making the thrust come from atop the cone, and thus making it much more stable in flight. You might also wish to change the Damping value on the rocket to a number like 0.1; this will reduce the chance that the rocket will spin as it is thrust upward, while still allowing orbital motion without much drag. When you now play back the animation, the rocket (if it has enough thrust) will smoothly rise and disappear from the screen.

At present, our rocket has infinite fuel, so it just keeps going. To make a more realistic flight, let's create a ballistic trajectory, allowing the rocket to rise for a time and then fall back to the planet.

To do this, keyframe the thrust (impulse) on and off. Select the Y impulse, set the Time Slider to the first frame, and RM select Key Selected. Now go out to about frame 15 and set the value of impulseY to 0 (the impulse will fall off from 5 to 0 over those 15 frames). When you play back the animation, the rocket should launch, rise, and then fall back to the planet.

Getting this sequence to work right will take a bit of tweaking the numbers. It is very easy to get the rocket stuck on the ground, or flying off at an amazing speed. If you are completely stuck, try opening the premade project (150rbit.ma) on the CD that accompanies this book.

We've now gone suborbital; it's time to get into orbit! To do that, we need to add an in-flight correction to make the rocket move sideways as well as up and down. Move the time indicator to frame 10, and key the impulseX (at 0) on this frame. Now move to frame 11 and key the impulseX to 5. Move the time to 39 and key impulseX back to 0 (again, you may need to change these numbers around to get good results). If all worked well, when you play back the animation, you will see the rocket orbit the planet (in a *very* scary looking, squashed orbit, but an orbit nonetheless). If you haven't given the rocket enough thrust, it will crash back into the planet in a pretty spectacular manner.

In order to get our orbit a bit cleaner, we need to add yet another in-flight correction. At around frame 90, set another key on impulseY (at 0). At about frame 95, set a key on impulseY to –2 (so it pushes down on the rocket). At about frame 115, set another key on impulseY, this time back to 0 again. If these numbers work for you, you should see the rocket following a much cleaner orbital path. If not, try adding a negative thrust to the X impulse around frame 150.

As an exercise, see how close you can get the orbit to circular. Can you keep the rocket from spinning around as it orbits the planet? With all the tweaking involved, you can see why they're called "rocket scientists"!

Converting (Baking) a Rigid Body Animation into Keyframes

Once you've got an orbital motion you like, you can "bake" the rigid body animation into keyframes, which you can then change into other sorts of motion. *Baking* is the term Maya uses for creating a set of keyframes that mimic the dynamic motion of a rigid body simulation. As we will see below, baking an animation allows you to adjust motion paths and keyframes for what was once a dynamic simulation (and thus did not allow this kind of adjustment).

If you may eventually wish to return to your rigid body simulation, save a different copy of your project before you bake the simulation. You can't go back once the simulation has been baked!

Select the rocket and choose Edit ➜ Keys ➜ Bake Simulation. The simulation will run, and when it's finished, you will have a baked animation (and a mess of keyframes in the Timeline).

Let's put this baked animation to good use, getting rid of that nasty rotation around the Z axis that the rocket developed. With the rocket still selected, open the Graph Editor (Window ➜ Animation Editors ➜ Graph Editor). On the left side, highlight the rotateZ channel, and then press F (to frame the selection). As in Figure 15.9,

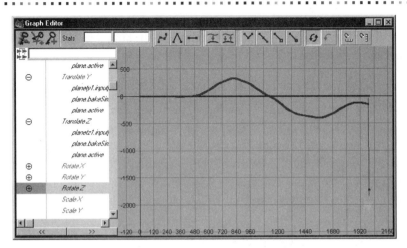

Figure 15.9 *The rocket's rotateZ curve in the Graph Editor*

you'll see a curve with hundreds of keyframes on it—a few more than we need for our animation!

To get rid of the cone's Z rotation problems, we could first attempt to simplify the curve. Choose Curves ➔ Simplify Curves from the Graph Editor's menu (or by RM selecting). Maya will remove many keyframes it considers unimportant to the curve. Unfortunately, even if you run the Simplify Curves command several times, the curve is still very heavy—and we don't want any of that motion, anyway! Let's just kill the whole curve.

Drag-select the entire curve and press the Delete key, and away it goes. Now when you play back the animation, the Z rotation is gone—all of it. To get some form of rotation, you'll need to first delete the rigid body from the rocket (so it doesn't interfere with your setting keyframes). In the Outliner or Hypergraph, choose Options ➔ Display ➔ Show Shape Nodes to reveal the rigid body nodes. Select the rigid body associated with the rocket and delete it. Now set a 0 keyframe on the Z rotation of the rocket at about frame 15 (just where it begins to tip over). Go to the end of the animation and set a keyframe of about –1080 for the Z rotation. (This is three full revolutions, which matches the number of times the rocket goes around in the 1500-frame example animation.) To get the rotateZ curve to look right, you'll have to adjust its shape in the Graph Editor. (See Chapter 9 for more information about the Graph Editor.)

For a finished project, see 15orbitBaked.ma on the CD-ROM that accompanies this book.

Throwing Dice: Working with the Dynamics Simulator

On a quick trip to Vegas, you might play craps, a game in which you throw two dice into a horseshoe-shaped pit and watch them bounce around (hoping for lucky 7). As you might guess, this is another great event to simulate in Maya using rigid bodies. Here, in a simplified version of the craps table, we will get to see how Maya's dynamics simulator handles a more complex, multiple-body collision.

First, build a NURBS plane and stretch it to the size of the grid. Now build a second plane and place it near the end of the first, at right angles to it. Figure 15.10 shows the initial scene.

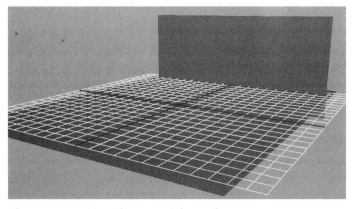

Figure 15.10 *Two planes at right angles*

Now add a cube of about default size, or a little smaller, and name it something like die1.

A NURBS cube is actually six pieces, or faces, and it is easy to choose only one of these faces by accident. A way to avoid choosing only a face is to be sure to name the cube itself (the parent level) something that you can easily recognize (like Die1, in this case). The simpler option is to create a Polygon cube, which is one body.

Add a second cube and name it die2. You can add a checker 2D texture to the dice to make them stand out better if you wish. (See Chapter 19 for information about basic texturing and other rendering techniques.) When the dice are textured and placed at the front of the "table," the scene should look something like Figure 15.11.

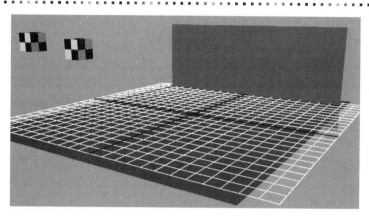

Figure 15.11 *Dice and a craps table*

Select both of the planes and choose Soft/Rigid Bodies → Create Passive Rigid Body. If you created NURBS cubes, use the Outliner or Hypergraph to choose the top level of each die. (Remember, it must be the top level, or you will get very strange results!) For polygons, you can just select each cube. Now choose Soft/Rigid Bodies → Create Active Rigid Body. Be sure both dice are still selected (or select them again) and choose Fields → Gravity.

When you play back the animation, you should see both dice fall and bounce off the table. If the dice break apart, you have created the rigid bodies on the sub-faces of your NURBS cubes, not their top levels, so you'll need to go back and try again. If you get stuck, try opening the file 15dice.ma on the CD.

To make life a bit more interesting, we need to give the dice some initial motion. Select one of the dice, click rigidBody1 in the Channel box, and set the initial velocity to –15 or so in Z. Repeat with the other die, but give this one a slightly different velocity. When you play back the animation, both dice should travel down the table and bounce off the far wall (if they don't, increase their velocities). You will notice, however, that they stay perfectly upright (that is, they don't rotate), which looks a bit odd. Give them an initial spin in X, Y, and Z or anything you like, and tweak the numbers until you get a nice-looking simulation. If the dice now bounce off the table, you can either scale the plane bigger or increase the plane's dynamic friction, which will make the dice "stick" to it more.

Finally, add a positive X velocity (maybe 5) to the left die, and a negative X velocity to the right die, making them collide in mid-air before hitting the table. You will probably need to adjust their velocities in both X and Z to get them to collide. Because of the complexity of the collisions between the spinning dice, you will notice a slowdown when the two collide, making it a bit difficult to determine if the motion looks good. To get a better idea of how the scene really looks, you can playblast it and watch it play back in real time (to playblast a scene, select Window ➜ Playblast). The Playblast tool will record the animation one frame at a time, and when it is finished, you will get a window with the completed animation in it.

A fully rendered version of the dice throw is available as a QuickTime movie (15diceFinished.mov) on the CD that accompanies this book.

Building a Chain: Adding Constraints to a Rigid Body

As a final example of rigid bodies, let's build something a bit more complex: a link of chains like a child's swing would have. Along the way, we'll learn how to add constraints and how to adjust the rigid solver to speed up some very difficult calculations.

Create a new scene, add a cylinder (named Bar), rotate it 90 degrees in X, and then scale it large on the Z axis so that it looks like Figure 15.12.

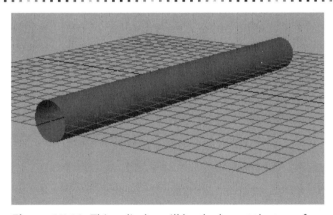

Figure 15.12 *This cylinder will be the bar at the top of our swing.*

Now create a torus (named EmbeddedLink) and stretch it into the shape of your basic chain link. Rotate the torus into position below the bar, as in Figure 15.13.

Once the first link is in place, duplicate it, rename it Link1, rotate it 90 degrees around the X axis, and move it into place. Do this three more times, until you get a link of chains that look like Figure 15.14.

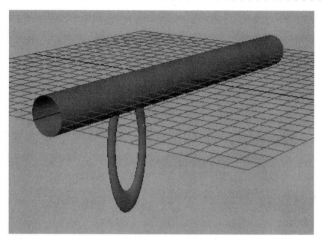

Figure 15.13 *A link added to the bar*

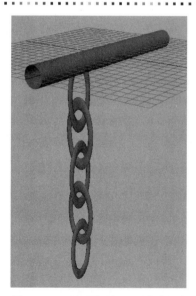

Figure 15.14 *The bar with five links*

Be sure there is a separation between each link (so they do not touch each other). Otherwise, when you create the rigid bodies, you will get an interpenetration error, and the simulation will break down.

After you create your first duplicate and then move and rotate it, you can use the Smart Transform option in the Duplicate options window to do the rest. Each duplicate will be rotated and moved into position automatically.

Now select the bar and the first link, and choose Soft/Rigid Bodies ➜ Create Passive Rigid Body. Next, choose all the other links and choose Soft/Rigid Bodies ➜ Create Active Rigid Body. With all the links still selected, add gravity to the scene (Fields ➜ Gravity). When you play back the animation, you should see all the links fall and then bounce off one another, finally coming to rest after about 200 frames (depending on how your bounciness settings are defined).

This is a good first step toward our chain link, but there are a couple of problems. First, the chains aren't in a "resting" position at the start of the animation, and second, they bounce all over the place when playback starts. Let's deal with problem two first (we'll deal with the first problem in a bit).

Our chains really don't need to bounce very much; in fact, bounciness just slows the simulation down. So we could either turn all the Bounciness attributes down to 0 or take care of the whole thing in one fell swoop by turning off the Bounce state attribute. Choose Solvers ➜ Rigid Body Solver, and in the attribute window, uncheck the Bounciness check box. This globally turns off all bounciness calculations and makes the remaining calculations run more quickly and smoothly. With the Bounciness calculations off, the links should just drop nicely into position when you play back the animation, coming to rest by frame 20 or so.

To finish our swing, we're going to add a weight to the bottom of the chain links. Create a sphere with a radius of about 3 (named weightBall), and position it just below the bottom link in the chain. (Remember not to allow the sphere to touch the link!) Looks a bit medieval, huh? First select the bottom link, and then Shift+select the sphere. Now choose Soft/Rigid Bodies ➜ Create Constraint ❏. This brings up a window that allows you to create a constraint between the two selected objects. Choose the Pin type of constraint, and leave the other settings at their default values. When you click the Create button, the sphere will be made into a rigid body, and a pin-type constraint will be added between it and the last link in the chain (as if the two were pinned together).

With the sphere selected, go to Window ➜ Relationship Editors ➜ Dynamic Relationships, and highlight gravityField1 (connecting it to the sphere). When you play back the animation, all the links plus the sphere should drop down (as before).

Now let's deal with the first problem from above: getting our links and ball into a resting position at the start of the animation so they will not fall into place to start every animation. Play the animation forward until the chain comes to a complete rest. Stop the playback, but don't rewind the animation. Choose Solvers ➜ Initial State ➜ Set For All Dynamic. This programs the current state of all dynamic objects into Maya as the initial state. When you rewind the animation now, it should remain in its current, rest position.

Great! We now have a completely lifeless simulation that does absolutely nothing! Let's make things a bit livelier. First, try adding an initial X velocity of around –10 to the ball weight. When you play back the animation, the ball (and the chain, following it) should swing out to the left and then pendulum back to the right, slowly settling back to stillness. You can try adding velocity in other directions to the ball, and even a rotation. When you have experimented a bit, reset all the initial velocities back to 0.

Instead of an initial velocity, let's now add an impulse of –4 or –5 in the X direction. When you play the animation back, the ball and chain will appear to be blowing in a wind from the right of the screen. (You could actually achieve the same effect by connecting an air field to the ball.) To allow the ball and chain to fall again, keyframe the impulseX back to 0 after 30 or 40 frames.

You may notice that the ball and chain get kinked up near the bar, and this slows the animation way down. To compensate for this, you might try adjusting the rigid solver settings. (Try a step size of 0.1 and set the solver to Runge Kutta—not Adaptive.) You might also get interpenetration errors, in which case you can reduce the step size a bit.

Finally, you might notice that the ball doesn't look very weighty in the way it is thrashed around by the chain. Try increasing the ball's mass to 50 or 100 (and set the impulse higher to compensate), and see how it looks now.

A rendered movie of a ball and chain (15ballAndChain.mov) is available in the Chapter 15 Animation folder on the accompanying CD.

All in all, the only real drawback to adding mass to objects is that it drastically increases calculation times.

Summary

In this chapter, we saw how easy it is (relatively speaking) to get Maya to do the work for us when simulating real-world events like falling and colliding objects. We also found that rigid bodies can be changed from passive (keyframable and not affected by fields) to active (not keyframable but affected by fields), and that, when a passive rigid body is made active, it inherits the motion it had before. This allows rigid bodies to work within a keyframed animation and with keyframed characters. Finally, we created more complex interactions, and we adjusted the rigid solver to give us realistic, but faster, simulations. In Chapter 17, we'll take the last example we worked on (the ball and chain) and automate the process of building it by creating a MEL script we can run from a single command.

Part IV
Working with MEL

In This Part

So far in this book, most of your interaction with Maya has been through its GUI (graphical user interface). Maya, however, is built upon a scripting language called Maya Embedded Language (or MEL for short), which allows you to control the program in very precise, powerful ways. As MEL is a scripting language (as opposed to a full-blown programming language), it is fairly easy to program, yet robust enough to accomplish complex tasks that would be difficult or time-consuming to do manually. What's more, you can use MEL's power even if you do not know how to program at all! Chapter 16 will show you how to cut-and-paste MEL commands to create buttons, hotkeys, and marking menus to perform a series of actions very easily. Chapter 17 will delve more into the programming aspects of MEL, showing you how to create a GUI using MEL, and also how to create full-blown, multiprocedure scripts that can do wonderful things. Included in Chapter 17 are several sample scripts that you can study and dissect to learn even more about how the language works.

While MEL is not as friendly as a push-button interface, it is remarkably easy to use given its power. A bit of time to getting to know MEL will open up a powerful new way of interacting with Maya.

MEL Basics

MAYA

Chapter 16

This chapter introduces Maya's embedded scripting language, MEL. You will learn how Maya uses MEL, and you'll see how you can increase your productivity by automating repetitive tasks and getting Maya to do exactly what you want it to do.

While MEL does require a bit of programming savvy, you really don't need to know a great deal about computer programming to use it—at least not at the basic level. If you have had some programming background, MEL's basic syntax will seem pretty straightforward. If you know the C or C++ programming languages, MEL's syntax will seem like second nature.

If you have never looked at a computer program before, MEL will at first seem baffling, but don't worry. Even if you never intend to do any real programming with MEL, you will find this chapter and the next one contain many nuggets of information that will allow you to use MEL to control Maya in powerful, high-level ways, often without the need for you to do any programming yourself.

Before reading this chapter, you should be familiar with basic Maya concepts, like interface conventions, how to create and animate objects, and how to move around Maya's windows and menus (see Chapters 1, "The Maya Interface," and 3, "Techniques for Speeding Up Workflow"). If you have some knowledge of computer programming, that will also prove helpful, but it is not necessary. This chapter features:

- MEL fundamentals
- The Script Editor
- Hands-on MEL: building lights automatically
- Hands-on MEL: creating, moving, and naming an object—with one keystroke
- Placing objects using a marking menu
- What's an attribute?
- Using expressions with MEL

MEL is Fundamental

MEL (Maya Embedded Language) is the ground from which you interact with Maya. When you open Maya, the program first runs several MEL scripts, which actually build all the windows you see—that's right: Maya itself has no interface whatsoever. You can even run Maya from your operating system command prompt by typing in **Maya –prompt**! Behind nearly everything you see in Maya is a MEL script.

What does this mean to the average Maya user? Simple: whatever the original programmers did, you also can do. You can write windows that have sliders, tabs, text fields, and buttons in them; you can create attributes in the Channel box; you can even add menu items to the main menu bar. The fact that Maya is built on MEL is one of the program's most powerful features.

What is a Scripting Language?

MEL is a scripting language, not a complete programming language (like Java or C++). A program written in a programming language is compiled and becomes an independent program (like the core program, Maya, which just runs off your computer's operating system). A scripting language, on the other hand, resides on top of another program (in this case, Maya), and is interpreted at every line rather than compiled. Because scripting languages are interpreted by the "mother" program, they are a bit slower than compiled programs—however, they require much less programming overhead than do compiled programs.

If you are a real "propeller head" and like to get into the guts of a program, Maya has its own API (application programming interface)—appropriately enough named Maya API—in which you can create plug-ins for the program itself, using the C++ programming language. MEL does just fine for 95% of the things most people want to do, however, and it isn't too difficult to learn.

Although the API is outside the scope of this book, you can contact Alias|Wavefront about using the Maya SDK to develop plug-ins for Maya.

The Script Editor

One of the best ways to get to know MEL is to use the Script Editor.

The Command line, which we discussed in Chapter 1, is just one input line in the Script Editor. Type a command in the Command line and you can see it appear in the Script Editor's History window.

MEL is a huge language (with over 600 commands and about 75 functions), but the Script Editor will clue you in on how different commands are used, and will allow you to "cut and paste" whole scripts together without the need to program a thing yourself. You don't even need to use the Command line to enter the MEL commands; operations you perform in the Maya interface are recorded as MEL commands in the Script Editor, so with no knowledge of programming, you can actually copy-paste together a fairly complex script.

You can bring up the Script Editor in either of two ways: either select Window → General Editors → Script Editor, or click the button, in the lower-right corner of the screen, that looks like a square with lines in it.

—Script Editor

When opened, the Script Editor will look like this:

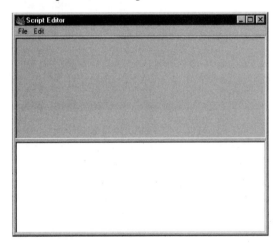

Notice that there are two windows in the editor. The top window is called the History window; the bottom, the Input window. With the Script Editor open, create a NURBS sphere (the easiest way to do this is to click the blue ball on the shelf tab at the top of the main window). Now look at the History window. The very last line of that window should read something like:

```
sphere -p 0 0 0 -ax 0 1 0 -ssw 0 -esw 360 -r 1 -d 3 -ut 0 -tol
0.01 -s 8 -nsp 4 -ch 1;
objectMoveCommand;
```

What you see in the top window is the command you told Maya to perform when you clicked the ball on the shelf. The sphere command is Maya's command to create a NURBS sphere; all the characters with dashes before them (-p, -ax, and so on) are "flags" that tell sphere how to build the sphere. For example, -p stands for pivot, which is the pivot point of the sphere (since it's 0, 0, 0, the pivot of the sphere is at the origin); -ax tells Maya which axis is the "up" axis for the sphere (in this case, the Y axis); -r stands for radius (the sphere's radius, in this case, is 1 unit); and -ssw and -esw are the start and end sweep (in degrees here). Finally, the semicolon at the end of the line tells Maya the command is finished. (Nearly every line of MEL code needs a semicolon at the end.)

As you can see, more characters will fit into the Input window than we can squeeze into the printed page, so the semicolon is also your guide to where one command actually ends and the next begins. As you enter commands from this book into the Script Editor, you generally need to press the Enter key only after semicolons.

Create a few more objects (like lights, cones, curves, etc.) and look at what appears in the History window of the Script Editor. You can see that every command you perform in the interface is relayed to Maya's core program via MEL commands. For ease of reading, you can clear the top window at any time. Go to the Script Editor menu and select Edit ➜ Clear History. The top window should now be cleared of all commands.

Now try opening one of Maya's windows (for example, the Hypergraph window: Window ➜ Hypergraph). What do you see in the History window? Probably nothing at all. To keep from cluttering the History window, Maya's programmers created a filter that blocks from view in the History Window many of the MEL commands programmers don't commonly need to see. Sometimes, however, it is very useful to see what's really going on in Maya. Close the Hypergraph, select Edit ➜ Echo All Commands in the Script Editor, and reopen the Hypergraph. Now you should see something like this:

```
hotBox;
buildObjectEdMenu MayaWindow|mainWindowMenu|menuItem138
tearOffPanel "Hypergraph" "hyperGraphPanel" true;
addHyperGraphPanel hyperGraphPanel1;
HyperGraphEdMenu hyperGraphPanel1HyperGraphEd;
createModelPanelMenu modelPanel1;
createModelPanelMenu modelPanel2;
createModelPanelMenu modelPanel3;
createModelPanelMenu modelPanel4;
buildPanelPopupMenu hyperGraphPanel1;
// Result: hyperGraphPanel1Window //
```

All these strange lines represent the steps by which Maya builds the Hypergraph window for you. (Actually, nearly all the words above, like `buildPanelPopupMenu`, are calls to other MEL scripts in the `\Maya3.0\Scripts\Others` directory. You can look through them to see how the window is actually constructed.) So you see, even the windows in Maya are created through MEL.

One other note worth mentioning about the lines above: the last line

```
// Result: hyperGraphPanel1Window //
```

is called the *result line*. The two slashes at the beginning of the line are a comment marker that tells MEL to ignore the rest of that line (you'll see these comment lines in all well-made MEL scripts). MEL then prints out for you the result of the operation (in this case, that it created the window as you asked). If there had been a problem making the Hypergraph window, the result line would have contained an error message instead of a result message.

Now let's take a look at the Input window (the window on the bottom half of the Script Editor window). First empty the scene of all objects and clear the History window of the Script Editor; then place your cursor in the bottom window and type in the following:

```
sphere -radius 1 -pivot 0 0 0 -name myBall
```

Press the Enter key on your numeric keypad (not the one on your main keyboard) or, alternatively, press Ctrl+Enter on your main keyboard. You should see the text disappear from the Input window and appear in the History window (you will also see another result line, telling you that the command was successfully completed). At the same time, you should see a sphere appear at the origin of your scene, named myBall. Congratulations, you have just executed your first MEL command!

 If you're wondering why you have to use the numeric keypad's Enter key or Ctrl+Enter, it's because the alpha Enter key is reserved for in-line returns. In other words, pressing the alpha Enter key just creates a new line in the editor window. To force the contents of the editor window to be evaluated (executed), you must use one of the two other options.

Now try this: delete the sphere from your scene, then triple-click the line in the History window that you typed earlier (`sphere -radius 1 -pivot 0 0 0 -name myBall`). Once you have the entire line highlighted, copy that line into the Input window (in Irix, simply MM click in the Input window; in Windows, Ctrl+C (copy) the text, click in the Input window, and Ctrl+V (paste) the line there). Now hit Enter. You should see the exact same sphere (called myBall) created at the origin of your scene, meaning that you have copied a command from the History window and made a mini-script (called a macro) out of it.

This was a very simple example, but consider the power this little cut-and-paste trick gives you: you can "record" anything you like from the History window and turn it into a MEL macro (or even a full-blown script). By storing this little script, you can return to it any time and, by cutting and pasting text, or even at the click of a button, make all those actions happen.

As noted in Chapter 3, you can create buttons for MEL commands simply by highlighting those commands, and then MM dragging the command lines up to a shelf.

Hands-On MEL: Building Lights Automatically

Let's put all this information to some use now. We're going to record several actions we perform to create a default lighting setup, copy those actions into a macro, and place that macro on a shelf. Once we've done that, we can automatically set up our scene lights for any scene we wish, at the click of a mouse.

1. Open Maya or begin a new scene.

2. Create a new NURBS plane object (Create ➜ Nurbs Primitives ➜ Plane), scale it to about the size of the Maya grid, and turn on hardware lighting (press the 7 key above the keyboard). This plane will help you see how your lights are affecting the scene.

3. Open the Script Editor and clear the History window.

4. Now create and place one or more lights in your scene. You can also set color, intensity, and name for each of these lights.

Refer to Chapter 20 for tips on best lighting setups. A three-light setup is a good choice, using spotlights in all cases: a key light, a fill light (both in front), and a rim light (in back).

5. Once you're happy with the lights' positions, colors, and other attributes, simply select everything in the History window and MM drag the highlighted text up to the shelf of your choosing. A new button will appear that looks like this:

Button Added for New Script

Let's see if it worked.

6. Select all in your scene and hit Delete (or to do the same thing you can actually type the following in the Script Editor: `select -all; delete;`).

7. Once your scene is empty, go up to the shelf and click your newly made button. After a couple of seconds, you should see your lights magically appear in the scene, just as you had set them up.

Not bad for a couple minutes of work and no programming! If you like, you can make several more lighting setups, each of which creates a different lighting arrangement for your scene.

One problem you might notice right away is that the default MEL shelf buttons all look alike. Fortunately, Maya can handle this problem quite easily.

1. From the main menu, select Window ➜ Settings/Preferences ➜ Shelves (or, alternatively, choose Shelf Editor from the Shelf menu, the black triangle at the left of the shelf icons). A window will appear that has three tabs.

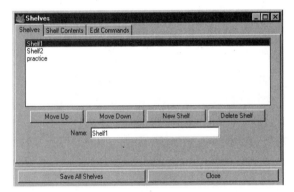

2. First, select the Shelves tab. In the main pane, you'll see listed all the shelves you currently have, along with buttons to add, delete, or move shelves up and down in the order they appear on screen. Click the New Shelf button, and a new shelf appears, entitled `shelfLayout1`. You can either rename this to create a shelf for you (like `myShelf`) or click the Delete Shelf button to remove the new shelf.

3. Now select Shelf1 from the list and click the Shelf Contents tab. In the main pane, you'll see a list of all the buttons on the selected shelf. Click the first item in the list (Curves With CVs) and look at the area below the main pane. Here, you'll see the Move Up, Move Down, and Delete Item buttons, as well as other buttons and fields:

- The Label text field contains the text you see in the window above (the internal label for the button).

- The Overlay Label field contains the text you see under the button in the shelf window. For the Curves With CVs button, this is blank, so there is no text on the shelf button. Try adding text and see what happens!

- The Change Image button allows you to find or create the bitmapped image that appears on the shelf—in the case of the Curves With CVs button, it's the image shown at left, stored in the \Maya 3.0\Bitmaps folder.

You can also navigate to the \Maya3.0\extras\icons directory and browse through many pre-built icons for your use in creating shelf buttons.

You can also create your own icons. In Windows, the icons can be in BMP, JPG, or XPM formats (BMP and JPG are supported by nearly all NT graphics editing packages). In Irix, you must save the image in XPM format (using Xpaint or another program). The icons are 32 × 32 pixels, and you should make your images that size. Note that if you wish to place text at the bottom of the image, you should leave a blank space to allow room for it, as the text and image both have to fit within the 32 × 32 area.

4. Now go back to the Shelves tab and select the shelf that contains your new light button.

5. Return to the Shelf Contents tab. Add a label and an overlay label to your button. Now change the image of the button to one of the images in \Maya3.0\extras\icons. (If you want text on your button, a good choice of icons is the UserMenuIcon group in this directory—they have room for text at the bottom of the button.)

The final tab, Edit Commands, is for more advanced users. This window actually allows you to rewrite the scripts for the menu buttons right inside the Customize Shelves window. The script for whatever item you had selected in the Shelf Contents tab will appear in the main window. You can then change any commands you wish, or add comments to the script.

To make these changes "stick," however, you *must* press the Enter key on your numeric keypad (not on your keyboard); otherwise, when you select another tab, all your changes will be lost! For practice, try adding a comment line like the following to your lights macro:

```
//This is my macro to make several lights in a scene.
```

Click another shelf button and then return to the Edit Commands tab. Did your changes hold? If not, try again, this time remembering to press the Enter key to make your changes stick.

Before leaving the Customize Shelves window, it is always a good idea to click the Save All Shelves button at the bottom of any of the tabs (assuming you want your changes to stick!). This button writes all the changes you just made to your `\Winnt\ Profiles\<user name>\maya\3.0\prefs\shelves` directory (for Windows), so that the next time you start up Maya, your shelves will look just as they do now.

In this example, you have learned quickly to record your actions, save them as a macro, place them in your shelves, and finally, change the text and image of the button to customize its look. Next, we will create a small script that will execute when we press a keyboard key.

Hands-On MEL: Creating, Moving, and Naming an Object—with One Keystroke

Let's say you often make a NURBS sphere, rename it to **ball**, and move it some distance from the origin (you can modify this to be a light, a plane, or whatever, but for now, we'll just do it with a sphere). Even though Maya has a very efficient workflow, it's a waste of your time to do the same things over and over, so let's make Maya do it for you at the press of a key.

1. Open the Hotkey Editor by selecting Window ➔ Settings/Preferences ➔ Hotkeys. This brings up a pretty scary-looking window, like Figure 16.1.

 New to Maya 3, navigating the Hotkey Editor is far more efficient: Commands are now grouped into categories, so you can find the one you're looking for more quickly. For example, if you are looking for the Quit command, it would logically be under the File category. First, in the Categories list, click File, then scroll down the list of Commands until you find Quit (the last command in this field). To see all commands, just click the List All button. Also, you can click the Restore Defaults button to change all keyboard shortcuts to their factory default settings.

2. Before we create a command, let's query a key first to see if it's free for us to use. In the Assign New Hotkey area, type **n** in the Key field, and check the Alt box in the Modifiers group below. You should get the following message just below the radio buttons:

   ```
   "Alt-n" is assigned to: nothing.
   ```

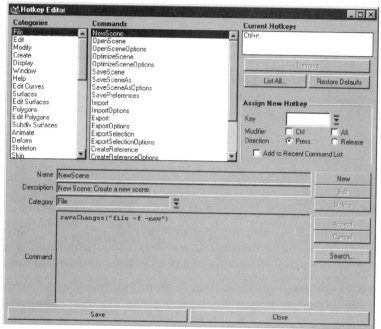

Figure 16.1 *The Hotkey Editor*

This means the key is available for your use (if it's not, try another key).

3. Now, scroll to the bottom of the Categories list and click the User category—you will see that the Commands list is now empty, as there are no user-defined commands yet. In the bottom portion of the window, click the New button on the right side; then, in the Name field, type **Sphere**, or something you find useful. In the Description field, type in something like the following:

```
Make and move a sphere.
```

Then, in the Command field, type the following (you could also paste commands from the Script Editor):

```
sphere -radius 4 -name ball -pivot 0 0 0 -ssw 0 -esw 360;
move -relative 0 5 0;
```

4. Click the Accept button. The Commands list at the top of the screen will now update, and you'll see your command text listed in the Command field of the window.

5. Return to the Assign New Hotkey section, where Alt+n should still be enabled (if not, type **n** in the Key field and select Alt). Now select the Press radio button, and click Assign. The Current Hotkeys pane will update, reflecting that your command has now been turned into a hotkey.

6. Click the Save button and close this window.

7. Now hold down the Alt key and press **n**. If you did everything right, you should see a sphere called "ball" sitting in your window and resting 5 units up from the grid on the Y axis.

Congratulations! You have now written some MEL commands and made them work simply by pressing a key!

If you don't get what you expected, check the Script Editor to see if there was an error. If so, go back to the Hotkey Editor and edit the command to make it work. If the Script Editor doesn't show anything happening at all, check that you mapped the command to the Alt+n key combination. If you're still having trouble, try typing the sphere commands into the Script Editor and get them to work properly, then copy them into the Command field.

If you now wish to delete this command, simply select it in the Hotkey Editor and press the Delete button (near the bottom right).

As a further exercise, try to take the commands used in the "create lights" exercise we did earlier, and map them to a hotkey of your choosing.

Placing Objects Using a Marking Menu

So far we have seen how to record MEL commands and make them into a button on a shelf, and we've seen how to issue MEL commands in text form and turn them into a hotkey. Now we will learn how to create a marking menu that performs any of several MEL commands.

Let's say that you wish to move a selected object (or objects) around in different directions simply by selecting an item from a GUI list. This is the perfect situation in which to use a Maya marking menu.

1. First, create a new NURBS sphere (or cone or whatever) at the origin of the grid. Now, in the Script Editor, type in the following:

```
move -r 0 5 0;
```

2. When you execute this command, the ball (or other object) should move 5 units up the Y axis (remember, -r stands for relative in this case, meaning that the object will move relative to its current position along the Y axis). To move the ball back to 0, type this:

```
move -r 0 -5 0;
```

The ball moves 5 units down, and goes back to 0.

3. Now open the Marking Menus window by selecting Window ➜ Settings/Preferences ➜ Marking Menus. The following window will appear:

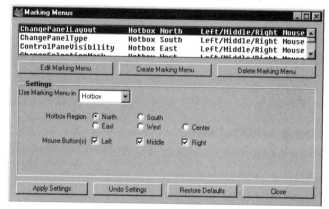

The top pane lists marking menus built into Maya (most are related to the hotbox), but of course you can build your own as well.

4. Simply click Create Marking Menu to bring up a window that will let you build a menu of your own.

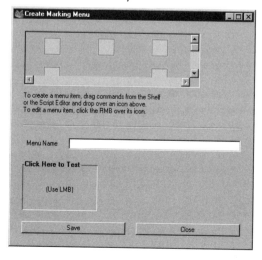

5. Under Menu Name, type in **MoveObject**. Now RM click the top-center yellowish button in the upper pane and select Edit Menu Item.

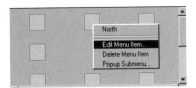

 In addition to the eight main marking menu positions (North, Northeast, East, and so on), there is a ninth position, at the bottom left of the window, called the "overflow" menu item. If you add a command to this item, another will be created just below it, allowing you to make the menu as large as you wish. Also, all menu items can have submenus, allowing you even greater flexibility in building a marking menu.

Edit Menu Item brings up a window in which you add the commands for the button.

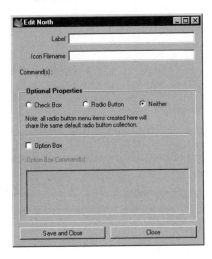

6. For Label, type **Move Up**, and leave the Icon Filename field blank (you can specify a path for an image that will appear in this position when the marking menu is accessed). In the Commands field, type in

```
move -r 0 5 0;
```

7. Leave Optional Properties set at Neither, leave the Option Box blank, and click Save and Close.

What you have just done is to create a marking menu item that will move a selected object up by 5 units.

8. To test how this action works, select an object in your scene and then press the LM button in the Click Here To Test area. Whatever you selected should move up by 5 units when you select the command.

9. Now, edit the East, West, and South marking menu buttons to the following, respectively:

```
move -r 5 0 0;
move -r -5 0 0;
move -r 0 -5 0;
```

10. Give them appropriate titles and test that they work as they should.

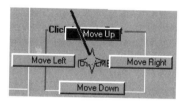

11. Once you're happy with how the menu buttons work, click the Save button and return to the Marking Menus window.

12. At the bottom of the list, you'll now see MoveObject listed. With this item selected, in the Settings pane, change the Use Marking Menu In field to Hotkey Editor (this allows you to make a hotkey for the menu you just made). Click the Apply Settings button and close the window.

13. Now, in order to use our new marking menu, we have to go back to the Hotkey Editor (Window → Settings/Preferences → Hotkeys) and make a hotkey for the menu.

14. Scroll to the bottom of the Categories list and click the User Marking Menus option. You'll see two new items in the Commands list: MoveObject_Press and MoveObject_Release. By mapping these two items, we will create a hotkey that will bring up our new marking menu (the release key must be mapped for marking menus, or the menu will just stay up even after the hotkey has been released!).

15. First, let's find an unmapped key. Query the Alt+o key to see if it's mapped (if it is, try another one).

16. Now, select the MoveObject_Press item in the Commands list, and click the Assign button. Maya will ask you whether you wish to assign the release key as well (a nice time-saver), so click Yes to the dialog that pops up. The MoveObject item should be updated to show that Alt+o is its new hotkey, and both press and release should be properly mapped (click the MoveObject_Release command to check that this has indeed happened).

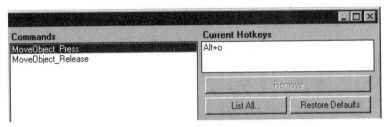

17. Click the Save button and close the Hotkey window.

18. Let's test our new marking menu: select an object in the scene window, press and hold the Alt and o keys, and press the left mouse button down. You should now see your marking menu, ready for action!

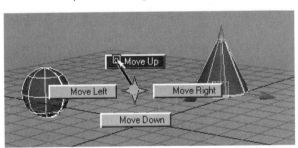

19. Move the object(s) you have selected around the screen to see how the new menu works.

You can take these steps and reuse them to create marking menus to do anything you like. For example, if you created several lighting setups in the work above, you could now create a marking menu to allow you to select any of these light setups very quickly and intuitively.

We've seen how we can record or type simple commands and place them on the shelf, in a hotkey, or even a marking menu. Now let's take a closer look at how MEL can work with the attributes of any object in your scene.

What's an Attribute?

As you likely understand from reading earlier chapters, an attribute (MEL uses the term Attr to refer to attributes) is any item that lives on a Maya node. (A Maya node is anything you can see in the Hypergraph, or the tabs at the top of the Attribute Editor.) This sounds a bit obscure, but it's really fairly straightforward: anything in the Channel Box, like rotateX, transformZ, or scaleY, is an attribute of an object (more specifically, an object's transform node).

When you build, alter, or animate an object, you're changing one or more attributes on one or more nodes in the object—and of course, all of these changes are just MEL commands, so you can make Maya do the work for you. In this chapter, we'll take a quick look at how MEL works with attributes; in the next chapter, we'll get into more detail about how to build complex scripts using attributes.

You may have noticed when you created the lights in the exercise earlier in this chapter that the Script Editor was filled with many statements that started with setAttr. The setAttr statement tells MEL to set a certain attribute to a certain value. Likewise, the getAttr statement gets (reads) the value of an attribute on a certain object so you can use that value in another MEL statement. The addAttr statement tells MEL to add a custom attribute to a certain item. Essentially, the setAttr statement is the same as going into the Attribute Editor window and changing a value in one of its fields (try changing a value in the Attribute Editor, and note that the Script Editor History window shows that a setAttr statement has been issued).

The syntax (the rules for what goes where) for an Attr statement is as follows:

```
setAttr [flags] objectName value;
```

Flags, as we've seen, are any special requests for MEL to complete; the object name is the name of the item's attribute to set (like nurbsSphere1.translateX); and the value is the value to set the attribute to. The getAttr and addAttr commands have similar syntax. For example, we could move a sphere called "ball" to 10 on the X axis by typing the following in the Script Editor:

```
setAttr ball.translateX 10;
```

Once you execute this command, your ball will move from where it is to 10 on the X axis. (Of course, if you have no object called "ball," you will get an error message.)

The way MEL (and Maya) references an attribute is similar to the way C++ and other object-oriented programs work: you reference the node, then a period, then the attribute: Object.Attribute. You must specify which node the attribute is located on, or you will get an error. For example, typing setAttr translateX 10; will generate an error message, rather than moving "ball" up 10 units.

Using the `setAttr` command to adjust the ball's position is pretty much like giving the `move` command: `move 10 0 0`. Unlike the `move` command, however, setting the attribute of `translateX` will not affect the other two attributes (the Y and Z translate attributes). Also, the `setAttr` statement is far more flexible than the `move` command, which can only translate an object.

As a quick example of how `setAttr` can work, let's make a ball and manually set several of its attributes. Type the following into the Script Editor's Input window:

```
sphere -n ball;
setAttr makeNurbSphere1.radius 4;
setAttr makeNurbSphere1.ssw 20;
setAttr makeNurbSphere1.esw 250;
setAttr ball.rotateY 90;
setAttr ball.translateX -5;
setAttr ball.scaleY 0.7;
```

Can you figure out on your own what each command does? Try highlighting each of these lines by itself and pressing the numeric Enter key to execute it.

Using the technique of highlighting one line at a time is a very useful way to figure out what's happening in a script—and to see where things go wrong!

Note that to change the way your sphere is constructed, you reference the make shape node (`makeNurbsSphere1`), not the transform node, which you have renamed `ball`.

The first line builds a sphere. The next six lines change many attributes, either on the shape node of the sphere (the `makeNurbSphere` node) or on the transform node (the `ball` node). After the `sphere` command, the next three `setAttr` statements change the radius, the start sweep angle, and the end sweep angle, respectively. The last three change the position and scale of the sphere's transform node (named "ball"). The finished product should look like this:

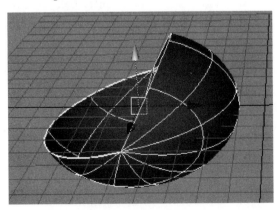

If, for some unknown reason, you needed to create a flattened half-ball over and over again in different scenes, you could just MM drag these commands to your shelf and you'd be able to make the object at the click of a button—quite a timesaver!

Using Expressions with MEL

Expressions are a specialized subset of the MEL scripting language which are designed to execute through time, not just when the command or script is called. Although MEL is evaluated only when the script or macro is run (except in special cases), expressions are evaluated at every frame, or after each interaction on screen (like moving an object). Expressions deal primarily with changing an object's attributes based on time, the current frame, or another attribute. Thus, expressions are well suited to calculating particle properties (see Chapter 24, "Using Particle Expressions, Ramps, and Volumes") or to creating relationships between scene objects in Maya. Unlike MEL, expressions do not require you to use a `setAttr` or `getAttr` statement, allowing their syntax to be somewhat simpler and making them very powerful aids to creating complex behaviors in your Maya animations. You can also embed expressions into MEL scripts, allowing you to create time-based expressions directly through MEL scripting (examples of using expressions in scripts are at the end of the next chapter).

In this section you'll find three examples that give you an opportunity to try out the Expression Editor. In the first, you'll make a cone move up and down by moving a sphere back and forth. In the second you'll make a ball move back and forth in rhythm as time elapses. In the last example, you'll use an expression to make a wheel "stick" to the pavement (a plane) so it doesn't slip.

The expressions we'll deal with here are fairly simple; however, if this kind of thing appeals to you, and especially if you like to work with particles and dynamics, there is a more advanced discussion on the use of expressions with dynamics in Chapter 24.

Transforming a Cone

Let's begin with a simple example: we're going to make a cone move up and down by moving a sphere back and forth on the Z axis.

1. First, make a new scene and create a sphere and a cone (call the sphere "ball" and the cone "cone"). Select the cone and open the Expression Editor (Window ➜ Animation Editors ➜ Expression Editor).

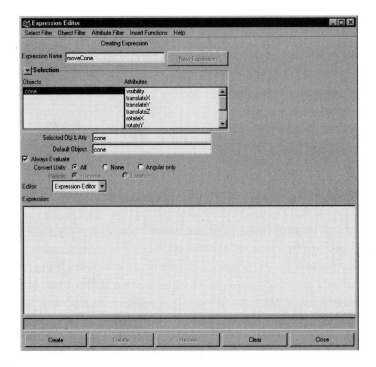

2. In the Expression Name field, type **moveCone**.

3. In the Expression field at the bottom, type the following:

```
translateY = ball.translateZ;
//to save time, you could also just type:
//ty = ball.tz;
```

Because the cone was selected, Maya knows to apply the translateY command to the cone (if the object is not selected, just type cone.ty = ball.tz;). Click the Create button. If you entered the information correctly, the feedback line (or the Script Editor's History window) will show

```
Result: moveCone
```

If not, you will get an error message.

4. Once the expression is accepted, move the ball back and forth in the Z axis, and watch the cone move up and down.

Though this is a simple example, it should indicate how you could solve some very complex interactions between objects more efficiently by using an expression instead of keyframing.

Rock the Boat

Now we're going to dust off those ancient memories of high school math class and put them to practical use—bet you thought you'd never hear that one! Using the sine function, we're going to get our favorite object, a sphere, to move back and forth over time.

1. Make a new scene in Maya, and add a NURBS sphere (called "ball").

2. Go to the Expression Editor and type in the following:

```
ball.tx = 5 * sin (time);
```

3. Set your time slider to about 400 frames and play the animation.

You should see the ball moving back and forth in rhythm as time (frames divided by frames-per-second, or the number of seconds that have gone by) progresses. The sine function takes an input number (the time of the animation) and converts it into a wave that goes back and forth between –1 and 1. Multiplying the sine function by 5 just makes it bigger (increases the amplitude). Starting from 0, this is what the sine function itself looks like:

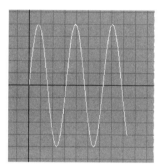

The X component of the sphere's motion just moves up and down (or back and forth) from –5 to 5 as time progresses. We can also make the ball go back and forth more quickly by typing in the following (and clicking Edit) in the Expression Editor:

```
ball.tx = 5 * sin (2 * time);
```

Here, the ball will go back and forth twice as fast, since time is being multiplied by 2. In general, you can alter the sine function's amplitude and frequency as follows:

Amplitude × sine (Frequency × Value)

The frequency component adjusts how fast the ball goes back and forth, while the amplitude adjusts how big the motion is. You can also put the frame number into the expression, as well as time:

```
ball.tx = 5 * sin (frame);
```

When you play back this expression, the ball will travel back and forth far more quickly than before, as the number of the current frame increases much more rapidly than does the time.

Now let's make the ball do something a bit more interesting, like move in a circle. Once again, edit the expression on the ball, this time to the following:

```
ball.tx = 5 * sin (time);
ball.tz = 5 * cos (time);
```

Here, the ball's X position is controlled by the sine function, while the ball's Z position is controlled by the cosine function. (Remember that the cosine is perfectly "out of phase" with the sine function. In other words, it begins at a value of 1 rather than 0.) When you play back the animation, the ball should move around in a perfect circle. How would you make the circle "squashed" (an ellipse)? Try changing one of the amplitude multipliers to 2 instead of 5. What happens when you increase the frequency of one of the positions? Try making ball.tz equal to 5 * cos (2 * time) and see what happens. What if the frequency number is 3 or 5? You can quickly see how you can make some very complex motion with relatively simple expressions.

As a further exercise in using expressions, try making the ball move around a three-dimensional sphere instead of just on the X–Z plane.

Wheels That Stick

As a last example of expressions, let's make something that can really come in handy: a way to make a wheel (in this case, our famous ball) "stick" to the pavement so as not to slip. If you've ever tried to keyframe a non-slipping wheel, you know what a pain it is to do; but with a simple expression, Maya will do it for you!

1. In an empty scene, create a sphere (or cylinder, if you prefer) with a radius of 1 unit and name it **tire**.

2. Create a plane and scale it big.

3. Now move the ball up by 1 on the Y axis so that it just rests on the plane (if you think you're ready, try making the plane and sphere, and then moving the sphere, all using MEL commands in the Script Editor).

4. Select the tire ball and open the Expression Editor. Name the expression **stickyTires** and then, in the Expression window, type the following:

```
tire.rz = - (tire.tx * (360.0 / (2 * 3.1415)));
```

This expression takes the `translateX` component of tire and turns it into an angle for the `rotateZ` component. The negative sign ensures that the tire actually rotates in the proper direction when the wheel is moved. The parenthetical expression just converts degrees to radians so that the two numbers will match up properly.

5. In the scene window, move the ball back and forth in the X direction and watch how the ball always rolls just the right amount to keep up with how far it moves.

In the next chapter, we'll briefly revisit this tire expression and make it more generally useful—and readable.

As a further exercise, can you make the ball roll properly as it's moved in the Z direction (be sure to set the X, Y, and Z positions back to 0 before you do this)? This is tougher than it sounds, so be forewarned!

Finally, let's use a nice little built-in MEL function called `noise` to make the tire move back and forth in the X direction as it sticks to the ground. The noise function creates a random, but connected, motion path (as opposed to the `rand` function, which goes all over the place). Compare the following two motion paths:

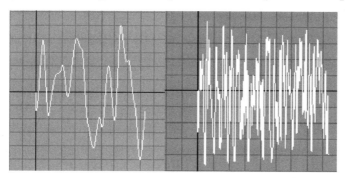

Although the `noise` function, on the left, is a random motion, it moves from point to point in a smooth path. The `rand` function, however, on the right, is very chaotic. There are cases where each has an advantage; here, we need to use the `noise` function to make the tire move smoothly back and forth. In the Expression Editor, type in the following to edit the expression you've already been working on:

```
tire.tx = 5 * noise (time);
tire.rz = - (tire.tx * (360.0 / (2 * 3.1415)));
```

As time increases, `noise` generates a new number for each new time, but each number is connected to the old one in such a way as to keep them relatively close together. When you play back the new tire animation, the wheel will move back and forth on the X axis, all the while "sticking" to the ground as it rolls. Considering how simple this expression is, it produces some very complex motion that would be difficult to reproduce in timely fashion using keyframes.

Summary

In this chapter, you have learned what MEL is and how Maya is constructed on it, and you have gained hands-on experience with some basic (yet powerful) ways to take advantage of scripting. You also learned how to make your scripts quickly available as buttons, hotkeys, or marking menus. Finally, you learned the difference between MEL commands and expressions, and how to create some basic expressions that do neat things.

In the following chapter, we will go into more depth about how to use MEL to create flexible procedures and complex scripts that can even have their own user interface. If this chapter was as far as you want to go with MEL right now, don't bother with the next chapter. If you're ready to learn how to really program the pants off Maya, just turn the page!

Programming
with MEL

MAYA

Chapter 17

The previous chapter introduced the Maya Embedded Language (MEL). You learned how to work with the Script Editor, create your own marking menus, and use expressions. This chapter takes you further into the language; it focuses on using MEL to maximize productivity, to create graphical user interfaces (GUIs, pronounced "gooeys"), and to create full-blown MEL scripts suitable for sharing with friends and family.

Although you can benefit from this chapter without any prior programming experience, it will be a big help if you already have some understanding of a programming or scripting language. If you'd like to try some programming first, you can avail yourself of a wealth of books, classes, and references for a dizzying array of programming languages. Otherwise, let's dig into the meat of MEL!

This chapter features:

- How to get Maya's help with MEL
- Debugging MEL scripts
- Variables, loops, and branching
- Creating a GUI
- Using procedures and scripts
- Commenting
- Learning from the masters

As Maya's syntax is very similar to that of the C and C++ programming languages, a good primer on one of these languages is your best preparation for MEL. The publisher of this book offers numerous titles on C and C++, including Visual C++ 6 In Record Time *by Steven Holzner (Sybex, 1998) and* Mastering Visual C++ 6 *by Michael J. Young (Sybex, 1998).*

How to Get Help with MEL

Before we delve too far into the more complex aspects of MEL, let's take a moment to examine the powerful Help tools Maya has available—and how easy they are to use.

First, you have Maya's internal Help function. Because there are so many MEL commands and functions (around 700), the Help function is a very quick and useful feature (you can even type in **help help** to get a look at how the Help command works).

To get help with a MEL command, just open the Script Editor and type the name of the command you want help with into the Input window (or just type it into the Command line below the main window). For example, to get help with the setAttr command, type in:

```
help setAttr;
```

Execute the command (press Enter on the numeric keypad, or Ctrl+Enter on the keyboard), and in the Script Editor's History window, you'll see the following result lines:

```
// Result:
Synopsis: setAttr [flags] Name[...]
Flags:
   -e -edit
   -q -query
  -av -alteredValue
   -k -keyable        on|off
   -l -lock           on|off
   -s -size           Index
 -typ -type           String
 //
```

These result lines give you a quick look at the setAttr command: a synopsis of its syntax (or how to use it) and a list of flags that you can use with the command.

If you're an experienced programmer, this information may be all you need in order to use the command. If you're just starting out, however, you'll probably want more guidance. In that case, try typing the following into the Input window:

```
help -doc setAttr;
```

When you execute this command, Maya will automatically bring up your browser of choice (usually Netscape Communicator or Microsoft Internet Explorer) and find the right HTML page in your online documents (contained on your hard drive) that contains the command you want help with. In the case of the setAttr statement, you get the following display (this is merely an excerpt—the actual page contains much more information):

Name
    setAttr
Synopsis
    SetAttr
        [flags] object.attribute value [value..]
ReturnValue
    None.
Description
    Sets the value of a dependancy node attribute. No value for
    the attribute is needed when the -l/-k/-s flags are used. The
    -type flag is only required when setting a non-numeric attribute.
    The following chart outlines the syntax of setAttr for non-
    numeric data types:
    {TYPE} below means any number of values of type **TYPE**, separated
    by a space
    [TYPE] means that the value of type **TYPE** is optional
    A|B means that either of **A** or **B** may appear

Examples
sphere -n sphere;
// Set a simple numeric value
setAttr sphere.translateX 5;
// Lock an attribute to prevent further modification
setAttr -lock on sphere.translateX;
// Make an attribute unkeyable
setAttr -keyable off sphere.translateZ;
// Set an entire list of multi-attribute values in one command
setAttr -size 7 "sphereShape.weights[0:6]" 1 1 2 1 1 1 2
// Set an attribute with a compound numeric type
setAttr "sphere.rotate" -type "double3" 0 45 90;
// Set a multi-attribute with a compound numeric type
setAttr "sphereShape.controlPoints[0:2]" -type "double3" 0 0 0 1
    1 1 2 2 2;

As you can see, a few examples can do a lot to clarify how a command is used.

You can also access the entire MEL manual online, for a more in-depth look at the structure of the program itself. In Maya, choose Help ➜ Library, and your Web browser will open to the main reference page. Choose the Using Maya/MEL link, and you will be presented with a menu of introductory material, frequently asked questions, and other resources for learning MEL. Between the internal Help files and the online help on your hard drive, you can access excellent reference material very rapidly.

Examining other users' scripts as guides for what you wish to do is another great way to learn more about MEL—you can even copy and paste portions of scripts for your own use (just be sure that you have the author's permission). See the last section of this chapter, or the new Maya Gems section of the online help, for some example scripts you can study.

Debugging MEL Scripts

If you were careful typing in the last chapter, you may have gotten away without seeing a MEL error; in the work ahead, however (and certainly as you begin building MEL scripts of your own), you will encounter errors, the most common of which is the syntax error. Every command has a particular structure or form that needs to be followed in order to execute successfully. Otherwise, the script interpreter won't know what to do with your command and will most often return a syntax error.

While debugging a script is a bit of an art form, there are a couple of ways you can help yourself. First, check the History window when you execute a script: if the last line of your script is the last line of the History window, the commands executed without an error. If, however, you get a comment line like the following:

```
setAttr tire 5;
//Error:  line 1:  No attribute was specified. //
```

you know that there has been at least one error in parsing the script.

Parsing is the programming term for the search the script interpreter does through the script to make sure all the commands are correct.

The Feedback line (at the bottom right of the screen) will also turn orange-red to indicate that the MEL interpreter has discovered an error in your code. One way to help you quickly identify where these errors might lie is by turning on the Edit ➜ Show Line Numbers option in the Script Editor menu. Generally, it's a good idea to keep this option on at all times, as it does not slow Maya down in any significant way and it provides useful information about where errors are occurring.

As you begin scripting, one error that will probably creep in is forgetting the final semicolon at the end of each line. This can be difficult to spot if you're not aware of the problem. If you are getting errors in your script that don't make sense, try looking at each line of code to be sure it finishes with a semicolon.

Finally, since MEL is an interpreted scripting language, you can execute a script one line at a time, rather than as a whole. This can be a very useful way to figure out where a problem is occurring in your program. A brief exercise will illustrate:

1. Type in the following, but don't execute it yet:

   ```
   print "hello, world!";
   print hello, world;
   ```

2. Now highlight the first line and execute it (by pressing the Enter key on your numeric keypad, or Ctrl+Enter on your keyboard). You should see `hello, world!` printed out in the History window.

3. Now highlight and execute the second line. You should see something like the following:

   ```
   // Error: print hello, world; //
   // Error: Line 1.12: Syntax error //
   ```

The first line executed properly, but the second had an error in it—the `print` command needs a string to work with, and you need to include quote marks to identify the string. In a two-line script, spotting the error would be simple; in a longer script, this method of going through the script one line at a time can be a great way of uncovering problem spots.

Great. We know how to get help and debug a script—now let's get down to business!

Variables, Loops, and Branching

If you've done any programming at all, you've probably been waiting for this point: the main reasons to program are (1) to create flexibility and (2) to do repetitive tasks. Flexibility comes through variables and branching, while repetition is made possible through looping.

Variables

It's actually much easier to see what a variable is than to talk about it. Type the following in the Script Editor:

```
string $myVariable;
$myVariable = "hi there";
print $myVariable;
```

When you execute these commands, you'll see that "hi there" is printed in the last line of the History window, indicating that when you told Maya to print $myVariable, it printed "hi there." The first line of the script, above, is called a declaration of the variable: string is the variable's type (a string is just text contained in quotes), and $myVariable is its name.

Types of MEL Variables

The other types of variables we'll be dealing with are

int   An integer number—used to represent a whole number, like 3 or –45.

float   A decimal number—used to represent a "real" number, like –35.4725.

vector   Three decimal numbers that make a vector number—used to represent a point on a three-dimensional grid, like (26, 31.67, 5.724). A vector number is very useful for three-dimensional information like position (X, Y, Z coordinates) or color (red, green, blue colors).

array   A list of numbers—used to store lists of either integers or floats. Arrays are useful for storing data about many similar items, like the color of each of a group of particles.

We'll examine vectors and arrays more closely when they are needed in the chapter.

Every MEL variable needs to start with the $ symbol, so MEL knows it's a variable. (This is easy to forget, and it causes strange errors—so remember your $ symbol!) The second line is called the assignment line: the text string "hi there" is placed into the variable (or placeholder) for future use. The last line is simply a print statement, telling Maya to print out what's inside the variable, $myVariable (which, in this case, is "hi there"). If we wished, on the following line we could type in

```
$myVariable = "goodbye";
```

which would change the data in the variable $myVariable to the word goodbye. As you may see, variables can be very useful, as they can store different data at different times in a program.

MEL has a convenience feature built into it for variables: you can declare and assign a variable in the same line. In other words, the script above could be written as follows:

```
string $myVariable = "hi there";
```

```
print $myVariable;
```

There is no real difference between the two scripts, except for less typing and a bit easier readability—you are free to use whichever method appeals to you (though most seasoned programmers opt to save keystrokes!).

Looping

Next, let's examine looping. Say you wish to create five spheres in your scene using MEL commands. You could either do this by typing in **sphere -r 1 -n ball** five times, or have MEL do it for you using the for loop. To build our five spheres, type in the following:

```
int $i = 0;
for ($i = 1; $i <= 5; $i++)
    {
    sphere -r 1 -n ball;
    }
```

Voilà, five spheres named ball 1 through 5. (However, you'll need to move them away from each other in order to see them as separate objects. We'll do that in a moment.)

MEL supports implicit variable declaration, so the int $i = 0 *line is not necessary. However, in most cases, it is preferable to declare all variables explicitly to avoid possible complications in the script.*

Note that there is no semicolon after the for statement: MEL expects there to be one or more commands (contained within the { } brackets) after the for statement, so it doesn't need a semicolon. Additionally, the closing bracket, }, functions as a semicolon, so there is no need for a semicolon on the last line either. The syntax for the for loop is as follows:

```
for (initial value; test value; increment)
```

The *initial value* is what the counting variable is set to at the beginning. The *test value* is how high (or low) the number can go before it tests negative—and thus how many loops the counter goes through. The *increment* is how quickly the counter increases in value ($i++ is a simple way of saying "increase the value of $i by 1 each loop").

To make this loop do a bit more for us, let's have it move the spheres on top of each other on the Y axis as it creates them:

```
for ($i = 1; $i<= 5; $i++)
    {
    sphere -r 1 -n ball;
    move -r 0 (2 * $i) 0;
    }
```

Now as the spheres are created, each one is moved up by twice the value of $i, placing them just atop one another.

Branching

The last basic program structure we'll look at is branching, a slightly more complex type of loop that allows MEL to ask a question and decide whether to do some further action given the answer (the for statement actually contains a branch in its *test value* statement). Let's use the same script as above, only this time let's put a conditional statement inside it:

```
for ($i = 1; $i <= 5; $i++)
    {
    sphere -r 1 -n ball;
    if ($i <= 3)
        {
        move -r 0 (2 * $i) 0;
        }
    else
        {
        move -r (2 * $i) 0 0;
        }
    }
```

What happens when you execute these commands? The first three balls are stacked up on the Y axis (when $i is less than or equal to 3), and the last two are stacked along the X axis (when $i is 4 and 5, and therefore greater than 3). In abstract, the syntax for the if statement is as follows:

```
if (test)
    {
    commands;
    }
else if (test)
    {
    commands;
    }
```

```
else
    {
    commands;
    }
```

The else if and else statements do *not* have to exist for the if statement to work. The else if statement, listed above, allows you to make as many tests as you like (there can be as many else if statements as you wish in your conditional statement), allowing you to test for multiple possibilities within one large conditional statement. The else statement must always be last in such examples, and is the "default" answer if no other conditions are met. Note that all the commands for an if, else if, or else statement must be enclosed in { } brackets. If we wish, we could increase the complexity of our create-and-move-ball code with an else if statement:

```
for ($i = 1; $i<= 10; $i++)
    {
    sphere -r 1 -n ball;
    if ($i<=3)
        {
        move -r 0 (2 * $i) 0;
        }
    else if ($i>3 && $i<=6)
        {
        move -r 0 0 (2 * $i);
        }
    else
        {
        move -r (2 * $i) 0 0;
        }
    }
```

Here, the balls will stack along the Y axis if $i is less than or equal to 3, along the Z axis if $i is between 4 and 6, and along the X axis if $i is greater than 6.

If there is only one line of commands after the if statement, you do not need the brackets. However, it's a good idea for readability to always include them anyway.

Now that we have all these time-saving functions at our fingertips, let's revisit a project from the last chapter and make it a bit more useful.

Using Variables, Statements, and Loops in Expressions

Not only can you use variables, conditional statements, and loops in MEL scripts, they can also be used in expressions. Let's take a quick visit back to that sticking tire expression we worked on in the last chapter.

If you don't have the scene saved, open a new scene, create a sphere, name it **tire**, and make a plane under it (scaled to about the size of the default grid, as in Figure 17.1). We're going to take the expression we had before, add variables to it, and add a conditional statement to do different things if the ball is being moved up the Y axis.

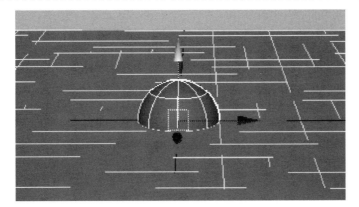

Figure 17.1 *A sphere and a plane*

One thing we haven't yet discussed, but is very important to our work, is the *reverse apostrophe*—the apostrophe that's above the Tab key on the keyboard and looks like this: `. Enclosing a statement in reverse apostrophes tells Maya to evaluate the statement inside them and pass the result on to the variable on the other side of the equation. The statement

```
float $myVariable = `getAttr tire.radius`;
```

returns the decimal (or floating-point) number representing the radius of the *makeNurbsSphere* attribute called tire. As you can probably tell, the ability to get the value of any attribute and read it into a variable is quite powerful. Just remember that this isn't the normal apostrophe that lives on the key with the double quote—type in that apostrophe and you'll get an error!

Now let's redo that expression:

```
float $radius = `getAttr makeNurbSphere1.radius`;
float $pi = 3.1415926;
float $deg = 360;
float $howHi = `getAttr tire.translateY`;
if ($howHi != $radius)
    {
    tire.translateY = $radius;
    }
tire.rotateZ = - (tire.translateX * ($deg / (2 * $pi *
$radius)));
```

The first four statements declare and assign values to variables. $pi is the value of π; $deg is the number of degrees in a circle. Having these variables in the expression just makes reading the equation below easier. The two variables $radius and $howHi are assigned values by using reverse apostrophes to enclose getAttr statements. The reverse apostrophes "evaluate" the getAttr statements and then read the sphere's radius and Y position into the variables. (Note that the attribute for radius belongs to the makeNurbSphere node, not the transform node.)

The conditional statement asks whether the Y position is different than the sphere's radius (!= is MEL's "not equal" operator). If so, it places the sphere directly on top of the plane (1 radius above 0). Also notice that the equation for Z rotation has been modified to take the sphere's radius into account now (the rotation angle being equal to 2πr, from high school math classes). With this equation, no matter how big or small the sphere is, it will always sit right on the plane and will roll without slipping!

Using variables and a conditional statement, we have reworked the simple one-line expression of the previous chapter into a flexible tool that can be used in varying situations.

We'll return to variables, looping, and branching as this chapter continues, but now let's turn to how to create a GUI in Maya.

Creating a GUI

While typing commands into the Command line or Input window of the Script Editor is very useful for simple tasks, it is often much more elegant (not to mention user-friendly) to create a graphical user interface window in your script to give users access to all the script's commands in a comfortable point-and-click environment. While creating these windows can be somewhat challenging, nearly all high-quality scripts use them, so it is good to learn at least the basics of GUI creation using MEL.

Windows in Maya can be very complex (just look at the Attribute Editor window for an example), but the basic way to create a window is fairly simple. At a minimum, you need three commands to make a window:

```
window -title "title" -wh 400 200 myWindow;
some kind of layout;
showWindow;
```

Executing the window command creates a window with a name that appears at its top (the -title flag), optionally a predefined width and height (the -widthHeight or -wh flag), and an optional name (the last item in the window command). Note that the title of a window and its name are *not* the same. Maya refers to the myWindow name, while a user would see the window's title.

The showWindow command makes the window appear on-screen (it will never appear if you forget this line)—this command usually resides at the end of a "make window" series of commands.

The layout commands specify what sort of layout the window will have. Some common types are columnLayout, scrollLayout, rowColumnLayout, and formLayout. The column layout creates a column, the scroll layout makes the window a scrollable window, the row-and-column layout makes a grid of rows and columns (like a table), and the form layout creates a flexible space that can be laid out in many ways. These layouts can also contain other layouts nested within them, creating the ability to make very complex windows relatively easily (the form layout is often the parent layout, with many other layouts inside it).

Let's create a simple window with one button and one slider in it. Type the following into the Script Editor:

```
window -t "The Big Window!" -wh 400 200 myWindow;
columnLayout -cw 200;
button -l "Click this button" myButton;
text " ";
attrFieldSliderGrp -l "Slide this around" -min 0 -max 10
theSliderGroup;
showWindow myWindow;
```

These commands create a window (which Maya knows as myWindow but, as you see in Figure 17.2, is titled "The Big Window!") with a width of 400 and a height of 200 pixels. A column layout is then set with a width of 200 pixels. Next, a button (labeled "Click this button" and known to Maya as myButton) is created; then a field-and-slider group is created (labeled "Slide this around" and known as theSliderGroup) with a minimum value of 0 and a maximum value of 10. The text command just puts a space in between the button and the slider group. Finally, we display the window via the showWindow command. Obviously it's not too difficult to create windows with buttons, sliders, or other objects in them.

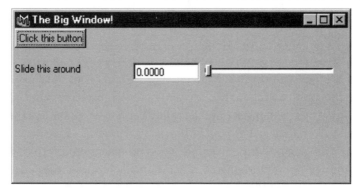

Figure 17.2 *The big window*

If you make some errors typing in the MEL script and then go back and try to run the script again, when you try to recreate the window, you may run into the following error: Error: Object's name is not unique: myWindow. *If you get this message, you need to delete the window* myWindow: *even though it doesn't appear onscreen, MEL has created a UI object named* myWindow *(note that the* showWindow *command is last, so an object can be created and not shown). Thus, while* myWindow *doesn't appear, it can exist in your scene, and it needs to be deleted. To do this, type* deleteUI myWindow *in the Command line or Script Editor and execute it. This is a very useful command to remember as you create GUI windows, so commit it to memory.*

Now let's make our buttons do something. Clear all objects in your scene and create a sphere called "ball." Edit your script to include the −command and −attribute flags, as follows:

```
window -t "The Big Window!" -wh 400 200 myWindow;
columnLayout -cw 200;
button -l "Press this button" -c "setAttr ball.ty  5" myButton;
text " ";
attrFieldSliderGrp -l "Slide this around" -min 0 -max 10 -at
("ball.tx") theSliderGroup;
showWindow myWindow;
```

The −c flag for button tells Maya to perform the quoted instruction each time the button is pressed. Thus, when this button is pressed, Maya sets the ball's Y position to 5 units. The −at flag in the slider group tells Maya to connect the slider and text field to the quoted attribute (in this case, the X position of the ball). When you click the button, the ball jumps up to 5 on the Y axis. When you slide the slider (or enter numbers in the text field), the ball moves back and forth between 0 and 10 on the X axis.

You can set the slider and text field to have different minimum and maximum values. The −fmn and −fmx flags give the field's min and max values. The −smn and −smx flags give the slider's min and max values. This allows the user to enter numbers outside the slider's bounds, which can be useful.

You can also create radio buttons and check boxes that perform functions when selected (see the MEL documentation for more information on these).

As an exercise, what command could you place on the button to make the ball move up 5 units every time the button is pressed? Hint: it's relative motion instead of absolute.

Now that you've seen how quickly you can create a basic window as an interface to your scripts, let's make a script that automatically creates a useful window for you. Make a new scene, and then create several lights and aim them at an object in the scene (you could use the "create lights" shelf button you made in the last chapter to do this for you automatically—or you could open a scene you have already created that includes several lights in it). Now enter the following in your Script Editor window:

```
string $sel[] = `ls -lights`;
string $current;
string $winName = "lightWindow";
if (`window -exists $winName`)
    {
    deleteUI $winName;
    }
window -title "Lights" -wh 600 300 $winName;
scrollLayout;
rowColumnLayout -nc 2 -cw 1 150 -cw 2 400;
for ($current in $sel)
    {
    text -l $current;
    attrFieldSliderGrp -min (-1) -max 10 -at ($current +
".intensity");
    }
showWindow $winName;
```

When you execute this script, Maya will automatically create a "light board" for you, allowing you to control the intensity of all lights in the scene from one floating window.

The most interesting portion of this script is the first line:

```
string $sel[] = `ls -lights`;
```

This line assigns to the variable string array $sel[] the name of every light in the scene. The [] after the variable name tells Maya this variable is an array, or list of variables, starting with the number 0. If there were three elements in the list, they would be $sel[0], $sel[1], and $sel[2]. By declaring one array, then, you get three (or four, or however many you want) variables for the price of one! The ls command tells Maya to list the items that come after (in this case, -lights means "list all lights in the scene"); then the reverse apostrophes tell Maya to evaluate this command (which returns the name of each light) and read the result into the array, $sel[].

Next, other variables are declared to store the "current item" ($current) and the window name ($winName), and the script checks to see whether the window already exists—if it does, the script kills the old window (using the deleteUI command) so it can write a new one. This little piece of code is good to include in all your GUI scripts, to ensure that you don't accidentally generate any errors if a window by that name already exists. Then a window is created with a scroll layout (so the window can scroll if it's too small) and a row/column layout (a table). Next the script performs a variation of the for loop, called the for...in loop. The for...in loop looks through an array (in this case, $sel[]) and does one loop for each item it finds, placing the value of $sel[number] in the variable $current.

The type of $current must therefore match the type of $sel[] (in this case, they're both strings).

As you can see in Figure 17.3, the loop then prints out the name of the light (in column 1) and makes a field slider group that's attached to the light's intensity setting (in column 2).

Figure 17.3 *A GUI window showing light controls*

If you only wanted the lights you have previously selected in the scene to be in the window, you could add the flag -selected to the ls command on the first line.

This little script should indicate how powerful a workflow-enhancer MEL can be: in just a few lines of script, you have created a way to control potentially dozens of lights in a complex scene in a completely simple, intuitive manner. If you needed to create just the right light levels on twenty lights in a scene, it could take hours navigating to each light and adjusting it individually. This script could make the job a ten-minute effort instead!

As an exercise, try creating sliders that let you adjust the light's colors as well as its intensity (hint: there are three attributes, colorR, colorG, and colorB, which control the red, green, and blue intensities). If you really want to get crazy, try placing each group of controls for each light in its own sub-window (so intensity, colorR, colorG, and colorB are all inside a window). You'll need to know about the setParent command, as well as how to make a frame layout with the flag -cll (collapsible) set to true (to make each window close by clicking its triangle). You could also add check boxes to turn off each light's visibility, so that you can see the effects of each light separately. You can find help for these commands in Maya's online reference documents, and if you get stuck, there is a finished MEL script listed at the end of this chapter and included on the CD.

Using Procedures and Scripts

In this chapter and the preceding one, we've touched on most of the basic elements of MEL. However, all the pieces we've created so far won't work very well if we try to give them to someone else or save them to our scripts directory. We haven't done anything to save the commands we've written in a format that Maya can read as a whole. Now, we need to learn how to make these bits of code into full-fledged ("stand-alone") scripts that you can port from one place to another and trade with others.

In this section we'll look at procedures and scripts. A *procedure* is the basic building block of a MEL script. At its most fundamental level, it's simply another declaration line that tells Maya that all the contained lines form one named function. A *script* is just a collection of one or more procedures.

Procedures

In abstract, a procedure would look like this:

```
proc myProcedure ()
{
```

```
commands
}
```

Maya will execute all the commands contained in the curly braces every time you type **myProcedure** into the Command line or the Script Editor's Input window. MyProcedure is the name of the procedure, and the parentheses can contain any number of declared variables that can either be called from another procedure or entered by the user when executing the procedure. As a simple example, let's make a procedure that will create a user-defined number of—you guessed it—spheres.

```
global proc makeBall (int $num)
{
int $num;
for ($i = 1; $i <= $num; $i++)
    {
    sphere -r 1 -name ("ball" + $i);
    }
}
```

Enter this text into the Script Editor, then execute it. You will notice that nothing happens in Maya. This is because the script as a whole has been "sourced" into Maya's memory. As the script now resides in memory, whenever you type **makeBall** into the Command line or Input window, followed by an integer number, you'll get that many spheres (called ball1, ball2, etc.) in your scene. Typing **makeBall 5**, for example, would make five spheres named ball1 through ball5 in your scene. We've made this procedure "global" so that Maya can reference the procedure from within your \Winnt\Profiles\<user name>\maya\scripts (for Windows) directory (more on this in a moment).

You know that a procedure is just a bunch of MEL commands contained in braces and given a name; so how would you turn our series of light-board commands into a procedure? If you can't guess, it would look something like this:

```
global proc lightBoard ()
{
string $sel[] = `ls -lights`;
string $current;
string $winName = "lightWindow";
if (`window -exists $winName`)
    {
    deleteUI $winName;
    }
window -title "Lights" -wh 400 300 $winName;
scrollLayout;
```

```
rowColumnLayout -nc 2 -cw 1 150 -cw 2 400;
for ($current in $sel)
    {
    text -l $current;
    attrFieldSliderGrp -min (-1) -max 10 -at ($current +
".intensity");
    }
showWindow $winName;
}
```

Once you source (enter) this procedure, each time you type **lightBoard** in the Command line, the procedure will run and you will get a light board for all your lights.

Scripts

What is the difference between a procedure and a script? A script is just a collection of one or more procedures. Thus, the lightBoard procedure we just wrote is actually a script as well. A true script is also saved as an external text file and given a name, which must end in .mel, and the name of the script *must* be the same as the name of the *last* (global) procedure in the script (plus the .mel extension). For our light-board example, we would save the script as lightBoard.mel, and store it in our \Profiles\<user name>\maya\ scripts directory (when you choose Save Selected from the Script Editor's menu, this is the default directory that shows up, so just save it there).

Now let's make a simple script that contains two procedures, to see how that's done.

```
//Source this script, and then type "makeBall <number>" in
//the Command line or Script Editor.  The procedure will make
//the number of spheres you specify, and call them "ball1,"
//"ball2," etc.
//Created by:  John Kundert-Gibbs.
//Last Modified:  October 24, 2000.
//Use at your own risk.

//makeIt creates the spheres and gives them names.
//This procedure is passed the number of balls you specify
//from the main procedure.
proc makeIt (int $theNum)
{
//$theNum must be redeclared internal to the procedure.
int $theNum;
for ($i=1; $i<=$theNum; $i++)
    {
```

```
    sphere -r 1 -name ("ball" + $i);
    }
}
//end, makeIt.

//makeBall is the main procedure you call.
//It just calls the procedure makeIt and passes it the number
//of spheres you specify.
global proc makeBall (int $num)
{
int $num;
makeIt ($num);
} //end, makeBall.
```

All we've done with this script is to create a subprocedure that will actually make the spheres. The main (or global) procedure merely calls the subprocedure (this is often the case with very complex scripts—just look at the end of a script, and you'll often find a very small procedure that simply calls all the other ones in the script). Note that the *last* procedure is the one that you call by typing **makeBall 5** in the Command line. This is (and should be) the only global procedure in the script—the makeIt procedure being a local procedure (and therefore not visible to Maya outside the script).

A Comment on Commenting

Notice that the script in the previous section is commented extensively (with all the // lines). At the very least, you should put in lines at the top of the script about what the script does, what arguments (inputs) it needs, who wrote (and modified) it, and when it was last modified. It's not a bad idea to also put in a "use at your own risk" line to indicate that some unforeseen problem could arise while using the script, and that the author is not responsible for any mishaps because of the script's usage (ah, the joys of a litigious society!). It is also a very good idea to comment the beginning and end of every procedure (so it's easy to read where they start and stop), and to comment any particularly tricky portions of a script.

You may think these comments are of use only to others and not yourself, and you'd rather not bother with them if you don't plan to distribute the script. But remember that two months after you create the script, you may need to modify it, and if you can't figure out what you did or why, you'll waste a great deal of time hunting through the script instead of getting right to your modifications.

Don't get lazy! *Always comment your scripts well (even the simplest ones). It's a habit (and for once, a good one), so get into it!*

Learning from the Masters

No matter how much you learn in these chapters, space and time simply aren't sufficient here for you to learn everything MEL has to offer. One of the best ways to continue learning MEL is, quite simply, to look at (and copy from) other people's scripts. If you can go through each line of a script and figure out what it does, you will learn a great deal. Better yet, if you can grab some code someone else wrote and modify it to do what you want it to, you can really start to put together some neat and useful scripts to solve your everyday work bottlenecks.

To begin your journey of discovery, let's take a quick peek at four scripts (they are all contained on the CD that comes with this book, so you don't have to type them in). So that you get used to reading commented scripts, all comments about the scripts are *inside* the scripts, rather than here.

There seems to be a problem with the way Maya "sees" (locates) some procedures and variables unless they are declared global. This is poor programming practice but apparently necessary, so many of the procedures and variables that follow are global.

The lightBoard Script

First is a reshaping of the lightBoard script we worked on in this chapter into a fairly robust tool for the user.

```
//script lightBoard
//Source this script; create and position one or more lights
//in your scene.  Then type "lightBoard" in the Command line.
//The script will generate a set of collapsible windows
//(one for each light) that control each light's intensity,
//RGB colors, and visibility.
//Created by John Kundert-Gibbs
//Last Modified: November 15, 1999.
//Use this script at your own risk.
//The check procedure just checks to see if the window already
//exists.  If so, it kills the old window.
```

```
proc check (string $theName)
{
string $theName;
if (`window -exists $theName`)
    {
    deleteUI $theName;
    }
} //end, check.

//beginning, lightBoard
//This is the script's main (global) procedure.
global proc lightBoard ()
{
string $sel[] = `ls -lights`;
string $current;
string $winName = "lightWindow";
string $main = "mainWindow";
int $count = 0;

check ($winName);

window -title "Light Board" -wh 600 300 $winName;

scrollLayout;
rowColumnLayout -nc 1 -cw 1 500 ($main);

for ($current in $sel)
    {
    $count++;

    //The -cll flag in the frameLayout command means that
    //the window will collapse when the user clicks the
    //triangle next to the window.
    frameLayout -cll true -w 400 ($current);
    rowColumnLayout -nc 1 -cw 1 400;

    attrFieldSliderGrp -min (-1) -max 10 -at ($current +
".intensity");
    text " ";
    attrFieldSliderGrp -min 0 -max 1 -at ($current + ".colorR");
    text " ";
    attrFieldSliderGrp -min 0 -max 1 -at ($current + ".colorG");
```

```
      text " ";
      attrFieldSliderGrp -min 0 -max 1 -at ($current + ".colorB");
      text " ";

      //The visibility slider group was intended to be a check
      //box for visibility.  However, the checkbox group doesn't
      //properly connect to attributes when it's created in a
      //for loop, so a slider group was created instead.
      //The -s flag set the step value to 1 (meaning an integer
      //jump) so the group is either 1 or 0.

      attrFieldSliderGrp -min 0 -max 1 -vis on -at ($current +
".visibility") -s 1;

      //The setParent command sets the focus of the window back
      //to the rowColumnLayout above.  Thus, the windows are
      //stacked below each other instead of inside each other.

      setParent $main;
      }
showWindow $winName;
} //end, lightBoard.
```

The setPose Script

The next script is a way to adjust all keyable attributes of a selected set of objects (for example, joints in an IK body), key each one individually, key all, record a "default" pose, and go back to that pose. Like the light-board script, this window can be a real time saver when it comes to keying complex motion.

```
//script setPose
//Source this script; select several objects, or joints in a
//character; type in "setPose" in the Command line.
//You will get a window that allows you to manipulate all
//keyable attributes on the selected objects.
//Additionally, you can record a "default" pose and go back to
//that pose.  You can also keyframe any or all attributes.
//Modified by John Kundert-Gibbs
//Last Modified: October 24, 2000.

//Procedure to perform a loop, keying all attributes in the
//window.
```

```
//This procedure is global because otherwise Maya won't see it.
global proc keyAll ()
{
global string $list[];
string $current;
string $Attr;

for ($current in $list)
    {
    string $attrLST[] = `listAttr -k $current`;
    for ($Attr in $attrLST)
        {
        setKeyframe ($current + "." + $Attr);
        }
    }
} //end, keyAll

//Procedure to record the current value of all attributes in
//the window. This creates a 'default' pose one can return to.
//This procedure is global because otherwise Maya won't see it.
global proc recDefault ()
{
global float $gDefault2[];
global string $list[];
string $current;
string $Attr;
int $j = 0;

for ($current in $list)
    {
    string $attrLST[] = `listAttr -k $current`;

    for ($Attr in $attrLST)
        {
        $gDefault2[$j] = `getAttr ($current + "." + $Attr)`;
        print ($current + "." + $Attr +"\n");
        $j++;
        }
    }
} //end, recDefault

//Procedure to return all attributes in the window to their
```

```
//default values, as recorded in the procedure above.
//This procedure is global because otherwise Maya won't see it.
global proc gotoDefault ()
{
global float $gDefault2[];
global string $list[];
string $current;
string $Attr;
int $j = 0;

for ($current in $list)
    {
    string $attrLST[] = `listAttr -k $current`;
    for ($Attr in $attrLST)
        {
        setAttr ($current + "." + $Attr) $gDefault2[$j];
        $j++;
        }
    }
} //end, gotoDefault

//Main procedure.
global proc setPose ()
{
global string $list[];
$list = `ls -sl`;
string $current;
string $Attr;
string $main = "mainWindow";

window -t "Set Pose";
scrollLayout;
columnLayout ($main);

text -l "Keyable Attributes";
text -l " ";

button -l "Record Default Pose" -w 200 -c "recDefault";
button -l "Go To Default Pose" -w 200 -c "gotoDefault";
text " ";
button -l "Key All" -w 100 -c "keyAll";
text -l " ";
```

```
for ($current in $list)
    {
    frameLayout -cll true  -h 380 -w 600 ($current);
    scrollLayout;
    gridLayout -nc 2 -cw 400;

    string $attrLST[] = `listAttr -k $current`;

    for ($Attr in $attrLST)
        {
        attrFieldSliderGrp -smn -100 -smx 100 -fmn -1000 -fmx
1000 -at ($current + "." + $Attr);
        button -l "Keyframe" -w 100 -c ("setKeyframe " + $current
+ "." + $Attr);
        }

    setParent $main;
    text " ";
    }

showWindow;
} //end, setPose
```

The makeChain Script

This script revisits the chain of rigid body links we made in Chapter 15, "Working with Rigid Body Dynamics." Here, instead of creating the links by coding MEL directly, we copied chunks of MEL output from the History window and reworked it into a flexible script that builds the links for you (with a heavy ball at the bottom). With all that goes on in this script, it appears pretty complex, but remember that we built this script up in pieces, mostly by modifying MEL output as we performed each command.

```
//script makeChain
//Source this script; then type "makeChain <number of links>"
//in the Command line.
//The script will generate a series of linked loops (like a
//swing chain) that are all connected and have gravity
//attached to them.  It also creates a ball called weight,
//at the bottom of the chain, and makes the ball (and chain)
//swing. There may be some rigid body interpenetration
//warnings, depending on how many links you have.
//Created by John Kundert-Gibbs
```

```
//Last Modified: October 18, 1999.
//Use this script at your own risk.

//Procedure that actually builds the chains
proc makeEm (int $num)
{
string $linkName = "linkNum";
float $moveNum = -5.160681;
float $offSetNum = 1.741263;
gravity -pos 0 0 0 -m 9.8 -dx 0 -dy -1 -dz 0 ;

cylinder -n mainBar -p 0 0 0 -ax 0 1 0 -ssw 0 -esw 360 -r 1 -hr 2
-d 3 -ut 0 -tol 0.01 -s 8 -nsp 1 -ch 1; objectMoveCommand;

setAttr "mainBar.rotateX" 90;
scale -r 1 5.995727 1 ;
scale -r 1 1.530854 1 ;

torus -n embeddedLink -p 0 0 0 -ax 0 1 0 -ssw 0 -esw 360 -msw 360
-r 1 -hr 0.2 -d 3 -ut 0 -tol 0.01 -s 8 -nsp 4 -ch 1;
objectMoveCommand;
setAttr "embeddedLink.rotateX" 90;
scale -r 1 1 2.188674 ;
move -r 0 -1.910194 0 ;

select -cl;
select -r mainBar embeddedLink;
rigidBody -passive -m 1 -dp 0 -sf 0.2 -df 0.2 -b 0.6 -l 0 -tf 200
-iv 0 0 0 -iav 0 0 0 -c 0 -pc 0 -i 0 0 0 -imp 0 0 0 -si 0 0 0 -
sio none ;

for ($i=1; $i <= $num; $i++)
    {
    select -cl;

    torus -n ($linkName + $i) -p 0 0 0 -ax 0 1 0 -ssw 0 -esw 360
-msw 360 -r 1 -hr 0.2 -d 3 -ut 0 -tol 0.01 -s 8 -nsp 4 -ch 1;
objectMoveCommand;
    setAttr ($linkName + $i + ".rotateX") 90;
    setAttr ($linkName + $i + ".rotateY") (90 * $i);
    scale -r 1 1 2.210896 ;
    if ($i == 1)
```

```
            move -r 0 $moveNum 0 ;
        else
            move -r 0 ((($moveNum + $offSetNum) * $i) - $offSetNum) 0;

        rigidBody -active -m 1 -dp 0 -sf 0.2 -df 0.2 -b 0.6 -l 0 -tf
200 -iv 0 0 0 -iav 0 0 0 -c 0 -pc 0 -i 0 0 0 -imp 0 0 0 -si 0 0 0
-sio none ;

        connectDynamic -f gravityField1 ($linkName + $i);
        }
} //end, makeEm

//Procedure to add the ball to the bottom of the chain
proc addBall (int $num)
{
float $moveNum = -5.160681;
float $offSetNum = 1.741263;
string $linkName = "linkNum";

select -cl;
sphere -n weight -r 2;
move -r 0 ((($moveNum + $offSetNum) * $num - $offSetNum - 5)) 0 ;
select -cl ;

//Now select the last link and the "weight" ball, and make a
//pin constraint.
select -r ($linkName + $num) ;
select -tgl weight ;
constrain -pin -i 0 ;
select -cl ;

//Make the sphere's weight 50, connect gravity to it,
//and create an expression to drive the weight back and
//forth in X (impulseX).
select -r weight ;
setAttr ("rigidBody" + ($num + 3) + ".mass") 50;
connectDynamic -f gravityField1 weight;

//The next line actually adds an expression to the weight
//ball, driving it back and forth.
//How cool is that?!
```

```
expression -s "impulseX = 5 * sin (2 * time);" -o ("rigidBody" +
($num + 3)) -ae 1 -uc all ;
} //end, makeBall

//Main procedure
global proc makeChain (int $numLinks)
{
makeEm ($numLinks);
//Comment out the following line if you don't want the ball
//at the bottom of the chain.
addBall ($numLinks);

select -cl;
select -all;
displaySmoothness -divisionsU 3 -divisionsV 3 -pointsWire 16 -
pointsShaded 4;

//Change some elements of the rigid solver so Maya
//doesn't choke on the data!
showEditor rigidSolver;
setAttr "rigidSolver.collisionTolerance" 0.0001;
setAttr "rigidSolver.bounciness" 0;
} //end, makeChain
```

The firecracker Script

The final script is a fun one: it creates a fully textured firecracker complete with burning fuse that explodes after a user-controlled amount of time, with a user-controlled force (power), and burns with a user-controlled density of sparks—and all of these controls are available after the firecracker is built. (Render the animation out to see the fuse burn down, because the OpenGL renderer cannot display the transparency properly. A rendered movie of the firecracker at work—17firecracker.mov— is on the CD.)

*This script includes some multiple-line expressions. To make these follow good MEL script form, we need new-line (\n) and tab characters. But a "tab" isn't going to show up in the book, so for the printed version we've inserted the word **TAB** in bold. Wherever you see **TAB** in bold, type a tab as you work with this script.*

```
//Script, firecracker
//This script builds an exploding firecracker with fuse
//according to your controls.
//Place this script in your <name>/Maya/scripts directory, or
//source it in the Script Editor, then type firecracker in the
```

```
//Command line.
//A window will open that allows you to control the fuse time
//(how long the fuse burns), the power of the explosion, and
//how many sparks the fuse will produce. Upon clicking the
//"build firecracker" button, the firecracker will be built
//(including basic textures, which you can later adjust), a
//light added to the scene, and the channel box will be set to
//the (invisible) locator which contains the timer, power, and
//sparks attributes.

//You can freely adjust these settings after running the script,
//so you don't have to relaunch the script if you wish to adjust
//any of the 3 settings after the firecracker has been built.

//Note:  The fuse acutally burns down when the firecracker is
//lit (the portion above the burning section becomes invisible).
//However, you cannot see this with the OpenGL renderer: you
//need to render the images out with the software renderer in
//order to see this effect.

//Note: This script will work properly _only_ with Maya 3 or
//higher (the random lifespan function for particles is only
//available with Maya 3).

//Copyright 2000 by John L. Kundert-Gibbs
//Anyone may use and modify this script, as long as credit is
//given to the author for the original script.
//Last Modified: October 24, 2000.
//Use and modify at your own risk.

//check checks for the build firecracker window. If it already
//exists, this procedure deletes it.
proc check (string $myName)
{
string $myName;
if (`window -exists $myName`)
    deleteUI $myName;
} //end, proc check

//build does most of the work of this script.  It creates the
//geometry, rigid bodies, fields, materials, lights, and
//expressions that become the firecracker.
```

```
//This procedure is global because otherwise Maya won't see it.
global proc build (string $theName)
{

//$framesps is set to 24, for film rate, by default.  If you
//use another frame rate for your scene (like 25 or 30),
//change this number to your frame rate.
//This procedure is global because otherwise Maya won't see it.
global float $framesps = 24;
string $theName;

//Build the components of the firecracker: two half cylinders
//(moved on the Y axis so the touch at 0), a curve, and then a
//circle which is extruded along the curve.

//First, build the two cylinders and display them at high
quality.
cylinder -p 0 0 0 -ax 0 1 0 -ssw 0 -esw 360 -r 1 -hr 2 -d 3 -ut 0
-tol 0.01 -s 8 -nsp 1 -ch 1; nurbsPrimitiveCap 2 1 0;
objectMoveCommand;
displaySmoothness -divisionsU 3 -divisionsV 3 -pointsWire 16 -
pointsShaded 4;
subdivDisplaySmoothness -smoothness 3;
setAttr "nurbsCylinder1.translateY" 1;
cylinder -p 0 0 0 -ax 0 1 0 -ssw 0 -esw 360 -r 1 -hr 2 -d 3 -ut 0
-tol 0.01 -s 8 -nsp 1 -ch 1; nurbsPrimitiveCap 1 1 0;
objectMoveCommand;
setAttr "nurbsCylinder2.translateY" -1;
displaySmoothness -divisionsU 3 -divisionsV 3 -pointsWire 16 -
pointsShaded 4;
subdivDisplaySmoothness -smoothness 3;
select -d nurbsCylinder2 ;

//Now build a curve and extrude a circle along it.
curve -d 3 -p 0.236052 2.424893 0  -p 0.262191 2.060595 0 -p
0.310557 1.386551 0 -p -0.956312 0.897331 0  -p -0.340486
0.319486 0  -p 0 0 0 -k 0 -k 0 -k 0 -k 1.053471 -k 1.905378 -k
2.907319 -k 2.907319 -k 2.907319 ;
setAttr "curve1.translateY" 2;
circle -c 0 0 0 -nr 0 1 0 -sw 360 -r 1 -d 3 -ut 0 -tol 0.01 -s 8
-ch 1; objectMoveCommand;
setAttr "nurbsCircle1.scaleX" .1;
```

```
setAttr "nurbsCircle1.scaleY" .1;
setAttr "nurbsCircle1.scaleZ" .1;
move -r 0 4.463519 0 ;
move -r 0.234772 0 0 ;
move -r 0 -0.0397919 0 ;
select -tgl curve1 ;
move -r 0 -0.106119 0 ;
extrude -ch true -rn false -po 0 -et 2 -ucp 0 -fpt 1 -upn 1 -
rotation 0 -scale 1 -rsp 1 "nurbsCircle1" "curve1" ;
select -cl ;

//Next, delete the circle, and smooth display the fuse.
select -r nurbsCircle1 ;
delete;
select -r extrudedSurface1 ;
displaySmoothness -divisionsU 3 -divisionsV 3 -pointsWire 16 -
pointsShaded 4;
subdivDisplaySmoothness -smoothness 3;

//Turn the two cylinders into rigid bodies.
select -r nurbsCylinder1 ;
rigidBody -active -m 1 -dp 0.2 -sf 1 -df 1 -b 0 -l 0 -tf 200 -iv
0 0 0 -iav 0 0 0 -c 0 -pc 0 -i 0 0 0 -imp 0 0 0 -si 0 0 0 -sio
none ;
select -r nurbsCylinder2 ;
rigidBody -active -m 1 -dp 0.2 -sf 1 -df 1 -b 0 -l 0 -tf 200 -iv
0 0 0 -iav 0 0 0 -c 0 -pc 0 -i 0 0 0 -imp 0 0 0 -si 0 0 0 -sio
none ;
select -cl ;

//Make the curve and extruded surface children of cylinder 1.
parent curve1 nurbsCylinder1;
parent extrudedSurface1 nurbsCylinder1;

//Create an emitter and move it into place.
emitter -pos 0 0 0 -type omni  -name exhaustEmitter -r 200 -sro 0
-nuv 0 -cye frame -cyi 10 -spd 10 -srn 0 -nsp 1 -tsp 0 -mxd 0 -
mnd 0 -dx 0 -dy 1 -dz 0 -sp 1 ;
particle;
connectDynamic -em exhaustEmitter particle1;
move -r 0 4.297956 0 ;
move -r 0.219112 0 0 ;
```

```
//Turn off visibility of the emitter-this is purely for
//aesthetic reasons, as the emitter gets double transformed
//once the upper cylinder begins to move.  As the double
//transform doesn't affect the rendered results, this was an
//easier fix than to remove the double transform.
setAttr "exhaustEmitter.visibility" off;
select -r particle1 ;

//Adjust a bunch of settings affecting how the particles look.
//The final result is a cloud (software) particle that looks
//something like sparks.  You can adjust the default volume
//texture to get a look you like better.
setAttr particleShape1.particleRenderType 8;
addAttr -is true -ln "betterIllumination" -at bool -dv false
particleShape1;
addAttr -is true -ln "surfaceShading" -at "float" -min 0 -max 1 -
dv 0 particleShape1;
addAttr -is true -ln "threshold" -at "float" -min 0 -max 10 -dv 0
particleShape1;
addAttr -is true -ln "radius" -at "float" -min 0 -max 20 -dv 1
particleShape1;
setAttr "particleShape1.radius" 0.3;
setAttr "particleShape1.threshold" 0.7;
setAttr "particleShape1.surfaceShading" 0;
setAttr "particleCloud1.color" -type double3 0.815 0.298418
0.17115 ;
setAttr "particleCloud1.glowIntensity" 0.40498;

//Adjust the particle lifespan to the new random range type.
//Works with Maya 3 or higher only!
setAttr particleShape1.lifespanMode 2;
setAttr "particleShape1.lifespanRandom" 0.7;
setAttr "particleShape1.generalSeed" 65485;

//Create gravity, connect it to the particles, then make the
//emitter a child of the fuse.
gravity -pos 0 0 0 -m 20 -att 0 -dx 0 -dy -1 -dz 0 -mxd -1 -vsh
none -vex 0 -vof 0 0 0 -vsw 360 -tsr 0.5 ;
connectDynamic -f gravityField1 particle1;
parent exhaustEmitter extrudedSurface1;
```

```
//Now create a path animation that makes the emitter travel
//down the fuse as it "burns".
select -r exhaustEmitter ;
select -tgl curve1 ;
pathAnimation -fractionMode true -follow true -followAxis z -
upAxis y -worldUpType "vector" -worldUpVector 0 1 0 -inverseUp
false -inverseFront false -bank false -startTimeU 0 -endTimeU
(`getAttr locator1.timer`*$framesps);

//Now we'll create an emitter that blasts out fragments when the
//firecracker explodes, and connect its particles to gravity.
emitter -pos 0 0 0 -type omni  -name blastEmitter -r 0 -sro 0 -
nuv 0 -cye frame -cyi 10 -spd 50 -srn 0 -nsp 1 -tsp 0 -mxd 0 -mnd
0 -dx 0 -dy 1 -dz 0 -sp 1 ;
particle;
connectDynamic -em blastEmitter particle2;
connectDynamic -f gravityField1  particle2;
select -cl ;

//Next, we create a volume shader for the blast particles,
//coloring them a similar color to the body of the firecracker
//(see below).
shadingNode -asShader particleCloud;
sets -renderable true -noSurfaceShader true -empty -name
particleCloud2SG;
connectAttr -f particleCloud2.outColor
particleCloud2SG.volumeShader;
setAttr "particleCloud2.color" -type double3 0.72045 0.75 0.30675;

//Select the particles and assign the material to them.
select -r particle2 ;
sets -e -forceElement particleCloud2SG;
select -cl ;

//Now adjust the render type to tubes, and adjust settings
//to create blast fragments.
setAttr particleShape2.particleRenderType 9;
addAttr -is true -ln "radius0" -at "float" -min 0 -max 10 -dv 1
particleShape2;
addAttr -is true -ln "radius1" -at "float" -min 0 -max 10 -dv 1
particleShape2;
```

```
addAttr -is true -ln "tailSize" -at "float" -min 0 -max 30 -dv 1
particleShape2;
setAttr "particleShape2.radius0" 0.3;
setAttr "particleShape2.radius1" 0.1;
setAttr "particleShape2.tailSize" 0.5;


//Now for some expressions to control burn time, power, etc.

//This expression is a cheat to allow the path animation's
//timing to be adjusted as the user changes the locator1.timer
//controls in the channel box.  If this expression were not
//included, the path animation would always be set at the
//original value, and it would not time out properly with any
//later adjustments the user made to the controls.
expression -s "if (time < locator1.timer)\r\nkeyframe -option
over -index 1 -absolute -timeChange (`getAttr
locator1.timer`*$framesps) motionPath1_uValue ;\r"  -o
exhaustEmitter -ae 1 -uc all ;

//This expression controls emitter rate for the fuse, turning
//it on and off at the proper time and having the emitter react
//to user controls for the amount of sparks emitted.
expression -s "if (time <
locator1.timer)\r\nTABexhaustEmitter.rate =
(locator1.sparks*10);\r\nelse exhaustEmitter.rate = 0;"  -o
exhaustEmitter -ae 1 -uc all ;

//This expression controls the emitter rate and speed for the
//explosion fragments, based on the locator1.power setting.
//Note that the time test (at the beginning) is not an equality
//(==) but rather a small range.  This provides for inaccuracies
//between exact frame time and the timer slider control time.
expression -s "if (time > locator1.timer - 0.05 && time <
locator1.timer + 0.05)\r\n{\r\nTABblastEmitter.rate =
(locator1.power*20);\r\n blastEmitter.speed =
(locator1.power);\r\n}\r\nelse blastEmitter.rate = 0;"  -o
blastEmitter -ae 1 -uc all ;
//These two expressions control the explosion, turning on a
//one-frame Y impulse (plus spin impulses in X and Z) at the
//specific time the fuse burns out.  Note that the time test
//(at the beginning) is not an equality (==) but rather a small
//range. This provides for inaccuracies between exact frame
```

```
//time and the timer slider control time.  Also note that the
//impulseY of the bottom rigid body is negative, as this piece
//should "explode" downward.
expression -s "if (time > locator1.timer - 0.01 && time <
locator1.timer + 0.01)\r\n{\r\nTABrigidBody1.impulseY =
(locator1.power*3);\r\nTABrigidBody1.spinImpulseX =
(locator1.power*rand(-1,1));\r\nTABrigidBody1.spinImpulseZ =
(locator1.power*rand(-1,1));\r\n}\r\nelse
\r\n{\r\nrigidBody1.impulseY=0;\r\nrigidBody1.spinImpulseX =
0;\r\nrigidBody1.spinImpulseZ = 0;\r\n}"  -o nurbsCylinder1 -ae 1
-uc all ;
expression -s "if (time > locator1.timer - 0.01 && time <
locator1.timer + 0.01)\r\n{\r\nTABrigidBody2.impulseY = -
(locator1.power*3);\r\nTABrigidBody2.spinImpulseX =
(locator1.power*rand(-1,1));\r\nTABrigidBody2.spinImpulseZ =
(locator1.power*rand(-1,1));\r\n}\r\nelse
\r\n{\r\nrigidBody2.impulseY=0;\r\nrigidBody2.spinImpulseX =
0;\r\nrigidBody2.spinImpulseZ = 0;\r\n}"  -o nurbsCylinder2 -ae 1
-uc all ;

//The next section creates and modifies several materials to
//give the firecracker its look.

//Create a shader for the fuse.
shadingNode -asShader phongE;
sets -renderable true -noSurfaceShader true -empty -name
phongE1SG;
connectAttr -f phongE1.outColor phongE1SG.surfaceShader;

//Connect the shader to the fuse.
select -r extrudedSurface1 ;
sets -e -forceElement phongE1SG;
defaultNavigation -cn -d phongE1.color;
createRenderNode -allWithTexturesUp "defaultNavigation -f true -
ce -s %node -d phongE1.color" "";
defaultNavigation -dtv -d phongE1.color;

//Now create and modify a cloth texture for the shader.
shadingNode -asTexture cloth;
shadingNode -asUtility place2dTexture;
connectAttr place2dTexture1.outUV cloth1.uv;
connectAttr place2dTexture1.outUvFilterSize cloth1.uvFilterSize;
```

```
defaultNavigation -f true -ce -s cloth1 -d phongE1.color;
setAttr "phongE1.specularColor" -type double3 0 0 0 ;
setAttr "place2dTexture1.repeatU" 6;
setAttr "place2dTexture1.repeatV" 0.5;
setAttr "place2dTexture1.rotateUV" 0;
setAttr "place2dTexture1.rotateFrame" 35.7;
setAttr "cloth1.gapColor" -type double3 0.134 0.0953788 0.022378;
setAttr "cloth1.vColor" -type double3 0.77686 0.77686 0.77686 ;

//Now create & modify a transparency ramp for the fuse material.
//This will be used to "erase" the fuse as it burns down.
createRenderNode -allWithTexturesUp "defaultNavigation -f true -
ce -s %node -d phongE1.transparency" "";
defaultNavigation -dtv -d phongE1.transparency;
shadingNode -asTexture ramp;
shadingNode -asUtility place2dTexture;
connectAttr place2dTexture2.outUV ramp1.uv;
connectAttr place2dTexture2.outUvFilterSize ramp1.uvFilterSize;
defaultNavigation -f true -ce -s ramp1 -d phongE1.transparency;

//Remove the middle color in the ramp, change the remaining
//colors, and set interpolation to none (so there is a hard
//break between visible and invisible).
removeMultiInstance -break true ramp1.colorEntryList[1];
setAttr "ramp1.colorEntryList[0].color" -type double3 1 1 1 ;
setAttr "ramp1.colorEntryList[2].color" -type double3 0 0 0 ;
setAttr ramp1.interpolation 0;

//Position the upper (black) color to the bottom.
setAttr "ramp1.colorEntryList[2].position" 0.001;

//Create an expression that controls the position of the black
//color entry over time, based on the value of locator1.timer.
expression -s
"ramp1.colorEntryList[2].position=(time/locator1.timer)+0.001;"
-o ramp1 -ae 1 -uc all ;
//Create a phong material, assign it to the cylinders,
//and modify its color to yellowish.
shadingNode -asShader phongE;
sets -renderable true -noSurfaceShader true -empty -name
phongE2SG;
```

```
connectAttr -f phongE2.outColor phongE2SG.surfaceShader;
select -d phongE2 ;
rename phongE2 "bodyPhong";
select -r bodyPhong ;
select -r nurbsCylinder1 ;
select -tgl nurbsCylinder2 ;
select -cl ;
defaultNavigation -source bodyPhong -destination
|nurbsCylinder1|nurbsCylinderShape1.instObjGroups[0] -
connectToExisting;
defaultNavigation -source bodyPhong -destination
|nurbsCylinder1|revolvetopCap2.instObjGroups[0] -
connectToExisting;
defaultNavigation -source bodyPhong -destination
|nurbsCylinder2|nurbsCylinderShape2.instObjGroups[0] -
connectToExisting;
defaultNavigation -source bodyPhong -destination
|nurbsCylinder2|revolvebottomCap2.instObjGroups[0] -
connectToExisting;
setAttr "bodyPhong.color" -type double3 0.719416 0.75 0.30675 ;
addAttr -is true -ln "colorRed" -dv 0.0 -at double
particleShape1;
setAttr -keyable true particleShape1.colorRed;
addAttr -is true -ln "colorGreen" -dv 0.0 -at double
particleShape1;
setAttr -keyable true particleShape1.colorGreen;
addAttr -is true -ln "colorBlue" -dv 0.0 -at double
particleShape1;
setAttr -keyable true particleShape1.colorBlue;
setAttr "particleShape1.colorRed" 0.9;

//Create and move a spotlight so we can see the rendered
//results.  This light may be further adjusted by the user.
spotLight;
move -r 9.75 10.8 14.6;
setAttr "spotLight1.rotateY" 30;
setAttr "spotLight1.rotateX" -30;
//A few final commands to clean up the interface a bit.
//First, close the render node window; then smooth shade the
//scene, and turn on lighting; next, pick the locator, so its
//controls are available in the channel box; and delete the
//build firecracker window.
```

```
window -e -vis false createRenderNodeWindow;
DisplayShadedAndTextured;
DisplayLight;
select -r locator1 ;
deleteUI $theName;
} //end, proc build

//firecracker is the main procedure in this script.  It creates
//an invisible locator with attributes for time, power, and
//amount of sparks, builds the window that you use to control
//the parameters of the firecracker. On clicking the "Build
//the Firecracker!" button, the build procedure is called.
global proc firecracker ()
{

//$winName is global because otherwise Maya won't see it.
global string $winName = "firecracker";
string $main = "mainWindow";

check ($winName);

//create a locator object, turn off its visibility, and add
//three attributes to it.
createPrimitive nullObject;
setAttr "locator1.visibility" off;
addAttr -ln timer -at double  -min 0 -max 100 -dv 5 |locator1;
setAttr -e -keyable true |locator1.timer;
addAttr -ln power -at double  -min 0 -max 100 -dv 20 |locator1;
setAttr -e -keyable true |locator1.power;
addAttr -ln sparks -at double  -min 0 -max 100 -dv 20 |locator1;
setAttr -e -keyable true |locator1.sparks;

//Now build the window interface, with controls for the
//three attributes on the locator, and a build button.
window -t "Build a Firecracker" -wh 600 300 $winName;

scrollLayout;
columnLayout ($main);

attrFieldSliderGrp -min (0) -max (100) -at "locator1.timer";
text " ";
attrFieldSliderGrp -min (0) -max (100) -at "locator1.power";
```

```
text " ";
attrFieldSliderGrp -min (0) -max (100) -at "locator1.sparks";
text " ";
button -l "Build the Firecracker!" -w 200 -c "build ($winName)";

showWindow $winName;
} //end, proc firecracker
```

If you got through these four scripts, and have a good idea what's going on in them, you are ready to start making scripts of your own! Use the online reference documents, build on other people's work, and make something really useful for yourself. Even better, share it with others via a Web site or an e-mail list server.

Two great places to get MEL scripts on the Web are www.highend3d.com/maya/mel/ *and* www.aliaswavefront.com/assistant_online/index.html.

Summary

In this chapter, we moved beyond the basics to discover just how powerful and complex MEL scripting can be. We worked with variables, loops, and conditional branches. You learned how to make custom GUIs for any purpose we wish. Finally, we created and examined full-blown MEL scripts.

Although big scripts look complex, the secret to writing them is to build them up from small pieces, and to grab chunks of code (either from the Script Editor's History window or from other Maya users' scripts) and modify them for your own use.

Advanced MEL scripting is not for everyone, but if you like this sort of work and get good at MEL, chances are you can land yourself a full-time job just scripting for Maya.

Part V
Rendering

In This Part

Part V of this book introduces the world of rendering in Maya. *Rendering* is an umbrella term for the many processes that actually create the images we see, such as setting up cameras to capture images, shading and texturing, lighting and shadowing the surfaces, and the actual creation of the image files. Rendering experts boast that 90 percent of all that we see in the final CGI output happens in rendering. The claim is justifiable. You can take poorly built models and still render out beautiful images with quality texturing, lighting, and camera work, but even the best models will end up looking terrible with poor rendering techniques. You will first learn the basics of rendering in Maya, and then learn to use the Hypershade in coloring and texturing surfaces through numerous examples and hands-on tutorials. Finally, you'll learn about creating proper lighting, shadows, and special light effects.

Rendering Basics

MAYA

Chapter 18

Rendering is a many-faceted process. First, you need a proper camera through which objects can be seen and captured into 2D images. You also need to decide on the quality and resolution of the image output. Then you can select how you want the surfaces to be lit—your choices include five different lights or incandescence. Next, you need to create materials and textures for the surfaces. You may also want to create an appropriate background, such as a stage set, an image plane with live footage, or an environmental texture. Alternatively, you could render the surfaces in layers, each layer being rendered with an alpha channel, and put them together with compositing software.

This chapter deals mainly with cameras, render settings, and using Maya's IPR (Interactive Photorealistic Rendering) tool. Shading and lighting will be covered more thoroughly in the following chapters. Topics include:

- Camera and resolution setup
- The Render Globals dialog box
- The Render View window
- Interactive photorealistic rendering
- Image planes
- Batch rendering
- Rendering techniques

Rendering an Object

As we've done in previous chapters, we will explore the rendering process by working through an example from beginning to end. To demonstrate rendering, we will use a beveled text letter. We will light it, texture it, and animate it to appear and disappear against a textured background. Then we will render the animation as a video-quality picture sequence.

Setting the Camera and the Resolution

First, we need to set the camera. As you've learned in earlier chapters, cameras are windows through which you look at things in Maya's world space. The default four views that you see when you start a new scene are actually four nondeletable cameras: one camera with a perspective view and three cameras with orthographic views, which we know as the front, side, and top views. Generally, the orthographic views are used for modeling, texturing, and animation purposes, and rendering is done only through the perspective view.

1. Create a beveled text letter *M* (using the Surface ➜ Bevel function), as we did in Chapter 5, "NURBS Modeling."

2. Create another perspective view by selecting Panels ➜ Perspective ➜ New. Persp1 camera is created.

3. In the Outliner, rename the view to Camera. Open its Attribute Editor, shown in Figure 18.1, and set Film Back ➜ Overscan to 1.1. Open Display Options and check Display Resolution. (You can also turn on Display Resolution by selecting View ➜ Camera Settings ➜ Resolution Gate.) In the camera view, you will see a box that shows you the exact area that will be rendered. The Overscan setting of 1.1 also shows a bit of the area just outside the box. Check the Display Film Gate setting (just above Display Resolution). This displays another box, representing the Film Gate, the camera setting for the medium in which you want to display the images. The default resolution size in Maya is 320×240 pixels, which gives us a width $\times$ height (*aspect*) ratio of 1.33333. If you see the Film Gate box overlapping the Resolution box imperfectly, there is an imperfect match between the aspect ratio of the pictures being rendered and the ratio used in the final display medium.

4. Go to the Film Gate setting in the Film Back section and select different media, such as 70mm projection, to see how the aspect ratio changes. Change the preset to 35mm TV Projection, as shown in Figure 18.1. This setting has the 1.33333 ratio for television. The Film Gate and Resolution boxes should now match perfectly. (See "Broadcast Standards" for more information on resolutions and ratios.)

You may want to render at a smaller size as a test render, but still maintain the correct (larger) aspect ratio, similar to the lock-aspect ratio feature available in Photoshop and other graphics software. Maya provides a setting for this in the Render Globals dialog box, discussed in the next section.

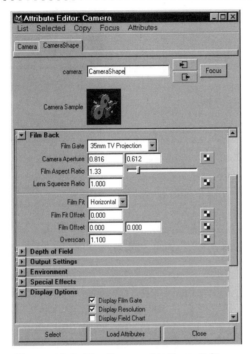

Figure 18.1 *The Camera Attribute Editor*

5. The default resolution setting is at 320 × 240, which you can see at the top of the resolution gate in the camera view, but you probably will want to render the pictures at a higher resolution. Select Window ➜ Render Globals and open the Resolution section. For our example, set the Render Resolution to 640 × 480.

6. Adjust the camera view, dragging and rotating the camera until you have the proper composition for the letter *M*. Then keyframe the Camera attributes. Now you will be able to switch back to the regular perspective window and test-render the camera view as you make changes to the lighting and textures.

As you saw in step 5, Maya provides many Render Resolution presets. For television and video productions, the most common resolution setting is CCIR 601, which is 720 × 486, Device Aspect Ratio 1.333, and Pixel Aspect Ratio 0.9. This means that the image will be 720 pixels wide and 486 pixels high, but it will be shown with a 4:3 width × height ratio because the pixel aspect ratio is not square. The 640 × 480 resolution that we are using has Device Aspect Ratio 1.333 and Pixel Aspect Ratio 1, and it is considered the minimum broadcast-quality resolution.

Broadcast Standards

Different broadcast standards are used in different parts of the world. The PAL (Phase Alternating Line) and SECAM (Sequential Color And Memory) systems are used in Britain and in Europe. The NTSC (National Television System Committee) system is used in North and South America and many Asian countries.

Unfortunately, these systems are incompatible in a number of ways. NTSC broadcasts 525 horizontal lines in a picture; PAL and SECAM broadcast 625 lines. NTSC transmits 30 fps (frames per second); the others transmit 25 fps. They also have different broadcast channel widths and types of signals. However, all of these standards broadcast pictures at a 4:3 image aspect ratio.

We render pictures at 640 × 480 resolution with square pixels, or 720 × 486 resolution with a pixel ratio of 0.9, in order to make them fit the 4:3 aspect ratio. A Device Aspect Ratio setting of 1.333 is another way of stating that images are being displayed at a 4:3 width × height ratio.

With the coming of HDTV (high-definition TV), these standards are changing. Although there still isn't a universal standard for DTV (digital TV), the accepted image ratio for HDTV is 16:9, which is the same ratio as the wide-screen format used for films. This ratio translates to 1.777 Device Aspect Ratio. The minimum resolution for HDTV is 1280 × 720. For film, 2:1 and 16:9 are currently the most commonly used image ratios.

Render Globals Settings

There are a few other things we need to set in the Render Globals dialog box. As shown in Figure 18.2, this dialog box offers many settings, but for now, we will set the quality, the output filename and format, and some frame rendering details.

1. Select Window ➜ Render Globals and open the Anti-aliasing Quality section. Set the Presets option to Intermediate Quality. You can change this setting to Production Quality when you are ready to render, but for test renders, the Preview or Intermediate Quality settings are usually good enough.

For production- or higher-quality anti-aliasing presets, Maya automatically turns on the Multipixel Filtering setting. Multipixel Filtering is good for situations where you see thin surface edges. If there are no thin edges to anti-alias, it's best to have this option turned off, because it can slow down the rendering process significantly.

2. Open the Image File Output section and type in a name for the picture sequence you will be rendering in the File Name Prefix field. If you don't enter a name, the rendered pictures will automatically be assigned the scene filename.

3. Set Frame/Animation Ext to `name.#.ext`. The animation settings become activated. If you leave the setting at `name.ext`, then only the current time frame will be rendered, unless otherwise commanded in a batch render.

4. Set End Frame to 60, because we will be rendering two seconds of animation.

5. The default Image Format is Maya IFF (.iff) picture format. Change it to something more widely acceptable, like the Targa (.tga) format.

6. Set the Camera to Camera to make it the renderable camera. Before closing the Render Globals window, check to make sure you have the settings shown in Figure 18.2.

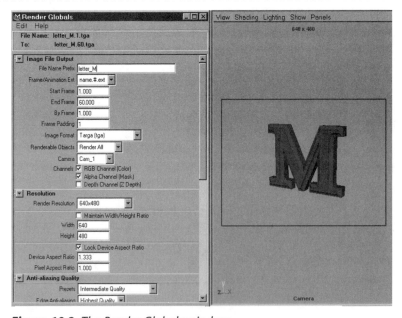

Figure 18.2 *The Render Globals window*

Here's a quick explanation of the Image File Output settings we've just made:

Image Format: Targa Formats such as JPEG or GIF are usually not used as image formats, because they do not carry alpha channel (mask) information, and alpha channel information is often needed for compositing purposes. Regular color pictures have 24 bits of color information for each pixel, stored in three RGB (red, green, blue) channels. A picture with an *alpha channel* has an extra 8-bit channel, which contains the masking information for each pixel of the picture. The information is stored in the form of a grayscale picture, which often turns out to be the outline of the objects being rendered. Compressed formats such as JPEG and GIF are also generally inappropriate for final renders because of potential data loss.

Channels By default, Maya renders the RGB channels and the alpha channel. You can also render the depth channel (Z-depth) by checking the Channels box. Z-depth is similar to the alpha channel in that it is represented as an 8-bit grayscale picture. As its name indicates, it stores the depth information of pixels to be rendered. Like the alpha channel, it is mainly used for compositing purposes. If the image format is the default IFF, then the Z-depth information is stored inside the image file being rendered, like other alpha channel information. If you are rendering in a format like TGA, Maya creates a separate Z-depth file for every image it renders.

Renderable Objects This option is set to Render All by default, but you can switch it to Render Active if you want to render only what you've selected. Using the Render Active option is also useful if you are rendering in layers.

Camera In the Render Globals dialog box, you see Camera as the only view that will be rendered. If you want to render multiple views, open the other view's Attribute Editor, go to the Output Settings section, and turn on Renderable. Now if you go to the Render Globals dialog box's Image File Output section and look at the Camera menu, you will see that the other view is also identified as Renderable.

Working in the Render View

Now we will set up some spotlights and take a look at our letter in the Render View window.

1. Create a default spotlight. Select Panels ➜ Look Through Selected, and move the spotLight1 view to something like (a) below.

2. Create another spotlight, and repeat the procedure to look something like (b) below. This is a very convenient and intuitive way to set lights. You do not need to fine-tune anything at this point—we will be doing that with the IPR tool soon.

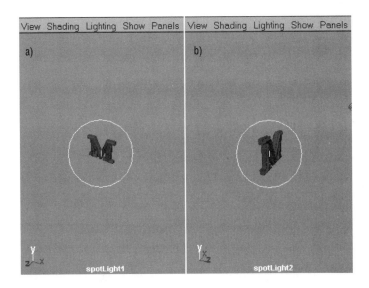

3. Select Window → Rendering Editors → Render View.

You can open many different images in the Render View window, and in Maya 3 you can also save an image in the format listed in the Image File Output section of Render Globals. Here are some of the other things you can do in the Render View window:

- Keep multiple images by selecting File → Keep Image or the Keep Image button in Render View for each picture you want to keep.

- Take wireframe snapshots of different cameras available for rendering, or select a region to render only that area.

- Zoom in and out and drag the image in the Render View window by using hotkeys and mouse buttons, just as you can in a modeling view.

- Use the options on the View menu to change the view. Frame Image shows an entire image, Frame Region focuses on just the selected region, and Real Size shows an image without any zooming. The Display menu list also allows you to see a rendered image as separate color planes, luminance, or its alpha channel (Mask Plane).

The toolbar in the Render View window includes buttons for the most often used functions. You can see what their functions are by placing the mouse arrow over the icons.

Using Interactive Photorealistic Rendering (IPR)

The Interactive Photorealistic Rendering (IPR) tool allows you to edit colors, materials, textures, lights, and shadows interactively. When you invoke IPR, Maya creates an image file that stores both the shading and the visibility information of surfaces. The size of an IPR file is considerably larger than a regular image file of the same resolution because it stores the extra visibility information. Then, when a tuning region is selected, Maya loads all the IPR information for the pixels in the region into memory. You can change the tuning region at any time, and the IPR will continue to load the pixel information for the new region.

We will use IPR to render our letter *M*, but first let's get a snapshot. It's always a good idea to take snapshots before you do any rendering, because it provides a quick view of what you are about to render. Taking a snapshot also sets the camera you've chosen as the active camera, and you can later use the Redo Previous Render and Redo Previous IPR Render icons to render the same camera view.

1. From the Options menu in Render View, turn off Auto Resize and turn on Auto Render Region.

2. Select Render ➔ Snapshot ➔ Camera. You can also RM click to access the menu in the Render View window.

3. Click the IPR button to start the IPR process. Once the letter *M* has been rendered, select a region to start IPR tuning, as shown in Figure 18.3.

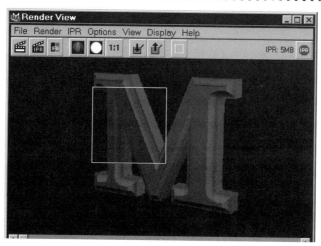

Figure 18.3 *An IPR rendering of the letter M*

If the image is actual size, the marquee box stays green. As soon as the image is zoomed in or out, the box turns red. Note that the IPR icon in the top-right corner becomes activated as well; clicking it will end the IPR mode. The indicator to the left of the icon shows how big the IPR file is. Now any changes you make to the lighting or texture information relating to the letter *M* will be updated within the tuning region automatically.

There are some neat things you can do within the selected IPR tuning region. You can Shift+click over any pixels within the region to find out which shades and lights are affecting them, and select those nodes. You also can drag materials and textures onto the objects within the region, and they will update accordingly. Any modification in the shading information is updated in the region with speeds comparable to that of a Hypershade swatch update, because the visibility calculations have already been made. (We will use the Hypershade window in the next section and examine it in detail in Chapter 19, "Shading and Texturing Surfaces.")

Having the visibility information already stored in the IPR file means that once the file exists, you can change the camera view and make changes in the surfaces without disturbing the IPR tuning region. Those changes are not recalculated until you start another IPR. While this allows you to get more mileage out of a single IPR file as you are editing lighting and shading, keep in mind that if the changes in the surfaces' visibility are significant enough, the IPR updates can go out of sync with how the surfaces actually look. If this happens, you should create another IPR file.

Shading the Object

Next, we'll use the Hypershade window to shade the letter *M*. As in the Render View window, you can zoom in and out and move around in the Hypershade window using the hotkeys and the mouse buttons. You can also zoom in and out of the Visor panel, which is essentially a rendering file browser. This may seem a bit weird at first, but it allows you to clearly see the swatches and the labels, which is a must when working with shaders. We will go through the steps to shade and texture our current example, without much explanation of the settings. You will learn more about the Hypershade in the next chapter.

1. Keep the Render View window open, and adjust the spotlights until you are fairly satisfied with the way the letter *M* is being lit in the tuning region. After you've shaded the letter properly, you can come back to this view and fine-tune the lighting.

2. Select Window ➜ Hypershade. Zoom in to the Visor panel that appears on the left side of the Hypershade window. Go to the Create directory and then the Materials folder under it (open the folder if it's closed), and MM drag the Blinn# material onto the Hypergraph, as shown below.

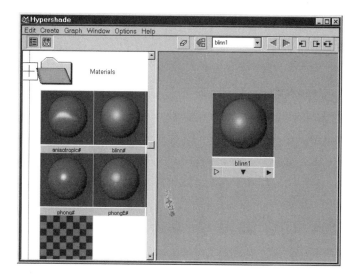

3. Go down to the Texture folder in the Visor panel and MM drag the Brownian# texture into the layout and over the Blinn material. A list of possible input connections pops up. Connect to Color, and you will see the Brownian texture come up on the Blinn material swatch.

4. Drag the same Brownian texture over the Blinn material to see the list pop up again. This time, connect to Bump Map, as shown below. You'll see the bump effect of the Brownian texture on the Blinn material, along with the creation of a Bump node.

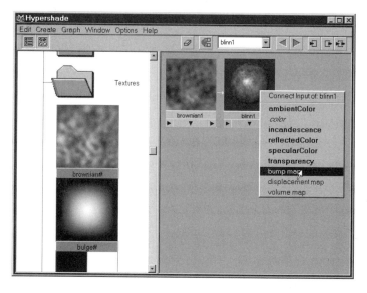

5. In the Hypershade window, RM choose Graph ➜ Rearrange Graph to sort the nodes, and then click the icon in the top-left corner to hide the Visor panel.

6. Bring the Hypershade and the Render View windows close to each other, and drag the Blinn material onto the letter *M* inside the tuning region of the IPR window. Since our letter *M* has two surfaces, you'll need to apply the material twice. The material, along with the Brownian color and bump, should update on the letter almost immediately, as shown below.

There are many other ways to apply the Blinn material to the letter M. One way is to drag the swatch onto the object inside the modeling window. Another way is to select the object, move the mouse over the Blinn swatch, and RM choose Assign Material To Selection.

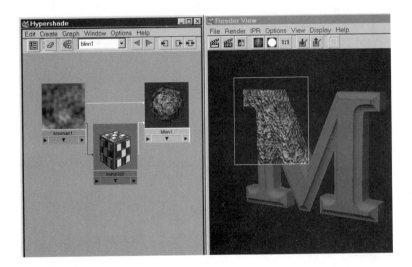

7. The default bump value is too high for our purposes. Either RM choose over the Brownian texture or double-click it to open its Attribute Editor; then open Color Balance and move the Alpha Gain slider down. You should see the bump on the letter *M* start to lessen in the IPR tuning region. Adjust the Alpha Gain value until you like what you see. To adjust the bumpiness in a different way, you can also try playing with the increment value slider in the Brownian Attributes section.

8. Work in the same way with Brownian's Color Gain and Color Offset values to adjust the color of the texture.

9. Go to the Blinn material and adjust Specular Shading by moving the Eccentricity, Specular Roll Off, and Specular Color sliders. (Specular Shading has to do with how the light is reflected from an object.)

10. Return to the spotlights and fine-tune the lighting, this time adjusting not only the angles, but also the Color, Intensity, and Dropoff values. You may also want to change the tuning region to different areas to make sure there are no hidden surprises. The updates we've made appear as shown in Figure 18.4. (You can also see this image in the Color Gallery for Chapter 18 on the CD-ROM.)

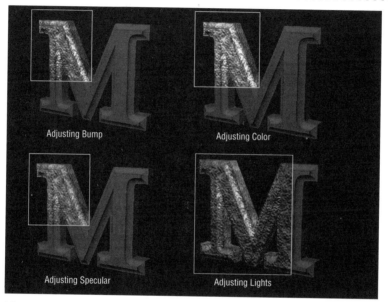

Figure 18.4 *IPR updates for shading and lighting*

If you have been experimenting with the other sliders and fields, you've seen that some of them do not affect the letter *M* at all and that some others should be left alone. It's very easy to play with the texture, material, and light attributes and get immediate feedback from the IPR tuning region. One of the best things about IPR is that it frees you to experiment with the attributes and think of other possibilities—there is less reason for number crunching and more room for artistic impressions.

If a single image is the goal, once you are satisfied with the way everything looks you can increase the Anti-aliasing setting to Production Quality and then click the top-left corner icon, Redo Previous Render, to render a final image. You can then save the image using the File ➜ Save Image command. But our example is for a sequence of images, which requires us to do a bit more work.

Making an Object Disappear

We would like the letter *M* to appear and disappear against a textured background. Before working on the background, we will make the letter appear and disappear. We can accomplish this by using the Transparency, Specular Color, and Set Key attributes.

1. In the Blinn material's Attribute Editor, slide up the Transparency value all the way to white. In the IPR region, the letter's surface disappears, but the specular highlights still remain. Notice that the alpha channel for the letter also becomes black, which you can check by clicking the Display Mask button.

2. To make the letter *M* become completely invisible, you need to turn down the Specular Color slider all the way to black. At frame 5, RM click over the Transparency attribute to get the pop-up menu, and choose Set Key to keyframe the value. Repeat for Specular Color.

3. Go to frame 15, turn down the Transparency value to black, raise the Specular Color value to white, and Set Key those attributes. The letter *M* now fades in over a ten-frame time interval.

4. Repeat the process in the opposite direction between frames 50 and 60 to make the letter disappear. Notice that as you move the current time indicator in the Time Slider, the IPR tuning region updates the changing transparency and the specularity.

5. In the Graph Editor, you can see the Blinn material's keyframed attributes, as shown below. Select all the curves and apply Tangents ➜ Flat to make sure the Transparency and Specular Color attributes stay constant between frames 15 to 50. The gradual slope of the keyframe curves also ensures the smooth appearance and disappearance of the letter *M*.

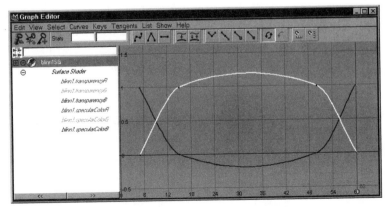

Adding a Textured Background

Our work on the letter *M* is done. Now let's add a background for the letter. The Create button in the Environment section of the camera's Attribute Editor lets you create an image plane. You can set the display to show the image only through the camera view or have it displayed in all views. When you are modeling, you will want to be able to see the image in different views. You can hide the image temporarily by setting the Display Mode to None. You can also load any image to use as the background by clicking the browser button beside Image Name, and you can place the image anywhere in the modeling window using the Placement and Placement Extras attributes. For our example, we will create a texture to use as the background.

1. Select Camera and open its Attribute Editor. Open the Environment section and click the Create button to create an image plane.

2. Click the Create button beside the Texture field to open Create Render Node, and select a solid fractal texture.

3. Because background textures do not show up in the IPR, you need to render the region to test how the solid fractal matches up with the letter *M*. Adjust the fractal texture's Color Gain, Offset, and Placement attributes to get it to look the way you want—something like the image shown below.

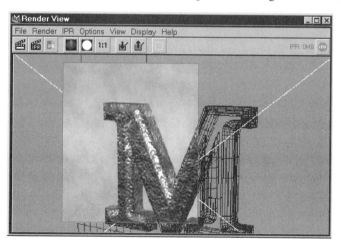

You can select the image plane in several different ways. One way is to first select the camera and then click the arrow beside the Image Plane Create button to get to it. Another way is to go into the component mode and click the question-mark icon, which enables image plane selection. A third alternative is to open the Outliner, RM choose to toggle off Show DAG Objects Only, and then scroll down to select the Image Plane node.

Batch Rendering

We are now ready to render. Before you save the scene, however, let's see where the rendered pictures will be placed.

1. Select File ➔ Project ➔ Edit Current. The Edit Project dialog box shown below tells you the location of the current project. Go to the Render File Locations section and look at the field beside Images. If this field's entry says Images, there is a default subdirectory in the current project called Images, and the rendered pictures will be placed into that directory by default. If nothing is in the field, the rendered images will be placed into the current project directory.

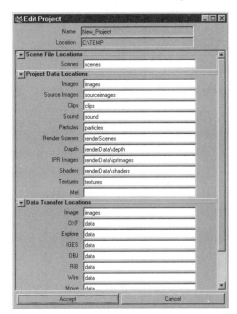

2. Save the scene, entering the name **letter_M**. You can exit Maya.

3. Open an MS-DOS Command Prompt window (if you are using SGI, open a Unix shell window). Go to the directory where you've saved your letter *M*, and you will see the file listed as `letter_M.mb`.

4. Type **Render –help** and press Enter. All the options that you can use with the Render command are listed.

5. For our example, enter a command like the following (substituting your own rendering project directory path):

```
Render -s 1 -e 60 -b 1 -rd D:\Mastering\Chapter18\Renders\
-n 2 letter_M.mb
```

The Maya Rendering program will take the file `letter_M.mb`, render frames 1 to 60 using two available processors, and put the rendered pictures into the directory listed in the path.

In this example, we used the most common Render command options: `-s` for start frame, `-e` for end frame, `-b` for by frame or step, `-rd` for the directory path in which to store rendered images, and `-n` for number of processors to use. If your machine has two CPUs, for example, you would want to make sure to use the `-n 2` option, as it will make the render go twice as fast. You also could leave out the `-rd` option, render the pictures into the default render directory, and move the pictures out of that directory later.

Other options, such as `-mb` for motion blur and `-sa` for shutter angle, can also be handy in certain situations. For example, let's say you've rendered a run cycle, and while checking the rendered pictures, you notice that frame 12 is looking very weird because of the motion blur. Rather than opening the file and fixing this, you can either render just that frame without the motion blur (`-mb off`) or reduce the motion blur by typing in a lower shutter angle value (`-sa 70`, for example).

Once the rendering is done, you can view the rendered pictures using the Fcheck utility. Fcheck allows you to view a single image or a sequence of images, check their alpha channels, view the different color planes, and see the Z-depth information. You can also save the images into many different picture formats. (If you are working with SGI machines, you can use the `imgcvt` command to convert images into different formats.)

You can reduce the time it takes to render your scenes by using some optimizing techniques. See Chapter 20, "Lighting," for some render optimization tips.

Using Other Rendering Techniques

So far, we've gone through the process of lighting, shading, and rendering a sequence of images for a simple beveled letter *M*. We've tried to keep the options as simple as we could, but rendering, by nature, is a rather complex endeavor. For the rest of this chapter, we will cover some other areas of rendering that you may find useful for your own projects.

Layer Rendering, Compositing, and Editing

What we've done with the letter *M* rendering is actually rather … dumb. Because the letter wasn't moving, the 60 frames of rendering were not necessary; only the first 10 frames were. In studio environments, where meeting deadlines and work efficiency are always paramount, this kind of rendering redundancy would have been frowned upon.

With any editing software, or with some renaming and renumbering script commands, you can extend frame 1 forward to frame 5, reverse the animation from frames 5 to 15 to make them frames 50 to 60, and hold frame 15 until frame 49.

Alternatively, we could have rendered the letter *M* separately from the fractal textured background. Since the background remains constant, only a single frame is necessary. Using compositing software, we could have composited the letter *M* onto the background.

In a production, the rendering pipeline is often set up to layer-render anything that can be layered. Figure 18.5 is a partial example of how the letter *M* can be rendered as multiple-layered render passes. The floor has been added to illustrate the shadow passes. (You can also see this image in the Color Gallery on the CD.)

Figure 18.5 *Render passes for different layers*

Although it's not included in the sample pictures, there can also be a separate render for the floor, with the accompanying alpha channel. To create just the shadows on the floor, select the letter *M* surfaces, go to the Attribute Editor's Render Stats section, and turn off Primary Visibility. To create the shadow mask, color everything white, make the lights black, and turn their shadow colors to white. Even if there are many lights, you will usually want two or three lights at most to create shadows. Separating these elements may seem like extra work, but it allows you much more control at the compositing stage, and it can ultimately save you time in terms of making changes or corrections in complex scenes.

You can increase or decrease only the specularity or you can change the colors on the letter *M*. You can darken or lighten just the shadows, or sharpen them or blur them. If you have the proper compositing software, such as Maya Fusion or Adobe After Effects, you can even transform and animate the different layer elements. If the rendering was being done in one pass, you would need to re-render the whole scene each time you wanted to make changes to any of these things. However, if you had rendered these items as separate elements, you would only need to re-render the elements you wanted to change. Ultimately, however, whether these refinements are worth the extra effort depends on your specific production situation.

Adding Depth of Field

Maya cameras also have the ability to imitate the depth-of-field functionality of real-world cameras. To be able to use this capacity in any practical way, however, requires some setup.

Open the `letter_M` file, select Camera, and open its Attribute Editor. Go to the Depth Of Field section and check Depth Of Field. Its attributes become active. The Focus Distance attribute does what it says—it sets the distance for the camera focus.

It would be useful to have a way of interactively controlling that distance in the modeling window, instead of punching in numbers. An easy way to do this is to open the Connection Editor with the Camera Shape loaded on both windows, and connect the Center of Interest output to the Focus Distance input. This constrains the focus distance to the camera's center of interest, which shows up as part of the Show Manipulator handle.

In Figure 18.6, the F Stop value may be a bit too low. Also, the blurring, a post-effect, is expensive (meaning it takes longer to render). However, because it is a 3D blur, it adds much more realism to the rendered image than any post-effect 2D blur can. If you want more control, or just need the camera's center of interest and the focus distance to be separate entities, you can connect the focus distance to a locator instead.

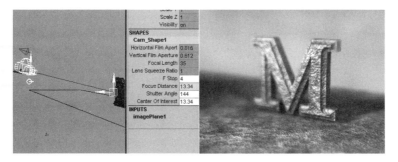

Figure 18.6 *Depth Of Field activated*

Importing Live Footage

When you want to match an animation with live footage, you need to animate the image plane. Let's assume we have 10 frames of footage properly numbered and with proper extensions. To bring in the sequence of images, display image plane's Attributes Editor and turn on Use Frame Extension in the Image Plane Attributes section. Click the browse button (the folder icon) beside the Image Name field to load the first frame of the footage. The result should look something like Figure 18.7.

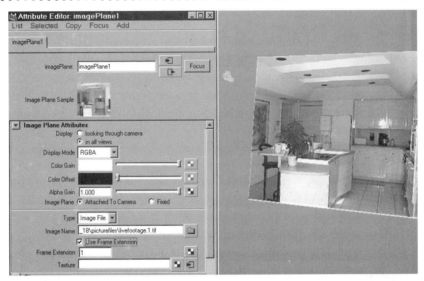

Figure 18.7 *The first frame of live footage loaded into the image plane*

Go to frame 1, enter **1** in the Frame Extension field, and RM choose Set Key to keyframe it. At frame 10, enter **10** in the field and keyframe that. Now when you move the Time Slider, the frames update. If you open the Graph Editor for the image plane, you can see a linear curve for the Frame Extension, as shown in Figure 18.8.

New in Maya 3 is a file texture node specifically for movie files. It works the same way as a regular file or the image plane, in that you have to keyframe the sequences, but instead of reading in separate pictures, it reads in the frames of an AVI movie file. Shown in Figure 18.9 is a movie file applied as a texture to a polygon face. The movie file is designed to play back live footage more efficiently than the regular image files, and it can be a great tool for animators to quickly reference an action sequence.

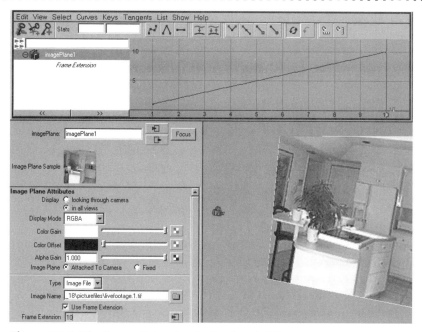

Figure 18.8 *The Frame Extension in the Graph Editor*

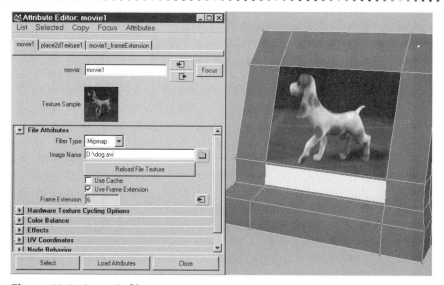

Figure 18.9 *A movie file texture*

Loading in picture sequences or movie files is easy. Camera tracking the live footage, however, is a tedious and time-consuming affair—usually frame-by-frame matching work. Once the tracking is done, matching up lighting and shading to the live footage is yet another grim task. But as we will see in the next chapter, using IPR can make the editing of lighting and shading an enjoyable process.

Summary

This chapter introduced you to the many and varied parts of rendering. You learned how to create and set up a camera and how to set the resolution and the format of the output in the Render Globals dialog box.

We also covered the Render View window and the IPR tool. Then we took a brief look at other topics, such as working with image planes and batch rendering. The Hypershade window and lighting were also introduced. These topics are covered in depth in the next two chapters.

Shading and Texturing Surfaces

MAYA

Chapter 19

Objects look different because they are made up of different materials. One way we can distinguish materials is by the way they reflect light. A metal object, for example, shines more than a wooden object. The brightest spot where the light is reflecting from an object is called the object's *specular highlight.* In Maya, materials are generally classified according to the way that specular light is calculated to represent them.

We can also identify objects by their color and texture. Maya has many default textures, such as wood, rock, leather, and so on. These allow you to quickly create easily identifiable everyday objects.

In this chapter, you will learn how to use these default materials and textures to create great-looking objects. We will use the dog, objects from the living room, and the human model from the previous chapters as examples. But first, you need to learn how to use the Hypershade. Topics include:

- Hypershade operations
- Surface coloring
- Shininess and bumpiness control
- Transparency, incandescence, and glow
- Texturing techniques
- Working with polygons and subdivision surfaces
- Hands-On Maya: Texturing a character

Using the Hypershade

Just as you can view and edit nodes and node network connections using dependency graphs in the Hypergraph, you can also work with them the same way in the Hypershade for rendering. The Hypershade differs from the Hypergraph in that it uses swatches, which give a level of visual feedback that the Hypergraph lacks. For viewing and editing render nodes such as textures and materials, the Hypershade is indispensable.

Working in the Hypershade Window

When you select Window ➜ Hypershade to open it, you see a rendering-based file browser, called the Visor panel, on the left side of the window. As you learned in Chapter 18, "Rendering Basics," the various folders in the Rendering directory display nodes for materials and other rendering elements. You can zoom in and out for a better view, and you can MM drag them onto the layout area on the right side of the window. The top-left button in the Hypershade window opens and closes the Visor panel, and the next button opens and closes the Hypershade layout area.

Let's briefly go over some of the menu functions available in the Hypershade window, illustrated in Figure 19.1. Then we will see how the nodes and networks work in the Hypershade.

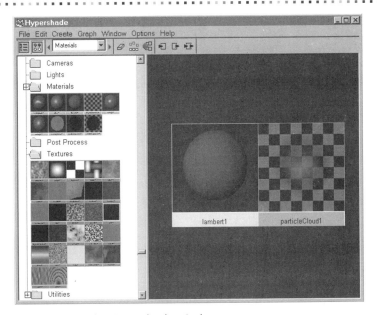

Figure 19.1 *The Hypershade window*

The Edit Menu

On the Edit menu, the Delete Unused Nodes function deletes all the nodes that are not assigned to geometry or particles in the scene. This is basically a cleanup command that you will want to invoke at the end of your session.

The Duplicate command has three options. The Blinn1 material with the checker texture and its placement node in the picture in Figure 19.2 form a simple network of render nodes we can use to demonstrate these options.

- Duplicate ➜ Shading Network produces the Blinn2 node network, an exact duplicate of the first.

- Duplicate ➜ Without Network produces just the Blinn3 node, which copies all the properties of the Blinn1 material, but not the network.

- Duplicate ➜ With Connections to Network produces Blinn4, which inherits the same upstream node network connections as the original Blinn1 node. The network connections are not duplicated, as in Duplicate ➜ Shading Network, but shared.

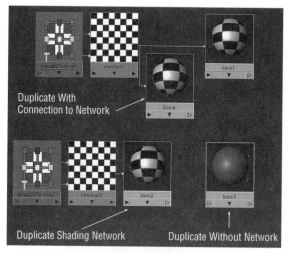

Figure 19.2 Duplicating the Blinn1 node

The Convert Material to File Texture function converts a material or texture into an image file. You can adjust the image size and turn on Anti-aliasing in the command's option window. The image will be placed into your current project directory. You can select material nodes, 2D or 3D textures, or projections for the conversion. If you select the Shading Group node, the light information will be baked into the image as well.

The Create Menu and Create Directory

Under the Create directory in the Visor panel, you will find the following folders:

- The Camera folder, containing the camera and image plane nodes.

- The Lights folder, containing the four standard lights and a new addition in Maya 3, the area light. (You'll learn about lighting in Chapter 20.)

- The Materials folder, containing nine materials. When you drag one of them into the layout area, a Shading Group is automatically created and linked to it.

- The Post Process folder, containing the opticalFX, which creates light effects such as glow, halo, and lens flare.

- The Textures folder, containing 2D and 3D textures, in alphabetical order.

- The Utilities folder, containing the Color, General, Particle, and Switch sub-folders.

On the Create menu, the Create Render Node command opens a window with tabs. For volumetric materials such as Env Fog, you need to use the Create menu or the Create Render Node window, because these materials are not listed in the Materials folder. Also, if you want to apply a texture as a projection or a stencil, you should use the Create Render Node window to change the setting from Normal to As Projection or As Stencil.

The Graph Menu

The Graph menu has several useful functions. The Graph Materials On Selected Objects command allows you to work with a select group of render nodes according to the surfaces you select. By moving the materials, textures, and networks that have been applied to selected surfaces into the layout area, this command provides an efficient way to isolate the render nodes you want to work with in complicated scenes. The Graph Materials On Selected Objects command also is available as a Hypershade window button.

The Clear View command clears the layout area, and it is also available as a button.

The Up And Downstream Connections command performs the same function as it does in Hypergraph, listing the nodes connected to the selected nodes in the layout area. The Upstream Connection and Downstream Connection commands can also be useful when you know which stream you want to view and edit, because they reduce the clutter in the work area when you are working with a complex scene.

The Rearrange Graph command cleans up the layout area and reorganizes the nodes for better viewing. This command is also available as a button placed next to the Clear View button. To see which button executes which command, keep the mouse pointer on the button, and the command label will appear as shown below.

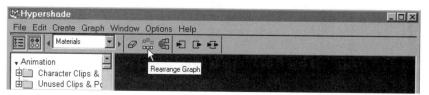

Other Menus

The Window menu gives you access to the Attribute Editor, Attribute Spread Sheet, and Connection Editor.

The Options menu's Swatches → Keep Fixed Size command keeps the swatch resolution to a fixed size, so that when you zoom in, the resolution doesn't update. This makes the swatches less accurate when closely zoomed in but increases their interactive speed.

The Layout menu enables you to switch the layout area to viewing only Shading Groups, Materials, Textures, Utilities, Cameras, or Lights. It also creates a new layer when you bring a new node into the layout area. Any subsequent nodes that you bring in stay in the same layout area so you can view their input/output relationships.

To create a separate layer for any node, select Graph → Clear View and drag the node into the work area. A layer is created with the node's name. Subsequent nodes that are brought in will stay in that layer.

Working with Nodes and Networks

To see how you can work with nodes, MM grab a Blinn node in the Materials folder and drag it into the Hypershade. Then try the following:

- RM choose over the bottom-left corner. You see a list of the attributes that can be connected with incoming information, as shown in Figure 19.3 (a).

- RM choose over the right-bottom corner. You see a list of the attributes that can go out to the other nodes, as in Figure 19.3 (b).

- MM drag a checker texture over the Blinn material. The default connection box pops up. In Figure 19.3 (c), this is the triple-channel connection. If the incoming information were a single-channel connection, a different box would pop up. Also, different nodes have different channels listed for their input/output connections.

- RM choose over the material node. A box pops up with a list of operations you can perform on the material node, as in Figure 19.3 (d). Graph Shader Network lists nodes that are connected to the material node. Assign Material To Selection assigns the material node to selected surfaces. Select Objects With Material selects all the surfaces that have the material node assigned to them. Frame Objects With Material selects and frames the surfaces with the material in the modeling window. You can also open the Attribute Editor for the material node or rename it.

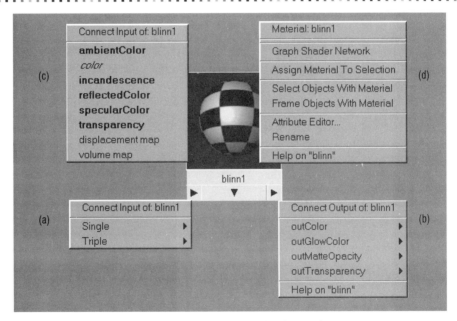

Figure 19.3 *Working with nodes in the Hypershade window*

You can assign different shading groups to different faces of a polygon object. For NURBS surfaces, only one shading group can be assigned to a surface.

Figure 19.4 is an example of a fairly simple network, which includes different swatches you will soon become very familiar with. (If you have a hard time seeing the lines of the diagram, it's also in the Color Gallery on the CD.) Working backwards (upstream) from the right, the Blinn1SG (Shading Group) is getting its shading

information from the Blinn1 material swatch and nurbsSphere node. The Blinn1 node is getting its color information from the checker1 node, which is also outputting its alpha channel information to a reverse node (reverse1). The reverse1 node, true to its name, reverses the information it's receiving and passes it on to the 2D bump node (bump2d1), which connects to the Blinn's bump channel input. The leather1 and brownian1 textures connect to the checker1 texture's color attributes, and there are placement nodes for each of the textures: a 2D placement node (place2dTexture1) for the checker1 texture and 3D placement nodes (place3dTexture1 and place3dTexture2) for the brownian1 and leather1 textures, respectively.

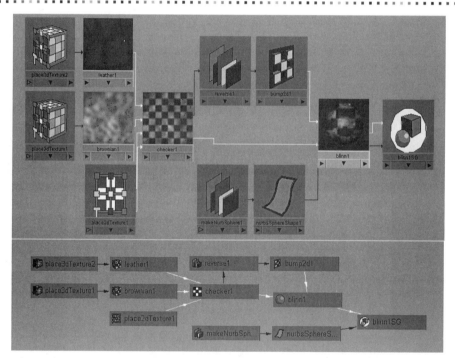

Figure 19.4 *A network of swatches in the Hypershade (top) and Hypergraph (bottom) windows*

Note that everything is arranged exactly the same way as in the Hypergraph node network. Like the Hypergraph, the Hypershade lets you move the mouse over the lines connecting the nodes to find out exactly what attributes are being connected.

- The green lines are triple attributes, such as the RGB color information or the world space (XYZ) coordinates.

- The light-blue lines are double attributes, such as the UV coordinates of a geometry surface.

- The dark-blue lines are single attributes, such as the 8-bit grayscale masking values of the alpha information.

To check or change these and other color designations, select Window ➔ Settings/Preferences ➔ Colors and go to the Hypergraph/Hypershade section.

MM dragging a node over another node opens the appropriate connection list. Ctrl+MM dragging a node over another one lets Maya choose the default connection automatically. If you want to use the Connection Editor to connect the two nodes, Shift+MM drag the node. You can also drag a node into another node's Attribute Editor.

The nodes and networks can also be imported or exported. To bring in a scene, use the File ➔ Import function or open your current project directory in the Visor panel and drag in the Maya scene you want. You can save specific nodes or node networks by selecting them and applying File ➔ Export Selection. The nodes will be saved as a Maya scene.

Using Shading and Texturing Attributes

Shading in Maya can be divided into the categories of color, shininess, bumpiness, transparency, and self-illumination. We will go through these "global" material properties first, and then proceed to cover some general texture properties.

Coloring Surfaces

When you create a material and open its Attribute Editor, you can find its default Color attribute in the Common Material Attributes section. The default is set as a gray color with zero saturation and 0.5 value in HSV, or 0.5 RGB. Maya provides many ways to adjust the color of the material:

- Use the Color Chooser. To access the Color Chooser, click the color box beside the Color attribute.

- Connect textures or image files to the Color attribute, typically by dragging them to the Color attribute in the Attribute Editor. The Diffuse attribute acts as a scale factor for the color values, with 0.0 being black and 1.0 being the original color values. The default Diffuse setting is 0.8. The image files can be single pictures, sequences of pictures, or a movie file (as you saw in the previous chapter).

- Map 2D textures or image files to a surface as normal UV textures or as one of many types of projections: planar, spherical, cylindrical, ball, cubic, triplanar, concentric, or perspective.

- Apply 2D textures as stencils.

- Map 3D textures as if they were solid objects occupying space in and around the surface.

- Use a Surface Shader for coloring a material node. Although it is stored in the Materials folder, a Surface Shader has the information for only the color, transparency, glow, and matte opacity of a material. When you want to use the same color for many different materials or textures, Surface Shader enables you to have one node control the color information of many nodes.

- Use the Shading Map tool to color a surface. Shading Map is typically used for non-photorealistic, or cartoonish, shading effects. It takes the colors sampled by a regular shader and replaces those colors with a simpler color scheme, using the brightness and hue of the original colors.

- Use the environmental shaders such as Env Sky texture or Env Sphere texture with an accompanying image file to simulate a surrounding environment, either as background image or reflections on surfaces.

Figure 19.5 illustrates some of the many ways colors and textures can be created on a simple sphere in the Hypershade.

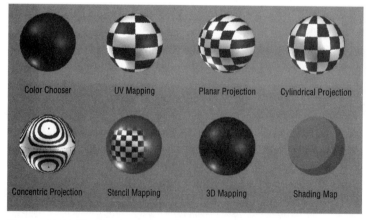

Figure 19.5 *Various ways to color a sphere*

In Maya 3, you can now assign textures directly to surfaces. RM click over the texture, and you can see a new command, Assign Texture's Material to Selection. When the texture is assigned this way, Maya creates a default Lambert material prefixed with the texture name.

Controlling Shininess

Different materials reflect light differently on their surfaces. Lambert material does not have any specular highlight. Blinn, Phong, and PhongE materials have different variables for calculating specular highlight.

Blinn has the softest specular highlights among the three, as shown in Figure 19.6, and is usually the material recommended for surfaces with bumps or displacements, because it tends to rope or flicker less than the Phong materials. Blinn and Phong are called *isotropic* materials, which means that they reflect specular light identically in all directions.

Anisotropic material reflects specular light differently in different directions, according to its Specular Shading settings. It more faithfully adheres to the way materials such as hair, satin cloth, feathers, or CDs reflect light unevenly.

Shading Map also calculates specular highlight, but in a non-photorealistic way, as mentioned in the previous section. The Use Background Material's Specular and Reflectivity variables work only with raytracing. The layered shader does not have specular variables, because it creates layered materials. See the "Applying Textures" section later in this chapter for more information about layered shaders.

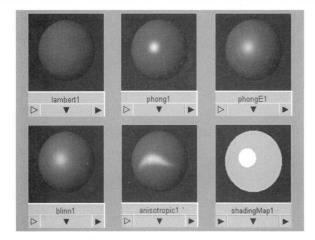

Figure 19.6 *Specular highlight properties of materials*

All the materials with specular highlight have Specular Color, Reflectivity, and Reflected Color attributes. You can use the Color Chooser to tint the specular color, or map textures or image files, in the same way that you can with material color. In Figure 19.7(a), the Specular Color attribute in the sphere with the anisotropic shader has been tinted to match the color of the material. In (b), the sphere has a checker texture mapped to Specular Color. You can also do the same thing with Reflected Color, and fake reflection in this way, although true reflection occurs only with raytracing. In (c), the sphere has an Env Sky shader with the floor texture mapped to its Reflected Color, making it appear as though the sphere is reflecting a sky environment. The sphere in (d) is raytraced; notice the reflections on the floor and in the sphere.

Figure 19.7 *Specular color and reflection*

Raytracing

Raytracing lets you create refractions and shadows through transparent objects. Although raytracing may be desirable and necessary when you want to create photorealistic images, it is also more expensive than the regular rendering. When the settings are set high, the render time can increase very dramatically.

To raytrace, you need to turn on Raytracing under Raytracing Quality in the Render Globals window. For refractions, you also need to open the material Attribute Editor of the selected surface and turn on the Refractions setting in Raytrace Options. To have raytraced shadows, you also need to open the shadow casting light's Attribute Editor and check the Use Ray Trace Shadows setting in the Raytrace Shadow Attributes section. We will discuss raytraced shadows again in Chapter 20, "Lighting." You also can control whether a surface is visible in reflections on other surfaces, by using its Attribute Editor to turn on or off its Render Stats ➜ Visible in Reflections setting.

· ·

Creating Bumpiness

There are two ways to create bumpiness on a surface:

- Apply a bump map to a surface, which fools the camera into believing that there are bumps on a smooth surface.

- Apply a displacement map, which actually moves the geometry to create the bumps.

There are advantages and disadvantages to both methods. Bump mapping is much more efficient to render, but it fails at the edges of a surface and cannot create the appearance of extreme bumpiness, as seen in Figure 19.8 (a). Displacement mapping does a better job of creating bumpiness because it actually displaces the geometry of the surface, but it takes longer to render. Also, the geometry's UV spans or its tessellation count often must increase before you see proper displacement, as shown in Figure 19.8 (b) and (c).

· ·

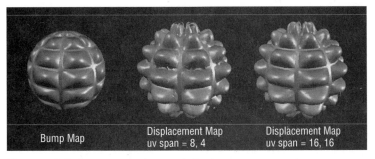

Figure 19.8 *Bump mapping and displacement mapping*

The displacement mapping algorithm has been significantly improved in Maya 3. The surface is displaced more efficiently, tessellating only in the areas that need the bumping, reducing processing time and making this method more practical to use. Also, displacement mapping no longer creates the additional bump node, which makes it much easier to place separate bump maps on the surface being deformed.

When you drag a texture over a material node and connect to its bump map, or drag to its Bump Mapping field in the Attribute Editor, a bump map node is created. If the texture is 2D, a bump2D node is created. If the texture is 3D, a bump3D node is created. Projection bumps also create a bump3D node. The texture's alpha value, which is a single-channel attribute, connects to the bump node's Bump Value attribute. The bump node then outputs a triple-channel outNormal to the material's normalCamera attribute, which creates the appearance of bumpiness on the material surface.

When you connect a texture to a material's Displacement attribute, a displacement node is created. It connects not to the material, but directly to the material's Shader Group node. You can also bump a displacement map to add more detail to a bump-mapped or displacement-mapped surface. In the example in Figure 19.9, we applied a ramp texture to a Blinn material as a displacement map, which we assigned to a plane, as seen in (a). We then connected a bulge texture to the middle color input of the ramp, adding detail to the displacement of the plane, as seen in (b). Another ramp texture with water texture as color input was then applied to the Blinn material as a bump map. The result appears in (c). The lower part of Figure 19.9 shows the whole sequence of connections in the Hypershade window.

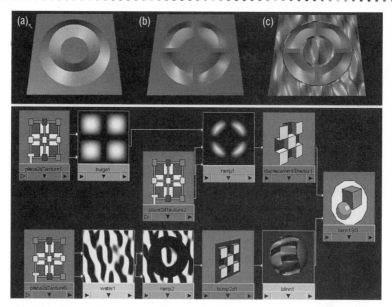

Figure 19.9 *Adding a bump map to a displacement-mapped surface*

Adding Transparency

Transparency is a triple-channel RGB color attribute, with black making the material opaque and white making it transparent. As with color and specular attributes, you can map textures or image files for transparency, as shown in Figure 19.10. Once a material becomes transparent, you can also turn on refraction for raytracing. The Refractive Index in the Raytrace Options section of the material's Attribute Editor controls how much the light bends as it passes through the transparent material. For the refraction to have any effect, there must be more than one layer of surface that the camera can see through. You can set up a simple example with a sphere and a textured floor to test how they raytrace with different Refractive Index settings, as shown below (and in the Color Gallery on the CD).

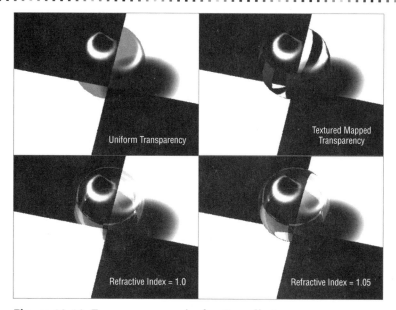

Figure 19.10 *Transparency and refraction effects*

The Refraction Limit setting is in the Raytrace Options section of the material's Attribute Editor, and it's also listed simply as Refractions in the Raytracing Quality section of the Render Globals dialog box. Both settings need to be adjusted; the lower of the two values will act as the maximum refraction limit for the material.

You can also use transparency to layer different materials and textures on top of others with a layered shader. For more information about using layered shaders, see the section later in this chapter dealing with texturing the eyes.

A related material attribute that needs a brief mention here is Translucence. A translucent object isn't completely transparent, but it does transmit light through its surface. Objects such as sheets of paper, leaves, clouds, ice, and hair are examples of translucent materials, as shown in Figure 19.11. (This image is also in the Color Gallery on the CD.)

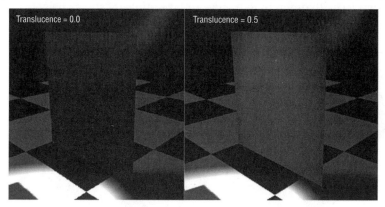

Figure 19.11 *Examples of translucence*

Adding Self-Illumination

You can add self-illumination attributes to materials through Incandescence, Glow Intensity, and Ambient Color settings.

Incandescence

Most materials have Incandescence under their Common Material Attributes. This attribute makes the surface appear to give off light on its own. Red-hot metal and neon signs would be good examples of noticeable incandescence.

Incandescence can also be used more subtly on many other surfaces. With an almost unnoticeable amount of incandescence, a person's eyes seem much brighter, and flower petals and tree leaves look much more like living things. You can also map textures or image files to Incandescence, and you can combine this attribute with Glow (discussed next) as shown in Figure 19.12. (A color version appears in the Color Gallery on the CD.)

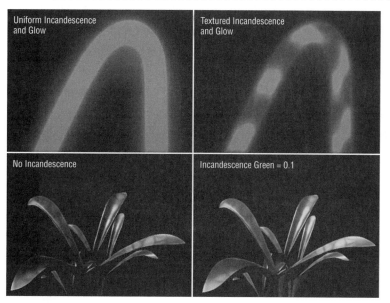

Figure 19.12 *Examples of Incandescence and Glow Intensity*

Glow Intensity

Materials can glow as well. Incandescence usually works better when it is combined with a bit of glow. Many materials have a Glow Intensity attribute under the Special Effects section in their Attribute Editor. When Glow Intensity is at zero, no glow is calculated; when the value is something other than zero, materials start to glow, as shown in Figure 19.13 (also in the Color Gallery on the CD). The Hide Source setting in the same section allows you to hide the surface with the material and show just the glow. Glow can be very effective in creating certain atmospheric effects with surfaces, such as a hazy moon, a warm sunset, or candlelight, as shown in Figure 19.13. You can edit the Shader Glow Attribute Editor to control the way the surfaces will glow in a scene. The Shader Glow swatch is located under the Post Process folder in the Visor panel. Halo Intensity works much like Glow Intensity, and the values you edit in Shadow Glow have global effect on the scene.

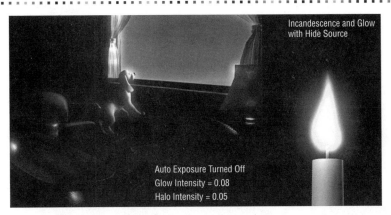

Figure 19.13 *Examples of Glow Intensity*

You need to be careful when using glow effects, because they can get tricky. Unlike the Incandescence attribute, glow is a post-process. It bases its calculations on the amount of light the surface is receiving from the light sources, including other objects that are glowing. In some circumstances, an object's glow intensity will visibly change when other glowing objects enter the scene, resulting in annoying flicker. In such a situation, you need to open the Shader Glow Attribute Editor, and turn off its Auto Exposure. This stops Maya from automatically calculating glow intensity in a scene. But you will have to readjust the Glow Intensity and the Halo Intensity in the Attribute Editor to get the proper glow look for the surfaces in the scene.

Another thing to watch out for with glow effects is that their intensity can change with changes in the render resolution. This means when you are test rendering with glow effects, you should test them with the same resolution as the final output.

Ambient Color

Materials also have Ambient Color. This attribute is similar to Incandescence in the way it lights the surface, but Incandescence illuminates the material, and Ambient Color instead illuminates the material's color or texture. Ambient Color is also different from Diffuse, which brightens the material color in areas where the light is hitting the surface; Ambient Color lights the whole surface. You could render a surface only with Ambient Color if you wished.

Applying Textures

Maya's Visor panel offers 26 textures: ten 2D textures, eleven 3D textures, five environment textures, and a new Layered texture. With the exception of Layered, all the textures get a placement node when they are created. Most textures also have a Color Balance section and an Effects section in their list of attributes.

Texture Placement

3D textures or 2D projections are placed much like real objects, as opposed to 2D textures, which occupy the UV space on the surface. You can transform them in the world space, and you can shear them as well. Be aware that rendering them generally takes longer than rendering 2D textures. You can convert 3D textures or projections to 2D image files using the Edit ➜ Convert To File Texture command in the Hypershade window, but you may lose some quality in the process.

Because of the nature of 3D texture placements, when a surface with a 3D texture deforms, the surface will seem to swim through the texture, as you can see comparing Figure 19.14 (a) and (b). To solve this problem, you can use Reference Object, which enables the 3D textures or 2D projections to deform with the surface. After you have assigned a 3D texture to a surface, select the surface and select Shading ➜ Create Texture Reference Object in the Rendering module. Maya creates a reference object, translated 5 units in the X axis by default. If you want the same 3D texture placement, either translate the reference object back to zero in the X axis or translate the 3D texture placement node 5 units in the X axis. Notice that the texture in Figure 19.14 (c) is squashed and stretched with the surface.

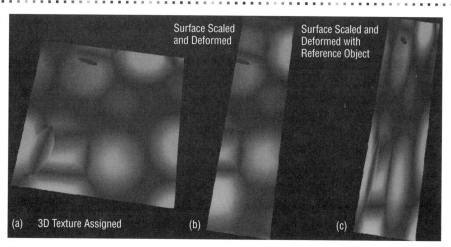

Figure 19.14 *Reference Object enables a texture to deform.*

A reference object must be created before any deformation or animation is applied to the original surface. A texture's placement is determined by its relationship to the reference object, not to the original surface being deformed.

By default, a place2dTexture node completely covers whatever surface it is assigned to. The Coverage attribute of the place2dTexture node lets you control the percentage of the surface area the texture covers, and Translate Frame and Rotate Frame transform the texture over the surface in UV. These attributes should not be confused with the UV Repeat, Offset, and Rotate attributes, which determine the way the texture is mapped within the coverage area. The examples in Figure 19.15 show how the various attributes affect the texture placement.

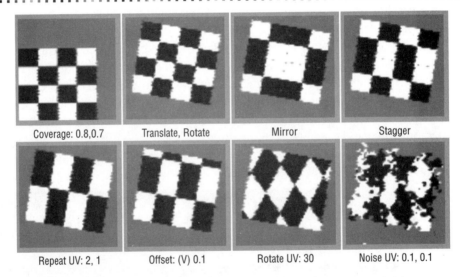

Coverage: 0.8,0.7	Translate, Rotate	Mirror	Stagger
Repeat UV: 2, 1	Offset: (V) 0.1	Rotate UV: 30	Noise UV: 0.1, 0.1

Figure 19.15 *The place2dTexture node with different placement variables*

Color Balance and Effects

A texture's Color Gain and Color Offset attributes are typically used to control its color and brightness. The Default Color attribute is the color of the surface area that is not covered by the texture. Usually, you wouldn't need to change this setting. However, if you are using the texture as a mask and the texture coverage is partial, you may at times need to turn the Default Color attribute to black or white.

The Alpha Gain attribute scales the alpha channel and is used for bump or displacement effects. The default value is at 1.0, which usually produces a bit too much bumpiness for most situations. Figure 19.16 is an example of the fractal texture, first with the default settings of gray for Default Color and 1.0 for Alpha Gain, and then with Default Color turned to white and Alpha Gain turned down to 0.3 to tone down the extreme bumping. The fractal texture's Threshold value was also pushed up to 0.7.

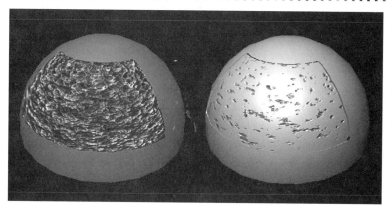

Figure 19.16 *The fractal texture with different Default Color and Alpha Gain settings*

To use the texture image as a bump map, turn on Alpha Is Luminance. When the image is calculated for bumping, the values are determined by a grayscale version of the image, with white bumping up, and black bumping down.

In the Effects section, many textures have Filter, Filter Offset, and Invert attributes. The Invert setting inverts the texture's colors and hue, changing white to black and vice versa. It also inverts the alpha channel, changing bumps into dents and vice versa.

The Filter and Filter Offset attributes blur textures, and they are useful for when the textures are too sharp or are aliasing. When a texture is too sharp, you may have shimmer or noise problems with the surface when the textured surface or the camera is animated. By blurring or smoothing the texture, you can usually make those problems disappear. Filter's default value is 1.0, but you can lower it to something close to zero. Filter Offset basically adds a constant value to the Filter attribute, and usually a tiny fractional value is sufficient to correct any excessive sharpness.

Figure 19.17 shows the same fractal texture as in Figure 19.16, but with Invert turned on, Default Color set to neutral gray, and Alpha Gain moved back to the default value of 1.0. The first half sphere has Filter set to 0.01, and it is a bit too sharp and may shimmer with a moving camera. The second half sphere has Filter Offset set to 0.005, and the bumps have been noticeably blurred, perhaps even a bit too much. But that much blurring has made the second surface safe from any problematic shimmering.

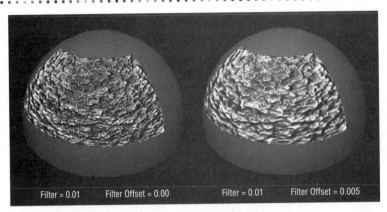

Figure 19.17 *The fractal texture with Filter and Filter Offset*

For 3D textures, the Effects section has three extra attributes: Wrap, Local, and Blend, shown in Figure 19.18 (and in the Color Gallery on the CD). Because a 3D texture is placed as a solid cube around an object, if the object is partially moved outside the cube, that area is colored by the Default Color attribute, as shown below. Wrap, which is on by default, enables the texture to extend to cover the whole surface. The Blend attribute mixes the Default Color to the texture color. It only works when Wrap is turned off. 3D textures are also by default applied globally, meaning that when a texture is assigned to three surfaces, those surfaces get different parts of the texture. When Local is turned on, the textures are applied locally, so that the three surfaces get the same texture placement.

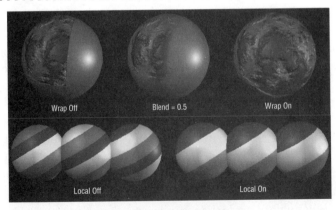

Figure 19.18 *Wrap, Local, and Blend effects*

Fix Texture Warp

For NURBS objects only, there's a Fix Texture Warp setting in the Attribute Editor, under the Texture Map section. Because of the parameterization of the UVs, NURBS surfaces sometimes warp the UV textures applied to them. Recall from Chapter 5, "NURBS Modeling," that chord-length parameterization of surfaces does a better job of mapping a UV texture to a surface than the Uniform method but is more difficult to model with. Fix Texture Warp calculates the NURBS surface in a way that decreases the warping, as shown by the bottles in Figure 19.19. The true advantage of the Fix Texture Warp function can be seen when the surface is being animated.

Figure 19.19 *Three bottles with textures*

Layered Texture

Our presentation of textures would not be complete without briefly introducing the Layered Texture node, a new addition in Maya 3. It works like the Layered shader node, except that it works directly with textures, not materials, and it has more options to composite the layers in different ways. Plane (a) in Figure 19.20 has a Blinn material with a Layered texture connected to the material's color. There is a single layer of Checker texture assigned to the Layered texture. When a Leather texture is added to the Layered texture (connected to input color[1]), it is mapped under the first checker texture, as seen in the Attribute Editor window. Different values of Alpha and Blend Mode in the Checker texture layer will bring out or hide the leather texture layer. The settings seen in the window produce plane (b). An Alpha of 0.5 with Difference Blend Mode results in plane (c). Plane (d) is created by applying a circular Ramp to the Alpha channel of the top layer, causing the Leather texture to show only through the middle circle. You can add as many layers as you want into the Layered texture.

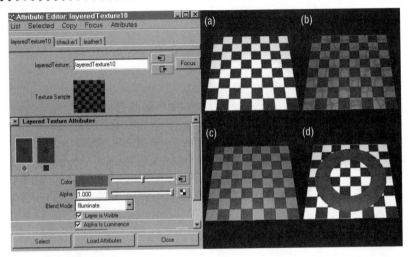

Figure 19.20 *Layered textures*

Using Shading and Texturing Techniques

Now we're ready to apply some of the shading and texturing techniques discussed in this chapter. We will work with the various models that we developed in previous chapters as examples.

Texturing the Puppy

In Chapter 8, "Organic Modeling," we constructed a dog model using many NURBS patches. If we had to texture each piece one by one, it would be a complicated and tedious task. One way to get around this is to apply a 3D texture and create a reference object for the dog. Here are the general steps:

1. Select all the patches of the dog, except for the eyes and the nose, and assign a Blinn shader. (You could also assign a Lambert or an anisotropic

shader, depending on the way you want the dog's fur to shine or not shine.) Adjust the specular settings until you are satisfied with the way the material looks.

2. Assign a leather texture as the color. You need to use a 3D texture, such as leather, for this example because a 2D texture will map differently to the different patches. Adjust the settings and the placement node until your dog looks something like the one shown in Figure 19.21 (and in the Color Gallery on the CD). Connect a solid fractal to Blinn's Bump attribute, and make it bump very subtly, as also shown in Figure 19.21. The Attribute Editor values on the left are only a rough guide. You will want to use the IPR tool to fine-tune the texturing.

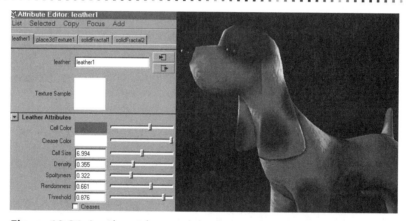

Figure 19.21 Leather values and the dog

Leather is a remarkably useful texture. It can serve as basis for a great variety of surfaces, such as spots on dog fur, human skin, grunge, plant leaves, or a field of stars, just to name a few examples.

3. When you are satisfied with the colors and the placement of the spots and their sizes, group all the patch surfaces under a group node, select the group node, and choose Shading ➜ Create Texture Reference Object. The reference duplicate of the dog is created five units away from the original dog. Translate the referenced duplicate back to the origin, and the texture placement on the dog should be the same as before.

When you're finished, test the dog's legs or head to make sure the spots move and deform with the surface.

Adding Textures to the Living Room

We created the living room model in Chapter 5 and added a lamp to it in Chapter 6, "Polygons and Subdivision Surfaces." Now we will add some textures to make the floor and wall appear old, and then refine the lamp with some texture and glow attributes.

The Floor and Wall Textures

Let's create a worn-out floor. It takes only a few more steps to go from a clean floor with a single texture to a more complicated dirty floor, but often the results (improvements?) can be startling.

1. Start with a Blinn material for the floor, and assign a marble texture to it as its color. Turn down the specularity quite a bit.

2. Create a 2D fractal texture and a brownian texture. Connect them to the Vein Color and Filler Color of the marble texture, respectively, as shown below (and in the Color Gallery on the CD). You can adjust the texture settings as you see fit. You may also want to connect the same fractal texture to marble as a bump map, and turn down the Alpha Gain setting to a very subtle level.

3. For an old wall, first we need an acceptable wall pattern. Start with a Blinn material and apply a checker texture as color. The placement node for the first picture shown below has a Repeat UV of 32 and 1. Connect a cloth texture to

Color1 of the checker attribute, and make its Repeat UV, 64 and 32. You should see something like the top-right picture below, and we have our wall pattern.

4. To create a worn-out look, you can use a handy technique called *smearing*. Take a brownian texture and connect its alpha channel to the Offset U and Offset V attributes of the placement node for the checker texture, as in the bottom-right picture below (and in the Color Gallery on the CD). Reduce the Alpha Gain value to keep the smear effect from being too drastic. The bottom-left picture is the result of a subtle smear.

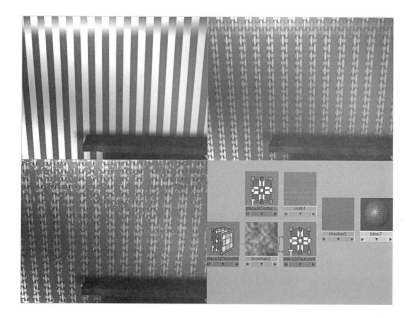

At this point, the colors themselves are still pretty clean, but there are many ways you can make the colors dirtier. You can map the Ambient Color attribute of the Blinn material or Color2 of the Checker attribute, tint the lights shining on the wall, or map their Color attributes. If you want complete control over the dirtiness of sections of the wall, you can reassign a layered texture to the wall, Blinn, and then add as many layers of dirt as needed.

The Lamp Textures

Let's try texturing the floor lamp we created in Chapter 5. The lamp stand, lampshade, and lightbulb need shading and texturing. We will use a ramp texture for the lamp stand, but first we need to briefly go over what a ramp texture is.

A ramp basically consists of layers of colors, and it is one of the most useful textures. By default, the ramp texture has three layers of RGB colors, which are called color entries. You can create additional color entries by LM clicking in the ramp. The circles that appear at the left side of the ramp allow you to drag the color entries, or you can type in a precise position value in the Selected Position field. The square boxes at the right side delete the color entries.

As you can see in the examples in Figure 19.22 (and in the Color Gallery on the CD), you can apply the ramp along the V isoparms, U isoparms, diagonally, radially, circularly, and so on. The color entries mix according to a set Interpolation type; if you set Interpolation to None, the color entries will not mix. You can also distort the ramp with waves and noise, and you can map other textures into any of the color entries.

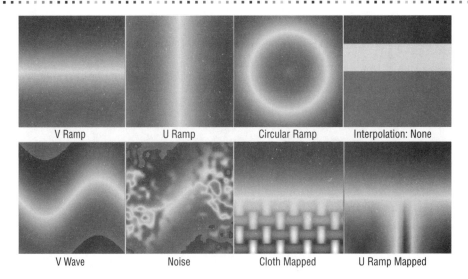

Figure 19.22 *Examples of different ramps*

Now let's add textures to the lamp.

1. Assign a Blinn material to the lamp stand. Add a ramp to its color. Delete one of the color entries in the ramp texture, and set Interpolation to None. Make the first color entry white and the second entry blue. Adjust the position of the blue entry until you see in the model window that the white is covering only the lamp base and the blue is covering the lamp pole, as shown next.

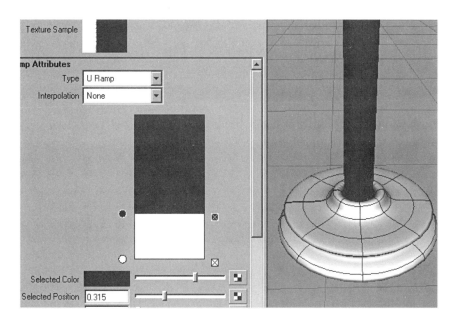

2. Apply a fractal texture to the ramp's white color entry, and apply a wood texture to the blue color entry. You could, for added effect, apply a subtle fractal bump on the Blinn material. You can use the same fractal texture for the bump mapping as you can control its Alpha Gain value without affecting its color values. Adjust the settings until you see something like the lamp stand in (a) on the following page. (This image is also in the Color Gallery on the CD.) A little glow was also added to the Blinn material.

3. We want the lamp cover to be thin and a bit transparent. Assign a Blinn material, then a checker texture as Color. The checker texture for this example has a Repeat UV of 16 and 32. In the Blinn material's Attribute Editor, increase the Transparency setting a bit, as well as the Ambient Color attribute; add a tiny bit of Translucence. Glow Intensity should be fairly strong, but not so strong as to wash out the texture. Play with the values in IPR until you see something like the lamp cover in (b).

4. For the lightbulb, assign a Blinn to the bulb, make the color dark orange, and choose a darker orange for the Incandescence setting. Raise the Glow Intensity setting and turn on Hide Source. Start an IPR process and adjust the settings until you see something like the lamp shown in (c).

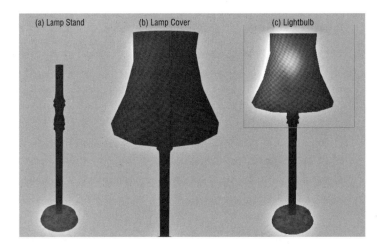

(a) Lamp Stand   (b) Lamp Cover   (c) Lightbulb

The glow on the materials will change slightly each time you introduce a new element into the scene, so don't spend too much time fine-tuning the glow until you have all the elements you want and know the resolution of the picture in the final render.

Shading and Texturing Polygons and Subdivision Surfaces

So far, we've worked only with NURBS surfaces. Shading works a bit differently with polygons, and unless you are firmly grounded in the basics, texturing polygonal surfaces can become confusing and frustrating. This is especially true of UV mapping in polygons. Texturing subdivision surfaces is essentially the same as texturing polygons, as you will see at the end of this section.

UVs in Polygons

As with NURBS surfaces, textures are mapped to polygon surfaces parametrically, with UV values. But UVs are not an intrinsic part of a polygonal surface. By definition, a NURBS surface has four sides and neatly arranged rows and columns of UV parameters. But because polygons have arbitrary topology, their UV information exists separately from the geometry, and must be mapped to the geometry. The default polygon primitives in Maya come with UVs already mapped neatly to the geometry, but they can be lost or replaced with new sets of UV mapping. Figure 19.23 shows examples of primitives and their default UV mappings above them. The pictures below the primitives show how the primitives can take on different UV maps.

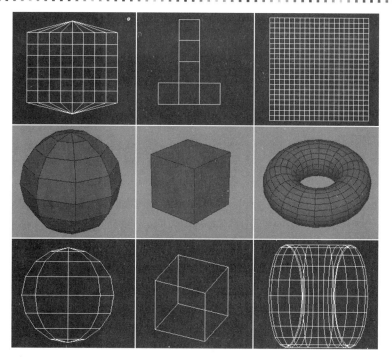

Figure 19.23 *Polygon primitives and UV mappings*

A polygonal surface can acquire UV values through various types of projections, normalization, or unitization. The best way to explain these concepts and the other tools you need to use for texturing polygons is to try out some examples.

Working in Texture View

The Texture View window allows you to work on UVs that are already mapped to a polygonal surface. In the modeling window, you can RM click over polygons to select UVs, which occupy the same position as vertices. When vertices are selected, they turn bright yellow, but when UVs are selected, they turn bright green. You can also select polygon components the same way in this window, but the shapes shown are flat 2D representations of UVs being mapped to polygon faces. You can work on UVs only in the Texture View: you can transform them, copy and paste them, and access the texture-editing functions to edit them.

First, let's create a polygon to work with in the Texture View window.

1. Start a new scene and select Window ➜ Texture View.

2. Select Polygons ➜ Create Polygon Tool ❑. Make sure that the Texture option is set to Normalize.

3. Go to top view and create a triangle, as shown below. Press Enter to complete the action, and you will see the triangle appear in the Texture View window.

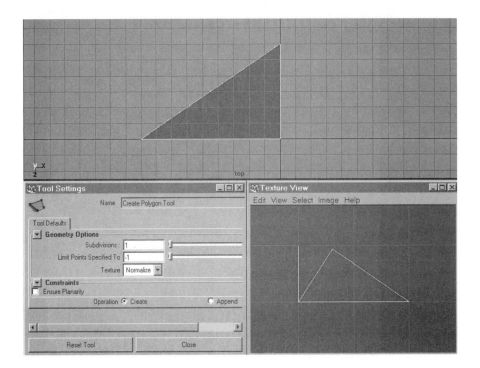

4. Create a Blinn shader in Hypershade, assign a Diagonal ramp to it with just two colors, and assign the shader to the triangle.

5. Press **6** to get into Textured Display mode, and select the triangle again. Your display should look something like the one shown next. Note that the triangle fits the texture horizontally in Texture View, which represents U parameterization from 0 to 1. Normalized UVs map the texture to the polygon surface in this manner.

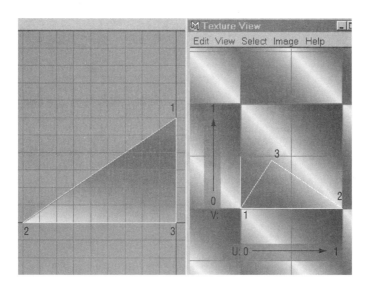

 It's a good idea to keep the Texture View window open when you are working with polygon textures. Most of the Texture submenu options can be accessed from this window, and we will use it throughout this section.

In the Texture View window, the texture image repeats according to the settings in Image Range; the default is 10 repetitions. If you find the default grid setting distracting, you can turn it off or change its display setting.

Transforming UVs

You can transform UVs in the Texture View window in the same way that you transform regular vertices. If the selected faces have a projection mapping, you can edit the Mapping manipulator as well.

1. In the Texture View window, select all the UVs and select the Move tool. A 2D Move manipulator appears. Move the manipulator, and you will see the texture in the triangular face update in the modeling window.

2. Select the Rotate tool, and a 2D Rotate manipulator appears. Rotate the UVs, and again, the texture inside the triangle updates accordingly, as shown below.

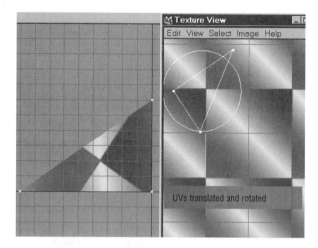

3. Append a quad face to the triangle. Open the Append To Polygon Tool window, turn off Ensure Planarity, and set Texture to Normalize. Select the right edge, switch to side view, and click the vertices up so that you end up with a diagonal face, as shown below.

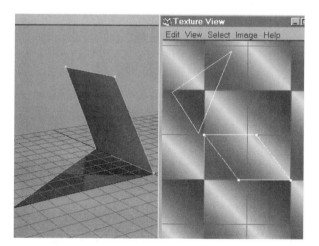

When it becomes part of the surface, the ramp texture is automatically assigned to the new quad face. As the UVs of the new face are normalized, the ramp texture is mapped to the diagonal face horizontally, from 0 to 1, as shown above.

Sewing Textures

In our example, although the faces are attached to each other with shared edges and vertices, the UVs are mapped separately. This creates a problem if we want a texture that will go across the two faces. To have the two faces share the texture mapping, you can *sew* the textures.

1. First, let's position the textures properly. In the modeling window, select the UVs on the edge that joins the faces.

2. In the Texture View window, take note of which two UVs of the triangle and the diagonal faces are selected. Select all the UVs of the diagonal face, and then rotate and translate them so that the two UVs of the triangle and the diagonal face are next to each other, as shown below.

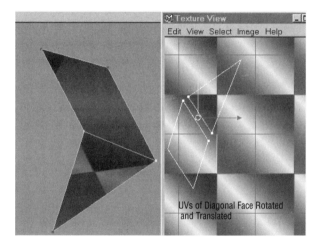

3. Select the common edge of the two faces and then, in the Texture View window, select Edit ➜ Sew UVs. The UVs of the triangle and the diagonal face snap to each other and become shared UVs. The Edit ➜ Cut UVs command performs the opposite function. It takes shared UVs and separates them, creating two new UVs per vertex.

Users of previous Maya versions will note that Cut UVs and Sew UVs are new Maya 3 names for the Cut Texture and Sew Texture commands.

Unitizing UVs

Now let's see what happens when we unitize our polygonal surface, which makes the UVs of the selected faces fit into a texture UV unit.

1. Open the Append To Polygon Tool window. Set Texture to Unitize and turn on Ensure Planarity.

2. In perspective view, select the longest edge of the triangle. When you see pink arrows, click the nearest edge of the diagonal face.

3. In front view, click a vertex straight up to the diagonal face's height. The new face is planar, and it should look something like the image shown below. The Unitized setting stretches the UVs for the new face to fit the texture UV unit.

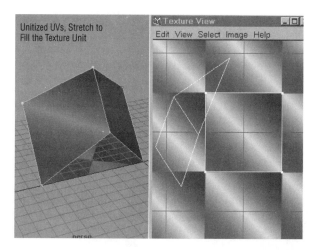

4. Repeat the sewing procedure: rotate and translate the unitized UVs to line up to the triangle and sew it. You should see something like the image shown under step 2 in the next section. Notice that now there is a smooth texture transition from the triangle to the unitized face.

Assigning UVs

From time to time, you will encounter models imported from other programs that carry no UV information with them. Or you may choose to delete the UVs of polygons you are working on. You will then need to assign UV values to those polygons before you can render them, following a procedure like the one outlined here.

1. Open the Append To Polygon Tool window again if you've closed it. Set Texture to None.

2. Select the top edge of the unitized face. When you see the arrows, select the top edge of the diagonal face. Press Enter to create a triangle, as shown below. Although it is part of the polygonal surface, this new triangle has no UV information, and therefore no texture is displayed. Notice that nothing new appears in the Texture View window.

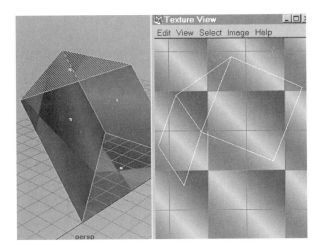

3. Select the face of the new triangle. Open the Normalize UVs option window from the Edit Polygons ➜ Texture submenu or the Edit menu in the Texture View window. The default setting will make the triangle stretch from 0 to 1 in both U and V, which is not what we want for this example.

4. Select Preserve Aspect Ratio, and it will normalize only one of the two values, in this case, U. Click the Apply button, and the texture should appear on the new triangle in the modeling window. Accordingly, the triangle, in its normalized UV points, should appear in the Texture View window.

5. Sew the new UVs to the diagonal face by rotating and translating the new triangle and then sewing the triangle and the existing rectangle edges, as shown below.

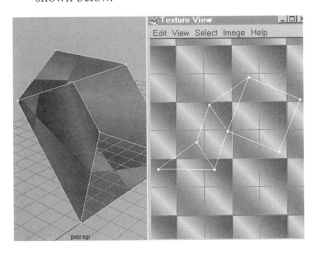

Projection Mapping

Maya has four types of projection mapping functions, which project textures onto the UV coordinates of the selected polygon surfaces, all available from the Texture sub-menu: Planar, Cylindrical, Spherical Mapping, and in Maya 3, Automatic Mapping. There is also a Create UVs Based On Camera function, which creates UV values of a planar mapping projected from the camera view. Let's try out the planar mapping.

1. Start a new scene and create a polygonal cube. With the cube still selected, open the Texture View window. You should see the cube UVs laid out as shown below. The default setting for the cube normalizes UVs, which means that each face will receive a whole texture, and the UVs are all connected for the whole object.

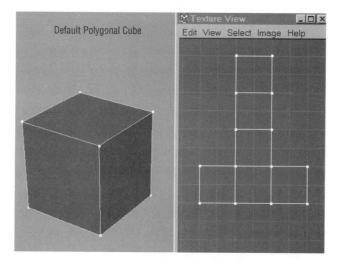

2. Rotate the cube on the Z axis 45 degrees. Then select its front face. Make sure that the Assign Shader to Each Projection function on the Texture sub-menu is checked, and apply Planar Mapping with the default settings. The Assign Shader to Each Projection setting automatically creates a default polygon shader with a checker texture and assigns it to the selected polygon. The default planar projection fits the texture to the bounding box of the selected object or face and projects the map along the Z axis.

3. The black and white checker colors are too intense for viewing in the Texture View window. In Hypershade, select the checker texture and assign dull blue to one color and green to the other. Note how the UV points are mapped as a square rotated 45 degrees in the Texture View window.

4. Select the cube. If you don't see the texture showing in the Texture View window, as shown below, select Image ➔ Selected Images ➔ texturedFacets ➔ pCube1.

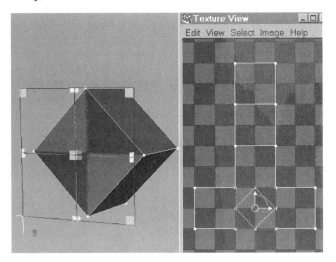

Do not confuse UV projection mappings for polygons with the texture projections for NURBS objects; they are completely different processes. When creating textures for polygons in the Hypershade, use the Normal setting, which creates UV textures. If you need to create a texture as a projection, the Interactive Placement button should be used only for NURBS objects, not polygons.

Mapping would be a bit harder if, for example, we selected the face at the top and rotated it in the Y and X axes to make it nearly perpendicular and diagonal, as shown in Figure 19.24. If we apply the default planar (Z-axis) mapping, we get stretched UVs (as in the top-left image). Note how the UVs are stretched in the Texture View window as well. If we set the option to Y-axis projection, again the result is not what we want (as in the top-right image). We could grab the manipulator handle and rotate and scale until the texture fits the surface straight, but that takes effort. Instead, we can set the option to Fit To Best Plane. The projection will extend in the direction of the surface normal, and as a result, we get a perfect fit (as in the bottom-left image). Another option is to apply planar mapping with camera direction (as in the bottom-right image). For the last example, we tried selecting the whole cube as an object, so all the UVs would become mapped exactly as the UVs you see through the camera in the modeling window.

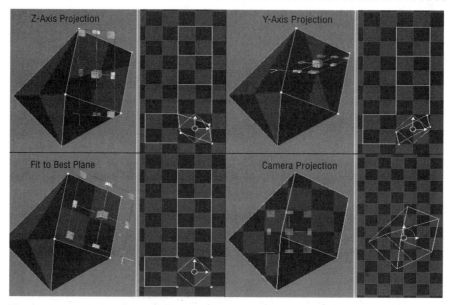

Figure 19.24 *Projections and corresponding Texture Views*

The Cylindrical and Spherical Mapping options are similar in principle to planar mapping, and they are applied in the same way. Often, the shape of the polygonal object will dictate which type of mapping is best suited for it.

One of the big difficulties with polygon UV mapping is that on complex models it is hard to get evenly spread out UVs. As the two examples in Figure 19.25 demonstrate, it's one thing to make a texture map evenly on a simple surface like a plane, quite another thing to map it evenly on more complicated surfaces.

Figure 19.25 *Mapping a ramp texture to a simple and a complex surface*

Let's look at the head more closely. Figure 19.26 shows the UV mapping that was applied to the head, which was a planar projection. When texturing the front part of the face, as shown in the middle picture, the UVs are evenly spreading the ramp texture. But when we try to map the ramp texture to the side of the head, we get stretching, as seen in the last picture. Getting rid of such texture stretching (or other problems, such as squashing or seams between faces) is often the more difficult part of working with polygons.

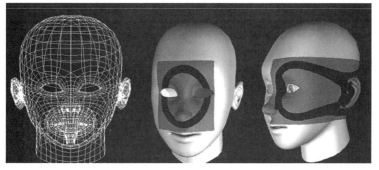

Figure 19.26 *UV mapping of a human head*

Creating Clean UVs

In order to avoid or reduce the stretching and overlapping of textures on polygon surfaces, we need to create clean UV coordinates. This usually means creating UVs that are neither overlapping nor stretched or squashed in relation to the actual surface areas of the corresponding polygon surfaces. Maya provides a variety of tools to help you to accomplish such a task.

Automatic Mapping

Automatic mapping, a feature added in Maya 3, can give us a starting point for creating a good UV map. The six projections of the head in Figure 19.27 illustrate this process. The first two UVs, (a) and (b), were created with Cylindrical Mapping and Spherical Mapping, and they are not at all practical for the head. As you can easily see, they will create overlapping textures that will stretch and squash. They will also create seams between some faces. UV map (c) was created using Automatic Mapping. Although this mapping creates many separate pieces of UVs, those pieces also reflect accurately the proportional sizes of the surface's faces. While picture (c) is not in itself a good UV map, it does give us a basis from which to start building one. In (d), two pieces of UVs, representing the front part of the face and the left side of the head, have been dragged closely together. Using Sew UVs or Move and Sew UVs command, we can sew together the two pieces. Picture (e) shows the sewing process. As the UVs are being sewn, there is inevitably some distortion of them. The final UV map that resulted from this process is shown in Figure 19.27 (f).

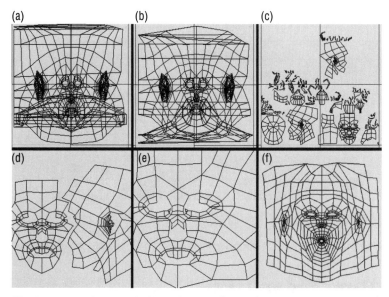

Figure 19.27 *Automatic Mapping produces the most accurate UVs, but the pieces must be sewn together.*

Automatic Mapping produces a UV map that lies within 0 to 1 texture space. This is important for texturing, especially if the texture will be created in a 3D paint program, because that space is where the texture will fit exactly once. If any of the UVs go outside the 0 to 1 boundary, it will map a repeating texture.

Move and Sew UVs

We've just seen that another new tool, Move And Sew UVs, is useful in working with UVs, especially if you create them with Automatic Mapping. In Figure 19.28, we have two separate UV patches, as shown in (a). If we apply the regular Sew UVs, we get stretching between the two pieces as their common edges are sewn, as seen in (b). But when we apply Move And Sew UVs, the smaller patch of UVs snaps to the larger piece, as shown in (c). This command can quickly sew together many separate patches of UVs while maintaining their proportional size and form.

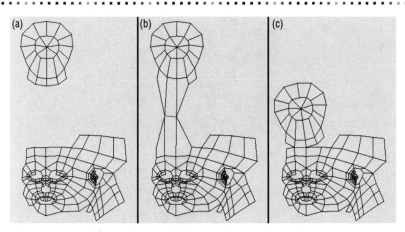

Figure 19.28 *Using the Move and Sew UVs command*

Maya 3 provides some other editing tools that we simply do not have space to get into, such as Relax UVs, Layout UVs, or Flip UVs. If you will be working with polygons frequently, you should explore the other commands in the Texture submenu on your own. One related command that we do need to cover, though, is Polygons ➜ Transfer.

Transferring UVs

The Transfer command, another new Maya 3 addition, copies vertex, UV, or Vertex Color information from the first selected polygon to the second selected polygon. As long as both polygons have the same topology, the command works. This enables us to create a clean UV map more easily on a smoothed-out version of a complex polygon surface, and then copy that UV map to the original complex surface. The smoothed version can be created by using the Artisan smoothing brush or the Average Vertices command. For example, face (a) in Figure 19.29 has a map in which the UVs around the nose and mouth areas are overlapping. Face (b) is a copy of the first, with the nose and mouth areas smoothed with Average Vertices. It may look ugly, but a planar mapping on this face creates a cleaner UV map, which then can be transferred to the first face, as shown in (c).

While the Transfer command is useful in working with polygons, it has a problem when copying UV information to subdivision surfaces. The next section has a more specific discussion of this issue, and the accompanying CD includes an original MEL script that overcomes this problem.

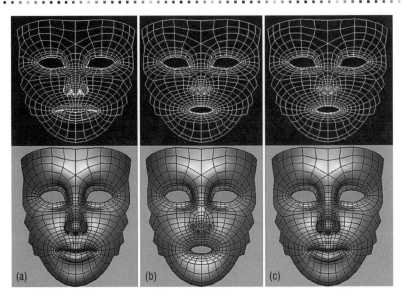

Figure 19.29 *Transferring smoothed UVs to a complex surface*

Texturing Subdivision Surfaces

Subdivision surfaces inherit the UV mapping from the polygon or NURBS surfaces they are created from. To edit subdivision UVs, first make sure the subdivision surface is in polygon proxy mode. Once the proxy polygon mesh is created, it can be edited just like any regular polygon surface. Any UV changes you make in the proxy polygon will be reflected in the subdivision surface. There are some things you need to watch out for, however.

Surface Stretching

The faces of subdivision surfaces are usually more stretched out than their proxy polygon counterparts. For example, the thin strip of black line going along the arm in Figure 19.30 was placed on the proxy polygon. When the same texture is applied to the subdivision surface, the line has become thicker.

This isn't so much a problem as something you just have to be aware of, even when you are modeling. And when you are texturing or painting on the UV map, you need to check where the colors will actually end up on the subdivision surface, not how they look in the Texture View window.

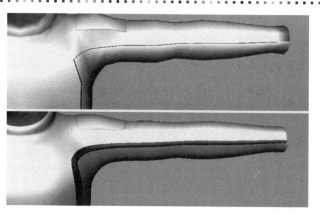

Figure 19.30 *Faces stretching out in a subdivision surface*

UV Editing Bound Subdivision Surfaces

Subdivision surfaces, once they are bound to a skeleton or a deformer, will not go into polygon proxy mode. How, then, can we edit the UVs, or work on the textures? One way to get around this problem is the approach we took in Chapter 12's Hands-On Maya tutorial for binding a character. We first put the subdivision surfaces into polygon proxy mode and then bound the proxy polygon meshes, not the hierarchical subdivision surfaces. This allowed us to continue editing the UVs after the binding.

Another technique for editing UVs of bound subdivision surfaces is to work with what are known as *intermediate objects*. In the Hypergraph, turn on the display of shape and invisible nodes. Under the bound subdivision surface node, you should see a shapeOrig node, which is an intermediate object. This node functions as a reference for the bound subdivision surface being deformed. Select that node and apply Deform ➔ Display Intermediate Objects. This enables you to edit the intermediate node. With the intermediate node still selected, RM click in the modeling window and you can enter polygon proxy mode. Once the proxy polygon node is created, you can edit its UVs, and the changes will trickle down to the bound subdivision surface.

Subdivision Surfaces and the Transfer Command Problem

One curious problem with UV mappings in subdivision surfaces arises with the Transfer command. As we saw earlier, the Transfer command copies UV mapping from one polygon object to another of the same topology. But when applied to a polygon proxy mesh, it destroys the hierarchical edit information of the subdivision surfaces. In Figure 19.31, a simple cube (a) has been turned into subdivision surfaces and edited in level 1.

Its UV mapping is shown above it. Cube (b) has a different UV mapping. When the cube (b) UV mapping is transferred to the polygon proxy mesh, the UV mapping is copied, but the edit information is also deleted, as shown in (c).

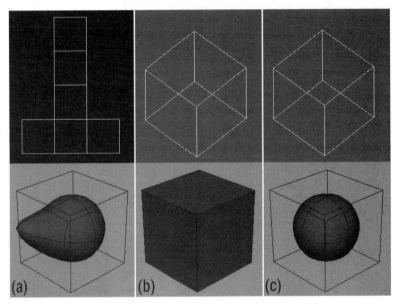

(a)   (b)   (c)

Figure 19.31 *An example of the Transfer command problem*

   The CopyUV MEL script in the Chapter 19 Working Files directory on the CD-ROM allows the UV mapping to be copied to the polygon proxy mesh without deleting the edit information of the subdivision surface.

Hands-On Maya: Texturing a Character

Let's now turn to texturing the human character we've been working with throughout this book. We will first deal with the hair and the eyes, which are NURBS surfaces, and then proceed to the subdivision surfaces—the head, body, hands, and feet.

Many image files were used to texture the character, and you can find them in the Chapter 19 Working Files directory on the CD-ROM. Note that the image files are all squares such as 256×256 or 512×512. Maya works better with square image files whose dimensions are powers of 2, such as 128, 256, 512, or 1024. It's also a good idea to start out with a bigger size than you think you need and then shrink the image later, instead of starting out with a size that may pixelate when rendered.

Texturing the Hair and the Eyes

Texturing the NURBS parts of the human character is fairly straightforward. While the following steps may not be the way to create the most photorealistic eyes and hair, they will give you good examples of how to work creatively with different render nodes.

1. Bring in the `character_bound.mb` file from the Chapter 12 Working Files directory on the CD-ROM. Make the subD_surfaces layer visible to see the hair. Assign an Anisotropic material to the hair strands and set SpreadX to 1.2, SpreadY to 1, Roughness to 0.1, and Fresnel Index to 3. You will probably change these settings as you refine the specularity of the hair later, but they will do for now. Apply a fractal to the color attribute and set the Repeat UV to something like 5 and 0.2. You should see the fractal stretch as in (a) below. Connect a Ramp to the Color Gain attribute of the fractal to get color variation to the hair, as shown in (b). Create an image file to connect to the Transparency attribute of the Anisotrpic material, and bring in the `hair_transparency.jpg` image from the CD-ROM. The hair should now look something like (c) below.

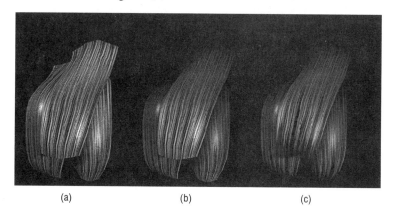

(a)   (b)   (c)

2. A few more steps need to be taken. Let's have a bit of bumping on the hair. Take the fractal node and connect it to the Anisotropic material's Bump Mapping attribute. The initial bump value is too high, so bring down the Alpha Gain value of the fractal to something like 0.6. The hair geometry is transparent at the bottom end, but the specular still shines on what's supposed to be empty space. We want only the hair strands to shine. Create a Reverse node from the Utilities ➡ General directory and connect it to the `hair_transparency` image file. Make a copy without a network of the fractal node, and connect the Reverse node to the Color Gain attribute of that copied fractal node. Then connect the copied fractal to the Specular Color attribute of the Anisotropic material. The specular now only shines where the hair is, as shown below. The hair shading network is also shown below for your reference.

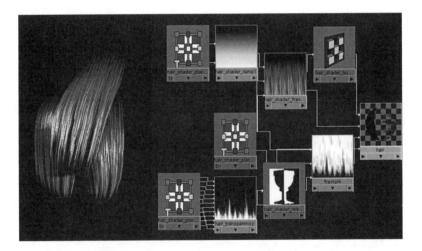

3. You can create good-looking eyes made of simple spheres and textures. In our example, however, the eyes are made of two spheres: an inner sphere for the pupil and the iris textures and a transparent outer sphere just for specularity. Start with a Layered shader, create a Blinn layer, and assign it to the inner sphere.

4. Start an IPR process to see how the values change as you work. Put a Ramp into the Color attribute of the Blinn material to create the pupil. Make the Ramp black and white and position the black color to start from the pupil area. Decrease the Blinn material's Eccentricity to 0.05, and increase Specular Roll Off to 1. Then push up the Specular Color's HSV value to 2.0. This will make the pupil shine with a tight and bright highlight, as shown in the first eyeball in Figure 19.32.

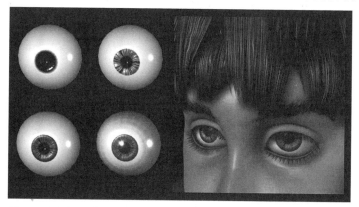

Figure 19.32 The eye-texturing process

5. Create another Blinn material over the pupil layer to texture the iris area, and map a fractal to its color and bump. Make the fractal's Repeat UV 0.02 and 3. Put a ramp into the layer's Transparency attribute and position the color entries so the ramp won't cover the pupil or too much of the eyeball area. It should look something like the second eyeball in Figure 19.32.

6. Create yet another Blinn layer over the third layer. This time, map a fractal just to its color, and make the fractal a bit darker. Put a ramp into its Transparency attribute so it will show up only at the edge of the iris, blending with the first fractal texture. You should see something like the third eyeball in Figure 19.32.

7. Assign a Blinn to the outer sphere and make it totally transparent. Decrease Eccentricity to 0.1, increase Specular Roll Off to 2, and push the Specular Color to totally white, or a value of 1. The outer sphere serves to make the eyes brighter with softer specularity, as you can see in the last eyeball in Figure 19.32, and it shows the convex shape of the eye lens.

Instead of using Layered Shader, we could use Layered texture. That would make the network much more efficient, but we wouldn't be able to enter different values for specular shading in different layers.

Texturing the Head and the Body

Since we are using image files to texture the character, almost all the difficulty in texturing its subdivision surface parts lies in creating the appropriate UV maps. The UV map created for the head, for example, is not perfect, as it stretches in certain areas, and squashes and overlaps around the ears. The artist who worked on creating the texture, however, dealt with the UV map well enough. Often, the artist has to make compromises to try to balance the quality of what she is doing with the realistic demands of the situation. This is especially true in painting good organic textures. Figure 19.33 shows the UV map for the head, along with the color image and the Texture View of the two together.

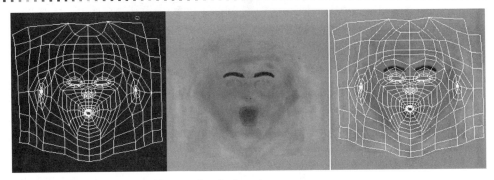

Figure 19.33 *UV map and image for the head*

1. Assign a Blinn material to the head, set its Eccentricity and Specular Roll Off to 0.3 and 0.5, and name it Skin. You can also give the material a tiny amount of Incandescence and a bit of Translucence to imitate the feel of living skin more closely. Connect an image file to Skin's Color attribute, and bring in face_C.jpg from the Chapter 19 Working Files directory on the CD-ROM. Then connect another image file to Skin's Bump Mapping attribute, and bring in face_B.jpg. As shown below (a), the default value for the bump map is too much. In the image file for the bump mapping, turn down the Alpha gain to about 0.2, and the bumping should seem more reasonable, as seen in (b). Also connect an image file to Skin's Specular Color attribute and bring in face_S.jpg from the CD-ROM. In this image file, bring up the Color Offset value to about 0.5, or gray color, and connect the bump map image file to its Color Gain attribute. This makes the specular shine only on the bumps. You should see something like (c) below.

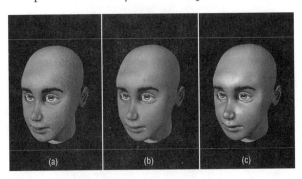

2. The body's UVs were collected into groups, as seen in (a) below. Then the artist mapped the appropriate textures on them: the body_C.jpg color file shown in (b), the body_B.jpg bump file in (c), and the body_S.jpg specular file in (d). Assign another Blinn material to the body, and connect the appropriate image files to the material. The specular intensity and the bump value should be fairly low.

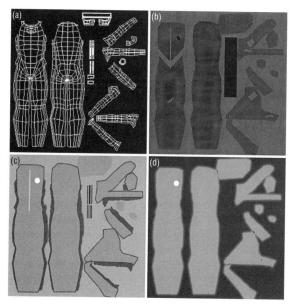

 The images for the head and the body are 1024 × 1024, which you may consider too large, but remember that it is always better to start big and then resize. For most purposes, these images could probably be resized to 512 × 512 without losing any quality.

3. Repeat the same procedure for the hands and the shoes. They each have three image files in the Chapter 19 Working Files directory on the CD-ROM, one for color, one for bump, one for specular. The artist has chosen to create separate files for the material's attributes, but one could easily use a bump map, adjusting its Color Gain and Color Offset, as a specular map as well.

4. The remaining image to be mapped is eyelashes.jpg, which should be applied in essentially the same manner that the hair_transparency image was used. Assign a Lambert material to the eyelashes, and then use the image file for both Color and Transparency attributes. You can see the finished images in the color insert section of this book.

Summary

In this chapter, you learned how to use the Hypershade and work with various render nodes. We covered materials and textures, their various properties and attributes, and how to work with them in shading a dog, parts of the living room scene, and a human character.

Shading and texturing, as we have seen working with our examples, can take the simplest objects and make them look good. But in creating the textures in this chapter, one essential part has been intentionally omitted from our discussion: lighting. In the next chapter, we will learn all about this other half of the equation in creating great-looking pictures.

Lighting

MAYA

Chapter 20

Although in this book we discuss lighting after modeling, animation, and shading, lighting is really a circular process, and it's difficult to confine it to any one stage in the production cycle. Before you can test-render anything, whether it's a model you are building or the textures of one you've already built, you need to set up proper lights in order to view the scene properly. At the same time, if you want to control precisely how the lights shine on the objects, you should not fine-tune your lights until all the animation is finished. We will discuss proper lighting techniques later in this chapter, and conclude with some tips on optimizing the renderer once lighting is set up, but first, let's go over the five Maya lights and their attributes. This chapter's topics include:

- Types of lights and their properties
- Shadows
- Light effects
- Lighting techniques

Types of Lights

You can light surfaces using Ambient light, Point light, Directional light, Spot light, or, in Maya 3, the new Area light. Usually you will combine different lights to get the effects you want. You can create any type of light from the menu by selecting it in the Lights menu in the Rendering module or by dragging it from the Visor panel in the Hypershade. Figure 20.1 shows the icons for the lights in the Hypershade and in the modeling window.

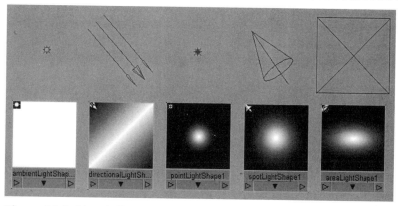

Figure 20.1 *Maya's five types of light in the modeling window (top) and Hypershade (bottom)*

Ambient Light

Ambient light can shine, as its name suggests, everywhere uniformly—bathing all the objects in the scene from all directions. You can get similar effects from a material shader by controlling its ambient color. But Ambient light can also behave as a simple Point light, which shines from a specific point and in a specific direction. You can combine omnidirectional and directional Ambient light using the Ambient Shade setting in the Attribute Editor. When the Ambient Shade is set to 1, the Ambient light behaves exactly like Point light; it lights a surface from a specific position. Ambient light can also cast shadows like Point light, but only when raytraced.

In Figure 20.2 (which also appears in the Color Gallery on the CD) you can see examples of different Ambient Shade values. The third picture is raytraced with Use Ray Trace Shadows turned on.

Figure 20.2 *Different Ambient Shade values*

Directional, Point, and Spot Lights

Directional light shines in the direction of its icon arrows. It imitates light coming from a distant source, such as the sun. Point light, by contrast, shines from a specific point to all directions evenly; it is ideal for imitating a light bulb or a candle. Spot light behaves exactly like a real-world spotlight, its direction defined by a beam of light that gradually widens. Spot lights are also good for imitating headlights or lamps. Figure 20.3 shows examples of these lights. Note how the Point and Spot light shadows are a bit bigger than the Directional light's. This is because the rays scatter for the Point and Spot lights, but not for Directional light. One significant difference between Point light and Spot light exists in the way they cast shadows. When Depth Map Shadow is turned on (see the "Shadows" section below), Point light creates multiple shadow maps by default, whereas Spot light creates only one.

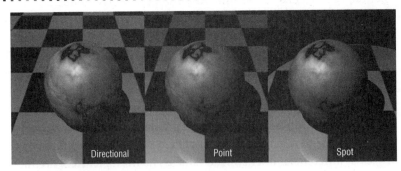

Figure 20.3 *Directional, Point, and Spot lights*

Ambient and Directional lights do not have Decay Rate attributes, whereas Point and Spot lights do. Spot light also has Cone Angle, Penumbra Angle, and Dropoff attributes as well. We will look at these and other light properties in the following sections.

You can change a light from one type to another in the Attribute Editor. When you do that, however, only the attributes common to both types will be retained. Other attribute settings will be lost.

Area Light

Area light behaves much like Point light, except that it shines from a flat rectangular area, which can be scaled like a regular plane. When you make the area larger, the light intensity increases proportionally. With Area lights you can create more realistic specular highlights, mimic radiosity better, and (when raytracing) create dissipating shadows.

Figure 20.4 (a) shows a shoe lit by a Spot light. Notice how the specular highlight is reflecting from the shoe. Picture (b) shows the same shoe lit by an Area light. The specular on the shoe is much more realistic. In (c), another Area light with low intensity was placed just behind the wall to imitate light reflecting off the wall and lighting the shoe. Again, the light seems to be bouncing off the entire wall, not just from a point.

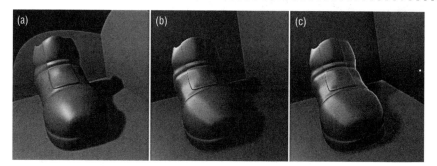

Figure 20.4 *Area light lighting a shoe*

Light Properties

For all types of light, you can control the basic properties of color and intensity. For Point, Area, and Spot lights, you can vary the intensity over distance by controlling the decay rate. Additionally, you can control the linkage between lights and the objects in a scene. Finally, Spot lights have some unique properties and attributes you can control. All of these controls can be accessed in the light's Attribute Editor.

Color and Intensity

As with shading, you can use the Color Chooser to tint a light (usually subtly) or map textures that will be projected onto the surface. When textures mask or filter certain areas of light, as in Figure 20.5 (a) and (b), the light is called a *gobo* light. You can also change the intensity, or brightness of a light. Negative intensity values will actually take away light, which can be useful for creating shadowy areas such as dark corners in a room, as shown in exaggerated form in (c). You can also make the light color black and the shadow color white to create shadow masks, as illustrated in (d). To create the mask, you also need to change the floor to plain white color and turn off the primary visibility of the shoe.

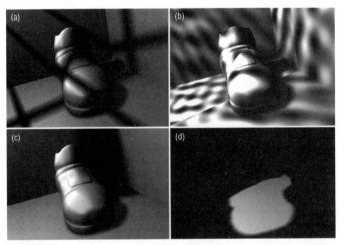

Figure 20.5 *The gobo, negative light, and shadow mask effects*

A shadow mask *is used in compositing to put shadows into a scene when objects in the scene are rendered separately. It is especially useful when computer graphic elements are being added to live footage. The shadow mask allows the compositor to blur the shadows, if necessary, and to adjust the HSV (hue, saturation, and value) settings of the shadow to match the shadows in the live footage.*

You can also control the intensity value of any light by mapping textures to it, which produces results similar to mapping texture to color. Figure 20.6 shows examples of a default grid texture mapped to the Intensity attribute of different lights with default settings. Note how the grids are translated to intensity values differently for each of these four lights.

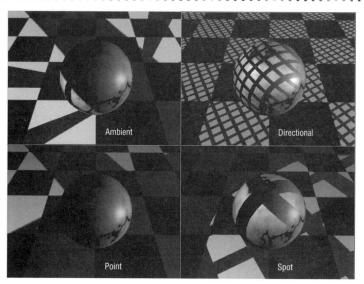

Figure 20.6 *A grid texture mapped to the Intensity attribute*

For Spot light only, you can also create Intensity and Color curves to control their values with respect to distance from the light source. To create the curves, click the Create buttons under the Light Effects section of the Attribute Editor. You can then edit the curves in the Graph Editor.

Decay Rate

You can make the intensity of Point, Area, and Spot lights decay over a distance by turning on Decay Rate. There are three decay rates to choose from: Linear, where intensity decreases proportionally to the distance; Quadratic, where intensity decreases proportionally to the square of the distance (distance × distance), which is how light intensity decays in the real world; and Cubic, where intensity decreases proportionally to the cube of distance (distance × distance × distance). In Figure 20.7 (and in the Color Gallery on the CD) you can see examples of each Decay Rate. Notice how the intensity value shoots up accordingly to light the sphere. You can hardly tell the differences in the sphere itself, but the differences are noticeable on the floor.

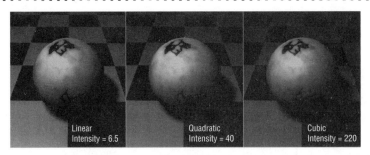

Figure 20.7 *Linear, Quadratic, and Cubic decay rates*

The Decay Rate setting begins to affect a light's intensity only at distances greater than one unit from the light source. Inside the one-unit radius, no decay of light intensity is possible.

Linking Lights and Objects

When a light shines on a surface, the two are said to be *linked*. All the lights have a setting called Illuminates By Default, which is turned on by default and makes the light shine on all objects; that is, the light is linked to all the objects in the scene. If the setting is off, the light will not shine on any object unless you manually link it to that object. You can also do the opposite and cut the link between individual objects and a light, so that the light will not shine on those objects. If you are working on simple scenes, you will usually leave things at default settings and let all lights shine on all objects. As soon as the scene gets fairly complex, however, it's a good idea to start linking lights only to the objects they need to light, because linking affects rendering time significantly.

The default light, with the Illuminates By Default setting turned on, used to be called Inclusive light. When the setting was off, it was said to be Exclusive.

You can link lights and objects, or sever the links, from the Lighting/Shading menu in the Rendering module. (Previous Maya versions had two separate menus: Lights and Shading.) Select the object(s) and light(s) in question. Select Make Light Links to link them or Break Light Links to sever them. You can also control light linking in the Relationship Editor. You can either open the Relationship Editor in what Maya calls a *light-centric* mode and link objects to a light, or open it in an object-centric mode and link lights to an object. Figure 20.8 shows examples of using a light-centric Relationship Editor to link objects to lights. On the left, the second and third spheres have been severed from pointLight1. On the right, the second sphere has been severed also from pointLight2, and as a result, is totally black.

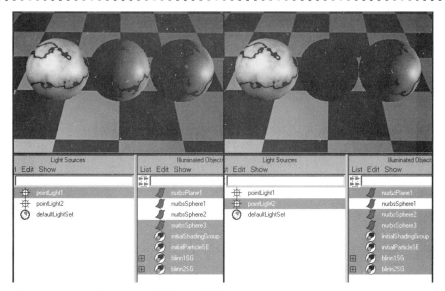

Figure 20.8 *Light-Centric linking of objects*

The Lighting/Shading menu also offers the Select Objects Illuminated By Light and Select Lights Illuminating Object commands. When you select a light and apply the first command, all objects linked to that light are selected. When you select an object and apply the second command, all lights linked to that object are selected.

Spot Light Properties

Unique to Spot light are the Cone Angle, Penumbra Angle, and Dropoff attributes. Cone Angle controls how much the beam will spread. It is usually sufficient to leave it at the default 40 degrees. Penumbra Angle, when given a positive value, blurs the area outside the cone to make the edge soft. With a negative value, it blurs the area inside the edge to make it soft. Figure 20.9 shows examples of different Cone Angle and Penumbra Angle settings.

Be careful not to spread the Cone Angle too much, as it will create problems with shadows.

Figure 20.9 *Examples of Cone Angle and Penumbra Angle settings*

Dropoff is similar to Linear Decay Rate, but instead of decaying over a distance from the light source, it makes the intensity drop off from the center of the cone to its edge. Its results are often similar to the Penumbra Angle with a negative value. Figure 20.10 shows examples of different Dropoff values and their effects on the Spot light.

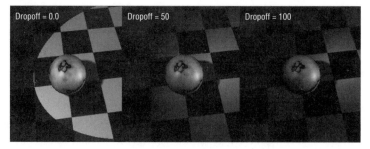

Figure 20.10 *Examples of different dropoff values*

Spot Light Effects

In the Light Effects section of the Attribute Editor, two more attributes of Spot light are worth mentioning: Barn Doors and Decay Regions. They are both turned off by default. Barn Doors act just like masks, or shutters, to cover the edges of the cone from four corners. You input values to set the angles between the Spot light's center and the barn doors. The Decay Regions option enables you to create regions within the Spot light beam where the light does not illuminate, as well as regions where it does illuminate. The example of Decay Regions in Figure 20.11 has light fog applied to it. (The effect is similar to a smoky nightclub. You'll learn more about fog effects later in the chapter.)

Figure 20.11 *Barn Doors and Decay Regions*

Shadows

The default light setting in Maya produces no shadows. This is because shadows can be very computationally expensive and, in general, you want only one or two main lights to be casting shadows. All lights can be set to produce either Depth Map Shadows or Ray Trace Shadows, with the exception of Ambient light, which can only produce Ray Trace shadows. To activate shadows, go to the Shadows section of a light's Attribute Editor, where you can check Use Depth Map Shadows in the Depth Map Shadow Attributes section, or check Use Ray Trace Shadows in the Raytrace Shadow Attributes section.

Depth-Map Shadows

Most of the time you will want to use depth-map shadows, because they are much more efficient than raytraced shadows. When a depth-map shadow is turned on, during rendering Maya creates a *depth map*, which stores the distance from the shadow casting light to the surfaces that the light is illuminating and uses this information to calculate shadows. The depth map, as you can see in Figure 20.12, is a Z-depth (see

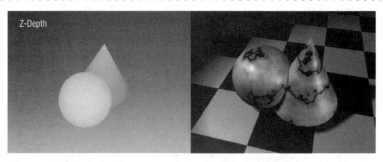

Figure 20.12 *A depth map and the resulting shadows*

"Render Globals Settings" in Chapter 18, "Rendering Basics") image file created from the light's point of view, and it enables Maya to calculate whether one surface is behind another surface with respect to the light. In this case, areas of the floor are found to be behind the sphere and the cone, and are thus rendered as shadows. A small area of the cone is also found to be behind the sphere and becomes a shadow as well.

Color

The default Shadow Color setting is black, but you may want to lighten it or tint it with other colors, or even map textures to it, depending on the look you want. Mapping into color can also be a good way to fake transparency. Depth map shadows do not recognize transparent objects; only raytraced shadows do. But for simple situations, you can often get away with clever use of Shadow Color, as in the examples in Figure 20.13 (also in the Color Gallery on the CD). On the left, a darkened version of the marble texture was connected to the Shadow Color; on the right, a ramp was used to create the more transparent upper area of the shadow.

Fog Shadow Intensity and Fog Shadow Samples

When the Light Fog attribute (discussed shortly) is applied to a light, you can control the intensity and the graininess of the fog shadow as well. The darkness of the shadow is controlled by the Fog Shadow Intensity setting, and the graininess is controlled by Fog Shadow Samples, as seen in Figure 20.14. Increasing the value in the latter increases the rendering time, so keep its values as low as is acceptable.

Dmap Resolution, Filter Size, and Bias

Dmap Resolution sets the size of the depth map that Maya creates. The default value is 512, which creates a square depth-map file 512 pixels in width and height.

Figure 20.13 Examples of faking transparency

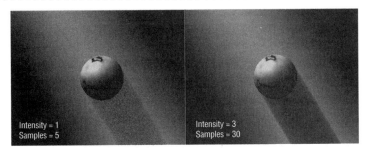

Intensity = 1
Samples = 5

Intensity = 3
Samples = 30

Figure 20.14 Fog Shadow Intensity and Fog Shadow Samples

If you need sharper shadows, you may need to increase the resolution, but for softer shadows, you can get good results with resolutions as low as 128 or even 64. The Dmap Filter Size blurs, or softens, the shadow edges. As with any filter, the higher the number the more expensive it gets, so keep the filter size as low as is acceptable. In Figure 20.15 are examples of various resolution and filter size settings and their effects.

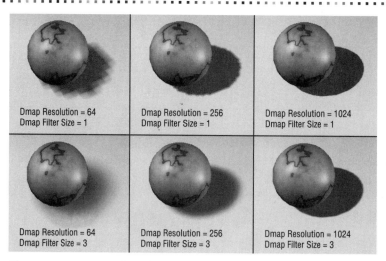

Figure 20.15 *Examples of Dmap settings*

Dmap Bias controls how much the shadow is offset from its source. It should generally be left at its default value, except to correct situations where the shadow placement seems off, as in the left image in Figure 20.16.

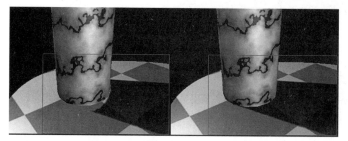

Figure 20.16 *Examples of Dmap Bias*

Disk Based Dmaps

The Disk Based Dmaps feature can make rendering go much faster when used properly. The default setting is Off, which means that every time Maya renders, it creates depth maps for shadow calculations. But since a depth map stores information about the distance between a light and the surfaces it illuminates, as long as the relative distance between the light and its linked surfaces in a scene does not change, you can reuse the depth map. Even if the camera and any other element in the scene are be animated, you can still reuse the same depth map.

Switch the setting to Reuse Existing Dmap(s), and other settings become active. The default Dmap Name is `depthmap`, and the Dmap Light Name is checked, which means that when the depth map is saved to disk, it will be assigned the name `depthmap` plus the name of the light generating the depth map. For example, for a Spot light named Spot, a depth-map file named `depthmap_SpotShape1.SM.iff` is created. The first time around, Maya looks for a depth map in the current project directories; and when it doesn't find one, it creates the depth map and places it in the current project directory, in the `\depth` subdirectory. The next time Maya renders, it uses this depth map to shadow the surfaces, thus reducing rendering time.

In cases where the distances between the light and its linked surfaces do change over time and you will be rendering the sequence more than once (as often happens with animation test-renders), you can still create a sequence of depth maps and reuse them by checking Dmap Frame Ext.

The other Disk Based Dmaps setting, Overwrite Existing Dmap(s), overwrites any existing depth maps. If you make positional changes to a light or any of its linked surfaces, you should overwrite existing depth maps. Once you've rendered and created new depth maps, change the setting to Reuse Existing Dmap(s) again.

Raytraced Shadows

Raytracing gives you better renders than depth-map shadows; the images have a clean, crisp feeling that regular rendering cannot completely match. For example, when you are creating shadows for transparent objects that have reflections and refractions, and you need photorealistic accuracy, raytraced shadows are the only way to go. The cost, however, is rendering time. For many situations, you can get almost exactly the same quality with depth-map shadows, with much more efficient render times.

To use raytraced shadows, you need to turn on Use Ray Trace Shadows in the individual light's Attribute Editor, and also Raytracing in the Render Globals.

When Use Ray Trace Shadows is turned on, Shadow Radius becomes active for Ambient light, Light Angle for Directional light, and Light Radius for Point and Spot lights. (This option is not available with Area light.) These different attributes all affect the softness of the shadow edges. Zero, which is the default setting, gives you sharp, hard shadow edges, and as the values go up, the edges become softer. The value range is different for different lights.

As the shadow becomes softer, the edges at the default setting become grainier, as in Figure 20.17 (a). The Shadow Rays setting blurs the graininess of the edges. Shadow Rays is render-intensive, so it is best to keep the values as low as you can.

Soft edge shadows can be much more efficiently created with depth-map shadows. Raytraced shadows are more useful for creating sharp, crisp shadows.

Ray Depth Limit sets the maximum number of times, minus one, that a ray of light can be reflected or refracted and still create a shadow. If the value of the Shadows attribute in the Raytracing Quality section of the Render Globals is lower than the Ray Depth Limit value, that lower value becomes the maximum limit. In Figure 20.17 (c) and (d) (and in the Color Gallery on the CD), a Ray Depth Limit of 1 isn't showing the shadow behind the transparent sphere. By contrast, a Ray Depth Limit of 3 shows it.

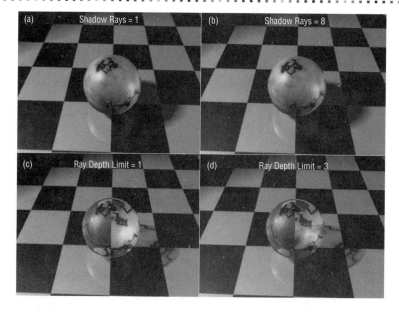

Figure 20.17 *Examples of Shadow Rays and Ray Depth Limit*

Raytracing with Area light can also give you dissipating shadows. The depth-map shadows on the left in Figure 20.18 are quite soft, but we still have a solid area of shadow. The raytraced shadow with Area light, in contrast, dissipates as it goes away from the object, as shown on the right.

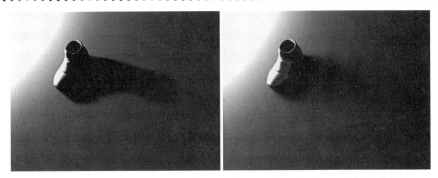

Figure 20.18 Raytracing can produce a dissipating shadow with Area light.

Light Effects

In addition to the properties we've looked at so far, Maya offers various special effects you can apply to lights. These include fog and various optical effects such as glow, halo, and lens flare. You can access these effects from the Light Effects section of a light's Attribute Editor.

Light Fog

The Light Fog attribute can be applied to Point and Spot lights. Point light fog is spherical, whereas the Spot light fog is cone shaped. When light fog is applied, a separate fog icon appears along with the light icon, which you can transform to create the size and shape of the fog you want. Figure 20.19 shows examples of Point light fog and Spot light fog with different scales.

The Fog Type and Fog Radius attributes are only available for Point light fog. Under Fog Type, the Normal setting lets the fog intensity remain constant regardless of the distance from the light source. The Linear setting decreases the fog intensity as the distance from the light source increases, and the Exponential setting decreases the fog intensity as the distance increases exponentially. Fog Radius determines the spherical volume of the fog. Figure 20.20 shows examples of Point light's Fog Type and Fog Radius settings.

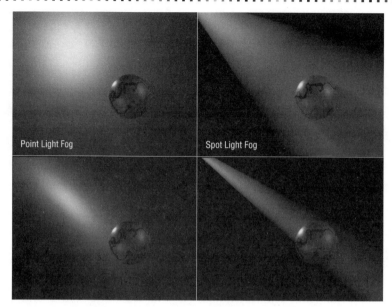

Figure 20.19 *Point Light Fog and Spot Light Fog*

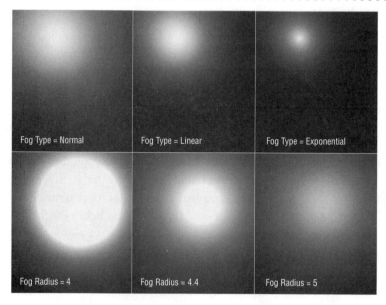

Figure 20.20 *Examples of Fog Type and Fog Radius*

Fog Spread is an attribute available only for Spot light fog. It functions very much like Spot light's Dropoff attribute. It determines the decrease in fog intensity as distance from the center of the cone increases, as in the examples in Figure 20.21. The decrease in intensity as the distance increases from the light source is determined by the Spot light's Decay Rate setting.

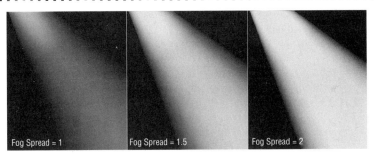

Figure 20.21 *Examples of fog spread*

You can go to the lightFog node and adjust the Color and Density attributes of the light fog, or combine light fog with light glow (discussed next) to produce a combination effect. When using light fog, you will often also want to map textures into the light's Color attribute to imitate smoke or bigger dust particles. The example in Figure 20.22 (also in the Color Gallery on the CD) has a solid fractal texture mapped to the Color attribute of Spot light and Point light.

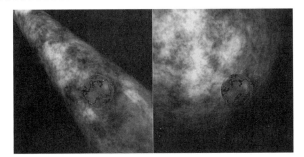

Figure 20.22 *Solid fractal mapped to light color*

OptiF/X

Maya has an optical light effects node (called OptiF/X), which can produce glow, halo, and/or lens flare effects for Point, Area, and Spot lights. The light effects are useful in imitating different camera filters, as well as stars, candles, flames, or explosions. The light sources have to be inside the camera view for the light effects to show, and the effects are all post-processes, applied after all the regular rendering is done. In the Light Effects section of the light's Attribute Editor, click the Light Glow box, and an opticalFX node is created. OptiF/X turns on when the Active box is checked and Glow Type and Halo Type are set to something other than None. For Lens Flare, you also need to check the Lens Flare box separately. Figure 20.23 shows examples of these three light effects.

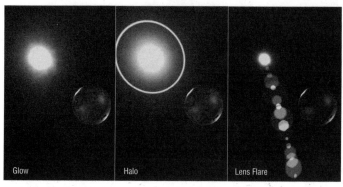

Figure 20.23 *Glow, Halo, and Lens Flare effects*

Glow and Halo

Both Glow and Halo have the same list of types: Linear, Exponential, Ball, Lens Flare (which shouldn't be confused with the OpticalF/X Lens Flare effect), and Rim Halo. Figure 20.24 (also in the Color Gallery on the CD) shows examples of the various types for glow and halo. For the glow examples, the halo type was set to None, and vice versa, but you would usually combine their effects.

Glow and Halo have same color and intensity attributes as regular lights, and you can change their sizes through the Spread attribute. Halo attributes are limited to those illustrated above in Figure 20.24. Glow, however, has the additional stars and noise attributes.

Working with glow effects can be confusing because these additional attributes are scattered in different sections of the Attribute Editor, with three of them in the Optical FX Attributes section, and some of the others in the Noise Attributes section. The pictures in Figure 20.25 (also shown in the Color Gallery on the CD) have glow beam effects with various settings. Starting from the top left, the Star Points setting determines how many regular beams will come out of the light source. Their sharpness, or width, is determined by the Glow Star Level setting, and randomness in the beams

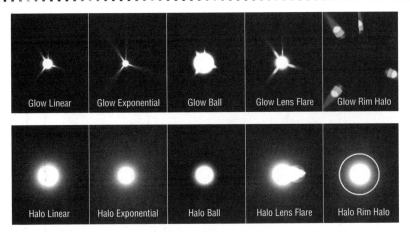

Figure 20.24 *Examples of glow and halo*

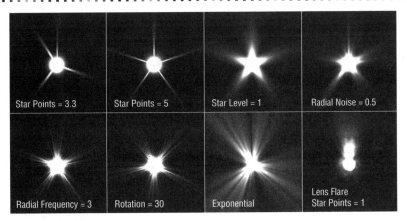

Figure 20.25 *Glow settings*

is introduced by Glow Radial Noise. Once you have a nonzero Radial Noise setting, you can adjust both the frequency of the random beams and their width by using the Radial Frequency attribute. The beams can be rotated with the Rotation attribute. The two last pictures show more combinations of different possible glow settings.

Noise attributes produce a fractalized look you can use to imitate a variety of effects such as fog or explosions, as you can see in Figure 20.26 (and in the Color Gallery on the CD). Glow Noise produces the fractalized glow, which should always be adjusted together with Glow Intensity and Glow Spread (among other settings) to achieve the desired look. The Noise section enables you to adjust the Noise Threshold, along with its vertical and horizontal Scale and Placement.

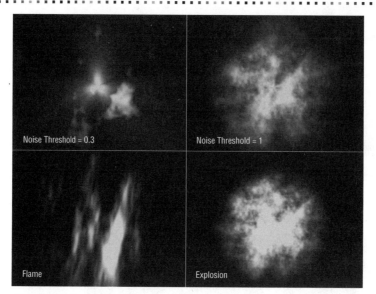

Figure 20.26 *Examples of noise*

Lens Flare

Lens Flare re-creates the effect of physical imperfections in an optical lens, which become particularly apparent as the lens is trained toward a light source. Color in Lens Flare works a bit differently from the regular Color attribute in that Lens Flare color is a spectrum of colors, the range of which is determined by the Flare Col Spread attribute. Flare Num Circles determines how many circles (hexagons if Hexagon Flare is turned on) will show in the lens flare beam, and Flare Length determines the length of that beam. The Flare Min and Max Size attributes limit the sizes of the smallest and largest circles, and Flare Focus can blur or sharpen the flare circles, as seen in Figure 20.27 (also in the Color Gallery on the CD). Lens Flare beam doesn't rotate but is placed in different positions with Flare Vertical and Horizontal controls.

As you've seen, lights in Maya can have many different properties and effects to manage, and a complex scene may have numerous lights. Chapter 17, "Programming with MEL," shows how to build a MEL script that creates a graphical interface window for controlling all the lights in a scene.

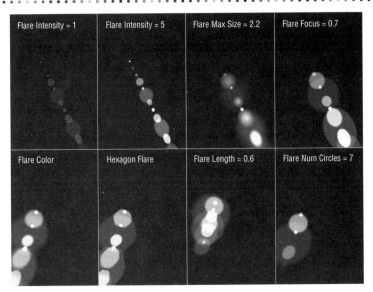

Figure 20.27 *Examples of lens flare with different attributes*

Lighting Techniques

The art of lighting is a whole world unto itself, and studies in painting or photography will certainly be of great help. We will be able to cover only the basics in the remainder of this chapter.

The Basic Rules

One of the first things to realize about digital lighting is that there must always be a proper mixture of the real and artificial. First, lighting has to be believable. If a character is in a room, for example, you need to think about what and where the light sources are. Is there a window? Sunlight or moonlight? Are there lightbulbs or fluorescent lights? You also need to create additional lights to imitate bounce lights, or reflected light. In Figure 20.28 (also in the Color Gallery on the CD), the light in (a) has problems because the character's face in the shadows is totally dark, even though the corridor is lit. Picture (b) is better, as it accounts for the bounce lights in similar brightness level as the rest of the corridor.

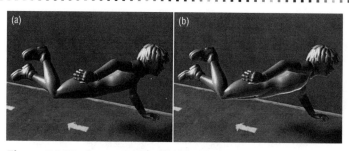

Figure 20.28 *An example of bounce light*

When you are dealing specifically with lights, you may find it better to get rid of textures for a while, as we did with the character in our examples. The absence of textures will enable you to think only about lights and shadows.

On the other hand, lighting is always an artificial endeavor. Stages and movie sets use many artificial lights to create the best possible lighting environment, setting the proper atmosphere and making sure the characters will be lit well. This often involves cheating reality, such as flooding characters with bright blue light for a night scene when in reality the light would be much darker, or creating a strong rim light (see Figure 20.29) on a character for a close-up, when the setting doesn't have any such strong light source coming from the character's backside. Good lighting often means that the dramatic needs of storytelling will override reality. But computer lighting also has the additional burden of making the overall result look as if real lights had been placed in the same spots. You need to make sure the shadows look proper, bounce lights exist, and colors don't get washed out. You also have to worry about issues like render time, transparent objects casting shadows, linking lights only to specific objects that need the lights, and so on.

Three-Point Lighting

When it comes to lighting a person, there are no hard and fast rules to good lighting—different light setups can serve different purposes, and experimentation is often the only sure rule. Generally speaking, however, *Rembrandt* lighting is considered a good starting point. This means light hitting a subject from an angle so as to bring out its contours, as in Figure 20.29 (a) (also in the Color Gallery on the CD). It creates a triangle of lit area on the dark side of the subject's face, as can be seen in many of Rembrandt's paintings. This light is usually called a *key light*. In our example, Spot lights and Area lights are

Figure 20.29 *Three-point lighting*

being used; but Point lights will work just as well. Another light is then placed to shine on the dark side of the subject, as in (b), usually from the side and lower in intensity. This light is called *fill light,* because it fills the dark shadowy parts of the surface with light. The general rule is that if the key light color is warm, the fill light color should be cool, and vice versa. The third light is usually placed at the back and shining down on the subject, creating an outline of the head and shoulders, as in (c). Its intensity can vary from soft to very intense, the latter creating a glow. This light is called *back light,* and it's good for separating the foreground character from the background. Some people use the term *rim light* to describe this light as well. These three lights make up what is known as *three-point lighting,* a standard lighting setup in photography. Because Maya does not automatically generate the bounce lights from these three lights, you may want a fourth light to act as a low-intensity second fill light shining from the front or the bottom to soften the dark areas between the key light and the first fill light, as also illustrated in (c). Then, as in picture (d), all the lights are combined to produce the final lighting.

A good technique for placing lights is to select the light and then, in the modeling window, select Panels → Look Through Selected. This lets you view the scene from the light's point of view. Then, as you move and rotate in the modeling window, the light position adjusts accordingly. It's also a good idea to work on one light at a time, as in Figure 20.29.

While three-point lighting will always give you a fairly satisfactory setup to work with, don't fall into the trap of making it the rule for all situations. Especially with lighting, the best examples are the ones that break the rules. (Of course, the same can be said of the worst examples.) Figure 20.30 shows some examples of extreme lighting setups. As a general rule, you do not want the key light to be shining directly from the front, as it makes the subject look flat, but it can produce a good live video camera effect if the intensity fall-off is carefully handled, as in (a). Hard light shining down as key light, or having two back lights as key lights, can also produce good dramatic effects, as in (b) and (c). And there's always the "I-am-the-spawn-of-hell" lighting, the key light shining almost vertically up from under the subject, as in (d).

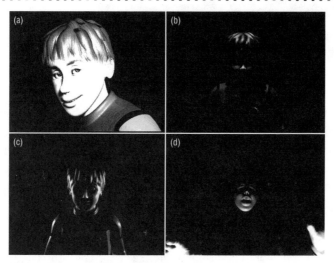

Figure 20.30 *More lighting examples*

Render Optimization Tips

You've read through the rendering information in this book, and you've set up your scene carefully. You've put in only the lights you really need, and you've set shadow casting for most of the lights. But your render times per frame are still through the roof! What's going on?

Most likely, the problem is that the render has not been optimized. There are many ways to do this, and modelers have their own ideas about where to compromise quality and to what extent. However, it's possible to optimize rendering without reducing the quality of your work. Here, we present some production-tested ideas to help make your scenes renderable in your lifetime.

First, and most important, you should link lights to the surfaces they will be illuminating, as discussed earlier. Linking lights causes the renderer to calculate only the rays necessary to illuminate the linked object and any shadows that are being cast by that linked object. The other objects in the scene are ignored.

For example, this technique might be helpful when you have a Directional light illuminating your objects. If this light is also raytraced, the light will cast shadows from *everything*, which could take a while (to say the least). An alternative would be to create a duplicate of the Directional light, exclusively link it to the objects that will not be casting shadows (don't link it to the floor, either), and make this copied light non-shadow casting. Now link the original raytraced light only to the objects that will be casting shadows (plus the floor). The result will be a faster render, with raytraced shadows for only those objects that need it.

Another way to optimize this scene would be to eliminate shadow casting for the floor itself, since we will never see the shadows it casts (which fall below the floor itself). Also, lowering the tessellation of distant objects will help conserve memory. Remember that a floor (unless curved) does not need to be highly tessellated!

Maya has the ability to selectively raytrace objects and surfaces (parts of objects), which you should use.

One of the best ways to reduce render times and give yourself more flexibility is to render in layers with alpha and depth channels. Then, if you need to make adjustments later, you only need to rerender the particular objects on a specific layer, not everything else, too. The real power comes later, during compositing, because you can tweak colors, lighting (to an extent), contrast balance, layer order, and so on. These things would take far too long to adjust and test in a full-scene render, but that isn't the case with a few intelligently rendered layers. You could render separate passes for the shadow, highlights, ambient color, reflection, and so on. Then later, in the composite, you can interactively tune these parameters to your specific needs. This takes some time to set up and initially results in longer render times. However, huge time savings can be earned when you are tuning a scene in real-time, changing the amount of reflection, highlight size, shadow color, and opacity—all in a compositor, not in the renderer. An excellent example of this can be found at Jeremy Birn's Web site, `http://www.3drender.com/jbirn/ea/Ant.html`. (Although this rendering was done in a program other than Maya, the principle applies to any 3D application.)

Here are some other render-optimization tips:

- Reduce bump maps, especially on objects far enough from the camera to not be noticed. An intelligently created color map, added to the base color map of your object's texture, can suffice to simulate the bump map from a distance, and it will greatly reduce render times.

- Only model what viewers will see. This is especially important if you are going to be raytracing—too much geometry to raytrace (in reflections and shadows on floors) will grind your render to a halt. The other reason to do this is to reduce the time you spend modeling, so that you can have more time for rendering! Don't spend time doing amazing things backstage where the audience can't see it.

- Limit your shadow map light's field of view to encompass only the objects casting shadows. This reduces the computations Maya must perform and allows that savings to be applied to a larger shadow map.

- Check that only your surfaces that are supposed to be reflecting are set to have some amount of reflectivity. If the shading group was created as a Phong, PhongE, Blinn, or anisotropic shader, these surfaces might be set to the default of 50 percent reflectivity.

- Selectively tune the render attributes of each object. Turn off Shadow Casting if you won't be seeing the object's shadow. Turn off Visible for reflections or refractions if that visibility isn't needed for the object. Turn off Motion Blur if the object doesn't move too fast (and if the camera doesn't fly past it too fast). Turn off Double Sided for enclosed objects that have no transparency.

- Test your render with the render diagnostics script. In the Render View window, select File ➜ Render Diagnostics. This will alert you to any problems immediately, and it's always better to know about problems sooner than later.

- Use environment reflection maps whenever possible. They should be a size that is divisible by 2, such as 256 × 256. These maps also don't need to be very high resolution, if the pixels that are reflecting don't take up much screen space. You can create animated environment maps if those are needed, since the render times wouldn't be very long for each frame at the small resolution. You also can simulate blurred reflections, by running the frames through a blur filter in a compositing program first.

- Use texture maps whenever possible, because they aren't as render-intensive as procedural maps are. Procedurals don't take up as much memory as image files, but this shouldn't make a huge difference if you keep a close eye on your texture map file sizes. Don't apply texture maps bigger than you need. This is especially true for output to television, because the color space and ultimate resolution are limited to begin with.

- Render frames with motion blur and not fields whenever possible. The hit you take with motion blur will rarely exceed the hit you take with rendering another whole field (or frame if you are going to interlace them later in a compositor).

- Use 2D motion blur whenever you can. It is smoother than 3D motion blur, almost as accurate (as far as the human eye can tell), and the render times are a fraction of those of 3D motion blur at the same quality level.

- Last but not least, read the release notes. They can warn you of problems or slow areas of the renderer before you start pulling out your hair!

Summary

In this chapter we went through the five types of light available in Maya, including the new Area light, their properties, the two ways of creating shadows, and the fog, glow, halo, and lens flare effects available for Point and Spot lights. We also discussed how to light characters in a scene using the standard three-point lighting setup.

This chapter completes the coverage of all the basic stages of producing character animation in Maya. We started with the interface in Part I and continued through the discussions of modeling techniques (Part II), animation (Part III), the MEL scripting language (Part IV), and rendering (Part V), of which this is the last chapter. In Part VI, we will move on to advanced effects in Maya, including Paint Effects, particles, and dynamics.

Part VI

Advanced Maya Effects

In This Part

I f you have worked through the book thus far, you are well on your way to high-level modeling, animation, scripting, texturing, and lighting skills. There is, however, another exciting facet of Maya that deals with large groups of objects. The effects available with both Paint Effects and particles require some practice, but once you understand the basics of working with large groups of objects, you can create stunning scenes with fire, water, clouds, flowers, and other elements. What's more, you can control both particles and Paint Effects strokes so that the effects you create happen as you wish.

In Chapter 21, you will learn how to paint grass, trees, hair, or other natural elements using Maya's powerful Paint Effects tools. Chapters 22 through 25 will walk you through particle basics, rendering with particles, using expressions to control particles, and finally using particle groups called soft bodies to create objects that appear solid but flow and collide like particles, thus enabling effects like water, jiggling fat, and other effects.

While Paint Effects, and especially particles, can be a bit more difficult to understand than single-object manipulation, the effort you spend learning these techniques will pay off in an ability to create physically realistic effects that will wow your audience!

Paint Effects

MAYA

Chapter 21

The dream of rendering a fully 3D natural environment or other organic object (like hair, plants, or food) has traditionally been an onerous task involving proprietary software and loads of difficult modeling and animation. It's little wonder that, until recently, most CG work has involved lots of space ships and desert planets! The complexity of the problem facing the computer artist in recreating nature's many wondrous sights has been daunting, to say the least; not only are there thousands of details to recreate, they must all look natural (e.g., no straight lines or simple repetitive textures) and, ultimately, they all need to move about in a realistic fashion. This bewildering array of technical and artistic problems has kept all but the bravest CG pioneers firmly in the land of artificial objects or simple backdrops.

With Maya's Paint Effects, released with version 2.5 and upgraded with new features and bug fixes for version 3, the rules have changed. Paint Effects is a brush-based paint program that lets you create both 2D and 3D objects—many of which can be animated as well! You can paint hair, trees, grass, corn stalks, pasta, or many other default Paint Effects brushes into your scene, or you can get really creative and start making your own brushes, either using the included brushes as a template or designing them from scratch. If you paint a 3D object into your scene and wish to alter its parameters (its texturing or how much it blows in the wind, for example), you simply select the node in your scene (Paint Effects brushes are node-based, just like the rest of Maya) and change whatever attributes you wish! It's hardly an exaggeration to say Paint Effects has changed the way many artists create their CG work; more importantly, it will give you a huge edge over your competition, who will have to pick their jaws up off the floor when they see your scenes!

Though Paint Effects can be a very complex tool, it is relatively straightforward to understand how it works, given some basic guidelines, which we lay out in this chapter. While you will not be an expert with Paint Effects after reading through the following pages, you should have a very firm grasp of how the tool works and how you can create and modify brushes to do what you wish—affording you the knowledge to experiment effectively. As you proceed through this chapter, you should play with Paint Effects as much as you can; you will discover that a bit of guided interaction with a particular brush is your best instructor. This chapter features these topics:

- Paint Effects theory
- Strokes and brushes
- Painting on a 2D canvas
- Painting a 2D texture on a 3D object
- Painting in a 3D scene
- Editing previous brush strokes
- Adding forces and animation to brush strokes
- Rendering
- Hands-on Maya: painting hair on a head

Paint Effects Theory

Paint Effects uses a "splat"-based (or tube-based)—rather than geometry-based—model for painting in both 2D and 3D. Thus, Paint Effects brushes can be rendered very quickly (compared to geometry) while still maintaining a high-quality look and texturing capabilities. Because the brushes are tubes (actually just curves) that can be rendered into three dimensions, you can work very interactively with the brushes (especially in wireframe mode) while producing astoundingly realistic effects. Also, because final rendering is done on the fly, you can freely move a camera (or the Paint Effects objects) in the scene, and the brushes will render properly from any angle. The combination of interactive "modeling" (though painting is closer to one's actual inter-action with Paint Effects), fully 3D renders, and high-quality texturing and shadowing make Paint Effects an eminently usable feature, right out of the box! Also, being able to add forces like turbulence, wind, and gravity to any Paint Effects brush means that you can animate your scene in a quick, intuitive manner that looks great.

The forces you apply to Paint Effects brushes are not actually calculated by Maya's dynamics engine, but are in fact expressions applied to the brush tubes. This means you can animate several trees, or the hairs on someone's head, with very little penalty in interactivity or rendering.

Paint Effects takes advantage of the depth buffer to do its rendering magic. The Paint Effects renderer uses the depth (or Z) buffer, in addition to six other buffers, to figure out where paint strokes should be placed in the 3D scene, then it splats the objects there, fully anti-aliased and rendered. The Paint Effects renderer is not a scan line–based rendering pass; it is actually a post process, meaning that all geometry is rendered first, and then the Paint Effects elements are added into the render. Although Paint Effects is a post process, it allows things like transparency (which is traditionally *not* possible in depth buffer effects), out-of-order draw, glowing paint strokes, depth of field, and motion blur (both 2D and 3D). The strokes are tubes that can be fully drawn along their length and separated by gaps, and nearly all Paint Effects elements (or attributes) can be keyframed or animated—or both.

If Paint Effects sounds fantastic, just wait until you see how easy it is to use. After reading the pages that follow, you should be up and running with this feature, which is worth the price of Maya Complete in and of itself. But enough superlatives, let's get painting!

Strokes and Brushes

Artists always begin by selecting their tools. To use Paint Effects, first you have to decide what line and effect you're going to produce—or, in this case, what your stroke and your brush should look like. Once you have a clear vision of the look you're after, you can create or modify the tools (strokes and brushes) to match what you want. Working with Paint Effects is a great deal like choosing a traditional paint brush and paint (the brush), and then setting down the appropriate line (or stroke) for the effect you're after.

Strokes

Strokes are the basic elements that underlie all that Paint Effects does. They are, in essence, curves drawn in real time by your mouse or graphics tablet, and they can take the form of curves on a canvas, on a 3D surface, between surfaces, or even on the Maya grid plane.

Wherever they are placed (or "painted on"), strokes are the curves that either define the shape of a brush directly (as in a stroke of air-brushed paint) or "emit" brush tubes from them (as in grass blades, hair, or entire trees). Although brush strokes are not particles, if they are set to emit tubes from their base curve, they can "grow" these tubes as you paint, the blades of grass, hairs, or branches of a tree sprouting up from the stroke curve. In the case of trees, for instance, the strokes can emit a base branch, then sprout further branches and sub-branches, then sprout leaves, buds, or flowers. Alternatively, if you have already created a curve, you can convert it into a Paint Effects stroke, and your selected brush will be applied to the curve. If the stroke uses only the base curve you draw, paint will be applied to the curve itself. If the stroke emits tubes, the original curve will render invisible, and the paint will be applied to the tubes emitted from the curve.

As tubes are emitted and grow (over time) from a Paint Effects brush, their growth can actually be animated as well as their other features. Thus you can create a field of flowers that grow up from the ground, or make a model's hair grow longer while the animation plays. We will explain how to animate growth later in this chapter.

Brushes

Brushes are a group of growth and render options (or attributes) you set for a given curve; more simply, they are the "paint" you choose to paint with. Thus, while strokes define the shape of the curve you paint (as in a painter's brush strokes), brushes define the look of the paint.

There are more than four hundred built-in brushes, including tube-shaped animals (snakes), animal elements (flesh, hair), natural phenomena (clouds, lightning, stars), traditional brushes (oil, felt pens, air brushes), metals and glass, plants of all varieties, and food (pastas, hamburger, corn). As you would expect from Maya, all these preset brushes are infinitely adjustable and animatable, allowing you to modify the built-in brushes to your fancy and save these new brushes for later use.

 There are also at least two Paint Effects brush exchanges online, at www.highend3d.com/maya/ paintfx *and* www.aliaswavefront.com/en/Community. *At both sites, you can look for new brushes, and at the* highend3d *site, you can also submit your own creations for others to use.*

Brushes are stored in the /Maya3.0/brushes folder (on NT, the path would likely be C:\Winnt\Profiles\<user name>\Maya3.0\brushes) and are accessible in Maya in the Visor window (Window ➜ Visor) or in the Visor subwindow of the Hypershade (Window ➜ Hypershade). On opening the Visor (or Hypershade), scroll down to the bottom of the window and click to twirl down the arrow next to the /Maya3.0/brushes text. This allows you quick access to Paint Effects' thirty-plus folders of brush presets, as shown in Figure 21.1.

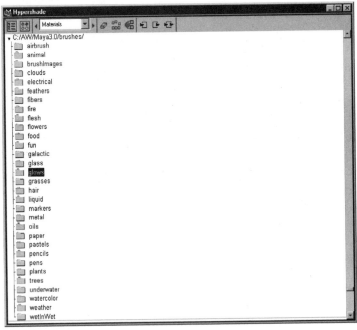

Figure 21.1 *Contents of the Paint Effects brushes folder in the Visor*

Open any folder, and inside will be brushes you can select simply by clicking the icon which represents it. If you roll the mouse over an icon, the name of the brush will appear. Select a brush (say, Delphinium from the Flowers folder) and note that your mode is now set to the Paint Effects tool in the toolbar and that your cursor has changed to a pencil icon with a red circle under it (again, similar to the Artisan cursor).

Paint Effects Brush tool

Click inside your Scene window and paint a stroke or two. You will see the outline of several flowers appear, as in Figure 21.2. As soon as you release the mouse button, the flowers will reduce to a rudimentary outline, and you will see the base curve (the actual curve you drew) highlighted on the scene grid. You may also notice that the flowers are painted on the Maya scene grid; this is because the Paint Effects tool defaults to painting on the scene grid (or the X–Z plane) if no other objects are selected and set to be paintable.

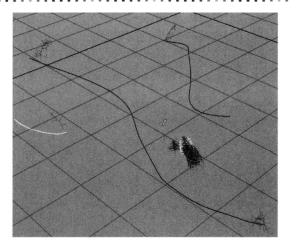

Figure 21.2 *Painting flowers in the scene window*

In order to keep the scene responsive to your input, Maya automatically reduces the complexity of the displayed curves and tubes it draws with the Paint Effects tool. You can adjust this reduction to your liking (see "Animating Brush Strokes" later in this chapter).

You may wonder why your brush strokes, while interesting, look nothing like a fully rendered flower. The answer is that, in order to see what your brush strokes will look like when they are rendered, you must either do test renders as you go or paint in a special Paint Effects window, rather than in the default Scene windows. You can define this window to be either a 2D canvas or to mimic the perspective (or other) camera in your scene. We will begin with painting on a 2D canvas in the next section, and then move on to painting in a 3D environment later in this chapter.

Painting on a 2D Canvas

At its simplest level, using Paint Effects on a 2D canvas looks a lot like traditional paint programs (Corel's Painter, for example). You simply paint on colors—or alter colors already present—and create a painterly image in two dimensions.

Start with a new Scene window (or erase the strokes you painted previously—choose Edit → Delete All by Type → Strokes), and then choose Window → Paint Effects to open a floating Paint Effects window. In this new window, you will probably see what appears to be your perspective view with a new set of icons at the top of the window. This is, in fact, the 3D environment for painting in Paint Effects. For now, we wish to paint on a canvas, so choose (from the panel menu bar, or RM choose) Paint → Paint Canvas. You will now see a large white canvas on which to paint, with icons at the top of the window (Figure 21.3) similar to the preceding set.

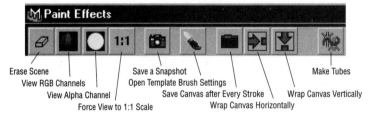

Figure 21.3 *Icons in the Paint Effects window*

To switch your main scene view window to the Paint Effects window and back, just press the 8 key on your keyboard (not on the number pad). As you will likely switch back and forth from the Paint Effects window to the Scene window(s) many times in a project, it is a good idea to memorize this shortcut. When you are in the Paint Effects window, you can momentarily access the Scene window (to pick an object, say) by holding down the Ctrl key and clicking in the window.

First, try painting on a few brush strokes. If you've been painting and have a brush still selected, you will see that brush painted on the canvas. If you have just opened a new session of Maya, you will see a black brush stroke (the default brush) painted on the window.

In the 2D view, you have just one level of Undo, and it can only be accessed via the panel menu (Canvas ➜ Canvas Undo)—not by the usual Z key. You can assign this function to a hotkey (like Ctrl+Z) via the Hotkey Editor (see Chapter 2 or 16 for more on assigning hotkeys). New with version 3, there is an Erase Scene icon so you can clear the entire canvas at once.

Once you have painted a few brush strokes, you may wish to clear the canvas, so you can paint on new strokes. To do so, choose Canvas ➜ Clear, or click the eraser icon in the toolbar, and the canvas will be reset to its initial color (probably white). To change the background color of the canvas, choose Canvas ➜ Clear ❑ and choose a new color for the canvas from the Clear Color color chip.

Clear your canvas, choose a new brush from the Visor, and paint something interesting! You may find that on a traditional canvas like this, the more traditional brush types (oil paint, pens, airbrushes, and such) look better than the organic brushes, but it's your canvas, so you get to decide. If you have a graphics tablet, you will find that many brushes have a built-in dependence on pressure, changing everything from color to size as you press harder with your stylus. You will also notice that as you move your cursor faster, many brushes will segment, not following your strokes in a continuous manner; this is because the brush strokes are merely a collection of "stamps" that the program places as you drag your mouse or stylus over the canvas. Thus, if you paint fast enough, you can "outrun" the spacing of the stamps and produce blank spaces in between. Sometimes this effect might be useful and sometimes not, so remember that Paint Effects is actually responding to the speed you draw your curves.

After you experiment a bit, clear your canvas once again (Canvas ➜ Clear or click the eraser icon) and turn on horizontal and vertical wrap. You can choose Paint Effects ➜ Paint Effects Globals ➜ Canvas and toggle on Wrap H and Wrap V, but it's simpler just to click the Wrap icons in the Paint Effects window toolbar.

Now that you have wrap on, try painting a brush stroke that goes beyond the edges of the canvas. You should see the stroke continue on the other side of the canvas, as if the canvas were wrapped into a ball where all sides meet together, like the canvas shown in Figure 21.4. This effect is, of course, extremely valuable for creating seamless tiles you could use as repeating textures in your Maya scene.

Figure 21.4 *Brush strokes wrapped in the horizontal and vertical directions*

If you wish to see how the edges of your canvas look for this, or any set of brush strokes, you can roll the canvas in any direction using the Canvas ➔ Roll ➔ <item> commands. You can, for example, roll the canvas halfway horizontally (by selecting Canvas ➔ Roll ➔ 50% Horizontal) in order to see the vertical seam in the middle of the canvas. Another roll of 50% Horizontal and your image is back to where you started.

If you have a texture that is not currently seamless (or just for other effects), you can change the brush mode from Paint to Erase, Smear, or Blur, and alter the paint that is currently on the canvas. Choose Paint Effects ➔ Template Brush Settings (from the Rendering menu set), or click the paintbrush icon in the toolbar to bring up the Paint Effects Brush Settings window, which allows you access to all of the brush's settings. For now, just change the Brush Type pop-up at the top of the window to Erase (or whatever you prefer) and paint over your image. You will see that the brush stamp is now painting on an erase (or smear or blur) effect, which can make for very intricate effects, as shown in Figure 21.5.

To save your image (if you wanted to use the image as a texture file, for example), you can either click the Camera (Save Snapshot) icon, or choose Paint ➔ Save Snapshot, and name the file. You can further modify the image in another program (like Adobe Photoshop) or use the file as a file texture on a scene object. (See Chapter 19, "Shading and Texturing Surfaces," for more information on using file textures.)

Figure 21.5 *Brush strokes, partially erased*

Modifying and Saving Brushes

In addition to simply using the presets Paint Effects gives you, you can alter just about every parameter for a brush, and then save this modified brush setting for later use. There are several ways to modify the look of a brush; we'll go from the simplest method to the one that offers the most control.

Using the Toolbar Sliders

To make basic adjustments to color and transparency, you can simply change the color chips or sliders that reside on the top-right side of the Paint Effects toolbar. Clear your canvas, then choose the puttyPaint brush from the Oils folder. Draw a few strokes onto the canvas to see what the default brush looks like.

You may wish to scale your brush up to see the strokes better. To do so, just use the same hotkey as the outer brush radius for Artisan: the B key. By holding down the B key and dragging your mouse left and right, the brush stamp size will interactively change on the canvas, allowing you to see how large your brush will be.

For the puttyPaint brush, you will only see two color chips and sliders in the tool-bar (one pinkish, which sets color, the other a dull gray, which sets transparency). Change the pinkish color to something else by clicking the color chip; then paint a few strokes to see your new brush in action. Next, increase the transparency (the gray color) by moving the slider to the right and paint some more. Your new strokes should look less solid (or more transparent) than before.

You may have noticed that changing a brush setting will not *affect your old brush strokes. Paint Effects strokes are each stored on a separate node (or, in the case of 2D work, they are just painted pixels) and thus will not automatically update when the brush profile is altered. In 3D scene painting, you can select and change old strokes, as we will see below.*

If you like the brush you have created and wish to use it again in future work, you'll want to save the profile so you don't have to make the same changes over again. You can either save the brush to a shelf or the Visor. To save the template, choose Paint Effects ➜ Save Brush Preset to bring up the dialog shown in Figure 21.6. In the Label field, name your brush (bluePutty, perhaps); in the Overlay Label field, type in any letters you would like to have printed on the icon overlay (this will only be visible if the brush is saved to a shelf). Choose either To Shelf or To Visor in the Save Preset box and, if you wish to save the brush to the Visor, type in the path to the directory where the brush will be saved. Finally, you can capture an image of the brush as an icon by clicking the Grab Icon button and then drawing a marquee around some strokes your brush made.

Figure 21.6 *The Save Brush Preset window*

Many users seem to prefer saving brush presets to a new shelf tab created just for brush presets, rather than to the Visor. This way, one can have ready access to different brushes in a convenient shelf. Of course, the choice of where to save brushes is completely up to you! For more information on creating shelves, see Chapter 2, "Your First Maya Animation."

Blending Brushes

For broader brush control than is available through the color and transparency sliders, you can easily combine two or more brushes into a third brush that shares the qualities of both parents. Reload your basic puttyPaint brush by selecting it again in the Visor. Now let's combine this brush with something natural, like the fernOrnament brush in the Plants folder. Be sure the puttyPaint brush is selected first, then roll your mouse over the fernOrnament brush and RM choose Blend Brush 50% (you will see several other blend modes, which you can play with as well). Now when you paint strokes onto the canvas, you will see that your brush has become a sort of hybrid between the putty and fern brushes. If you continue to RM choose Blend Brush 50% from the fern brush, you will continue blending the brush toward the fern look, and your strokes will look more and more like the basic fern preset. An in-between state of the brush is shown in Figure 21.7.

Figure 21.7 *A brush blended from the putty and fern brushes*

For even more control over the blending of shape and shading between two brushes, choose Paint Effects ➜ Preset Blending and adjust the two sliders, as shown in Figure 21.8. If you choose another brush preset, it will be blended in with the other brushes according to the percentages you set. This way, in just a few minutes of experimentation, you can create completely new, unique, and fun brushes for your own use. Try some blend of ferns, grass, and hair, and see what you come up with! To remove the blending effect, simply close the Brush Preset Blend window, and the next brush you pick will be loaded at 100%.

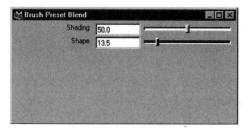

Figure 21.8 *The Brush Preset Blend window*

Using Brush Settings

The final way to adjust brushes is to use the Paint Effects Brush Settings window (Paint Effects ➜ Template Brush Settings, or click the paintbrush icon in the Paint Effects toolbar). Here you have access to the "guts" of any Paint Effects brush, with control over everything from brush profile to lighting and shadowing effects to animation and forces. There are literally hundreds of settings you can adjust here (try twirling down some of the arrows to see how many nested menus there are!), so there is simply no way to cover all of them here. If you need information about a specific setting, look in *Using Maya: Paint Effects,* either in its printed or online form. You may also find that simply altering a setting and examining the resulting look of the brush will give you enough feedback about the setting's purpose that you need look no further.

For the purpose of becoming familiar with brush settings, let's take a look at a few settings, and you can experiment with others as you go. It is no understatement to say that getting to know the Template Brush Settings window is paramount to becoming a skilled Paint Effects user. This window is where all the action is, and you need to understand enough to make intelligent changes to the settings in this window to control how your brushes will look.

Let's start with a simple brush. Choose the markerRed brush (in the Markers folder). Paint a few strokes to see what the marker looks like in its default setting, then clear the canvas. Open the Brush Settings window (either click the paintbrush icon in the toolbar or choose Paint Effects ➜ Template Brush Settings) and twirl down the Brush Profile settings. From this group of controls, you can set, for example, the Brush Width, Softness, and Stamp Density of the brush (how frequently the brush creates a new stamp of its image as you drag your mouse). Try setting the Brush Width bigger, the Softness very small, and the Stamp Density to a large number (like 10). You should end up with a series of large, distinct circles, maybe something like the one in Figure 21.9— a very different-looking brush from the default marker! The Stamp Density placed the circles very close together, the Brush Width (obviously) increased the size of the stamp, and reducing Softness created sharply defined circles instead of a blurred stroke.

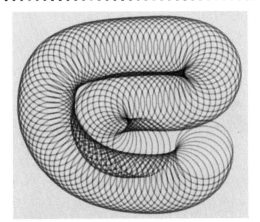

Figure 21.9 *An altered marker brush*

Under Shading, you can adjust the color, incandescence, and transparency of the marker brush. Illumination allows you to "light" the strokes (when Illumination On is checked), choose the light's direction (the Real Lights setting will not function properly in Canvas mode), and add effects like specular highlights to the brush. By setting Fake Shadow to On under Shadow Effects, you can add either a 2D offset shadow (a drop shadow) or a 3D cast shadow (the 3D cast works best in scene painting mode). Under the Glow tab, you can set several Glow attributes. You can set Gaps in your brush, so it appears more like a dotted line than a continuous curve, via the Gaps submenu. Finally, under Flow Animation, you can actually animate your brush strokes (more on this in the 3D painting section, below). Experiment with any or all settings and see what your brush ends up looking like. Figure 21.10 shows a sample of a further modified marker brush.

If you have a graphics tablet and want to map brush properties to stylus pressure, go to the Paint Effects Tool Settings window (Paint Effects ➜ Paint Effects Tool ❑). In this window, you have control over any three attributes you wish to map to pressure. Simply pull down the mapping pop-up, choose an attribute to map, and set the min/max values.

Now let's try a growing tube-based brush, to see how we can actually alter the attributes of the tubes that grow from a brush like this. From the Plants folder, select the fernOrnament brush, draw a few test strokes, and then open the Brush Settings window. You can, of course, alter any of the color, lighting, shadow, and other settings

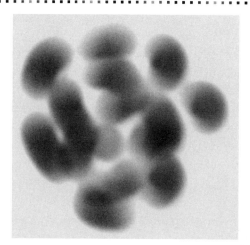

Figure 21.10 *A new look for the marker brush*

we discussed above, but here let's look at the Tubes attributes. Twirl down the Tubes settings, then twirl down the Creation sub-menu. If you set the Tubes per Step very high (like 7 or 8), you will no longer get individual fern fronds, but a mass of fern-looking things, as in Figure 21.11.

Figure 21.11 *A bunched fern brush*

While interesting, this density is calculation-intensive, so reset the Tubes per Step to a low value (like 0.2). Just a sample of the controls you have in the Creation section includes making your ferns very long by adjusting the Length Max setting, changing the tube start and end widths by adjusting the Tube Width1 and 2 settings, altering the number of Segments for each tube (more segments means more of a flowing curve) and, of course, randomizing the Tube or Width settings, so each fern doesn't look identical to its neighbor.

Creation is just the start, however; under the Growth settings, you can turn any of the following on or off, and adjust settings for them as well: Branches, Twigs, Leaves, Flowers, and Buds. The default fern only has leaves and buds turned on, so try turning on branches, twigs, and flowers, and see what happens. Without even changing the default settings, just turning on these options creates a rather interesting shrub-like brush, shown in Figure 21.12 (there's a color version of this art in the Chapter 21 Color Gallery on the CD).

Figure 21.12 *Fern with Flowers*

Inside each of these Growth sections, you have control over how many items will be created, at what angles they split off from their parent tubes, whether all tubes will have children (the Dropout rate), whether the new tubes will twist (and how much), how large they will be compared to their parent tubes, and several specialized settings for each element. As an experiment, let's create something that looks like a flowering wild rose tree. Our leaves and flowers are obviously too large for a tree, so we'll have to modify our Growth settings. The settings we chose for different aspects of the brush were done mostly by trial and error; we made adjustments and painted strokes until we were happy with the look of the tree. Table 21.1 lists a collection of settings that produces the rose you see in Figure 21.13.

Table 21.1 Settings for a Wild Rose Tree

Aspect	Setting	Value
Branches	Num Branches	4
	Branch Dropout	0.15
	Middle Branch	on
Twigs	Twigs in Cluster	4
	Num Twig Clusters	2
	Twig Dropout	0.3
	Twig Length	0.25
	Twig Base	0.9
	Tip Width	0.7
	Twig Start	0.4
	Twig Angle 1	107
	Twig Angle 2	45
	Twig Twist	0.3
Leaves	Leaves in Cluster	4
	Num Leaf Clusters	4
	Leaf Dropout	0.25
	Leaf Length	0.1
	Leaf Base	0.05
	Tip Width	0.001
	Leaf Start	0.7
	Leaf Angle 1	105
	Leaf Twist	0.5
	Leaf Flatness	1
	Leaf Size Decay	0.48
Flowers	Petals in Flower	10
	Num Flowers	5
	Petal Dropout	0.14
	Petal Length	0.03
	Petal Base	0.03
	Tip Width	0.01
	Petal Twist	0.1
Buds	Bud Size	0.02
	Bud Color	a muted red

Figure 21.13 *The fern brush turned into a rose tree brush*

Be sure to experiment with all these settings as you go, and draw on the canvas to see how your changed settings are affecting the brush.

Of course there are a multitude of possibilities here; although we can't cover the effect of all of these options, here are a few highlights. Twig Start sets how high up the tree the twigs will begin appearing. Leaf Start determines how high up a tree its trunk and branches are bare. For the buds, choose a color that stands out from the branch color. You can also change the two base leaf colors and how the two colors are randomized—try setting the randomization values very high and see what happens. When you are finished, you should have a shrub-like tree with large reddish flowers on it. The color version of Figure 21.13 can be found in the Chapter 21 Color Gallery on the CD.

Because tubes are drawn using recursive, fractal algorithms, where each layer of tubes depends on the settings for the previous layer, all tube sizes, lengths, and such are relative measures, not absolute ones.

In addition to color, you can actually map texture files onto flowers, leaves, and the main object tube itself. To map the main tube, go to Shading ➔ Texturing, click the Map Color check box, set Texture Type to File, and choose an image to map in the Image Name text field (to browse textures, click the folder icon to the right of the Image Name field near the bottom of the Texturing section). To texture Leaves and Flowers, twirl down the Leaves (or Flowers) section, uncheck the Leaf (or Flower) Use Branch

Tex(ture) check box, then choose an image in the Image Name field (or browse textures by clicking the folder icon). See the birchBlowingLight texture in the Trees collection for a demonstration of texture-mapping colors on a brush.

Painting a 2D Texture onto a 3D Object

If you would like to create a texture map for a scene object using Paint Effects, the process is fairly straightforward. First, create a side-by-side layout (Panels → Layouts → 2 Side by Side), make the right side the Perspective view, and the left side the Paint Effects window (still set to Paint on Canvas mode). In the Scene window, create an object you'd like to paint a texture on—for the example shown in Figure 21.14, a simple sphere will suffice.

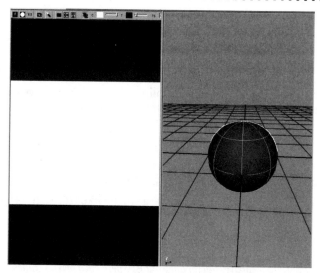

Figure 21.14 *A split view with a sphere object*

  For information on creating, modifying, and saving layouts, see Chapters 3 and 16.

Next, open a Hypershade window, create a new material, and assign a file texture to its color channel. (For more on how to create textures, see Chapter 19.) From the Hypershade window, first MM drag the material onto your scene object (to assign the material to it), then MM drag the file texture onto the Paint Effects canvas. A dialog box will appear, as in Figure 21.15, allowing you to assign the name and size (in pixels) of your texture.

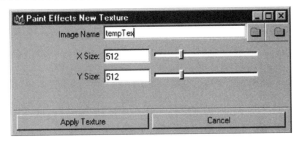

Figure 21.15 *The New Texture dialog box*

Click Apply Texture to File, choose Yes to save the file, and save it in your /sourceImages directory. Before painting on the canvas, choose Canvas ➜ Auto Save to turn on Save After Each Stroke. When you release the mouse button each time, you will see your texture updated on the scene object(s) to which the material is being applied. Try painting with several brushes onto the canvas and see how your texture map updates. Remember, you may wish to turn on Wrap Horizontal and Vertical to allow your map to be seamless as it wraps around the objects in your scene. Figure 21.16 shows how wrapping appears on your canvas, and can be found in the Chapter 21 Color Gallery on the CD.

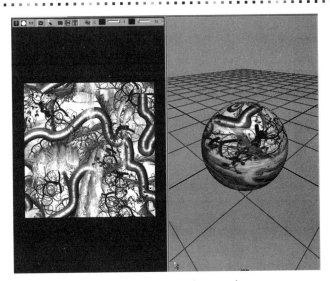

Figure 21.16 *File texture applied to a sphere*

The current version of Paint Effects has a "feature" in it that can cause a few headaches if you're not aware of it: if you choose Canvas ➡ Clear while painting a texture map, the canvas will become disconnected from the material, and you will have to assign the texture to the canvas again. To erase a canvas, then, you need to use the Erase feature of Paint Effects (under the Template Brush Settings) to erase unwanted strokes. (The reason for this feature is to keep people from accidentally erasing their file textures: with Save After Each Stroke on, clearing the canvas automatically erases the file texture, which apparently upset some Paint Effects beta testers.)

Painting in a 3D Scene

Now that we understand strokes and brushes, and how to use them in 2D, let's get on to the really interesting aspect of Paint Effects: painting in three dimensions. As all Paint Effects brushes are 3D curves that can (optionally) create tubes, you can paint in a scene as easily as on the canvas. If you open a new scene, choose a Paint Effects brush, and start painting, you will automatically paint on the scene grid (as we noted at the start of this chapter). This can work very well if you wish to paint trees, grass, or other elements on the "ground." If you wish to paint on an actual scene object (or multiple objects), however, you need to select that object and then tell Paint Effects that the object is paintable.

In a new scene, create a NURBS Cylinder (be sure to cap the cylinder). In the Scene window, select the object and choose Paint Effects ➡ Make Paintable. (Remember, holding down the Ctrl key in the Paint Effects window momentarily enables the Scene window so you can select objects in the Paint Effects window as well as in the main Scene window.) If you're not in the Paint Effects window, press the 8 key on your keyboard to choose that mode. If you are still in Canvas mode in the Paint Effects window, choose Paint ➡ Paint Scene to toggle on display of your scene.

We could choose to paint some hair on this object, but we'll wait on this until the hands-on project later in this chapter. Instead, let's paint some other brushes on, like one of the grasses, an oil paint, and a waterfall (under the Liquid folder). Remember that you can alter the scale of the brush by pressing B and dragging the mouse.

Many of the Paint Effects brushes require real lighting to appear, so you may need to add one or more lights to your scene to see your brushes in all their splendor.

Because painting on an object simply creates curves on the object's surface, you can select, move, modify (alter individual CVs), or offset these curves from the surface, giving you a great deal of control over the look of each curve.

If you tumble the Paint Effects window, you will notice that the brushes revert to an outline of their fully rendered selves in order to speed up redraw, so you don't have to wait for the full effect of the brushes to render each time. To change how Paint Effects simplifies the *display* of your strokes (not the actual strokes themselves), open the Template Brush Editor, open the Tubes section and then the Creation section, and alter the Simplify Method. If you choose Tubes per Step, the redraw will remove many of the initial tubes from display (this is good for elements like hair, which have many tubes). Choosing Segments removes portions of each tube object, but retains the initial tube for each one (this is good for trees, flowers, and the like). Choosing Tubes and Segments will (of course) reduce display of both. You can also force Paint Effects to redraw the entire window each time you move in the scene (Stroke Refresh ➜ Rendered in the Paint Effects window), but this will slow your interaction with Paint Effects down a great deal. To force a redraw of the window after you have painted many strokes, click the Redraw Paint Effects View icon in the toolbar.

Redraw Paint Effects View

After some painting, your cylinder will probably look a great deal more interesting than it did in the first place; an example of what you might create is shown in Figure 21.17.

Figure 21.17 *A cylinder with multiple brush strokes applied to it*

While painting in the Paint Effects window is great for getting the look of brushes down, it is often far more interactive to paint in the Scene view for large-scale jobs. When you switch over to the Scene window, you will be limited to painting in wireframe, but the painting will go much faster. One workflow example might be to create an interesting look for a tree brush or two in the Paint Effects window, save these (in the Visor or on a shelf), then switch to the Scene window and paint a forest of these trees. When you create the forest, you already know what the trees look like—you just wish to paint them into the scene quickly and interactively, and the Scene window is better suited to this than the Paint Effects window.

If you wish to delete the last stroke you made in 3D paint mode, the normal Undo feature works fine. To delete selected strokes, simply select them (in the Scene or Hypergraph window) and press the Backspace or Delete key. To delete all strokes in one fell swoop, simply choose Edit ➔ Delete All by Type ➔ Strokes, and all your brush strokes will magically disappear!

Take some time now to play with different brushes (altering them as you wish, or just using different defaults) and get a feel for how various brushes act in a 3D scene as opposed to a 2D canvas.

If you wish to create a curve first, and then attach a brush to the curve, select the curve in your Scene window and then choose Paint Effects ➔ Curve Utilities ➔ Attach Brush to Curve. In this manner, you can "multipurpose" curves for brushes and other functions within your scene.

Editing Previous Brush Strokes

As you experiment with brushes, you may find yourself wishing you could go back and alter strokes you've already laid down (remember that each new stroke is a new node, so changing a brush will normally not affect older strokes). Because Paint Effects strokes are just curve nodes in a 3D scene, you can choose these curves and alter any attributes you wish via the Attribute Editor.

As an example, let's choose one of the strokes you created on your scene object and modify it. You can try to select a curve via the Select tool, but you will likely choose many curves at the same time; the Hypergraph is a better way to choose an individual curve (you can also zoom in very close to a stroke and select it that way). When you open the Hypergraph, you will see dozens of nodes named *stroke<item><number>*, where <item> is the name of the brush and <number> is the number of that brush's stroke. Figure 21.18 shows some sample strokes in the Hypergraph window.

Choose one of the Grass strokes (for example), then open the Attribute Editor (Ctrl+A). Under the grass*<type><number>* tab (the second tab from the right), you will

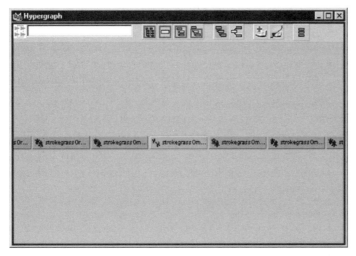

Figure 21.18 Hypergraph showing Paint Effects stroke nodes

have access to all the settings that were available via the Template Brush Settings window, only this time the changes will be made to the existing stroke. Try adding some flowers to the grass (under /Tubes/Growth), and change the color of the grass to something other than green (/Shading/Tube Shading). As exemplified in Figure 21.19, you have complete control over your brushes, even after you create them!

Figure 21.19 Altered grass brush strokes

If you have several strokes that you wish to vary all at once, you can elect to "group" them so that they share one brush setting. This way, as you make adjustments to one brush, all the strokes will update simultaneously—a real time-saver. To accomplish this, select all the strokes you want to have share one brush. These strokes can have any brush attached to them, but be sure to select *last* the stroke with the brush shape you want to assign to all of them, because the last stroke selected supplies the shared brush. Next, choose Paint Effects ➜ Share One Brush to make them all share the same brush settings. If you now open the Attribute Editor and change the attributes of the current brush, all the strokes you had selected will update together. If you had chosen, for example, to share the vineLeafy2 brush (in the Plants collection), you could change the default brush settings to include twigs, and all your strokes would come out looking something like Figure 21.20.

Figure 21.20 *Altered vine look on the cylinder*

To remove sharing between strokes, simply select the strokes, and then choose Paint Effects ➜ Remove Brush Sharing.

Adding Forces to Paint Effects Brushes

If creating still lifes isn't enough for you, don't worry: you can add dynamics to your Paint Effects brushes (at least the tube ones) and animate the brushes over time.

Paint Effects brushes actually don't use dynamics (as do particles and rigid bodies) but use recursive expressions on the tubes nodes. While expressions aren't quite as wide-ranging as Maya's dynamics engine, using them was a very clever trade-off between speed and natural motion. Using Maya's built-in dynamics engine, even a single tree could take minutes per frame to update, whereas the expression solution allows for very fast updates, and even allows you to scrub the animation back and forth, which dynamics simulations cannot handle.

To see how to add dynamics, let's create some grass that blows in the wind. In the Visor, select the grassClump brush (in the Grasses folder) and, using the Paint Effects Template Brush Settings window, change the grass's Length Max (under /Tubes/Creation) to about 4, so there's a lot of grass to blow around. (There are, of course, preset grasses that include wind, but by starting with a grass that has no forces applied to it, you can build your own.) Paint a single stroke on the ground plane. If you play back the animation now, you will see that the grass stays perfectly still as the animation plays. While you could adjust your brush settings in the Brush Settings window, and then paint a new stroke each time, it is easier to simply select the stroke and go into the Attribute Editor and make changes. Your "sample" stroke will then update as you make changes, allowing you to see the effects of what you are doing.

You will find it far more interactive to switch to the Scene window (by pressing the 8 key) rather than trying to watch animation play back in the Paint Effects window.

With the stroke selected, click the grassClump1 tab in the Attribute Editor, and open the /Tubes/Behavior subsection. There are several menus under this: Displacement, Forces, Turbulence, Spiral, and Twist (Paint Effects is a deep plug-in with lots of controls!). Feel free to play with any of these behavior modifiers, but we will concentrate on just a couple as examples.

First, twirl down Forces and adjust the Gravity setting. You will notice that the blades of grass bend over as if they're growing heavier and heavier as you adjust this setting. Due to the relatively few segments on the grass blade, the grass will bend at sharp angles when gravity is applied. (Of course you can change this by altering /Tubes/Creation/Segments to a higher number, like 20.) You can also make the grass stretch under gravity by setting the Length Flex to a number greater than 0. While a heavy, stretchy look might be great for some items, it's not particularly appropriate for grass, so set the Length Flex back to 0. Still, we can make the grass a bit heavier by setting gravity to about 0.12. As all Paint Effects brush behaviors are based on expressions, you can either type a value for most attributes, or create an expression or a Set Driven Key to control that attribute. To create an expression or to set keys, RM choose Create New Expression (or Set Key) for an attribute; in the case of an expression, you would then write an equation that alters the value of said attribute. Try this simple equation to make the grass "do the wave." With your cursor over the Gravity setting, RM choose Create New Expression, then, in the expression window, type in the following:

```
gravity = sin (time);
```

When you play back the animation, your grass should wave up and down.

Several of the other controls in this block (like Path Follow and Attract) will be discussed in the hands-on section at the end of the chapter.

Now let's add some wind to our grass. First, delete the gravity expression from the expression editor, or RM choose Delete Expression over Gravity. Twirl down Turbulence, and choose Grass Wind from the Turbulence Type pop-up menu. Leave the Turbulence Interpolation set to Smooth over Time and Space (or feel free to experiment with the other settings), and try adjusting the Turbulence, Frequency, and Speed settings while your animation plays back. At their default settings, the grass will wave back and forth a bit, fairly quickly. To make it wave more slowly, set the Turbulence Speed to a small number. To make the grass blow more strongly, change the Turbulence slider to a large number. Turbulence Frequency controls how much space the turbulence field will vary across the stroke. In other words, setting the Turbulence Frequency to 0 will make every blade of grass blow just the same, while setting Turbulence Frequency to 1 will make them all blow independently. If you now go back and adjust the /Forces/Length Flex to 1, you'll get grass that stretches as it blows—an interesting, if unrealistic, effect.

If your playback speed is set to Free, you may find your animation runs too quickly, giving the illusion that your objects are moving around much faster than they will in the final render. To compensate for this, you might try setting the playback rate to Normal (Window → Settings/Preferences → Preferences, then choose the Settings/Timelines section); or if your scene is complex (slowing down playback) or depends on Free playback for dynamics, just playblast the animation (Window → Playblast) to get a better idea of its output speed.

Finally, once you get just the brush you were looking for, you will probably want to save it for later use. With your brush stroke still selected, choose Paint Effects → Get Settings from Selected Stroke, and then save the brush to your shelf or the Visor.

The center color insert and CD contain a still and an animation of a water fountain we will create in the next several chapters; this fountain includes Paint Effects trees, grasses, moss, and such (see 21fountain.mov for the movie file). This animation shows off just a small portion of the possibilities Paint Effects opens to your modeling and animation endeavors.

Animating Brush Strokes

In addition to animating the tubes on your brush strokes, you can also animate the appearance of your strokes over time, enabling you to "grow" hair on a head, or flowers in a field. Let's do the latter, using the brush flowerTallRed (in the Flowers folder). First, make a nice long stroke in your Paint Effects or Scene window, as Figure 21.21 shows, so you have a nice bunch of flowers to work with.

Figure 21.21 *A curve of flowers painted in the Scene window*

First, we need to change the simplification mode of the flowers (so we can see them better as we animate their growth). With the stroke selected, click the flowerTallRed1 tab in the Attribute Editor and, under Tubes/Creation, set the Simplify method to Segments. Now twirl down Flow Animation to get at the settings for animating brush growth. Set the Flow Speed to a number greater than 0 (drag the slider, or, if you wish, you can set a value greater than 1 by typing in the number field). Next, check the Time Clip box, set the start time to 0 and the end time to a larger number (the default is 1,000), and play back the animation. You should see all your flowers rise out of the ground at the same time, growing to full height over 100 or so frames. Figure 21.22 shows a still from this animation process.

Setting the start time to a number greater (or less) than 0 allows the objects to begin growing after (or before) the animation starts. Setting the end time to a small number (like 1 or 2 seconds) will make the objects "decay" after that much time: they will disappear, starting at the roots. While this effect isn't quite right for flowers, it could be used in other instances (as in water drying up at its source, or streaks from fireworks) to good effect.

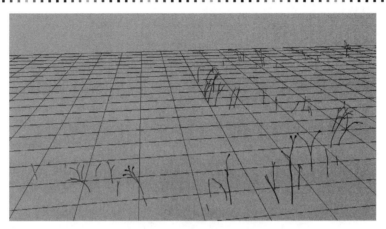

Figure 21.22 *Flowers half grown all together*

Having all the flowers appear at once may not be what you're after. If, instead, you would like the growth pattern to follow your brush stroke, simply click the Stroke Time check box to enable the brush to remember the direction of your strokes. With both Time Clip and Stroke Time enabled for various brush strokes, you can create a field of grass and trees, or grow hair on a model's head, just as easily as drawing the curves! The flowers shown in Figure 21.23 are growing at different rates.

Figure 21.23 *Flowers growing at different rates*

Instancing Brush Strokes

New to Maya 3, you can instance brush strokes as particles, allowing you to, for example, rapidly create a field of flowers (by instancing flower strokes to a grid of particles), or—as we'll do here—make a showering fountain of feathers. Obviously, some uses of instancing are more realistic than others! (Particles are covered in depth starting with Chapter 22, "Particle Basics." For the purposes of this chapter, we'll just work with basic particle emitter and field settings.)

In a new Scene window, open the Particle Emitter Options window (Particles ➜ Create Emitter ❑ from the Dynamics menu set). Set the Emitter Type to Directional, the rate to 50, the DirectionY to 1 (set X and Z to 0), the spread to 0.4, and the Speed to 20 (you will have to twirl down the first three subsections of the window to find these settings). When you have the proper options set, click the Create button. Play back the animation; you should see little purple dots shooting up into the air. Select these dots (not the emitter) so they turn green, and then choose Fields ➜ Gravity ❑, choose Edit ➜ Reset Settings in the Gravity Options menu, and click the Create button. Now when you play back the animation, you should see the particles shoot up, and then fall down again as they succumb to gravity's influence—you may need to zoom your view out to see the particles better.

If you don't see the particles falling back down, select the particles again and open the Dynamic Relationship editor (Window ➜ Relationship Editors ➜ Dynamic Relationships). Click the gravityField1 text to the right (highlighting it pale orange), and your particles should be connected now.

Now that we have a fountain, let's instance a Paint Effects feather to it. In the Visor, choose a feather brush (down3, for example), and, anywhere in the Scene window, paint a short stroke until you see a single feather. With the feather still selected, Shift-select the particles (not the emitter) and choose Particles ➜ Instancer (Replacement). Now, when you play back the animation, you should see the basic fountain *and* a fountain of feathers, offset from the emitter, as in Figure 21.24. You can then hide the original fountain and move the first feather wherever you wish the fountain to go. You have a great deal of control over how the instanced geometry interacts with the particles by clicking the instancer1 tab in the Attribute Editor—however, you may find it easier to adjust settings by using the Instancer Options window when you first create your particles.

Rendering

While Paint Effects is a very deep program with a great many controls, rendering is a relatively transparent process. To render a scene with Paint Effects brushes in it, all you

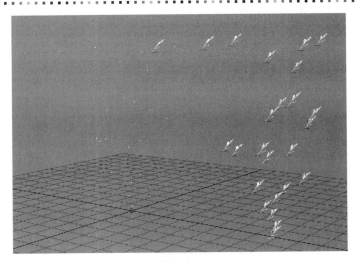

Figure 21.24 *A fountain of feathers*

need do is batch render (or test render into the Render View Window) as you would normally. When a render including Paint Effects brushes is launched, Maya first renders all the geometry in the scene, and then, in a post-render process, adds the brushes, fully rendered. Though Paint Effects rendering is a post-render process (after all geometry), the renderer is intelligent enough to place Paint Effects brushes properly in 3D space. In other words, a brush that is partially behind some geometry (like a cube, for instance) will render with that portion hidden from view. This way, though Paint Effects rendering is done after normal rendering, you don't generally have to deal with the difficulties of masking and compositing the two elements together; Maya does this for you. The hands-on tutorial that follows covers the issue of partially occluded Paint Effects brushes in more detail.

There is an exception to the rule that Maya precomposites Paint Effects brushes with geometry renders: refractions (for semitransparent objects) and reflections. If you render a raytraced scene with refractions or reflections, you will not see the Paint Effects brushes in the objects that are refracting or reflecting. In order to circumvent this problem, you must render out your geometry and the Paint Effects brushes in separate passes and composite them together in a compositing package (such as Maya Composer, Maya Fusion, or AfterEffects). The fountain animation on the CD (21fountain.mov), as well as the still from this animation in the center color insert, use compositing to get the appropriate reflections and refractions in the water.

While most of the controls in a Paint Effects brush that have to do with rendering are fairly self-explanatory (color, textures, illumination, and so forth), two items are worth noting here. First, there is a Translucence setting (under Illumination in the Paint Effects Template Brush Settings window) for brushes (high translucence allows diffuse light to pass through an object), which can be very useful for plants, tree leaves, and hair. Second, you have two choices for shadowing (under Shadow Effects): a 2D offset shadow (the drop shadow we discussed earlier in the chapter) and a 3D cast shadow. The 3D cast shadow is a "fake" shadow and thus might need some adjustment to have proper size and density in your scene. The following hands-on section discusses this issue further.

You can quickly enable or disable Paint Effects strokes in your renders (or choose to render only Paint Effects strokes). In the Render Globals window is a section for Paint Effects with Enable Stroke Rendering and Only Render Strokes check boxes. With Enable Stroke Rendering on, Paint Effects brushes are rendered. When off, only the geometry of the scene will be rendered. If Only Render Strokes is on, geometry in the scene will be hidden, and only Paint Effects brushes will be rendered. In such a case, you need to have previously rendered out your geometry and included a depth map image with your render—you then choose this depth map (under Read This Depth Map) to inform the Paint Effects brush strokes where to render. Using these render features can be very valuable when you wish to use a compositing program to adjust and assemble render passes.

A few exceptions notwithstanding, rendering Paint Effects brushes is a very painless (and quick!) experience. With your basic understanding of the principles of rendering in Maya, you will find yourself producing great-looking images right from the start.

Hands-On Maya: Painting Hair on a Head

Until now, the boy we created earlier in the book has been stuck with somewhat plastic-looking hair. While you could explain his hairdo away as an overzealous use of hairspray, a better option would be to just give him some "real" hair, which is where Paint Effects comes in. (To see a different way to animate the boy's hair, see Chapter 25, "Dynamics of Soft Bodies.")

Start by opening one of your head models or the included scene file 21hair.mb. The included project defaults to a close-up of the boy's bald head.

Bring up the Side window full-screen. You should be in shaded, textured mode. The hair is not very graphics-intensive, so we will be able to run at a fairly high window-display setting. This is good, because we will need the fine details to decide how and where to paint the hair. Select the head object and press the 3 key to increase the display quality.

In the Visor, go to /AW/Maya3.0/brushes and open the Hair folder. Select the hair-BlondeNoShape brush. Now, since the boy actually has black hair, we will blend the shading of the eyeBrowBlack brush at 100%. With your mouse over the eyeBrowBlack icon, RM choose Blend Shading 100%, as shown in Figure 21.25.

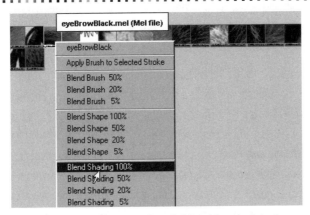

Figure 21.25 *Creating a brush blend for dark hair*

Because Paint Effects brushes cannot be applied to polygon or subdivision surfaces, we first need to make a skull cap of NURBS curves on which we will paint (this cap will then be hidden after the hair is applied). With the head selected, choose Subdiv Surfaces ➜ Extract Vertices, set the Level to 1, be sure the Original Object is set to Show, and click Extract. In the Hypergraph or Outliner window, find the original head (and eyes) model and hide it. Now select the extracted vertices and choose Modify ➜ Make Live to allow you to draw curves on the head's surface. Starting around the hair line, draw curves around the head, each one getting closer to the top of the head. When you have all your curves drawn, just select them all (in order from bottom to top) and choose Surfaces ➜ Loft to loft a skull shape, as shown in Figure 21.26. Next, select the lofted surface and choose Edit ➜ Delete By Type ➜ History, and then delete all the curves you used. Finally, delete the polygon head (not the original subdivision surfaces head!) and redisplay the original head again, if you wish.

The skull cap has been completed for you in the `21hair.mb` *file on the CD. If you wish to create the curves on the head using this file, simply erase the lofted surface and make them yourself.*

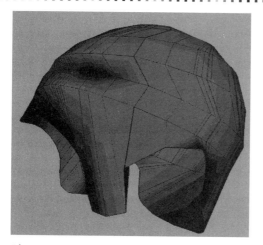

Figure 21.26 *A NURBS skull cap on which to use the Paint Effects hair brush*

With the skull selected, choose Paint Effects ➔ MakePaintable. Now let's try a few strokes; click and hold down the mouse while drawing a line on the head (remember, only the skull-cap portion will be paintable). You will instantly see hair sprouting from the head, although it will probably not be long enough to give the impression that this child has much of a hairstyle. We need to change the brush size.

Interactively resize the brush with the B key (as shown previously in this chapter). You may have to experiment to get a size that works for you. Try painting different brush sizes, and once you get the hair size you want, delete all the strokes to start fresh (Edit ➔ Delete All by Type ➔ Strokes). You now have a clean head and a properly sized hair brush.

The next step is to decide how the hair will be added to the child's head. There are quite a few ways to accomplish this. For this exercise, many options were explored for getting hair on the head. It turns out that the most obvious, in this case, seemed to work the best for us: just paint the hair following the topology of the head model from front to back.

With that in mind, let's start giving this poor boy something to comb. We will start on the left side of the boy's head. Start your first stroke from the sideburn area and paint up and around the ear, to where the hair would naturally stop growing, as shown in Figure 21.27. The reason for starting here is that the more hair we add, the harder it will become to see the strokes as we make them. The area around the ear is the most critical (as it has to match the boy's sideburn and ear line), so we begin here.

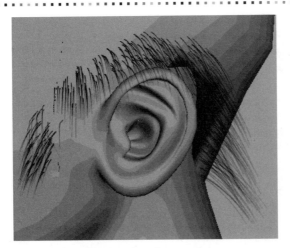

Figure 21.27 *Hair painted around the ear area*

If you are painting a huge model, or one with very intricate curves, you can select your brush and, before you paint, select Paint Effects ➜ Paint Effects Tool, and change the Display Quality to 0. You will still see the hairs as you paint them, but when you lift your finger from the mouse button to get another stroke ready, they will disappear. You will be left with only the curves on surface visible, showing you where you painted without slowing your work down. Remember, this setting only affects the display, not the rendering of the strokes.

If you have a tablet, now is the time to use it. You will find that painting the boy's hair will be much easier with a tablet than a mouse!

We are now going to set things up so that from this point on the hair will be shaped to the head as we paint. (The brush actually isn't shaping itself to the head, as much as following the direction of the curve that we are painting.)

With the hair brushstroke still selected, open the eyeBrowBlack1 tab for this brush in the Attribute Editor, twirl down the /Tubes/Behavior/Forces triangles, and find Path Follow. Path Follow defaults to 0 for this brush because hairBlondeNoShape is controlling our hair's shape, while eyeBrowBlack is in control of the shading. Because we need something a little different, change the value to 0.7.

Now you will notice that the hairs that are already on the model's head have nicely aligned themselves to the shape of the head (actually the curve we painted), as in Figure 21.28. Feel free to play with values in this field to get different results.

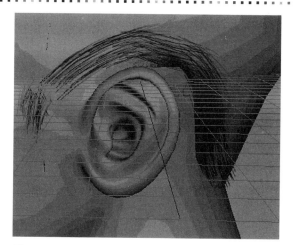

Figure 21.28 *Hair following the curve of the head*

After you have a shape you like for your hair stroke, select Paint Effects → Get Settings from Selected Stroke. This will ensure that as you paint each new stroke, the settings you have changed on the stroke you already have painted will be used for each subsequent stroke. Give it a try. It makes painting the hair and designing the shape of the hair style much more intuitive.

If you also change the value of Path Attract to a non-zero number, the hairs will tend to "lean" toward the curve as well as follow its direction. This can be particularly useful when you paint braided hair and you want the hairs to be more compressed to the head in evident rows. You can also enter a negative number, to repel the hair and get an "Einstein" look.

Now start working your way up the head, drawing slow, even strokes from the front of the head toward the back. You will notice that the hair sticks straight up and has no real defined shape. This is by design, since we picked the hairBlondeNoShape brush. The reason we did this is to allow us to shape the hair after we painted it, to give us more eventual control over the hair, and faster feedback while drawing, without all the added dynamics that are built into some of the other hair presets. You should end up with somewhere between 10 and 15 brush strokes, which can be seen as curves on surface and show up in the Hypergraph window as strokeeyeBrowBlackShape1, strokeeyeBrowBlackShape2, etc. Figure 21.29 shows the results.

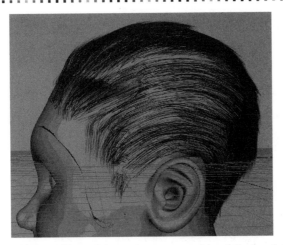

Figure 21.29 *Hair strokes on one side of the boy's head*

Now rotate your view and repeat the process for this side of the head. As Figure 21.30 indicates, our boy now looks as though he has a premature case of male pattern baldness, because we haven't yet painted the top of his head.

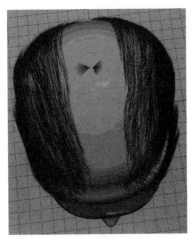

Figure 21.30 *Missing hair on top of the boy*

Switch to the Top camera (or rotate your perspective view again) and start at the forehead, painting toward the back of the head. Finally, rotate your view to the back and finish the job. You may wish to swirl the boy's hair around the crown of the head, imitating the way hair grows there. Figure 21.31 shows a completed head of hair.

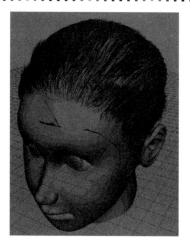

Figure 21.31 *A head full of hair*

Now, add a light or two and do a test render. Notice anything wrong? More than likely, the specular highlights on the hair strands are very blown out. This can be controlled for the entire head by selecting Edit ➜ Select All by Type ➜ Strokes. With all the strokes selected, go to the Channel Box and open up the Inputs for the brushes. Change the following settings, to affect the specularity: Specular to 0.085 (this sets the brightness of the specular highlight, based upon the specular color settings) and specular Power to 10 (this is the size of the specular highlight, where a larger number means a tighter highlight).

Do another test render. Much better! However, the hair is looking a little gray, so change the Color 1 and Color 2 settings to the following: color1 R, G, and B to 0.01 each; color2 R, G, and B to 0.02 each.

Now with another test render, you should notice more natural-looking hair color and specularity. You will find that different lighting conditions may warrant changing these settings, so feel free to experiment with them.

There still seems to be something missing here, though; the boy is looking like a fairly cheap hair-transplant recipient. This is because the default settings for density on the original brush weren't high enough.

To change this, select all the strokes and, in the Channel box under Shapes, change the Sample Density value to a larger number, like 5. This will give you a thicker head of hair, shown in Figure 21.32, as the brush stroke is more densely populated by hairs along its path. Now make everything visible on the boy model and do a test render.

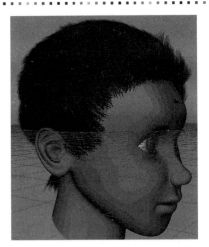

Figure 21.32 *Same boy, but the hair has a higher density*

For even more control of the hair shape, change the number of segments for the tube (under Inputs for the stroke) to a higher number. This will cause the hair shape to not only look more realistic, but act more predictably as you paint.

If you look closely at the render, you will notice that the hair is also casting nice fine shadows onto the boy's head. These are fake shadows, caused by Maya placing additional black strokes on the surface of the head to simulate shadows. It guesses where the surface is in 3D space, and draws a shadow paint stroke where it thinks the surface lies. This method isn't perfect, but it allows nice fine shadow details when it works. To prevent the hair from casting shadows onto other objects, or to give yourself another type of shadow option when the fake shadows aren't working, set Fake Shadow to None in Attribute Editor (remember to select all your strokes first!).

Alternatively, you can also change the shadow setting to 2D offset, but this is for creating a drop-shadow effect. While it works well for ferns that are painted on the side of a brick building, it isn't very good for hair on a curvy surface like a head.

With Fake Shadow set to None, scroll up to the top of the Inputs section and check Cast Shadows to On. Make sure your light is set to cast Depth Map Shadows. The Cast Shadows setting only works with Depth Map Shadows, as none of the Paint Effects elements can be raytraced. Compare the various shadow types shown in Figure 21.33.

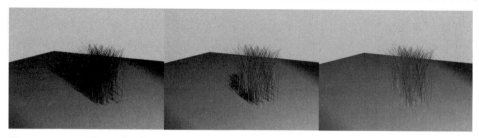

Figure 21.33 *Three shadow types. (left) Shadow mapped shadows (with Cast Shadows on); (center) 3D cast shadows; (right) No shadows*

Though they cannot be raytraced, all Paint Effects brushes can be motion-blurred, both in 2D and 3D. Most people will opt to use 2D motion blur, as it's usually faster and smoother than 3D. Also note that there will probably be some visibly chunky lines near where a brush stroke (hair or otherwise) is occluded by the geometry. This is because the hair is rendered into place using the Depth Buffer, and therefore there can be no anti-aliasing of the edge where they meet; depth is either true or false for a given depth. As Duncan Brinsmead (co-creator of Paint Effects) stated, "We don't have the notion of an anti-alias for the depth. It's sort of an on or off thing. It's either at that depth, or it's at a different depth for that whole pixel in the Depth Map." You must therefore take steps to compensate for this problem if it is apparent in your renders.

To alleviate this edge, we suggest you render your geometry first without the Paint Effects elements, then render the Paint Effects elements without the geometry (remember what we said previously about rendering in passes). Using various compositing tricks, such as blurring and shrinking the elements slightly, you should be able to eliminate these chunky lines. They are really only a problem in very close shots, or when there is little to no motion. Another quick way around aliasing problems is to use 2D motion blur, which we found almost totally hid these areas.

Now that you have given your model a full head of hair with shadows, take away some of his dignity and have some fun with your brush. Select all the strokes and, in the Visor, with your cursor over the Hyacinth brush (in the Flowers folder), RM choose Apply Brush to Selected Stroke. Do a test render, as in Figure 21.34, and enjoy the boy's fancy new 'do. Have fun with these experiments, and try applying several different brushes to your strokes to see what they look like.

Figure 21.34 *A head of flowers!*

Summary

While there is no way to fully explore the depths of Paint Effects in just one chapter (that could be the subject of another book!), this introduction should enable you to grasp the underlying elements of the Paint Effects tool set, and you should now be comfortable enough with this feature of Maya that you can experiment intelligently, using the built-in presets, or creating your own unique brushes. You have learned how to paint in both two dimensions (on a canvas) and three (in a scene), how to interactively create texture maps, how to animate your strokes, and what many of the Paint Effects options do. Furthermore, you went through a "real-world" example of using Paint Effects to create hair on a head—a process you might repeat often in a production environment. By now, you should have an appreciation of both the depth of Paint Effects and how it can help you accomplish tasks that were heretofore too difficult or time consuming to attempt.

Paint Effects is a great deal like Artisan: you will likely need to experiment with it creatively for a while before you will feel comfortable. However, you should now have enough knowledge to use simple Paint Effects elements in your scenes right away, and to understand how to experiment with the package to create more complex and interesting effects in the future. With Paint Effects—and Maya as a whole—you should have fun recreating reality, or creating anything you can imagine.

In the next several chapters, we turn to another area of advanced effects work: particles. Using particles (introduced briefly in this chapter), you'll be able to create a number of effects—from dust clouds to jiggly, "fleshy" bodies—that would be very difficult to create in any other manner.

Particle Basics

MAYA

Chapter 22

This chapter introduces Maya's built-in particle dynamics engine, which can be used to simulate everything from dust motes in the air to hordes of rocket ships battling in space. This tool both simulates the physics of the real world and is able to handle huge volumes of particles; even millions of particles can be simulated. As a result, it is one of the most powerful tools you have in Maya for producing exciting and visually appealing work.

We will begin with elementary particle systems and work our way up to more complex simulations, including particle interaction with rigid bodies. If you have not read Chapter 15, "Working with Rigid Body Dynamics," you should do that first. Particles and rigid bodies share many underlying features, so understanding one can help with understanding the other. Although we use relatively simple examples to demonstrate working with particles, this is a difficult area for most animators to grasp. Be prepared to spend some time working through the examples in this chapter and experimenting on your own. Topics include:

- The Particle tool
- Particle emitters
- Fields as forces on particles
- Particle collision collections and events
- Particle lifespan
- Particle and rigid body interactions

What Are Particles?

Essentially, particles are little points (like dust or confetti) that you can place in your animations manually or have emitted by a particle emitter. Particles, like rigid bodies, are physics simulations, not animation in the traditional sense; so you cannot manipulate them directly. To control particles, you must adjust their attributes (or the attributes of their emitters) in the Channel box or Attribute Editor. Particles can be affected by collisions and fields, and they can have their attributes altered by expressions. You can render particles in many ways, including simply as points, and they can even make up collective bodies (called soft bodies).

 This chapter covers using collisions and fields with particles. Expressions, render types, and soft bodies are discussed in the next chapters.

Like (active) rigid bodies, particles themselves cannot be keyframed (although their parent emitter object can). If particles are not keyframable, and you need to use numbers to alter their behavior, why bother? As we will see, particles are a great way to create random or very large-scale behavior that would be nearly impossible to produce by traditional keyframing. Items ranging from rocket exhaust, to leaves, to human hair can be simulated using particles. If you need a plasma cannon or a fountain (our first two projects), particles come to the rescue.

Because particles (like active rigid bodies) depend solely on their attributes, you need to bring along a sense of adventure to your work with particles. The best way to get to know how to do things with particles is to play (and play and play) with the numbers in the Channel box or Attribute Editor. Oddly enough, although particle simulation is based on science, getting the particles to do what you want is really an art.

Creating Particles

Before we begin making things with particles, let's figure out how to create the particles themselves. There are a couple of basic ways to make particles: You can simply draw them in the scene using the Particle tool, or you can create an emitter to shoot them into the scene. In the brief examples in the following sections, you'll try both methods.

Drawing Particles in a Scene

To draw a particle in a scene, create a new scene in Maya and choose Particles ➜ Particle Tool ❏ from the Dynamics menu set. This brings up the Particle tool's Tool Settings window, as shown in Figure 22.1.

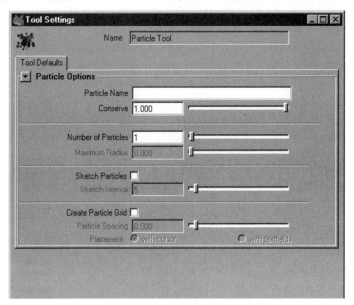

Figure 22.1 *Particle Tool options*

In this window, there are settings for creating single particles, multiple particles, random particles, and particles in grids. Let's see how they work.

1. Leave the Particle tool at its default settings and LM click anywhere in the scene. You should see a red cross (a little bigger than a dot) indicating where you have just created a particle. Click a few more times to create several particles in the scene; you can rotate your view to get the particles in different places. Then press Enter to turn this bunch of particles into a group. Particles in a group all live on the same node and will share the same fields, collisions, and render types.

2. Let's create clumps of particles instead of individual ones when we click. Delete all the particles you just created, and reselect Particle Tool ❏. In the Particle Options section, set Number Of Particles to 10 and Maximum Radius to 5. Click in the scene. You see a clump of 10 particles created in an imaginary sphere 5 units in radius, as shown in Figure 22.2. If you continue to click, the new clumps will be part of your current particle node. If you press Enter between clicks (and then Y to return to the Particle tool), you will create a new particle node each time.

The easiest way to delete particles is to LM drag over them using the Select tool (Q on the keyboard or the arrow in the menu) and then press Delete. You can also RM choose Select All and delete them, but the particles must be unselected first.

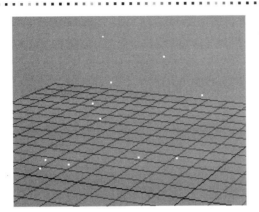

Figure 22.2 *A clump of new particles*

3. Now try sketching particles in a line. Delete your particles once again and press Y to bring up the Particle tool's window again. Click the Reset Tool button to return to the default Particle tool settings. Then check the Sketch Particles box. In your scene window, LM drag to create a line of particles, as in Figure 22.3. Next open the Particle tool window and reset Number Of Particles to 10 and Max Radius to 5. Sketch in the window again. You see a kind of "tube" of particles, created with a radius of 5. Note that if you don't hit Enter, both the curve and tube of particles will share the same particle node, so the same forces will affect them.

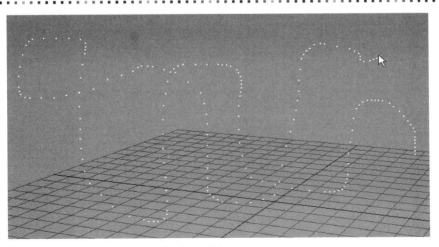

Figure 22.3 *A curve of sketched particles*

4. Finally, let's have Maya create a grid of particles for us. Delete the old particles and reset the Particle tool. Check the Create Particle Grid check box (you can adjust the spacing between particles here as well, if you wish). LM click once in the scene window, where the lower-left corner of the imaginary box around your grid should be, click again in the upper-right corner, and then press Enter. You'll get a two-dimensional grid like the one shown in Figure 22.4. If you would rather have a 3D "box" of particles, click the With Textfields radio button and enter the coordinates of the corners in XYZ space.

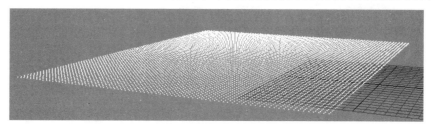

Figure 22.4 *A grid of particles*

You now know how to create groups of particles by placing them with the Particle tool. The other technique for dispersing particles is through an emitter, as described in the next section.

To see the difference between one particle of many parts and several smaller particle groups, try selecting one particle only. If you have created one giant particle node, all the particles in the scene will be highlighted. If you created several smaller particle nodes, only those in that particle's group will be highlighted.

Emitting Particles

Now let's see what a particle emitter does.

1. Clear your scene again and choose Particles ➜ Create Emitter ❑.

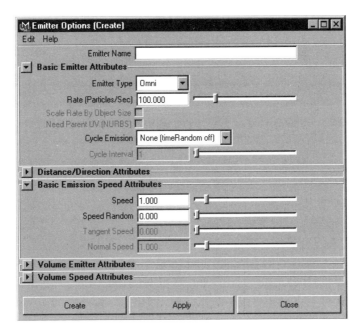

2. In the Basic Emitter Attributes section, select Directional for Emitter Type. In the Distance/Direction Attributes section, change DirectionX (the direction in which the particles will be emitted) to –1. In the Basic Emission Speed Attributes section, increase the Speed setting to 5. Then click Create.

3. You'll see a small ball in the scene window and attribute options listed in the Channel box. Play back the animation. You should see a purple line extending out from the particle emitter, as shown in Figure 22.5.

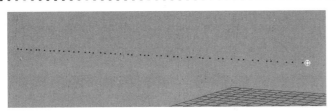

Figure 22.5 *A particle emitter emitting a line of particles*

To play back an animation, use the VCR-like controls at the bottom-right of the screen, or use Alt+V to play (and stop) the animation. But remember that you must always *rewind your animation before playing it when dynamics are involved. Because all dynamics simulations are calculated based on information from the last frame, failing to rewind will result in bizarre playback behavior (as will scrubbing through the animation). To fix this, simply rewind and play the animation from the beginning. Use the Rewind button on the Playback bar or Alt+Shift+V to rewind the animation.*

In order for more complex dynamics animations to play back properly, you need to set Maya's playback rate to Free. To do so, click the Animation Options button (at the far right end of the Range Slider bar) or choose Window ➜ *Settings/Preferences* ➜ *Preferences and choose the Settings/Timeline category. Then, in the Playback section, set Playback Speed to Free.*

4. To see the individual particles a bit more clearly, try turning down the Rate attribute in the Channel box from its default 100 to about 10 or so. Now you should see little peas shooting off into the distance.

Now that you've tried both methods for creating particles, let's see how to use them in your projects.

Working with Particles

As we've done throughout this book, we'll introduce you to the basics of particles by going through a couple of examples. In the following sections, we will build a plasma cannon and a fountain.

Making a Plasma Cannon

Every good science-fiction battle game needs at least one plasma cannon. This weapon of mass destruction shoots a blast of plasma—a collection of charged particles—toward the bad guys. While a plasma cannon is not something you want to have pointed at you, it's a good workout for Maya's particle dynamics engine.

1. If you don't have an emitter from the previous example, create one with emission DirectionX set at –1, Rate at 10, and Speed at 5.

2. To make our cannon, we're going to keyframe the emitter on and off, making the particle stream "pulse," rather than emit particles continuously. Set Rate to 0 in the Channel box (or Attribute Editor), and be sure you are at the first frame in the Timeline.

3. With the word "rate" (to the left of the number field) selected in the Channel box, RM choose Key Selected to set the first key for the rate (at a rate of 0, which means it emits nothing). Move to about frame 10 and key another frame at rate 0.

4. At frame 11, set a keyframe for the rate at 50 (or more, if you want a thicker stream). At frame 18, set another keyframe at 50. At frame 19, set a keyframe at 0 again (turning off the emitter again).

If you turn the Auto Key function on (click the button at the lower-right corner of your screen, so it turns red), Maya will automatically create the keys for you as you go—after you manually create the first keyframe.

5. Rewind and play back the animation. You should see a pulse of particles move away from the emitter.

6. To make the cannon pulse on and off, select all the keyframes you have made and copy them down the Timeline several times. You should see a pulsed stream of particles, as shown in Figure 22.6. (If you don't see the particles playing back properly, remember to set your playback speed to Free in the Animation Preferences dialog box.)

To copy keyframes, Shift+select the keyframes in the Time Slider, and then RM choose Copy. Move the Timeline to another frame (like 25 in this case), and RM choose Paste ➜ Paste.

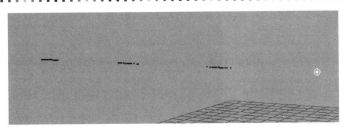

Figure 22.6 *A pulsed stream of particles*

7. Let's give these pulses a bit of spread, so they're not all lined up perfectly. With the emitter still selected, set the spread attribute to 0.05. (A spread of 0 is a straight line; a spread of 1 is a 180 degree half-sphere around the emitter.) You may also wish to increase the rate of particle emission for your keyframes to

make a thicker cloud. (Just be sure to set all your non-zero keyframes to the larger number.) Now when you play back the animation, the particles should look more spread out, as in Figure 22.7.

 The easiest way to change several keyframes at once is to use the Graph Editor (Window ➜ Animation Editors ➜ Graph Editor). With the emitter selected, you can select all the nonzero keyframes and type in a new value for the rate (or interactively move the values up or down). See Chapter 9, "Animating in Maya," for more about using the Graph Editor.

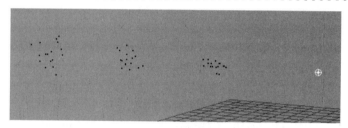

Figure 22.7 *The pulsed stream of particles with spread*

8. You will notice (if your window is large enough and if your frames are set high enough) that the particles appear to go on forever. As any true science fiction fan knows, a plasma cannon creates blasts with limited range (in other words, the particles must die off after a certain time). To make this happen, you must select the particle shape node itself (not the emitter). Play back your animation for a few seconds, until you see particles. Now select the particles themselves, as shown in Figure 22.8.

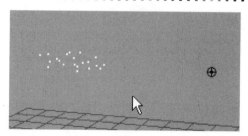

Figure 22.8 *The pulsed particles selected*

9. With the particle shape selected, open the Attribute Editor. In the Lifespan Attributes section, change the Lifespan Mode from Live Forever to Random Range, then set the Lifespan to 3 (seconds), and change the Lifespan Random from 0 to 1. Now the particles will all die off in a range from 2 seconds (3 – 1) to 4 seconds (3 + 1) after they are emitted from the "gun" as shown in Figure 22.9.

Figure 22.9 *Emitted particles with random lifespan; the first group of particles has only half its original particles.*

If you have used particles in previous versions of Maya, you will recognize that the new Lifespan Attributes section for particles is a real time-saver compared to the older way of controlling particle lifespans using expressions. We will work further with both methods of controlling lifespan in these chapters.

10. Although we have created a fully functional plasma cannon, let's improve it by having it emit streaks of light rather than just particle specks. Select the particles (not the emitter) and open the Attribute Editor. Near the center of the window is a Render Attributes section that allows you to select how you want your particles rendered. Choose MultiStreak from the pop-up window, which makes each particle into a clump of streaks instead of a single point.

11. In the Current Render Attributes section of the Attribute Editor, click the Current Render Type button. This adds controls for new attributes associated with the MultiStreak particle type. Adjust these numbers to get a satisfactory-looking streak of particles. The settings that produced Figure 22.10 are Line Width = 2, Multi-Count = 12, Multi-Radius = 0.165, Normal Dir = 2, Tail Fade = –0.5, and Tail Size = 10.5. (We also colored the particles orange, so they would stand out better, as you can see in the Color Gallery on the CD).

Figure 22.10 *The plasma canon with multistreak particles*

12. Save this project (name it `plasmaCannon1` if you can't think of anything more original). We will use it again in the next chapter.

As you saw in step 10, there are many choices for particle styles. We will use some other types in the next examples. For a full discussion of the various types, see Chapter 23, which addresses the topic of rendering particles.

Adding Motion to Particles with Fields

In Chapter 15, you learned how to use fields with rigid bodies. Fields can also be used with particles; they simulate forces affecting the motion of particles. To demonstrate how this works, we will build a fountain using particles and fields.

1. Create a new scene in Maya. Create an emitter. In the Emitter Options window, Channel box, or Attribute Editor, make the emitter Directional, set the emitter's Rate to 500, DirectionX to 0, DirectionY to 1, Spread to 0.3, and Speed to 10. When you play back the animation, you should see something like the image shown in Figure 22.11.

Figure 22.11 *A shower of particles shooting straight up*

2. You will notice that this image lacks an important element to make it look even remotely like a fountain: gravity. To add this element, choose Fields ➜ Gravity. Then select Window ➜ Relationship Editors ➜ Dynamic Relationships. In the Dynamic Relationships Editor, select particle1 on the left and highlight Gravity on the right. Now when you play back the animation, the particles will fall, as in Figure 22.12.

Figure 22.12 *The particle shower with gravity*

If you select the particles (not the emitter) before creating gravity, the two will be connected automatically, and you can skip the extra step of connecting them through the Dynamic Relationships Editor.

3. Add a plane and scale it across the grid. You'll see something like a fountain in a pool of water. (OK, it's rough right now—we'll make it look better over the next few chapters!) To get a slightly better look for the water, change the render type of the particles to spheres. (Select the particles, open the Attribute Editor, and choose Spheres from the Particle Render Type pop-up menu in the Render Attributes section.) Click the Current Render Type button, and then change the radius of the spheres to about 0.25 (so the spheres are smaller).

4. This is looking better, but everything is too smooth. To fix this, let's add a turbulence field to the fountain. Select the particles (spheres)—just grab any of the particles, and all of them will be selected—then choose Fields ➜ Turbulence.

5. With the Turbulence Field selected, in the Channel box or Attribute Editor set Magnitude to 30, Attenuation to 0.5, and Frequency to 60. Now when you play back the animation, the spheres should move in a more random pattern, as in Figure 22.13.

Figure 22.13 *The particle shower with spheres and turbulence*

In this example, we've set three of the attributes for the Turbulence field:

- Magnitude sets how powerful the field is.

- Attenuation sets the falloff of the turbulence field as particles get farther from it.

- Frequency sets how often the irregularities change.

Experiment with the settings for these attributes and discover how changing each one affects the playback.

Save your file (call it `fountain` if you can't think of anything better) for later use.

Using Collisions to Make a Splash

In the example we just finished, you probably noticed that the spheres pass right through the plane, which makes the fountain seem a bit unreal. We need some splashing of water as our fountain operates. Fortunately, Maya comes to the rescue again, by providing particle "collisions." Let's see how to make particles collide.

1. Move the emitter (not the particle shape node) just a bit above the surface of the plane (otherwise, the spheres will be "trapped" in the plane and will not emit properly).

2. Now select the particles (not the emitter) and Shift+select the plane. Choose Particles ➡ Make Collide ❑. Set the Resilience (bounciness) to 0.9, and the Friction to 0.1; then click the Create button. This creates a collision connection between the particles and the plane. (In the Dynamic Relationships Editor, you can see this connection under the Collisions radio button—and you could break it if you wanted to). Play back the animation. The spheres should bounce off the plane now.

3. We have a collision, but we need something more interesting for our splashes. We need to create a bunch of smaller "splash" particles. Choose Particles ➡ Particle Collision Events. As shown in Figure 22.14, select particle1, set All Collisions on, Type to Emit, Random # Particles on, Num Particles to 5, Spread to 0.5, Inherit Velocity to 0.5, and Particle Dies on. Then click the Create Event button.

4. We now have a second group of particles, called particles2, which will "emit" when the first particles hit the plane (between 1 and 5 will be created). Now set the second particle group's Render Type to Sphere, and set its Scale to 0.12 or so (so these particles are smaller than the spheres in group 1). Connect the gravity and turbulence fields to the second group of particles (see step 2 in the previous section).

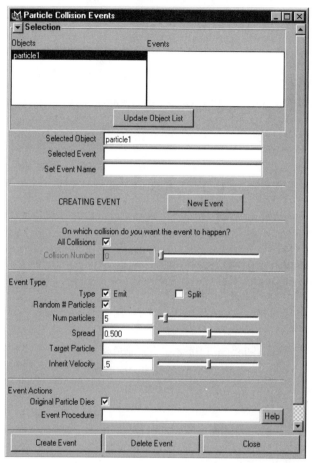

Figure 22.14 *The Collision Events option window for particle1*

5. When you play back the animation, you will see the second group of particles created, but they will simply fall through the plane, just as particle1 did at first. We need to create a collision event between these particles and the plane as well. We could use the same method as in step 2, but let's try another way: open the Dynamic Relationships Editor, select the second group of particles on the left, click the Collisions radio button, and highlight the plane in the right window.

6. Once you have connected the collision, go back to the Particle Collision Events dialog box and set the particle2 event (be sure particle2 is highlighted) as

shown in Figure 22.15. Most options are set as they were for the first particle group, but the number of particles will only be 3 this time.

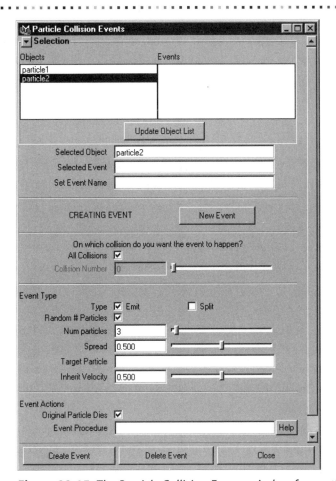

Figure 22.15 *The Particle Collision Events window for particle2*

7. Return to the Dynamic Relationships Editor and connect the new particles you've just created (the particle3 group) to gravity, turbulence, and the collision with the plane. Note that here we can leave the render type as Point— these are the little splashes.

8. You could continue adding collisions and new particles, but you've probably noticed by now that playback is getting very slow because of all the calculations Maya needs to do for so many particles. Let's just make one more collision event to "kill" all the particles in group 3 when they collide with the plane. In the Particle Collision Events dialog box, select particle3 and check the Original Particle Dies box in the Event Actions section at the bottom. At the top of the Event Type section, turn off both Emit and Split (this makes sure no more particles are created). When you play back the animation, it should look something like the picture shown in Figure 22.16.

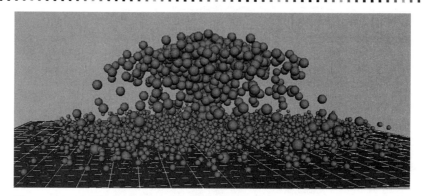

Figure 22.16 *The fountain with three sets of particles*

9. Save this project (as `fountain1.ma`, or something like that). In the next chapter, we'll make the particles look a lot more like water.

This example should give you a basic idea of how to create effects with particle collisions. Just keep in mind that we used multiple collisions and did the following for *each* collision:

- Connected the particles to the collision surface (the plane)

- Connected the particles to our fields (gravity and turbulence)

- Created a collision event that created new particles and/or killed the old ones

As long as you take these steps one at a time, it's amazingly simple to create complex simulations with particles. As usual, you should play with the settings in the Particle Collision Events dialog box and watch what happens in your scene.

Tips on Speeding Up Playback

It probably became apparent in our fountain example that playback can get really bogged down as you add elements, especially those requiring complex calculations. You may want to increase playback speed, even if it sacrifices some degree of accuracy. The most obvious way to speed up the playback of our fountain example is to change all the render types to simple points. (You can change it back to whatever shape you wish just before you do a render.) This will save a great deal of time, because Maya doesn't need to calculate the shapes of the particles.

Short of changing the particle render type, there are a few other things you can do to speed up playback. If you would like your fountain to be going full force at the beginning of the animation, play it back until it is going at full volume, stop it, and type in that frame number in the Animation Start Time text field in the far-left corner of the screen (below the Time Slider). When you rewind and play now, you do not need to wait to see the fountain to "run-up" to its full-volume state. However, you do need to start your animation at that frame.

To set the state of the objects at the current frame so you can rewind to the beginning of the animation and they will retain their state, select Solvers ➜ Initial State ➜ Set For All Dynamic. This will set the current state of all dynamics objects to be their initial values when you rewind the animation to frame 1. The one problem with this method is that you can't undo it.

A better solution—especially for scrubbing—is to enable scene caching (Solvers ➜ Memory Caching ➜ Enable). It may take a while to cache the frames, but once they are cached, you can scrub back and forth in the Timeline and play back the animation at much faster speeds. This solution is especially useful if there are other elements in the animation. For example, if the fountain is a background element in a character animation, not having Maya calculating the fountain's state at every frame can be a real time-saver.

Under the particleShape1 tab in the Attribute Editor, you can also reduce the Max Count and Level of Detail to reduce the number of particles being emitted. A Max Count of 100, for example, will limit the number of particles emitted to 100. (The emitter will cease to emit particles until the number in the particle group falls below 100.) A Max Count of −1 (the default) means there is no limit to the number of particles in a group. The Level of Detail setting randomly removes particles based on the percentage you enter in the box (a number between 0 and 1). If, for example, you emit 100 particles per second and set the Level of Detail to 0.3, the emitter will emit about 30 particles per second. These two settings are a great way to lower particle counts, but be sure to reset them to default levels before rendering if you want the render to contain the original number of particles.

You can also temporarily disable all dynamics calculations in a scene, thereby speeding up playback of other scene elements. Simply select the particle object you wish to disable and turn isDynamic off in either the Channel box or the Attribute Editor.

If you wish to see your spheres flowing, but don't want to wait for the slow speed of Maya's playback, you can try to adjust the tessellation factor to speed up playback. Select any particle shape, and then select the GeoConnector1 tab in the Attribute Editor. Change the tessellation factor from its default of 200 to something low, like 10, and see if it makes any difference in your playback speed.

Adding Particles to Objects: Plop, Plop, Fizz, Fizz

So far, we've painted particles into the scene and used emitters to make our particles for us. Another technique is to add particle emitters to objects. When you create a stand-alone emitter, it is just a point that sprays out particles; when you add a particle emitter to an object, you can tell the emitter to emit the particles from the actual surface of the object. To examine how to do this, let's re-create an image from a famous ad for a fizzy antacid: a tablet dropping in water and then bubbling.

Creating the Objects and Bubbles

We won't worry too much about our models right now—we just want to get the feel here.

1. Create a new scene in Maya. Create a large cylinder (the water glass) and a smaller, squashed one (the tablet). For the glass and tablet cylinders, choose Create ➜ Nurbs Primitives ➜ Cylinder ❏. To cap the ends of the cylinder for the tablet, choose the Cap Both radio button. For the glass, select the Cap Bottom button.

2. You can make the glass bluish and the tablet white if you wish. At the least, set X-ray mode on by selecting Shading ➜ Shade Options ➜ Xray. (For information about texturing objects, see Chapter 19.) Your two objects should look like those shown in Figure 22.17 (which is also in the Color Gallery on the CD).

Figure 22.17 *A basic glass and antacid tablet*

3. Before we add our bubbles, let's animate the tablet falling into the water. Place the tablet a distance above the glass and keyframe all translate and rotate channels. At frame 15 or so, place the tablet just where the water starts (or at the top of the glass) and keyframe all values again. At about frame 55, place the tablet near the bottom of the glass and rotate it about. Feel free to tweak this animation as much as you wish, but at least get this basic motion. (For information about how to create a keyframed animation, see Chapter 9.)

If you don't want to bother with this animation, you can get an already animated file (`22glassAnimated.mb`) on the CD that accompanies this book.

4. Now we'll *add* (instead of create) a particle emitter to the top surface of the tablet. In the Hypergraph or Outliner, be sure Show Shapes is enabled (Options ➜ Display ➜ Shape Nodes in the Hypergraph). Then, from the shape nodes below the tablet shape, select the revolveTopCap2 node and choose Particles ➜ Emit From Object ❑. In the option window, change the Emitter Type to Surface, the Rate to 100, the Speed to 1, the Speed Random to 0.3, the Normal Speed to 1, and the Tangent Speed to 1.3, as shown below. Then create the emitter and close the window.

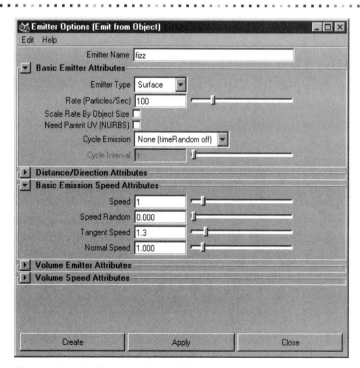

Figure 22.18 *The Emit From Object option window*

5. Because we've added an emitter to the top of the cylinder and set its emitter type to Surface, the entire surface of the top of the tablet will act as an emitter. When you make the tangent speed of the surface emitter greater than 0 (1.3 in this case), the surface will emit particles parallel to the tablet's surface, rather than just straight out from it. (Try playing with the settings in the Channel box, and watch the results.)

6. In the Attribute Editor's particleShape1 tab, select Spheres as the particle Render type, with a Radius of about 0.1 (for small bubbles).

You can add emitters to the side and bottom of the tablet as well. However, for this example, emitting from only the top surface will suffice. To add emitters to all surfaces at once, you can drag-select all the tablet's surfaces and add particle emitters to them using Particles ➔ Emit From Object.

7. If you have already played back the animation, you probably noticed that the particles emit very slowly and mostly just hang around. To make them rise a bit faster (as if they were air bubbles escaping from water), we'll create a weak gravity field that actually pulls the particles up instead of down. Choose Fields ➔ Gravity ❑. Set its strength to 1 or 2 instead of 9.8, and make its Y direction +1 instead of −1 so that it pulls the particles up instead of dragging them down. Then assign the gravity field to the bubble particles in the Dynamic Relationships Editor.

Adjusting the Particles' Lifespan

There are a few other problems with our particles: They start emitting immediately, and they don't die! Both of these problems can be handled by keyframing either the rate or the lifespan of the particles. If you get stuck, a finished version of this scene is available on the CD-ROM that accompanies this book, (22glassComplete).

1. Before we adjust the particles' lifespan, let's make sure we start emitting the particles after the tablet has fallen into the water. Select the emitter (not the particles), and set a keyframe on its rate to 0 at the start frame. Create another keyframe a little after the tablet enters the water and set it to 0 as well. (We don't want the particle to begin emitting just at the frame where it enters the water—the tablet needs time to begin dissolving.) Then, at frame 35 or 40, set the rate to about 100, so the tablet is bubbling at full strength by then.

2. If you play back the animation now, you will see the particles begin emitting at the right time. However, they come shooting out of and around the glass! First, let's take care of those pesky bubbles that are escaping from the sides of the

glass by making a collision between the glass and bubbles. Create a collision link between the particles and the glass, as described in the "Using Collisions to Make a Splash" section earlier in this chapter.

3. By creating a collision connection, we keep the bubbles inside the sides of the glass. However, they bubble right out of the top of the glass—talk about a head on your root beer! To keep the bubbles from popping out of the glass, we need to keyframe the lifespan of the particles. Because the lifespan of the particle controls how long it lives, adjusting the lifespan will change how far the particles can rise before they disappear. Getting the lifespan keyframed just right will take a bit of doing. First, change the Lifespan Mode of the particles (under Lifespan Attributes in the Attribute Editor) to Constant. Then try keying the resultant Lifespan attribute as follows:

- At 19 frames, lifespan = 0
- At 20 frames, lifespan = 0.5
- At 35 frames, lifespan = 1
- At 50 frames, lifespan = 2
- At 85 frames, lifespan = 2.5

Unless you copied everything exactly, your mileage will vary, and you'll need to adjust your keyframes to get a good result.

4. Save this animation (as `glass`) for use in the next two chapters.

After you finish adjusting the lifespan of the bubble particles, you should have a fairly nice animation, although it's by no means perfect yet. Fear not, however; over the course of the next two chapters, we'll turn our fizzing antacid tablet into a really nice-looking sequence.

Colliding with Rigid Bodies

You might wonder whether rigid bodies can react to particles, in addition to particles reacting to other scene objects. Because all these objects are dynamic, they can interact to produce interesting and useful behavior. To examine how particles and rigid bodies interact, let's create a simple plane rigid body and turn a fire hose of particles loose on it.

1. In a new scene, make a plane, scale it out to about grid size, and rotate it 90 degrees in the Z axis (so it stands upright).

2. Create an emitter that is directional, with a speed of about 10 and a spread of about 0.2. When you play back the animation, it should look something like in Figure 22.19. It doesn't look much like a hose, but it's good enough for our purposes.

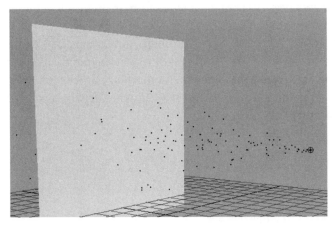

Figure 22.19 *Emitted particles shooting at a plane*

 After the work we've already done, it's a good idea to reset the options on the emitter when you create it. Just open Particles ➜ Create Emitter ❑ and choose Edit ➜ Reset Settings to reset the emitter.

3. Make the plane a rigid body (select it and choose Soft/Rigid Bodies ➜ Create Active Rigid Body). When you play back the animation, it still won't show any interaction between the plane and the particles. That's because you must also create a collision event (just as in the fountain example) before the two will interact.

4. Select the plane and then the particles (not the emitter), and choose Particles ➜ Make Collide. During playback, you now see the particles ricochet off of the rigid body. This would be great, except that the rigid body isn't moving.

 In order to see the plane and particles better, you can adjust the plane's color (in the Hypershade) to white, and you can change the particles' color to black by creating a per-object Color attribute in the Attribute Editor. You will learn more about particle render properties in the next chapter.

5. There is one last "switch" we need to throw before the rigid body will react to the particles. In the Channel box (with the plane selected), open the Rigid

Body section and set Particle Collision on. When you play back the animation now, the plane goes shooting off with the first particle.

6. To reduce the motion of the plane, we need to do a few things: reduce the number of particles emitted, reduce the emitter's speed, and increase the mass of the rigid body. In the Channel box for the emitter, set the speed down to 1 or 2, and reduce the rate to 40. With the plane selected, change the mass to 1000 to make it heavier. Play back the animation, and you will see that the plane rotates but does not move away as quickly, as in Figure 22.20.

Figure 22.20 *Particles colliding with the plane*

Because playback of these animations can be slow, try using playblast to see your work in real time (select Window ➜ Playblast).

As you can imagine, in addition to creating something like a fire hose, particle/rigid body collisions also can be useful for many other simulations—for example, space ships reacting to fire or meteors striking buildings (the buildings being made up of many smaller rigid bodies).

As an exercise, try to balance a ball on a fountain of water (remember to include gravity). It's no easy task! To make things easier, try setting the initial state of the fountain after it's running at full volume.

Attaching Fields to Objects

As a final example of basic particles (if there is such a thing), let's try attaching a field to a scene object and then have that object affect particles in the scene. Specifically, we'll make a UFO kick up some dust on the desert floor.

If you don't wish to build and animate this scene, just load `22UFOAnimated` *from the CD-ROM that accompanies this book.*

1. In a new scene, create a cone, flip it on its side, and squash it a bit (or use any UFO model you have handy). Next, place a plane a little beneath the UFO, as in Figure 22.21.

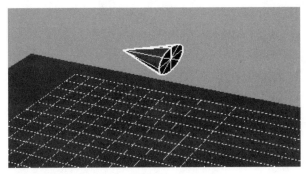

Figure 22.21 *A simple UFO model and plane*

2. Animate the UFO to make a flight path across the plane. For good measure, throw in a loop and a few up-and-down moves.

3. Create a grid of particles that will be blown around by the UFO's speedy rush through the desert. Open the Particle tool's option window (select Particles ➜ Particle Tool ❑), check the Create Particle Grid box, and set Particle Spacing to 10. (Adding any more particles really slows down playback later.)

4. Choose the top scene view and scale out so you can see the whole plane. Click the lower-left and upper-right corners of the plane and press Enter. You should get a grid of particle points across the plane.

5. In the Attribute Editor, click the Current Render Type button and set the point size to 10 (so the particles are easily visible), and then move the particle grid up on the Y axis until the particles are a bit above the plane.

If you have a very fast computer, you can increase the density of particles in your grid. Be aware, how-ever, that very dense grids can choke Maya, so save a backup copy of your scene file.

6. Now we have our UFO and particles. All we need to do is make a field to help the two interact. Select the UFO and choose Fields ➜ Air ❑.

7. In the Air Options window, click the Wake button, and then try the settings shown in Figure 22.22. Setting Direction X, Y, and Z to 1 enables the UFO to interact with the particles in all directions. Turning on Inherit Rotation allows the curving motion of the UFO to "suck up" particles. Decreasing the Magnitude to 0 means only the motion of the UFO will affect the particles, not any constant "wind" force created by the field. Increasing Max Distance to 25 allows the field to displace particles farther away from it. (The Max Distance setting is actually not necessary when a volume field type is chosen, as in step 8. However, it will not cause any problems in the simulation, and for complete-ness' sake we've included it here.)

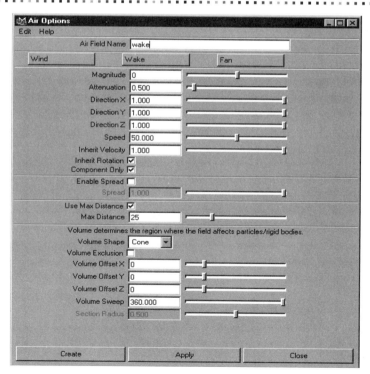

Figure 22.22 The option window for creating the Air field

8. In Maya 3, you can now create a volume area in which field forces are applied. In the bottom section of the Air Options Window, set the volume shape to Cone, and leave the other settings as is. Click Create to create the field. As always, try playing with these numbers to see what happens.

9. Now, let's connect the new field to our UFO, using another new Maya 3 technique. Select the Wake field, and then (in the Hypergraph or Outliner) select the NurbsConeShape node (on the revolveBottom node) and choose Fields ➜ Attach to Selected Object as Source. You will see the cone attach itself to the UFO, as in Figure 22.23.

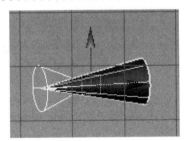

Figure 22.23 *The cone of the Wake field is attached to the UFO.*

10. Deselect everything in your scene, and then select the wake cone (so you don't move the UFO at the same time), and rotate and scale the cone until it shoots out from the back of the UFO like an exhaust plume, as Figure 22.24 illustrates.

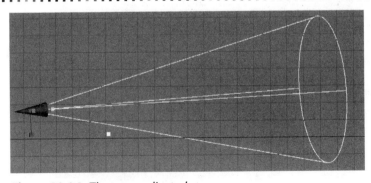

Figure 22.24 *The cone, adjusted*

11. To connect the field to the particles, use the Dynamic Relationships Editor as described earlier in the chapter. Then play back the animation, and the dust particles should move around after the UFO.

12. To make this simulation look a bit more realistic (or at least appear as realistic as giant blocks moving around can), we need to add a gravity field and allow collisions between the particles and the plane, so they don't just fall down. Select the particles, and then choose Fields ➜ Gravity (be sure Gravity is in the negative Y direction for this example). You will need to drastically reduce the effect of gravity here, so the particles float back to earth as if they were light. Try setting Gravity to 2 and see what happens.

13. Select the particles, and then Shift+select the plane. Choose Particles ➜ Make Collide ❑, and set resilience (or bounciness) to 0.2 and friction to 0.5. The frictional force will make the particles stop moving when they collide with the ground. If all worked well, you should see the dust whirl after the UFO as it passes by, as seen in Figure 22.25 (and also in the Color Gallery on the CD).

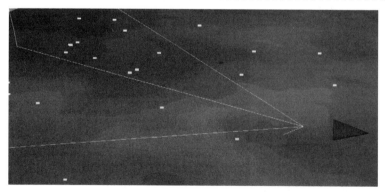

Figure 22.25 *The UFO whips up dust particles as it passes.*

Finding the proper settings for gravity and the collision took quite a bit of tweaking. Try experimenting with the numbers and see what happens (remember to save a clean version of the project first).

14. Save your project (as UFO) for more work in the next chapter.

If you notice that the particles bounce off the desert floor and then settle when the animation starts, you may wish to set the initial condition for the particles to be their state after coming to rest on the plane. First, turn off the Air field (set its Speed to 0), and then run the animation until the particles have settled onto the plane. Then select the particles and choose Solvers ➜ Initial State ➜ Set For Selected.

If you want the dust to look better, try setting the render type to MultiStreak, increasing the number of particles (the Multi Count), and increasing the Multi Radius. The neat thing about streaks is that they exist only when they are in motion, which means that they disappear back into the desert when they collide with the floor. This can make for a much nicer animation, although it's a bit hard to see. (This effect is too subtle to be seen as reproduced in print; to see the flying dust in action, check out 23UFO.mov on the accompanying CD-ROM.)

As an exercise, try making a jet trail of particles for your UFO. Will it be affected by wind and gravity? How fast will it go? Will it be constant or pulsing?

With particles, it is often very useful to create sparsely packed particles that are big and blocky. This saves a great deal of time in setting up an animation. When you are ready to render the particles, simply increase the particle density and make them look more presentable.

Summary

In this chapter, we worked with particle dynamics, getting to know how to create and emit particles. You learned how to change the look and lifespan of particles, how to get them to interact with fields, how to get them to collide with objects—either standard objects or rigid bodies—and finally, how to attach fields to objects that then affect particles.

At this point, you know most of the basic elements of creating and using particles in your work. Over the next two chapters, we will take the work we started here (plus some other examples) and learn the intricacies of rendering them, as well as how to add expressions to them. So save your work and get ready to go—it just gets better from here!

Particle Rendering

MAYA

Chapter 23

This chapter continues the work we started in the preceding chapter, "Particle Basics." We will examine several methods of rendering particles; specifically, we will look at how hardware rendering and software rendering differ. We will also discuss situations in which various types of rendering are appropriate.

Because of the special nature of hardware-rendered particles, this chapter also touches lightly on compositing techniques. If you have not read Chapter 22, "Particle Basics," you should be familiar with creating and using particles in a variety of situations before proceeding with this chapter. Also, if you are not acquainted with basic rendering using Maya, you should first read Chapter 18, "Rendering Basics."

This chapter covers the following topics:

- Hardware rendering
- Hardware rendering and compositing
- Software rendering
- Using sprite particles in particle rendering
- Fine-tuning your particle rendering

Particle Rendering in Maya

When you work in Maya's workspace, you use your computer's built-in OpenGL graphics card, which supports flat shading in real time. (OpenGL is a standard specification that practically all graphics cards comply with; see www.opengl.org for more information.) When you tell Maya to render into a new window (Render ➜ Render into New Window) or to batch render (Render ➜ Batch Render), you are launching a separate module of the program that will render shadows, reflections, and refractions, and will generally produce a smoother, more realistic image. But all this is at the cost of lengthier rendering times. In general terms, unless you are a game producer, you work in Maya's workspace and then produce your final images in the rendering module of the program.

In Chapter 22, we examined how to create particles in the Maya workspace; here in Chapter 23 we will take particles to the next step of creating images suitable as final products.

One thing to keep in mind throughout this chapter is that rendering is truly in the eye of the beholder. You should always tweak your materials until you get a rendering you are satisfied with—even if it is quite different from our suggested material. What pleases our collective eye may not please yours, and vice versa.

And in This Corner: Hardware vs. Software Rendering

If you have previously used Maya particles for production work, you already know that one of the most confusing aspects of Maya's implementation of particles is the issue of hardware rendering versus software rendering. In the Render Attributes section of the Attribute Editor for a particle shape, you'll find options to set Particle Render Type to Blobby Surface (s/w), Cloud (s/w), or Tube (s/w). That "s/w" indicates that the corresponding particles are software rendered. Other particle types (such as Point and MultiStreak) are hardware rendered.

What does it mean that some particles are hardware rendered and some are software rendered? Isn't all rendering part hardware and part software? If these questions seem confusing, take comfort—there is a reasonably simple explanation. *Software rendering* is the type of final rendering you are already familiar with (i.e., rendering with the full power of Maya's rendering module). *Hardware rendering*, on the other hand, uses the power of your computer's graphics card to create quick, flat-shaded images of your particles. (If your card is not OpenGL-compliant, hardware rendering will work but very slowly.) Perhaps the main obstacle to understanding hardware rendering is its name, because you don't use only hardware to render the particles. Rather, you use a combination of Maya's software and the graphics card's OpenGL processing to create the images. It may be easier for you to think of this type of rendering as *hybrid rendering*. It's a bit of a cross between the default shading you see in your workspace and the images produced by Maya's batch-rendering module.

To do hardware rendering, Maya first creates a flat-shaded image of your particles (taking into account your preferences for rendering), and then actually performs a screen capture to "grab" the image just created. Because of this nifty trick, hardware-rendered particles can often be rendered in near real time. Software-rendered particles, in contrast, can take a very long time to render.

Because hardware rendering uses a type of screen capture to create its images, you must not *allow anything to come in front of the render window (including a screen saver). Be sure not to move any windows in front of the render window, and remember to turn off your screen saver if you are about to start a potentially long hardware rendering.*

The primary difficulty with hardware rendering is that you need to know and use a *compositing program* (such as Alias|Wavefront's own Composer for IRIX, or Fusion or AfterEffects for Windows NT) to combine software and hardware renderings. This can also be a big advantage, however, because you can control the look of your particles independently from the way the rest of the scene works. Indeed, compositing is such an effective and timesaving way of working with 3D animation that many animators also render software particles separately from their scenes. Some basic compositing techniques are discussed later in this chapter (see "Hardware Rendering and Compositing") to give you some insight into the power of this technique.

Hardware Rendering

Let's now take a closer look at hardware rendering, using as an example the handy plasma cannon that you created in the last chapter. If you don't have a finished copy of the plasma cannon from Chapter 22, you can use `22plasmaCannon` on the CD-ROM that accompanies this book.

Open your saved project (or the one included on the CD-ROM), and play the animation until it reaches a frame where you can see some of the particles. Now open the Hardware Render Buffer window by going to Window ➜ Rendering Editors ➜ Hardware Render Buffer. This window, shown in Figure 23.1, will open with the current frame from the workspace loaded. You will have at your disposal several menus from which to adjust render options. The Render menu has options for test and final renderings, the Cameras menu lets you render from any camera in the scene (including an orthographic camera), and the Flipbooks menu allows you to choose or clear any flipbooks you create.

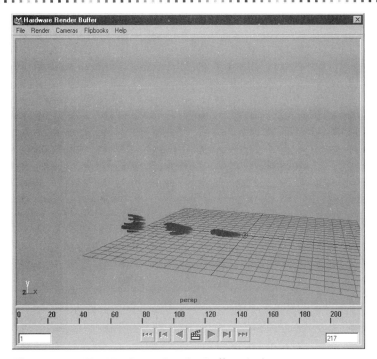

Figure 23.1 *The Hardware Render Buffer window*

A **flipbook** *is Maya's term for a sequence of hardware-rendered images that are created in the* `projectName\images` *directory by default. Remember to set up your project before you begin rendering images, or you won't know where they're going as they are rendered. See Chapter 1, "The Maya Interface," for more on creating and setting projects.*

Give the hardware renderer a whirl:

1. Select Render ➜ Test Render (or click the clapper board icon below the Time Slider). You should see your particles against a black background.

2. Now let's adjust the render attributes for the Hardware Render Buffer. Select Render ➜ Attributes; the Attribute Editor will open, and you will have several options for modifying your hardware rendering.

For now, we will only look at the first section of the Attribute Editor: Image Output Files, shown in Figure 23.2. Here, just as in the Render Globals window for software rendering, you can set the filename, extension numbering (including the number of zeros in the name), start and end frames, image file type, and resolution. You can also

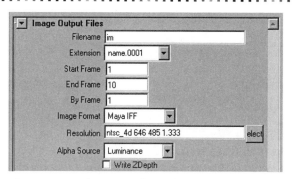

Figure 23.2 *The Image Output Files section of the Render Attribute Editor*

set alpha channel information here. The Alpha Source list box offers choices of None (for no alpha channel), Hardware Alpha, Luminance, and any of the RGB channels. (See the "Alpha Channels" sidebar for more information.)

3. Leave Alpha Source set to Off (the default), but keep in mind that you'll need to turn it on (that is, use Hardware Alpha, Luminance, or one of the other settings) for final renderings that you wish to composite later.

4. Before you leave the Image Output Files window, be sure to set your start and end frames to the start and end frames of your animation, and give your rendering a filename.

You also have the option to write the Z depth (or the distance of each object from the camera) into your images. You can use this information to help you composite the image, but the method is complex and beyond the scope of this book. See your compositing program's user manual for information about whether it supports Z depth compositing and how it works.

5. To see your particle animation run in the scene portion of the window, choose Render ➜ Render Sequence from the Hardware Render Buffer window.

6. After the sequence is rendered, you can play back the animation in a separate (Fcheck) window by choosing Flipbooks from the Hardware Render Buffer window and then selecting your animation name. (See Chapter 18 for a look at the Fcheck utility.)

If you wish to stop the hardware rendering before it is complete, simply press the Esc key on your keyboard.

Alpha Channels

An *alpha channel* (also known as a *mask* or *matte channel* or *layer mask*) is an outline of the rendered elements of your scene. Everything within the outline is visible in the final image; everything outside it is invisible. (In addition, there are semitransparent parts at the edges of the outline, which partially show those pixels.) Think of an alpha channel as a cookie cutter that slices out the rendered pixels of an image, allowing you to place the cut image on top of another image in a compositing program. You can learn more about alpha channels from your compositing program's documentation.

If you can, use Hardware Alpha as the alpha channel setting for your renderings. In the Hardware Render Buffer window (Window ➡ Rendering Editors ➡ Hardware Render Buffer), select Render ➡ Attributes and set Alpha Source to Hardware Alpha. If your graphics card doesn't support Hardware Alpha, you will see an error message in the feedback line when you try to select this option. In that case, you will generally want to set Alpha Source to Luminance to create your alpha channel.

After watching the animation, you might discover that the particles are the wrong color or that they are moving too slowly or too quickly. To remedy these problems, tweak your animation for speed, tail size, and color. When the particles are moving too slowly, select the emitter and change the speed to something like 20 instead of 5. To compensate, shorten the particle's tail size a bit by selecting the particles, changing to the Attribute Editor, and setting the tail length to, say, 2. So far, so good; the particles should now have a bit more zip to them. You can try rerendering in the Hardware Render Buffer for verification of your work, and, of course, tweak it some more if you are not happy with the results.

With speed and tail size under control, you can now modify the color to your liking. Make sure the particles are still selected. In Attribute Editor for the particle shape, click the Color button in the Add Dynamic Attributes section, and the Add Per Object Attribute option in the Particle Color dialogue—this option will be grayed out if you have previously adjusted the particle color. Once you have added your per-object color, you will see the following listed in the Render Attributes section of the Attribute Editor: Color Red, Color Green, and Color Blue, along with the other attributes that pertain to the currently selected Particle Render Type. Try changing the color boxes (Red/Green/Blue) to suit your tastes. We've done this in Figure 23.3, which you can find in the Color Gallery on the CD. We used a fiery orange, with values of 0.9, 0.2, and 0.1, respectively. Then you can rerender the sequence to see if you like what you have done.

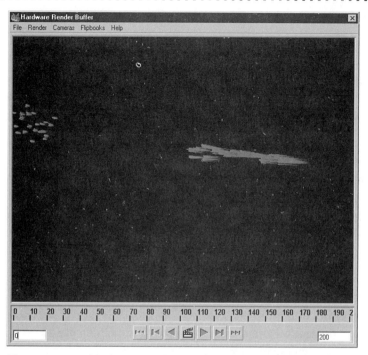

Figure 23.3 *A hardware rendering of the updated plasma cannon particles*

 When rendering, if you keep your image sequence name the same, Maya will write over your last sequence for you, saving disk space. If you wish to keep a sequence for later use, rename your rendering something else in the Attribute Editor.

You may have noticed when you did the test render that you did not need a light in the scene to make these particles show up. If you do not have any lights, Maya provides a default light to emphasize the particles—thus they appear in your scene even if you haven't yet placed a light into it. Of course, you may prefer to use your own. From the Hardware Render Buffer window, select Render ➔ Attributes. In the Attribute Editor's Render Modes section, you can set Lighting Mode to Default Light, All Lights, or Selected Lights. Feel free to play with some lighting setups now and see how they affect the plasma cannon's appearance. (You may find that the choice of lights used with a particular particle or streak rendering type makes no difference.)

Save your rendering of the plasma cannon for use in the next chapter.

Hardware Rendering and Compositing

Now that you have a good feeling for the basics of hardware rendering, let's create an example where we can composite the particles on top of a software-rendered scene. Open your UFO project from Chapter 22, and add a few lights to the scene (if you haven't already).

If you didn't complete or save the UFO project in the preceding chapter, use `22UFOComplete` from the CD-ROM.

1. If your particles in the UFO project are still large blocks, select them. In the Attribute Editor, change their type to MultiStreak in the Render Attributes section.

2. Click the Current Render Type button, and set the render attributes. Aim for something similar to the following: ColorRed 0.8, ColorGreen 0.6, ColorBlue 0.2, Line Width 2, Multi Count 20, Multi Radius 1, Normal Direction 2, Tail Fade 0, and Tail Size 1. You can choose to turn on Use Lighting, but you will need to reduce the colors on your particles, or they will appear almost white. Feel free to experiment until you have the look you want.

3. Open the hardware rendering window (Window ➜ Rendering Editors ➜ Hardware Render Buffer). Specify a filename for the image sequence in the Attribute Editor, set your beginning and ending frames, and choose to use All Lights in the Render Modes section.

4. Run a test sequence, and you will get an image sequence that essentially looks like a clean playblast rendering. (If your geometry is not included in the rendering, be sure the Geometry Mask check box is not highlighted.)

In this situation, it is best to have a software rendering of the geometry (the plane and UFO) rather than a hardware rendering of the entire scene. In order to do this, you will have to render out two individual sequences for the animation—a hardware rendering of the particles, and a software rendering of the rest of the scene—and then composite them. If you do not have a compositing software package, you can still follow along until the last step.

5. If you've closed the Attribute Editor, open it again (in the Hardware Render Window, select Render ➜ Attributes). Set it to the default globals for hardware render.

6. Go to the Image Output Files section. Set your alpha channel (Alpha Source) to either Hardware Alpha (if your graphics card supports this) or Luminance.

7. In order to mask out the geometry (so you can use a software rendering for it), check the Geometry Mask box in the Render Modes section.

8. Render the sequence again in the Hardware Render Buffer window, and the geometry will no longer appear. You'll see only the particles.

Although it may not be obvious in this sequence, the geometry of the plane will still mask the particles even though it does not appear in the rendering. If, for example, the particles pass beneath the plane in this scene, they will be blocked out and not rendered. This feature is very useful for later compositing.

Adding Multi-Pass Render and Motion Blur

One thing you may have noticed previously in testing particle- and streak-rendering types is that the particles and streaks are very sharply defined. For the desert dust being blown around by our UFO, it would be better to have a slightly more diffuse look for the particles. Fortunately, Maya has two features that can help here: Multi-Pass Render and Motion Blur.

When Maya does multi-pass rendering, it renders out a number of frames *in between* the frames of the animation, based on the number you select. If, for example, you select 3, the Hardware Render Buffer will render three "in-between" images for each frame and then average them together. This makes for a much smoother and subtler particle rendering—but it also takes much longer to render (three times as long for three rendering passes, five times as long for five, and so on).

Motion Blur simulates the period of time a camera shutter is open during a picture's exposure, producing a blurring of quickly moving objects. The larger the Motion Blur number (between 0 and 1), the more blur there will be. It is often useful to keep this number small when rendering and then add a bit more motion blur when compositing.

To try out these two options, go to the Multi-Pass Render Options section of the Attribute Editor. Select the Multi-Pass Rendering check box. Below it, a pop-up menu with a number (3, by default) will be enabled, allowing you to select how many Render Passes to make for each frame. Choose a fairly low number here (5, for instance). You can also add a bit of Motion Blur (say 0.1 or 0.2).

Render the sequence again, and this time you may find the dust effect too subtle (that is, indiscernible). To make the dust stand out more, you can adjust the number of passes, the color of the dust, the transparency of the dust, or the motion blur factor. Or you can make these adjustments in your compositing package—a much faster and more versatile method of tweaking your rendering.

When working with composited layers, you'll often have to rework render settings to make elements a bit bolder in their rendered look, in order to provide more choices when it comes time to composite. You can easily reduce the visibility of a layer in a compositing package, but it is extremely difficult to make a layer more visible.

When your test renders look good, select Render ➜ Render Sequence to render an image sequence out to your images folder. You can then import these images into your compositing package and combine them with your software-rendered sequence. (If you need help with the process of software rendering, read "Software Rendering" later in this chapter. Also, see Chapter 18.)

Once your hardware-rendered sequence is finished, you need to render your geometry in a separate, software-rendered image sequence. Open the Render Globals window (for software renderings, choose Window ➜ Render Globals). Set your start/end frames, and set the image format to be the same as your particle-rendered sequence—Maya IFF (iff) is the default. Then batch-render the sequence.

Watch out—do not give your geometry render sequence the same name as your particle render sequence. If you do, the geometry rendering will erase the particle-rendered image sequence.

To reduce render times, you can render out the UFO ship and ground plane in separate passes, taking just one "still" image of the ground plane, because it doesn't change throughout the render. See the following section for more on how to do this.

Once you complete your hardware and software render sequences, import them into your compositing package, and be sure to place the particle layer (with its alpha channel) as the top layer of your composition. Then, in the compositing package, adjust the brightness, opacity, and/or transform mode of the particles (and geometry) to get a high-quality final product, as illustrated in Figure 23.4 (a color version of this shot is available on the CD-ROM). Save your Maya project (as UFOParticles, perhaps) for use in the next chapter.

For a finished example of this UFO sequence, see 23UFO.mov on the CD-ROM. (Due to the small movie size, the dust has been somewhat exaggerated for visibility's sake.)

Figure 23.4 *A shot of the UFO kicking up dust*

Hardware Rendering and Compositing, Take Two

Before we leave the subject of hardware rendering and compositing, let's quickly revisit our antacid tablet project from Chapter 22. The particle-rendering techniques we've just discussed will allow us to create much more subtle, realistic bubbles for our tablet.

Open your saved file from that project (or use the `22glassComplete` file on the book's CD-ROM). Recall that we used the sphere rendering type for our bubble particles. The sphere type, because it's hardware rendered, doesn't support transparency, but we can make the bubbles transparent in the compositing package since they are being rendered separately. We will render all three elements (glass, tablet, and bubbles) in turn. Then we will composite the bubbles with a still shot of the glass (instead of rendering out many frames of the same shot of the glass—a nifty, time-saving trick), plus the animated tablet.

Instead of the sphere rendering type, you can also use the cloud (software) rendering type. If you're curious, you can experiment with the cloud type to see how it compares with sphere.

Rendering the glass, tablet, and bubbles is a bit more complex than what we did with the UFO project, because the glass is supposed to be semitransparent; thus, using the geometry mask will not work. Fortunately, we need to add only one extra step to this process to make it work properly: We hide the geometry selectively.

Before doing that, let's first perform a little trick to save some time in the rendering process.

1. Rewind to the first frame of the animation, select the tablet, and choose Display → Hide → Hide Selection (to hide the tablet).

2. Change your render globals to whatever you intend to use for your tablet rendering. For example, in the Resolution section, set Render Resolution to 320 × 240

(the default); under Anti-aliasing Quality set Edge Anti-aliasing to Medium Quality; and turn Motion Blur on. Then set your start and end render frames to 1.

3. Now batch-render the "sequence" (actually just one frame), naming it something like **glass**. By rendering only one frame with the glass (which doesn't move during the animation, and which takes quite a while to render), we save substantial time and disk space for this element of the tablet sequence.

4. Now we can take up the process of hiding geometry selectively. Reopen the Render Globals window, and leave everything the same except for the end frame. Set that to the final frame in your animation. Close this window.

5. Select Display ➜ Show ➜ Show Last Hidden to make your tablet visible again. Then highlight and hide the glass by selecting the glass and choosing Display ➜ Hide ➜ Hide Selection.

6. With only the tablet now showing, render out the complete animation, calling it something like **tablet**. You now have your software-rendered sequences, and it's time for the bubbles.

7. From the Hardware Render Buffer window, select Render ➜ Attributes. In the Image Output Files section, set Alpha Source to Hardware Alpha (if your computer supports it) or Luminance. Be sure the Geometry Mask check box is checked, and name the sequence something like **bubbles**. In the Multi-Pass Render Options section, turn Multi-Pass Rendering on. (Creating a multi-pass rendering will smooth out the bubbles just a bit.)

8. Render the sequence.

Once the rendering is finished, import all three pieces of your project (glass, bubbles, and tablet) into your compositing package. Here, you have many options for combining the pieces. We chose to place two copies of the glass into our composition—one on top, set to low opacity and with some color adjustments; and one on the bottom, a more opaque version of the glass that makes it look solid in the final composite. We then sandwiched the bubbles and the tablet between the glasses, with the bubbles above the tablet so they're visible. The bubbles' opacity (or visibility) can be reduced to give them a "see-through" look. You can also create an opacity ramp for the bubbles so that they fade out as they rise through the water.

 Figure 23.5 (in color on the CD-ROM) shows a still from the animation sequence. A finished version of the animation is available as 23glass.mov on the CD-ROM.

Figure 23.5 *A still shot from the glass animation, showing compositing techniques in action*

Some Compositing Guidelines

When you work with Maya in conjunction with your compositing package, you will surely encounter a number of problems—both artistic and technical. It is difficult in the context of this book to be specific about compositing Maya renderings because there are a number of available software packages that perform this function, and all of them work a little differently. Nevertheless, we can offer you a few rules of thumb:

- Do early testing of single frames of your animation in the compositing package. This way, you only have to render one frame for each composition layer to see whether the composition will work, saving you time in renderings.

- Always use alpha channels, even for layers that you expect won't need them. It's better to be prepared than to have to rerender.

- Render particles to be highly visible in Maya rather than going for the subtler look you intend to get in the end. Having more data (visibility) to work with can only help in the long run, and it's very easy to blur or reduce the opacity of particles in your compositing package as a last step.

- Be sure to test-render some images in the resolution of your final project. Often you'll get excellent results at 320 × 240 pixels, only to get an inferior product when you do your final compositing at 640 × 480.

- Don't be afraid to try new ways of combining layers in your compositing package. Just as in Maya, you may discover a much more interesting look by doing a bit of experimentation.

Never move your render camera! If you move the camera between renderings, your particles and geometry will not match up and the results will be awful. It is often a good idea to create a separate camera (not the default perspective camera) to use for renderings. Using a separate camera reduces the chance of accidentally moving the camera as you work.

Although multiple renderings and compositing may at first seem a confusing waste of time, stick with it. Once you begin to see how creatively (and often easily) you can alter the look of a particle-rendered sequence, using Maya plus a compositing package for particle sequences (and in general) will likely become your preferred method of working.

Save this project (as `glassFizz2`*, perhaps) for use in the next chapter.*

Software Rendering

Now that we've covered hardware rendering, let's take a look at Maya software-rendered particles and see where they might be useful. In general, Maya uses hardware rendering for speed when rendering simple points and shapes. When it comes to complex render types, however, such as clouds, water, or fire effects, Maya sacrifices speed for the power of the software renderer. The result is a photorealistic image.

Software rendering can be very slow. While doing the work for this section, you may wish to reduce the quality and size of your renderings in order to keep waiting time reasonable. Temporarily reducing the number of particles emitted, while adjusting particle properties, can also be useful. Working with just a few particles will give a good suggestion of the final product, without requiring you to endure overlong rendering times.

The three types of software rendering are Tube, Blobby Surface, and Cloud.

- *Tubes* are, of course, tubes—they can have beginning and ending radii that differ, and can be rendered with several special effects added. Tubes are useful for everything from hair to laser beams, similar to Figure 23.6.

Figure 23.6 *Some Tube particles*

- *Blobby surfaces* are known as metaballs, spheres that blob together like drops of mercury. Blobbies can be used for water, lava, or a range of other liquid materials (see Figure 23.7 for one example).

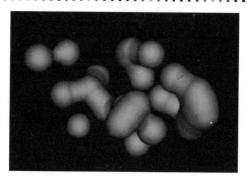

Figure 23.7 *Blobby Surface particles*

- The *Cloud* type, as illustrated in Figure 23.8, is a blobby surface that is blurred or semitransparent. Clouds are very useful for airy effects such as fire, smoke, and (not surprisingly) clouds.

Remember that IPR renders (discussed in Chapter 18) do not at present work with particles, even software particles. You must rerender each image (or section thereof) manually while adjusting the look of software-rendered particles.

Figures 23.6, 23.7, and 23.8, which demonstrate the software render types discussed just above, are all are available in the Color Gallery on the CD.

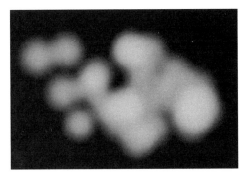

Figure 23.8 Cloud particles

As an exercise, let's see how blobby surfaces can be used to create the effect of water.

1. Open either your fountain project from Chapter 22, or use the 22fountain project on the CD.

2. Depending on the speed of your computer, you may wish to reduce the number of particles (currently spheres) being emitted by the fountain emitter, because blobby surfaces render very slowly with even a few particles. We found a rate of about 200 to be sufficient for the purposes of experimentation, although using more particles allows for a smaller radius for each particle and increases the watery look. Choose whatever you find is a good compromise between speed and final quality.

3. After adjusting the particle emitter, select the particles emitted (the particle1 group, which the emitter directly emits). Now we can set the render type. Display the Attribute Editor for the particle shape (particleShape1) and, in the Render Attributes section, set Particle Render Type to Blobby Surface (s/w). Alternatively, you can assign this type using the Channel box.

4. Click the Current Render Type button to display attributes for the blobby surface render type. You can set two controls over blobby surfaces: the Radius attribute (the size of each individual surface) and the Threshold attribute (which controls how the spheres blob together). The two controls work complementarily. As you increase the threshold from 0 (no interaction—the spheres just act like spheres) to 1 (complete meshing—spheres that are not connected will disappear), you will need to increase the radius because the apparent size of the particles will decrease.

Setting the threshold of blobby surfaces to 0 is a good way to produce software-rendered spheres, allowing you to adjust materials and transparency much more carefully than hardware-rendered spheres. Longer rendering times is the price you pay for software-rendered spheres.

Like almost all other areas of Maya dynamics, a good deal of experimentation is required to get the right effect for blobby surfaces. After some tweaking, we were satisfied with a radius setting of 0.6 and a threshold of 0.9 for the particles. Your tastes may differ, of course, so try out some settings yourself. You will need to render test images as you go, so be sure to add a light or two to the scene so you can see your results.

Surface Types and Other Enhancements

Another element of blobby surfaces (like any geometry) that greatly affects the quality of the rendering is the surface type. To get something approaching a watery appearance, we used a phongE shading group, made it a very unsaturated blue and transparent, and gave it a small but very bright specular highlight. A version of the project with this texture is on the CD-ROM (23fountain).

Now let's adjust the properties of the second set of particles produced by the fountain (the ones that appear after the first particle group's collision event). Open the Attribute Editor with the particles selected, click the Current Render Type button, and set the render type to Blobby Surface (s/w). For starters, try a radius of 0.5 and a threshold of 0.8 for these particles. You can then take the same material you created for the first set of particles and use it for the second one—or make up a new material if you prefer.

Recall that we set the third group of particles (those emitted when the second group collides with the plane) to be points. You can either leave them like this and composite them in later, or change their type to Blobby Surface and then render them all together, or even leave them out entirely. We found the smallish splashes created by a multipoint particle to be a nice contrast to the blobbies of the other two-particle types. So we composited them into the final rendering, producing the 22fountain.mov movie on the CD-ROM. A still from this animation is shown in Figure 23.9 (and the color version is on the CD-ROM).

As an exercise, try redoing your plasma cannon project using a Particle Render Type setting of Tube (s/w). Adjust the radii (that is, the Radius0 and Radius1 attributes, which are added after you click the Current Render Type button) to make the blasts grow in size as they move away from the emitter.

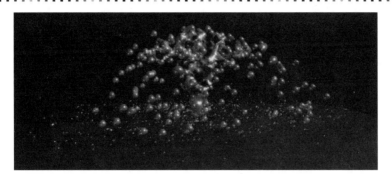

Figure 23.9 *The Fountain with blobby surfaces for water*

As with hardware rendering, there are countless ways to tweak and perfect software rendering. Although you can achieve decent results with software-rendered particles very quickly, getting just the right look with them can be a tricky and time-consuming affair—especially if you don't have much experience creating them. You probably already know, from attempting the fountain example, that even minor changes to a particle's attributes or an emitter rate often result in highly altered renderings. Additionally, the interaction of textures, particle types, emitter rates, and so forth creates a complex chain of interrelated variables that can prove frustrating to even an experienced user.

Apply two rules to get your software particles to do what you want:

- Be a perfectionist. "Close enough" usually isn't.

- Be patient. You want the best results, so give yourself the time and freedom to make mistakes.

With a critical eye and some practice, you can get excellent results with Maya's software particles. Experiment with the Cloud and Tube render types, now that you have an understanding of what software particle rendering can do. Try creating a fuzzy beam of light with Tube, or a dissipating puff of smoke with Cloud. If you have difficulty understanding any of the settings, don't forget that Maya's electronic documentation (especially Chapter 14 of the *Dynamics* manual) is an excellent source of information.

Save this project (as `fountain3`, perhaps) for use in Chapter 24, "Using Particle Expression, Ramps, and Volumes."

 Don't forget: It's often very useful to render software particles in a separate pass, just as must be done for hardware particles. It gives you a great deal of control over how the particles interact with the rest of the scene.

Pictures from Outside: Using Sprite Particles

Before moving on, we'll discuss a particle rendering type that falls somewhere between hardware and software rendering: the *sprite*. Sprites are simply placeholders for an image you create somewhere else—it can be another 3D rendering, a computer-based image, or a scanned photograph. The image is mapped onto a two-dimensional rectangle (the sprite), and, for each particle, an instance of the image is created in the hardware renderer. Although sprites are 2D images, they are always oriented toward the camera, so they appear to have depth. You can also choose to use either one image or several images in a sequence (or animation) to map onto your sprites.

We will discuss mapping of image sequences to sprites in Chapter 24.

As an example of how to use sprites, we'll revisit the UFO project—this time changing our streak particles to sprite images of leaves that the UFO can blow around.

1. To begin, open your UFO project (or 23UFO from the CD-ROM). In the Hypergraph, select the particle group. In the Render Attributes section of the Attribute Editor, change the Particle Render Type to Sprites.

2. The Sprite render type has several attributes, accessed by clicking the Current Render Type button in the Attribute Editor. For our purposes, check Use Lighting, and then set the Sprite Twist (or rotation about the Z axis) to 90. This will lay the leaves on their sides. If you desire, you can also change the Sprite Scale X and Sprite Scale Y values, altering the size of the sprites in the scene.

3. The sprites now look like little boxes, so we need to create a texture for them. First, create a Lambert shader group. (Because Lambert shaders have no specularity—or shine—to them, they work well for sprites.) To create a Lambert shader in the Hypershade, open the Hypershade window (Window ➜ Hypershade), and from the menu bar (or RM choose), select Create ➜ Materials ➜ Lambert. Click anywhere on the right-hand side of the window to place the new material group.

4. Select the Lambert materials group, and open the Attribute Editor (Ctrl+A). In the Common Material Attributes section, click the button that looks like a checkerboard to the right of the Color swatch and slider.

5. In the Create Render Node window, under the Textures tab (the default), click the File button in the 2D Textures section. This creates a texture that places an image you specify on whatever object the material is applied to. Close this window.

You can also create your own image(s) for the file texture. Just be sure you include an alpha channel in your image in order to cut it out from the background. If you don't, you will be able to see the edges of the sprite rectangle when you apply the Lambert shader to the sprite.

6. The Attribute Editor is now focused on the file1 texture, with an Image Name text field and a Browse folder icon under the File Attributes section. Click this folder icon, find the `23leaf.tif` file on the CD, and choose it for your file texture. You should see something like Figure 23.10 in your Attribute Editor.

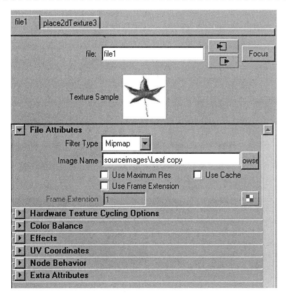

Figure 23.10 *A leaf texture mapped to a file texture for the particle sprites*

It is a good idea to transfer your images into your `scene/sourceimages` folder, where Maya will look for them by default.

7. Now that you have a shader and a sprite, you need to connect the two. In the scene window (or Hypergraph), select the particle group. Then, in the Hypershade, highlight the new Lambert shader you just made. Click just below the image of the material (or on the image sphere itself), and RM choose Assign Material To Selection (see Figure 23.11). If all went well, you should now see Figure 23.12: a bunch of leaves spread across your desert floor. Both Figures 23.11 and 23.12 are also in the Color Gallery on the CD.

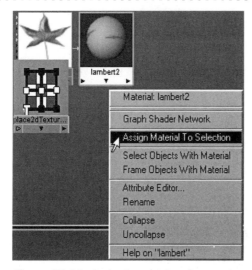

Figure 23.11 *Assigning the Lambert texture to the sprites*

Figure 23.12 *Sprite leaves on the desert floor*

If you now play back the animation (or if you just look at the first frame, depending on how high you have placed your particles), you will see that the leaves fall halfway through the plane before they stop. This is because the sprites detect a collision with the plane only when their *center points* hit the plane (that is, when they are halfway through it). To get around this problem, we need a bit of trickery.

You may have noticed this same problem when rendering the Sphere particle type for the tablet-and-glass animation. The same solution will work for that situation, as well.

8. Select the plane that is the current floor, and duplicate it (Edit ➜ Duplicate).

9. Move the original plane up until it just covers the top edges of the leaves.

10. Now deselect the plane and select the leaves, and move the leaves up until their middles are just above the original plane.

11. Finally, select the original plane and hide it (Display ➜ Hide ➜ Hide Selection), revealing the duplicate plane below. The leaves will now collide with the original (invisible) plane but will stay above the visible plane.

12. Save your project for use in the next chapter.

To add a bit more turbulence to this version of the animation (these are leaves blowing around, after all!), we altered the Magnitude and Direction attributes of the Wake field (attached to the UFO). We set the Magnitude to –7, and the X, Y, and Z directions (the way the force is directed) to 0.5, 1, and –0.5, respectively. For even more fun, you can try adding a turbulence field to the animation, forcing the leaves to rock as they travel through the air.

When you now run your animation, the leaves should blow around in the wake of the passing UFO. You can either render this project out in hardware or just create a hardware rendering of the leaves blowing. (In the Hardware Render Buffer window, select Render Attributes. In the Image Output Files section, be sure Alpha Source is set to Hardware Alpha or Luminance, not to Off. In the Render Modes section, be sure Geometry Mask is on.) You can use this new image sequence with your *old* UFO software rendering to make a new animation, saving the time and disk space of another rendering. A final composite movie is available on the CD-ROM as 23UFOSprite.mov. Figure 23.13 (a color version of which is in the Color Gallery of the CD) shows a still from this animation.

Figure 23.13 *A still from the UFO sprite animation*

Can you use sprites for the antacid tablet project? Try to create an image of a bubble (with alpha chan-nel), and map this to your particles. Does this method work better for this animation?

Fine-Tuning Particle Rendering

While rendering the UFO leaf animation in the preceding section, you may have noticed that the leaves lacked a realistic twirling motion as they were blown around by the UFO. This is because the sprites are always pointed at the camera. To get around this problem, you can use Maya's new Particle Instancer feature (Particles ➜ Instancer) to replace your particles with one or more geometric shapes (see *Dynamics:* Chapter 15 of the Maya reference manuals for details). You can then create a box or rectangle, map onto it an image of a leaf, and use the script to replace the particles with that geometry and shading group. The leaves will blow around more naturally.

You probably ran into a problem when you tried to composite your particles on top of your software-rendered sequence, especially if you used the Luminance alpha channel: the particles were probably close to invisible in your composition. This occurs because Luminance alpha takes as its alpha value the brightness (or lumi-nance) of each particle. This is fine when the particles are very bright, but when they are darker, the alpha channel will be mostly dark, too, making the particles very dim. Although it's a bit of a pain, there is an old and very effective trick to solving this problem. First, make a new copy of your scene so you won't mess up your good version. Next, create a new (Lambert) shading group, and assign it to all your hard-ware-rendered particle groups. In the Attribute Editor, change the Lambert group's color to pure white, and increase its incandescence to full. The sample should show all white.

If you are using sprites, create a file texture for the sprites with the alpha channel copied into the RGB channels of the image. (Call this `spriteImageWhite.tif` *or something similar.) This step, combined with the complete incandescence of the shading group, will produce a good alpha channel for a sprite group.*

The particles assigned to the new shading group should now all be pure white. When you do a new hardware rendering, using Luminance to create the alpha channel, you will get a version with white particles in exactly the same places as your colored particles from before. (Be sure to give the two sequences different names!) Finally, in your compositing package, use the newly rendered sequence as an alpha matte for your other, colored particle layer. (See your compositing software's manuals for more on how to do this.) You will now have a much more visible set of particles to work with!

Summary

In this chapter, we took the first steps toward creating finished animations using particles. Using either hardware or software particles and employing many different techniques (and a few tricks), we were able to produce high-quality renderings. We also used multiple renders for hardware and software particles to separate the elements of an animation, so that we could then combine them in a compositing package. Although certainly not exhaustive on the subject, this chapter gives you a good start into the difficult but rewarding area of particle renderings.

In the next chapter, you will learn how to use expressions and ramp generators to create complex per-particle (rather than group-level) effects. So make sure you've saved your work from this chapter, and let's move on!

Using Particle Expressions, Ramps, and Volumes

MAYA

Chapter 24

In the previous two chapters, we created, tweaked, and rendered Maya's dynamics particles. For the most part, however, we have only worked with these particles as entire groups. Now it's time to dig a little deeper into the power of Maya's dynamics and learn how to control Maya particles in very specific ways—as individual particles as well as intact groups. The tools for particle manipulation are expressions, ramps, and volume emitters and fields.

This chapter covers the following topics:

- Using volume emitters
- How expressions and ramps work in Maya's particle dynamics
- Changing the color, lifespan, and radius of particles
- Moving particles around in a volume field and with expressions
- Employing collision events and expressions
- Using transparency ramps
- Creating emitter expressions
- Changing opacity and rotation with motion

Particle Manipulation in Maya

You've worked briefly with all of the particle manipulation tools in earlier chapters, and here in Chapter 24 you'll see much more of what you can accomplish by developing your skill with these tools. As we began exploring MEL in Chapter 16, you got a glimpse of how the Expression Editor helps define the mathematical formulae that control object behavior. Ramps, introduced in Chapter 19, are akin to the gradients you may have created in a program such as Adobe PhotoShop. And in the UFO project from Chapters 22 and 23, you worked with a volumetric wake field. The particle manipulation tools have some overlap in functionality, but each has its own strengths, as you will see during the course of this chapter.

After a general introduction to volume emitters, particle expressions, and ramps, we'll try out various modifications of expressions and ramps. Then we'll explore some new opportunities for emitting and affecting particles, provided by volumetric emitters and fields. Although the complexity of particle manipulation tools can at times be daunting, the power and control they bring to particle systems make mastering these tools truly worth your effort.

Volume Emitters

New to version 3 of Maya are *volumetric emitters* and *volume fields*. Volume emitters provide an effective way to emit particles from a volume of space, rather than from a single point or from the surface of an object. (Volume fields allow substantial control over, and visual feedback for, the effects of a field. Setting volume fields is often far quicker and more intuitive than trying to adjust the Displacement and Max Distance attributes of a field.)

Emitting particles from a volume lets you produce particle groups with true depth. That's because volume emitters, as opposed to surface emitters, create particles throughout the entire body of the emitter, not just on the surface. For example, volume emitters are excellent for creating moving star clusters, antibody cells in an animation of a human artery, or even the appearance of blood drops "sweating" from a knife (see the "Bloody Knife" image in the color insert). As with most elements of Maya, what you can produce with this type of emitter is limited only by your imagination.

Volume emitters come in five shapes: Cube, Sphere, Cylinder, Cone, and Torus. You cannot create any arbitrary volume shape for an emitter, but you can scale and rotate all five primitive shapes. You'll be able to achieve a great variety of looks, giving you great freedom in setting the form your emitter will take.

We're going to work through these next examples rather briskly. So if you aren't comfortable with the steps for particle creation, you may wish to go back and work through Chapter 22 before you continue with this chapter.

For a quick look at the effects of volume emitters, let's create a simple disk-type galaxy using the Torus-shaped emitter.

1. Open a new scene in Maya, and choose Particles ➜ Create Emitter ❑.

2. Set the following for your emitter:

   • Under Basic Emitter Attributes, set the Emitter Type to Volume, and the rate to around 500.

   • Under Distance/Direction Attributes, set Direction X, Y, and Z to 0 (this reduces the linear velocity of the particles to 0).

   • Under Basic Emission Speed Attributes, set Speed Random to 0.7.

   • In the Volume Emitter Attributes section, set the volume type to Torus, and set the section radius (the thickness of the torus) to around 0.3.

   • In the Volume Speed Attributes section, set Away From Axis to 0, Along Axis to 1, Around Axis to 0.5, and Random Direction to 0.2.

3. Click Create. The settings you've just made adjust the particles' circulation around the torus emitter—feel free to play with the settings and watch how the particle attributes change. Then scale the torus emitter shape outward until it looks something like Figure 24.1.

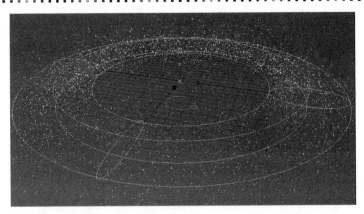

Figure 24.1 *The scaled torus emitter, with particles*

4. Select the particles, choose Fields ➜ Newton ❑, and set the following attributes: Magnitude = 2, Attenuation = 0.2, and Use Max Distance turned Off. Click Create and press Play, and you should get a disk of particles that spiral in on the origin, similar to a galaxy or a spiraling dust cloud. See Figure 24.2.

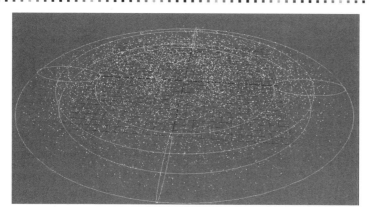

Figure 24.2 *A disk of particles*

This is a very simple example, but consider how difficult it would be to create the same effect using point or surface emitters. Volume emitters have a valuable place in the dynamics animator's toolbox, because they can turn out effects that would be very problematic for traditional emitter types.

Later in this chapter, we will work with volume fields, another very useful new tool for working with particles.

A Simple Expression and a Simple Ramp

To explore how expressions and ramps work in Maya's particle dynamics, let's begin with a very simple example of each. Start by creating a default directional point emitter that shoots point particles straight up, give it a bit of spread (say 0.3), and set a fairly slow speed with a high degree of speed randomness. To create an emitter:

1. Select Particles➜ Create Emitter ❑.

2. In the Emitter Options (Create) window, set Emitter Type to Directional.

3. In the Distance/Direction Attributes section, set Spread to 0.3, directionY to 1, and both directionX and directionZ to 0. With these settings, the particles will shoot straight up along the Y axis of the workspace.

4. In the Basic Emission Speed Attributes section, set Speed to 1 or 2 for a fairly slow speed, and set Speed Random to about 3.

Now, to make our emitter a little more interesting, we will vary the particles' lifespan using an expression based on their initial speed (which has been randomized by the Speed Random setting). Then we will vary the particles' subsequent velocity in an unusual manner by using a ramp.

Particle Expressions: Controlling Lifespan

Maya 3 gives you substantial control over random ranges for the life of particles (their *lifespan*)—without having to resort to expressions. By setting the Lifespan Attributes' Lifespan Mode to Random Range, you can control how long particles live, with a minimum and maximum particle life. If, for example, you set the Lifespan to 2 seconds and the Lifespan Random to 1 second, you get particles that live between 1 (2 − 1) and 3 (2 + 1) seconds. (See Chapter 22 for more on creating particles with random lifespans.) You can also set a constant lifespan for all particles (by choosing Constant from the Lifespan Mode menu, or just setting the Random Range to 0). Or you can have the particles live forever (the default state).

Sometimes, however, using expressions gives you the most exact control over the lifespan of particles, far more exact than working with the basic random lifespan settings. In our example here, we will control the lifespan of each particle based on its initial speed as it is emitted.

Be sure you have set your emitter's Speed Random (in the Basic Emission Attributes section) to a high number relative to its Speed setting. Otherwise, you will have a hard time seeing the effects of the expression you will create in this exercise.

Defining a Particle Expression

Before we can use an expression to control how a particle lives and dies, we first need to tell Maya that we wish to control the lifespan attribute ourselves. You may have noticed a setting in the Lifespan Mode menu called LifespanPP Only (PP stands for Per Particle). Select this option now, and your particles will live forever, since we have not yet defined their lifespans using an expression (you can test this by playing back your animation and noting that the particles never die).

You can switch lifespan settings at any time by choosing another Lifespan Mode setting.

Now that you have control over your particles' lifespans, let's get to work creating an expression for them. With the particles still selected, scroll down to the Per Particle (Array) Attributes section. With your mouse in the text field next to LifespanPP, RM choose Creation Expression, as shown here:

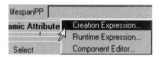

The Expression Editor now opens up (Figure 24.3), ready for you to create an expression to control the lifespan of each particle.

Context-sensitivity is a convenient feature you may not have noticed when you worked with the Expression Editor in Chapter 16, "MEL Basics." Here in this exercise, because we're launching the Expression Editor from the particle array section of the Attribute Editor, it automatically loads the proper object (particleShape1) in the Objects window, as shown in Figure 24.3.

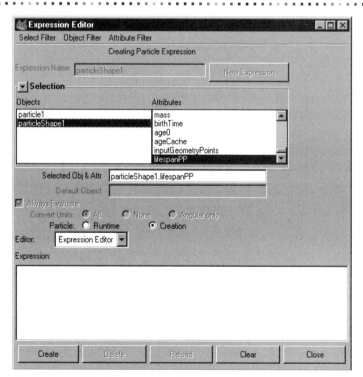

Figure 24.3 *The Expression Editor, with particle1 lifespanPP loaded*

Creation vs. Runtime

What's the difference between a creation expression and a runtime expression? A creation expression runs once for each particle (on its birth frame). A runtime expression runs for every frame (except the birth frame) for each particle.

- When a particle is first created (when its age is 0 frames—that is, at its creation frame), you can have an expression that will execute once for each particle, but *only* for that frame. In other words, if a particle is created at frame 21 (the particle's frame 0 or birth frame) and you have a creation expression for it, the creation expression will run *for that one frame*. Then the particle will go on its merry way.

- If you make a runtime expression, it will execute for that particle for each frame *except* the birth frame. It will execute starting at frame 1 for the particle, or frame 22 in our example.

In some cases, as in setting particles' lifespans, it is better to just run the expression once at the particle's birth (so it just has one lifespan value). In other cases, it is better to use a runtime expression. In yet other situations, you must use *both* a creation and runtime expression. As you proceed through the chapter, you will see more of how these two types of expression work together.

Also notice that the Expression Editor has two radio buttons for particle expressions that allow you to select either creation or runtime expressions. You therefore don't need to close and reopen the Expression Editor to create each type of expression.

In the Expression area at the bottom of the Expression Editor window, type in the equation

```
lifespanPP = 2 * velocity;
```

and then click the Create button. If you entered the expression correctly, you will see the following message in the feedback line (or Script Editor): Result: particleShape1. If you see an error message instead, examine your expression for errors. The velocity is a Per Particle attribute (even though it does not have the PP moniker at the end), and the expression simply assigns each particle (as it is created) a lifespan equal to its velocity, times two.

When you now play back the animation, you can see that the more rapidly moving particles live longer than the slower ones, as in Figure 24.4. (You may need to look carefully, or make the particles' Point Size bigger, in order to see them.)

For a bit more fun, try changing the expression to

```
lifespanPP = 2/velocity;
```

Figure 24.4 *Particles with lifespan set to their initial velocities*

Now the slower particles will live longer than those with a quick initial velocity. Figure 24.5 shows how the particle fountain looks slightly different with the new settings (note that the top area of this figure is filled with more particles than in Figure 24.4). Additionally, the fountain will now appear to move much more slowly than it did with the former expression, since most visible particles are now moving at low, rather than high speed.

Figure 24.5 *Particles with lifespan set to the inverse of their initial velocities*

To edit an expression, just retype it and press the Edit key. If you do not see your expression in the editing window, choose Select Filter → By Expression Name from the Expression Editor menu, and click on the particleShape1 name under the expressions list.

When you reopen the Expression Editor after creating your expression, you will see that Maya has updated the expression to read as follows:

```
particleShape1.lifespanPP = 2/particleShape1.velocity;
```

Because you previously selected the particleShape1 node before opening the Expression Editor, Maya knew to apply the lifespanPP expression to this node. Had you not selected the particleShape1 node first, you could still create the expression, but you would have to use the full name of the attribute (such as `particleShape1.lifespanPP`).

Particle Ramps: Controlling the Velocity

Pretty neat stuff—using a simple formula, we've quickly and (almost) painlessly made our particles die off after a time determined by their initial velocity. Next, instead of using velocity as an input in an expression, let's create a ramp to control the velocity of the particles, making them move around in a circle. (Because velocity is simply position-per-unit time, controlling particle velocity will control the particle's position in space at any given time.)

1. First, we need to get rid of the expression that's currently controlling the lifespan, so that the lifespan per object will control how long the particles live. Reopen the Expression Editor, select the expression, and click the Delete button. Alternatively, you can select the particles and choose Constant from the Lifespan Mode menu; set the lifespan to somewhere around five seconds.

2. Now return to the Attribute Editor. In the rampVelocity text field, in the Per Particle (Array) Attributes section, RM select Create Ramp ❑, as shown in Figure 24.6. The options window that pops up allows you to control how and where the ramp is applied (see Figure 24.7). We'll use the default options here: Input U set to None, Input V set to Particle's Age, and Map To set to New Ramp. (You should get familiar with these options, in case you wish to map the ramp to a different set of attributes.) After checking these settings, close the window by clicking OK.

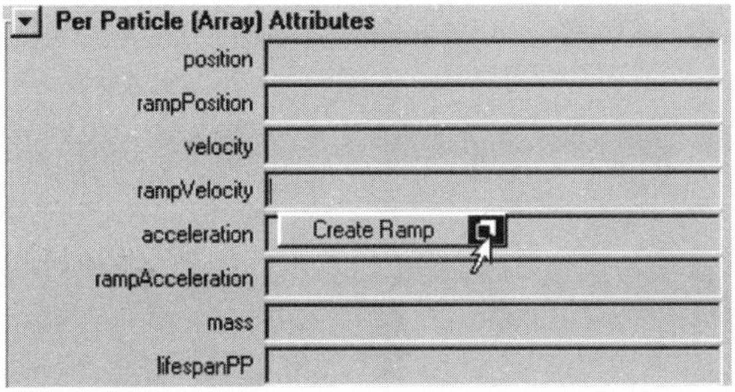

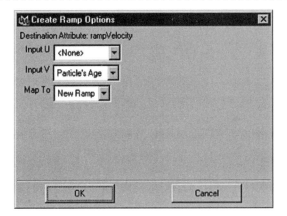

Figure 24.6 *Choosing the Create Ramp option*

Figure 24.7 *The Create Ramp Options window*

3. Return to the Attribute Editor and, from the rampVelocity text field, RM select ArrayMapper1.outColorPP ➜ ArrayMapper1.outColorPP ➜ Edit Ramp. This will focus the Attribute Editor to the ramp you have just created, as in Figure 24.8.

In the top section of the Ramp Editor (not shown in Figure 24.8) is the name of the ramp (currently ramp1), along with a texture swatch that is updated as you change the values in the section below. The swatch is set to a ramp between red, green, and blue. For velocity, position, and acceleration values, don't think of red, green, and blue as colors, but as values on a given axis: red is the X direction/velocity/acceleration, green is the

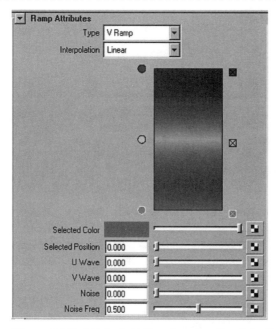

Figure 24.8 *Attribute Editor showing the default ramp*

Y value, and blue is the Z value. (The scene window uses these colors to represent the X, Y, and Z axes.) As the particles age, their velocity values move up the ramp, going from red (out the X axis) to green (up the Y axis) to blue (out the Z axis). If you play back the animation right now, the particles will move to the right, then up, and finally toward you, and then die. (This is based on the Constant lifespan you assigned in Step 1. To change the speed at which all this happens, set the lifespan value to a greater or lesser value.)

If you have Lifespan Mode set to Forever, you will not get correct behavior out of your ramp. You must have a per-object or per-particle lifespan set in order for particles to "age" properly and thus move up the ramp.

To make the particles travel in a circle, we'll need to change the default ramp. But first we must remap the array because currently no particle can travel less than velocity 0 (no negative values). In order for our particles to travel in a circle, they must be able to go in a negative as well as a positive direction.

4. The array mapper is the part of the ramp group that tells Maya how to interpret the gradient. To focus on the array mapper, click the right-arrow box next to the Focus button at the top of the Attribute Editor:

- The Min Value field tells Maya what the minimum value for the ramp will be. For our purposes, let's make this value −1, so the particles will travel at a velocity of −1 when a certain ramp color value is 0.

- Leave the Max Value set to 1, so the particles will travel at a velocity of 1 when a color value is 1.

Because of this remapping, a value of 0.5 for any color will translate into a velocity of 0, which is halfway between −1 and 1. This remapping may be a bit confusing, but stay with it here; things will get a bit clearer when we edit the ramp. If you want, try playing back the animation now and note that the particles travel in a very different path.

5. Now that the ramp has been remapped, it's time to edit the ramp. From the Attribute Editor's menu, choose Focus ➡ ramp1 (or just click the ramp tab) to return to the ramp. Set the first color swatch to RGB values of 0.5, 1, 0.5. To do this, first click the green dot at the bottom-left of the gradient, then change to RGB mode (instead of HSV) in the color chooser (the menu for this is located just below the alpha setting). Finally, enter the values 0.5, 1, and 0.5 in the R, G, and B channels. The particles will now start life moving straight up the Y axis—remember that 0.5 on the color ramp equates to a 0 velocity, so there will be no motion in the X or Z directions.

6. To make a circle, we need five points on our ramp:

- Somewhere between the bottom and middle points, click in the ramp to create a new point. With the new point selected, change the Selected Position to 0.25 (one-fourth of the way up the ramp). Then change the R, G, and B values of this point to 0, 0.5, 0.5, respectively. At this point (one-fourth of the way through the particle's life), the particle will be travelling in the negative X direction.

- Now click the middle point, be sure its Selected Position is set at 0.5, and set its RGB colors to 0.5, 0, 0.5 (traveling straight down).

- Next, click above the middle point in the ramp to create a new point, set its Selected Position to 0.75, and set its RGB values to 1, 0.5, 0.5.

- Finally, pick the top point and set its RGB values to 0.5, 1, 0.5.

When finished, your ramp should look like Figure 24.9 (there is a color version of this image on the CD).

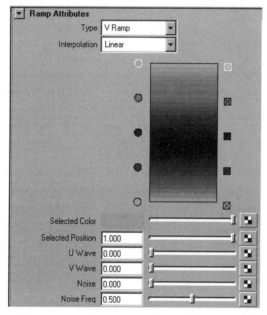

Figure 24.9 *The ramp used to make particles move in a circle*

Now when you play back the animation, the particles will travel around in a circle, as in Figure 24.10—a pretty neat effect! You can, of course, play with the ramp values to get different effects. Also, try randomizing the lifespanPP values so that all particles do not have the same age. As you can see, the ramp mapper allows you to create some very interesting graphical effects.

You can also edit points on the ramp by dragging the circle (on the left side) up and down. To delete a point, uncheck its box on the right side of the ramp.

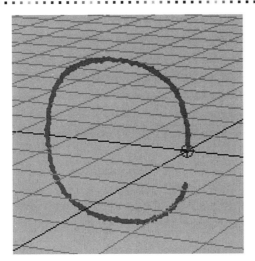

Figure 24.10 *Particles traveling in a circle*

With this introduction to volume emitters, particle expressions, and ramps under our belts, we'll devote the rest of the chapter to trying out various modifications of these basic techniques. Sometimes we'll use one technique or another, but often we'll use two together. The common thread in all these exercises is that we'll be using the power of Maya to achieve more realistic—or at least more interesting—animation. This chapter's samples are meant only as an introduction, however, to the range of possibilities available with these controls. As you work through the examples, consider what other effects you might be able to produce with similar techniques. Then—using what's in this chapter as a guide—try to create what you envision.

Moving Particles Around in a Volume Field

Volume fields—new to Maya 3—are a very useful, interactive way to visualize the fields you create and use with particles and rigid bodies. Unless you plan to employ a universal force that applies evenly everywhere (such as a gravity field), you will likely find a volume field more intuitive than setting the range of a field's effects using only the maximum distance settings. Volume fields can also produce special effects not easily done with traditional fields. Let's take a look at two effects we can create using volume fields and the new Volume Axis field.

The Volume Axis field pushes, pulls, and rotates particles (and rigid bodies) within its volume area, allowing effects such as particle obstacles and tornadoes (the two examples we will create), as well as a number of other possibilities. First, let's force a stream of particles to flow around a volume field.

1. Create a directional particle emitter that emits in the X direction, with a rate of 100, a spread of 0.3, and a speed of about 2.

2. Begin the animation, select the particles, and then create a Volume Axis field (Fields ➜ Volume Axis ❏). Use the following settings: Magnitude = 3, Attenuation = 0.1, Volume Shape = Torus, Away From Axis = 1; set everything else to 0 and click Create.

3. Move the torus a bit to the right, scale it outward some, and rotate it so it is partially in the path of the particle stream, as in Figure 24.11.

The Magnitude of the Volume Axis field sets the amount of force applied by the field. Attenuation sets how rapidly this force decreases away from the center ring of the torus (slowly, in this case). The Away From Axis setting is the speed the force is applied on an axis radiating from the torus—note the arrows in Figure 24.11 that point out from the center of the torus. You also have controls for circulating particles around the axis and along the axis; additionally, you can add a constant force in one or more directions using the Directional Speed and Direction (X, Y, Z) attributes. Try playing with the different settings and see how your altered settings change the particle's motion.

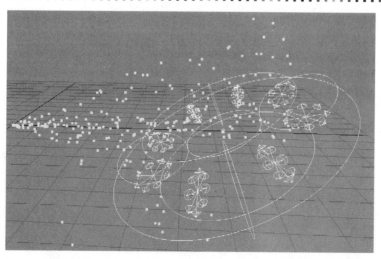

Figure 24.11 *Particles dividing around a toroidal Volume Axis field*

With the settings you've just arranged for the Volume Axis field, the particles in this scene move partway through the torus before they are "pushed" out and away from the center ring. To create more force, you can alter the magnitude of the entire Volume Axis field, reduce the attenuation so the field is applied out toward the edge of the torus, or increase the Away From Axis value. This last method of increasing the Volume Axis force is very useful, because you can control the field's force specifically in the Away, Along, and Around Axis directions.

Now let's create a tornado effect using the Volume Axis field.

1. Create a new scene, and make a volume emitter of type Cylinder with a rate of about 500, a directionY of 1, and an Along Axis speed of 5.

2. Scale this to be a good size for the bottom of your tornado.

3. Run the animation forward and select the particles (note that they all run straight up the Y axis and out of the cylinder).

4. Choose Fields ➜ Volume Axis ❏, and set Magnitude to 50, Attenuation to 1, Shape to Cylinder, Around Axis to 0.75, Along Axis to 0.5, and Away From Axis to –4; then check the Invert Attenuation box.

These settings pull the particles up the axis (Along Axis), spin them around (Around Axis), and pull them back into the cylinder (Away From Axis with a negative setting). Enabling the Invert Attenuation option makes all these forces more extreme at the edges of the cylinder, rather than in the center (you'll immediately see the difference if you try running the animation with Invert Attenuation turned off). When you finish, you should end up with an effect similar to Figure 24.12.

Figure 24.12 *Whirling particles in a tornado within a Volume Axis Field*

The settings we achieved in Figure 24.12 took quite a bit of tweaking to get right. You are welcome to play with the settings, but you will find it is fairly difficult to keep the particles trapped within the cylinder.

Obviously, any number of effects can be achieved using volume fields. As an exercise, try creating a mushroom cloud using the Volume Axis field in a sphere shape. You'll need to place the emitter inside the sphere, and turn on Invert Attenuation to get the right look.

Changing Color per Particle

Our next technique uses expressions and ramps. We'll make the blasts from the plasma cannon we've been working on in the last two chapters more realistic (or, at least, more visually appealing), by modifying the color of the plasma.

Open your saved plasma cannon project from Chapter 23, or use the 23plasmaCannon project from the CD-ROM.

If you have not previously set the plasma particles to have a random lifespan, or if you want to give the rand function a try, you can use an expression to control the lifespan. Only one thing is missing from our cannon to produce the perfect blast: The color of the particles should fade from a bright blue-white to a duller orange as the energy of each blast lessens. A ramp is a good way to accomplish this.

With the particles selected, click the Color button in the Attribute Editor. Check the Add Per Particle Attribute check box, and add the attribute. Next, create a ramp for the newly created rgbPP attribute at the bottom of the Per Particle (Array) Attributes section. Then edit the resulting default ramp (follow the earlier steps for "Particle Ramps: Controlling the Velocity" if you get lost).

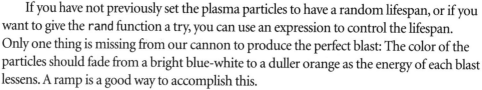

Now let's change the colors, starting at the bottom. First, click the round red button to the left of the gradient; then click the red color swatch below it to bring up the color picker. Choose a nearly-white blue (or whatever color you wish) for your first color. Choose the next point up, and make it a yellowish color; then make the top color a darker red/orange. One point is still missing—add a point between the yellow and red points (by clicking in the gradient), and make it an orange that's less saturated than the top color. When you are finished, you should have something resembling Figure 24.13 (see the Color Gallery on the CD for a color view).

Play back your animation. You should see the particles change color as they shoot across the screen, as in Figure 24.14 (also in color on the CD).

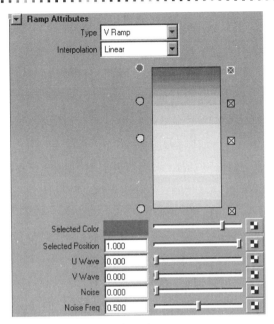

Figure 24.13 Particle color ramp

Figure 24.14 The plasma cannon with changing colors for the blast

Forcing a Complete Ramp Cycle

Advanced Maya users may be aware that, because particle lifespans are random, many of the particles will not cycle through a complete color ramp. To force all particles, regardless of their lifespan, to go through a complete color range, you can use the following expression for both the creation and runtime expression for rgbPP, instead of a color ramp. (Copy this expression into both the creation and runtime expressions.)

```
$howOld = smoothstep (0, particleShape1.lifespanPP, particleShape1.age);
particleShape1.rgbPP = <<1.5 - $howOld, $howOld/1.2, $howOld/1.5>>;
```

The smoothstep function creates a smooth ramp from 0 (at time 0) to 1 (at time lifespan) for each particle. The rgbPP components (red, green, blue) are then assigned values between 1 (1.5, actually) and 0, based on the particle's age compared to its full life expectancy. The numbers (1.5, 1.2, and 1.5) are just ways of adjusting the colors to make for a nice transition, as shown here and in the Chapter 24 Color Gallery on the CD.

Changing Radius by Position

Now let's see how we can change particle shape by using expressions. Create a directional emitter that shoots particles up in the air, and then assign the particles a Sphere render type. Next, keyframe the emitter to move from 0 up to about 10 on the Y axis over about 200 frames—we'll use this motion to change the particles' radii. If you wish, give the particles a random lifespan between 4 and 10.

We are now going to create an expression that ties the radius of each particle to the birth position of the emitter. First, we need to create a radiusPP attribute for the particles. To create the radiusPP attribute, click the General button in the Add Dynamic Attributes section of the Attribute Editor for your particles, as shown in Figure 24.15. In the window that pops up, select radiusPP, click Add, and close the window.

Now open the Expression Editor window by RM choosing Creation Expression from the radiusPP field. In the creation expression, type the following:

```
particleShape1.radiusPP = emitter1.ty/10;
```

This simple expression gives each particle a radius based on where the emitter is at the moment of creation (the radius equals the Y position of the emitter, divided by 10). When you play back the animation, you should get something like Figure 24.16.

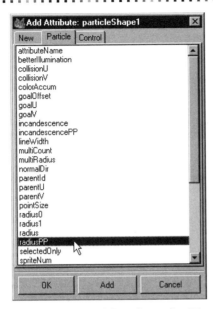

Figure 24.15 *Adding the radiusPP attribute*

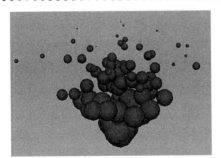

Figure 24.16 *Particles with varying radii*

To see the difference between creation and runtime expressions, cut your script (Ctrl+X) from the creation expression, and then click the radio button to select Runtime instead of Creation. Then just paste the line you cut from the other expression into this new one, and click the Create button. Play back the animation again, and you will see the radii of all particles increase as the emitter moves up the Y axis (Figure 24.17). Because the runtime expression is evaluated at *every* frame (except the first one), the particles' radii will constantly increase—in synch, no less—as the emitter rises.

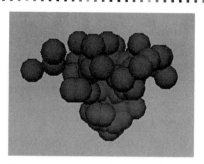

Figure 24.17 *Particles with the same increasing radius*

Moving Particles Upward in a Spiral

If you're familiar with *Using Maya: Expressions* in the old Maya 2 manual, you might recall seeing a picture of particles rising in a spiral from the ground. This may appear to be a complex effect, but we're going to create it here with a fairly straightforward run-time expression. We'll use the Sine function to place particles into a loop and push them up at the same time, so they form a spiral.

If you are unfamiliar with the Sine function, see Chapter 16 (or a trigonometry book) for more information on what it is and how it works. (The Maya 3 manual, too, contains an explanation and several examples of using the Sine function—see Maya Expressions: Functions, Chapter 7, or look in the online help.)

First, create an emitter that emits roughly five particles per second (about one for each five frames). Make the render type Sphere, and set the velocity to 0. Using an expression, we're going to place the spheres in a position based on their age, and, by virtue of the Sine function's properties, the position of the particles will form a moving spiral. In the Attribute Editor (with the particle shape selected), RM choose Runtime Expression in the Position field. Copy the following expression into the editing window.

```
$pX = 15 * sin(particleShape1.age);
$pZ = 15 * cos(particleShape1.age);
particleShape1.position = <<$pX, particleShape1.age, $pZ>>;
```

This expression first declares the variables pX and pZ (for position X and Z), and then assigns them a value based on the Sine of their age (which starts at 0 when they are born, increasing from there).

For more on variables, see Chapter 17, "Programming in MEL."

Because Sine function values range only between −1 and 1, we multiplied the function by 15 to get a wider range (from −15 to 15). Note that pZ uses the Cosine function instead of the Sine function. This is because the Cosine is perfectly out-of-phase with the Sine function (that is, it is 0 when the Sine is 1, and vice versa), and when the two are combined this way, they will make the particle travel in a circle on the X-Z plane.

The final statement of the expression does all the real work: It assigns to the X, Y, and Z positions of each particle the value of pX, the age of the particle (forcing the spheres up in the Y direction as they age), and pZ. As all these values change on every frame, the particles move in a nice spiral, shown in Figure 24.18.

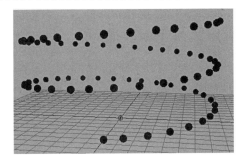

Figure 24.18 *Particles in a spiral*

You may notice that there is a flickering at the origin as you play your animation. This is the sphere being created (at 0, 0, 0) on its first frame of life because the runtime expression does not work for a particle's birth frame. To get rid of this annoying problem, simply cut and paste the runtime expression into the Creation Expression window (switch over to the Creation Expression window using the Creation/Runtime radio buttons in the Expression Editor).

As a last step, see if you can figure out how to make the spheres' colors change as they spiral up, as shown in Figure 24.19 (and in color on the CD). You can use the same Sine (and Cosine) function to alter colors as well.

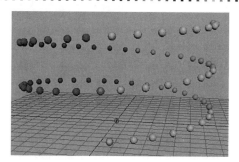

Figure 24.19 *Spiral particles with color*

If you get stuck, try looking at this code to help you out:

```
$pX = 15 * sin(particleShape1.age);
$pZ = 15 * cos(particleShape1.age);
$cX = ($pX + 1) / 2.0;
$cZ = ($pZ + 1) / 2.0;
particleShape1.position = <<$pX, particleShape1.age, $pZ>>;
particleShape1.rgbPP = <<$cX, 0.5, $cZ>>;
```

The new variables (*$cX* and *$cZ*) reset (more properly, they "renormalize") the *$pX* and *$pZ* variables to between 0 and 1 (they originally ranged from –1 to 1). The *rgbPP* statement just assigns these variables (plus 0.5 for green) to the spheres' red and blue color channels.

Here, with just a few lines of code, you have created an animation that would be next to impossible using traditional keyframe methods.

Collision Events and Expressions

For particles, not only does Maya keep track of color, age, and other attributes; it also tracks events such as the number of collisions a particle has experienced.

Create a new scene with a fountain shooting spheres up in the air. Add gravity, create a plane, and create a collision plane. (If you don't want to go to the trouble of setting this up, just open the 24collide project on the CD-ROM.) Now let's create a runtime expression that will change each particle's color based on the number of times it has collided with the plane.

We will use the event attribute (which is a per-particle attribute, even though it doesn't end in PP) to determine how many collisions each particle has been through. Then we'll use an if – else if – else statement to assign a particular color to the particle, depending on how many collisions it has been through. To add the event attribute, you have to create a particle collision event: Select the particles—not the emitter—and choose Particles ➜ Particle Collision Events. Click the Create Event button. Several new channels will be added to the particleShape1 node, and the event attribute will be listed in the Expression Editor's Attributes box. (If you are not familiar with `if - then` statements, see Chapter 17 of this book, or a basic programming text.)

Create a per-particle color Attribute (if none exists yet), and RM select a runtime expression for the rgbPP of the particles. Type the following expression into the Expressions Editor, and click the Create button when you are finished:

```
if (event == 0)
    rgbPP = <<0,1,0>>;
else if (event == 1)
    rgbPP = <<1,0,0>>;
else if (event == 2)
    rgbPP = <<0,0,1>>;
else rgbPP = <<1,1,1>>;
```

This expression executes on every frame (except the birth frame), checking the number of collisions each particle has had. If the number is 0 (no collisions), the expression assigns a green color to the sphere. If the number of collisions is 1 (after the first bounce), it assigns the color red to the sphere. If the number is 2 (after the second bounce), it assigns the color blue to the spheres. In all other cases (when the particle has bounced more than twice), the expression assigns a white color (all 1s) to the sphere.

Note that the test condition is specified by a double *equals sign (*`event == 0`*), not a single equals sign. A single equals sign tells Maya to assign a value to the left-hand side of an equation (as in* `rgbPP = X`*); a double equals sign tells Maya to test whether the two sides of the equation are equivalent.*

You can also use a `switch` command in expressions like that above, rather than the `if - then - else`. A `switch` and an `if - else` statement perform the same function but in a slightly different way. For more information about the `switch` command, see the *Using Maya: Expressions* Manual in Maya's online documentation.

Play back the animation and watch each sphere; you will see that the individual particles change color each time they bounce, ending with a white color after they have bounced more than twice, as shown in Figure 24.20 (in color on the CD). You may also notice that the spheres are emitted as completely black objects—this is (again) because a runtime expression is not evaluated on the birth frame of the particles. To solve this problem, simply copy and paste the expression into a creation expression for the rgbPP of the spheres.

In the Maya documentation, see Using Maya: Dynamics *for more information about creating particle collision events (Chapter 4, "Particle Collisions") and the event attribute (Chapter 15, "Advanced Particle Topics").*

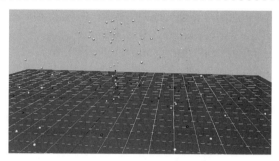

Figure 24.20 *Colored bouncing particles*

Transparency Ramps: Disappearing Bubbles

One problem with our antacid tablet from Chapters 22 and 23 is that the bubbles rising from the tablet have a continuous opacity (unless, that is, you created an opacity ramp in your compositing package). Let's take care of that deficiency in Maya, using a transparency ramp and particles with blobby surfaces.

First, open your antacid project from the last chapter or open the 23glass file on the CD-ROM. For a little different look, let's change the bubbles to software-rendered ones. In the Attribute Editor, set the particle type to Blobby Surface, and set the threshold to 0. (Remember that setting the threshold of a blobby surface to 0 makes the spheres noninteractive and, thus, just spheres. For bubbles, this is exactly what we're after.) With particles selected, add a per-particle radius attribute to the bubbles, then create and edit the ramp of radiusPP to look something like Figure 24.21.

You'll probably find that the bubbles created with this ramp range in size too much, overall, so remap their sizes using the Array Mapper (RM choose radiusPP ➜ arrayMapper1.outvaluePP ➜ arrayMapper1.outvaluePP ➜ Edit Array Mapper). A minimum value of 0.1 and a maximum of about 0.3 give a much subtler effect, as shown in Figure 24.22.

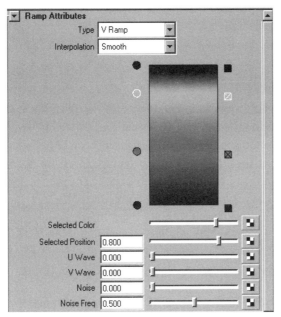

Figure 24.21 *A radius ramp for the bubbles*

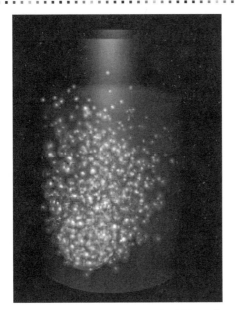

Figure 24.22 *A glass with bubbles of varying radii*

The bubbles in this image have a material attached to them—a phongE material with high specularity and low opacity. This, of course, improves the look of the bubbles tremendously.

Emitter Expressions

So far, we have created several ramps and expressions for particles, but we have yet to create expressions for particle emitters. You can either create a default emitter for this example, or reopen your fountain project from Chapter 23 (or 23fountain on the CD). Because it's easier to see the effects of this particular expression in a simpler project, it might be advisable to first create a simple emitter. Then, after you see how the expression works, you can copy it into the fountain project.

Although emitters are random in their particle output, they tend to produce a "constant" randomness (a kind of even spread) over time. To get the emitter to create a widely varying number of particles, and a wide range of spread, we could keyframe these values—or we could simply create a two-line expression using the noise function.

We could also use the rand function, but noise produces a more connected randomness (as opposed to the rand function's jumping from value to value). With noise, the look is more like the varying water pressure we might see in a fountain. For more on the noise function, see Chapter 16.

With the emitter (not the particles) selected, open the Expression Editor and type in the following expression.

```
emitter1.rate = ((noise (time) + 1) * 200) + 20;
emitter1.spread = ((noise (time) + 1)/4) + 0.1;
emitter1.speed = ((noise (time) +1) * 5) + 3;
```

In essence, each line of this little expression tells the emitter to vary its rate (or spread amount, or speed) according to a random amount as defined by the noise function, which uses time as its input to create its numbers. The other numbers in the script are simply to get the value output by noise into a good range for each attribute. Because noise varies between –1 and 1, we added 1 to both lines so the result would vary between 0 and 2. For the rate, we wanted the value to range between 20 and 420, so we multiplied the results of noise by 200 (giving a range of 0 to 400) and added 20. For the spread, a good range seemed to fall between about 0.1 and 0.6, so we divided by 4 (giving a range of 0 to 0.5) and added 0.1. Finally, we adjusted the speed of the emitted particles as well, multiplying the noise function by 5 and adding 3 to the results. As your results should show, the noise function is a very powerful way to create a more "live" look to your particles.

The result of this expression applied to the fountain project is on your CD-ROM as `24fountain.mov`. If you compare this to the previous fountain movie (`23fountain.mov`), you'll see the fountain's dramatically improved realism (like one of those shooting fountains).

Changing Opacity with Motion

We're now going to create a nice little effect using expressions: increasing the opacity of a particle based on its motion—in other words, the more it moves, the more opaque it is. To test this out, open your UFO project from Chapter 23 (or use `23UFO` on the CD-ROM).

With the particles selected, change their render type to MultiPoint, reduce the point size to 2, and increase the Multi Radius to about 2. Next, create a per-particle opacity attribute (Add Dynamic Attributes: Opacity). Then open the Expression Editor and type in the following simple runtime expression.

```
if (particleShape1.velocity != 0)
    particleShape1.opacityPP = (particleShape1.velocity / 2.0);
else
particleShape1.opacityPP = 0;
```

All we're doing here is testing whether the velocity is not 0 (the ! sign in front of a comparison operator means "not"). If the particle is moving, then its opacity is based on its speed. We divided by 2 to get a more gradual fade-up of opacity—you can try other numbers if you like. If the particle is at rest (the `else` statement), its opacity is defined as 0, or invisible. Thus, the "dust" is invisible when it is resting on our desert floor. As the UFO picks it up and moves it around, the dust becomes visible; then, as it falls back to the ground, it disappears again.

A movie of this new UFO sequence is on the CD-ROM: `24UFOFade.mov`, and Figure 24.23 shows a still from this movie.

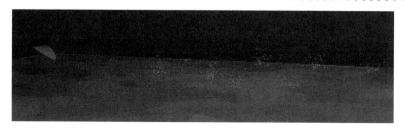

Figure 24.23 *The UFO and semi-opaque dust*

Changing Rotation with Motion

Now that we have dust appearing and disappearing, it seems only natural to visit the UFO project we did in the last chapter with sprites. This time, instead of simply pulling the leaf sprites along in the UFO's wake, we'll make them rotate based on their motion (so they aren't just sliding across the desert floor).

Either open your UFO sprite project or use the one on the CD-ROM (23UFOSprite). With the particles selected, add a spriteTwistPP attribute (click the General button in the Attribute Editor, scroll down to spriteTwistPP, highlight it, and click the Add button). In the text field next to the new spriteTwistPP attribute, RM choose New Expression; and in the Expression Editor, type in the following runtime expression:

```
float $speed = particleShape1.velocity;
if (particleShape1.velocity != 0)
    particleShape1.spriteTwistPP = particleShape1.spriteTwistPP
    + ($speed * noise(time) * 2);
```

The essence of this expression is the same as the one for changing opacity in the preceding section. If the velocity isn't 0, we rotate the leaves. Some of the details have changed, however.

- First, we created a variable (note that it is a `float`) called `$speed`, which receives the *magnitude* of the particle's velocity.

- The second line checks to see if the sprite's velocity is *not* 0; if that's the case, the spriteTwistPP of the particle is changed by the value of `$speed`. The multipliers (`noise` and 2) are there to make the motion of each leaf different from the others. Essentially, the value of `$speed` is multiplied by a randomly changing number between –2 and 2, making the leaves spin in both directions by varying amounts. You will notice that there is no `else` statement here—if the leaf isn't moving, its rotation should just stay where it is, not suddenly jump back to some other number (like 90 degrees).

Figure 24.24 shows a still from a movie of the leaves, which is available on the CD (24UFOSpriteSpin.mov).

Figure 24.24 *The UFO with spinning leaves trailing*

Converting Data Types in MEL

The velocity variable is a vector quantity (with X,Y,Z values), but $speed is a scalar (just one number). When Maya sees an assignment operator (a single equals sign), Maya always forces the value on the right to fit that on the left if it can. In the case of a vector's being converted to a float, Maya takes the magnitude of the vector (the square root of each element squared and added together), which is a single number, and assigns that number to $speed. Whew—enough math for one day!

More Expressions: Animated Sprites

As one last example of using expressions, let's create a more interesting, animated array of plant life for our UFO to pass over. The leaves in our desert were pretty boring, so let's remedy that situation and make them less uniform. Open the 23UFOSprite project (or your saved one). You can use the one we just worked on, too, although the results will be a bit harder to see with all that spinning.

Select the Lambert shader that controls the sprite shape (the one with the leaf on it). In the Attribute Editor, click the Focus button next to the Color attribute (the triangle in a square) to bring up the file1 attributes. Now you need to open the `LeafSequence` subdirectory (you will see about 50 files in the sequence). You can get this from the CD or the directory on your hard disk where you've saved the `Working_Files` directories, or you can copy the `LeafSequence` folder to your project's `sourceimages` folder. Choose any file from `LeafSequence`; then be sure to check the Use Frame Extension box below the Reload File Texture button. This will assign the first leaf in the sequence to the shader.

Hardware texture cycling is extremely *picky about your numbering and tagging of the files you wish to use. You must* not *use any frame padding (that is, leading 0s), and you cannot have an* .xxx *extension at the end of your filename. This is especially challenging in the Windows world, where the filename extension is usually hidden from view. To get around these traps, it's generally best to use a good file-naming utility (such as SiliWin for Windows).*

Now, in the Hardware Texture Cycling Options, check Use Hardware Texture Cycling. Set the Start Cycle Extension to 1, the End Cycle Extension to 50 (for 24leaves1 and 24leaves50, respectively), and the By Cycle Increment to 1.

The By Cycle Increment controls how many images are skipped before the next one is shown. For an animation (of, say, a bird flying, or a rendered animation sequence you've made previously), you would set the increment to 1. For a choppier look (skipping some of the images, thus producing a "stop motion" look as the sequence plays), an increment of 2 or 3 would work.

You might be realizing at this point that sprite sequences can be extremely useful. For instance, you could play back a movie (saved as an image sequence) in sprites, creating a dazzling array of moving images in your final scene.

If you play back the animation now, you won't see anything different. That's because we have to write an expression to alter the look of each sprite. First, add a new attribute: spriteNumPP (click the General button in the Attribute Editor and add it). Then RM choose a new runtime expression and type in the following:

```
particleShape1.spriteNumPP = ((frame/10) % 50) + 1;
```

The % is the modulus (or remainder) function—whatever number remains from dividing one-tenth of the frame number by 50 is returned (plus 1 so that the number is never 0, for which no sprite is defined). The division by 10 simply ensures that the leaves change color more slowly. For example, on frame 1, `1 % 50` returns 1 (the remainder of 1 / 50). The second frame returns 2, and so on. At each frame, a different spriteNumPP is defined. We could also write a `noise` function to get each sprite to randomly change colors, instead of having all of them changing in synch. Either way, we get to see all the fall colors in very short order!

Figure 24.25 (in color on the CD) shows a still from the movie, `UFOSpriteColors.mov` (also on the CD).

Figure 24.25 *The UFO trailing colored leaves.*

As an exercise, try creating a new emitter that produces leaves of different colors that then stay the same color for the rest of their lives. You'll need to use a creation expression this time, instead of a run-time expression.

Summary

In this chapter, you have discovered how to unlock the power of particle dynamics by using volume emitters and fields, ramps, and expressions. With volume emitters and fields, you gain fine control over particle emission as well as the interaction of forces with particles in space. Using ramps, you can produce large-scale effects—opacity, color, or even velocity—that occur over the lifetime of each particle. In contrast, expressions are best at breaking down groups of particles into their constituents, and you learned how an expression allows you to control each particle in a different but related manner. None of the expressions you studied were more than a couple of lines long, yet they produced impressive results, ranging from positioning particles based on the Sine curve to varying opacity based on the particles' rate of movement.

If you have a fairly good grasp of the techniques covered in Chapters 22 through 24, you are now ready to create some very sophisticated effects in (most importantly!) a relatively short time. The next chapter, on soft bodies, is the final chapter on particle dynamics and in the book. You'll see that the term *soft bodies* is a slight misnomer—they are actually collections of particles that act as bodies. And these past three chapters are just the primer you need for creating these complex and challenging objects. When you're ready, turn the page to begin exploring soft bodies!

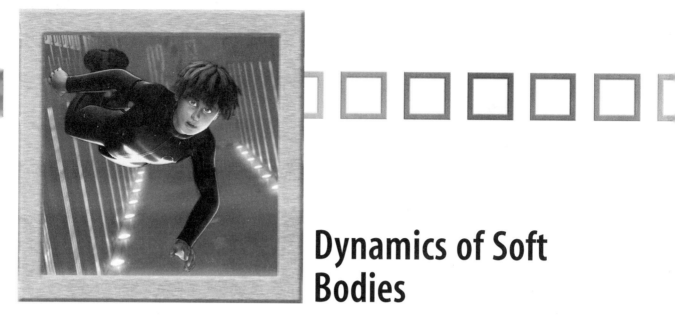

Dynamics of Soft Bodies

MAYA

Chapter 25

I n this final chapter, you'll learn what soft bodies are, how to use them, and where you can use them to create amazing special effects. Along the way, you'll revisit two projects begun earlier: the boy's head, improving the appearance of the hair; and the fountain, this time concentrating on the plane below the fountain. You'll also have a chance to work through an advanced use of soft bodies to create an effect similar to the famous "water head" scene in the film, *The Abyss*. In these and other exercises, you will see how soft bodies are the culmination of Maya's particle dynamics and how they allow you, the animator, to create a whole new realm of animation. Many animation effects you have avoided in the past because of their difficulty are now within easy grasp. The ability to use soft bodies to create flexible, fluid objects is indeed one of Maya's most powerful features. Topics include:

- What are soft bodies?
- Creating a basic soft body
- Adjusting goal weights
- Using goal weights to create fluid motion
- Adding springs to soft bodies
- Faking a bounce
- Denting soft bodies
- Creating flexible hair with soft bodies
- Adding ripples to the fountain project
- Creating a watery body and face

What Are Soft Bodies?

At heart, soft bodies are simply collections of particles. There are a few differences, however, between standard particles and soft-body particles. For one thing, soft-body particles are connected to hold a shape. For another thing, they appear on the screen (and in the final render) as a solid shape rather than as a collection of points. Because of these two properties, soft bodies are special: they can appear to be a solid piece of geometry but react like a bunch of particles when forces and motions are applied to them. Although working with them can be quite complex, creating soft bodies in Maya is easy: you simply select your model and tell Maya to make a soft body out of it.

Creating a Basic Soft Body

To begin working with soft bodies, create a basic NURBS sphere in a new scene. Then take the following steps:

1. Select Soft/Rigid Bodies ➔ Create Soft Body ❑ from the Dynamics menu set. The Soft Options window will appear with options for creating a soft body.

2. In this window, be sure that Make Soft (the default option) is selected from the Creation Options pull-down menu, as shown in Figure 25.1.

3. Now click Create and then Close.

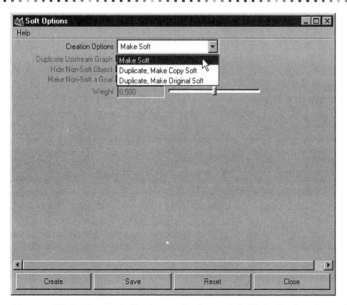

Figure 25.1 *The Soft Options window with Make Soft selected*

That's about it! You have just converted your original geometry (the sphere) into a soft body. You will see what looks like your original sphere, surrounded by a cloud of points (or particles) that actually define the shape. The number of isoparms (or polygon faces) in your original geometry determines the number of particle points. If you want more points (for higher-resolution effects), create your original shape with more isoparms. To see how this works, select the makeNurbSphere1 node and change the number of spans (or sections) to 8. You will see the number of soft-body particles change to match.

Don't try adding or subtracting spans or faces after you begin animating. You will end up with bizarre, uncontrollable soft-body effects!

Understanding the Structure of the Soft Body

Before we actually use this soft body, let's take a quick look at its structure in the Hypergraph.

1. Open the Hypergraph and choose Options ➜ Display ➜ Shape Nodes. Your Hypergraph window should show something like Figure 25.2.

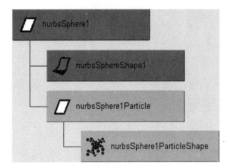

Figure 25.2 *The Hypergraph representation of a soft body*

2. The highlighted nodes (nurbsSphere1Particle and nurbsSphere1Particle-Shape) are your new soft-body transform and shape nodes that have been attached to your old sphere (and replace it). If you highlight the nurbsSphere1ParticleShape node and look in the Channel box (or Attribute Editor),

you will see that the attributes listed there—shown in Figure 25.3—exactly match the attributes you'd find if you created a standard particle shape. When you finish examining the structure of your soft body, close the Hypergraph.

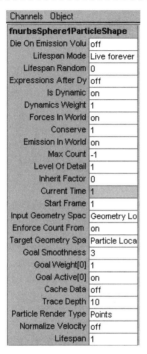

Figure 25.3 *The Channel box showing the particle shape node of a soft body*

Using a Soft Body

Now that we have created a soft body, what can we do with it? First, let's create a gravity field to affect it.

1. Select the sphere and then choose Fields ➡ Gravity. Notice the gravity field now displayed in the center of the workspace. When you play back the animation, the ball drops under the influence of gravity (just as a rigid body would).

2. Now rewind the animation, move the ball up, and add a plane to the scene. (Be sure to scale it large enough so that the ball will fall on it.)

Remember that you always have to rewind a particle animation before playing it back. If you do not, you will see bizarre actions when you play back your animation.

3. Select the sphere, Shift+select the plane, and then choose Particles ➜ Make Collide. Now, as gravity forces the soft body to fall, the *particles that make up the soft body* will collide with the plane. When you play back the animation, you should see something like Figure 25.4.

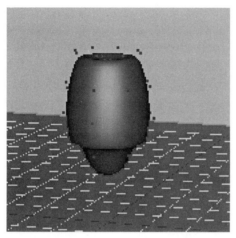

Figure 25.4 *A soft-body ball collides with a plane*

You can see that the soft-body collision is different from a rigid body collision. First, rigid bodies (assuming they use the same rigid solver) will automatically collide with one another; for a soft body, you have to define the collision, as you do with standard particle groups. Second, each particle—not the solid surface as a whole—collides with the plane at a different time, giving rise to the sphere's distortion.

As when you created standard particle collisions (in Chapter 22, "Particle Effects"), you have control over how the soft body collides with the plane. Both the soft-body shape and the plane (in its geoConnector node) have controls for resilience (bounciness) and friction (how much the objects "stick" when they collide at an angle) for the collision. You cannot adjust the soft body's resilience and friction apart from the plane's: they are constrained to be the same values via the geoConnector.

1. To see how resilience works, try changing the plane's Resilience attribute to a number larger than 1 (such as 1.2). When you play back the animation, the particles will bounce higher and higher (as, on each bounce, they rise to 120% of their last height—impossible in our world, but not in Maya's). If you decrease resilience to 0, the particles will simply stick to the plane when they strike it.

Maya also supports negative resilience. With a negative value, your soft body will move through the plane and then bounce back toward it from underneath. If you use this feature with gravity, however, the particle will continue to fall (as gravity continues to pull on the object). To counteract this problem, you can keyframe gravity to change directions.

2. Now move Resilience back to 0.8 or so and be sure that the friction value is 0.6 or so. If there is no sideways movement to the particle (no movement tangent to the plane), you will see no difference.

3. Try, however, adding a bit of shear to your gravity; make the directionX value of gravity 0.2 or so (select the gravity node at the center of the Maya grid or in the Hypergraph, and set directionX to about 0.2). When you play back the animation, you will see the ball move sideways under "gravity"; then, as it collides with the plane, it will slow on each collision. If the ball slides off the plane, just make the plane bigger (or enjoy the spill!). If you set friction to a large value, such as 4, the ball particles will actually bounce *backward* when you play back the animation because friction is greater than 100% (which is, again, impossible in the real world). If you make friction negative, the ball particles will be pulled forward on each collision.

If you try to keyframe the ball's motion, you may potentially run into a nasty little problem called double transforms. *Because each point is being transformed twice what it ought to be, you will see the particles jump out ahead of the ball shape. To counteract this problem, simply group the soft body to itself (select the shape, and then press Ctrl+G), and keyframe the position of the ball using this new node (called group1 by default).*

Adjusting Goal Weights

Now that we've created a soft body, let's make one that isn't so squishy. Goal weights are a way to control how closely a soft body mimics its original shape (the shape you used to create the soft body). The closer a goal weight is to 1, the more closely it maintains the original shape, whereas if the weight is 0, it does not follow the original shape at all. Adjusting goal weights properly can create everything from gelatin-like jiggles to pouring water.

1. Create a new scene like the last one—a sphere above a plane. (Be sure to turn collisions on again by choosing Particles ➜ Make Collide once you have created your soft body.)

2. Now open the Make Soft Body options window (choose Soft/Rigid Bodies ➔ Create Soft Body ❏). Choose Duplicate, Make Copy Soft from the pull-down menu, check Make Non-Soft A Goal, and create the object. (Note that there is a slider for an attribute, Goal Weight, that is now enabled—be sure this is set to about 0.5.) Highlight the sphere, and create gravity. If you look in the Hypergraph now, you will see the original geometry (nurbsSphere1) and the duplicate soft body (copyOfnurbsSphere1 plus the particle node).

Generally, you want to hide the original geometry (by selecting that check box in the Create Soft Body options window). Here, we're leaving it visible so that we can see how the soft body and original geometry interact.

3. Play back the animation. You should see the sphere "sag" and then bounce back into nearly spherical shape. Soft-body particles are being pulled down by gravity, but they have a "goal" to stay as close as possible to their original shape—the original sphere. Thus, they sag a bit and then try to bounce back to their original shape. We can alter how strongly attracted to its original shape a particle is simply by adjusting its goal weight.

4. Select the particle node (you may need to do this in the Outliner or Hypergraph), and find the goalWeight[0] and goalActive[0] attributes listed there. They should be set to their default 0.5 (or 50%) and "on" settings, respectively. If you turn the goalActive attribute to "off" (by typing that in the text field), the soft body will fall away from the sphere when you play the animation, just as in our first example. Why? Because turning that attribute off tells Maya to pay no further attention to the goal weight.

5. Now turn goalActive[0] back on.

GoalActive[0] can be keyframed, meaning that you can animate whether the soft body will attempt to match its original shape or simply follow the forces applied to it. The [0] for goalActive and goalWeight is a note that these attributes are for the first element in the particle array (they thus apply to the whole group).

For more subtle control of goal weights, you can adjust the goalWeight[0] from its default 0.5. If you turn the goal weight up to 1, the soft body will no longer sag; it will now perfectly match the original shape. If you turn the goal weight down to 0, the soft body will fall away from the sphere; this is the same as turning off the goalActive attribute. Low numbers will make the soft body react strongly to gravity; high numbers will make it hold its original shape well. Try changing goalWeight's numbers, and then see how this changes playback.

Changing the Shape of a Soft Body

Now let's try changing the original shape and see how the soft body reacts.

1. Be sure your goal weight is about 0.3.

2. Be sure you select the original shape (nurbsSphere1—not nurbsSphere1Copy!), and scale this shape out in the X axis. When you play back the animation, you will see the soft body stretch to fit the new shape of the sphere; it will overextend, however (as its goal weight isn't 1), and will "jiggle" back and forth until it finally nears the sphere's new shape, as shown in Figure 25.5.

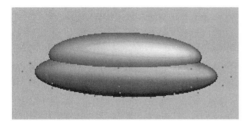

Figure 25.5 *A soft body (below) trying to match the shape of a distorted sphere*

3. Change the scale of the original shape back to 1, and then keyframe a Z rotation to the original sphere (try rotating it about 500 degrees in 40 frames). Now, as the animation plays back, the soft-body shape will "balloon" out, as shown in Figure 25.6, because each particle is being forced away from the original shape by centrifugal force. When the original sphere stops rotating, the soft-body shape will oscillate until it adjusts back to the goal shape.

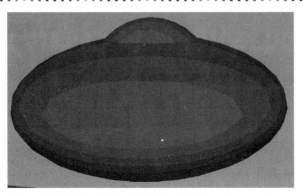

Figure 25.6 *A soft body (below) ballooning out from a spinning sphere*

If you think this image looks like a UFO, and wish to save out the soft body (and original sphere) as a model, simply select the sphere and soft body, choose Edit ➜ Duplicate ❑, make sure the Duplicate Upstream Graph option is not on, and duplicate the object. See "Denting Soft Bodies" later in this chapter for more detail on how to model using soft bodies.

By now, you should start to see what a fun and powerful tool soft bodies can be, so let's kick things up a notch. Not only can you adjust the soft body's goal weight as a whole, you can do it on a per-particle basis.

First, set your object goal weight (goalWeight[0]) to 1. With the particle node selected, in the Attribute Editor's Per Particle (Array) Attributes section, you will see a new per-particle attribute called goalPP. This attribute controls the goal weight of each particle individually, just as the other per-particle attributes do.

You need to set your object goal weight to 1 because the object goal weight is multiplied by the particle goal weight. (If a particle goal weight is 0.5 and the object goal weight is 0.6, the final goal weight of the particle will be 0.3.) If the object goal weight is not 1, there will be some "play" in the entire object, and you will not see the results pictured in the next section.

Adjusting Goal Weights Using the Component Editor

Let's explore how to adjust goal weights using the Component Editor with our spherical soft body.

1. In the text field next to the goalPP attribute, RM choose Component Editor (you can also find this editor under Window ➜ General Editors ➜ Component Editor). A window pops up that lets you control the value of any selected attributes.

2. With the Component Editor open, move back into the scene window, and then switch to Select by Component mode and turn off all components but points.

To change to Select By Component Type, click the Component Type button on the top toolbar (a cube with an arrow pointing at it), or press the F8 key. To turn off all types but points, choose All Components Off in the pop-up menu next to the button, and then click the Points button next to the menu (the black square), or RM choose Surface Point with the cursor over the sphere.

3. Your sphere should now have a cloud of blue-purple points around it. Select half the points on the sphere (the top, say), and, under the Particles tab, select the entire goalPP column (Shift+click the top and bottom entries), and change all entries to a value such as 0.2, as shown in Figure 25.7. When you play your animation, the top half should spin away from the original sphere while the bottom half stays put, as in Figure 25.8.

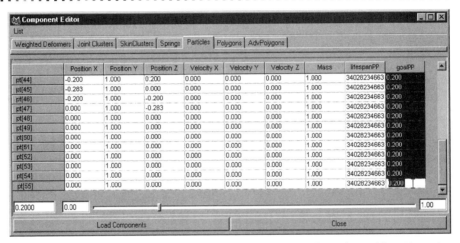

	Position X	Position Y	Position Z	Velocity X	Velocity Y	Velocity Z	Mass	lifespanPP	goalPP
pt[44]	-0.200	1.000	0.200	0.000	0.000	0.000	1.000	34028234663	0.200
pt[45]	-0.283	1.000	0.000	0.000	0.000	0.000	1.000	34028234663	0.200
pt[46]	-0.200	1.000	-0.200	0.000	0.000	0.000	1.000	34028234663	0.200
pt[47]	0.000	1.000	-0.283	0.000	0.000	0.000	1.000	34028234663	0.200
pt[48]	0.000	1.000	0.000	0.000	0.000	0.000	1.000	34028234663	0.200
pt[49]	0.000	1.000	0.000	0.000	0.000	0.000	1.000	34028234663	0.200
pt[50]	0.000	1.000	0.000	0.000	0.000	0.000	1.000	34028234663	0.200
pt[51]	0.000	1.000	0.000	0.000	0.000	0.000	1.000	34028234663	0.200
pt[52]	0.000	1.000	0.000	0.000	0.000	0.000	1.000	34028234663	0.200
pt[53]	0.000	1.000	0.000	0.000	0.000	0.000	1.000	34028234663	0.200
pt[54]	0.000	1.000	0.000	0.000	0.000	0.000	1.000	34028234663	0.200
pt[55]	0.000	1.000	0.000	0.000	0.000	0.000	1.000	34028234663	0.200

Figure 25.7 *The Component Editor showing the goal weights adjusted for selected particle points*

Figure 25.8 *The top half of the soft body (with lower goal weights) balloons out, while the lower half (with high goal weights) stays fixed on the original sphere.*

As an exercise, try using what you learned in the previous chapter to create an expression that randomizes the goal weight. If you can't figure it out, check below.

Using Goal Weights to Create Fluid Motion

One of the primary benefits of using soft bodies is the ability to create realistic flexion in objects. Rather than have to keyframe individual points on a model to get this illusion, you can simply manipulate the goal weights of a soft body to do so. Let's put aside our sphere test project for a moment, and create a new one.

Save the sphere project for use later in the chapter.

1. In a new scene, create a nice, long, skinny cylinder (a tentacle, if you will), turn it on its side, be sure that it has about 20 spans, and animate it to move back and forth on the Y axis. (Try to make the motions happen at different speeds, including some very rapid motions.) Then make the cylinder a soft body, this time hiding the original object and setting the Goal Weight to 1. You should end up with something that looks like Figure 25.9.

Figure 25.9 *A soft-body tentacle*

2. When you play the animation, the (invisible) cylinder will move, forcing the soft body to follow. Because the soft body's Goal Weight is currently 1, it will move in perfect synch with the original shape—not very exciting yet. Now let's create an expression to alter the goal weights based on where each particle is. RM choose Creation Expression in the text field next to the particle's goalPP attribute.

3. In the Expression Editor, type the following:

```
float $scaling = 0.9;
float $offset = 0.1;
```

```
vector $pos = copyOfnurbsCylinder1ParticleShape.position;
float $posY = $pos.y;

copyOfnurbsCylinder1ParticleShape.goalPP = ((($posY + 1)
/ 2) * $scaling) + $offset;
```

Most of the components of this expression are simply variable definitions. The one line that actually does something (the last line) tells Maya to assign each particle its goal weight based on how far to the right it is on the cylinder. The first two lines define a scaling and an offset constant. These variables adjust the range of values that the bottom equation will produce (in this case, 0.9 adjusts the range of goal weights to 0–0.9 instead of 0–1), and the offset of the values (in this case, the range will be 0.1–1.0 instead of 0–0.9). The next two lines read the (vector) particle position into a variable, *$pos*. This variable's Y component is then read into another variable, *$posY*. The reason we read in the cylinder's Y position instead of its X position is that, although the cylinder is lying on its side, its Y axis is still along its long axis, and thus the Y axis of the cylinder is the X axis in world space.

You cannot directly read a single element (such as the Y component) of a vector attribute (such as position) into a scalar (float) variable. Thus, you must first read the value into a vector variable and then take that variable's Y component and read it into another, scalar, variable.

The final line of the equation grabs the relative position of each particle (which is always between –1 and 1) and renormalizes it to a range of 0 to 1. The scaling and offset values are then used to further refine the range of goal weight values. When you run the animation, on the first frame, each particle is assigned a goal weight between 0.1 and 1, and then, depending on your cylinder's animation characteristics, the tentacle or "tail" will waggle more the farther to the right you go on the cylinder, as in Figure 25.10.

Figure 25.10 *A soft-body cylinder with variable goal weights*

You can also paint goal weights directly onto objects like this tail using Artisan's Paint Attribute Tool. For more information on this tool, see Chapter 7, "Working with Artisan," or the advanced tutorial on hair at the end of this chapter.

4. If your Component Editor is still open, you can look at the value of each particle by highlighting it (in component mode), choosing the Particles tab, and reading the goalPP value in the last column.

We could, of course, have manually adjusted all the goal weights using the Component Editor, but it's sometimes nice to have Maya do the math for us. In this case, it would probably be just as fast to use the Component Editor to change the goal weights, but our expression gives us the ability (via the *$scaling* and *$offset* variables) to quickly play with the numbers to get the characteristics we want. Additionally, given a more complex shape with more points that are closer together, the above expression would be far faster than adjusting goal weights by hand. In short, use whichever way will prove faster and more flexible for your situation.

For more on expressions, see Chapter 24, "Using Particle Expressions, Ramps, and Volumes."

Adding Springs to Soft Bodies

If you created violent motion on your cylinder in the last section, you probably noticed that, when you played back the animation, the right end of your "tentacle" looked more like a flimsy piece of clay than a tail or octopus arm, because it stretched all over the place. In more formal terms, the soft body did not maintain its length or overall volume; it didn't have a kind of "bone" structure inside it, helping it to maintain these two properties. Even more obvious, each part of the tentacle looked separate; what was going on at the bottom had no effect on the middle or top—not a good simulation of a tail! This is where Maya *springs* come in. They act (for the most part) just like little springs between each particle, helping them to maintain their shape better under the stress of violent motion and allowing the motion of one particle to affect the motion of others.

Use your project from the last section (or, if you're not happy with that project, open the 25tentacle file on your CD-ROM).

1. Select your soft-body shape in the scene window, and then choose Soft/Rigid Bodies ➜ Create Springs ❑ to open the Spring Options dialog box, shown in Figure 25.11.

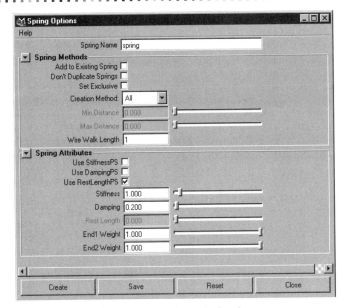

Figure 25.11 *The Spring Options dialog box*

2. In the Spring Methods section, set Creation Method to All (all particles are connected). You can leave all the other areas of this dialog box in their default state. Click the Create button, and then close the window.

You can create per-spring (PS) attributes for Stiffness, Damping, Rest Length, and End Weights. If you don't create per-spring attributes, Maya uses per-object attributes, just as with particles. Though we won't discuss modifying springs on a per-spring basis, the method is the same as for per-particle attributes, and the results can be extremely subtle and beautiful.

The Wire Walk Length setting controls how much structure there is to your object. A walk length of 1 sets springs to each particle's closest neighbors on all sides. A walk length of 2 sets springs between the two closest neighbors on all sides. At higher settings the object will have more structure, but there will be an added calculation cost because of the higher number of springs.

3. You will see a huge mess of dark dots (springs) covering your cylinder. As you play the animation, you will see the springs stretching and contracting to keep the cylinder moving in a more natural, connected motion, as in Figure 25.12.

Once you see how the springs work, you may want to hide them to prevent screen clutter.

Figure 25.12 *A soft-body cylinder with springs*

With springs selected, you can (in the Channel box or Attribute Editor) adjust the stiffness of the springs (how resistant to bending they are) and their damping (how quickly they come back to rest after they've been moved). While very low stiffness and damping values make the tail play back as if no springs are attached, increasing stiffness and damping can often create the rigidity that makes an object like ours appear to have a constant length.

4. Try moving the Damping up to about 0.4, and set the Stiffness to 1 or a bit higher to get the tentacle to bend a bit more stiffly and not stretch as much. If you're lucky, you'll see your animation play back as it should. If not, you'll see the simulation go out of control, as in Figure 25.13.

Figure 25.13 *A soft-body cylinder with misbehaving springs*

This bizarre behavior happens because Maya can't calculate the solution given its sampling rate (once per frame is the default). The solution is to increase the sampling rate to allow Maya to better calculate the motion of the springs.

5. From the Dynamics menu set, choose Solvers ➜ Edit Oversampling or Cache Settings. The Attribute Editor opens with one option: Oversampling Rate (which should currently be set to 1). Try setting this number to 2 and see if that fixes the simulation. If not, move up to 3, and so on. Once you have an animation that doesn't break, try playblasting it to see how much like a tentacle your cylinder looks.

Increase the oversampling rate slowly—it will affect your playback times! While Maya 3 appears to work much more quickly with high sampling rates, the number you put in the field is still related to how many times longer the simulation will take to play than if the rate were set to 1. So first increase by 1, and see if the simulation works; if not, increase it again by 1, and so on. Generally, very high values for Stiffness and Damping are not desirable anyway, so alter these numbers slowly as well.

As you can see, springs can really contribute to more realistic motion for soft bodies, so keep them in mind when your soft bodies look a bit too much like stretched clay!

Faking a Bounce

While you can use rigid body objects as goals for soft bodies, there are times when, for control and accuracy (not to mention playback speed!), creating a bit of keyframed "dynamics" on your own can be advantageous.

The method for creating a soft body with a rigid body goal is the same as the one outlined earlier for normal geometry, except that you have to check the Duplicate Upstream Graph check box in the Create Soft Body Options dialog box. If you don't do this, the soft body will just go along for the ride, as if it had a goal weight of 1.

1. Create a new scene with a ball and a plane, and then type the following expression for motion into the Expression Editor (or just use the 25bouncingBall file on the CD).

```
NurbsSphere1.translateY = 1 + (10 * (1 - linstep(0, 300,
    frame)) * abs (cos(time)));
```

This equation makes the ball bounce (using the Cosine function) lower and lower, until the ball comes to rest (using the linstep function).

The linstep function (and the similar smoothstep) is useful. You give it a starting and ending value (the start and end frame) and the "unit" it will be using (frames), and then the function moves between 0 and 1 over that range. In this example, the value output by linstep increases from 0 to 1 over the range of 0 to 300 frames.

Now we have a bouncing-ball motion. Let's add a soft body, adjust its goal weights, add some springs, and see what happens.

2. Add a soft body to the sphere (use the Duplicate, Make Copy Soft and Hide Non-Soft Object options) and set its Goal Weight to 1.

3. Using the Component Editor (or the expression for goal weights given earlier), set the top points of the sphere to have a goal weight near 0.5, and set the bottom points to have a goal weight near 0. Keep playing with the values until you get a look something like Figure 25.14.

Figure 25.14 *A deformed bouncing ball*

In playing back the animation, you should see the ball (the bottom especially) jiggle quite a bit. Although this could be a useful effect in itself, let's add some springs to it to give the whole ball a more connected look.

4. Select the soft body sphere and add springs to it. (You might try increasing the walk length to 2 here to give the ball more structure.)

When the ball bounces now, it reacts more connectedly, its sides moving in as the ball bounces away from the plane (thus imitating real life squash and stretch by preserving volume), as shown in Figure 25.15. Additionally, the ball now wiggles much less, because the spring dampens the extra motion—of course, this is adjustable via the Damping and Stiffness controls.

One last thing to check out with these springs is using the Rest Length setting (available in the Channel box or Attribute Editor). First, be sure the restLengthPS check box is set to off, and then try adjusting the rest length. If you set the number to 0, the ball will shrink dramatically; whereas if you set the value to 5 or 6, the ball will expand. The rest length tells the springs how far apart they should be when "resting" (in other words, when they're not being moved by forces or collisions), so the larger the number in the field, the bigger the distance between springs (and thus points), and thus the larger the sphere.

Figure 25.15 *A deformed bouncing ball with springs*

One great feature of springs is the ability to place them between standard particles (not just soft bodies). You can connect a stream of emitter particles to form an interacting group, enabling you to produce anything from a simulation of molecules in a room to a "blob" that can shoot across the screen. For more information on adding springs to standard particles, see the "Springs" topic in the Maya online reference. The accompanying CD-ROM also includes 25cloudSprings.mov, an animation of particles connected by springs.

Denting Soft Bodies

To see how we can use soft bodies for modeling as well as animation, we're going to look at two ways to create an asteroid: first by using a Turbulence field to distort a sphere, and then by using an emitter to bombard the sphere with particles.

1. Open a new scene and create a sphere with about 32 spans and sections (so that the soft body will have lots of points on it). If you wish, you can stretch the sphere up a bit, as shown in Figure 25.16, since no one ever heard of a perfectly round asteroid!

Save this project now as a separate file, because we'll use the sphere again when we create the asteroid using a particle emitter.

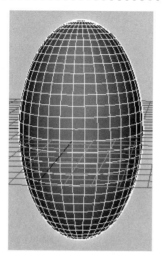

Figure 25.16 *A scaled sphere with 32 spans*

2. With the sphere selected, choose Soft/Rigid Bodies ➜ Create Soft Body ❑. In the Soft Options dialog box, set the Creation Options to Make Soft and create the body. Choosing Make Soft tells Maya to convert the object to a soft body (there will no longer be any original geometry). Because there is no goal object, there is no goal weighting for this type of soft body.

3. Now, with the new soft body selected, choose Fields ➜ Turbulence ❑. Reset the defaults (Edit ➜ Reset Settings), set Magnitude (the force of the turbulence) to about 5 and Frequency (the number of "waves" of turbulence) to about 20, and create the field. As you play the animation, you will see the sphere distort under the influence of the Turbulence field. Since there is no goal weight to bring the sphere back, the sphere will distort too much if the animation plays back too long. Try a few settings for magnitude and frequency, and stop the animation at a frame where you like the look of your new asteroid, as in Figure 25.17.

4. Now that you have the shape, getting it to be a permanent model is as easy as duplicating the object. With the soft body selected, choose Edit ➜ Duplicate ❑. In the option window, reset the default values, making sure Duplicate Upstream Graph is *off*, and then duplicate the object by clicking the Duplicate button. Voilà, one ready-built asteroid!

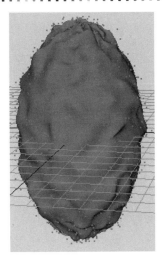

Figure 25.17 *A sphere distorted by turbulence*

If you were to duplicate the upstream graph (the input connections), Maya would create another soft body that would then change with the Turbulence field. By turning this option off, you create the model as a standard node with no history.

If you see a group of points when you move your duplicate copy (the duplicate soft-body points), you can simply delete them.

5. You can now either delete the original shape or alter its shape and the magnitude and frequency of the Turbulence field to make a few more asteroids.

You can also turn lattices into soft bodies. As an exercise, try adding a lattice shape to your original sphere, turning the lattice into a soft body and then adding a Turbulence field to the lattice. How does this alter the way the distorted sphere looks? You might like the results better.

Now that we've used a field to create an asteroid, let's try using an emitter plus a field (emulating lots of little meteorite collisions) to do the same thing.

1. Open your original sphere, and make it a soft body, using the Duplicate, Make Copy Soft option, checking the Make Non-Soft a Goal box, and setting the goal weight to some low number like 0.2.

2. Create an emitter that shoots particles at a rate of about 50 toward the sphere. Figure 25.18 shows the particles being shot at the sphere.

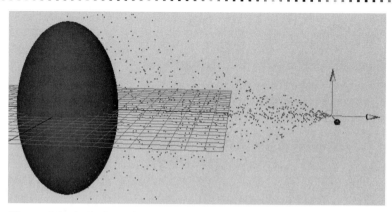

Figure 25.18 *Emitter shooting particles at a sphere*

3. Choose Fields ➜ Air ❑. In the options window, click the Wind button, and then set the Magnitude to 20 and the Directions X, Y, and Z to –1, –0.1, –0.1, respectively. Be sure Use Max Distance is on, and set it to 1; then click Create.

4. With the field still selected, Shift+select the particles and choose Fields ➜ Attach To Selected Object As Source. Next, select the sphere soft body, open the Dynamic Relationship Editor (Window ➜ Relationship Editors ➜ Dynamic Relationships) and highlight the Air field, connecting it with the particles. You will now have an Air field that is owned by the particle group (the icon will move along with the particles if you play the animation). However, if you now play back the animation, you will notice that the Air field affects the particles on the sphere only as the actual fan icon passes by, which is not what we're after here.

5. To alter this behavior, select the Air field, and, in the Attribute Editor, open the Special Effects section and check the Apply Per Vertex option, which now attaches the wind to each particle, rather than to the particle group as a whole. Because the Use Max Distance setting is on and because the distance is only 1 unit, each particle will create a little "ball" of wind around it that will affect any object connected to it.

The Apply Per Vertex option is new in version 3 of Maya. Previously, you would have used the Fields ➜ Add Air option to apply an Air field to each particle automatically. The new method is a bit more hidden, but it gives you the option of attaching fields to entire groups of objects or to individual points (or particles), which can be useful.

Because the particles now strike the sphere, it will distort—probably more than you want it to! Never fear; we can use random goal weights to fix that problem.

6. With the soft body again selected, open the Expression Editor and type in the following expression.

```
goalPP = rand (0.3, 0.6); //try adjusting these numbers for
    different effects
```

This expression simply sets the goal weights of the soft body's particles to a random number between 0.3 and 0.6. Now, as the particles (plus their Air field) pass through the sphere, different parts of the sphere will react in differing amounts to the Air field, creating a more interesting look to the distortion.

You will need to set the per-object goal weight to 1 for this effect to work properly. Also, you will need to increase the Magnitude of the Air field to about 500 to see results.

7. To get an even spread of dents, try rotating the sphere around its Y axis twice (720 degrees) over about 200 frames. (Select the sphere, and then key its Y rotation value between 0 and 720.)

One last adjustment we can make is to force the particles to collide with the sphere. You may have noticed that, now, the particles pass through the sphere and dent it outward on the far side of the object—not what a meteorite collision would do!

8. Select the emitted particles first, Shift-select the sphere, and then choose Particles ➜ Make Collide. Now, when the particles strike the sphere, they bounce off, creating only dents, not stretches in the sphere.

You can make a couple of adjustments to fine-tune your collisions: (1) try increasing the magnitude of the wind force to about 1000; (2) change the value of the resilience for the collision, and see what different values produce. A low resilience will keep the particles around the sphere longer, creating deeper pits.

Although playback can be a bit slow with fields and collisions turned on, you can do millions of years of damage to your asteroid in just minutes! Figure 25.19 shows a banged-up asteroid.

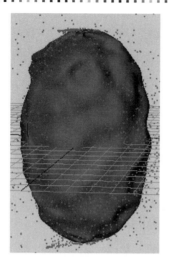

Figure 25.19 *An asteroid dented by particles*

To create a permanent model from your new asteroid, simply stop on a frame you like and duplicate the object, as we did earlier. As you can see, soft bodies can be a fast way to create organic, or beat-up, shapes.

Hands-On Maya: Painting Goal Weights on Hair

In earlier chapters of this book, we created a head complete with locks of hair. As you may have noticed, however, this hair did not move around very realistically if you moved the head about. To solve this problem, we're going to create soft bodies out of all the strands of hair, and then paint on appropriate goal weights to each strand to get the ends to flow around as the head moves.

1. Open your head project file, or 25hair off the CD-ROM. If you open your own project, make sure all the elements of the head are children of the main head node, and then animate the head so it rotates around a couple of axes. (We'll use this motion to see how our hair reacts as we adjust it.) If you use the CD project file, some animation is already included—feel free to alter this in any way you wish.

2. Rather than create and paint each soft-body strand of hair separately, we're going to save some time by working with the whole head at once. Using the Hypergraph, select all the hair on the left side of the model (all the nodes beneath the hair1 node), as below. Do *not* just select the hair1 node, or you will not be allowed to create a soft body.

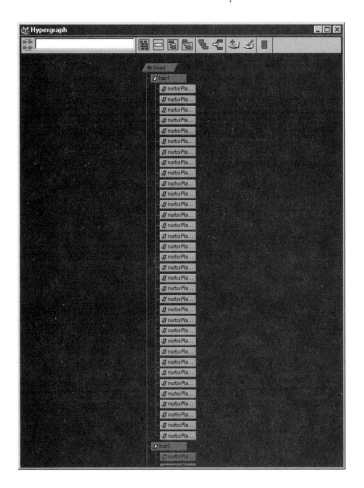

3. Now Shift+select the hair strands on the other side of the head, and then choose Soft/Rigid Bodies ➜ Create Soft Body ❏. Select the Duplicate, Make Soft option, hide the original geometry, and set the goal weight to 1. You will see a mess of bounding boxes, as below. Maya has created a soft body for each hair strand.

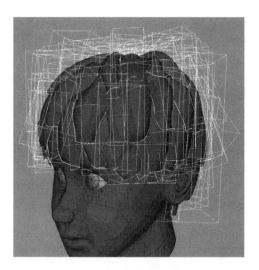

4. With all the soft bodies still selected, choose Deform ➜ Create Cluster, creating a cluster that contains all the soft-body particles.

According to the Maya manuals, creating a cluster is not necessary for painting weight attributes. We have found, however, that the next series of steps will not work if a cluster is not created first.

5. Now return to the Hypergraph and drag-select all the soft bodies plus the cluster. (This will involve zooming way out in the Hypergraph, as there are now dozens of soft-body nodes.) Once you have all the elements selected, choose Modify ➜ Attribute Paint Tool ❑.

6. In the Tool Settings option window, click the Attr tab, open the Particle text under the Paintable Object Type section, and click on the goalPP item. This will select all the particle groups and place them in the Selection window, below. Finally, click the double arrow, as shown next, to load all the particle goal weights into the Selected box to the right.

See Chapter 7, "Working with Artisan," for more on how the Artisan Options window works.

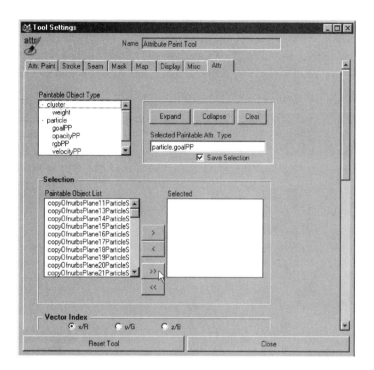

7. If the boy's hair turns white, you are almost ready to begin painting on goal weights. If not, choose the Display tab, turn Show Active Lines off, and turn on Color Feedback and Disable Lighting in the Values section (also be sure the Min and Max Colors are set to 0 and 1 respectively).

A tablet can be very useful for painting weights. If you have one, set the Stylus Pressure to Both (radius and opacity) in the Stroke tab.

8. We're almost ready here! Choose the Attr. Paint tab, set the opacity of the brush to a low value like 0.4, set the Value to around 0.7, and set the Operation to Replace. When you paint now, your brush will (slowly, because of the opacity setting) change the particle goal weights from 1 (solid white) to a minimum of 0.7 (a light gray). A goal weight of 0.7 is still fairly high, so the hair will not flop around greatly. You can, of course, go back and set Value lower (or higher) and repaint as you wish to get the effect you're after.

9. Go to the scene window now, and paint a darker color (lower goalPP value) onto the tips of the hair strands around the boy's head, as shown below. If,

after you have painted around the head, you discover that you have trouble getting to a hair that's underneath others, you can deselect the group of soft bodies, then select only the hair you want (plus the cluster node) and paint that strand of hair. Remember that you're going for subtlety here: you don't want big chunks of hair that are a very dark color, or they will fly off the head and stretch in odd ways. Just a little gray (lower goalPP values) goes a long way toward making effective hair. Remember to test-animate and repaint hair as necessary.

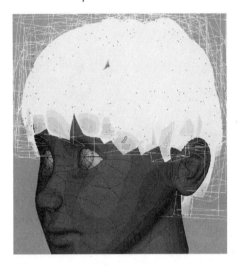

 If you start deselecting and reselecting soft bodies, you are likely to run into a "feature" of the Paint Attributes tool: the attribute being painted (in this case, the goalPP attribute) becomes deselected when you switch the objects you paint on. You need to return to the Attr tab and reselect the goalPP attribute from each strand's particle node before you can return to painting.

If you are happy with the hair you have working now, feel free to leave the project as it currently is. If you want to try a few more tricks to get even better hair, you can add gravity to the scene (be sure the soft bodies are selected first) to make the hair fall toward the ground. You can also create a collision between the head and strands of hair, so the hair won't penetrate the head. Finally, you can add springs to the hair, which will give each strand more structure—you may find you need to paint on lower goal weights when springs are applied. Also, bear in mind that adding collision detection and springs will substantially increase the calculations required and thus slow down playback. The best advice (as always) is to try the simpler methods first, and add in more complex elements like collisions and springs only as needed.

You can check out a render of the boy and hair (including springs, collisions and gravity) on the CD: 25hair.mov.

Advanced Hands-On Maya: Adding Ripples to the Fountain Project

If you thought we were finished with the fountain project after the previous three chapters, guess again. We have been leaving out an important part of our animation: the plane that the water drops strike. In real life, of course, the water in a fountain is agitated from the water that constantly falls on it—not like our flat and unassuming plane at all. To correct this, we'll make the plane a soft body and let the particles "collide" with it by having them carry an Air field with them, just as we did earlier with the asteroid.

Creating the large number of particle collisions in this project can be time consuming. If you don't have a fast computer, you might want to just read through this section—or just attach an Air field to the first group of particles.

1. Open your fountain project from the previous chapter (or use 24fountain on the CD-ROM). Select the plane, go to makeNurbsPlane1, and then increase the U and V patches to about 50 so there will be more points for the soft body you will create. For a more accurate simulation, you can increase this number, but remember that Maya will slow to a crawl on all but the fastest computers, even at this setting. It's going to have to do a ton of calculations for each point on the grid!

2. Once your plane is subdivided, make a soft body out of it, using the Duplicate, Make Copy Soft option and setting the Goal Weight to 0.4. Once the plane is a soft body, you need to add an Air field to particles 1 and 2. Select each particle group, and then create an Air field that is attached to the particles. Do this using the Apply Per Vertex option as described in "Denting Soft Bodies" earlier in this chapter. Set the Magnitude of this field to about 500, the X and Z directions to 0.5, and the Y direction to –1. Be sure the Use Max Distance check box is on, and set the Max Distance for particle1 to about 1; set the Max Distance for particle2 (the smaller ones) to about 0.5 so that they will make smaller "splashes." Once the Air fields are created, link them to the soft-body plane. (Choose Windows ➜ Relationship Editors ➜ Dynamic Relationships; then highlight the air fields.)

3. You can now play back your animation. You may find, however, that the playback speed is so slow that it is difficult to see the motion of the particles and

waves. To compensate for this, either playblast (choose Windows ➜ Playblast) or hardware-render the scene.

4. When you can view the motion of the plane, you should see reasonably good results. Each collision "dent," however, simply exists on its own; the waves don't connect and move. To solve this, we need—you guessed it—springs. (As if play-back weren't slow enough already!) Here is where the real compromises begin. It would be ideal to create springs between all particles, using a large walk length (such as 3 or 4); however, unless you have a beastly computer with lots of RAM, this will not be possible, because the process of creating springs will generate a memory error (there is not enough memory to create all the springs needed). Instead, try creating springs with a wireframe setting and a walk length of 1 or 2 (so that each particle is connected only to its nearest neighbor or two).

If you have a fast computer with lots of RAM (512MB or so), try using a Min/Max setting, with a mini-mum spacing of about 0.1 (or just 0) and a max of about 2. This will produce better results, because more particles are connected, but it will be slower than the wireframe choice.

5. The waves will not propagate outward fully now, but the effect will still be better than it was. Set the Damping value of the springs very low (at 0.05 or lower) so that the waves continue moving after the collision, and set the Stiffness to a middle value such as 0.6. When you look at your playblast or hardware render of the scene, notice how the waves interact with one another and with the particles. If they don't look good enough to you, try adjusting the springs' stiffness and damping, as well as Air field Magnitude and Max Distance. With some patience and experimenta-tion, it is possible to get good-looking results.

A final render of this scene, complete with Paint Effects trees and rocks is available on the CD-ROM (25fountain.mov), and a still frame of this shot is included in the color insert.

When creating complex dynamics simulations involving soft bodies—and espe-cially springs—the art of a successful project often lies in compromising between the best settings and those that aren't quite as accurate but get the job done on deadline. If, for example, this fountain was a background element of your scene, it would make no sense to create such a time-consuming, accurate simulation. Simply make the plane a soft body, and add a Turbulence field to simulate ripples. By contrast, if the fountain will be the center of attention, it is probably worth the effort to create this effect, because the inaccuracy of a simple Turbulence field will call attention to itself. You, the artist, must decide where perfection and efficiency meet in these situations.

Advanced Hands-On Maya: Creating a Watery Body and Face

For the final advanced tutorial, we're going to use a long neck with a face attached to the end of it. In the steps that follow, we're going to make this figure a soft body and then animate the face and goal weights, creating an effect similar to the groundbreaking effect in the film, *The Abyss*. The techniques we use here are a culmination of many of the particle and soft-body lessons you have learned throughout the past four chapters, and can be applied to a number of similar animation scenarios.

1. Open the file 25abyssDeformed on the CD-ROM. If you play back this scene, you will see the "pseudopod" move in a bending path toward you, the face finally ending up looking at you.

2. Let's now use some blend shapes to alter the face's expressions (two blend shapes are built into the CD-ROM file). As the face moves through the tube, shut its eyes, and give it a neutral expression. When it stops (after about frame 160), have it go through two or three more expressions, and then return it to neutral by the end of the animation (about 400 frames).

If you want your file complete with blend shapes and lighting, use the 25abyssBlended *file on the CD-ROM.*

3. Now for the soft-body stuff. We're going to turn the whole pseudopod into a soft body, adjust the goal weights on it, add a Turbulence field to it, and then animate the goal weights to make the face pop out of the pseudopod. First, drag a selection marquee around the entire body; then make it a soft body with Duplicate, Make Copy Soft, and a Goal Weight of 1. (We'll adjust individual goal weights later—if you opened 25abyssBlended, this step is done for you already.) Test the soft body to be sure it animates properly. (If it doesn't, go back to the saved version and try again.) Because the Goal Weight is currently set to 1, the animation should look pretty much the same as before.

4. This is where things get tricky (it's an advanced tutorial, after all). Because the head is constructed of several (eight, to be exact) objects and because we need to vary the goal weight, we need to control all of them via an expression that we'll cut and paste into each particle shape's goalPP attribute. First, however, find the two cylinder pieces, and change their global Goal Weight values to 0.5. They will be at this goal weight constantly, so we don't need to do anything further with them.

5. Now, type the following into the Expression Editor, and copy it so that you can paste it into all eight `goalPP` runtime expressions.

```
float $goalStart = 0.6;
float $goalUp = (0.6 * smoothstep (181, 190, frame)) +
    0.25;
float $goalDown = (0.6 * (1 - smoothstep (361, 385,
    frame))) + 0.25;

if (frame <=180)
    {
    goalPP = $goalStart;
    }
else if ((frame >180) && (frame <=360))
    {
    goalPP = $goalUp;
    }
else goalPP = $goalDown;
```

This expression sets the goal weight of each particle based on the current frame. Early in the animation (during the pseudopod's motion), the goal weight is lower. In the middle, during the facial expressions, the weight is higher, rising using a `smoothstep` function. At the end, again, the weight is lowered back down using a `smoothstep` function.

You could also control the goal weight for each segment of the face by keying the per-object goal weight. This technique is more intuitive, but it requires keyframing eight objects. Use the method that seems easier to you.

6. Now that the goal weights are animated, let's add a bit of turbulence. Drag-select all the soft bodies, and then choose Fields ➔ Turbulence ❑. Set Magnitude to about 60, Attenuation to 0, Frequency to a high number such as 100 or so (this will make for smaller waves), leave Phase at 0, and set Use Max Distance to off. As a final touch, we parented the Air field to one of the head soft bodies so that the turbulence would travel along with the form. You might like the turbulence to stay in one place while the figure moves through it; try both ways and see which you prefer.

7. If you like your animation, all that's really left is to create and apply a water texture. Try creating a PhongE shader with a pale blue color (almost white), slightly roughened, but tight and bright specular colors, and a good deal of transparency (only the highlights of water really show well). You might also

add a background image or geometry and set the shader to have a refraction and reflection so that it looks more like water.

A finished movie is available on the CD-ROM as `25waterHead.mov`, and you can see a rendered still in the color section of this book.

For more on how to create materials, see Chapter 18, "Rendering Basics."

This animation (like the fountain we developed earlier) should take you a good deal of time to get right. These projects are the culmination of your understanding of the entire Maya dynamics package, so, when you finish, congratulate yourself on a job well done!

Summary

In this, the final chapter of the book, you learned what soft bodies are, how to create them, and how to use them for everything from simple animation effects to modeling, to adding the final touches to complex projects. As a group of particles that act as a whole, soft bodies are a unique blend of form and motion, allowing us to create effects that would otherwise be so difficult to do correctly that we probably wouldn't. Although this and all the chapters in this section have only begun to reveal the power of Maya dynamics, we hope that you now have enough knowledge and the confidence to continue experimenting and working on your own. Think of something you always wanted to animate that has clouds of dust or jiggling, organic figures in it. Now go on and create that animation!

Interviews

MAYA

Appendix

This appendix features interviews with three luminaries from the digital graphics world. Perry Harovas spoke with Alias|Wavefront Ambassador Mark Sylvester, and Industrial Light and Magic artist Habib Zargarpour. John Kundert-Gibbs interviewed Craig Lyn, Technical Director for Industrial Light and Magic.

Mark Sylvester: Ambassador, Alias|Wavefront

Mark Sylvester was one of the original founders of Wavefront Technologies, one of the first animation software developers, in 1984. He initially helped to develop The Advanced Visualizer, a 3D-computer animation system first used at Universal Pictures. In helping to create Wavefront, Mark took a leadership role in establishing global customer support activities, which included educational relationships and user groups.

In 1995 Wavefront merged with Silicon Graphics and Alias Research, and Mark now serves as Ambassador for Alias|Wavefront. In this role, he works closely with the development organization and the product marketing teams as a liaison between customers and the company, ensuring a close relationship between artists and developers.

Before founding Wavefront, Mark was a private chef and helped to build several restaurants in the Santa Barbara area, where he currently lives with his family. In this interview conducted in December, 1999, for *Mastering Maya 2 Complete,* Mark gave us an incredible amount of his time to try to give readers a deeper understanding of Alias|Wavefront, and the tools that make up Maya.

Perry Harovas What was the reason for creating Maya, and what were your most important goals for its first release?

Mark Sylvester Maya is the result of an effort that was undertaken immediately upon the merger of Alias and Wavefront. At the end of 1994, Alias Research was in the midst of a next-generation, very secret product development. Wavefront, in conjunction with TDI, because we had merged with TDI three years earlier, were in the midst of a next-generation product development ourselves. The code bases at that time were about ten years old and in dramatic need of complete ground-up rewrites. Things that we did in the very beginning were a result of only being able to run on 64MB—not even that, 16MB—systems with limited graphics capabilities. The operating environment of Unix at the time and the graphics library environments caused us to do a lot of different tricks that we didn't really need anymore, so we were suffering from the inefficiencies at an architectural level. That is why we had started those rewriting efforts. Because of the merger, we were faced with a couple of issues. One was a business problem which was, can we continue to effectively support and put research and development dollars into the Advanced Visualizer, which was Wavefront's product line, Explore, which was the TDI product line, and PowerAnimator, which was the Alias product line. Management at the time said, "You know that really doesn't make sense because not only would we have those three lines, we have a next-generation effort at Wavefront and a next-generation effort at Alias. So that's really several teams that are working, and that's painfully expensive. Let's figure it out." The president at the time challenged the technical team to come up with a unified product agenda that would unify the requirements of the Wavefront users, the Alias users, and the TDI users into one next-generation product that we could deliver in a year. Absolutely overly ambitious, but I believe our heart was in the right place.

So you had this really interesting challenge because the Alias developers really knew how to think along the lines that they had been accustomed to thinking for 10 years as the same was with Wavefront developers and the Parisian developers. The first year was really spent understanding the requirements of the various installed bases because they were all very, very different. We also spent a great deal of time learning how to work together, across continents and language barriers.

It is somewhat interesting that three graphic systems were all started within three months of one another in 1984. They all had modeling, animation, rendering, and display capabilities. They all attracted a certain kind of user. There was the Californian approach, there was the Canadian approach, and there was the Parisian approach. They had their own zealots who felt that their given approach was the right way to do it. Yet, at the end of the day, we all made pictures and got pixels up on the screen.

Perry Harovas How did you get to be known as "The Ambassador"?

Mark Sylvester My role at the company has always been interesting. At the merger, the management was predominantly Alias management and they did not believe in titles for people. So, at the merger, we found out that there would be no titles; no one would have a title. I was going to Japan two weeks later to head up a delegation that was going to assure all of our customers in the Pacific rim that everything was going to be fine and the merger was going to be good for them; just to kind of calm them down. I said, "Listen, I cannot go to Japan without a title. It's not acceptable. They will not know how to deal with me. It's a culturally significant issue." They said, "OK, that's fine." So they called me one day and said, "We think we have got a title. How does "Ambassador" sound?" And instantly, it hit me chemically. I said, "That's it. That's absolutely it." And while we were on the phone I jumped on the Net and looked up the definition of "ambassador" and in reading it, I thought that's a perfect job description for me because it would allow me to exercise the kind of mission that I've always had, which focuses more on back-channel kinds of relationships. A role that is clearly focused on customers. My favorite line was when I was meeting with a vice president at NBC. He likes to walk me through (the facility) and as he introduces me, he loves to give my title and he says that I am the only guy he knows that outranks an entire room of vice presidents.

Perry Harovas What area of Maya do you think doesn't get enough attention?

Mark Sylvester Wow, that's a great question! Boy, that's a hard one. My first thought is the dynamics. I think that that's the most unexplored territory. I think people naturally gravitate toward particle system work and they're starting to understand the soft body dynamics more. But I think the whole area of dynamics gives a look to modeling that there's no other way to achieve; and it gives a feel to standard keyframe animation that's exquisite and can produce effects in the renderer that are impossible any other way, yet none of it is readily apparent. It does take experimentation and so I'm very sensitive to the fact that most users don't have a lot of time to experiment—they're busy! They're busy getting work done and it's hard enough to learn what the software does as it's designed to do, much less to say, "what would happen if I did this; if I hooked up this emitter to the transparency feature in a shader?" You know, that kind of thing. "What would happen; what if?" That's the part of the software where I spend most of my time; I like to get in and play with the dynamics almost exclusively. I just think you can get to unusual looking images quicker than any other way. I see myself artistically as a surrealist, not a photorealist.

Perry Harovas Are there tangible results from relationships with places like ILM, Pixar, and Santa Barbara Studios?

Mark Sylvester Oh, absolutely. The relationship that we have with these customers is what we call "Design Partnerships." It goes beyond beta testing and it precedes beta testing by at least a year. We work with customers, not just in film but video, game development, and industrial design, to help us understand what the new requirements are that they're starting to see from *their* customers. Remember, we're tool builders, and the best tool builders are the ones that have forged strong relationships with the people who use the tools. They're the ones that are sitting in the meetings with the visionaries and the directors and the avant-garde designers and the game developers saying, "Wouldn't it be cool if we could do this?" And then they look at the software to determine whether they can do that or not.

It takes a long time to develop software, and places like ILM are going to want to be able to respond to their own customers' requirements as quickly as possible. Now, they can come back to us and say, "we need to be able to do this," whatever it is and we will take that under advisement, as we do with all requests, and we can produce those requests at a given speed—a given rate of innovation. That's where open architecture comes in and that's where an API that's extremely robust and touches all aspects of the code becomes probably the single most important feature for those customers. Because it allows the customers to add these features themselves, especially if they do not have time to wait for us.

I think it's the most important aspect of Maya for the high end of the market. It's certainly not the most important part to the low end of the marketplace. The high end of the market wants to be able to open the hood and fine-tune the engine. The lower end of the market just wants to get in the car and go to the store. They don't want to understand the ignition system; they just want to turn the key and go.

Perry Harovas And they want to do it fast!

Mark Sylvester Exactly! I would say we probably have an order of magnitude of work to do in the ease-of-use, ease-of-learning piece of Maya in the next couple of years.

Perry Harovas What do you see as the single most important thing to tackle next?

Mark Sylvester I'm going to say ease of learning. I think that continuing education in a software package is extremely underrated as to its importance. Software is not static, and so once or twice a year you get a major update of software and you have a challenge in front of you, which is to be able to assimilate that technology into your pipeline, your workflow, into the way that you produce images. We don't produce gratuitous features. We produce features that are specific to solving problems, and yet we'll find that once someone gets a version update, they tend to load the CD into the computer, the software gets loaded, the manual goes onto the bookshelf, and sometimes doesn't even get opened. Maybe the release notes will get read. But to be able to assimilate that newly installed software takes an investment of time in what I call "continuing education." You constantly have to be thinking about improving your skills and learning more about the software that you already have. So, given that condition, I think that's the next major area that has to be resolved.

I'd like to also say that the other area that I think is ready—and it's one of our goals—is to create *Synthespians*. Jeff Kleiser coined that term 10 years ago. We have created photorealistic humans and creatures; we've created surrealistic humans and creatures, aliens and the like, and they move realistically and they look realistic, but they're dumb as rocks! I think there is a real opportunity to build intelligence into these characters that would absolutely help our ability to tell stories if we didn't have to worry about hand-animating walk cycles. Yet, you want to have the individuality that every organic creature has. Nothing walks the same or flies the same.

So you can't really solve this problem with motion capture and you can't really solve the problem with procedurally generated motion, and I don't really know how to solve the problem. I think one of the great things about audacious goals is that you don't really know how you're going to solve it, but I would love to have directable characters. I would love to be able to feed a script into the system and be able to direct the system by voice, much as a director would, and not have to be concerned as much with hand-animating walk cycles.

Perry Harovas Yet one of the difficult things for artists is changing the way they work, especially when it comes to doing the same thing they have always done, but approaching it in a vastly different way.

Mark Sylvester Yes. That is very hard. It takes openness and willingness, and people are very resistant to change. That is a core human condition. No matter how high-tech we envision ourselves, no matter how advanced and cutting edge we think we are, we don't like to change. This whole ability to just have your eyes opened to the idea that there might be another way of doing it. And again, I don't know how to do that yet. I'm looking at it. I'm trying to figure out how can I help capture the little stolen moments in a day and use those for education. While you're waiting for a render to happen or you're waiting for a file to load, could you get a little three-minute lesson on lighting or could you listen to someone during lunch? Could you download a 10-minute brown bag lesson by some lighting director? I think it's an area that we haven't spent as much time as I think we need to, and I know for sure that Alias|Wavefront is devoting a tremendous amount of time now to this whole area of continuing education. It's clear that we're not completely meeting the needs of the broader professional market until we have a level of ease that will show users how to learn online, quickly and easily.

Perry Harovas It's very interesting that applications like 3D Studio MAX and Lightwave, which are obviously very complex programs in their own right—although compared to Maya, a percentage of Maya's complexity—have all this education out there to explain them! Then you have all these users of Maya that are scratching their heads saying, "I don't know what I'm going to do next; I guess I'm out here on my own trying to figure this out." A main sore point with Alias|Wavefront has always been the Web site and the amount of information that's on the Web site to help people. Recently the LISTSERV has been probably the most fertile ground for some of this stuff, but I think there needs to be something else.

Mark Sylvester The importance of continuing education; the importance of ease of use and ease of learning is one of the number-one priorities for the Maya team.

We will not have the success that we need in a broader professional market and with casual users and with this coming tidal wave of new users unless we address this specific issue. These users, they know all the features are there but like you said, it's access to help, access to information, access to tips and tricks, that kind of stuff. We know that historically we've not been as successful in this area, so I expect that to change, probably not dramatically at first, but with real strong incremental steps along the way.

Perry Harovas Well that's good to hear. Who do you see as your primary competition in the 3D world?

Mark Sylvester Oh, Studio MAX, without a doubt!

Perry Harovas So, was that what you had up on your bulletin board when you were developing Maya?

Mark Sylvester No, at the beginning it was SoftImage. I think neither Alias nor Wavefront had strong character animation tools. SoftImage did, and as the trend toward character animation grew, so did their business. So that was one of the principle areas that we wanted to focus on in 1.0, which we did—the whole character-building/character-modeling, IK, puppetry, the digital puppets, all of that stuff. All of it was to be able to respond to the needs that our customers had, which was for strong character animation tools. We wanted to break the paradigm of "model in Alias, animate in Soft, render in Renderman." That had to go away. So now many shops are strictly Maya. We want to be able to have the entire workflow be within Maya. So that was one goal. I think after 1.0 we absolutely hit that target dead on. And consequently Softimage is not the main competitor anymore.

Perry Harovas In terms of specific tools, what would you like to see Maya do better, as a user?

Mark Sylvester My personal weakness is in modeling and so anything that we can do in the area of making it easier to do will be appreciated. I think that one of the goals as a visual artist is to create very complex worlds, with scenes and environments that tend to require lots of detail. Look what Paint Effects has done. I mean, try modeling a palm tree and try modeling it within a year. It's a lot of work to make it look real. Yet, we can do a palm tree in what amount of time with Paint Effects? Two seconds, three seconds—with dynamics on it even! So tools that help us model complexity are very important because to make things visually interesting, they've got to have a lot of detail in them and that can be very, very time consuming, especially for someone who is not real gifted as a modeler, and that's certainly me!

Perry Harovas I've always said, I don't know if it's the Moore's law of 3D graphics—I haven't come up with a name for it yet—but this is the core idea: once you get a new tool that lets you do something that you've never been able to do before, all of sudden you're excited and then you're interested in doing things which you never would have attempted, and it becomes voracious and you start to attempt things that slow down your system again and you work toward the point where you can actually get back up to functionality. The systems come up to speed again and then another tool is introduced which bogs you down again. And I don't think with the complexity of what we're trying to do as artists, we're ever going to have the computing horsepower to achieve everything we can see in our heads.

Mark Sylvester Right. Absolutely! It's the same with disk space; you never have enough. I had thought that one of the things that we could invent that would be really helpful would be a, I don't know what you would call it, but it would be a Complexity Meter that you could have turned on, and as you are doing things the Complexity Meter starts to rise so that you know that that thing you just did just added 33% more to the render time, for instance. You put the shadow button on in a shader and this meter goes up another 50% or whatever.

This is something that I've talked with our broadcast clients about. They would like to be able to say, "I need to get something done in an hour…just bam, bam, bam, get it done!" Now I want to turn up the quality knob by another 50%. What does that mean? Now I can use this level of shaders; I can add this much more geometry and this many more lights and now…because that means it doesn't have to be ready until the 6 o'clock news I can turn the quality meter up again. It's going to be something that's going to go on a weekly event that's going to happen and I've three or four more days so I can turn that quality knob up even more.

How many times have you just start working, you're doing this, doing that, and all of a sudden you've got a one-hour render and you're like, "Oh-h-h!" As I was working, had this, whatever that meter was, had it shown me as I was glibly adding more and more complexity, that's where I think we can help users. That isn't on the planning boards anywhere. But it is a great idea and would really be helpful. Especially, to help us in the case where you are bidding a job—to be able to say that I can complete this job and keep my quality meter on at 2 and be able to deliver it at so many dollars a second. And if the budget goes up I can crank, crank, crank it up and now I know I can add volumetric clouds or hundreds of lights and still make my budget.

Perry Harovas Well it becomes very easy to do things like paint in complexity with Paint Effects where it's casual. It's kind of going back to the other statement I made where you would never even think that you could paint a field of grass, yet I've done at least six animations of fields of grass, with trees and every blade of grass casting shadows. I mean…

Mark Sylvester You never would have done it.

Perry Harovas I would have laughed in your face if you would have even suggested it to me and now you just casually do it, so you keep adding complexity to it and now all of a sudden you're surprised when you see an hour-long render! Look at things like radiosity. People want to have radiosity or global illumination and don't care how long it's going to take if it's a choice between a long render time or not having it at all. Of course they'd rather have less render time *and* the feature, but they don't want to be limited at all. That must be very difficult for you when you decide what features to put in there; when you have to balance it against how much time and money it's going to take to develop this and how much return on your investment you are going to get.

Mark Sylvester Correct. That's absolutely correct. When we look at any given release there's three big audiences that have to be appeased. One of them is our own developers. There are things that need to be done in any given release that are architectural or are things that are done under the hood that never show up on a list of new features added. And there are things that you didn't get done in a prior release or things that you know that you need to do to get ready for the next release. Or it's just under the hood kind of stuff that if you ignore, it will come back and bite you *bad* in a release or two down the road. Because you will have no flexibility. That's very important, to listen to those engineers when they say, "We've got to do this."

The second group is the marketing group. They're out there talking to new customers about things that need to be in the software that aren't there. They're looking at the competition; seeing what the competition is doing; what they're working on; what their future stuff is going to be; to make sure that we're competitive on a check-list basis and that we don't lose business because we don't have the key features for given markets that we're trying to grow into. If you don't grow your business, you go out of business and then no one is happy.

The third group is customers. And customers are just users—me and you. Our needs and our focus are all on what we're doing right now, today, our current projects and the projects in our immediate future. That's really what our whole field of view is, really focused on the job that we're doing day to day. We're the ones that are going to report bugs because we're the ones that are using the software most aggressively. We're the ones who probably use competitive packages as well and can say, "Well, I really like the way this package handles this particular problem."

So, you've got that group's advice and suggestions as well, but you can't listen to any one of those groups exclusively or to the exclusion of the others. The trick is to come up with a balance—and a good balance so that you add new features, fix bugs, put things in to remain competitive, and also work on your architectural underpinnings. This becomes a real balancing act because you have to add a business wrapper on that whole topic and say, "OK, that looks good. Now how much of that can we do in a short enough time to continue our momentum, and not so long that we get out of phase?"

So, that's one of the hardest things to do as a software company is to figure out what do you do now, what do you do later? What do you put on the list for later? How do you make your dates? Making your dates or not being late is something that we've intermittently been very good at and very poor at. I think we are much better at time commitments now than we've ever have been in the past. I think it's due to maturity in the team and a commitment to keep our commitments. So, it will be the case that not everything gets in but releases get out on a regular basis.

Perry Harovas I think you as a company need to let the users, the people on the LISTSERV who are very vocal and maybe are or are not coming from an informed view, know your struggles and why certain things are in there and why certain things aren't. Why you're making these engineering leaps and they're "under the hood," as you say, and nobody even knows about them. I think people's assumptions are that the majority or all of your work is spent on new tools. So naturally they start to say "Why isn't tool X in this new release of Maya?" I think there is a lack of that knowledge for the casual users. ILM certainly is aware of it, but Joe Animator doesn't know what your challenges are as Alias|Wavefront and what you have to do day in and day out, so that might be an area to work on.

Mark Sylvester Maybe you can help by getting a little bit of that flavor in the book.

Perry Harovas I would love to. Just to give them an idea, and not to shut them up, certainly, but just to get them more informed so that…

Mark Sylvester Yes, exactly. Don't shut them up at all. That's where we get our best ideas! But we get our ideas lots of different ways. That's what is important. If I just listened to one guy, then what do I do about my guys at NASA? What do I do about my guys at NBC? What do I do about my guys at Pixar, or the ones that are just a few guys in a garage working on feature films?

That's the deal. And how do we keep it up? Even though we've gotten to be a pretty good-size company, I don't want to lose that kind of interaction. We're actively listening to customers. We're paying attention to these kinds of things. I hope that we never get too big where we don't have that personal touch. We can't get out and get to every customer, but I know that we are extremely proactive in going out on customer visits in all areas of the company. And that once we do have a chance to have these kinds of conversations people will come away with a strong appreciation for the challenges we have and a respect for the way that we go about running our business. At least, I hope so.

Habib Zargarpour: Artist, Industrial Light and Magic

Habib Zargarpour of George Lucas's visual effects firm Industrial Light and Magic (ILM) has been instrumental in helping to create some of the most stunning visual effects ever seen on film. His credits include *Dragonheart, Twister, Mighty Joe Young,* and *Star Wars: Episode One, The Phantom Menace.* He is a Maya enthusiast, giving speeches two years in a row at the Alias|Wavefront Global Users Association meetings during the SIGGRAPH convention. He is also one of the nicest and most knowledgeable people working in visual effects today. For *Mastering Maya 2 Complete,* Perry Harovas spoke with him in December 1999, about the way Maya was used in *Star Wars,* and how it integrated into the ILM production pipeline.

Perry Harovas The things you've done with Maya are amazing! How long have you been using Maya?

Habib Zargarpour I'm actually coming onto two years with Maya.

Perry Harovas And did you start from nothing? Were you going through the tutorials and all that, or did you just dive in?

Habib Zargarpour I kind of dove in and tried to figure things out. I'm more like a self-hacker rather than reading manuals. So, unfortunately that means that sometimes there are a lot of features that I don't find out about until other people tell me, but I do look at online documentation a lot. I like doing searches through the documentation, the global index, and especially the MEL commands. So, that stuff is really helpful.

Perry Harovas What version of Maya did you run on *Star Wars?*

Habib Zargarpour We started with Maya 1.0 and then we were able to get additions like the emit command, which we use heavily in animation, and the curve emitter, so then it was called version 1.1 Alpha 3, which is pretty much like the 1.5 release.

Perry Harovas Did you have any trepidation about upgrading the software in the middle of production?

Habib Zargarpour We had a concern, but it went very painlessly. We got the new version and basically switched over lunch. It was fine.

Perry Harovas How did Maya get implemented into your pipeline at ILM, with all the other applications that you use, all having to talk to each other?

Habib Zargarpour When we started out, we wanted to look at rigid body dynamics to use on the show and also to replace any particle effects we had to do instead of using Dynamation. But the particular application for me was to use the pod crashing with it, and as we were doing R&D for that, we tripped into doing the pod flying with it, which is simulating how they fly and animate. So, we ended up making a really nice setup where all the pod animations were, for the most part, done as rigid body simulations in Maya, and in the same scene we were able to set up the animation for dust for the pods and exhaust animations for the pods. Sometimes pods affecting each other, or hitting each other.

Animators were trained to use the package and to use the dynamic controls that they needed. If they wanted to keyframe they could go ahead and keyframe shots. And then we created a Maya pipeline that would take the Maya scene through our in-house software so that we can render it in Renderman. So, it was actually a pretty smooth set-up, and the replacing of the geometry to higher resolution was done in our in-house pipeline.

Perry Harovas Did you have any problems converting Maya's scene files, animations, and things like trims that are specific to Maya, over to Renderman to render?

Habib Zargarpour We did have a problem initially, through the in-house pipeline, dealing with NURBS because we were previously just dealing with B-Spline surfaces from Softimage. Other than that, I believe trims made their way through okay and all the other kinds of geometry made their way okay. We wrote our own converter so that so we could add things that were missing or we could decide what would happen to certain types of nodes that weren't recognized.

But I think as far as the use we had for it, it kind of started growing from when we were doing the pods to doing things like bubbles in the underwater sequence or suspended algae, doing the effect in the underwater city when Jar Jar and Obi Wan walked through the membrane.

We used it for doing some flock animation of different places and then, of course, eventually it got used for doing the people animation in the stadium—people sitting on the seats and also in the end battle sequence where the Gungans and Droids are battling. That whole choreography of the simulating and running the crowds was all used. So as we started out, we didn't think we would end up with such a large usage of the software, but because of the expandability and the way we could put our own plug-ins into it, we could make it fast and efficient. We were able to take advantage of it for a lot of uses. And I have to say, it's thanks to our supervisor John Knoll, who's open to new ideas and new methodologies and not afraid to dive into doing that.

Perry Harovas Was there extensive testing going on to decide what you were going to do in what specific application and what you were actually going to shoot on-set as a real element to comp in?

Habib Zargarpour Yeah. Each sequence supervisor was using their own experience to decide what elements should be filmed and what should be CG. But sometimes George would have an opinion about that and he would want it one way or the other.

But the scope of the project and all the different shots that had to be accomplished was really vast, so a lot of times approaching it wouldn't be as obvious as you would think because you would say, "Well this might make sense normally to shoot an element, but then we'd need hundreds of them from different angles." The Rotunda is an example, with all the people sitting in the boxes, trying to get that kind of footage.

Perry Harovas I know that multicolored Q-tips were photographed in the models of the stadium to simulate thousands of people in the stands. Were all those shots eventually replaced with CG?

Habib Zargarpour No. There were shots where the Q-tips were left in. Mostly shots where you were not within the stadium or from a distance. The shots where you can see people waving their arms, those pretty much were replaced with CG crowd or footage with a compositing technique.

Perry Harovas I believe I remember you saying at the Alias|Wavefront Users Group that you can make them do the wave if you wanted to! Did you do any shots where you just had fun with them?

Habib Zargarpour We actually had blooper takes of them doing very funny stuff. But we had some people running blooper shots on their own. What I wanted to do was have a Battle Droid riding one of the pod engines.

Perry Harovas How did the MELBots get started?

Habib Zargarpour We were doing all kinds of work with dynamics and expressions, and a couple of in-house people were experimenting with them. I started using them for the pods, and that year I think the real robot wars got canceled. So in the back of my mind I was always saying, "It's really sad because John Knoll also participates in that, in the robot world, you know, the robot he built in the lightweight category." So the real stuff was always in our minds, so it was only a matter of time to connect the virtual stuff. I think Mike Ludlum had run some preliminary tests of just robots—they weren't robots, but they were rigid bodies that moved around.

So I took that idea and took the real robot world idea and I thought, hey if you could build robots actually with rigid bodies, then they'll have expressions so they can fight each other. Then we actually made a sample case with it. We were having a riot with how fun it was to watch these things go at it. I had some really preliminary tests where they would just attack a cube or something. It grew from there to build more intelligence in them. Like, the first arena I had didn't have a border, so they kept falling off the edge. So I had them build in that experience so that they avoided the edges.

Perry Harovas Does it ever threaten to be addictive?

Habib Zargarpour Oh yeah, definitely! Each time we start doing the medleys or the FLU little parts, people start piling up and looking and cheering for one side or the other. If you had a new robot, you'd want to run some test battles first and fine-tune your expressions and then you'll be ready. It's kind of like an evolution thing; it grows. With more experience you can improve your robot. It would be pretty unfair if you didn't have battle experience and you just put it in there. You'd probably get run over pretty quickly!

Perry Harovas I like the rules: you can't delete your opponent, you can't change your robot's size on the fly, and things like that.

Habib Zargarpour Right. I still have people coming up to me saying, "Hey you know you can do this…" and then you think, "Well, that's cheating." The rules are getting longer and longer.

Perry Harovas Have you ever just said, "You know what, I'm going to stay here late, I'm going work on something just for fun because it's what I want to do and nobody else has to have a say on how it looks or how it moves"? It doesn't have to be anything big or anything anybody ever sees, but just something that makes you happy as an artist.

Habib Zargarpour I find myself thinking constantly about things that are possible to do or things I want to be able to do and it becomes like a little test pilot. Kind of like if you're in a restaurant and you have a napkin and you find yourself sketching on it, but as ideas come you think to yourself, "I wonder if I can make something like *this* and hook it up to *that?*"

To me the interesting part of the package is when you have these different modular features in it, then you can combine them. You can combine rigid bodies with particles; you can combine relational modeling with animation. All these different things can talk to each other, so then you start thinking in your head about tinkering with different inventions, basically, building them in Maya and that's the curiosity factor for me. You build things to see if you can make them work a certain way. Or someone else can throw you a challenge, saying, "I bet you can't make a locomotive drive chain with an IK skeleton" or something like that, you know? I have lots of scenes that are just little proof-of-concepts of different effects or inventions.

Perry Harovas And I'm sure all of those end up getting funneled back into production when you need an idea and you remember you did something six months ago for fun?

Habib Zargarpour Yeah, absolutely. And that's where good naming conventions come in. You want to name something *exactly* what you think it should be called when you want to look for it again.

Perry Harovas What do you see as the most difficult part of using a commercial application like Maya in production?

Habib Zargarpour That's a heavy question (pause). Learning it, I guess.

Perry Harovas Having the time to learn it or just learning it in the first place?

Habib Zargarpour Both. I think there's so much there that you want to be able to continuously learn. That's true with any package, but specifically, to really harness the power you need good training on a package like Maya to be aware of all the different possibilities. And also to take advantage of the expressions.

I think it is a voyage of discovery. You cannot be afraid of going into different places or menus. I think that anyone who has fear of what's new is going to have trouble in general in the land of computer graphics. Things change so fast that you have to accept that change is going to happen. I went through this when I had learned Alias and then Softimage came around and I had to [learn that]. Initially I was really angry and bitter that here's a whole new thing I have to learn after becoming good with Alias. I think at that point I decided to accept change and decided that if there's something new, I'm going to dive into it. You just have to change your attitude around.

Perry Harovas When you open yourself up to things like that, sometimes there's the danger of being into everything new and it affects what you're trying to do if you're excited about the new thing and get lost in it. I imagine you have to scale yourself back sometimes so that you can meet your schedules?

Habib Zargarpour Yeah. You don't jump into everything that's new; you have to use your judgment to say, "This particular thing looks very promising, so it seems like it's worth checking out." As you check it out, you find out pretty quickly if you made a good decision or not. You know, at some points it was more fun to make the [MEL] scripts than to do the work. I think that's the danger with Maya—it's really fun to make those buttons and make the icons for them and make them do stuff! I thought that was just extremely fun. We have over 200 of them, some of which I've made and some of which the rest of the crew did. I think we've been very successful in integrating it into our pipeline, customizing it to what we do.

Perry Harovas There is only so far you can go with MEL and at some point you have to do a plug-in either for speed or just to get it done at all. Did your R&D department write a lot of plug-ins as well?

Habib Zargarpour Yes. Actually, our R&D TD's (Technical Directors) would write plug-ins; the software department would handle things like big projects.

Perry Harovas Are you able to write at that level of programming or are you happier and most confident in things like expressions and MEL?

Habib Zargarpour I have a software background in mechanical engineering. I learned it there and I have been writing code on various platforms, as well as some custom code on Twister and some of the programs we use in-house. I wouldn't say I'm totally confident with it. I'm much better at editing than writing it from scratch, and I'm certainly much more comfortable with the scripting language, having done a lot of Dynamation work before. Thanks to the speed [Maya] has, there are very few times you need to go to the plug-in level. The cases where you have to go to the plug-in level are if you want to create a primitive and have it deform and have it all be part of the pipeline, the live relational things. I'm most likely to hand that stuff out to people that are more capable than me and much faster than me in the actual programming language.

Perry Harovas Maya Fur and Maya Cloth are part of the package and they're really well integrated, but I imagine that there was some reason that you made a decision not to use those, and to instead use your own in-house tools for those things?

Habib Zargarpour Those weren't decisions I had to make, as I wasn't working on that creature portion of the show. The people that were doing the creatures were developing in-house cloth and were open to using any other packages' cloth that was available to test, but it just so happened that we finished our cloth and made it very robust before the Maya cloth was ready. At that point, when the Maya cloth was ready and we saw it, I think our dynamics were still ahead in terms of robustness and realism. They still had improvements to make, which they did by SIGGRAPH last year. The people who were deciding which methodology to use were happy with what we already had.

In terms of Fur, we've had a long history of doing fur kinds of projects here, and they've been going through different evolutions with every show. The first use, I think, was in *The Flintstones,* believe it or not. Then we used it on the monkeys in *Jumanjii,* and on the lion. Then the latest resurrection of it is in *Mighty Joe Young* with the gorilla fur, where we added dynamics to it.

Perry Harovas Is it the same in-house renderer as your particle renderer?

Habib Zargarpour It used to be separate, but now they are the same. I don't know if the people responsible for doing that work had a chance to look at Maya Fur or not. Certainly, what they saw with the Paint Effects, they were very happy with this year at SIGGRAPH.

Perry Harovas Did you get a chance to see Paint Effects after your speech at the Alias|Wavefront User's Group?

Habib Zargarpour Unfortunately not. I'd seen it last year, but it was an independent unit; it wasn't integrated into the package and I don't think he [Duncan Brinsmead] had all the animation features. But I heard people talk about it. It sounded really promising.

Perry Harovas At SIGGRAPH, ILM presented a technical paper which described how you were able to keyframe the dynamics, which is a fascinating concept. Have you tried to implement any of that in Maya?

Habib Zargarpour We implemented that concept. In the rigid bodies, we were using impulses to add our own guidance into what we wanted to do. In some ways, the way pod rigs were set up was pretty much that you have human input into a dynamics system to guide it, to tell it where to go. But basically, the bottom line would be that the simulation is going to decide where it's going based on its own characteristics of mass, momentum—all these different things. So, in a way, that set-up is entirely an input into a dynamic system, as opposed to letting it run purely based on fields, like we do on particles. With particles, there are so many of them that you have to come up with *global* controls.

Perry Harovas So the cage you set up, with the different springs attached to the engines of the pods, that was your input device, by keyframing that, then letting the dynamics of the springs on top of it take over under that?

Habib Zargarpour Exactly.

Perry Harovas How, if you can tell me this without killing me, did you implement denting in the pieces of the engine that hit the ground?

Habib Zargarpour (Laughs.) We had several different R&D projects at the same time looking into that, and one of the methodologies was to take expressions and use lattices to deform them based on impact. To deform the object, you have to do all kinds of tricky things to the rigid bodies for them to recognize that they got deformed, but I won't go into that! It was a combination of what's in the package and some expressions and plug-ins that we managed to get the airframe technique working so it would automatically dent as a hit and whatever object it was, it would start to deform.

It was very exciting for us, for example, to get the front ring of the engine hitting the ground. If that was a solid piece, it would just hit the ground and fly out, whereas if it's an airframe, the bottom starts to take the impact and work backward, and causes a distortion to go through it. It behaves more like a piece of metal would, that could deform, as opposed to a hard piece that would just fly off.

The last technique was something we had developed as a plug-in, which was a deformation node. We could hand-place and animate them as a live relational node in the hypergraph. We would just dial in just how much deformation we wanted. That technique was used when the wrench goes into the engine, for example. You see dents coming out of the different spots on the engine. That way, it was real easy for us to just place them in different spots, and if George wanted more or less of them or different timing on them, [we could do that]. So it was very easy for us to place the deformers manually and just hand-animate them coming on. Because they were relational it was animatable, so it wasn't like we were permanently deforming it.

Perry Harovas Were there any instances where the dynamics were not working, or taking much too long to calculate?

Habib Zargarpour There were a few shots where the animators were trying to get the pod rigs to move a certain way, and there would be, maybe some really fast turn that they couldn't do, or a specific action. So for the most part, they would make the simulation so that most of the pieces were moving physically correctly, and then they could go in and hand-edit some of the keyframes. Like, if an engine went a little too high in a certain frame, they could bring it down and basically post-edit it as if it were motion capture. But that didn't happen very often—very, very rare.

Perry Harovas How long did it take you to develop the cages that surrounded the pods and engines?

Habib Zargarpour That's a good question. That process took about three to four months. And the reason being that it was basically an engineering project trying to make an airplane and fly it. You need test pilots and you need mechanical configurations. We ran into all kinds of interesting discoveries, like dealing with moving rigid body hierarchies. It was not only a matter of building it, but also making tools that could handle it. In Maya 1.0 you couldn't do rigid body hierarchies, so we had to come up with a way to do the hierarchies and then a way to move them and rotate.

But it wasn't four months of full-time work for me. As I was doing the pod crashes, I was also doing this research. As an example, if you were real precise with your rope configuration, let's say like where the pins would go, you would end up with some high-frequency problems at high speed causing the cockpit to break off or something. That's why I keep saying it's like dealing with a real craft—it physically has to function that way. A lot of the time was spent trying to get the right configuration. What is the best way to grab an engine? Do you grab it from the front, which is the first thing we tried, or do you grab it from all four corners? Each decision has its own repercussions and efficiency.

One of the difficulties in doing the pod race that was that we weren't able to tell them any details about what we were doing with the rigid bodies. We just had to say, "Look, we're trying to go really fast and it's misbehaving or doing this or that."

Not having the luxury of sending [Alias|Wavefront] a scene and ask, "Why doesn't this work?"—that's always a frustrating thing, not to be able to do that.

Perry Harovas I think it's maybe everybody's misperception that ILM has a really, really fast machine on everybody's desk.

Habib Zargarpour Right, that's what I thought before I came here!

Perry Harovas Were you given something that could do the calculations in our lifetime so that you wouldn't have to be there all day and all night to wait for the simulation?

Habib Zargarpour I just used my O[S]2. What you had to do is use the tools in the package to make efficiencies happen. If two objects are really heavy, you put them on different layers. Those kinds of things you have to constantly watch for and take advantage of. But yeah, it would be really nice if they multi-threaded the package as far as dynamics go, not just rendering, so that you could run the simulation on an Origin or do massive parallel processing on fast machines. Nowadays, even desktops are coming with four processors!

Perry Harovas Is there a concern about using commercial packages, which change often, and sometimes go away?

Habib Zargarpour Yeah, that's always a concern. I feel like we need to take full advantage, as much as we can, of vendor software because there are so many developers involved with it. There's only so much manpower you have in-house, and we do have amazing programmers here. But I find that if we are able to harness some or both of those rather than making it exclusive, there are huge benefits in that kind of relationship. As users, we end up benefiting from developers and dedicated companies who make tools for you. And more and more, I guess, packages are opening up with APIs and plug-ins, and it's creating this interesting gray area where code is code, and its almost like it doesn't make any difference what its called or where its running. Put one package into another or vice versa. But then what's important is the user interface and the design, right?

Perry Harovas Do the other users of Maya out there ever benefit from things that you've developed in ILM, or do they just not let anything go to Alias|Wavefront?

Habib Zargarpour That's a good question. We have a lot of suggestions for them on improving the package, and most of those changes get put into the official package.

Perry Harovas Thank you for a such a wonderful conversation, and for all your thoughts and ideas and excitement.

Habib Zargarpour You're welcome!

Craig Lyn: Technical Director, Industrial Light and Magic

Craig Lyn has been a Technical Director at Industrial Light and Magic for over three and a half years. His filmography includes *Amistad, Deep Impact, Star Wars: the Phantom Menace, Mission to Mars, Galaxy Quest,* and *Pearl Harbor.* He's also the author of *The Macintosh 3D Handbook* (Charles River Media, third edition 1999), a guide to 3D graphics on the Mac platform. A prolific writer, modeler, animator, and texture artist, Craig has perfected the look of many a shot from the films mentioned above.

John Kundert-Gibbs Like many people, you came to Maya from a very different software package. What was this other package, and how long did you use it before moving to Maya?

Craig Lyn Well, because of NDAs (non-disclosure agreements), I can't really say what the other package was, but I used it for about five years before coming to Maya. In fact, I used the other software for quite a while before coming to ILM.

John Kundert-Gibbs What did you do before coming to ILM?

Craig Lyn Well, mostly freelance work, and of course writing three editions of *The Macintosh 3D Handbook.*

John Kundert-Gibbs Do you still use this other software now?

Craig Lyn Not at all at work. A bit at home, but I don't really do that much animation on my own anymore.

John Kundert-Gibbs A busman's holiday, right?

Craig Lyn Exactly. I have plenty to do at work, so I'm not too interested in working during my off hours!

John Kundert-Gibbs How long have you been using Maya now?

Craig Lyn About two years now. My group first used Maya doing animatics for *Galaxy Quest,* and it sort of went on from there.

John Kundert-Gibbs What made you (and ILM) move to using Maya?

Craig Lyn Well, Maya has great animation tools, for one thing. And it's just great for particles and dynamics—everybody just loves the dynamics engine. ILM uses Maya all over the place, actually.

John Kundert-Gibbs What about you? What do you like best about—or what's made easier for you by—Maya?

Craig Lyn Everything! Specifically, I love the integration Maya brings. I model in [Alias|Wavefront's] Studio Tools, and it's just seamless to bring in geometry to Maya. It accepts all different surface types, and even the Studio layers are transferred intact. I also really like the scriptability of Maya. Maya's like PhotoShop: it's a great program on its own, but the ability to add plug-ins, and especially to write your *own* MEL scripts makes Maya an indispensable tool. And again, everything's integrated: I can model, do particles, and animate, all in one environment. I actually really enjoy the experience of working with Maya. Of course, every package has its shortcomings…

John Kundert-Gibbs Speaking of that, what do you wish Maya would do better?

Craig Lyn Rendering. The rendering engine needs more work. For example, I'd like to do a diffuse render pass with no speculars, but I can't do that now. This isn't so much a problem for a large studio like ILM, since we have proprietary tools to cover texturing and rendering, but for a small company that needs an all-around package, this is a real problem.

John Kundert-Gibbs What sort of work are you doing now with Maya?

Craig Lyn Oh, lots of things. Mostly modeling and deformation work right now. I'm also doing some scripting with animation.

John Kundert-Gibbs Sounds like a whole bunch of different jobs.

Craig Lyn That's the life of a TD [Technical Director]!

John Kundert-Gibbs What other tools are you using in conjunction with Maya on these projects?

Craig Lyn Proprietary. Mostly proprietary. Our proprietary paint system works well with Maya. We also use Studio Tools because its modeler is more exacting— you know, they use it to build cars and things!

John Kundert-Gibbs So do you actually build real models out of Studio Tools using CAM [Computer Assisted Manufacturing] software?

Craig Lyn Actually, several models for SW1 [*Star Wars, Episode I*] were machined from virtual models.

John Kundert-Gibbs That's a pretty nice time saver: build it once and use it twice.

Craig Lyn Yes, and it solves some continuity problems too, since the real model looks like the virtual one.

John Kundert-Gibbs Does Maya fit in well with the proprietary tools in your pipeline?

Craig Lyn Yes. We use it to do everything from animatics to particle systems. The data input/output is really easy, so Maya can be integrated at many points in the pipeline.

John Kundert-Gibbs Let's look into the future for a few minutes: where do you see Maya evolving in the next few years?

Craig Lyn I see them [Alias|Wavefront] really focusing on games. That's the real hot area right now for 3D software.

John Kundert-Gibbs There's certainly a lot of money out there for games.

Craig Lyn Yes, and Maya's scriptability is real power for game developers. I see a lot of people—both in gaming and in the film business—looking very closely at Maya these days because of its power. Everybody wants Maya to knock out quick animations for previz, since it's so fast and flexible. Frankly, coming from the other software I had used, I was just blown away by Maya's animation tools. And their NURBS modeling package is great, too—it's nice to see a company actually do NURBS right, not like a lot of other software that just pretends to do NURBS. Oh yeah, and I think—or hope—they'll work on the renderer in the next couple of years!

John Kundert-Gibbs Do you think Maya will still fit into ILM's pipeline in a couple of years?

Craig Lyn That's hard to know. I sure hope so, since not many other 3D packages are going that way.

John Kundert-Gibbs Do you think the market for 3D is shrinking as a whole?

Craig Lyn Not really shrinking; I'd say consolidating. This isn't so good for competition, but I guess it had to happen.

John Kundert-Gibbs Yes, we seem to have lost a lot of the "low-end" 3D applications over the last few years.

Craig Lyn Yeah, there really aren't any hobbyist applications left. Just middle- and high-end packages, and there seem to be less of these as well.

John Kundert-Gibbs If you could give the Alias|Wavefront developers one piece of advice for developing Maya, what would it be?

Craig Lyn Well, from my *personal* point of view (we have specific needs at ILM that are different from the general user's), I think Maya should make the task of the animation easier for individual artists. For example, Maya should be optimized to handle really big scenes well. The developers should go out and see how artists work, and use that to develop Maya further. How do artists work? What is important for them on a day-to-day basis? Things like low-res/hi-res model swapping and multipass rendering should be easier to do.

John Kundert-Gibbs Yes, these are possible right now, but take a lot of work.

Craig Lyn Exactly. They need to improve scene management tools to simplify redundant tasks. Artists have to do too much work sometimes on things that could be automated, or at least made a lot simpler.

John Kundert-Gibbs Do you have any other thoughts on using Maya in a multi-tool workflow?

Craig Lyn I generally really like Maya. It's flexible; it handles polys really well. And how many packages can really handle NURBS? Not many. I think what I like best is that, for the most part, the developers decided to do things *right* the first time with Maya, and that makes things a lot nicer for us.

John Kundert-Gibbs Thanks very much for your time.

Craig Lyn Not a problem.

Index

Note to the reader: Throughout this index **boldfaced** page numbers indicate primary discussions of a topic. *Italicized* page numbers indicate illustrations.

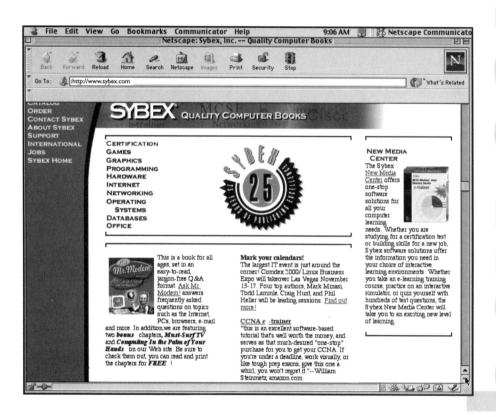

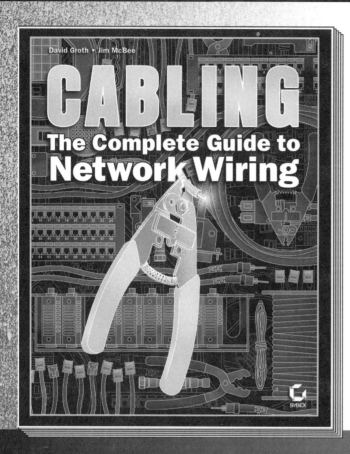